Human Societies

A Macrolevel Introduction to Sociology

Human Societies

A Macrolevel Introduction to Sociology

Gerhard Lenski

DEPARTMENT OF SOCIOLOGY
UNIVERSITY OF NORTH CAROLINA

McGraw-Hill Book Company

NEW YORK   ST. LOUIS   SAN FRANCISCO   DÜSSELDORF
LONDON   MEXICO   PANAMA   SYDNEY   TORONTO

COVER SCULPTURE

"City Square" by Giacometti
Used by permission of Morton G. Neuman.

HUMAN SOCIETIES: A Macrolevel Introduction to Sociology

Library of Congress Catalog Card Number 73-100804

37166

1 2 3 4 5 6 7 8 9 0 VHVH 7 9 8 7 6 5 4 3 2 1 0

This book was set in Optima by Progressive Typographers, and printed on permanent paper and bound by Von Hoffman Press, Inc. The designer was Barbara Bert; the drawings were done by Edward Malsberg. The editors were Ronald Kissack and Helen Greenberg. Peter D. Guilmette supervised the production.

TO
Jean
Bob
Kathy
and Dick

Preface

Introductory courses are notoriously difficult to teach well, and introductory sociology is no exception. Despite the best efforts of thousands of talented teachers, the course too often fails to be a rewarding intellectual experience for both students and instructors. To some extent this is because of overly large classes, inadequate facilities, and other administrative shortcomings. But beyond that, and more basically, I believe that there are serious problems with the content and basic conception of the course itself. Among the criticisms one hears, the following are so common that they can hardly be ignored: the course is not sufficiently challenging, especially for today's students, who come better prepared than predecessors of twenty years ago; the materials of the course are poorly integrated and fail to add up to any meaningful body of knowledge; the course devotes too much attention to terminology and too little to the explanation of social phenomena; the course presents a largely static, structural view of society despite the fact that we are living in the midst of a social revolution; the course overemphasizes the systemic qualities of society and slights the crucial processes of social conflict; the course concentrates too much on *micro*level phenomena (i.e., social psychological and institutional materials), too little on *macro*level (i.e., total societies); the course tends to be ethnocentric, focusing chiefly on American society despite the increasing need of students for training that will help them understand other societies; and, finally, the course has not kept up with basic changes in sociology, especially the recent shift from structural-functional to evolutionary theory.

Naturally, not all these criticisms apply everywhere. However, my conversations with teachers around the country lead me to believe that these problems are sufficiently widespread to justify the belief that the introductory course is in need of a basic overhaul. And that is precisely what this volume undertakes.

The key innovation which this text offers is a shift from structural-functional to evolutionary theory. By making this one change, it becomes possible to deal far more effectively with all the other weaknesses mentioned above. To begin with, the evolutionary approach brings the phenomenon of social change to the center of the stage where it properly belongs, especially in our day. Second, it automatically directs attention to macrolevel phenomena, since basically it is societies, or sociocultural systems, which evolve. Third, the evolutionary approach naturally employs a comparative approach which forces students and teacher alike to consider societies other than our own. Fourth, this approach inevitably directs attention to social conflict. Fifth, evolutionary theory is far more concerned with explanation than with definition. Sixth, because it is explanatory, it integrates the materials of the field and facilitates the accumulation of knowledge. Seventh, for all of these reasons, evolutionary theory provides a greater challenge to students. Finally, the evolutionary approach brings the introductory course into line with the newer trends in theory.

There is still one other gain that deserves note. The evolutionary approach provides a remarkably effective vehicle for pulling together not only the scattered materials of sociology, but the basic findings of biology, anthropology, history, political science, and economics as well. This is no small contribution in the modern multiversity, where the fragmentation of knowledge has become such a serious impediment to learning. Sociology may never become "the queen of the sciences," as some nineteenth-century sociologists hoped. But the evolutionary approach may yet make it "the integrator of the social sciences."

Some teachers will undoubtedly wonder why I have not devoted more space to the various subspecialties within sociology. Twenty years' experience in teaching introductory sociology has convinced me that it is a serious mistake to try to do a little of everything in this one course; it is better to do a few things well than many things poorly. In my opinion, *the basic task of the introductory course in any field is to provide a comprehensive and meaningful framework for thinking about the subject matter of that discipline.* This framework will be of lasting value to the student whether he takes only a single course or goes on to major in the field.

Two areas often stressed in introductory sociology are deliberately deemphasized in this text: methods and social psychology. This does not indicate a lack of interest in them. On the contrary, my appreciation of their significance leads me to doubt the advisability of a brief and therefore necessarily superficial treatment. Methods and social psychology each deserve a full course of their own.

But some would argue that they should be presented first. I disagree: that puts the cart before the horse. Methods of research are the tools which are used to answer questions raised by theory, and asking meaningful questions is one of the most critical parts of research. To train students in methods before we introduce them to theory will produce, at best, technicians. Such an approach may be appropriate to a trade school, but not to a university. The question of whether microlevel studies should precede macrolevel is more debatable; obviously a case can be made for either approach. But for thirty years or more we have been using the microlevel approach in introductory sociology, and the result, as we have seen, has been less than satisfactory. It would seem to be time to try the other. I have been doing this in my own teaching for the last twelve to fifteen years and have been extremely pleased with the results—and so have others who have tried it. One reason is that sociology has so much more that is new and not self-evident to offer at the macrolevel. (Social-psychologized introductory courses, by contrast, are highly vulnerable to the "Mickey Mouse" charge because every intelligent student is already a social psychologist of sorts.) In addition, I believe that a macrolevel approach sheds more light on, and therefore leads more naturally into, microlevel phenomena than the reverse.

Teachers who are accustomed to building the introductory course around the definition of terms will also find this volume requires some readjustment on their part. But a sociology that is largely a matter of definitions does not deserve a place in the curriculum of a modern university or college. I have deliberately played down terminology, simply defining terms as they are introduced and supplying a Glossary for subsequent reference. Some students will require more, but I believe it is wiser to leave this problem in the hands of the instructor. If his students need additional explanation and discussion, he will know it and he can provide it. But to build it into the text is not necessary and will only alienate the abler students, who resent books that elaborate the obvious and talk down to them.

Because the evolutionary approach is new to most present-day instructors, I have prepared a Teachers' Manual which is something more than the usual catalog of exam questions. It calls attention to films and supplementary readings which I have found helpful and to topics which lend themselves to fruitful class discussions. I believe that this will make the transition much easier for teachers used to the traditional approach.

Gerhard Lenski

Acknowledgments

In the preparation of this book, I benefited tremendously from the help of a number of people. First, scholars in several fields were kind enough to read part or all of the original manuscript. My only complaint is that they had so many valuable suggestions that the preparation of the book took much longer than I had planned. (In fact, had I tried to incorporate them all, I would have had to make this my life's work!) I am sincerely grateful for their help, and I know that the present version is far superior to the earlier draft because of the contributions of Alfred E. Emerson, Walter Goldschmidt, Amos Hawley, Norman Storer, and Everett Wilson.

I also owe a special debt to Ronald Kissack, McGraw-Hill's sociology editor. His skillful assistance and constant support have been invaluable, and his good humor and enthusiasm made our collaboration a pleasure.

A skillful typist is also a tremendous asset, and it was my good fortune to have an excellent one—Mrs. Harold McFarland—in preparing both drafts of the manuscript. While I have worked with a number of able typists in the past, she is easily the best.

Finally, I owe the greatest debt of all to my wife. She and I have discussed the contents of this book more hours than either of us can remember. Her criticisms and suggestions have influenced the manuscript at every stage in its development. In recent months she has been working full time, "translating" what I had written in sociologese (an obscure dialect stylistically akin to pidgin English) into comprehensible, contemporary English. If she was not completely successful, the fault is mine, since I stubbornly insisted on veto power and the right of retranslation. Because of the magnitude of her contribution, both substantively and stylistically, I wanted her to agree to coauthorship, but she too modestly refused. I have reluctantly accepted her decision, but readers should realize that if they find something of value in the pages that follow, no small part of the credit is hers.

Gerhard Lenski

Contents

Preface   vii
Acknowledgments   xi

PART I: GENERAL INTRODUCTION TO HUMAN SOCIETIES

1/An Introduction to Sociology   5
Human societies: their place in nature
A definition of societies
The basic function of societies
Man's threefold relation to the biotic world
Excursus: A brief history of sociology

2/The Structure and Functioning of Human Societies   27
Human needs and human nature
Basic elements of sociocultural systems
Appendix: A further note on human nature

3/An Introduction to Evolutionary Theory   48
The new synthetic theory of organic evolution
Organic and sociocultural evolution compared
Basic outlines of a theory of sociocultural evolution

                                                                           xiii

4/Sociocultural Continuity, Innovation, and Extinction   71
  Sociocultural continuity
  Sociocultural innovation
  Sociocultural extinction

5/Basic Evolutionary Trends   95
  Sociocultural diversification
  Sociocultural progress
  Other patterns of change
  Appendix: Further notes on technology and ideology

6/The Types and Varieties of Societies   118
  Classifying human societies: earlier typologies
  A current typology
  Societal types through history
  Correlates of societal type: Some basic patterns
  Technological determinism?

PART II: PREINDUSTRIAL SOCIETIES

7/Hunting and Gathering Societies   147
  The archaeological evidence
  The ethnographic evidence
  Archaeological and ethnographic evidence compared
  Appendix: Hints from ethology

8/Horticultural Societies   192
  Simple horticultural societies in prehistoric Asia and Europe
  Advanced horticultural societies in prehistoric Asia and Europe
  Horticultural societies in prehistoric America
  Horticultural societies in the modern era
  Horticultural societies in evolutionary perspective

9/Agrarian Societies   237
  Simple agrarian societies
  Advanced agrarian societies

10/Specialized Societal Types   290
  Fishing societies
  Herding societies
  Maritime societies
  Preliminary recapitulation

PART III: INDUSTRIAL AND INDUSTRIALIZING SOCIETIES

11/The Industrial Revolution   311
The concept of the Industrial Revolution
Causes of the Industrial Revolution
Causes of the continuing Industrial Revolution

12/Industrial Societies: Part 1   340
The technological base
Demographic patterns
The system of social organization: Introduction and overview
The polity

13/Industrial Societies: Part 2   369
The economy
Social stratification

14/Industrial Societies: Part 3   410
Knowledge and beliefs
Kinship
Student communities and their subculture
Intratype variation: Trends and prospects
Progress and problems

15/Industrializing Societies   430
Industrializing agrarian societies
Industrializing horticultural societies

16/Retrospect and Prospect   468
Looking back: The long view
Distortions
Progress reconsidered
Looking ahead

Glossary   495

Appendix: Notes on Murdock's Sample   503
Picture Credits   508
Index   511

Human Societies

A Macrolevel Introduction to Sociology

Part I
General Introduction to Human Societies

Chapter 1
An Introduction to Sociology

Sociology is a relatively new field of study. Because of this, many people are unclear about its aims and purposes. Some confuse it with social work. Others think of it as the study of social problems. A few even associate it with socialism and similar movements which seek to reform society.

Sociology is none of these things. Rather, it is an academic discipline, and its goal, like that of history, economics, or chemistry, is *the acquisition of knowledge*.

As one of the social sciences, sociology shares with anthropology, political science, economics, and social psychology an interest in the ways of men. The actions of individuals and groups are the data which sociologists and other social scientists study and analyze and on which they base their theories.

Though all the social sciences have this common interest in human behavior, each discipline has grown up around a core of problems peculiarly its own. The problems central to sociology are those which concern the *social* aspects of human life. Man is a social animal, and sociology is dedicated to the exploration of the many implications of this fact. This means that sociology is much concerned with the various kinds of groups men have formed—their families, communities, churches, political parties, governments, business organizations, and the like. But even more, sociology is interested in the larger social systems of which these groups are merely a part, such as American society, French society, Soviet society, and the others, both past and present. For this reason, sociology may be defined as *the study of human societies*.[1]

Few subjects deserve more careful study. These large and complex social

---

[1] For a definition of this and other technical terms, see the Glossary, pp. 495–502.

systems into which the human family is divided are immensely important both for us as individuals and for mankind as a whole. To a far greater degree than most of us realize, our lives and even our personalities are molded by the society of which we are part. Being raised as a member of American society is a very different experience from being raised in Brazilian, Turkish, Pakistani, or Samoan society and has very different consequences. If we are to obey the ancient injunction "Know thyself," we must know the society of which we are a part. The study of human societies is no less important if we hope to understand our fellow men.

The study of human societies has a special urgency at the present time, because we are living in the most revolutionary era in history.[2] Never before have so many aspects of human life changed so rapidly for so many of the peoples of the world. No area of life has escaped: art, science, religion, morality, education, politics, the family, the economy—all are affected. Even in the inner recesses of our personalities we feel the impact of the modern social revolution, as new experiences, new knowledge, new relationships, and new opportunities transform our hopes and fears, our beliefs, and even our conception of ourselves.

This revolution necessarily raises questions in the mind of any thoughtful person. What has caused it? Why has it spread so rapidly? Can it be controlled and directed, and if so, how? Where is it taking us? To a world of plenty and freedom for all, or to Orwell's *1984* or an atomic holocaust?

In many ways, we are like travelers on a rocket hurtling through space to an unknown destination, with only the most limited knowledge of the vehicle, i.e., our society, in which we are traveling and on which our lives depend. Under the circumstances, it is not surprising that men are more concerned than ever before with the study of human societies and are turning increasingly to sociology and the other social sciences for answers to their questions. Not that we have answers yet to many of these vital questions. Indeed, some we may never be able to answer. Human societies are among the most complex phenomena in the whole world of nature, and the social sciences are still very new. But if answers are to be found, it is clear they will be found only through systematic, disciplined study.

The aim of this volume is to provide an introduction to the results of sociological efforts to date. Naturally, no single volume can present more than a small part of the knowledge sociologists have gained about human societies, but this one will cover the most basic findings, leaving the more detailed and more specialized to subsequent courses.

In sociology, as in any large and active field of study, there are many controversies. Not all sociologists share the view of human societies presented in this volume. As indicated in the brief history of sociology at the end of this chapter, the discipline is currently in a period of transition. One view of human societies, the

---

[2] It has been said that every generation imagines its own era is the most revolutionary. While there is some truth to this, it is also true that our own generation has the best grounds for thinking so. Evidence to support this claim will be presented in later chapters.

structural-functional, which was dominant from the 1930s to the early 1960s, is slowly giving way to the ecological-evolutionary view presented here. The latter promises to become the dominant perspective in the years ahead and therefore is the view presented here.

HUMAN SOCIETIES: THEIR PLACE IN NATURE

Though human societies are an important and familiar part of the world we live in, their relation to other parts of the world of nature is not always clearly understood. In fact, many people think of them as somehow set apart from the rest of the natural world. While it is true that human societies *are* unique in a number of fundamental ways, it is also true that they share many essential characteristics with other parts of the natural world. Therefore, it is important to establish at the outset the place of man's societies in the natural order, and to spell out the consequences of this relationship.

As many scholars have observed, the world of nature is structured much like a system of wheels within wheels, with all the parts ultimately related. Thus, when we examine any object carefully, we find that it is made up of various differentiated parts and that these parts, in turn, are made up of still smaller parts. In the same way, we find that our original object is a unit within some larger, more inclusive system, and that this system is, in turn, part of a still larger and more inclusive system.

As a starting point for our analysis of human societies, it is helpful to see where they are located in this complex hierarchy. Fig. 1/1 provides a somewhat over-simplified view of the matter. Subatomic particles, such as electrons and protons, form the lowest level in the hierarchy of organization. These are combined in various ways to form atoms, such as carbon and radium. Atoms, in turn, are organized to form molecules, such as water, salt, amino acids, and proteins. Though Fig. 1/1 does not show it, molecules constitute more than a single level in the hierarchy since certain of the simpler molecules, the amino acids, for example, are the building blocks for more complex and more inclusive molecules, such as the proteins.

Once we go beyond the level of molecules, we encounter the important division between living and nonliving things. Since our concern is with human societies, we need not examine all the levels in the hierarchy of nonliving things. Suffice it to note that this hierarchy leads by degrees to the level of the giant galaxies, or star systems, that wheel through space, and it appears to end with the universe itself.

Societies, by contrast, are part of the biotic world, the world of plants and animals. More specifically, they are one of the forms of organization found in that world. From the standpoint of inclusiveness, they are between the level of the multicellular organism and the level of the species. In other words, some species are divided into territorially bounded subunits known as societies, and these societies, in turn, are made up of individual organisms.

As Fig. 1/1 suggests, relations among the various levels and types of organiza-

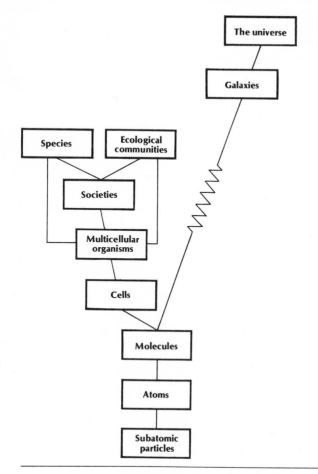

Fig. 1/1   The hierarchy of organization

tions in the biotic world become rather complex once we go beyond the level of the multicellular organism. For one thing, not all species are divided into societies (as the direct line from organism to species, bypassing the societal level, denotes). For another thing, species and ecological communities are two different, but overlapping, forms of organization on essentially the same level of inclusiveness.[3]

For our purposes, however, these complications are not important. What *is* important is that we begin to think of human societies as a part of the world of nature, especially the biotic world, and that we come to recognize what this has meant in the life of man and his societies.

---

[3] The term "ecological community" refers to a population of plants and animals of diverse species that occupy a given territory and are bound together by ties of mutual dependence. Species and ecological communities are placed on the same level of organization in Fig. 1/1 since neither subsumes the other. A species usually includes portions of a number of ecological communities and vice versa.

A DEFINITION OF SOCIETIES

Up to this point, we have discussed societies without actually defining them. We have identified two of their basic characteristics, however. Specifically, we have seen that a society is a territorially distinct organization and that it is made up of animals of a single species. To complete the definition, we must add three further criteria.

First, a society is a form of organization involving *relatively sustained ties of interaction among its members.* Occasional contacts are not enough. Thus, we would not say that the species of wasp known as the mud dauber maintains societies, since interaction among members of this species occurs only for brief intervals at the time of mating and reproduction. On the other hand, the criterion is clearly met in the case of the many varieties of social insects which maintain sustained contacts with others of their kind throughout their lives.

Second, a society is a form of organization involving a *relatively high degree of interdependence among its members.* That is to say, the survival and well-being of each member depend to a great degree on the actions of others. A colony of ants with its division of labor among workers, soldiers, and queen provides a good illustration of this.

Third, and finally, a society is a form of organization characterized by *a high degree of autonomy.* In other words, a society is not subject to the control or regulation of any outside organization to a significant degree. Applying this criterion, we see that the American nation constitutes a society but that the individual families, communities, churches, and other groups found within it do not.

Bringing together the various parts of our definition, we can now say that *a society exists to the degree that a territorially bounded population of animals of a single species maintains ties of association and interdependence and enjoys autonomy.* As this definition indicates, the world of animal organizations cannot be neatly divided into those that are societies and those that are not. Rather, there is a scale or continuum along which organizations are ranged, and between those that obviously are societies and those that obviously are not, there is a gray area of organizations that possess the qualities of a society in varying degrees.

The position of a group on this scale is not immutably fixed. Over a period of time, some groups take on more of the qualities of a society while others lose them. A good example of the latter are the many American Indian groups during the past several hundred years. Prior to contact with Europeans, each group was autonomous, and its members were bound together by strong ties of interaction and interdependence. Following contact with the Europeans, and later the Americans, these Indian groups gradually lost most of their autonomy and were brought increasingly under foreign control. Eventually, the ties of intragroup interaction and interdependence began to break down as individuals established more and more ties with the surrounding American population. Thus, over the years these groups gradually lost the properties of a society. As such cases illustrate, it is often difficult to say with certainty whether, at a specific point in time, a given population does or does not constitute a society. If the reasons for the difficulty are clearly understood, however, the problem should not be too troublesome.

THE BASIC FUNCTION OF SOCIETIES

Societies have not always been present in the biotic world. Rather, they are a form of organization that emerged during the long course of evolutionary history. Some years ago, one writer referred to their appearance as "one of the great steps in evolution" and compared it in importance with the emergence of the cell, the multicellular organism, and the vertebrate system.[4] As he pointed out, society is a form of organization that has evolved not once, but a number of times, independently, and in widely separated animal lines. It is found not only among humans, but also among many species of mammals, birds, fish, and even insects. Furthermore, those species that have adopted the societal mode of organization have generally prospered and multiplied.

What function does this form of organization perform that might account for its widespread occurrence? The answer that emerges from the study of both human and other societies is the same: *the societal form of organization is a mode of adaptation whereby certain types of organisms have increased their chances of surviving and multiplying.* In essence, therefore, the societal mode of organization may be thought of as a functional counterpart of other familiar adaptive mechanisms in the animal world, such as speed, strength, bodily weapons and armament, instinctive response sets, intelligence, and so forth.

The importance of this can hardly be exaggerated, since it has far-reaching implications for our whole approach to the study of human societies. Above all, it reminds us once again that the study of human societies cannot be divorced from the study of the rest of the biotic world. More than that, it suggests that we would do well to adopt an evolutionary approach in our study of human societies, since it is only in these terms that adaptive mechanisms can be fully understood. This is not to say that the study of human societies should be swallowed up by the biological sciences, but it does mean that as students of human societies we must have a clear understanding of man's relation to the biotic world and of the ways in which basic biological forces influence human life.

---

[4] Kingsley Davis, *Human Society* (New York: Macmillan, 1949), p. 27. See also a similar statement by a leading zoologist, Alfred E. Emerson, in "Human Cultural Evolution and Its Relation to Organic Evolution of Insect Societies," in Herbert Barringer et al. (eds.), *Social Change in Developing Areas: A Reinterpretation of Evolutionary Theory* (Cambridge, Mass.: Schenkman, 1965), pp. 50–51.

MAN'S THREEFOLD RELATION TO THE BIOTIC WORLD

The nature of man's relation to the biotic world has long been a source of confusion and misunderstanding. Much of the difficulty has been caused by two sharply contrasting views of man. The first view was popularized by some of Darwin's more enthusiastic followers in the nineteenth century. They argued that his work proved that man is essentially an animal and can best be understood if he is studied solely, or largely in biological terms.

Though this view still has its supporters, most scholars now reject it on the grounds that it involves what some have called the "nothing but" fallacy. As George Gaylord Simpson, a leading paleontologist, explained:

> To say that man is nothing but an animal is to deny, by implication, that he has *essential* attributes other than those of all animals. This would be false as applied to any kind of animal; it is not true that a dog, a robin, an oyster, or an ameba is nothing but an animal. As applied to man the "nothing but" fallacy is more serious than in application to any other sort of animal, because man is an entirely new kind of animal in ways altogether fundamental for understanding of his nature. It is important to realize that man is an animal, but it is even more important to realize that the essence of his unique nature lies precisely in those characteristics that are not shared with any other animal.[5]

In reacting against the excesses of the "nothing but" fallacy, many sociologists and other social scientists in recent decades have backed into the opposite camp. By tending to ignore, or give perfunctory treatment to, the biological bases of human society, they almost seem to have adopted the position of those who deny man's animal heritage. The chief reason for this is probably the failure to see clearly that our choice is not limited to these two opposed positions. There is a third possibility—one which recognizes that man has some qualities that are uniquely his, and others that he shares with other forms of life. This position can be summarized in three simple propositions:[6]

1. Man shares some attributes with *all* living things.
2. Man shares some additional attributes with certain other forms of life, but not with all.
3. Man has still other attributes which he does not share with any other form of life.

Once we accept these three propositions, the risks in viewing man and his societies as part of the biotic world become minimal, and are far outweighed by the advantages.

---

[5] George Gaylord Simpson, *The Meaning of Evolution* (New Haven, Conn.: Yale, 1951), pp. 283–284. Quoted by permission of Yale University Press.

[6] For a parallel statement about individuals, see Clyde Kluckhohn and Henry Murray, *Personality: In Nature, Society, and Culture*, rev. ed. (New York: Knopf, 1965), p. 53.

Fig. 1/2a   Man shares the need for food, light, and air with all living things

Fig. 1/2c   Religion is unique to man

Fig. 1/2b   Man shares the societal form of organization with some living things

The universals

When we first survey the great diversity of living things, it is easy to suppose there are no universals, no properties common to all. The differences between man and the ameba are immense and obvious. Yet underlying these differences are certain uniformities, and these are tremendously important if we are to develop a meaningful perspective on human societies.

This fundamental unity first became evident in the work of Darwin, more than a century ago. Since then, biological research has served to strengthen Darwin's basic insight. As one biologist recently expressed it:

> The world of living things is [now] seen as far more of a unity than was conceivable a hundred years ago. The post-Darwinian era in research has tended, on the whole, to break down the barriers between phyla and between individual disciplines. The same fundamental principles are [now] seen to be operating to a very large extent throughout the animal and plant kingdoms.[7]

Much the same point was made earlier by George Gaylord Simpson when he wrote:

> The first grand lesson learned from evolution was that of the unity of life . . . all living things are brothers in the very real, material sense that all have arisen from one source and been developed within the divergent intricacies of one process. Man is part of nature, and he is kin to all life.[8]

What, then, are these universals that apply to all living things? The following are among the most important relevant to the study of human societies. Other, less relevant ones could easily be added.

1. All living things require food, water, and air to survive.
2. Because of these needs, all living things are involved in intimate interaction with, and are dependent on, their physical and biotic environments.
3. All living things have a capacity for reproduction which, in the long run, exceeds the environment's capacity to sustain.
4. So long as living things reproduce freely, sustenance is in short supply.
5. So long as sustenance is in short supply, there is competition for it.
6. Living things usually reproduce true to kind, but owing to the occurrence of mutation and recombination of genes by means of sexual reproduction, genetic variation can be expected in all large populations.
7. So long as there is competition for sustenance and differences within and between species, a process of natural selection occurs, favoring organisms

---

[7] W. H. Thorpe, *Learning and Instinct in Animals*, 2d ed. (Cambridge, Mass.: Harvard, 1963), p. 467. Quoted by permission of Harvard University Press.

[8] Simpson, *op. cit.*, p. 281. Quoted by permission of Yale University Press.

and species with the following characteristics: high fecundity (i.e., a capacity for high rates of reproduction), strength and offensive weapons, defensive armament, speed, social organization, intelligence (i.e., the capacity to learn), camouflage, the capacity to utilize unusual foods, the capacity to survive in generally unfavorable environments, behavioral flexibility, and genetic flexibility (i.e., a moderate rate of mutation).[9]

8. So long as variation and natural selection occur, there will be organic and behavioral evolution (i.e., a nonrandom, or progressive, development in the directions indicated in item 7 above).

With respect to the last point, it should be noted that no single species could possibly evolve in all these directions simultaneously. Rather, they are alternatives, with the result that some species survive through the development of high rates of reproduction, others through the development of great speed, and still others through the development of powers of learning. Of necessity, there are built-in incompatibilities between many of these solutions to the problems created by competition. For example, great speed and elaborate defensive armament (e.g., the turtle's shell) tend to be incompatible, since the weight of armament necessarily reduces speed. Similarly, high fecundity and high intelligence tend to be incompatible, since large numbers of offspring cannot be cared for by the parents during the prolonged period of maturation that is necessary for the learning potential to be fully realized. Hence, different species follow different evolutionary paths.

The implications of this list of universals for man and his societies are clear. Individually and collectively, man requires food and water, and for this he is dependent on the environment. However, because of his omnivorous nature and his intelligence, he has been able to adapt to almost every terrestrial environment and even, to a limited extent, to marginal marine environments. As with other animals, his capacity for reproduction exceeds the capacity of the environment to sustain life, and, as a consequence, food has usually been in short supply. Hence competition for it has been a recurrent feature of human life, and most persons have died well before the end of their potential life-span. Though the relevance of points 6, 7, and 8 above has been quite limited since the emergence of Homo sapiens, or biologically modern man, a curious, but vitally important, functional equivalent has developed. We shall examine this shortly (see *Specialties* below).

The semispecialties

Some years ago, the author and humorist Clarence Day wrote a book entitled *This Simian World* speculating about the kind of civilization that might have developed had man evolved in the feline, rather than the simian, or primate, line, he wrote:

---

[9] On the adaptive value of a *moderate* rate of mutation, see W. C. Allee, A. E. Emerson, O. Park, and K. P. Schmidt, *Principles of Animal Ecology* (Philadelphia: Saunders, 1949), pp. 600 and 684.

A race of civilized beings descended from the great cats would have been rich in hermits and solitary thinkers. The recluse would not have been stigmatized as peculiar, as he is by us simians. They would not have been a credulous people, or easily religious. False prophets and swindlers would have found few dupes. And what generals they would have made! what consummate politicians!

. . . They would never have become as poised or as placid as—say-super-cows. Yet they would have had less insanity, probably, than we. Monkeys' . . . minds seem precariously balanced, unstable. The great cats are saner. They are intense, they would have needed sanitariums: but fewer asylums. And their asylums would have been not for weakminded souls, but for furies.

They would have been strong at slander. They would have been far more violent than we, in their hates, and they would have had fewer friendships . . .

The super-cat-men would have rated cleanliness higher. Some of us primates have learned to keep ourselves clean, but it's no large proportion; and even the cleanest of us see no grandeur in soap-manufacturing, and we don't look to [manicurists] and plumbers for social prestige. A feline race would have honored such occupations; . . . the rich Vera Pantherbilt would have deigned to dine only with [manicurists].

None but the lowest dregs of such a race would have been lawyers spending their span of life on this mysterious earth studying the long dusty records of dead and gone quarrels. We simians naturally admire a profession full of wrangle and chatter. but that is a monkeyish way of deciding disputes, not a feline.

It is fair to judge peoples by the rights they will sacrifice most for. Super-cat-men would have been outraged had their right of personal combat been questioned. The simian submits with odd readiness to the loss of this privilege. What outrages him is to make him stop wagging his tongue. He becomes most excited and passionate about the right of free speech, even going so far in his emotion as to declare it is sacred . . .

In a world of super-cat-men, I suppose there would have been few sailors; and people would have cared less for seaside resorts, or for swimming . . .

Among them there would have been no anti-vivisection societies:

No Young Cats Christian Associations or Red Cross work:

No vegetarians:

No early closing laws:

Much more hunting and trapping:

No riding to hounds; that's pure simian . . .

They would have had few comedies on their stage; no farces. Cats care little for fun. In the circus, superlative acrobats. No clowns.

In drama and singing they would have surpassed us probably. Even in the stage of arrested development as mere animals, in which we see cats, they wail with a passionate intensity at night in our yards. Imagine how a Caruso descended from such beings would sing.[10]

Fanciful as this is, it points to a basic truth we cannot afford to ignore: *human societies bear the special mark of man's primate ancestry.*

---

[10] Reprinted with omissions, by permission of Alfred A. Knopf, Inc., from *This Simian World* by Clarence Day. Copyright, 1920, by Clarence Day. Renewed 1948 by Katherine B. Day.

Much has been written about the significance of this for us *as individuals*. From our primate ancestors we inherited such important physical characteristics as our upright posture and flexible arms, our flexible hands with the separated fingers and opposable thumbs, our excellent vision, our year-round sexual readiness, our prolonged period of immaturity, our enlarged cerebrum, and our complex central nervous system. Because of these and other physical features that reflect our primate ancestry, our patterns of action as individuals differ from those of other animals. The further removed other animals are from the primate line, the greater the difference. Thus we have more in common with the primates (and especially the suborder of anthropoids, which includes monkeys and apes as well as man) than with other mammals; more with other mammals than with other vertebrates; and more with other vertebrates than with invertebrates or plants.

For present purposes, however, we are concerned less with the implications of our ancestry for us as individuals than with its implications for *human societies*. For a crucial point emerges here: the societal mode of organization itself is something man inherited, not something he developed on his own. Recent research has made it clear that all anthropoids live in societies.[11] While it is remotely possible that human and other modern anthropoid societies are independent developments, the weight of evidence is strongly against this. Not only are societies universal in the anthropoid line, they are also, in varying degrees of development, widespread among other mammals. Furthermore, there seems to be an evolutionary progression which culminates in human societies, the most complex of them all. Thus, though evidence for the thesis that man inherited the societal mode of existence is circumstantial, it is compelling.

The close association between mammals and the societal form of organization brings us back to a question we dealt with briefly and in very general terms earlier: what is the function of societies? At that time we limited ourselves to saying that it is an adaptive mechanism which certain species have adopted, thereby enhancing their chances of surviving and multiplying.

Because societies differ so much from one phylogenetic line to another (e.g., compare insect and mammalian societies), this is as much as can be said in general terms. When we limit our discussion to mammalian societies, however, or better yet to primate societies, we can be much more specific. This was shown recently by two scholars in the important new subdiscipline of primate behavior. At the conclusion of a volume reporting the findings of a number of recent studies, they pointed out that all species of monkeys and apes live in social groups, and then posed the question of why this should be so. They concluded that the chief reason is that *the societal mode of organization enhances opportunities for learning*. As they observed, "The group is the locus of knowledge and experience far exceeding that of the individual member. It is in the group that experience is pooled."[12] The same

---

[11] See Sherwood L. Washburn and David A. Hamburg, "The Implications of Primate Research," in Irven DeVore (ed.), *Primate Behavior: Field Studies of Monkeys and Apes* (New York: Holt, 1965), p. 612.

[12] *Ibid.*, p. 613.

answer could be given in the case of human societies, where, as we shall note in the next section, the opportunities for learning are vastly greater than in other anthropoid societies.

Learning may be defined as *that process which manifests itself by changes in behavior (usually adaptive in nature) based on prior experience.*[13] As this definition indicates, learning is not an end in itself. Rather it is a tool that aids men and animals in the attainment of their goals. This is what makes it so important.

The ability to learn enables an organism (or a species) to adapt more quickly to diverse or changing circumstances. Instinct (or what we, today, might call the genetic programming of behavioral responses or response sets) is the only alternative to learning that nature has devised. But because instincts are genetically determined, the process of adaptation is far slower and the outcome, therefore, far less certain.

To contrast learning and instinct in this way may seem to suggest that learned behavior is independent of genetics. However, such is not the case. Though learned behavior is not genetically programmed, the ability to learn has a definite genetic basis. As a consequence, some species have a highly developed capacity for learning, while others have little or none.

The marked capacity for learning evident in mammals is clearly linked with certain genetic peculiarities of this class of animals. For example, it is definitely linked with the advanced development of the brain and central nervous system. Less obvious, but no less important, is the prolonged physical immaturity of mammalian offspring that necessitates prolonged contact between them and adults and greatly increases their opportunities for learning. Thus, even learned behavior has a genetic basis.

The importance of this becomes evident when we compare the various species of mammals. Here we find a pattern indicating a definite evolutionary progression. Among the various orders, the primates are distinctive both genetically and be-haviorally. Genetically, they are remarkable in the ways we noted previously. Behaviorally, they are remarkable for the strong social bonds that unite them, as well as for their singular dependence on learned patterns of behavior. For example, studies have shown that among many species of primates, even the sex act must be learned. Both genetically and behaviorally, the differences separating the primates and other mammals are most pronounced in the case of the anthropoids, that part of the primate order which includes man. From this we can only conclude that man belongs to a part of the animal world whose very survival depends on a complex combination of the societal mode of existence and learned forms of behavior.

The specialties

We do not need the tools of modern science to show us that man is different. We need only look around us. Men build skyscrapers, compose symphonies, set off

---

[13] Thorpe, *op. cit.*, p. 55. Occasionally learning can be maladaptive for the individual, as in the case of the person who learns to rely on patent medicines or medical quacks rather than on competent prac-titioners, but this is the exception not the rule.

atomic explosions, philosophize and moralize, travel in outer space, and do a thousand other things that no other animal can do. Such patterns of behavior suggest that genetically man differs profoundly from all other forms of life, since modern biology has shown that usually behavior and genetics are closely linked. The surprising fact is, however, that man is not nearly as distinctive genetically as his behavior suggests. The physical differences that separate him from the other anthropoids are minor compared to the differences separating these anthropoids from most other animals. *Behaviorally*, however, the picture is reversed: apes and monkeys have far more in common with most other animals than with man. It looks as though some critical threshold was crossed when man evolved, with only a few, modest genetic changes opening the way to a major behavioral breakthrough.[14]

The explanation for this curious development lies in man's immense capacity for learning—a capacity far exceeding that of even his closest kin among the anthropoids. This has made it possible for man to develop a unique mode of adaptation to his environment, one that social scientists refer to as *cultural*. Because this cultural mode of adaptation is such a crucial feature of human life, it is important to understand it clearly. The problem is complicated because the word "culture" has been used in a number of different ways. In popular usage, for example, it has long referred to the refinement of taste and manners that results from special training. In the social sciences, however, the term has a much broader meaning.

The classic definition for social scientists was formulated by the pioneer anthropologist E. B. Tylor at the end of the last century. He defined culture as "that complex whole which includes knowledge, belief, art, morals, law, custom, and any other capabilities and habits acquired by man as a member of society."[15] More recently, others have sought to sharpen the definition to take account of our modern understanding of the basic difference that sets man apart from the rest of the animal world. To this end, one contemporary anthropologist defined culture as "an organization of phenomena—acts (patterns of behavior), objects (tools; things made with tools), ideas (belief, knowledge), and sentiments (attitudes, 'values')—*that is dependent upon the use of symbols*."[16] The great virtue of this definition is that it links the concept "culture" to the concept "symbols."

For our purposes, we can simplify and clarify the definition of culture even further. Everything essential is present if we define culture simply as *mankind's symbol systems and all the aspects of human life dependent on it*.[17] This raises the question of what is meant by "symbols" and "symbol systems," which brings us

---

[14] For a more detailed discussion of this point, see A. L. Kroeber, *Anthropology*, rev. ed. (New York: Harcourt, Brace, 1948), chap. 2, especially pp. 70–71.

[15] E. B. Tylor, *Primitive Culture* (New York: Holt, 1889).

[16] Leslie White, *The Science of Culture* (New York: Grove Press, 1949), pp. 139–140. Emphasis added.

[17] Not only is this definition brief and therefore easy to remember, but also it makes clear that symbols themselves are a part of culture.

directly to the basis of the breakthrough that sets man apart from all other living things.[18] All mammals are able to communicate with others of their species, but except for man, they are limited to the use of *signals*. Man, however, uses symbols as well as signals.

Both symbols and signals are *vehicles of the transmission of information*. But there is one important difference. The relationship between a signal and its meaning is wholly or largely fixed from the genetic standpoint (i.e., it is a genetically determined response to a particular stimulus). The relationship between a symbol and its meaning, by contrast, is not fixed in this way.

A classic example of a signal is the cry of pain uttered by an injured animal. This cry is largely an involuntary response, and within a single species it is not subject to much variation except in intensity. A member of the group responds instinctively to this sound, or else learns through observation and experience to associate it with the moods and actions of his fellows. He then adjusts his behavior accordingly. Hence, though they lack variety and flexibility, signals are extremely useful in ordering social relations within a group.

Not all signals are of such a primitive nature. Anticipatory signals illustrate the ability of certain animals to use signals to anticipate a sequence of events. For example, if one deer in a herd is frightened by an unexpected sound, it is likely to bolt, and this action normally warns others to do the same. Thus, by its action the first animal transmits vital information and saves its fellows from potential harm.

This example illustrates several important characteristics of signals. First, they are not merely responses to experiences, but may actually anticipate them. Animals can learn to associate experiences and, by means of signals, communicate essential information. Second signals are not always vocal in character; in fact, in the animal world most are not. Body movements and glandular secretions are both common methods of signaling, and recent research shows that signaling often involves a combination of several methods. Third, signaling is often involuntary and not necessarily intended to be a method of communication. The animal that bolts when frightened by an unexpected sound may be concerned only with its own safety, but its action serves as a warning to other, less attentive, members of the group. Finally, the example illustrates the relatively inflexible character of signals. Though the bolting action of the animal is sometimes a learned response, the range of his possible responses to sudden fright, or any other stimulus, is apparently determined by his genetic heritage and is severely limited.

Symbols, by contrast, are not limited in this way. Because they are not determined genetically, they can easily be modified. We see abundant evidence of this in the history of every language, wherein countless symbols have changed while their meanings remained unchanged, and vice versa. Hundreds of examples of the former can be found in the unrevised version of Chaucer's *Canterbury Tales* or the

---

[18] For a more extended discussion of this subject, see White, *op. cit.*, pp. 22–39.

King James Version of the Bible. Examples of the latter abound in the kaleidoscopic world of slang, the very essence of which is the modification of the meaning of traditional symbols.

The genetic independence of symbols can be illustrated in yet another way. When we examine the symbols we currently use, we find that many have a variety of unrelated meanings. For example, consider the sound we designate in our written language by the letter *c*. This single sound may refer to the third letter of the alphabet, the act of perceiving, the jurisdiction of a bishop, or a large body of water. To Spanish-speaking people, the sound means "yes"; to French-speaking people it means "yes," "if," "whether," or "so." Obviously there is no logical connection between these varied meanings, nor is there any genetically determined connection between the meanings and the sound. All of them are simply arbitrary usages that the members of certain societies have adopted.

Because they are not genetically determined, as signals are, symbols can be combined and recombined indefinitely to form *symbol systems* of fantastic complexity, subtlety, and flexibility. As a consequence, *there are no intrinsic limits to the amount or variety of information they can handle.* The only limits are those set by their users' physical limitations (e.g., the number, type, and accuracy of their senses, and the efficiency and capacity of their brains and nervous systems). With the aid of a symbol system, even these limitations can be partly overcome. For example, the substitution of written records for human memory greatly increased man's capacity for storing information. Similarly, the invention of tools that supplement man's senses (e.g., microscopes and telephones) greatly increased his capacity for acquiring and transmitting information.

In technologically advanced societies today, the volume of information transmitted from generation to generation has become so great that no single individual can master it. Thus, while individual men and women are the bearers of culture, a culture in its totality is the property of a society.

Basic analogue To speak of symbol systems as mechanisms for the handling of information is to point the way to one of the most important relationships in the biological world: *symbol systems are the functional analogues of genetic systems.* Both are mechanisms that facilitate the behavioral adaptation of populations to their environment through the acquisition, storage, transmission, and use of relevant information.[19] Genetic systems accomplish this by the slow, and always costly (in

---

[19] Modern studies of genetics, especially studies of deoxyribonucleic acid (DNA) and ribonucleic acid (RNA), have done much to clarify the information-handling function of genetic systems. For a brief summary of this work, see Emerson, *op. cit.*, pp. 56–58. For a discussion of this subject among a group of scientists, see Sol Tax and Charles Callender (eds.), *Evolution After Darwin: The University of Chicago Centennial* (Chicago: University of Chicago Press, 1960), vol. III, pp. 79–86. Note that the only objection to the idea that genetic systems serve an information-handling function comes from Hermann Muller, and he objects solely on the grounds of the association of the word "information" with the idea of *conscious* knowledge. In an era of computers, the risk of confusion because of this traditional connotation should be minimal.

Fig. 1/3 Symbol systems are the functional analogue of genetic systems. Both are mechanisms that facilitate the behavioral adaptation of populations to their environment through the acquisition, storage, transmission, and use of relevant information. The figure on the right is a model of the structure of the DNA molecule, the famous double helix

terms of lives), method of *organic evolution;* symbol systems accomplish the same thing by the swifter, and usually less costly, method of *sociocultural evolution.* For the first time in evolutionary history, major behavioral changes can occur without corresponding genetic and organic changes. Only the forms of social organization and the culture need change.

Through the creation of symbol systems, our prehistoric forefathers laid the foundation for a major evolutionary breakthrough—a breakthrough that has enabled their descendants to modify their behavior and achieve progressively more efficient adaptations to their environment without recourse to organic evolution. *The nature and consequences of this development will be our primary concern in this volume.*

A caution Although we speak of symbol systems as mechanisms for the mobilization of information, we must be careful not to think of culture merely as a tool that men manipulate in a calculating, rational way to achieve their goals. This is a dangerous half-truth. In certain respects, culture has the qualities of Frankenstein's monster—that is, once it has been brought into being, it possesses a life of its own and often forces its creators to respond to its demands. To a considerable degree, the members of a society become prisoners in the cultural system they have created.

There are many reasons for this, but the most important is that cultures outlive their creators. Each of us is born into a society with an established culture, and it is only through the mastery of this culture that we are able to satisfy our needs and desires. But in the process of mastering the culture, the culture tends to master us and make us its creatures. To a great degree, it even defines our goals in life and shapes the patterns of our thought.

The problem is further compounded because men often find it difficult, even painful, to unlearn what they have once learned. New information can threaten an individual's entire view of life and it may be easier for him to ignore it than to restructure his thinking. This problem is especially acute among older people; yet they are the very ones who occupy most of the seats of power in society. Hence elements of culture often persist long after the conditions that gave rise to them have ceased to exist.

These are matters to which we will return in Chapter 4. For the present, suffice it to say that if culture is to be compared to a tool—and this is legitimate—it is wise not to compare it to a hammer or saw or any other simple tool that can be used and set aside as men wish. Rather, we should compare it to an artificial kidney or to some other marvel of modern medical technology that is, for those who need it, a vital part of the life process—a tool, yes, but a tool that cannot be set aside or manipulated at will to suit the passing whims of its beneficiaries.

Excursus: A brief history of sociology

Before going further in our analysis of human societies, it may be well to pause and take a look at sociology itself—its origins and history, its recent trends and current status. This brief excursus will also provide an opportunity to consider the relationship between sociology and the various other social sciences.

Though sociology is a relatively recent addition to the scholarly world, its roots extend at least as far into the past as the writings of Plato and Aristotle. In their day, philosophers were already speculating about their own societies, comparing one with another and trying to understand the forces which shaped them.

Without denying the contributions of these early scholars, sociologists usually think of their discipline as beginning—at least in its modern form—in the middle decades of the last century. The key development at that time was the emergence of the idea that the basic principles of science, as developed in the physical and biological sciences, could be applied to the study of human societies. This idea and its implementation marked the transition from traditional social philosophy to modern sociology.

Credit for the founding of modern sociology is usually given to a French scholar, Auguste Comte (1798–1857). As early as the 1830s, Comte argued persuasively for the formation of a new science which he named "sociology." The basic task of the field, as he envisioned it, would be to develop a scientific body of knowledge about human societies, consisting of (1) a theory of social order (i.e., a theory to explain the cohesion of societies), and (2) a theory of societal progress or evolution.

The work which Comte began was continued by

Fig. 1/4 Auguste Comte (1798–1857), founder of modern sociology

many others, of whom the most important was the famous English scholar Herbert Spencer (1820–1903). Through his writings, Spencer brought the new discipline to the attention of the educated classes in the English-speaking world. Like Comte, Spencer was profoundly interested in societal evolution, believing it to be closely linked with organic evolution, a subject that had become of great interest because of Darwin's revolutionary work.

Ironically, though the origins of sociology were in Europe, the new discipline found more rapid acceptance in the United States. Professorships were established at a number of leading American universities even before the turn of the century. By the early decades of the present century, separate departments of sociology were established in many institutions. During the period between the two world wars, sociology became predominantly an American enterprise, partly because of attacks on the field by totali-

tarian governments in Europe and partly because of the greater resistance to change and innovation by the faculties of European universities.

Following World War I, sociology underwent a number of important changes. Under American leadership the discipline became increasingly concerned with contemporary society, and even more narrowly, with contemporary American society. Interest in other societies declined, as did interest in the historical dimension of human life. To a large extent these changes reflected the desire of a new generation of sociologists to make the discipline more scientific. The result was a greatly heightened interest in empirical research, especially studies of local communities and their problems—crime, poverty, divorce, juvenile delinquency, illegitimacy, prostitution, the adjustment problems of immigrants, and so forth.

With this shift in the focus of interest, sociologists

gradually abandoned the earlier evolutionary approach. In part, this was because of criticisms leveled against it, but primarily it was because the older approach seemed irrelevant to the concerns of the newer generation. As a result, sociologists were forced to find a substitute for evolutionary theory—some other theoretical approach that could organize the growing, but diffuse, body of sociological knowledge. By the late 1930s, this was found in what came to be known as the *structural-functional* approach.

The structural-functional approach to the study of human societies is, in effect, the sociological counterpart of the anatomical and physiological approaches in biology. Like anatomists, structural-functionalists are concerned with the identification and labeling of the different parts of the things they study and with the structural relations among these parts (e.g., the structural patterns formed within business organizations, families, etc.). Like physiologists, they are interested in the functions each of the parts performs. For example, just as physiologists are concerned with the functions of organs, such as the liver, heart, and spleen, structural-functionalists are interested in the functions of institutions, such as the family, and of moral rules, such as the taboo against incest.

Since World War II, sociology has enjoyed substantial growth not only in the United States, but in Europe, Japan, and Canada as well.[20] In other parts of the world, too, it has begun to take root. One significant development has been the changing attitude of Communist authorities in Eastern Europe. During the Stalin era and for some time thereafter, sociology was regarded as subversive and was forbidden in most Communist nations. Today, however, restrictions are being removed and interest in the subject is growing.[21] The development of sociology in other countries has helped greatly to reduce the unhealthy concentration

of the discipline in the United States that characterized the decades of the 1930s and 1940s.

Another notable development has been the movement of sociology beyond the confines of the academic community. Prior to the 1940s, sociologists were employed almost entirely by universities and colleges. Beginning in World War II and continuing to the present, there has been a steadily rising demand for their services by government, industry, and other kinds of organizations.

Intellectually, too, sociology has made substantial progress. In this respect, two of the most important developments have been the increasing use of quantitative techniques and the revival of evolutionary theory. The first of these was a natural outgrowth of the efforts of sociologists to achieve greater precision in their descriptions of social phenomena and greater rigor in their analyses. This trend was given an enormous boost by the invention of computers, which enable researchers to handle large volumes of data and carry out complex statistical analyses that otherwise would be impossible or prohibitively slow and costly.

The more surprising of the newer trends has been the revival of interest in evolutionary theory. Thirty years ago, evolutionary theory seemed as dead as the dodo. Even a decade ago, the structural-functional approach seemed solidly entrenched as the dominant theoretical orientation. Today, however, it is definitely on the decline. Criticism of this approach increases with each passing year, and even some of those who were leading spokesmen for it only a few years ago are now turning to evolutionary theory.[22]

The chief reason for this shift has been a growing recognition that the structural-functional approach does not provide an adequate basis for understanding two crucial aspects of human life—*change* and *conflict*. Though these have been important features of human

---

[20] See, for example, Charles Modge, "From Small Beginnings," *The Times Literary Supplement*, April 4, 1968, pp. 337ff., on the recent growth of sociology in England.

[21] See, for example, Alex Simirenko (ed.), *Soviet Sociology* (Chicago: Quadrangle, 1966), especially pp. 19–35, on the Soviet Union.

[22] See especially Talcott Parsons, "Evolutionary Universals in Society," *American Sociological Review*, 29 (1964), pp. 339–357, or *Societies: Evolutionary and Comparative Perspectives* (Englewood Cliffs, N.J.: Prentice-Hall, 1966).

life in most eras, they have never been more important than in our own day. Events in recent years—the civil rights struggle, the war in Vietnam, the exploration of space, and the continuing technological revolution—have all contributed to the growing dissatisfaction with the structural-functional approach.

The new approach might best be described as the *ecological-evolutionary* approach. As its name suggests, it too has links with two of the basic approaches in the biological sciences. Since this is the approach we shall use in this volume, its nature will become evident in later chapters. Suffice it to say here that this approach shares with the evolutionary approach in biology an intense interest in the processes of change—especially basic, long-term, developmental, and adaptive change—and in the related processes of competition and conflict. With the ecological approach in biology, it shares an interest in the ties of interdependence within and between populations and in the relations between populations and their environments.

Despite their criticisms of the older approach, proponents of the ecological-evolutionary approach do not ignore structural and functional relations within societies. On the contrary, they regard them as very important. However, the identification and description of these relations is no longer the sole or primary concern in sociological analysis. Rather, structural and functional relations are studied within the larger and more inclusive framework provided by the ecological and evolutionary perspectives. Thus, we could legitimately label our approach *structural-functional-ecological-evolutionary*, since it incorporates all the essential elements of both. For the sake of convenience, however, it is usually referred to simply as the *evolutionary* approach, and this is the practice we will follow most of the time.

Sociology and the other social sciences

The study of human societies has never been exclusively a sociological concern. All the social sciences have been involved in one way or another. Most of the others, however, have focused on some particular aspect of the subject. Economics and political science limit themselves to a single institutional area. Human geography studies the impact of the physical and biotic environments on societies. Social psychology is concerned with the impact of social organization on the behavior and personality of individuals.

Only sociology and anthropology have been concerned with human societies per se. That is to say, only these two disciplines have interested themselves in the full range of social phenomena, from the family to the nation, and from technology to religion. And only these two disciplines have sought to understand societies as entities in their own right.

In matters of research, there has been a fairly well established division of labor between these two fields. Sociologists have, for the most part, studied modern industrial societies; anthropologists have concentrated on primitive preliterate societies of both the past and present. This division of labor has made good sense, since the skills needed to study a remote tribe in the mountains of New Guinea are very different from those needed to study a modern industrial society such as our own.

From the standpoint of teaching and the development of theory, however, such a division is far less satisfactory. There are many problems that can be understood only if one takes into account the findings of both disciplines. This is especially true of long-term, evolutionary processes: to ignore the findings of either discipline is likely to result in incomplete or biased interpretations and conclusions. As a consequence, there has been a long tradition of intellectual "borrowing" between sociology and anthropology, and this volume follows in that tradition.

With the revival of evolutionary theory,[23] scholars in these fields have come to recognize that both disciplines were neglecting agrarian societies—those societies that occupy the middle range in the evolutionary scale between primitive preliterate societies and modern industrial societies. In recent years, there-

---

[23] The revival of interest in evolutionary theory is even more pronounced in anthropology than in sociology. See, for example, the work of Leslie White, Walter Goldschmidt, Elman Service, Marshall Sahlins, Robert Carneiro, and Marvin Harris.

fore, both sociologists and anthropologists have begun research in southeast Asia, the middle East, and Latin America.

The growing concern for agrarian societies has also led to increased contact between sociologists and historians. Since history is the study of written records of the past, historians have been the experts on agrarian societies of earlier centuries. Much of the older work by historians, with its heavy emphasis on the names and dates of famous men and events, was of limited value for the student of human societies. But that discipline has been changing too, and historians today are increasingly concerned with the basic social patterns and processes that underlie the more dramatic but usually less significant events on which their predecessors focused. As a result, the relationship between history and sociology is growing in importance.

This trend toward interdisciplinary cooperation is evident today in all the social sciences, and even beyond. Scholars are coming to recognize that no discipline is sufficient unto itself. To the degree that any field cuts itself off from the others, it impoverishes itself intellectually. Conversely, to the degree that it enters into communication with other disciplines, it enriches itself and them. This is especially true of such fields as sociology and anthropology, which are concerned with all aspects of the life of human societies. Human societies are such fantastically complex phenomena that we need to draw on the resources of every discipline whose work sheds light on the subject. This is why the present volume draws as heavily as it does on research and theory outside sociology. Though this may offend a few disciplinary purists, it is the only responsible course for those whose goal is the understanding of human societies.

*T*he Structure and Functioning of Human Societies

Chapter 2

Human societies are basically adaptive mechanisms. They are, in other words, instruments which men use to satisfy their needs. This might well be called the first principle of sociology, for it is the foundation on which all sociological analysis builds.

To understand human societies, therefore, we must understand men's needs, especially those that move them to act in social ways (i.e., that bring them into relations with others). Some of these needs are obvious, some are not; but all of them contribute in one way or another to the structure, functioning, and evolution of human societies. In the present chapter, our goal is to see how human needs, and men's efforts to satisfy them, influence the *structure* and *functioning* of human societies. In the next chapter, we shall move on to the more complex problems of societal evolution and change.

HUMAN NEEDS AND HUMAN NATURE

As we saw in Chapter 1, man stands in a threefold relation to the biotic world. Some of his attributes he shares with all living things, others he shares with his nearer kin in the animal world, still others are uniquely his own. The same is true of man's *needs*. Some are common to all living things, some man shares with a part of the animal kingdom, and some he shares with no other living creature. Each of these needs influences the structure and functioning of human societies. Or we can turn this around and say: the way societies are structured and the way they function are the result of men's efforts to satisfy these needs.

27

Elemental individual needs

Whatever else men may be, they are animal organisms that depend for their survival on the continuing satisfaction of certain basic biological needs. These include the need for light, warmth, oxygen, food, moisture, sleep, and physical safety (i.e., protection against other men, animals, germs, and physical and chemical processes of various kinds). In addition, most humans have a need for sexual gratification, but their survival *as individuals* does not depend on its satisfaction. Some of these needs can be satisfied by individuals with little or no effort, and acting entirely on their own. Light and oxygen, for example, are readily available to everyone. With respect to these needs, we live in a Garden of Eden.

The satisfaction of other needs, however, requires effort on our part, and the outcome is much less certain. Even when men make a vigorous effort, there is no guarantee that they can satisfy these needs. For example, there is only a finite quantity of food available at any given time, and the human population, with its infinite capacity for growth, can easily become larger than the current food supply can sustain. When this happens, and it often has, some men's needs go unsatisfied and they die.

A comparable situation exists with respect to men's need for safety. Again, there is no guarantee that their efforts will be successful. There are many hostile forces which are capable of destroying men, no matter how clever or vigorous they may be.

Because these two needs have been so difficult to satisfy, they have always loomed large in human life. The culture of every society contains a wealth of information relevant to the problems of food production and safety, and many man-hours are invariably spent trying to provide for these needs. More than that, these needs give rise to cooperative activities and thereby lay the foundation for societal organization. In the process, however, they generate a host of derivative needs which become as compelling and demanding as any of our elemental, individual needs.

Derivative social needs

It is one of the great ironies of human life, yet also one of its great fascinations and challenges, that in solving one set of problems we so often create others. This has clearly been true in the case of man's reliance on the societal mode of organization. From one standpoint, societal life can be viewed as a means of satisfying certain basic needs. From another standpoint, however, it looms as one of the chief *sources* of mankind's problems and needs. Many of our needs arise only because we live in societies. If Homo sapiens were a solitary species like the mud dauber, men would have far fewer problems and far fewer needs. For societies, once they are formed, develop needs and problems of their own. Certain conditions must be met if the

Fig. 2/1   Derivative social needs

Functional requisites of societies:

a system of communication

a system of production

a system of distribution

a system of defense

a system of member replacement

a system of social control

organization is to survive *as an organization*.[1] Sociologists usually refer to these as the *functional requisites* of societies.[2]

The first functional requisite of every society is *a system of communication.* This is the *sine qua non* of every social organization, whether animal or human. The members must be able to exchange relevant information. In subhuman societies, communication systems employ signals;[3] in human societies, a mixture of signals and symbols is used. The more complex a society, the more important is the problem of communication, and the more complex the system of communication must be.

The second requisite of societies is *a system of production.* If societies are to survive, they must develop techniques to provide their members with the material necessities of life. Though men satisfy some of these needs individually, production is largely a social process in species that have adopted the societal mode of exist-ence. Among insects and other lower animals, productive techniques are, for the most part, genetically determined, but among man and other mammalian species, these techniques are usually behaviors which the individual learns through partici-pation in the group. Sometimes these learned behaviors can be applied by the individual working alone, but more often a cooperative effort is required, as in the case of a pack of wolves running down a deer or a group of men building an automobile.

The third requisite of societies is *a system of distribution.* Whatever is produced must be gotten into the hands of those who will consume it. Producers and con-sumers are never entirely the same in any society, and in complex societies (i.e.,

---

[1] The survival of its individual members is no guarantee that an organization will survive. If the members of a society are scattered and their social ties broken, the group has been destroyed though every in-dividual survives.

[2] See, for example, D. F. Aberle et al., "The Functional Prerequisites of a Society," *Ethics*, 60 (1950), pp. 100–111; or Talcott Parsons, *The Social System* (Glencoe, Ill.: Free Press, 1951), pp. 26–36.

[3] See, for example, the fascinating work of Karl von Frisch on communication systems among bees, in *Bees: Their Vision, Chemical Senses, and Language* (Ithaca, N.Y.: Cornell, 1950), or "Dialects in the Language of Bees," *Scientific American* (August, 1962), pp. 3–7.

those with considerable specialization in production) there is little overlap between the producers and consumers of a given product. At the very least, producers must transfer a portion of what they produce to children and others who are unable to provide for themselves. Where there is specialization, there must be mechanisms of exchange among producers themselves. These must provide not only for the technical problems of moving goods and services about, but also for the potentially explosive social problem of determining who gets how much of what.

The fourth requisite of societies is *a system of defense.* Every society must develop techniques to protect its members, individually and collectively, against hostile forces. No society is completely successful in this: sooner or later, all of us die. What is necessary for a society's survival is simply that enough of its members live long enough, and in good enough health, for the work of the society to be carried on and the next generation raised to adulthood. As this implies, systems of defense include both military and medical components.

Since death is the eventual fate of every member of society, the fifth requisite of societies is *a system of member-replacement.* This need is basically satisfied by the mechanism of biological reproduction. In some societies, it is supplemented by voluntary immigration or by the involuntary incorporation of captives taken in war or slaves purchased in international markets.

Sixth, and finally, societies require *a system of social control.* This need stems from the fact that, though they live in societies, men have few if any social instincts. They have, however, a capacity for *learning* to conduct themselves in socially responsible ways. Systems of social control develop as a "mechanism" for transforming this potential into a reality. Analytically, systems of social control can be divided into two parts. First, there must be a system of rules and values to define right conduct and a system of beliefs to provide a rationale for these rules and values. Second, there must be a system of rewards and punishments to motivate individuals to act in socially approved ways. As sociologists have long noted, no system of social control can operate effectively if sanctions are imposed upon an individual only by others. To a large degree, each individual must assume responsibility for policing his own conduct. This is achieved through *socialization,* a complex social-psychological process that begins at the moment of birth. Its objective is to so mold the individual that he will take the standards and beliefs of his society for his own and govern his behavior accordingly. Though no society is ever completely successful in this, every group must approximate this goal to a minimum degree. The only alternative is anarchy and the speedy dissolution of the society as a viable social system. Because of its great importance, we shall examine the socialization process in more detail later (see pp. 74–76).

Derivative individual needs

In one sense, man's individual needs are few. We named them earlier: light, warmth, oxygen, food, moisture, sleep, and safety. If these needs are met, the individual can survive. But if *only* these needs are met, the individual will not become a human being in the full sense of the term. He will remain a helpless, animal-like creature with few of the skills or qualities of personality we normally associate with humans. This has been well documented in several cases. In one instance, an illegitimate child and her deaf-mute mother were isolated in a dark room for the first six and a half years of the child's life.[4] When they were finally discovered by authorities, the child was unable to speak and could not walk properly; when confronted with strangers, her behavior "was almost that of a wild animal, manifesting much fear and hostility." At first, it was thought the child was feebleminded, but with intensive training, and through association with normal people, she became a completely normal child within a two-year period.

Cases like this serve as reminders that *the qualities that are most distinctively human emerge only as a result of our association with others.* The potential is there in every genetically normal individual; but the potential is *realized* only when the individual shares in the life of society—especially in the crucial early years of life. This is a fact we easily overlook, since few of us ever meet individuals who have been cut off from society in this way.

Involvement in the life of society and exposure to the socialization process equip the individual with the skills that make it possible for him, in his adult years, to satisfy his elemental needs—at least to the degree that the environment permits. At the same time, however, it creates, or activates, in him a whole series of further needs. He becomes a person who is no longer content merely to eat and sleep and have his basic needs satisfied. He is now concerned about such things as his relations with others—whether they like him, whether they respect him, whether they love him, and whether they will do what he wants them to. In other words, he develops the need for affection, for respect, for love, and for power. Not all individuals develop these needs to the same degree. For a variety of reasons which we are only beginning to understand, their intensity varies considerably from one person to the next, but most of us develop all of them to some degree. When someone does not have these needs, it is usually because of deficiencies in his early socialization experience or because of later experiences which destroyed all hope of their fulfillment.

Many efforts have been made to catalog men's various needs, but none has been completely satisfactory. Though the following list is incomplete, it suggests the diversity of the needs which are generated by our involvement in society. Not all these needs are found in every society, and certainly not all are present in every individual, but all of them occur with considerable frequency:

The need for love and affection
The need for the respect of others

---

[4] See Kingsley Davis, "Extreme Social Isolation of a Child," *American Journal of Sociology,* 45 (1940), pp. 554–565, and "Final Note on a Case of Extreme Isolation," *ibid.,* 52 (1947), pp. 432–437.

The need for self-respect[5]

The need for power (either as a means of satisfying other needs or as an end in itself)

The need for material possessions and wealth (either as means or end)

The need for manual and mental skills

The need for the satisfaction of intellectual curiosity

The need for peace of mind

The need for salvation

The need for aesthetic satisfaction

The need for new experience and/or variability of experience

The need for creative opportunities

One could easily add to this list, but even in this form it serves as a reminder of the complexity of the human animal and of the magnitude of the problems human societies face as they strive to satisfy human needs.

The nature of human nature

Our primary concern in this chapter, as elsewhere in this volume, is with human societies. However, as we have seen, the study of human societies cannot be divorced from the study of human individuals—which brings us to the troublesome, but important, subject of human nature.

This concept has had a very checkered career in the history of social thought. Much of the difficulty stems from the uncritical use of the term in earlier times by many laymen and some social scientists, who equated human nature with the behavioral patterns of their own society or, perhaps, the Western world. If the people they knew regarded eating snails as repulsive and infanticide as reprehensible, they assumed that such reactions were simply expressions of "human nature."

Most social scientists quickly came to realize that such attitudes are not shared by people in all societies, and therefore cannot be the expression of a universal human nature. Rather, they are reflections of the culture of particular societies. Misgivings about the usefulness of the concept were reinforced as anthropological studies showed how variable mankind's behavior patterns actually are. Under the influence of a school of anthropologists known as the "cultural relativists," it became fashionable to argue that *all* patterns of human behavior are socially determined.[6] The newborn infant was often likened to a completely blank slate awaiting the markings of his society.

This view of man was highly attractive to many people for ideological reasons. If there is no such thing as human nature, mankind is infinitely malleable. This means

---

[5] See especially the work of Charles Horton Cooley and George Herbert Mead on this important subject: Cooley's *Human Nature and the Social Order* (New York: Scribner, 1922); and Mead's *Mind, Self and Society* (Chicago: University of Chicago Press, 1934).

[6] See especially Ruth Benedict, *Patterns of Culture* (Boston: Houghton Mifflin, 1934), a volume which did much to popularize cultural relativism.

that all of man's nasty practices, such as war, crime, exploitation, and cruelty, can be eliminated if only the powers of societies are used correctly. With the right kind of schools, the right kind of government, or the right kind of economy, men could create a new social order in which peace and justice would prevail forever.

In recent years, however, a reaction has set in against this optimistic, relativistic view of man. Events of the twentieth century have cast grave doubts on theories that proclaim the extreme malleability and perfectibility of man. Despite many vigorous efforts to eliminate economic injustice, political tyranny, and war, these evils all remain a part of the human scene.

The findings of psychology and the biological sciencies reinforce the lessons of history. Modern psychology has shown that the newborn infant is anything but a blank slate. He comes equipped with imperious needs and a determination to satisfy them without regard to the cost to others.[7] If, later, he learns to be more considerate of those around him, it is not because he has lost interest in satisfying his own needs. Nor has he become an altruist who loves others as much as he loves himself. Rather, he has learned that maximal satisfaction of his own needs depends on his willingness to take the needs of others into account to some extent, and that enlightened self-interest is more rewarding than unenlightened self-interest.[8] In addition, he may also come to love a few people enough so that he is willing to sacrifice his own safety and happiness for theirs, but the number included in this circle tends to be extremely small.

In striving to satisfy their needs, humans seem to be governed by an "economizing principle." That is to say, they use as few of their resources as possible in the effort to satisfy any specific need. This is because few, if any, individuals have sufficient resources—time, money, energy, strength, etc.—to satisfy fully *all* their needs.[9] Economizing, therefore, is a necessary corollary of their desire to achieve maximal satisfaction.

The newer sciences of ethology and genetics help us understand the biological basis of these elements of human nature. Comparative studies of animal societies show that individuality tends to be suppressed in insect and other societies in which genetic mechanisms regulate the social life of the group. By contrast, individuality is

---

[7] See, for example, L. Z. Freedman and Anne Roe, "Evolution and Human Behavior," in Anne Roe and George Gaylord Simpson (eds.), *Behavior and Evolution* (New Haven, Conn.: Yale, 1958), pp. 455–479. See also Dennis Wrong, "The Oversocialized Conception of Man in Modern Sociology," *American Sociological Review*, 26 (1961), pp. 183–193.

[8] Elman Service makes a similar point when he speaks of the evolution of culture as "redirecting [man's] selfishness," rather than as overcoming or eliminating it. See *The Hunters* (Englewood Cliffs, N.J.: Prentice-Hall, 1966), p. 32. See also Gerhard Lenski, *Power and Privilege* (New York: McGraw-Hill, 1966), pp. 26–31, for a more detailed treatment of this subject.

[9] Not only are men's needs numerous, they also tend to expand: the more we have, the more we want. For discussions of this important point, see A. H. Maslow, *Motivation and Personality* (New York: Harper, 1954), especially chap. 5; Thorstein Veblen, *The Theory of the Leisure Class* (New York: Macmillan, 1899); or Lenski, *op. cit.*, p. 31.

fairly pronounced in mammalian societies, where social unity depends so much more on learned behavior. Hence, there is a fair degree of intragroup conflict in most mammalian societies, and human societies are no exception. The recent discovery of DNA, RNA, and the genetic code help us see more clearly the ways in which, and the degree to which, these patterns are rooted in the genetic heritage of different species.

Gradually a new view of human nature is emerging. It is now clear that the term cannot refer to most of the specifics of human behavior—how people dress, how they marry, what they eat, and the like. These are merely customs, socially determined and highly variable. When the term "human nature" is used today, it should be only with reference to basic behavioral tendencies rooted in our common genetic heritage. Specifically, this means (1) man's basic biological needs; (2) his inborn, genetically programmed motivation to satisfy them as fully and as economically as possible; (3) his genetically based dependence on sociocultural systems; and (4) his genetically based culture-building potential.

When we spell out the nature of human nature this way, we see the tension that is built into the very fabric of human life: man is, at one and the same time, a social animal and an individualistic, self-seeking animal. It is this, above all, that creates the uncertainties in human life, as well as the drama, and it is this which justifies the description of human societies as systems of "antagonistic cooperation."[10]

BASIC ELEMENTS OF SOCIOCULTURAL SYSTEMS

In seeking to satisfy their needs, men have created sociocultural systems of amazing complexity. One of the major tasks of sociological analysis, therefore, has been to identify and sort out the various constituent elements. A number of ways of doing this have been proposed, but none has yet gained general acceptance. We shall follow a slightly modified verson of a method of classification developed some years ago by Leslie White, a leading anthropologist.[11] This method has several virtues. First, it is simple—easy to understand and easy to remember. Second, it makes relations among the various elements clearer than most alternative methods. Finally, it is more useful than the alternatives in dealing with the important problems of societal change and evolution.

For purposes of analysis, sociocultural systems may be divided into four basic components:

Language   Technology   Social organization   Ideology

As we examine each of these, we shall see that they can be broken down into subcategories, and that some of these subcategories can be divided even further. All of

---

[10] William Graham Sumner, *Folkways* (New York: Mentor, 1960, first published 1906), p. 32.

[11] See Leslie White, *The Science of Culture* (New York: Grove Press, 1949), pp. 366ff.

these parts are extremely important in sociological analysis, for not only are they the basic building blocks of sociocultural systems, they are also *basic tools of sociological analysis.*

Language

Every human society requires a system of communication. To some extent, this need is met through the use of signals. For example, we make a face when we taste something bitter and we cry out when we are badly startled or hurt. But this is not enough. Even the simplest human society must have a language, that is, *a system of symbols capable of transmitting and storing information.*

The core of every language is a system of spoken sounds which have distinctive meanings attached to them. These meaningful sounds are combined in customary ways which constitute the grammar of the language. Languages differ not only in the sounds they use and the ways they combine them, but also in the way experience is divided into the units of meaning we call words. When we first begin to study foreign languages, we have the illusion that other languages must have an exact counterpart for every word or phrase in our own. But we soon learn otherwise—some words have no exact counterpart in other languages. This can be a source of considerable confusion, as Americans and Russians discovered in talks between President Kennedy and Chairman Khrushchev some years ago.[12] At their meeting in Vienna, Kennedy repeatedly told Khrushchev that he should not *miscalculate* the will and intentions of the American people. Every time this word was translated into Russian, Khrushchev flushed angrily. Kennedy learned later that there is no true Russian equivalent of "miscalculate" and that the translator had fallen back on a Russian expression meaning "inability to count." Thus it seemed to Khrushchev that Kennedy was implying he was too stupid to add two and two! Similarly, Khrushchev used a colloquial Russian expression to state his conviction that the Soviet system would outlast the American. When translated literally, he was quoted as saying, "We will bury you," which in English, where there is no comparable colloquial expression, suggested a deadly threat.

Languages, like other parts of culture, are subject to change. Sounds acquire new meanings, usually by a process of association with traditional meanings. For example, the word "tap" originally meant "something cut out."[13] Later, it came to mean a plug that was cut out of a piece of wood and used to stop up a hole. In time, the word was applied to the stoppers used to control the flow of beer from a keg. Since these "taps" were knocked into place by a light blow, the word came, by extension, to be used with reference to any light blow. In England, the word has also

---

[12] Fred Blumenthal, "The Man in the Middle of the Peace Talks," *The Washington Post,* July 14, 1968.

[13] These examples are from Charlton Laird's popular and stimulating introduction to linguistics, *The Miracle of Language* (Greenwich, Conn.: Premier Books, 1953), pp. 54ff.

come to be applied to valves or faucets regulating the flow of any liquid (as in the kitchen sink or bath tub) and, since these taps are threaded on the inside, the instrument used to cut threads on the inside of pipes has also come to be called a tap.

Obviously, there is a large element of chance involved in this process, and it is very unlikely that the same pattern will repeat itself in its entirety in two societies. Even if exactly the same vocabulary is used by two different societies, as when a small group splits off from the parent group to settle in a new territory, it is certain to become differentiated as time goes by unless there is a *very* high degree of communication between their members.[14]

In addition to the spoken language, most societies have what might be called an *unspoken* language made up of conventional gestures and facial expressions. These should not be confused with signals, such as the facial grimace we make when we taste something bitter. That is a reflexive movement and biologically determined. Symbols, whether spoken or unspoken, are *socially* determined. A good example of an unspoken symbol is the shrug of the shoulders which Americans and some other peoples use to express indifference, uncertainty, or a lack of relevant information (the meaning intended is usually evident from the context or from other gestures).

Unspoken language is especially effective in communicating emotional reactions, which is one reason many people avoid the telephone when they have an emotionally sensitive message to deliver (e.g., in reporting a death). In a face-to-face situation they can communicate their own feelings more effectively and read the responses of the other person more clearly, because they have a combination of spoken symbols, unspoken symbols, and signals to guide them.

In technologically advanced societies, *writing* is yet a third form of language. The earliest function of the written language was to provide a durable record of contractual agreements between Mesopotamian temple authorities and their business associates.[15] Later, it was used to record royal decrees, sacred traditions, judicial decisions, military triumphs, and anything else too important to entrust to human memory or requiring an exact and durable record. Writing also provided a means of communication for people separated by barriers of distance and time, and was a way to reach large and scattered audiences. Finally, it came to be used as a medium of artistic expression and for the purposes of education and entertainment.

After its invention five thousand years ago, the written language gradually gained in use and importance relative to the spoken and unspoken languages. More recently, the trend has been reversed, as the telephone, radio, movies, television, and other electronic devices have largely overcome the ancient barriers of distance and time. This reversal will probably continue, but it is unlikely that the written language will be replaced, any more than it could replace spoken or un-

---

[14] Good examples of this are the differences which developed between the German and British Saxons and later between the British and Americans. Recent reports suggest similar differences are beginning to appear between East and West Germans.

[15] See V. Gordon Childe, *Man Makes Himself* (New York: Mentor, 1951), pp. 144ff.

spoken language. Each means of communication performs multiple functions, and no single method could prove superior for all of them.

When we first think about language, it seems to be merely a neutral and passive vehicle for exchanging information. But as political leaders, propagandists, advertising men, and others have long recognized, many words have powerful emotional connotations which make rational responses by their hearers difficult. Terms like "Fascist" and "Communist," for example, have powerful negative associations for most Americans. Therefore, to pin one of these labels on an individual is to discredit him in the eyes of many people who will respond unthinkingly to the emotional content of the symbol.

The emotional loading built into words is not always negative. On the contrary, many words have strong positive connotations, and these can also be used to manipulate emotions. Kinship terms which can be linked with organizations and individuals are particularly useful in stimulating positive responses. Several examples that come readily to mind are the use of the term "mother," as in "Mother Russia" or "Mother Church," or the use of the term "uncle," as applied to the late North Vietnamese leader, "Uncle Ho," or the mythical symbol of this country, "Uncle Sam."

A leading linguist of the last generation, Edward Sapir, went so far as to claim that the "real world," as men understand this term, "is to a large extent unconsciously built up on the language habits of the group," and that because of this, different societies live in different worlds, "not merely the same world with different labels attached."[16] Though most modern scholars would not go this far, they would almost universally agree that language is by no means the simple, neutral, passive vehicle for exchanging information which we so often imagine it to be.[17]

Technology

Technology refers to *the information, techniques, and tools by means of which men utilize the material resources of their environment to satisfy their varied needs and desires.* In effect, it is a kind of cultural extension of the organic equipment with which we are endowed: our hands, our eyes, our ears, our legs, and all the rest. Like language, it is an essential element in every sociocultural system; without it, most human needs could not be satisfied.

Each set of needs tends to give rise to its own distinctive technology. Thus, we can speak of the technology of production, the technology of defense, the technology of communication, and so forth. In modern, technologically advanced societies, the number and variety of technologies is extremely large; no single individual is able to master more than a small fraction of them.

---

[16] Edward Sapir, *Selected Writings in Language, Culture, and Personality,* ed. by David Mandelbaum (Berkeley: University of California Press, 1949), p. 162.

[17] See, for example, Dell Hymes, "Linguistics: The Field," *International Encyclopedia of the Social Sciences* (New York: Macmillan and Free Press, 1968), vol. 9, pp. 367–368; or William Bright, "Language: Language and Culture," *ibid.,* vol. 9, p. 22.

Sometimes it is helpful to speak of a single society as having a number of different technologies or technological systems. Usually, however, we speak of a society's technology in the singular. In part, this is a semantic convenience. But is is also the reflection of an underlying unity. To a considerable degree, the basic elements in the different technologies are shared. If, for example, a society has discovered the techniques of metallurgy in its effort to solve one problem, this information is likely to be applied before long to other problems. In short, there is a common core of techniques and tools in every society which are applied to a wide range of problems. The differences are in the more superficial area of application (e.g., the techniques of metallurgy are applied in slightly different ways to make such varied things as tractors, guns, musical instruments, etc.).

For some purposes, a distinction is drawn between technology and science. "Science" is used to refer to the search for general information about the natural world, without regard to its immediate practical uses. "Technology," in contrast, is used to refer to the pursuit of information for specific practical ends and to the application of scientific information to practical problems. This distinction can be quite important in sociological analyses of modern industrial societies, where the question often arises as to the relative proportion of the gross national product which should be invested in each of these competing forms of activity. For our present purposes, however, most of science can be subsumed under the more general heading of technology, to avoid the unnecessary multiplication of basic categories.

Of the four major components of sociocultural systems, technology is often thought of as the most prosaic, and it has interested social scientists less than any of the others.[18] As we shall see, however, its influence on societal evolution and change has been out of all proportion to the recognition accorded it until fairly recent times.

Social organization

Social organization is a rather general term that refers to *any structured system of relationships among people*. It may, for example, be used to refer to an entire society. It can also mean any of the various systems of relations found within a society, such as the relations among the members of a family or the members of a labor union. Finally, the term may mean the system of relations within some international or intersocietal organization, such as the Roman Catholic Church. In the present context, however, we are concerned only with the second meaning, that is, the systems *within* human societies.

Individuals   The two basic building blocks in every system of social organization are (1) the individuals who enter into social relations with one another and (2) the roles which they fill. Little need be said about the former except that the number of

---

[18] See, for example, Robert S. Merrill, "Technology: The Study of Technology," *ibid.*, vol. 15, p. 576.

individuals involved may be no more than two, as in families and cliques. At the other extreme, an organization may include millions of individuals, as in the case of large metropolitan communities, large religious groups, or large political parties.

Roles The concept "role," as the term suggests, has been borrowed from the theater. In sociology, as in the theater, it refers to *a position which can be filled by an individual, and to which distinctive behavioral expectations and requirements are attached.*[19] Thus, just as a person may play the role of Polonius in *Hamlet*, so he may "play" the role of doctor in his community, or elder in his church.

The key feature of a role is that it involves a set of behavioral expectations and requirements to which anyone who fills it must adapt. Roles vary greatly in the degree to which these obligations are spelled out. In some they are fuzzy and ill-defined, in others they are spelled out clearly and precisely. In the latter case, when the role is a position in a formal organization (e.g., a church or a governmental agency) and is held in special honor or entitles the incumbent to exercise authority, we speak of it as an *office*. Offices, in other words, are a special type of role.

To say that a role entails a set of behavioral expectations and requirements is not to deny the possibility that these can be changed by the individuals who occupy it. This takes effort, however, and incumbents generally find it easier to accept their obligations than to change them. A person's chances of changing them varies greatly, depending on the nature of the role. For example, if it is a role which he shares with thousands of others in a large organization (e.g., the role of student in a large state university), it will be much more difficult to change than if it is a unique role in a small and informal organization (e.g., the role of president in a small student club).

As an alternative to changing the obligations associated with a particular role, an individual sometimes has the option of switching to another. For example, if a college student finds the requirements of this role too difficult or too tedious, he can take a job or join the armed services. Some roles, however, cannot be changed legitimately, as in the case of age, sex, race, and ethnicity. These are known as *ascribed* roles; those which can be changed legitimately through the effort, or lack of effort, of the individual are *achieved* roles.

Roles serve many functions in societies, but four are of crucial importance. First, roles encourage specialization, which tends to increase the efficiency of human labor. Second, role specialization has an integrative effect: the more men divide up the tasks necessary to their survival and well-being, the more dependent they become on one another. Third, roles function as a mechanism of social control: they harness people's energies and guide them into the performance of tasks that the group as a whole, or its more powerful members, regard as necessary and desirable. Finally, roles function as a mechanism for the transmission of traditions from one generation

---

[19] For a more detailed discussion of the important subject of roles, see Ralph Turner, "Role: Sociological Aspects," *ibid.*, vol. 13, pp. 552–557.

to the next: individuals die, or leave the group for other reasons, but roles can persist indefinitely. Unlike humans, they are not mortal. The role of rabbi, for example, has existed for over 2,500 years, contributing immeasurably to the survival of the Jewish group and the preservation of its cultural heritage.

Groups In most societies, the members are divided into a variety of functional units we call groups.[20] These range from small family units and cliques to giant corporate entities of various kinds. In popular usage, the term "group" is sometimes applied rather indiscriminately to any aggregation of people, regardless of their other characteristics. Sociologists, however, limit the term to *those aggregations whose members (1) act together in a common effort to satisfy common, or complementary, needs; (2) share common behavioral expectations; and (3) have a sense of common identity.*

As this definition suggests, human aggregations differ in the *degree* to which they have the quality of "groupishness." While some aggregations clearly qualify as groups (e.g., the United Auto Workers Union) and others just as clearly do not (e.g., all the redheads in the United States), many are on the borderline (e.g., Americans of Irish descent). As this last example reminds us, the degree of "groupishness" of an aggregation is not permanently fixed. Aggregations may take on more of these qualities, or they may lose them: their members may come to work together more closely; develop new, stronger, and more generally shared behavioral expectations; and acquire a stronger sense of common identity; or just the opposite may occur, as in the case of the Irish-Americans.

Despite the exclusion of aggregations like redheads, the concept "group" still includes such a wide variety of organizations that it is often necessary to differentiate among them. The most familiar way is by their primary function. Thus, we differentiate between families, religious groups, educational groups, political groups, and so forth.

For many purposes, sociologists also differentiate among groups on the basis of their size and the nature of the social ties among their members. Small groups in which face-to-face relations of a fairly intimate and personal nature are maintained are known as *primary groups.* Larger, more impersonal groups are known as *secondary groups.* Primary groups are of two basic types, *family groups* and *cliques.* In other words, some are organized around ties of kinship, others around ties of friendship. The category of secondary groups also contains two basic types, associations and communities. An *association* is a formally organized secondary group which performs some relatively specialized function or set of functions. Political parties, churches, labor unions, corporations, and governmental agencies are familiar examples. *Communities,* by contrast, are less formally organized and perform a wider range of functions.

---

[20] There are a few exceptions—societies made up of a single family that lives autonomously—but they are rare. See Service, *op. cit.,* p. 7.

Fig. 2/2 Types of human groups

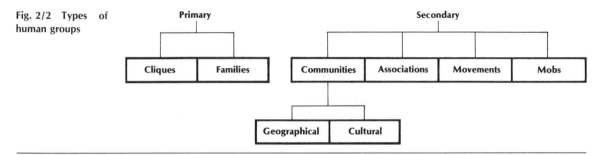

Basically, there are two types of communities, geographical and cultural. *Geographical communities* are those whose members are united primarily by ties of spatial proximity, such as neighborhoods, villages, towns, cities, and regions (e.g., the South). *Cultural communities* are those whose members are united by ties of a common cultural tradition, such as racial and ethnic groups. This category may include members of a religious group if they are closely bound together by ties of kinship and marriage and if the group has also developed a distinctive subculture of its own.[21]

As this last example indicates, associations may give rise to communities. And, it should be added, communities may give rise to associations. Black militant groups are good examples of the latter process. When either of these possibilities occur, membership in the community and the association overlap to a considerable degree. Usually, however, the community is larger, since its membership requirements are less stringent (often membership is automatic by virtue of birth).

In addition to associations and communities, there are several other types of secondary groups, the most important of which are *social and political movements.* These are loose-knit groups that try to change the existing social order in some way. If they are successful in developing a following, a more tightly organized association is usually formed and this becomes the nucleus of the movement. A good example of this was the rise and spread of the socialist movement in nineteenth-century Europe, with the eventual formation of socialist parties in most countries.

Mobs are another type of secondary group. Like movements, they tend to be hostile to the existing social or political order but, unlike movements, they are very short-lived, localized groups, often violent or threatening violence, and usually much less effective.

Statuses Up to this point in our discussion of social organization, we have considered only the "horizontal" dimension of societies, the functional differences between individuals, roles, and groups. There is a second dimension, however, a *vertical* dimension. Individuals, roles, and groups can be ranked in a variety of ways, such as by income, wealth, education, or other culturally defined standards. This is

[21] See, for example, Gerhard Lenski, *The Religious Factor* (Garden City, N.Y.: Doubleday, 1961), pp. 17–19 and 301–302.

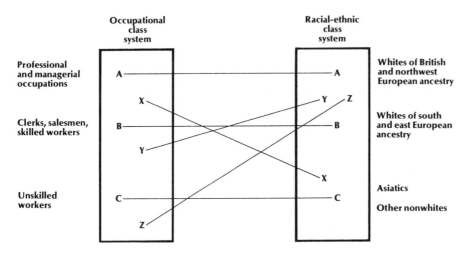

Fig. 2/3 A comparison of consistent and inconsistent statuses in the United States

Status combinations A, B, and C are consistent; combinations X, Y, and Z inconsistent.

said to be the *status* of the unit in the society. The term "status" may be used to refer either to a ranking based on a *specific* criterion (such as income) or to the *overall* ranking of the unit. Sociologists are especially concerned with statuses that reflect the power, privilege, or prestige of units, since these are extremely important in the structure and functioning of socieites.

Usually the various statuses of a unit are fairly consistent. People who are wealthy and well educated also tend to be powerful and to enjoy considerable prestige. There are exceptions, however, and these are interesting and important. A leader of the Mafia, for example, may enjoy great power and wealth in the community at large but, at the same time, have little prestige except in the Mafia itself. A person, a role, or a group exhibiting such characteristics is said to have *inconsistent status.*

The status of a unit often changes with the passage of time. When this occurs, we say that the unit is *upwardly mobile* or *downwardly mobile.* For example, when an individual is promoted, he is upwardly mobile; when a family fortune is gradually dissipated, the family is downwardly mobile.

Classes Like status, the term "class" is also used in two different, though related, ways. Sometimes it refers to an aggregation or group of people whose *overall* status is fairly similar. In this case, we usually speak of an upper, middle, and lower class; or we may divide the hierarchy more narrowly into upper-middle, lower-middle, and so on.

The term "class" is also frequently applied to an aggregation or group of people who stand in a similar position with respect to *some specific resource,* such as wealth, education, occupation, or anything else that affects their access to power, privilege, or prestige. Used in this way, the term is applicable to the nobility and peasantry of the past, as well as to the rich and poor today. Similarly, one may speak of a propertied class, a managerial class, a working class, or a governing class. Generally, this usage of the term "class" is the more accurate and precise.

Taken together, all the classes of a given type (e.g., all the occupational classes in a society) form what is known as *a system of stratification*.[22] Taken together, all the systems of stratification in a society (e.g., the occupational system, the racial-ethnic system, the property system, etc.) form what is known as *the system of stratification* or *the distributive system* of that society.

As the latter term suggests, the basic function of these systems is to distribute the things of value which men produce in their life together in societies. These include not only the material products of the economy, such as food and clothing, but also intangible products, such as prestige and power. Such a system is imperative, since these things are usually in short supply (i.e., not enough is produced to satisfy the desires of all the members of the society), and when men produce things through cooperative efforts, as they do in societies, there is no one obviously right way to distribute the product. For example, it is equally reasonable to argue that the products of the group's efforts be distributed on the basis of (1) the needs of individuals for these products, (2) the amount of effort individuals expend in their production, or (3) the degree of skill contributed by the producers. Even if a group settles on one of these principles, further disputes are likely. For example, if the members decide to apply the principle of effort, they still must decide how to measure effort. Shall it be measured by the number of hours spent on the job, or by the foot-pounds of energy expended? Or, should they select a different criterion, how does one compare a statesman's skills with those of a surgeon? In short, there is no one right way to handle this problem. Societies have to impose arbitrary standards. The only alternative is anarchy, given the natural tendency of individuals to put the satisfaction of their own needs ahead of the needs of most other people.

One question which naturally arises in any discussion of systems of stratification is whether or not classes are groups. The answer is both "yes" and "no." Many times, classes are simply human aggregates whose members stand in a similar position with respect to some resource, but who lack a sense of common identity and common behavioral expectations and do not act together to satisfy their common, or complementary, needs. For example, this seems to be true of office workers, an occupational class in our society. On the other hand, American Negroes, a racial-ethnic class, have long been a cultural community as well. More than that, the community has given rise to a great number of associations (Negro churches, etc.) and to a major social movement that includes many whites (i.e., the civil rights movement). Thus, classes constitute a fertile seed bed from which groups of many kinds are likely to spring.

---

[22] Classes are sometimes called strata, and a system of classes, or strata, is therefore called a system of stratification. It may also be called a *class system*.

Summary   By way of summarization, we can say that systems of social organization are built on two basic principles: (1) the principle of the division of labor and (2) the principle of stratification. Because it is more efficient and more rewarding for men to divide up the tasks that are necessary for their survival and well-being, a system of functionally differentiated roles and groups gradually evolves in a society. But as this process of *functional* differentiation takes place, it is accompanied by a process of *status* differentiation. Thus, individuals, roles, and groups come to be differentiated in terms of status, as well as in terms of the function they perform; this, in turn, leads to the formation of classes. In some human societies, these possibilities have been realized in only the most limited way, but in others, systems of social organization have become immensely complex.

Ideology

The last basic component of sociocultural systems is ideology. This term refers to *a society's basic belief systems and their applications to daily life.* The ideology of a society is made up of three important elements: (1) world views, (2) values, and (3) norms.

World views   Culture makes it possible for men to ask the question, "Why?" "Why do some people enjoy greater success in life than others?" "Why must my child die?" "Why do the rains not come and our people starve?" By the asking of these questions, men express their culturally generated need for meanings.

To some extent, these questions are answered by what we call science, at least in modern industrial societies. "The child died because it contracted a disease known as leukemia." "The rains did not come because of the presence of a high-pressure system in the area and a stationary front to the west." But even though such answers may be correct, they invite further questions. "Why did *my* child contract the disease?" Or, "Why was there this high-pressure system and this stationary front?" In other words, it is possible for us to ask questions in an infinite regress. At some point, however, men weary of explanations of explanations of explanations and ask questions about the *ultimate* nature of reality. "What is really real in this world?" "What are the forces that ultimately control the life of man?"

These are questions science cannot answer and never will. The answers men give to these questions are answers based on faith.[23] This is not to say that reason plays no part in shaping them. Intelligent men draw their inferences from observation and experience as carefully and as rationally as they can, but in the last analysis they are forced to make the leap of faith and say "I believe . . . ."

One might suppose that the immense variability of human experience combined with this need for an act of faith would result in an almost infinite variability

---

[23] See also Lenski, *Religious Factor*, pp. 300–302; or Peter Berger, *The Sacred Canopy: Elements of a Sociological Theory of Religion* (Garden City, N.Y.: Doubleday, 1961), chap. 1.

in world views. While it is surely true that they vary greatly, there are forces at work promoting agreement. From the standpoint of the individual, it is not reassuring to have a wholly unique view of the world and one's place in it. From the standpoint of society, too much divergence in this area can undermine the unity of the group.

In most societies, at most times in the past, a single world view has tended to be dominant. Frequently there were variations on it, as in the medieval world where the educated classes had a somewhat different view from that of the illiterate peasant masses. In the modern world, however, a variety of circumstances have created a situation in which a much larger number of conflicting world views compete for men's loyalties. As a result, most modern industrial societies lack this former source of integration. In the nineteenth and early twentieth centuries, many people thought that science might replace all the existing ideologies and provide a final, definitive world view. Today, however, as the nature of science, and its limitations, come to be better understood, this possibility has gone aglimmering. Today, we realize that while the findings, the method, and even the outlook of modern science are data that an educated person must take into account in his effort to define his own world view, science alone cannot create one, since it explicitly avoids pronouncements on the *ultimate* nature of reality.

Values The beliefs that make up the ideology of a society include not only men's world views, but also their values. This term refers to *the generalized moral beliefs to which members of a group subscribe.* These include such things as the belief that lying, stealing, and murder are wrong, and qualities such as generosity and bravery commendable

Values tend to be tied to world views, with the world view usually providing a justification or rationale for the values, as well as for the actions these values encourage. Thus, Communists have long justified revolutionary violence on the grounds that feudalism and capitalism are doomed and that revolutions shorten the period of oppression and exploitation under the old order and speed the coming of the glorious new era of the classless society. Similarly, nineteenth-century Europeans justified the spread of the colonial system in Asia and Africa on the grounds that it was the white man's burden to be the carrier of civilization to these benighted lands.

As these examples suggest, one of the major functions of ideologies is to *legitimize* courses of action men want to follow. Ideologies have long been used in this way to justify economic and political exploitation. This has been extremely important in countries with marked social inequality. Pronounced differences in power and privilege have an explosive potential. Unless the poor and downtrodden are given some acceptable explanation for the practices that keep them poor and downtrodden, they are likely to revolt. Usually some kind of explanation has been found to justify these practices, and the poor have suffered in silence.

Sometimes, however, rebels have been shrewd enough to see the need for a counter-ideology to fight the official one. While this is not likely to persuade members of the class in power, it is essential if the energies of the common people are to be mobilized behind a revolutionary program. So long as the common people accept the old world view, they are psychologically immobilized. Marx saw this much more clearly than most men, and his success in creating a new world view is largely responsible for the appeal and power of Marxist movements in many parts of the world today.

In this relation between world views and values, it is sometimes difficult to determine which is the chicken and which is the egg. Logically, one would expect that men would derive their values from their world views. But few men are logicians, and even the few who are, are self-interested logicians. That is to say, most of us have special interests to defend and, as a result, we find it convenient to make our world view serve our interests, rather than the other way around. Not that this is always done consciously. Probably it is not in most cases, but the result is the same. Perhaps the best way to summarize what we know about this subject is to say that there seems to be a dialectic—a two-way exchange of influence—between world views and values, with each influencing the other.

In discussing values, it is important to distinguish between two sets of values which are often lumped together and treated as though they were the same. These are (1) pragmatic values and (2) ideal values.[24] Pragmatic values are at the core of all popular moral codes and are based on the recognition that members of the group need one another. Therefore, they condemn those kinds of actions that threaten to undermine the unity of the group (e.g., dishonesty, violence against fellowmembers, etc.) and encourage those actions that enable the group to satisfy its needs (e.g., hard work, honesty, etc.). Ideal values go much further. They define how the ideal man should act, but it is taken for granted that few, if any, group members will be able to live up to this standard (e.g., the Christian Church has always taught that men should love their neighbors as themselves).

Since ideal values are so seldom realized, one might argue that they are of little social significance. This is not true, however, because their purpose is achieved if they stimulate men to go even a little way beyond the minimum level of performance called for in their group's pragmatic values. Ideal values are important in the crucial process of transforming individuals from the totally self-interested animals they are at birth to the partially group-oriented humans they must become.

Norms Values are always stated in general terms; they take no account of circumstances. Norms, by contrast, are the application of these general rules to specific circumstances. They are *behavioral prescriptions and proscriptions for the incumbents of specific roles in specific situations.*

Earlier, we defined roles as positions to which certain distinctive behavioral expectations and requirements are attached. As is now evident, "norms" is the technical term for these expectations and requirements.

There are two basic types of norms. Those that are written down in an official

---

[24] Lenski, *Power and Privilege, op. cit.*, p. 30.

code of some kind and systematically enforced by a governing authority are usually called laws or regulations or, in some cases, simply rules. Contrasted with these more formally defined standards, every group and society also has many customary standards which, though unofficial and informal, are nonetheless regarded as important.

Some norms prescribe a single action in a certain situation and proscribe all others. Other norms define a range of alternative behaviors which are acceptable: these may all be defined as equally acceptable, or some identified as preferred.

Violations of norms tend to generate guilt feelings on the part of the offender and reactions on the part of others. These responses are due to the socialization process, which we shall examine more fully in Chapter 4. For now, the important point is that violations of norms are usually punished, while conformity tends to be rewarded. This system of norms and their related rewards and punishments are the core of every system of social control.

Appendix: A further note on human nature

One aspect of the problem of human nature that has been much debated, and often quite unprofitably, has been concerned with human values. Many scholars have taken the position that it is impossible to attribute any common set of values to mankind the world over —other than, perhaps, the very general self-seeking tendency noted previously. It is argued that some men seek physical comfort, some fame and honor, others aesthetic gratification, and so forth. Given these great differences, they argue, human nature can have nothing to do with the matter.

Recently, however, a psychologist, A. H. Maslow, has developed a theory of human motivation that shows how such diverse goals and motivations might all spring from a common source. In a volume entitled *Motivation and Personality*, Maslow argues that men have a common inborn hierarchy of needs.[25] The most basic are physiological (the need for food, water, sleep, protein, etc.). Next most basic are the safety needs. These are followed, in turn, by the "belongingness and love needs," the esteem needs, and the need for self-actualization. According to Maslow, the more basic needs are normally dominant until such time as they are satisfied. The closer they come to

being satisfied, the stronger the higher needs become. In the case of individuals in whom the physiological and safety needs are fully met, the higher needs are usually dominant. In referring to one or another set of needs as dominant, Maslow does not claim that they alone are active. On the contrary, he suggests that several needs are likely to be operative at the same time, though all are not likely to be equally compelling.

Though Maslow's theory can hardly be called definitive, it is suggestive. Above all, it points the way to a resolution of the apparent paradox of diverse motivations and a common human nature. Also, as noted in Chapter 16, this theory may have special relevance for evolutionary theory and its application to contemporary social change. Thanks to the continuing industrial revolution, a number of societies are now, for the first time in history, in a position to satisfy most of the physiological and safety needs of the majority of their populations. If Maslow is correct, this could result in a major shift in patterns of individual action, and this, in turn, could have far-reaching consequences for societies. This is a subject that deserves more attention than it has yet received from either sociologists or social psychologists.

---

[25] Maslow, *op. cit.*, especially chap. 5. The brief summary of Maslow's theory given in this short note does not do justice to his highly sophisticated and carefully qualified presentation. Hence, the reader is urged to read Maslow's argument firsthand.

Chapter 3
An Introduction to Evolutionary Theory

In Chapter 2, the structural-functional approach provided an introduction to the anatomy and physiology of human societies. This was an important first step, but we must go further. We need to understand the forces that cause change in societies —long-term, large-scale, nonrecurrent evolutionary patterns of change. For this, we must go beyond the structural-functional approach, just as biologists have had to go beyond the study of the anatomy and physiology of organisms.

Sociologists can learn a lot from the experience of biologists, especially from the development of what has come to be known as *the new synthetic theory of evolution*.[1] The great achievement of this theory is that it has brought together, in a single framework, the basic findings of many diverse, and previously separate, subdisciplines. These include genetics, ecology, physiology, anatomy, paleontology, embryology, ethology, and biochemistry.

Though this theory has only limited application in the study of human societies, it is nonetheless of considerable interest to sociologists. Because of the analogous nature of many aspects of organic evolution and sociocultural evolution, the new synthetic theory contains many sociologically suggestive hypotheses. Even more

---

[1] For major statements of the new synthetic theory, see Julian Huxley's pioneering study, *Evolution: The Modern Synthesis* (London: G. Allen, 1942); George Gaylord Simpson's more recent volume, *The Major Features of Evolution* (New York: Columbia, 1953); or Ernst Mayr's still more recent volume, *Animal Species and Evolution* (Cambridge, Mass.: Harvard, 1963). For the views of a number of other scholars, as well as further statements by the three authors above, see Sol Tax (ed.), *Evolution After Darwin: The University of Chicago Centennial* (Chicago: University of Chicago Press, 1960), especially vols. I and III. For a short summary, see G. G. Simpson, "The Study of Evolution: Methods and Present Status of Theory," in G. G. Simpson and Anne Roe (eds.), *Behavior and Evolution* (New Haven, Conn.: Yale, 1958), p. 14. For a very readable, recent paperback statement, see John Maynard Smith, *The Theory of Evolution* (Baltimore: Penguin, 1958).

48

important, it provides a "model" that illustrates how the scattered and unorganized findings of the *social* sciences may be brought together within a single theoretical framework. Also, if we accept the postulate of the essential unity of nature, recognizing that human societies are a part of the natural world and that sociocultural evolution is an extension of organic evolution, then it follows that the theory of human societies and their evolution must eventually be linked with basic biological theory. For all these reasons, then, we should study the new synthetic theory to see how it can contribute to our understanding of human societies.

THE NEW SYNTHETIC THEORY OF ORGANIC EVOLUTION

Four basic facts of life

The primary objective of the new synthetic theory is to explain, within a single unified framework, what might be called the four basic facts of life. These are:

1. Organic *continuity*
2. Organic *innovation*
3. Organic *extinction*

Collectively, these give rise to the fourth, and most basic of all:

4. Organic *evolution*

Phenotype, genotype, and environment

To understand the new synthetic theory, we must understand at the outset several basic terms and their relationship to one another. These are (1) phenotype, (2) genotype, and (3) environment. *Phenotype* is a term developed in recent years to refer to the totality of organic and behavioral characteristics of an individual organism or population of organisms. It includes such things as its (or their) size, shape, color, eating habits, reproductive patterns, learned behaviors, and so forth. *Genotype* has a much more restricted meaning. It refers to all the genetic materials found in an individual organism or population of organisms. *Environment* refers to everything that is external to an organism or population and affects it in anyway. Thus the environment of a particular animal includes other animals and plants, as well as inorganic elements.[2]

The distinction between phenotype and genotype is extremely important, because it lays the foundation for a clearer understanding of the crucial relationship

---

[2] Some scholars now add a third environment to the traditional two. For example, Ernst Mayr writes, "To the two well-known classes of environment, the physical and biotic environments, we must add a third, the genetic environment. A given gene has as its genetic environment not only the genetic background of the given zygote on which it is temporarily placed, but the entire gene pool of the local population in which it occurs" (*op. cit.*, pp. 278–279). For some purposes, this seems a useful addition, for others not.

between an organism and its environment. This relationship can be stated quite simply: *The phenotype of an organism, or a population of organisms, is determined by the interaction of its genotype with its environment.* To be more specific, in this interaction the genotype sets the limits—sometimes broad, sometimes narrow—for phenotype variation, while the interaction of environment and genotype determines exactly where within these limits the phenotypic pattern is established. For example, the genotype for each of us sets upper and lower limits on our possible height, but where within those limits we wind up depends on the interaction of environmental influences and genetic characteristics.

Populations of organisms

One of the key elements in the new synthesis is the recognition that *populations of organisms*, rather than the individual organism, should be the basic unit of analysis in evolutionary theory. As one scholar puts it, "the thing that is actually evolving, is a population."[3] The nature of these populations varies somewhat, depending upon the problem under study, but they are always units whose members share a common ancestry and a common gene pool. Among the higher forms of life, the crucial population unit is usually *the species.* In modern usage, this is defined as "an evolved or evolving, genetically distinctive, reproductively isolated, natural population."[4]

With this shift from the individual to the population as the basic unit of analysis, modern biologists have developed a much clearer understanding of the process of speciation, and hence of the process of genetic differentiation. Though Darwin's name will forever be linked with the phrase "the origin of species," this is a process he never really understood. As Ernst Mayr, a leading proponent of the modern synthesis, put it, "Although he demonstrated the modification of species in the time dimension, he never seriously attempted a rigorous analysis of the problem of the multiplication of species, of the splitting of one species into two."[5] Mayr added that the chief reason for this was Darwin's lack of understanding of the nature of species, a consequence of the lack of knowledge of genetics at that time.

In the modern view, the key to the process of speciation is found in the concept of reproductive isolation. Quoting Mayr once more, "The mechanisms that isolate one species reproductively from others are perhaps the most important set of attributes a species has, because they are, by definition, the species criteria."[6] Recognition of this has led to a greatly increased interest in the causes of reproductive isolation. These are of two types, genetic and environmental. Genetic factors work in a

---

[3] Simpson, "The Study of Evolution," p. 14.

[4] Alfred E. Emerson, "Biological Species," *Encyclopaedia Britannica*, 1967 ed., vol. 20, p. 1149.

[5] Mayr, *op. cit.*, p. 12.

[6] *Ibid.*, p. 89. For a more recent discussion of the subject of speciation, see M. J. D. White, "Models of Speciation," *Science*, 159 (1968), pp. 1065–1070.

variety of ways. Some completely prevent reproduction by members of different species, while others substantially reduce the success of reproductive efforts. Environmental factors are equally varied. The important point, however, is that a species is created by anything that effectively isolates a population of organisms as far as the flow of genetic materials is concerned. *Isolation, therefore, is the key to genetic differentiation.*

Organic continuity

Within a population of organisms, organic continuity is achieved through the processes of reproduction, whereby sets of chromosomes are passed from parents to offspring. In the case or organisms that reproduce asexually (e.g., many plants and some of the lower animals), the parental set is simply passed on, usually unchanged. When sexual reproduction is involved, two homologous sets[7] are received, one from each parent. In either case, the genetic mechanism insures a high degree of organic and behavioral continuity from one generation to the next.

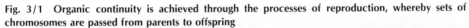

---

[7] In other words, two sets that are genetically similar because of the common evolutionary ancestry of the mating pair.

Fig. 3/1 Organic continuity is achieved through the processes of reproduction, whereby sets of chromosomes are passed from parents to offspring

Organic innovation

Curiously, the same genetic system responsible for stability and continuity is also responsible for all *heritable* innovations. This apparent paradox is partly resolved if we keep in mind that in sexual reproduction there are always some genetic differences between the two parents. Sexual reproduction, therefore, always results in the creation of new combinations of genetic materials, a process known as *recombination*.[8] Contrary to popular opinion, most of the variation within species is due to this process.[9]

Though recombination is one of the basic processes of innovation, it does not produce any new genetic materials. This can occur only through the process of *mutation*. This term includes changes in the number of chromosomes, changes in the internal structure of chromosomes (other than by crossing over in meiosis[10]), and changes in the internal structure of the genes themselves. All of these kinds of changes may be inherited.

One might logically suppose that these two innovative processes are the cause and explanation of evolutionary progress. Nothing would be more reasonable than to infer that all, or most, of the newer forms resulting from mutation and recombination are superior to the older forms they replace. But this is not the case. Modern research has shown that neither of these processes by itself produces a progressive pattern. In the case of recombination, the harmful innovations are as numerous as the beneficial. In the case of mutations, *most* are harmful or regressive.[11] Hence, though the innovative processes make some contribution to evolutionary progress, we must look beyond them for the major explanation.

Organic extinction

Surprising as it may seem, the search for the major explanation of evolutionary progress leads directly to the subject of organic extinction. When we first consider the matter, it seems that progress and extinction must be antithetical. Darwin and his successors have shown, however, that this is not true.

We can better appreciate the potency of the forces of extinction when we consider the estimate of modern biologists that more than 99 per cent of all the species that have appeared in evolutionary history are now extinct. Those species alive today constitute "a good deal less than one per cent of those that have ever existed."[12]

---

[8] Recombinations may involve either the recombination of genes by crossing over in meiosis or the recombination of chromosomes by conjugation of gametes with unlike chromosomes.

[9] Simpson, *The Major Features of Evolution*, p. 62.

[10] The process by which the chromosome number is reduced by half to compensate for the chromosome-doubling effect of fertilization.

[11] W. C. Allee, Alfred E. Emerson, Orlando Park, Thomas Park, and Karl Schmidt, *Principles of Animal Ecology* (Philadelphia: Saunders, 1949), p. 600.

[12] Mayr, *op. cit.*, p. 620.

Fig. 3/2 Two forms of organic innovation: mutation (two-headed calf) and recombination

Just as there are two basic processes giving rise to organic innovation, there are two responsible for organic extinction. The first of these is *genetic drift,* or random fluctuations in the distribution of genes within a population. Genetic drift occurs because the gene pool of a population is distributed differently among its members. No single individual possesses all of the genes found within his population group, and, since all the members of the population do not have equal numbers of offspring, there is bound to be some change in the composition of the population's gene pool from one generation to the next. Certain genes become a bit more common, others a bit more rare.

In large populations, genetic drift rarely leads to the extinction of any widely distributed gene. In small populations, however, or in the case of rare genes in large populations (e.g., a gene resulting from a recent mutation), the situation is different: genes can quickly be lost as a result of the failure of only a few individuals to reproduce. The greater danger in small populations and in the case of rare genes can be proven statistically. The situation is analogous to one in which two boys match pennies. If one starts with a thousand pennies and the other with only two, the statistical probabilities are far greater that the boy with two pennies will lose all of his than that the boy with a thousand will.

Important as the process of genetic drift is, it does not give rise to progressive evolutionary change. Like recombination, it is a random process from the standpoint of the adaptation of organisms to their environment. True evolutionary change—that is, change that contributes to a sustained advance in the adaptation of a population to its environment—comes about only through the process of *natural selection.* Because of this, biologists sometimes call it "the keystone of evolution."[13]

Natural selection refers to the processes by means of which environmental influences contribute to the multiplication of certain populations of organisms and to the decline and extinction of others. Of all the natural processes producing biological change, it is the only one that operates in a *non*random fashion, and it is this which is responsible for the patterned character of evolutionary change. As its name implies, natural selection is the unplanned, spontaneous counterpart of man's practice of selective breeding, or artificial selection.

The basic cause of natural selection is the inherent tendency of all forms of life to reproduce in numbers greater than environmental resources can sustain. Modern biology is indebted for this insight to a pioneer social scientist, the Reverend Thomas Malthus. In his early analysis of the cause of poverty, Malthus concluded that it was basically the natural tendency of human populations to increase more rapidly than resources for their support could be increased.[14] Human populations, he argued, tend to double every twenty-five years unless checked by war, famine, or disease. This means a potential for growth at the geometric rate of 1, 2, 4, 8, 16, etc. By

---

[13] *Ibid.,* p. 185.

[14] See Thomas Malthus, *Population: The First Essay* (Ann Arbor, Mich.: University of Michigan Press, 1959, first published 1798).

contrast, he argued, the means of subsistence cannot be increased at more than the simple arithmetic ratio of 1, 2, 3, 4, 5, etc. In a brief aside, he spoke of the similar tendency of plants and animals to reproduce in greater numbers than the environment can sustain, and of the inevitable consequences of this tendency.

Both Darwin and Wallace, the cofounders of modern evolutionary theory, read Malthus and attributed to him their basic insight concerning the process of natural selection.[15] Modern studies of the reproductive rates of plants and animals have made the inevitability of the selective process abundantly clear. In some species, such as the herring, the potential increase per generation may be as much as a millionfold.[16] Obviously, all of the offspring cannot survive. Even with man's modest reproductive potential, if no Malthusian checks (i.e., war, famine, etc.) had operated, the living descendants of the 10 million persons estimated to have lived seven thousand years ago would now be so numerous that they would weigh more than the combined weight of all the visible stars.[17] This inherent tendency to overreproduce under normal conditions seems to be both a necessary defense against occasional disasters and a necessary requirement for evolutionary progress (see below). Without it, evolutionary progress would have been impossible, and probably survival as well.

One of the important developments associated with the rise of the new synthetic theory has been the reestablishment in biological theory of the significance of the environment in evolutionary change. Today, biologists refer to it as the "principal agent of natural selection."[18] In saying this, they are not reverting to the pre-Darwinian view that environmental change itself induces modifications directly into the genotype of an organism. Rather, they mean that on the level of populations, environmental conditions which favor the survival and reproduction of certain genes and genotypes are simultaneously handicapping others and causing them eventually to become extinct.[19]

Prior to the rise of the new synthetic theory, it was generally assumed that the process of natural selection operated solely on the individual level, causing the multiplication of individuals with environmentally favored characteristics at the expense of other, less favored individuals. Now, however, it is recognized that the process of natural selection also operates on the population level, and its operation on this level tends to counterbalance the effect of the selective process on the indi-

---

[15] See, for example, Loren Eiseley, *Darwin's Century: Evolution and the Men Who Discovered It* (Garden City, N.Y.: Doubleday Anchor, 1961), p. 182, or Julian Huxley, "The Emergence of Darwinism," in Tax, *op. cit.*, vol. I, p. 5.

[16] Smith, *op. cit.*, p. 33.

[17] Harrison Brown, *The Challenge of Man's Future* (New York: Viking Compass, 1956), p. 68.

[18] Mayr, *op. cit.*, p. 7.

[19] Adherents of the new synthetic theory prefer to define natural selection in terms of reproductive success rather than in Darwinian terms as survival. The distinction seems at times a bit of a quibble since they invariably sneak survival in by the back door. Perhaps in time they will come to talk about "population maintenance" or some similar term that embraces the idea of both fertility and mortality rates.

Fig. 3/3 The bald eagle, one of many species of birds and mammals currently threatened with extinction via natural selection

vidual level, since populations having considerable genetic diversity are favored over populations that are genetically more uniform. This means that the long-run chances of survival of a population are *enhanced* by the presence of a certain number of individuals with inferior endowments, as judged by the population's *current* needs. The reason for this is that genetic diversity increases a population's flexibility, or ability to respond successfully to rapidly changing environmental conditions. A population whose members are all highly adapted to current environmental conditions is extremely vulnerable to environmental change—and environmental change (e.g., changes associated with the various ice ages), like biotic change, is a basic fact of life on this planet.

Recognition of the continuous nature of environmental change has been greatly enhanced by the incorporation of the basic insights of ecology into the new synthetic theory. So long as environment is thought of merely in terms of climate and other physical factors, we can regard the environment of most species as fairly stable for long periods of time. Once we take into account the existence of ecological communities, however, with their complex ties of interdependence among species, it becomes evident that environmental stability is the exception rather than the rule. As man has discovered in recent years, as his impact on the biological world has increased, the disappearance or decline of a single species of plant or animal can sometimes set off a long chain of repercussions that may affect adversely many other species.

Before leaving the subject, it should be emphasized that natural selection is not a simple process operating at a single point in the life cycle, or at a single level in the biotic realm. On the contrary, it operates in every situation involving an organism's or a population's chances of survival and reproduction, and it operates simultaneously on both the individual and population levels. Furthermore, natural selection often involves the operation of counterpressures which limit the degree of development possible in a certain direction. As we noted in Chapter 1, the unlimited addition of bodily armament might prove advantageous from the standpoint of protection against predators, but at some point this development would begin to interfere with the processes of mating, reproduction, and sustenance. This interdependence of phenotypic traits explains why so few evolutionary trends are carried to their possible extremes.

Despite the multiplicity of selective forces at work in the biological world, some biologists insist that these forces have not all been of equal importance in shaping the course of evolution. In particular, a strong case has been made in recent years for the great importance of sustenance problems and pressures. According to one prominent biologist, differences in food-getting behavior have been the crucial factor responsible for the differences between the major phyletic groups (i.e., orders, classes, and phyla rather than mere species). In his words:

> Major groups of animals—orders, classes, phyla—are to a surprising extent distinguished by structural or behavioral [characteristics] that, in one way or another, turn around food habits. This, among mammals, is reflected in such ordinal names as "Carnivora," or, for that matter, in the word "Mammalia" itself.[20]

Though this thesis is not universally accepted as part of the new synthesis, it is consistent with the rest and likely, in time, to find acceptance. As its author himself points out, he is carrying the analysis a step beyond the currently fashionable level of *micro*evolution—where the species is the basic unit of analysis—to the level of *macro*evolution—where the divisions between the major phyletic groups are the central problem.

---

[20] Marston Bates, "Food-getting Behavior," in Simpson and Roe, *op. cit.*, p. 209.

Organic evolution: the basic trends

Up to this point in our review, we have focused on the specific processes of continuity and change that form the warp and woof of organic evolution. Though these have been important concerns of adherents of the new synthesis, their interests do not stop there. Like Darwin and the other early evolutionists, contemporary biologists are concerned with *the total process.* As George Gaylord Simpson put it, "Evolution is an incredibly complex but at the same time an integrated and unitary process," and it is a great mistake to allow the details to obscure the basic pattern.[21]

Basically, organic evolution has meant two things: (1) *organic diversification and* (2) *organic progress.* On the first point there is no argument. All biologists agree that biotic history involves a fairly continuous, long-term multiplication of species and therefore a corresponding increase in organic diversity. The term used to describe this trend is *adaptive radiation.* This is the process whereby populations become organically diversified in order to take advantage of all available environmental niches or settings. A classic case is provided by the marsupials of Australia, which, because of the absence of most groups of placental mammals of that continent, radiated into many of the niches occupied elsewhere by the latter.

If diversification were the only basic pattern in the biotic world, the term "evolution" might have been dropped long ago. That we continue to speak of evolution reflects our awareness that *progressive change* is also involved. Biologists have found, however, that it is easier to speak of evolutionary progress than to define it. Many simply avoid the problem by treating the concept as though its meaning were self-evident.

A few, however, have sought to work out a defensible definition. One of the more noteworthy efforts was by Sir Julian Huxley, a pioneer in the development of the new synthetic theory. In an important study, *Evolution: The Modern Synthesis,* Huxley defined evolutionary progress as "a raising of the upper level of biological efficiency, this being defined as increased control over and independence of the environment."[22] By limiting the definition to a raising of the "upper level" of biological efficiency, Huxley sought to take account of the continuing presence in the modern world of many of the most primitive forms of life. Clearly, evolution has not meant their elimination, and this fact must be reckoned with in any definition of progress.

Those who have found fault with Huxley's effort have not challenged him on this aspect of his definition. Rather, they have criticized his attempt to equate evolutionary progress with "increased control over and independence of the environment." One critic suggested that progress be defined instead as an "increase in the range and variety of adjustments of the organism to its environment."[23] He went

---

[21] Simpson, *The Major Features of Evolution,* p. 377.

[22] Huxley, *op. cit.,* 1963 ed., pp. 564–565.

[23] C. J. Herrick, "Progressive Evolution," *Science,* 104 (1946), p. 469.

on to say that this involves "increase in the complexity of structure, ensuring sensitivity to a greater variety of environing energies and more refined sensory analysis, elaboration of more varied and efficient organs of response and more complicated apparatus of control."

Each of these definitions contributes something to our understanding of evolutionary progress, but each leaves something to be desired. A better definition might be built around the concepts of energy and information, both of which have come to assume considerable importance in a growing number of scientific fields. Specifically, evolutionary progress might be defined as *a raising of the upper level of the capacity of populations to mobilize energy and information in the adaptive process*.

The term "information," as used in this definition, has a much broader meaning than that attached to it in popular usage. As biologists have begun to use it, and as we are using it here, the term refers to information stored in the genes as well as to information stored in the memory. Biologists now recognize that both are basic adaptive mechanisms, both are internal mechanisms which regulate "behavior,"[24] and both are precious products which populations extract from their experience with the environment. In short, learning is simply a very specialized and very complex extension of the process of genetic adaptation.

Variable concepts and probabilistic theory

Finally, the new synthetic theory has involved a shift from *categoric* to *variable* concepts, and from *deterministic* to *probabilistic* formulations of theory. Categoric concepts are framed in simple either-or, black-and-white, terms. For example, using categoric concepts we would divide the various species of animals into those that are capable of learning and those that are not. By contrast, variable concepts permit us to take account of the important differences in *degree* among those that are able to learn. Some species have an extremely limited capacity; others, such as man, a very great capacity. If we ignore this, as we automatically do when we rely on categoric concepts, we have an oversimplified view of the world.

The increasing use of variable concepts is reflected in the growing concern with measurement, quantification, and statistics in biological theory and research. This change is largely due to the shift in focus from the individual to the population, which we noted earlier. The characteristics of an individual can be described in categoric terms much more satisfactorily than can those of a population. Analyses of populations necessarily require the use of variable concepts, since so many important attributes are found in varying frequency or varying degree, and the magnitude of these variations is often of the greatest importance.

In addition to the growing reliance on variable concepts, older, deterministic formulations of theory are gradually being replaced by newer, probabilistic formula-

---

[24] The term "behavior" is used broadly here to include the growth patterns and physical development of plants and animals as well as their movements in space.

tions. This has become essential as the many unpredictable aspects of the evolutionary process have become evident. For example, although we can learn the rate at which certain kinds of mutations occur in nature, it is impossible to predict *which individuals* will be the mutants. Similarly, though accurate estimates can be made of the percentage of herring that will survive to the age of reproduction, it is impossible to predict which ones these will be. Since the larger evolutionary processes depend on the outcome of these smaller processes and so many of the latter contain unpredictable elements, it has become evident that the process of organic evolution as a whole is not rigorously predictable in the sense which many hoped for in an earlier era.[25] The scientific and philosophical significance of this shift in thought can hardly be exaggerated.

ORGANIC AND SOCIOCULTURAL EVOLUTION COMPARED

Similarities

Similarities between organic and sociocultural evolution were first recognized more than a century ago. No one did more to direct attention to them in the nineteenth century than the pioneer English sociologist, Herbert Spencer. Unfortunately, early efforts to develop sociological theory in this way proved largely abortive, with the result that the subject of sociocultural evolution, as well as its relation to organic evolution, was generally ignored for many years.

One reason for the failure of these early efforts was the tendency of some evolutionary theorists to exaggerate the degree of similarity between the two types of evolution. Clearly, there are many remarkable similarities. In fact, it is now evident that *sociocultural evolution is, in essence, an extension of the process of organic evolution.* There are differences, however, as well as similarities between the two processes. Both deserve the most careful consideration if we are to avoid the dangers of exaggeration in either direction.

The major similarities between organic and sociocultural evolution should be reasonably apparent by now. To begin with, as we pointed out in Chapter 1, the symbol systems developed by human populations are functional analogues of genetic systems (though it should be emphasized that they *supplement*, rather than supplant, man's genetic system). Like genetic systems, they are "mechanisms" for handling information relevant to the adaptation of the population to its environment. Second, in light of the analysis developed in this chapter, we can now see that human societies are functional analogues of species. Like a species, a human society is an "isolated"[26] population whose members share a pool of information and are

---

[25] Mayr, *op. cit.*, p. 184.

[26] In human societies, the degree of isolation is usually much less than in species. See the discussion of diffusion which follows on pp. 67 and 84.

therefore bound to a common evolutionary path. Third, sociocultural evolution, like organic evolution, involves a complex interaction of the processes of continuity, innovation, and extinction. Finally, sociocultural evolution, like organic evolution, is a complex process of change of long duration, characterized by the progressive emergence of organizations which possess ever greater capacities for the mobilization of energy and information.

Differences

Side by side with these similarities are differences of equal importance. To begin with, symbols are *not* genes despite the fact that they perform the same basic function. We get an indication of what this means when we compare the content of genetic and symbol systems. Much of the information contained in symbol systems has no counterpart in genetic systems. This is especially true of the evaluative and interpretive components. Symbol systems, therefore, have made it possible for man to develop moral codes, aesthetic standards, philosophies, and religions—all elements uniquely his in the biotic world.

There are also differences between symbols and genes in the patterns of flow of information. The flow of genetic information is virtually halted by species boundaries.[27] Though hybridization occurs occasionally, it is rare, and even then it occurs only between species whose common ancestry is not too remote. By contrast, the flow of symbolic information across societal lines is substantial. Despite the lack of any recent common cultural ancestry, American Indians and Europeans exchanged symbolic information of great value almost from the moment of the latter's arrival in the New World. The same thing has occurred in almost every instance of societal contact.

Because the flow of symbolic information between human societies is so much greater than the flow of genetic information between species, the process of information diffusion, or *cultural diffusion*, as it is called, is of central significance in sociocultural evolution, while its genetic counterpart, hybridization, is rather unimportant in organic evolution.[28] Because of the relative ease of cultural diffusion, the boundaries between human societies are not as sharply defined or as easily maintained as the boundaries between species. As a consequence, there is good reason to believe that with improved methods of transportation and communication, societal boundaries will eventually be eliminated and there will be but one human society. In organic evolution, by contrast, the multiplication of species promises to continue so long as there are unfilled ecological niches.

---

[27] There is, of course, some "sharing" of genetic information across species lines as a result of the transmission of such information from common ancestors. This is the basis of the semispecialties discussed in Chapter 1 (see pp. 14–17).

[28] See V. Gordon Childe, *Social Evolution* (London: Watts, 1951), pp. 168–175; or Julian Huxley, *Evolution*, pp. xlvi–xlvii.

The differences between genes and symbols have still other important consequences. Since information stored symbolically can be revised so much more easily and rapidly than information stored genetically, sociocultural evolution has a potential for rates of change that far exceed the potential of organic evolution, at least among higher animals where the period between generations is a year or longer.[29] Related to this, the ease with which adaptive information can be transferred between human societies eliminates the necessity for step-by-step, stage-by-stage sequential evolution of the type that is inevitable in the rest of the biological world. By borrowing key cultural elements from more advanced societies, the less advanced can skip over many intermediate steps in the evolutionary process.[30]

Another important difference between the two types of evolution is that the adaptive process represented by sociocultural evolution is sometimes a *conscious and deliberate* process, while its organic evolutionary counterpart never is. This means that sociocultural evolution can, to some degree, be controlled and even planned. Organic evolution obviously cannot, at least not apart from the actions of men utilizing their sociocultural resources (i.e., in breeding new strains of plants and animals).[31]

Finally, sociocultural evolution, unlike organic evolution, is able to incorporate adaptive "phenotypic" responses to the environment directly into the system of heritable information. At one time many biologists believed that this was also possible in the organic realm. In fact, this was the basis of the pre-Darwinian theory of evolution. Lamarck, Darwin's predecessor, argued that environmental conditions cause the formation of appropriate habit patterns and that these habit patterns, in time, produce heritable structural changes in organisms. It has long been clear that this is not the case in the organic world, but in the cultural world of man, a kind of Lamarckian pattern does prevail. Environmental conditions cause the formation of habit patterns, and these patterns then become part of the society's cultural heritage.

In view of the substantial differences between sociocultural and organic evolution, it is clear that no simple borrowing of concepts and hypotheses is possible. At the same time, the similarities are too great to permit students of human societies to ignore the substantial achievements of the new synthetic theory. As a consequence, our wisest course will be to utilize the synthetic theory, both as a model of theory construction (owing to the many remarkable parallels in the nature of the problems involved) and as a source of potential insights in the formulation of specific hypotheses. Someday, perhaps, we may even reach the point where we are able to link up the bodies of theory. But that is beyond the scope of our concern here.

---

[29] Huxley, *op. cit.*, p. xlvii.

[30] Donald Campbell, "Variation and Selective Retention in Sociocultural Evolution," in Herbert Barringer et al. (eds.), *Social Change in Developing Areas: A Reinterpretation of Evolutionary Theory* (Cambridge, Mass.: Schenkman, 1965), p. 42.

[31] George Gaylord Simpson, *The Meaning of Evolution* (New Haven, Conn.: Yale, 1949), pp. 289–290.

Organic Evolution

Continuity **via reproduction**

Innovation **via recombination and mutation**

Extinction **via genetic drift and natural selection**

Evolution, **meaning organic diversification and the raising of the upper level of the capacity of populations to mobilize energy and information**

Sociocultural Evolution

Continuity **primarily via socialization**

Innovation **via invention, discovery, alteration, and diffusion**

Extinction **via intra- and intersocietal selection**

Evolution, **meaning the raising of the upper level of the capacity of human societies to mobilize energy and information**

Fig. 3/4   Organic and sociocultural evolution compared

BASIC OUTLINES OF A THEORY OF SOCIOCULTURAL EVOLUTION

Four basic facts of human life

In our review of the new synthetic theory of organic evolution, we began by noting that this theory has been designed to explain within a single unified framework several basic facts of life. A parallel task confronts students of human societies. Here, too, there are certain basic facts of life that require an explanation which should be within the framework of a single, unified theoretical system. Moreover, the parallel does not end there. The facts confronting the student of human societies are direct analogues of those confronting the biologist. Specifically, they are:

1. Sociocultural *continuity*
2. Sociocultural *innovation*
3. Sociocultural *extinction*
4. Sociocultural *evolution*

Sociocultural genotypes?

The starting point for the new synthetic theory of biology is, as we have seen, the important distinction between genotype and phenotype, plus the conception of the role which they, together with the environment, play in the process of evolutionary change. By identifying the genotype and the environment as the only autogenous (i.e., self-generating) sources of change, biologists have greatly simplified their task. For them, the many phenotypic characteristics of species become secondary factors —mere agents transmitting the influences which stem from these other, more basic, sources.

Unfortunately for sociologists, the situation with respect to human societies is not so simple. Here, too, the environment is an autogenous source of change, but there is no exact analogue to the relationship between genotype and phenotype. In other words, there is no single limited source of autogenous change within societies. At the same time, however, there is reason to believe that all the parts of sociocultural systems have not been equally important as sources of change, especially as sources of the major social and cultural revolutions that several times in history radically transformed the conditions of life for much of mankind. Language, for example, has never played this kind of role. Languages change, it is true, but largely in response to previous changes in technology, social organization, or ideology. Even when this is not the case, as when gradual changes occur in the pronunciation or spelling of words, there is nothing to suggest that this leads to significant change in other parts of the sociocultural system. Each of the other basic elements of sociocultural systems has, at one time or another, apparently been an autogenous source of change, triggering change in the others. However, the record indicates that *technology* has played this role more often than either social organization or ideology.[32] This is a subject to which we will return in Chapter 4.

Population

In sociocultural evolution, as in organic, the evolving units are populations, not individuals. Furthermore, from the standpoint of the exchange of information, they

---

[32] The view presented in this section is still a subject of considerable controversy among sociologists and other social scientists, many of whom deny that technology plays a distinctive role. The importance of technology is more often recognized by those who take a broad evolutionary view of human societies and human history than by those whose interests are more specialized and whose perspective therefore is more limited. Also, the unusual role of technology is more likely to be recognized by scholars and statesmen who have wrestled with the difficult problems of development in the world's underdeveloped countries, where the need to find the most effective levers of change is most urgent, than by those whose concern is limited to American society.

In recent years, the view that technology plays a distinctive role in the processes of societal development has found significant support in a number of systematic quantitative studies. Studies which have applied the technique of factor analysis to data on contemporary societies at different levels of development have found repeatedly that technological differences are at the core of the most powerful factor or factors. See, for example, Brian Berry, "An Inductive Approach to the Regionalization of Economic Development," in Norton Ginsburg (ed.), *Essays on Geography and Economic Development* (Chicago: University of Chicago Press, 1960), pp. 78–107; Leo Schnore, "The Statistical Measurement of Urbanization and Economic Development," *Land Economics*, 37 (August, 1961), pp. 229–245; Alvin Gouldner and Richard Peterson, *Notes on Technology and the Moral Order* (Indianapolis: Bobbs-Merrill, 1962); and Jack Sawyer, "Dimensions of Nations: Size, Wealth, and Politics," *American Journal of Sociology*, 73 (September, 1967), pp. 145–172. Though none of these studies *prove* the causal dominance of technology, they are far more consistent with this hypothesis than with the alternatives.

are isolated, or partially isolated, populations. Paraphrasing the statement of the biologist quoted earlier, we can say, "The mechanisms that isolate one society from others are perhaps the most important set of attributes a society has because they are, by definition, the societal criteria." In the case of human populations, however, these isolating mechanisms are political and cultural, not reproductive and genetic.

Sociocultural continuity

With a population of organisms, intergenerational continuity is achieved wholly or largely through the process of reproduction. In human societies, a number of factors help to preserve sociocultural continuity, but the most important and the most distinctive is the process of *socialization*. As we have seen (page 30), its objective is to mold individuals so that they will take the standards and beliefs of their society as their own and govern their behavior accordingly. It is, therefore, both a mechanism to promote continuity and a mechanism of social control.[33]

---

[33] A rudimentary form of socialization is also found in many subhuman societies, especially among mammals. Here, parents teach their offspring certain essential behavior patterns by means of signal systems (e.g., techniques of hunting).

Fig. 3/5 Sociocultural continuity is achieved primarily by means of the socialization process. Formal education is but one of many techniques of socialization

In the past, this term was often used to refer to the process whereby the cultural heritage of a society is transmitted to children. While this is still regarded as the most crucial aspect of socialization, the phenomenon known as "adult socialization" has also come to be recognized. This is simply a continuation of the process into the adult years. Adult socialization is especially important in modern industrial societies where the rate of change is so rapid and where children are largely cut off from the adult world of work and therefore have no opportunity to learn many things that will be extremely important in their adult years.

Sociocultural innovation

Turning from continuity to innovation, we find both similarities and differences. The new synthetic theory of evolution, it will be recalled, recognizes two basic processes of innovation: mutation and recombination. Each of these has one or more sociocultural counterparts. Recombination, or the regrouping of genetic materials in new patterns, is a rough functional counterpart of *invention;* mutation, or the production of new genetic materials, is paralleled by *discovery* and *alteration.* In addition, there is a fourth sociocultural process, *diffusion,* which is roughly analogous to hybridization.

Not much need be said about invention and discoveries, since both are familiar aspects of human life. The chief point is that the term "discovery" refers to innovations that provide men with new information (e.g., the discovery of a new continent or a new principle of physics), while "invention" is reserved for useful new combinations of already existing information.[34] The automobile provides a good example of the latter, since all the things that went into the construction of the first car (e.g., gasoline engine, running gears, drive shaft, carriage body, etc.) were existing elements of the culture. The "only" new thing was the total combination of elements.

Alterations, the third form of innovation, resemble discoveries in that they involve the introduction of new elements into the cultural tradition. Unlike discoveries, however, alterations have no identifiable adaptive value. They are merely changes, not an increase in the store of useful information. They are frequently a result of the fallibility of the mechanisms of transmission. When men have been forced to rely on oral transmission, as was the case throughout most of human history, mistakes often occurred. What the younger generation learned from its elders was not always just what the elders had learned from their parents. Linguists have shown, for example, how the pronunciation of words has gradually changed with the passage of time. A good instance of this is the diversity of words for "mother" now used in the various Indo-European languages; yet all derive from the same root. Similar changes have occurred in legends, songs, and other aspects of culture.

Alterations also occur as the result of conscious intent. Slang, for example,

---

[34] For one of the earliest statements of this distinction, see F. Stuart Chapin, *Cultural Change* (New York: Century, 1928), p. 345.

involves the deliberate distortion of words to create a distinctive vocabulary. Changing styles in art seem to reflect a similar process.

The fourth, and final, form of sociocultural innovation is diffusion. It involves the transmission of information from one society to another,[35] or from one subdivision of a society to another subdivision. Like invention and discovery, it usually has adaptive value for the receiving society; unlike them, it adds nothing to the total store of human information. Nevertheless, as we shall see in the next chapter, the ease with which diffusion occurs helps account for the greater rapidity of sociocultural evolution compared with organic evolution.

We find yet another difference between these two forms of evolution when we consider the relation of innovations to progress. As we have seen, most mutations are regressive, and recombinations are, in balance, neither progressive nor regressive. Inventions and discoveries, two of the basic forms of sociocultural innovation, are, by contrast, largely progressive and hence contribute directly to sociocultural advance.

Sociocultural extinction

Turning to the process of extinction, we find that the analogue of genetic drift has been of such minor importance in sociocultural evolution that it does not even have a name.[36] There are a few documented cases in which valuable culture traits have been lost to a particular society because of the failure of certain family lines to reproduce, but these are rare. In one society, knowledge of the technique of canoe building was lost in this way, in another the technique of making stone adzes.[37] In both instances the loss occurred because the technique was the preciously guarded secret of certain families or groups that died out without transmitting their secrets to others. Except in small, extremely isolated groups, such losses are virtually impossible, owing to the relative ease with which cultural information is transmitted both within and between societies. Therefore, we can largely ignore the process of what might best be called *sociocultural drift*, since its effects on human societies have been very minor indeed.

By contrast, sociocultural selection, the analogue of natural selection, is of major importance. Like its counterpart, it is largely responsible for the progressive character

---

[35] It is in this respect that it resembles hybridization, since it involves the transmission across basic population boundaries—in one case the boundaries defining species; in the other, the boundaries defining societies.

[36] The nearest approximation is "cultural regression," but that term usually includes the results of natural selection as well as the results of drift. It cannot be equated with the term "cultural drift" as used by Herskovits and Eggan, since they have used it to refer to change that has a directional character. See Melville Herskovits, *Man and His Works* (New York: Knopf, 1948), chap. 34; or Fred Eggan, "Cultural Drift and Social Change," *Current Anthropology*, 4 (1963), pp. 347–355.

[37] A. L. Kroeber, *Anthropology* (New York: Harcourt, Brace, 1948), p. 375.

Fig. 3/6   A case study of intra-societal selection: automobiles replacing horse-drawn vehicles

of the evolutionary process. There is one important difference, however. In the organic world, the process of selection operates entirely without regard to the wishes of the individuals and populations involved. It is a blind, spontaneous process. This is why Darwin called it *natural* selection (i.e., to contrast it with the conscious, rational process of *artificial* selection used by plant and animal breeders).[38] In the sociocultural world, blind, spontaneous processes of selection are also operative, but they are supplemented to some extent by rational, conscious selection. Especially in *intra*societal selection, men are able to choose between alternatives. They can use their powers of reason to make a conscious choice between a stone axe and a metal axe or between a horse and buggy and an automobile. This has given men a tremendous advantage in the interspecies competition for survival and dominance.

But while conscious choice is an important and distinctive feature of socio-cultural selection, we must be careful not to exaggerate its significance. The fate of specific cultural patterns as well as entire cultural systems often depends on power struggles rather than on rational decision making. When this happens, it is military, political, or financial power that determines the outcome. In wars, for example, no one can sit back, compare the contestants, and decide that it would be better for one society to survive instead of another. The result is determined by a process directly analogous to that operating in the rest of the biotic world.

---

[38] See *The Origin of Species* (New York: Mentor, 1958), especially pp. 47ff., 73ff., and 87ff.

Earlier we noted that natural selection is not a simple process operating at a single point in the life cycle, or at a single level in the biotic realm. The same is true of sociocultural selection. It operates continuously, and it operates at every level— from the individual to the intersocietal—where choices are made or where the spontaneous operation of social forces leads to the extinction of some sociocultural patterns and the preservation of others. Multiple criteria are at work in sociocultural selection, just as in natural selection, and these often conflict with one another. These selective cross-pressures are extremely important, and will be examined more carefully in Chapter 4. Suffice it to repeat here that sustenance problems and pressures are of major importance in sociocultural selection, just as in organic, and this is one of the reasons why technology is such a crucial factor in the evolutionary process.

Environment plays a major role in sociocultural selection, just as it does in natural selection. In both instances, the environment is the thing to which the unit is adapting. In both instances, the environment includes not only the inorganic world of sun, soil, and all the rest; it also includes other species and other societies. In fact, in the case of human societies, other human societies have come to be one of the most important elements to which they must adapt. Once we recognize this, we can never again think of environment as a stable and unchanging entity to which some final, perfect, and stable mode of adaptation can be achieved.

Sociocultural evolution: The basic trends

Following the model developed in biology, our attention is ultimately directed to the total process of sociocultural evolution and the overall patterns of development. Here, as elsewhere, we find both similarities and differences.

As we have seen, the two basic trends in organic evolution are toward diversification and progress. These are paralleled by comparable trends in sociocultural evolution. The first of these, the growth of social and cultural diversity, is obvious to any student of history. There are reasons to believe, however, that this trend will not continue much longer. Forces at work in the modern world promise to reverse it.[39] Even now we may be on the threshold of such a reversal. When it occurs, it will provide yet another important distinction between organic and sociocultural evolution.

Though the trend toward sociocultural diversity is hard to deny, many people challenge the thesis that there has been progress in human history. They insist that it is impossible to show that modern man is happier or more moral than his prehistoric ancestors. This is a serious misunderstanding, however, of what modern evolutionists mean by progress. When evolutionists use this term today, they are referring primarily to *technological* advance, and secondarily to certain other very

---

[39] For further discussion of this subject, see Chapter 5, pp. 95–110.

specific and limited forms of organizational and ideological advance that are by-products of technological advance. We could, in fact, paraphrase our earlier definition of biotic progress to fit this modern conception of sociocultural progress. In other words, sociocultural progress may be defined as *the raising of the upper level of the capacity of human societies to mobilize energy and information in the adaptive process.* So defined, sociocultural progress is indisputable. This approach, of course, distinguishes technological and organizational progress from progress in morality and human happiness, and makes no assumption that they are necessarily linked. Their relationship remains an open question requiring further study.[40]

Variable concepts and probabilistic theory

Finally, the new synthetic theory of organic evolution provides a useful model by virtue of its shift from categoric to variable concepts, and from deterministic to probabilistic formulations of theory.[41] Categoric concepts need not be wholly abandoned by sociologists, since there are many situations in which they are appropriate or at least convenient. When they are used merely as a convenience, however, we must keep in mind the essentially noncategoric nature of the phenomena involved. In this way we can avoid some of the difficulties of the nineteenth-century theories of evolution.

A postscript on validity

Before concluding this brief introduction to evolutionary theory, it should be emphasized that we will use the new synthetic theory of organic evolution only as an aid in constructing a theory of sociocultural evolution. The *validity* of the two theories is in no way related. If our theory should prove faulty, this would not discredit the new synthetic theory in biology. Similarly, should the latter someday be proven less than 100 per cent correct, this would have no bearing on the validity of our theory. The *logic* of the two theories is parallel, but the *content* is quite distinct, and their validity, therefore, is in no way linked.

---

[40] We shall return to this subject in Chapter 15.

[41] See pp. 59–60 for an explanation of these terms.

Chapter 4
Sociocultural Continuity, Innovation and Extinction

The three processes of continuity, innovation, and extinction, are, as we have seen, the basic building blocks of evolutionary theory. Without an understanding of them, we cannot hope to understand the evolutionary process as a whole. In this chapter we shall examine each of these important processes more closely in an effort to see not only how they contribute to the larger evolutionary process, but also how the structural-functional and ecological-evolutionary approaches can be knit together.

SOCIOCULTURAL CONTINUITY

Of the three basic processes, continuity, at first glance, appears to be least essential to evolutionary theory. In fact, it might even seem antithetical, since evolution means change and continuity can be thought of as the antithesis of change. When we think about it more carefully, however, we realize that evolution is change of a very special kind. It is change that implies continuity because, in essence, it is *cumulative* change. It involves the addition of new elements to a continuing base of elements rather than the constant abandonment of existing elements and their replacement by new ones. Because of this, we cannot ignore the fact of continuity in any theory of sociocultural evolution.

Evidence of social and cultural continuity is all around us. The modern processes of papermaking, printing, and bookbinding used in producing this book, for example, contain numerous elements that originated hundreds of years ago. The more basic elements such as the alphabet and the very concept of books are over three thousand years old. Other elements in our culture such as the calendar, the concept of God, certain tools and techniques of cultivation, the basic techniques of metallurgy, and the concept of justice, to name but a few, are even older.

Habit and custom: two levels of sociocultural continuity

Sociocultural continuity manifests itself on two levels in human societies. On the level of individual behavior, we see it in what we call habits; on the level of group behavior, in customs. Our primary concern here is with customs, but since they depend, in part, on the existence of habits, we must start there.

In popular usage, the term "habit" often refers to any recurring pattern of action in the life of an individual. The term has a more precise meaning, however, one which reflects our modern awareness of the important psychological processes underlying most of these recurring patterns. Thanks to the contributions of psychologists as diverse as Pavlov, Freud, and Skinner, we have come to recognize the importance of *conditioning on the subconscious levels.* Such conditioning is the functional equivalent of instinct in human life and action. In other words, habits provide the individual with a programmed set of responses to recurring problems.

On first thought, it might appear that these conditioned responses subvert the adaptive value of learning, which is presumably a more flexible means of solving problems than genetic programming or instinct. In a sense this is true: subconsciously programmed responses, even though learned, *are* relatively inflexible. But flexibility of response is not an unmitigated blessing, as any child learning to walk, or young person learning to drive, can attest. Flexibility can be enjoyed only at the price of tying up much of our limited span of consciousness and expending much of our limited store of emotional energy. At the conscious level we can normally do only one or two things at a time, but thanks to subconscious conditioning, we can often carry on a variety of activities simultaneously. Thus, despite their built-in inflexibility, habits greatly enrich our behavior patterns, and ultimately our lives as well.

When we compare the habits of members of the same society (e.g., speech habits, eating habits, etc.), we find a great deal of similarity. This is no coincidence: most habits are learned from others. Sometimes this is the result of deliberate efforts to promote desired patterns of behavior, as in the training of children; often it is simply the result of conscious or unconscious imitation.

Habits which are shared by the members of a group and persist over a period of time are known as *customs.* The term covers not just shared habits, however, but *any durable pattern of action common to the members of a group,* including those that operate primarily on the level of consciousness. From the functional standpoint, customs may be regarded as traditional solutions to recurring problems. Certain problems arise repeatedly in every society. It would require an impossible expenditure of time and energy for every individual to work out his own solution to them. Furthermore, most of the solutions would be less efficient than the standardized group solution that evolves over a period of time. Sometimes, too, no particular solution is intrinsically superior; yet a standardized solution is necessary. A good example of this is the problem of which side of the road automobiles should drive

Fig. 4/1 British laws require that vehicles travel on the left-hand side of roads and highways

on. It makes no difference whether they stay on the right or the left, but it *is* imperative that all drivers in a particular nation follow the same practice.

At this point, the question naturally arises as to how customs are related to norms. Norms, it will be recalled, are the rules defining correct behavior in specific situations. Customs, by contrast, are the ways people *actually act* in those situations. Norms and customs are usually similar, but they are seldom identical, since certain violations of the norms tend to be customary. For example, driving somewhat in excess of the speed limit is the rule on certain stretches of highway in this country, even though this is clearly in violation of a legal norm. Similarly, the practice of "cooping," "huddling," or "going down" (i.e., sleeping on duty) has long been customary on many police forces, especially during the midnight to 8 A.M. shift.

The causes of sociocultural continuity

Not surprisingly, a process as common and as basic as sociocultural continuity is due to a variety of factors. Some of these involve deliberate, conscious efforts to promote continuity and avoid change; others operate spontaneously, without conscious intent on anyone's part. Some depend on highly complex organizational arrangements; others operate in a very informal way. We must consider them all if we are to appreciate the magnitude of the forces responsible for continuity.

Some of the most powerful forces stem from man's basic nature. As we have seen, men appear to have an inborn, genetically programmed motivation to satisfy their needs as economically as possible. In most instances, this is best achieved by adhering to customary practices. Change is not only risky; it usually requires new learning, and learning requires two of men's most precious commodities, time and energy. After providing for the necessities of life, most men have little left of either. As a result, men usually cling to traditional ways of doing things except in cases where the anticipated benefits of change clearly outweigh the anticipated costs, or in trivial matters where nothing of value is at stake. Even the great revolutionaries of history have recognized the impossibility of *total* change and have never advocated it.

The process of aging is another important barrier to change. Older people, because they usually possess more wealth and power than younger ones,[1] stand to lose more from change. Also, learning is more difficult for them than for younger people,[2] and they have stronger emotional ties with traditional practices. Thus, the most powerful members of a society—those who control a disproportionate share of the economic and political resources that could underwrite the cost of change—are the very ones who have the least propensity for change.

Another basic aspect of human nature that contributes to sociocultural continuity is *the prolonged helplessness of the human infant.* Unlike the offspring of most other species, the newly born human is incapable of satisfying even his most basic needs, and he remains in this condition not for days or weeks, but for years. To survive into adulthood, he must master the traditional culture of his society, since it alone provides the resources he needs to cope with the problems of existence. Language is a good illustration of this. Until a child masters the linguistic symbols of his society, he is largely dependent on others; once he masters them, he has an invaluable resource at his disposal. This applies to all of the basic elements of his group's culture: *it pays the child to master them.* Thus the desire of the older generation to preserve the traditional culture and transmit it to their offspring is more than matched by the desire of the younger generation to master it.

The process by which an individual learns the culture of his society is, as we have seen, the socialization process. The key to this process lies in the system of rewards and punishments which surrounds each of us from infancy on. Each person has, at birth, a potential for developing in a variety of different ways. More than that, in the early months and years of his life he explores many of these possibilities. Some he finds are rewarding, while others result in unpleasant experiences. The normal individual responds by repeating those actions that have been pleasant or rewarding and abandoning those that were not.

Figure 4/2 is a graphic representation of the situation in which most of us find ourselves. The larger circle represents the full range of potentialities open to us.

---

[1] See Gerhard Lenski, *Power and Privilege: A Theory of Social Stratification* (New York: McGraw-Hill, 1966), pp. 105, 136, and 406–407.

[2] See, for example, H. G. Barnett, *Innovation: The Basis of Cultural Change* (New York: McGraw-Hill, 1953), p. 386.

Fig. 4/2 The sanction system surrounding the individual

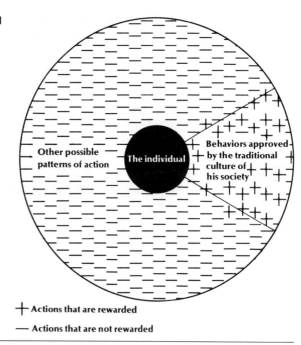

Other possible patterns of action

The individual

Behaviors approved by the traditional culture of his society

╋ Actions that are rewarded

— Actions that are not rewarded

The wedge represents the more limited range of behavior patterns approved by the culture of our society. When we experiment with actions that lie within the approved limits, we find that we are usually rewarded; when we go beyond these limits, we usually find the opposite. Sometimes, however, we are punished when we act in accord with the norms and rewarded when we violate them. For example, a student who cheats on an examination and is not caught may receive a higher grade than one who is honest. Some instances of this are inevitable in almost any society, since those who do the sanctioning are not omniscient. In general, however, conformity with the norms is rewarded, deviance punished. As a result, by a process of conditioning that begins in infancy and continues throughout our lives, we gradually become habituated to those patterns of action that are customary in our society and approved by it.

Figure 4/2 may be slightly misleading in one respect. It shows the limits of approved behavior for a single individual and may appear to suggest that the same boundaries apply for all members of that society. Actually, this is not the case. As we saw in Chapter 2, norms are rules of behavior governing the conduct of the incumbents of *specific roles.* What is correct for the incumbent of one role is not necessarily correct for the incumbent of another. For example, the norms of dress for women are quite different from those for men in our society. Similarly, there are marked differences in the norms of conduct for members of the upper and lower classes. The total range of behaviors that are approved by a society for incumbents of all the various roles, then, is far greater than the range approved for any single role. Even so, the total range of approved behaviors falls far short of what is possible.

To a considerable degree, every system of sanctions reflects *conscious and deliberate* efforts to promote continuity. The older generation naturally uses its resources to encourage adherence to the cultural standards it believes right, and to discourage deviance from them. These standards are, after all, an important part of the precious residue of information gleaned by the group from generations of experience. If each generation had to start afresh and build a culture from its own experiences, mankind would never have escaped the Stone Age.

The socialization process is not only a matter of deliberate efforts, however. Some of the most effective socialization occurs in situations where no conscious effort is being made to train or influence others. Many of the "rewards" and "punishments" experienced in everyday life are simply spontaneous by-products of normal social interaction. It is human nature to respond positively to actions we appreciate and value, and negatively to those we do not. Since our values reflect our training

Fig. 4/3 Some of the most effective socialization occurs in situations where no conscious effort is made to train or influence others

and experience, we tend to respond positively to actions consistent with the traditional culture of our group and negatively to those that are not. While there are exceptions to this, they are just that–exceptions.

We cannot fully appreciate the power of the socialization process, however, so long as we think of it as an external force to which men respond more or less reluctantly. It is, rather, an external force that so transforms our inner nature that it gradually becomes an internal force as well. As one writer puts it:

> What happens in socialization is that the social world is internalized within the child. The same process, though perhaps weaker in quality, occurs every time the adult is initiated into a new social context or a new social group. Society, then, is not only something "out there,". . . but it is also "in here," part of our innermost being. Only an understanding of internalization makes sense of the incredible fact that most external controls work most of the time for most of the people in a society. Society not only controls our movements, but shapes our identity, our thought and our emotions. The structures of society become the structures of our own consciousness. Society does not stop at the surface of our skin. Society penetrates us as much as it envelops us.[3]

As a result, the socialized individual shares in the traditional culture of his society with a minimal sense of constraint. What is more, by his own actions, both deliberate and spontaneous, he reinforces the system of sanctions which surrounds others, thereby making his own contribution to sociocultural continuity.

The conservatism inherent in the socialization process is greatly reinforced by most ideologies. One of their chief functions is to preserve for future generations the basic insights of the past. For this reason, ideologies invariably acquire a sacred and conservative character if they survive and win popular acceptance. Ironically, this has been true even of revolutionary ideologies, such as Marxism. Once they win acceptance, they too acquire an aura of the sacred and become a force for continuity–and against change.

Still another factor contributing to sociocultural continuity is *the systemic character of sociocultural systems*. Most of the parts of these systems are linked to other parts in such a way that a change in one necessitates changes in others. For example, when the Swedes decided to drive on the right side of the road a few years ago, this "simple" change necessitated hundreds of others and took months of planning. Cars and buses had to be redesigned, traffic signals moved, highway billboards relocated, and traffic laws rewritten. The changeover cost literally millions of dollars. Similar linkages are found throughout every sociocultural system. As a consequence, there are many changes that cannot be made without numerous additional changes, and while the benefits of the initial change may outweigh its costs, this may no longer be true when the costs of the additional changes are added.

---

[3] From *Invitation to Sociology* by Peter L. Berger. Copyright 1963 by the author. Reprinted by permission of Doubleday & Company, Inc.

Benefits and costs of continuity

Until the modern era, most men accepted without question the principle that traditional ways of doing things are usually best. To say that a practice had been customary for centuries was necessarily to praise it. Today, however, we are less sure of this. Though many still prefer "the old ways," many others prefer change. Attitudes on the question of tradition versus change have become a divisive force in politics, economics, religion, art, scholarship, and many other fields. Conservatives emphasize the virtues of tradition, while liberals stress the advantages of change. Though we cannot hope to resolve such controversies, we can, perhaps, achieve a better understanding of the basic issue by examining both the benefits and the costs associated with continuity.

On the positive side, it is clear that sociocultural continuity yields a number of major benefits without which human life would be impossible. As we have noted, the development of habits greatly increases people's efficiency. If every problem had to be worked out again each time it was encountered, mankind would not survive for long. Similarly, if children did not inherit ready-made solutions to most of life's problems, they could not survive.

Beyond these individual benefits, there are social ones. Men cannot live alone; they are dependent on society. But a social system can function only if the actions of its members are mutually predictable, and sociocultural continuity is a requisite of predictability. The costs of unpredictable behavior patterns are dramatically illustrated by the many tragic misunderstandings that developed between the early European explorers and the natives of both Africa and the New World.

Finally, as mentioned earlier, evolutionary progress is built on the foundation of cumulative change, and cumulative change presupposes the continuation of advantageous elements from the past. To express it somewhat differently, a sociocultural system incorporates the best solutions that the members of a society have found for their recurring problems. To ignore these solutions simply for the sake of change would be to abandon the group's chief resource in its struggle for survival.

Yet having said all this, we still must recognize that sociocultural continuity can be costly. In the realm of technology, innovation usually leads to greater efficiency in the use of man's time and energy, a higher standard of living, and the opening of a wider range of options in many areas of life. Much the same is true in the realm of social organization.

Sociocultural continuity is likely to prove especially costly in a changing world. Either a society changes in response to changes in its environment, or the adequacy of its adaptation declines. This is inevitable in a world where societies compete for land and other essential resources, as technologically primitive peoples have discovered, to their regret, in recent centuries. To repeat a point made earlier: in *a changing world, no final, perfect, or ultimate form of adaptation to the environment is possible.*

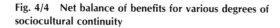

Fig. 4/4   Net balance of benefits for various degrees of sociocultural continuity

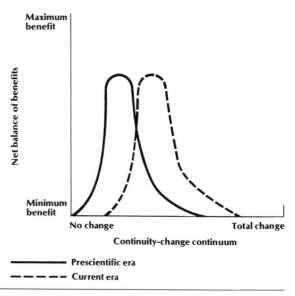

To summarize, sociocultural continuity, entails both benefits and costs. The net balance of benefits is smallest at the two extremes on the scale of continuity and change (see Fig. 4/4). The most rewarding course for a society appears to be somewhere between the two extremes. Prior to the Industrial Revolution and the rise of modern science, the most rewarding course was probably much closer to the "no change" pole than it is today, since fewer innovations were likely to be successful and environmental conditions were more stable. Today, however, societies that include a larger component of change almost certainly come out ahead.

SOCIOCULTURAL INNOVATION

The basic causes of innovation

Many factors contribute to innovation within a society, but for purposes of analysis, they may be divided into two categories: (1) environmental factors, and (2) internal factors.

By now it should be clear that the relationship between a society and its environment is extremely important. The environment is not only a society's source of sustenance, but its various characteristics act as a set of conditions to which the society must adapt. Changes in the environment, therefore, force compensatory changes in the society.

Several times in history, societies have had to make major adjustments in response to changes in their physical and biotic environments. The ending of the Pleistocene Ice Age, for example, necessitated drastic changes in the sociocultural systems of Europe, which were then based on the highly specialized hunting of reindeer on open plains.[4] With the warming of the climate, forests began to spring up across Europe, and the reindeer retreated toward the arctic regions where they are found today. When new varieties of plants and animals appeared, societies had either to innovate or perish.

The environment to which a society must adapt also includes the other societies with which it has contact. Any major change in one usually has consequences for the rest, frequently triggering a chain reaction of countless adjustments and innovations. In the last 5,000 to 10,000 years, the social environment has usually been much less stable than the physical and biotic and, as a result, has been a much more frequent source of change.

If environmental change were the only source of innovation, however, the rate would have been much lower than it has been. Innovations are also the result of forces rooted in man himself. There is an *inner dynamic* within human societies that prevents them from becoming completely stable.

To begin with, as we have seen, men do not always learn perfectly everything their elders try to teach them. Errors occur in the process of transmitting the cultural heritage from one generation to the next, giving rise to alterations of various kinds. But in addition to this, men are apparently motivated by their very nature to deliberately try new patterns of action. Sometimes they experiment with alternatives because they have become bored by overly repetitive routines and feel the need for new experiences. Sometimes the motivation is curiosity, a trait found among many of the higher animals, but intensified by culture. At other times, the motivation may simply be material self-interest. Given men's desire to maximize their rewards, experimentation and innovation are inevitable.

Man has been exploring his environment and experimenting with new methods of doing things from the earliest times. In the ensuing processes of discovery and invention, purposive behavior and accident, or chance, have often been curiously intermingled. For example, the great scientist Pasteur discovered the principle and technique of immunization only after he accidentally injected a stale bacterial culture of chicken cholera into some animals. When, unexpectedly, they survived, it occurred to him that a weakened culture might immunize against the disease.[5] Similarly, a key problem in the development of photographic techniques was solved when Daguerre put a bromide-coated silver plate into a cupboard where, unknown to him, an open vessel of mercury was standing. When he returned the following day, he found the latent image had begun to develop and surmised that fumes from the mercury were responsible.

Even though chance has played a major part in the process of innovation, *knowledge, intelligence,* and *purpose* have also been essential. An appreciation of

---

[4] See, for example, Grahame Clark, *The Stone Age Hunters* (London: Thames and Hudson, 1967), chaps. 3 and 5.

[5] For a discussion of a number of interesting examples, including those here, see A. L. Kroeber, *Anthropology* (New York: Harcourt, Brace, 1948), pp. 353–355.

the value of new information presupposes both intelligence and knowledge, and often purpose as well. It was *more* than accident that led Pasteur to discover the process of immunization, and Daguerre the process of developing pictures. Both men had already acquired the knowledge which enabled them to appreciate the import of their accidental discoveries. Furthermore, both were actively seeking new knowledge. Thus, in these cases as in most others involving chance, the outcome was due to the *combination* of chance, knowledge, intelligence, and purpose.

Given man's evolutionary history, this is exactly what we should expect. Man stands in an evolutionary line that has relied on learning as one of its basic means of adaptation, and the chief function of learning is to enhance the value of experience. He acquires experience through chance occurrence as well as by purposive action.

In the earlier stages of human history, chance was probably much more important in the innovative process than it is today. Accidental alterations were far likelier before the invention of writing and other methods of record keeping increased the accuracy with which information could be transmitted. Moreover, though we have no record of how important discoveries of the past occurred (e.g., fire-making, animal domestication, plant cultivation, etc.), it seems likely that chance played a significant part.

The rise of science, with its systematic methods of research and organized store of information, has further reduced the role of chance in the last century. Many modern inventions (e.g., submarines and rocket ships) were predicted years in advance of the construction of the first workable model. Similarly, most of the "newer" elements in the periodic table were predicted long before their actual

Fig. 4/5 In his novel <u>Twenty Thousand Leagues Under the Sea,</u> Jules Verne wrote about the submarine almost thirty years before it was invented

discovery. This decline in the importance of chance and the corresponding increase in the importance of purposeful action are natural by-products of the steady growth in the store of man's useful information.

The rate of innovation

Though innovation occurs in every human society, its *rate* is highly variable. In some societies, during some periods, the rate has been so low as to be virtually imperceptible; at other times, or in other societies, it has been extremely high. To understand the major trends in evolutionary history, we first must understand what is responsible for these variations.

Amount of information Of all the factors involved in the rate of innovation, probably none has been more important than the magnitude of the existing store of information in the group.[6] The reason is simple. Invention, as we have seen, is one of the basic processes of innovation, and inventions are essentially *recombinations of existing elements of the culture.* It follows, therefore, that a society's potential for invention is a simple mathematical function of the number of elements available for combination. This is easily illustrated. Table 4/1 shows the number of combinations that are possible for various numbers of units or elements. While two units can be combined in only one way, three units can be combined in four ways, and four units in eleven ways. In other words, *the addition of each new unit more than doubles the number of possible combinations.*[7] Thus a mere fivefold increase in the number of units from 2 to 10 leads to a thousandfold increase in the number of possible

---

[6] For an early discussion of this point, see William F. Ogburn, *Social Change* (New York: Viking, 1922), chap. 6.

Table 4/1 Numbers of combinations possible for various numbers of units

No. of units	2 at a time	3 at a time	4 at a time	5 at a time	6 at a time	7 at a time	8 at a time	9 at a time	10 at a time	Total
				Total number of combinations						
2	1	0	0	0	0	0	0	0	0	1
3	3	1	0	0	0	0	0	0	0	4
4	6	4	1	0	0	0	0	0	0	11
5	10	10	5	1	0	0	0	0	0	26
6	15	20	15	6	1	0	0	0	0	57
7	21	35	35	21	7	1	0	0	0	120
8	28	56	70	56	28	8	1	0	0	247
9	36	84	126	126	84	36	9	1	0	502
10	45	120	210	252	210	120	45	10	1	1,013

combinations! To show how rapidly the number of combinations increase it may help to raise the number of units to 20:

Table 4/2 Number of combinations possible for units from 10
to 20

Number of units	Total number of combinations
10	1,013
11	2,036
12	4,083
13	8,176
14	16,365
15	32,744
16	65,503
17	131,022
18	262,061
19	524,140
20	1,048,299

Of course, many of the elements of a sociocultural system cannot be combined in any useful way. For example, it is difficult to imagine a useful combination of the hammer and the saw. The number of *possible* combinations, therefore, is much greater than the number of fruitful ones. Also, we should note that the units in the tables are basic, or uncombined, units. This means that inventions add nothing to a society's *potential*; only discoveries do this. Nevertheless, despite these qualifications, *the amount of available information* is certainly a major factor in a society's rate of innovation.

Size of population   A second cause of difference in the rate of innovation is the size of societal populations.[8] The more people looking for a solution to a problem, the quicker it will be found, other things being equal. Since societal populations vary

---

[7] To be exact, the addition of the nth unit increases the number of possible combinations twofold plus, n-1. If one society has x times as many units as another society, and if there are c possible combinations in the latter, then the number of possible combinations in the former society equals slightly more than c^x. For example, if society A has 10 units of information, which makes possible a total of approximately 1,000 combinations, and if society B has 20 times as many units, then the number of combinations possible in society B equals approximately $1,000^{20}$. This method of estimating the effects of additional units of information becomes more accurate the larger the number of units. The error involved always results in an *under*estimation of the true magnitude of the difference. I am indebted to William Postl, a former student, for bringing this relation to my attention.

[8] Ogburn mentioned this factor briefly in his study, but did not stress it. See *op. cit.,* 1950 ed., p. 110.

so greatly (by ratios as high as 30,000,000 to 1), this is a factor of considerable importance.

Extent of intersocietal contact A third factor influencing the rate of innovation, and one of the most important in the modern world, is the extent of intersocietal contact. The greater the contact one society has with others, the greater its opportunities to appropriate their discoveries and inventions. In short, sociocultural contact enables a society to take advantage of the brainpower and cultural heritage of other societies.

The importance of this was beautifully illustrated by Ralph Linton, a leading anthropologist of the last generation. Analyzing American culture, he wrote:

> Our solid American citizen awakens in a bed built on a pattern which originated in the Near East but which was modified in Northern Europe before it was transmitted to America. He throws back covers made from cotton, domesticated in India, or linen, domesticated in the Near East, or wool from sheep, also domesticated in the Near East, or silk, the use of which was discovered in China. All of these materials have been spun and woven by processes invented in the Near East. He slips into his moccasins, invented by the Indians of the Eastern woodlands, and goes to the bathroom, whose fixtures are a mixture of European and American inventions, both of recent date. He takes off his pajamas, a garment invented in India, and washes with soap invented by the ancient Gauls. He then shaves, a masochistic rite which seems to have been derived from either Sumer or ancient Egypt.
>
> Returning to the bedroom, he removes his clothes from a chair of southern European type and proceeds to dress. He puts on garments whose form originally derived from the skin clothing of the nomads of the Asiatic steppes, puts on shoes made from skins tanned by a process invented in ancient Egypt and cut to a pattern derived from the classical civilizations of the Mediterranean, and ties around his neck a strip of bright-colored cloth which is a vestigial survival of the shoulder shawls worn by the seventeenth century Croatians. Before going out for breakfast he glances through the window, made of glass invented in Egypt, and if it is raining puts on overshoes made of rubber discovered by the Central American Indians and takes an umbrella, invented in southeastern Asia. Upon his head he puts a hat made of felt, a material invented in the Asiatic steppes.
>
> On his way to breakfast he stops to buy a paper, paying for it with coins, an ancient Lydian invention. At the restaurant a whole new series of borrowed elements confronts him. His plate is made of a form of pottery invented in China. His knife is of steel, an alloy first made in Southern India, his fork a medieval Italian invention, and his spoon a derivative of a Roman original. He begins breakfast with an orange, from the eastern Mediterranean, a canteloupe from Persia, or perhaps a piece of African watermelon. With this he has coffee, an Abyssinian plant, with cream and sugar. Both the domestication of cows and the idea of milking them originated in the Near East, while sugar was first made in India. After his fruit and first coffee he goes on to waffles, cakes made by a Scandinavian technique from wheat domesticated in Asia Minor. Over these he pours syrup, invented by the Indians of the Eastern woodlands. As a side dish he may have the egg of a species of bird domesticated in Indo-China, or thin strips of the flesh of an animal domesticated in Eastern Asia which have been salted and smoked by a process developed in northern Europe.

When our friend has finished eating he settles back to smoke, an American habit, consuming a plant domesticated in Brazil in either a pipe, derived from the Indians of Virginia, or a cigarette, derived from Mexico. If he is hardy enough he may even attempt a cigar, transmitted to us from the Antilles by way of Spain. While smoking he reads the news of the day, imprinted in characters invented by the ancient Semites upon a material invented in Germany. As he absorbs the accounts of foreign troubles he will, if he is a good conservative citizen, thank a Hebrew deity in an Indo-European language that he is 100 per cent American.[9]

Environmental stability A fourth factor affecting the rate of innovation is the stability of the environment to which the society must adapt. The greater the rate of environmental change, the greater the pressure on the society to modify either its technology or its system of social organization. As we noted before, the *social* environment usually changes much more rapidly than the biophysical. Especially important are events that upset the balance of power among neighboring societies, such as large-scale migrations, the building of empires, and similar developments.

Fundamental discoveries and inventions Fifth, the rate of innovation is greatly influenced by "fundamental" discoveries and inventions. Not all discoveries and inventions are of equal importance; a few open the way for literally thousands of other innovations, while the majority have no such effect.[10] The steam engine is a good example of a fundamental invention in the recent past. Examples from earlier periods include the discovery of the principles of plant cultivation, animal domestication, and metallurgy, and the invention of the plow.

Sometimes a fundamental innovation will cause the rate of innovation to rise because the principles involved can be applied, with minimum effort and imagination, to hundreds, even thousands, of problems. This was true of both the steam engine and metallurgy. Sometimes, however, an invention or discovery earns the label "fundamental" because it so drastically alters the conditions of human life that hundreds or thousands of other changes become either possible or necessary. This was certainly the case with the discovery of the principles of plant cultivation, which, as we shall see in a later chapter, led to a host of major sociocultural changes.

Before leaving the subject of fundamental innovations, we should note that they have an impact that follows the pattern of the so-called S-curve, or logistic curve, shown in Fig. 4/6. In other words, their immediate effect is a period during which derivative innovations occur at an accelerating rate. In time, however, the rate of innovation begins to decline as the number of possible derivative innovations begins to be exhausted. How soon this happens depends on the nature of the fundamental innovation. Some have a much more limited number of possible derivatives than others. In every case, however, the long-term trend involves some approximation of the S-curve.

---

[9] From: *The Study of Man* by Ralph Linton. Copyright, 1936, by D. Appleton-Century Company, Inc. Reprinted by permission of Appleton-Century-Crofts.

[10] Ogburn, *op. cit.*, 1950 ed., p. 107.

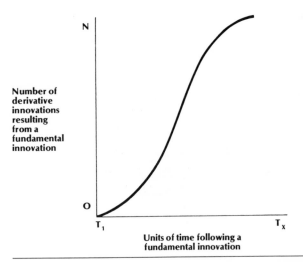

Number of derivative innovations resulting from a fundamental innovation

Units of time following a fundamental innovation

Fig. 4/6   S-curve pattern of derivative innovations resulting from a fundamental innovation

Attitude toward innovation   A sixth and final major factor influencing the rate of sociocultural innovation is the society's attitude toward innovation. In some societies, innovation has been positively valued, at least in certain areas of life. Contemporary American society is a case in point: Innovation or creativity is highly valued in art, science, technology, philosophy, entertainment, and recently even in theology. Sometimes in our society, it seems that an innovation can even be inferior to what it replaces and still be applauded. In most societies, however, traditional patterns have been highly valued, especially in the areas of ideology and social organization, and the idea of innovation for innovation's sake has been entirely alien.

Though the problem has not been studied as systematically as it should be, a society's attitude toward innovation is apparently greatly influenced by its prior experience with change. A society that has undergone an extended period of change and benefited from it will almost certainly favor innovation more than a society that has not had this experience. A society's attitude toward innovation may also vary in response to religious or other ideological influences. Some ideologies generate a very conservative and anti-innovational outlook; Confucianism was a classic example of such a faith. Judaism, Christianity, and Communism, by contrast, have been much more receptive to sociocultural innovation and change.

The "multiplier effect" in innovation

Up to this point we have considered each of the factors influencing the rate of innovation independently. Actually, however, *most of the factors stimulating innovation are mutually interdependent.* The nature of this interdependence is shown graphically in Fig. 4/7. As indicated by the doubleheaded arrow linking size of population and size of the store of useful information, each of these factors affects the other. The greater the store of useful information, the larger the population that can be supported in a given geographical area and the larger the area that can be controlled by

Fig. 4/7 Relations between factors responsible for variations in the rate of innovation

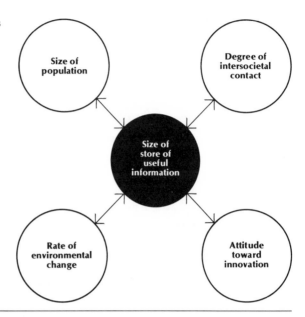

a single society. Conversely, the larger the population working on problems, the more rapidly the store of useful information tends to grow.

A similar relation exists between the size of the store of information and the degree of intersocietal contact. A greater store of useful information means more ''leisure'' time (i.e., time free from the demands of providing daily sustenance) that can be devoted to intersocietal contacts, and it may also mean better means of transportation and communication to facilitate such contacts. Conversely, the more contact a society has with other societies, the greater its own store of information will become.

Similarly, a society's store of information and changes in its environment are related. An increase in the former will usually result in changes in either the physical or social environment. Such changes, in turn, create the need for further change in the society and in its store of information, or else the level of the society's adaptation to the environment will decline.

Finally, the more useful information a society possesses, the more favorable its attitude toward innovation (because of rewarding experiences with innovations), and conversely, the more favorable its attitude toward change, the greater its store of information. In short, the size of the store of information is linked to each of these other factors in a reciprocal relation.

Because of these interrelations, a single innovation often gives rise to a whole series of others. Something analogous to the economist's multiplier effect seems to operate.[11] An increase in the store of useful information can easily contribute to

[11] For a discussion of the multiplier effect in economics, see Paul Samuelson, *Economics*, 6th ed., (New York: McGraw-Hill, 1964), pp. 231ff.

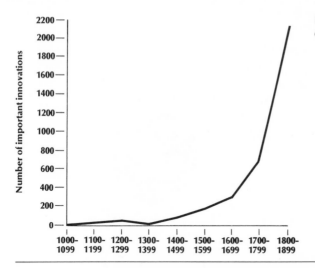

Fig. 4/8 Number of important inventions and discoveries, by century, from 1000 A.D. to 1900 A.D.

increases in population, in the degree of intersocietal contact, and in the rate of environmental change, and to an improvement in attitudes toward innovation. These changes, in turn, are very likely to contribute to a further increase in the store of useful information.[12]

The long-term rise in the rate of innovation

One of the striking facts of human history is the tremendous increase in the rate of innovation since early prehistoric times. Though one might suppose that this is largely due to recent developments, such is not the case. On the contrary, the trend has been going on for tens of thousands of years. Figure 4/8 shows the pattern for the past nine hundred years and, as we shall see in Chapter 7, archaeological evidence traces the trend to man's earliest history.[13]

This is not to say there has been a constantly accelerating rate in every society, or even that there has been an accelerating rate for the world as a whole in every century. At several points in history the rate of innovation remained fairly stable, or even declined, for a period. Nevertheless, the rate invariably turned upward again and became greater than ever before.

The reasons for this should be evident by now. As we have seen, technological information is cumulative, and each new bit of useful information increases the probability of gaining additional information. More than that, technological advance

---

[12] Normally the multiplier involved in the innovation process is considerably less than 1.0. This means that the derivative effects of the initial innovation become smaller and smaller in magnitude until eventually they disappear. For example, if we imagine an initial innovation with an adaptive value of 100 and a multiplier effect of .5, the first derivative effect would have a value of 50, the second of 25, the third of 12.5, and so on until the effects become imperceptible.

[13] See Table 7/1, p. 148.

makes possible larger populations, and larger populations mean more people looking for solutions to problems. It also leads to increased contacts between societies and to the more rapid diffusion of knowledge. Finally, the benefits resulting from all of these developments gradually undermine historic prejudices against change and contribute to the emergence of new ideologies more favorable to innovation.

Where will this trend end? No one can really say at this time. We can say only that sooner or later acceleration must cease. At some point, any further increase in in the rate of innovation will almost certainly prove psychologically, and perhaps economically and politically, intolerable. Sometimes it seems we are already approaching that point. When we think about the situation more carefully, however, we realize that considerable acceleration is still possible simply because so many innovations in today's highly specialized societies require little or no adjustment on the part of most people. With the extreme division of labor that has developed during the last century, an individual is seriously affected by only a small proportion of the many inventions and discoveries being made. In short, sociocultural evolution appears to increase a society's ability to tolerate higher rates of innovation.

SOCIOCULTURAL EXTINCTION

Sociocultural extinction, like genetic extinction, has two components, as noted in Chapter 3. The first, the analogue of genetic drift, has been of very minor importance in human history, affecting only a few small, isolated societies. The reason for this, as mentioned earlier, is the ease of transmitting cultural information, which makes the unintentional loss of useful information an uncommon occurrence. We will focus, therefore, on the vastly more important process of *sociocultural selection*, dividing it, for purposes of analysis, into two parts. The first deals with *intra*societal selection, the second with *inter*societal.

Intrasocietal selection: The selection of elements within societies

As a result of the process of innovation, the members of human societies are often confronted with alternative solutions to problems. The choice a group makes in such a situation often leads to the extinction of one or more of the alternatives. Many factors influence men when they make such choices—the facts available to them, their judgments concerning the probable benefits and costs of the various alternatives, and, above all, their values. In keeping with the economizing principle stated earlier, men strive to follow the course of action that promises the greatest rewards for the least expenditure of resources.

This does not mean that men are strictly rational in making these choices. Decisions are often made on the basis of unexamined assumptions, and emotional factors frequently play a significant role. Furthermore, as we noted earlier, many human actions are primarily conditioned responses, with little or no conscious component.

In many areas of human activity, it is extremely difficult to determine which of several possible alternatives is likely to prove the most rewarding. This is especially true in matters of ideology. Technology, for reasons we have discussed, poses less of a problem, with the result that the process of selection in that area moves more swiftly. To a lesser degree, this is also true of systems of organization, especially organizations created for a single purpose, such as to make a profit or to defend a nation. Here, as with technology, alternatives are subjected to recurring tests, and their relative efficacy can be judged by a single standard (where multiple standards are involved, as in organizations with diverse functions, it is much more difficult for men to agree on the relative efficacy of alternatives). Thus, with the passage of time, the sequence of choices made by the members of a society produces a definite progression of organizational forms, just as choices among technological alternatives produces a definite progression of technological forms.

One of the great ironies of evolution is the fact that the process of intrasocietal selection does not necessarily increase a society's chances of survival.[14] It may even reduce them. The explanation of this paradox is that the principles governing the selective process on the intrasocietal level are different from those that operate on the intersocietal level. Within societies, choices are made on the basis of the maximization principle as applied by individuals and groups like families, businesses, and labor unions. These decisions are based on what each judges to be its own best interests, and these often conflict with the best interests of the society as a whole, at least when judged from the standpoint of its chances of survival. For example, most American families prefer to spend their resources on things that contribute to their own immediate comfort and pleasure rather than on things that strengthen the nation economically, militarily, or morally.[15]

Human societies as imperfect systems

This brings us to a characteristic of human societies that is frequently overlooked: though human societies may quite properly be called systems, they are very *imperfect* systems. A human society lacks the degree of coordination among its parts, and the degree of coordination between the parts and the whole, found in most of the things to which we apply the term "system."

Too often this term is used categorically: either something is a system, or it is not. Like many other concepts, however, it becomes more meaningful when it is used as a variable. For purposes of definition we should say that a system exists *to*

---

[14] See Walter Goldschmidt, *Man's Way: A Preface to the Understanding of Human Society* (New York: Holt, 1959), p. 128. For the biological parallel, see Konrad Lorenz, *On Aggression*, trans. by M. K. Wilson (New York: Bantam, 1967), pp. 36–38.

[15] See John Kenneth Galbraith's discussion of this problem in *The Affluent Society* (Boston: Houghton Mifflin, 1958), especially chap. 18.

the degree that the actions of the parts are coordinated with one another and with the actions of the entity as a whole. Defined in this way, it is clear that human societies are less perfect systems than most of the other things to which this term has been applied. For example, there is much less internal conflict within insect societies than within human societies. Though insect populations are divided into different castes, they exhibit nothing comparable to the struggles between castes and classes within human societies. Similarly, the coordination between the actions of the parts and the whole is much greater in insect societies, and in organisms and mechanical systems, than it is in human societies. In fact, there are few phenomena to which we apply the label "system" which show systemic properties less clearly than do human societies.

This suggests that we must use the term with considerable caution if we are not to distort our image of social reality. As we observed in Chapter 1, the cultural tools we create to serve us can easily become our masters and end up shaping our perception of the world we are trying so hard to understand, preventing us from seeing it as it really is.

Intersocietal selection: The selection of societies

While the selective process goes on within societies, eliminating first one, then another, of the elements of sociocultural systems, a similar process is taking place in which societies themselves are the units whose survival is at stake. No adequate understanding of evolutionary history is possible if we ignore this second mode of selection.

The two processes differ from one another in a number of ways, but the most important difference is in the basis of selection. In intersocietal selection, the basic determinant has usually been *military power*. To survive, a society has had to be strong enough to protect its territory and its resources against the attacks of aggressive neighboring societies. Those that have been too weak to defend themselves have usually been destroyed.

If this seems an unduly harsh view, one need only examine the historical record. Thousands of societies that once flourished no longer exist. If we look for the reason, we find that the great majority of them were simply unable to defend themselves. Defeated in war, they were absorbed, destroyed, or so crippled that they could not survive as autonomous units. The hundreds of Indian tribes that once flourished in North and South America and the many independent city-states that once dotted the Mediterranean world and the Middle East are good examples.

One of the widespread misconceptions of the modern era is that peace is the normal state of relations between societies, and hostility and war abnormal conditions. Much as we might wish this were true, the historical record indicates otherwise. A study of eleven European countries, covering periods of 275 to 1,025 years, found that the incidence of war ranged from a low of 28 per cent of the years in the

Fig. 4/9 A doomed society: Navajo Indians of the American Southwest

case of Germany to a high of 67 per cent in the case of Spain.[16] The mean was 47 per cent, indicating that on the average these eleven countries were engaged in some kind of military action almost every other year. Though we lack such systematic data for more primitive societies, the evidence we have suggests that warfare and fighting are common among them too.[17]

There are a number of reasons why wars and other struggles have been so common. Throughout most of history, the basic cause seems to have been the same one that underlies competition in the rest of the biological world, namely, *the*

---

[16] Pitirim Sorokin, *Social and Cultural Dynamics* (New York: Bedminster Press, 1962 ed.), vol. III, chap. 10 and p. 352.

[17] See, for example, L. T. Hobhouse, G. C. Wheeler, and M. Ginsberg, *The Material Culture and Social Institutions of the Simpler Peoples* (London: Routledge, 1965 ed.), p. 232, or Quincy Wright, *A Study of War* (Chicago: University of Chicago Press, 1942), chap. 6.

scarcity of resources.[18] As Malthus and Darwin recognized, a *finite* supply of resources, no matter how great, will never suffice for a population with an *infinite* capacity for growth. Unless its growth is checked somehow, every population, human or animal, eventually exhausts its supply of resources. In that situation, it will encroach on the territories and resources of neighboring populations. But since these resources are essential to the latter, they cannot permit it. Conflict thus becomes inevitable, and in time the weaker groups are destroyed. In many ways, evolutionary history has been like a deadly game of musical chairs in which a succession of contestants have been eliminated because of their inability to defend their territorial base.

In the case of man, the problem has been complicated by his possession of culture. To begin with, the problem of scarcity is more acute because culture multiplies human needs and desires enormously. The wants of animals are limited, but the more men have, the more they usually want. Thorstein Veblen, a pioneer American social scientist, saw this clearly. In his famous work, *The Theory of the Leisure Class,* he developed the thesis that once a society is able to produce more than the necessities of life, its members strive to acquire nonessential goods and services because of their prestige value.[19] Since prestige is always a relative matter (i.e., it is a measure of one's standing only in relation to others), it is impossible to satisfy the demand for goods and services which it generates, and scarcity is therefore inevitable no matter how much technology is improved or production increased.[20] Many wars have been fought to provide not the necessities of life for the masses, but glory and luxuries for their leaders.

Although military power has been the basic determinant of societal survival, other factors are involved, if only because they influence military power. For example, the greater a society's supply of manpower, the stronger it tends to be militarily. Similarly, the more advanced a society is technologically, the greater its military power. A society's size and level of technological development, therefore, are major determinants of its chances of survival.[21]

---

[18] This is not to deny other causes of conflict between societies. Sometimes, however, what appear to be other causes partly or wholly disappear when we examine them, just as a close examination of the Crusades indicates that religious motivations were far from dominant for most of the leaders. Political and economic motives loomed large in the minds of nobles and clergy alike.

[19] Thorstein Veblen, *The Theory of the Leisure Class* (New York: Macmillan, 1899), now available in various paperback editions.

[20] A similar conclusion is suggested by the provocative work of certain contemporary psychologists who have come to view human motivation as an unfolding or emerging process in which the satisfaction of one set of needs creates an awareness of further, previously hidden, needs. See especially A. H. Maslow, *Motivation and Personality* (New York: Harper, 1954), especially chap. 5.

[21] While other factors, such as the morale of soldiers and the skill of their leaders, help account for the success or failure of a particular society at a particular time, they are of little importance in explaining the basic pattern of evolutionary history. They may explain, for example, why one Indian tribe defeated another Indian tribe, but they are irrelevant to the ultimate victory of the Europeans over all the hundreds of Indian tribes in the New World. That was a matter of superior technology and superior numbers.

Nonmilitary forms of power, too, sometimes affect societal selection. Recent studies in India, for example, show that Hindu society has been gradually destroying, through cultural absorption, scores of primitive societies along its borders.[22] In most instances, members of these tribes, or their leaders, are envious of the advantages afforded by membership in Hindu society. This leads them to adopt Hindu ways and to abandon the traditional culture of their own group. Even when only part of a tribe does this, it can be enough to undermine the autonomy of the group and bring about its eventual destruction. This pattern is likely to occur only when a small, primitive society comes into contact with a large, advanced one.

Nonviolent extinction can occur in still other ways. A number of American Indian tribes, for example, were destroyed by smallpox epidemics. Other groups have disappeared because of internal struggles that resulted in schism. Currently another nonviolent form of societal extinction seems to be developing. This is the elimination of small nations that are unable to compete economically with the mass markets of larger nations, and their resulting low unit costs of production. The formation of the Benelux union in Western Europe could well be the prototype of a new pattern of societal merger and extinction.

Before concluding this discussion of societal extinction, we should note one more important difference between sociocultural and organic evolution. In organic evolution, extinction always means death for the members of the population involved. In sociocultural evolution, this is not necessarily the case. Thanks to the greater flexibility of this peculiarly human mode of evolution, the members of a society that has been destroyed can be absorbed into the ranks of another society even if their sociocultural heritage is completely wiped out.

---

[22] See, for example, F. G. Bailey, *Tribe, Caste, and Nation* (Manchester; England: Manchester University Press, 1960).

Chapter 5
Basic Evolutionary Trends

Someone once said that the study of history is nothing but the study of one damned thing after another. And often it does seem that this is true—that human history is just a tangled web of events, lacking any meaningful patterns and trends. But if we look more closely and if we take a broader time perspective, we soon discover that there *are* significant patterns. This chapter is concerned with two of these, the trend toward sociocultural *diversity* and the trend toward sociocultural *progress*.

SOCIOCULTURAL DIVERSIFICATION

Earlier we saw that one of the basic trends in organic evolution is the increasing diversity of genetic materials and adaptive patterns. Over the long course of evolutionary history, the number and variety of plant and animal species have multiplied enormously, and the adaptative patterns of living things have grown more and more diverse.

Sociocultural evolution provides a direct analogue of this: over the course of human history, the number and variety of societies have increased greatly, and the adaptive patterns of mankind have grown more and more varied. There is one important difference, however, between the process of organic diversification and its sociocultural counterpart. Organic diversification has been chiefly dependent on the multiplication of the number of species. Major differences in the plant and animal world have usually been *between* species, not within them; intraspecies differences have usually been relatively minor.

A parallel situation used to prevail in sociocultural evolution. Throughout most of human history, sociocultural differences were largely due to the spread of mankind to new territories and the resulting increase in the number and variety of societies. The more pronounced sociocultural differences were *between* societies (e.g., between primitive societies in the Arctic and primitive societies in the tropics), not within them. In the last 5,000 to 10,000 years, however, the situation has been changing. With technological advance, societies have become both larger and more differentiated internally. Now, sociocultural differences *within* societies are almost as great as those between societies. Looking to the future, there will probably be a sharp decline in both the number and variety of human societies, and sociocultural diversity will be largely a matter of *intra*societal differences. Whether this will mean a reversal in the historic trend toward greater sociocultural diversity overall is a question we will want to examine after we have reviewed the developments that have brought societies to where they are today.

The first phase: diversification through the multiplication of societies

Exactly when human history began is a much debated question. Modern research indicates that man became differentiated from his primate cousins and the rest of the animal world by a process that extended over a million years or more. Given the gradual, evolutionary character of the process, it is rather arbitrary and misleading to say that human history began at this point or that. A much more realistic approach is to identify certain critical developments in the total process and establish as best we can their approximate dates.

From the sociocultural standpoint, the first important development was the emergence of tool-making primates. Research on this problem is still in an unsettled state, partly because certain of the major findings are so recent and partly because so many of them are susceptible to a diversity of interpretations. At the present time, however, there is fairly general agreement among archaeologists that tool-making primates first appeared two million years ago.[1] Whether or not these creatures are classified as human depends entirely on the stringency of our definition, since they meet only the most minimal requirements.

A second and more crucial development was the emergence of symbols and language. Unfortunately, the first symbols our ancestors used were almost certainly verbal, and verbal symbols leave no mark. To infer their existence from the rudimentary stone tools found with primate remains, as some have done, is very hazardous.[2] We cannot safely infer the use of symbols prior to the appearance of the first burial remains approximately 100,000 to 150,000 years ago.

---

[1] See, for example, C. Loring Brace, *The Stages of Human Evolution* (Englewood Cliffs, N.J.: Prentice-Hall, 1967), chaps. 6 and 9.

[2] As one writer puts it, "In the Lower Palaeolithic period the hand-axe, although it was gradually improved, remained in use as the dominant tool form for over a quarter of a million years. It has been argued, and cogently, that this almost unimaginable slowness of change demonstrates a lack of inventiveness that could only survive among societies without fully articulate speech." From Jacquetta Hawkes, *Prehistory*, vol. I, part 1, of the UNESCO *History of Mankind* (New York: Mentor, 1965), p. 172.

The third and most recent step in the evolutionary emergence of man was taken when sociocultural adaptation finally replaced genetic adaptation as the *dominant* mode of human adaptation. One could well argue that man, in the fullest sense of the term, did not exist until this critical point was reached. Though again precise dating is impossible, it appears that this occurred about 35,000 years ago, when modern man (Homo sapiens sapiens) emerged as the dominant type of hominid. Prior to this, cultural change had been painfully slow, even slower than genetic change in the hominid line.[3] After this, *major* genetic changes came to an end (i.e., Homo sapiens sapiens remained the dominant type), and major cultural changes began (see Chapter 7). *At this point, sociocultural adaptation became the primary mode of human adaptation to the environment.*

On the basis of our current knowledge of hunting and gathering societies,[4] we know that the early growth and spread of the human population involved a continuing multiplication and diversification of human societies. Prior to the horticultural revolution that occurred less than ten thousand years ago, man was incapable of establishing large multicommunity societies of the type we take for granted today. In hunting and gathering societies technology is too primitive and inefficient to provide the resources needed to support political institutions of the kind found in modern industrial societies. As a result, in societies at this level of development each local community is normally autonomous. Occasionally somewhat more complex organizations emerge, but these are always small and usually short-lived.[5] Though these conclusions are based on observations of societies that have remained at the hunting and gathering level of development until modern times, there is no reason to suppose that in this respect their prehistoric predecessors were more favorably situated.[6]

Until recently, *societal fission* was a basic feature of human life. Because of population growth, each society would reach the point where the resources of its territory could not support any more people. The only alternative to starvation was a reduction in the size of the group through the migration of some of its members. Migration was a natural solution to the problem for people already accustomed to the nomadic way of life (this is a normal characteristic of most hunting and gathering societies). Furthermore, so long as habitable, unoccupied land was available, the choice was not an onerous one.

This growth in the number of human societies in the earlier phase of evolutionary history was undoubtedly accompanied by a growth in social and cultural diversity. As groups of people spread out over an ever wider area, they encountered

---

[3] See Table 7/1, p. 148.

[4] See Chapter 7 for a detailed analysis and description of this type of society.

[5] I am ignoring groups, such as the Plains Indians and the Northwest Coast Indians, that cannot be regarded as true hunting and gathering societies for reasons that will be developed in Chapter 7.

[6] For a discussion of the methodological issues involved here, see Chapter 7.

a variety of new environments to which they were forced to adapt. Unlike more advanced societies, they were not able to compensate for deficiencies in the local environment by transporting the missing elements from remote areas within their boundaries, and trade with members of other societies was quite limited. For the most part, each society had to make do with the resources found in its own immediate area. As a consequence, groups that migrated to subarctic areas developed very different cultural patterns from those in tropical or subtropical areas. Similarly, differences developed between societies in rainforests and desert areas, in mountainous regions and lowlands, in woodlands and open plains. In short, the descendants of what was once a small, homogeneous population gradually became more and more diversified as their numbers grew and as they occupied ever more varied environmental niches.

The increased geographical separation of societies also contributed to societal differentiation. As modern biologists recognize, reproductive isolation, by preventing interbreeding and the sharing of genetic information, is the basic cause of speciation. Societal separation and isolation have a similar effect. By reducing opportunities for sharing cultural information, they foster social and cultural differentiation.

Language differences are excellent indicators of the influence of societal separation and isolation. These differences are certainly not the result of environmental variation:[7] no one has ever claimed, for example, that phonetic or grammatical differences are the result of climate. But the *magnitude* of the differences between languages (e.g., the relative similarity of the Romance languages versus the great disparity between these languages and Chinese) makes sense only in terms of the variations in the degree of isolation between the groups which developed them.

Because of the importance of social contact and communication, major geographic features have played a significant role in human history. Oceans, deserts, mountains, and other barriers to transportation and communication have created many basic sociocultural cleavages. It is very doubtful that the languages, technologies, ideologies, and modes of social organization found in the European countries would have differed so greatly from those which evolved in Africa, Asia, or the New World had Europeans been in as close contact with these other peoples as they were with one another. Similarly, it is unlikely that each of these other groups would have developed their own distinctive sociocultural patterns had they not been so isolated for so long.

The second phase: diversification through intrasocietal differentiation

Prior to the discovery of the techniques of plant cultivation and animal domestication approximately ten thousand years ago, men everywhere were forced to rely on the

---

[7] Studies do show, however, that some differences in vocabulary are related to environmental differences. For example, Eskimos have an unusually large number of words to differentiate various kinds of snow. See, for example, E. Adamson Hoebel, *Anthropology: The Study of Man*, 3d ed. (New York: McGraw-Hill, 1966), p. 35.

uncertain bounty of nature. Wild animals were hunted and wild plants collected, but men had no control over their food supply.

The discovery of the new techniques of food production proved to be the basis for the first major social revolution in human history. Populations began to grow larger and settlements became more permanent. With less time and energy consumed by the basic task of finding food, men found more time to cultivate the arts of government and warfare, to practice the fine arts, to develop religious ritual, and to produce new kinds of goods and services. In short, social and cultural patterns became increasingly complex, and societies became internally differentiated to a degree that had never been possible before.

This trend has continued down to the present day. Subsequent technological advances freed men even further from their ancient bondage to the elemental task of finding food and opened the way to new and more varied patterns of life. Today, food production takes only a small fraction of the time and energy of a modern industrial society. As a result, the social and cultural differences found *within* one of these societies are at least as great as those found *between* a number of hunting and gathering societies in very different environments. Compare, for example, the way of life of an advertising executive living in a modern metropolis like New York with that of an illiterate migrant farm worker in Texas or California. The differences

Fig. 5/1 Two members of a single society: an example of social and cultural differentiation in modern industrial societies

between these two people, both members of the same society, are every bit as great as those between hunting peoples of the Arctic and hunting peoples of the tropics.

Adding to the diversity of social and cultural forms, the older modes of life developed in hunting and other primitive societies have survived down to the present, alongside the newer modes of life developed in industrial societies. As a result, there are at least three major bases of diversity in the world today:

1. Differences between simple societies, due to isolation and to diverse environmental influences
2. Differences within complex, modern industrial societies
3. Differences between the simple and the complex societies

In view of this, we can safely say that social and cultural patterns are more varied today than they have ever been before.

Although one is usually tempted to predict the continuation of current trends, it would be unrealistic in this instance. Technological developments have reached the point where the survival of hunting and gathering societies and other simple societal types is seriously threatened. During the past 5,000 to 10,000 years, thousands of these societies were absorbed or destroyed by more powerful and technologically more advanced neighbors. Nevertheless, many groups managed to survive in such remote and relatively inaccessible areas as New Guinea, Australia, the New World, the Arctic, and Africa. In recent centuries, even these areas have been invaded one after another by more advanced societies. Now, in our own day, the last sanctuaries are falling, and it is doubtful that the social and cultural patterns of these simpler societies will survive much longer. By the end of the century probably only industrial and industrializing societies will be left.

Technological advance may also reduce the differences *within* societies. Modern techniques of heating and air conditioning have already greatly reduced the differential effects of living in New England and the South, and there will surely be further advances of this kind. Radio, television, and the other media of communication have largely destroyed the differentiating influences of distance and the isolation it once created: today, people living thousands of miles apart share a more similar culture and maintain closer contacts than people of the past who lived only a hundred miles apart. Finally, the great abundance of goods and services produced by the economies of industrial societies, together with the discovery of better techniques for controlling population growth, make it possible to reduce considerably the tremendous social inequalities that have been a characteristic feature of more advanced societies for the last five thousand years.

In short, the effects of technological advance in the centuries ahead are likely to prove very different from its effects in the past, at least insofar as social and cultural diversification is concerned. Instead of increasing diversification, technological advance is likely to reduce it.

SOCIOCULTURAL PROGRESS

Sociocultural progress, as we noted earlier, is an often misunderstood term. As used by modern evolutionists, it has nothing to do with moral progress or with an increase in human happiness, as desirable as these are. Rather, it refers to *technological* advance and to certain specific forms of organizational and ideological change that are by-products of technological advance.

Although sociocultural progress in this sense is one of the basic trends in human history, it does not follow that every society has progressed continuously or that all societies have taken the same evolutionary path. With respect to the first of these points, the historical record provides clear evidence of technological regression in a number of instances and of technostasis (i.e., the absence of either advance or regression) in many others.[8] With respect to the second point, research shows that there is no single pattern of development, or sequence of stages, through which all, or even most, societies move.[9] In fact, as we shall see in Chapter 6, *no* society has ever survived intact while evolving across more than a fraction of the total evolutionary scale.

Technology's distinctive role in sociocultural progress

As we have seen at a number of points in our analysis, technology plays a distinctive role in the process of societal evolution. Compared with the other basic elements in sociocultural systems (i.e., language, social organization, and ideology), it is far likelier to be an autogenous source of change, and it also causes change in them much more often than they change it.

Walter Goldschmidt, an American anthropologist, has pointed out some of the kinds of change that are likely to result from a society's technological advance. In his volume *Man's Way: A Preface to the Understanding of Human Society*, he lists five fundamental changes of this kind.[10] First, technological advance means a more efficient utilization of the environment, and this usually leads to *population growth*. Second, technological advance reduces the need for migration, and *settlements become more permanent*.[11] Third, technological advance leads to *an increased*

---

[8] For examples of regression and technostasis, see pp. 112–116.

[9] At the same time, it should be recognized that there are certain orderly patterns in societal development. See, for example, Linton Freeman and Robert Winch, "Societal Complexity: An Empirical Test of a Typology of Societies," *American Journal of Sociology*, 62 (1957), pp. 461–466; or Robert Carneiro, "Scale Analysis: Evolutionary Sequences, and the Rating of Cultures," in Raoul Naroll and Ronald Cohen (eds.), *Handbook of Method in Anthropology* (forthcoming).

[10] *Man's Way: A Preface to the Understanding of Human Society* (New York: Holt, 1959), p. 115.

[11] In the most primitive societies men are usually obliged to move their settlements with some frequency, since the supply of wild animals and edible plants is quickly reduced to the point where it cannot support the group. Similarly, horticulturalists find that their methods of cultivation so deplete the fertility of the soil that they are forced to move every few years. For a more extended discussion of these topics, see Chapters 7 and 8.

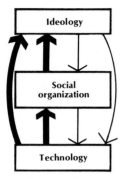

Fig. 5/2 Relations among three basic elements of sociocultural systems from an evolutionary perspective

---

production of goods and services, with all that implies (e.g., the possibility of greater economic and political inequality). Fourth, technological advance fosters *greater specialization and division of labor and increased organizational complexity.* Fifth, technological advance makes possible *increased "leisure"* (i.e., time not consumed in providing for such basic material needs as food and shelter), which can be used for a wide variety of other activities—art, religion, politics, the production of non-essential goods and services, etc.

From an evolutionary perspective, the relationship between technology, social organization, and ideology resembles the movement of traffic on a two-way street where the flow is heavier in one direction than the other.[12] As Fig. 5/2 indicates, the dominant flow of influence is from technology to social organization and ideology; the flow in the opposite direction is not only less frequent, it is also less important.[13]

It is interesting to speculate why this is so. Apparently, a number of factors are involved. For one thing, in matters of social organization and ideology, men have usually been more conservative, more eager to preserve traditional patterns. Generally, these possess an aura of the sacred, and questioning them is discouraged. Societies usually make changes in these areas only when forced to do so.

Technology, by contrast, is the least sacred of the three (though even it is sometimes tinged by the quality of sacredness). It is the aspect of sociocultural systems in which men have the least emotional investment, and therefore they tend to regard it more pragmatically. One reason for this difference of attitude seems to be that it is so much easier to compare the effects of alternative tools or techniques than it is to compare the effects of alternative systems of social organization or alternative ideologies. For example, one can demonstrate the superiority of one

---

[12] Language is omitted here, since it never seems to be an autogenous source of change. See pp. 63–64.

[13] From a more limited perspective, the picture would not necessarily be the same. For a single nation at a certain point in its history, or even for a group of nations over a rather extended period, the impact of organizational and ideological change on technology might be greater than the reverse. Fig. 5/1 shows the relationship only from a broad evolutionary perspective on a global scale.

method of making steel over another far more easily than one can demonstrate the superiority of one system of government over others, or of one religious doctrine over another. Furthermore, technology is more *instrumental* in nature; it involves the *means* men use to attain their goals, not the goals themselves. And men are naturally more flexible and pragmatic with respect to means than to ends.

Ironically, therefore, because men are *less* attached to the specifics of technology than to the specifics of social organization and ideology, technology has been *more* important in shaping the course of sociocultural evolution. To understand this paradox, we must keep in mind the interdependence of the various parts of socio-cultural systems. A change in one part of the system usually fosters change in other parts. Thus, when the technology of a society changes (as it more often does because of its less sacred, instrumental nature), compensating adjustments frequently become necessary in social organization and ideology. New forms of technology often open up new possibilities in these other areas and sometimes undermine the basis for old patterns.

To put the matter differently, *a society's solutions to its technological problems tend to function as a set of prior conditions that limit the range of possible solutions to its organizational and ideological problems.*[14] Thus, a society which is dependent on a primitive hunting and gathering technology could never develop large com-munities with thousands of residents, religious organizations led by elaborate hierarchies of priests, complex legal systems, factories, labor unions, or any of dozens of other organizational systems which members of an industrial society take for granted. Neither could it develop complex and abstract ideologies or belief systems, such as modern Christianity, communism, or humanism. One can go even further and say that a society's system of technology helps determine which of the possible organizational or ideological patterns open to that society it will, in fact, adopt. For example, as we shall see in a later analysis, both monarchical and republican governments are possible in agrarian societies, but for societies at that level of technological development, the monarchical pattern is, under normal conditions, much more likely.

To say that technology exercises an important influence on social organization and ideology is not to deny that causal influences also flow in the opposite direction. Social organizations and ideologies, once established, *can* influence technological systems. Their chief effect, however, has been to influence the *rate* of technological

---

[14] Technology sometimes plays this role even with respect to art. E. Power Biggs, the noted organist and student of organ music, reports that organ compositions have varied greatly depending on the type of instruments available to the individual composer. Handel's music, for example, was written for eighteenth-century English organs, noted for their bright and gay tones. Bach's famed Toccata in D minor was ap-parently written to display and employ the massive power and range of the organ at the Johanniskirche in Lueneburg, where he was a student in his early years. Spanish organ music was for many years thought to be of inferior quality when played on the instruments of northern Europe and this country, but these com-positions "take on zest and splash of color" when played on Spanish instruments. See E. Power Biggs, "Dr. Schweitzer's Intuition Confirmed," in *Saturday Review*, August 31, 1968, pp. 41–43.

Fig. 5/3 A society's solution to its technological problems tends to function as a set of prior conditions that limit the range of possible solutions to its organizational and ideological problems: Bushmen distributing meat after a kill

innovation. Some systems of social organization and some ideologies have been conducive to high rates of innovation, while others have had the opposite effect. To a lesser degree, systems of social organization and ideologies influence the *content* of technological innovation, stimulating technological advances in some areas at the expense of others (e.g., advances in military technology taking precedence over advances in subsistence technology). These influences are important, as we shall see in later chapters; but as Fig. 5/2 suggests, over the total course of history their effect on technology has been less potent and less important than the reverse.

As a consequence, technological criteria have usually been employed as the basis for taxonomies (i.e., systems of classification) of human societies, especially for those that cover the whole range of societies from the most primitive to the most complex. Social scientists use technological criteria for the same reason biologists use genotypic rather than phenotypic criteria in classifying plants and animals: each provides the most efficient basis for classifying the materials.

There are some indications, however, that the relative influence of technology, social organization, and ideology on the processes of change has been altered somewhat during the course of societal evolution.[15] In particular, the relative

[15] See, for example, Talcott Parsons, *Societies: Evolutionary and Comparative Perspectives* (Englewood Cliffs, N.J.: Prentice-Hall, 1966), p. 114; or Gerhard Lenski, *Power and Privilege: A Theory of Social Stratification* (New York: McGraw-Hill, 1966), pp. 436–437, for other statements of the thesis that evolution causes changes in the operation of the evolutionary process itself.

importance of ideological factors seems to have grown in modern times. From the standpoint of theory, this is not surprising since cultural and other resources steadily increase with technological advance. The leaders of modern industrial societies, therefore, have far more resources at their command, and far more options open to them, than the leaders of less advanced societies ever dreamed of. Thus they are freer to base their decisions on ideological principles, to choose, perhaps, more costly solutions to problems but solutions more in keeping with their world view and values (see the appendix following this chapter for a further discussion of this subject).

Explanations of sociocultural progress

The evolutionary explanation of sociocultural progress should, by now, be reasonably clear. Admittedly, it is not a simple explanation: the causes are numerous and their interrelations complex. They involve many of the most basic elements in human nature and many of the most basic features of our world. They include man's self-seeking nature; his great capacity for learning and communicating; the highly varied and expandable nature of his needs and desires; his limited supply of time, energy, and other resources and his resulting tendency to economize; the natural tendency of the human population to multiply; the finite supply of land available to man; the expandable, but limited, capacity of the environment to satisfy his needs; and the inevitable fact of scarcity (i.e., man's demands are always greater than his current technology and the resources of the environment can satisfy). Collectively, these conditions give rise to the crucial processes of innovation and extinction, which together are responsible for sociocultural progress.

Over the years, some have sought to modify this explanation, or even replace it with alternative ones. Though none have found lasting acceptance in scholarly circles, several have won wide acceptance among laymen and therefore merit attention. Three in particular fall in this category: (1) racialist explanations, (2) geographical determinist explanations, and (3) "great man" explanations.

Racialist explanations   In the nineteenth century, racialist theories enjoyed widespread support among both scholars and laymen. In recent decades, scholarly support has almost disappeared and lay support, too, has declined. Nevertheless, racialist theories are still popular enough to merit consideration.

Two basic observations gave rise to them. First, as a result of greater contact between the races in recent centuries, Europeans became increasingly conscious of their own technological and military superiority. Second, in the United States and certain other nations in which immigration had produced racially heterogeneous populations, people of European extraction enjoyed higher status than those of African or Asian descent. Recognition of these patterns naturally led many people to the conclusion that Europeans are genetically superior.

This conclusion was reinforced for a time by the publication of the early results of intelligence testing conducted by the American army during World War I. Tests of draftees showed that, on the average, whites scored substantially higher than Negroes.[16] Further analysis of these tests, however, revealed that Negroes from a number of Northern states had higher average scores than whites from a number of Southern states, indicating that the scores were determined, at least in part, by social influences.[17] Subsequent research has confirmed this. In studies made of Negro children in New York and Philadelphia, for example, the average IQ scores increased the longer the children were in these communities and the briefer their exposure had been to segregated southern schools.[18] Other studies have shown that the IQ scores of Negroes, like those of whites, vary substantially according to the class position of the family in which a child is raised.[19] These and other findings have made it clear that IQ tests do not measure what they were originally designed to measure, namely, the innate ability, or genetic potential for learning, of the individual. Rather, they measure innate ability in conjunction with socially differentiated opportunities for learning.[20] Since the latter cannot be fully controlled in experimental studies, it is impossible to draw valid conclusions concerning racially based differences in learning potential.

On the societal level, the evidence regarding racial abilities is no less complex, especially if we take earlier centuries into account. Prior to the modern era, there was little if any evidence of the technological superiority of the European peoples. During the Dark Ages following the fall of Rome, when Western Europe reverted to a very primitive agrarian level, societies in this area were technologically and organizationally much inferior to Chinese society, and even as recently as the twelfth century the superiority of Western European societies over certain west African societies was not great. One distinguished anthropologist of the last generation wrote that "in their arts and crafts these societies were little, if at all, inferior to medieval Europeans, while in the thoroughness of their political organization and skill with which social institutions were utilized to lend stability to the political structure, they far exceeded anything in Europe prior to the sixteenth century."[21]

---

[16] See R. M. Yerkes (ed.), "Psychological Examining in the U.S. Army," *Memoirs of the National Academy of Sciences*, 15 (1921); or Carl Brigham, *A Study of American Intelligence* (Princeton, N.J.: Princeton University press, 1923).

[17] See William C. Bagley, "The Army Tests and the Pro-Nordic Propaganda," *Educational Review*, 67 (1924), pp. 179–187; or Otto Klineberg, *Negro Intelligence and Selective Migration* (New York: Columbia University Press, 1935), Table 2, p. 2.

[18] Klineberg, *op. cit.*, graph 6, p. 27. See also Everett S. Lee, "Negro Intelligence and Selective Migration: A Philadelphia Test of the Klineberg Hypothesis," *American Sociological Review*, 16 (1951), pp. 227–233.

[19] See, for example, M. Deutsch and B. Brown, "Social Influences in Negro-White Intelligence Differences," *Journal of Social Issues*, 20 (1964), pp. 24–35.

[20] Recent research has begun to show how complex and also how subtle the influence of the social environment can be. For example, recent studies show that dietary deficiencies during the first year of life can cause irremediable damage to the learning mechanism.

[21] Ralph Linton, *The Tree of Culture* (New York: Vintage Books, Knopf, 1959), p. 170.

Though this statement is an exaggeration, it is closer to the truth than most Europeans or Americans realize. In any case, when we enlarge our perspective to include the evidence of other centuries than our own, the basis for the racialist theory is seriously weakened. In view of what we know at this time, it appears that racial differences have had very little, if any, effect on the course of sociocultural progress. The sweeping claims made by racial theorists are simply not supported by the data.

Geographical determinist explanations Geographical determinist explanations were also much in vogue in the nineteenth century and these too have now been largely abandoned, at least by serious scholars. One of the last important advocates of geographical determinism was Ellsworth Huntington, an American geographer of a generation ago. Huntington sought to prove that climatic factors were the chief determinants of sociocultural progress.[22] To do this, he compared indices of progress with indices of climate. This led ultimately to the preparation of the two maps on the next page, which show a striking correlation between climatic conditions and the level of societal development in his day.

Unfortunately for Huntington, critics quickly tore his theory to shreds. They asked, among other questions, why the northeastern quarter of the United States, which had one of the most favorable climates in the world, was inhabited throughout most of history by extremely primitive peoples, and why Greece, once one of the centers of civilization, should now be ranked among the underdeveloped nations, despite the absence of any substantial climatic change. Huntington's inability to provide satisfactory answers to such questions led to the theory's speedy rejection.

Nevertheless, social scientists do recognize the significance of geographical factors in evolutionary history. For though every society's natural environment contains possibilities for development, the possibilities are not equally distributed. Climatic differences, while not as important as Huntington sought to make them, are certainly significant, especially in extreme cases (e.g., arctic conditions). Topographical factors have probably played an even greater role by shaping patterns of intersocietal communication. Such features as oceans, deserts, and mountain ranges have prevented or seriously impeded the flow of information between societies, while other features, such as navigable rivers and open plains, have facilitated it. Considering the importance of cultural diffusion, quite substantial differences in sociocultural development can be explained by this factor.

Certain types of environments apparently limit indigenous development and may even prevent progress by diffusion. Since desert and subarctic areas cannot support primitive horticultural societies, for example, the normal evolutionary progression from hunting and gathering to horticulture has been impossible in many places. The experience of the Incas of South America shows how such factors can even block diffusion. Despite the fact that they were able to build, in the central Andes, an advanced empire covering approximately 350,000 square miles, the

---

[22] See especially Ellsworth Huntington, *Mainsprings of Civilization* (New York: Wiley, 1945).

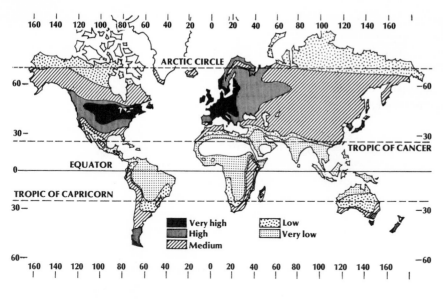

Fig. 5/4 The distribution of human health and energy on the basis of climate, according to Ellsworth Huntington

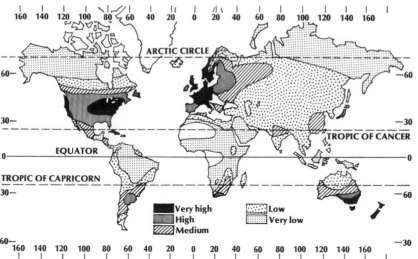

Fig. 5/5 The distribution of civilization, according to Ellsworth Huntington

Incas never could extend it into the tropical forest region only a few miles east of their capital city. As one anthropologist put it, "This suggests that the subsistence resources of the lowlands were so meager that they could not support such an advanced culture even when it brought with it well-developed techniques for the mass production and distribution of food."[23]

Finally, variations in the distribution of critical natural resources have been important in societal evolution. The presence of mineral resources, for example,

---

[23] Betty Meggers, "Environmental Limitation on the Development of Culture," *American Anthropologist*, 56 (1954), p. 808.

or differences in their accessibility, undoubtedly influenced the course of development for many societies.

In summary, geographical factors have been much more important than racial ones. Far from contradicting the evolutionary explanation, they are an integral part of it. Problems arise only when enthusiasts like Huntington seek to establish a deterministic explanation which ignores or minimizes the role of other factors that must be taken into account.

"Great man" explanations   For a long time, the discipline of history was largely a chronicle of the achievements and disasters wrought by a handful of famous men. To people schooled in this tradition, nothing was more natural than to suppose that the progress achieved by certain societies was due largely to a few men of genius, and that without them these societies would never have risen above the others.

Social scientists, as well as the newer breed of historians, reject this view. Basically their rejection is due to advances in our understanding of the nature of intelligence and the innovative process. One of the most damaging pieces of evidence against what has been called "the great man theory of history" was the discovery that many of the most important innovations of modern times were made almost simultaneously by two or more individuals working completely independently of one another. Following is a list of just a few of these simultaneous inventions and discoveries:

Sunspots: Fabricius, Galileo, Harriott, Scheiner, 1611
Logarithms: Napier, 1614; Bürgi, 1620
Calculus: Newton, 1671; Leibnitz, 1676
Nitrogen: Rutherford, 1772; Scheele, 1773
Oxygen: Priestley, Scheele, 1774
Water as H_2O: Cavendish, Watt, 1781; Lavoisier, 1783
Telegraph: Henry, Morse, Steinheil, Wheatstone and Cooke, 1837
Photography: Daguerre and Niepce, Talbot, 1839
Neptune: Adams, Leverrier, 1845
Natural selection: Darwin, Wallace, 1858
Telephone: Bell, Gray, 1876
Phonograph: Cros, Edison, 1877
Rediscovery of Mendel's Laws: De Vries, Correns, Tschermak, 1900
South Pole: Amundsen, December, 1911, Scott, January, 1912[24]

Half a century ago, 148 of these simultaneous innovations had been identified, and since then others have been added to the list. In a number of instances as many as three, four, or more men produced the same innovation with no knowledge of the

---

[24] Adapted from William F. Ogburn and Dorothy S. Thomas, "Are Inventions Inevitable? A Note on Social Evolution," *Political Science Quarterly*, 37 (1922), pp. 93–98, and A. L. Kroeber, *Anthropology* (New York: Harcourt, Brace, 1948), p. 342.

others' work. While not denying the ability of the men involved, this finding suggests that few of those who have contributed most to the advance of knowledge were indispensable. In recent years, simultaneous inventions and discoveries have become so common that they are a serious matter for scientists. Since many are working on the same problem and since the rewards for running second are few, scientists often go to great lengths to be first and to establish their claims to being first.[25]

The modern understanding of inventions as recombinations of existing elements of culture not only explains the frequency of simultaneous inventions, it also makes understandable the great da Vinci's inability to design a successful flying machine in the fifteenth century when lesser men succeeded four centuries later. Even Leonardo's genius was no substitute for the advances in technology that took place in the intervening period and were available to the Wright brothers and others in the late nineteenth century. None of this is meant to deny the ability of inventors, but only to indicate that few if any of them have been indispensable and that sociocultural progress depends not on the actions of any small handful of great men, but rather on the accumulation of information by society as a whole.

OTHER PATTERNS OF CHANGE

In addition to the two master trends of diversification and progress, there are several other important patterns of change in societies. These include various cyclical and semicyclical patterns, as well as certain static and regressive patterns. Each of these must be considered if we are to avoid an oversimplified view of evolutionary history.

Cyclical change

In the controversies that surrounded evolutionary theory earlier in the century, it was sometimes made to appear that one must choose between a progressive, evolutionary theory of human history and an essentially cyclical, nonprogressive theory. Today we see that this was a false choice, and one that we are not obliged to make on the grounds of either logic or empirical evidence.[26] History clearly shows that certain aspects of man's activity conform to the progressive evolutionary pattern, while others conform to a cyclical or semicyclical pattern.

This fact was recognized long ago by some of the more astute social theorists. For example, this wedding of evolutionary and cyclical theory is evident in the work of Herbert Spencer, the foremost social evolutionist of the nineteenth century. In his famous three-volume work, *Principles of Sociology,* Spencer argued vigorously for

---

[25] See Warren Hagstrom, *The Scientific Community* (New York: Basic Books, 1965), or James D. Watson, *The Double Helix* (New York: Atheneum, 1968).

[26] See, for example, Wilbert Moore, *Social Change* (Englewood Cliffs, N.J.: Prentice-Hall, 1963), chap. 2.

the evolutionary view of history; yet in his treatment of political institutions, he offered an interesting cyclical subtheory. Spencer argued that the energies of societies have been directed throughout history toward the two goals of profit through war and profit through peaceful industrial pursuits and economic activity.[27] While both patterns are normally present in most societies, there are frequent shifts in their relative emphasis. Sometimes the militant element is stronger than the industrial, at other times the reverse. This is not a matter of short-term trends obscuring long-term trends. In this area, Spencer could find no long-term evolutionary trend, only a cyclical pattern.

When we look for patterns of this kind, we have no trouble finding them. They range from small patterns of little importance, such as changing fashions, to some of great importance, such as political cycles. They include patterns found only at certain levels of societal development (e.g., the business cycles of industrial and industrializing societies) as well as patterns present in all or most societies (e.g., the annual cycle of seasonal activities). Finally, they include patterns that are neatly symmetrical (e.g., commuter traffic patterns) and others with no symmetry at all (e.g., patterns of war and peace).

Many of the most interesting and important cyclical patterns occur in the political area. These patterns have been noted since the days of Plato and Aristotle, who discussed at length the factors responsible for the shifts from one form of government to another.[28] Neither was able to find any enduring progressive or evolutionary pattern in these shifts.

In the modern era, too, a number of scholars have called attention to the cyclical character of many basic political changes. None has expressed this more poignantly than Robert Michels. In the closing paragraph of his famous work, *Political Parties*, published during World War I, Michels wrote of one of the more basic cycles of political history:

> The democratic currents of history resemble successive waves. They break ever on the same shoal. They are ever renewed. This enduring spectacle is simultaneously encouraging and depressing. When democracies have gained a certain stage of development, they undergo a gradual transformation, adopting the aristocratic spirit, and in many cases also the aristocratic forms, against which at the outset they struggled so fiercely. Now new accusers arise to denounce the traitors; after an era of glorious combats and inglorious power, they end by fusing with the old dominant class; whereupon once more they are in their turn attacked by fresh opponents who appeal to the name of democracy. It is probable that this cruel game will continue without end.[29]

---

[27] Herbert Spencer, *The Principles of Sociology* (New York: Appleton, 1897), vol. II, chaps. 17 and 18.

[28] See, for example, Plato, *The Republic* (New York: Modern Library, n.d.), especially book VIII; or Aristotle, *Politics* (New York: Modern Library, 1943), especially book V.

[29] Robert Michels, *Political Parties: A Sociological Study of the Oligarchical Tendencies of Modern Democracy*, trans. by Eden and Cedar Paul (New York: Dover, 1959, first published, 1915), p. 408.

In subsequent chapters we will have occasion to observe many other cyclical patterns. Viewing the total process of social and cultural change, one might say that these cyclical patterns provide the counterpoint which combines with the basic evolutionary patterns to produce the fascinating complexity and richness of human history.

Technostasis[30] and regression

Despite the overall rise in the capacity of societies to mobilize energy and information, many individual societies have shown little evidence of this for long periods, and some have even regressed. Perhaps the best examples of technostasis are provided by the various hunting and gathering societies that survived into the modern era. Though the cultures of these peoples have certainly changed in a number of respects, their basic technology appears to be much as it was ten thousand years ago or more.[31]

Archaeological research indicates that technostasis was also characteristic of most hunting and gathering societies throughout most of the prehistoric era. By modern standards, the rate of technological advance was unimaginably slow.[32]

Technostasis was also common among agrarian societies. The rate of progress in these societies was so slow that our country's Founding Fathers and their European contemporaries would have found themselves far more at home, from the technological standpoint, in Roman society at the time of Christ than in present-day America.

Sociocultural regression is a much less common pattern, but it does occur. In our earlier discussion of sociocultural drift (page 67), we had occasion to refer to one form of regression. A more serious pattern of regression is associated with the breakdown of political institutions in more advanced societies. A classic example is provided by the events which followed the collapse of the Roman Empire. This was not the usual case in which one society was conquered by another on the same level of development. Rather, the Roman state was destroyed by technologically less ad-

---

[30] In an earlier version of this chapter, I used the word "stagnation" where I now use "technostasis." As one reviewer pointed out, this word has many negative connotations, suggesting among other things an unhealthy condition. He proposed "stability" as an alternative. Unfortunately, this word is just as loaded with unsuitable connotations, though of a different kind. "Stability" implies a desirable state. In searching for a truly neutral term, I could not find one that was not cumbersome and awkward (e.g., "changelessness"). Thus I was forced to look for a Greek or Latin substitute. The Greek word *stasis* (literally, standing still) seemed the best. However, since the term has been used in other ways in biology, and occasionally creeps into sociology, I linked it with the stem "techno-" in order to avoid any possible ambiguity or confusion. As I shall use the term, "technostasis" refers to a society (or other group) that is standing still from the technological standpoint.

[31] See, for example, Frank Hole and Robert Heizer, *An Introduction to Prehistoric Archaeology* (New York: Holt, 1965), who write that "in many areas of the New World there was no discernible 'development' over the whole time of occupation. That is, economy, being in fine adjustment with the physical and cultural environment, remained stable. The changes that could be seen were stylistic . . ." (p. 242).

[32] See Chapter 7.

Fig. 5/6   The collapse of the Roman Empire was the basis of one of the most striking examples of sociocultural regression

vanced peoples.[33] As a result, it was replaced by a number of much smaller, less advanced, and less efficient states. The well-articulated economy that had emerged under Roman aegis was disrupted, trade and commerce declined greatly, and the whole economy moved toward a pattern of local self-sufficiency. As a consequence, urban populations were drastically reduced, and many industries disappeared or were severely restricted. For example, the once numerous copper mines of Western Europe were all or nearly all shut down by the beginning of the sixth century and were not reopened until the tenth century; brass, an alloy of copper and zinc, seems not to have been manufactured again until the fifteenth century.[34] From the end of the sixth to the end of the tenth century, such ores as were mined (chiefly iron) were taken at much shallower depths, by much more primitive methods, and in much smaller quantities than in earlier periods.[35] Regression was also evident in most other fields of production.

---

[33] The success of the barbarians was due in no small measure to the internal conflicts that racked the Roman Empire.

[34] John Nef, *The Conquest of the Material World* (Chicago: University of Chicago Press, 1964), p. 8.

[35] *Ibid.*, p. 7.

The causes of technostasis and regression

These cases of technostasis and regression pose an interesting problem. They demand an explanation, but it must be one that is consistent with the explanation of progress.

We have already identified five distinctive patterns of technostasis and regression. Since there is no reason to suppose that all are due to the same forces, we must consider each in turn:

1. Technostasis in hunting and gathering societies that survived into the modern era
2. Technostasis in most hunting and gathering societies in the prehistoric era
3. Technostasis in most agrarian societies
4. Limited regression in some very small and isolated societies
5. General regression in a few large, developed agrarian societies such as Rome and its successor states

We have already found an adequate explanation for categories 2 and 4. As we saw in Chapter 4, the hunting and gathering societies of the prehistoric era were poorly situated from the standpoint of technological advance. Above all, they lacked a large store of accumulated information on which to build. In addition, their small populations and their relative isolation put them at a disadvantage. Finally, throughout much of the prehistoric era the ready availability of new lands prevented population pressures from building up and thus slowed the deadly, but progressive, process of intersocietal selection.

In the case of limited regression (i.e., the loss of certain specific elements of technology) in small and isolated societies, the explanation is simple when the lost traits were secrets held by a single family. In other instances, the loss can be explained by the migration of a society to a new territory where some essential raw material was unavailable. For example, the case is reported of a group of Eskimos who moved into an area so far north that there was no driftwood. By the time European explorers discovered them some generations later, the group had lost all knowledge of how to build seaworthy kayaks.[36]

With respect to technostasis in contemporary hunting and gathering societies, the explanation is partly the same as for hunting and gathering societies of the prehistoric era. The same factors that kept those societies at the primitive level for countless thousands of years also prevented advance in the surviving remnant during the last 8,000 to 10,000 years. From an evolutionary perspective, this extra several thousand years is not a long period of time.

One may ask, however, why these few surviving hunting and gathering groups did not benefit from cultural diffusion as did so many others, and evolve into some more advanced type of society. The answer seems to be that most of them were too

---

[36] Kroeber, *op. cit.*, p. 376.

remote from the centers of technical advance to be affected by those developments. A recent survey of ninety-two hunting and gathering societies revealed that 85 per cent of them were located in either the New World or Australia, areas cut off from the main stream of evolutionary development until the last several centuries.[37] Most of the rest were in such remote, isolated areas of the Old World as the Kalahari Desert, Arctic Asia, and the jungles of Malaysia.

The two remaining categories (3 and 5) involve agrarian societies. These pose a somewhat more difficult problem, which we will examine in detail in Chapter 9. For the present, however, we may note that both technostasis and regression in these societies are linked with certain basic developments in social organization. In the case of technostasis, the cause apparently lies in the emergence in agrarian societies of a highly exploitative social order in which few of the rewards for work or innovation accrued to the worker or innovator. Rather, they were monopolized by the members of a small, powerful, and wealthy elite that knew little about technology and cared less.[38] Under these conditions, people's natural inclinations to maximize their rewards were diverted into other channels. Potential peasant innovators knew that they could seldom hope to benefit from inventions or discoveries they might make. And the elite were so unfamiliar with the mundane world of technology that they were incapable of making any significant contribution.

Finally, the occasional instance of general regression, exemplified by Western Europe after the collapse of the Roman Empire, points again to social organization as a major contributing factor. The immediate cause of the decline was the breakdown of government. Because the government was unable to protect them, merchants could no longer move safely from town to town, and trade became increasingly unprofitable and dangerous. With the curtailment of trade, the supply of many specialized products declined or disappeared, and skilled artisans were forced to turn to other activities to earn a livelihood. With the reduction in numbers or elimination of merchants, artisans, and governmental officials, the economic base of most urban communities was so badly undermined that they declined in size, or even disappeared. The result was a reversion to a much more primitive form of agrarian society.

A somewhat similar pattern occurred in the Indus river valley two thousand years earlier. Beginning shortly after 3000 B.C. and continuing for more than a thousand years, an impressive civilization flourished in this area[39] Between 1500 and 2000 B.C., however, the cities in which this civilization was centered were destroyed

---

[37] These figures are adapted from Allan Coult and Robert Habenstein, *Cross Tabulations of Murdock's World Ethnographic Sample* (Columbia, Mo.: University of Missouri Press, 1965), p. 9. The societies referred to are those in which hunting and gathering were the dominant or codominant means of subsistence.

[38] For a classic statement of this, see V. Gordon Childe, *Man Makes Himself* (New York: Mentor Book, 1953), chap. 9. See also Thorstein Veblen, *The Theory of the Leisure Class* (New York: Modern Library, 1934, first published 1899), for an outstanding analysis of the logic underlying the actions of such elites.

[39] For a good description of this civilization, see Stuart Piggott, *Prehistoric India* (Harmondsworth: Penguin Books, 1950), chaps. 5 and 6.

or abandoned and a period of technological and social regression set in. It was not until twelve hundred years later that writing was again used in India, so far as we know today.[40]

These developments in agrarian societies (i.e., both general technostasis and occasional regression) underline the importance of the thesis that there is a *two-way* relationship between technology and social organization. Though the flow of influence from technology to social organization may be more important in the long run, the feedback from social organization to technology can also be tremendously important in the short run in one or more societies.

Appendix: Further notes on technology and ideology

To understand the changing relationship between technology and ideology, it is important to keep in mind that the greater cultural resources of the more advanced societies mean greater economic resources. Thus, these societies can afford alternatives that less advanced societies cannot. Graphically, the situation resembles that shown in Fig. 5/7. Spread out along the horizontal axis are all the conceivable solutions (A to Z) to a hypothetical problem. The vertical axis measures costs and resources. The curved line (line 4) is a

---

[40] *Ibid.*, p. 252. It is possible that writing was practiced during some part of this period and the remains have not yet been discovered, but the basic fact of regression seems indisputable in light of the evidence, currently available.

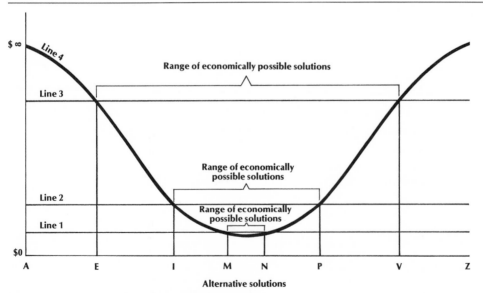

Line 1: Resources available in technologically primitive society
Line 2: Resources available in technologically intermediate society
Line 3: Resources available in technologically advanced society
Line 4: Costs of alternative solutions

Fig. 5/7 Influence of technological advance on the range of possible solutions to problems

measure of the cost of each of the conceivable solutions to the problem; the straight lines (lines 1, 2, and 3) are measures of the resources available to societies at different levels of technological development. The more advanced a society technologically, the more it can afford to spend to solve a given problem. As Fig. 5/7 indicates, each increase in the level of technological development results in an increase in the number of solutions that are possible. For the most primitive society (line 1), the only possible solutions are M and N. By contrast, in the case of the most advanced society (line 3), the range of possible solutions includes all of the alternatives from E to V. Even though solutions M and N remain the least costly (a condition that would not necessarily hold true in all cases, but which is assumed here to simplify the discussion), ideological considerations might dictate a preference for one of the more costly alternatives. In this way,

ideological factors are able to play a greater role in the more advanced society than in the more primitive.

This approach to the problem may help explain the long-standing controversy among social scientists over the relative importance of ideology and technology (see Chapter 3, footnote 32). Those who argue for technology are, perhaps, taking a broad, evolutionary view of the problem; those who emphasize ideology may be thinking largely in terms of recent history and the more advanced societies. If so, both are correct.

This serves as a reminder that evolution often involves not only change in the phenomena in question (e.g., organisms or societies), but *change in the operation of the evolutionary process itself*. Failure to recognize this has been responsible for many sterile debates over evolution in the past.

*T*he Types and Varieties of Societies

Chapter 6

Every branch of science is built on a foundation of comparisons. To understand anything in the world of nature—a plant, a star, a society, a rock formation—we are forced to compare it with other things, noting how it resembles them and how it differs.

Over the course of history, this process of comparison has gradually led to the discovery of many orderly patterns. This, in turn, has laid the foundation for a variety of classificatory systems—the Linnaean taxonomy and its successors in biology, the periodic table in chemistry, the typology of market systems in economics (i.e., perfect competition, oligopoly, monopoly, etc.), and others.[1]

Classification systems are essential in every field of study because they enable us to order and organize our kaleidoscopic welter of experience. Without this ordering, it would be impossible to develop general propositions about the world of nature —propositions which help us anticipate, and sometimes even control, the forces of nature and the behavior of living things.

CLASSIFYING HUMAN SOCIETIES: EARLIER TYPOLOGIES

During the past two centuries, there have been a number of attempts to develop a systematic classification of human societies. The initial impetus behind these efforts came largely from the philosophers of the eighteenth-century Enlightenment, who did so much to stimulate interest in social and cultural progress. The new outlook which they fostered led naturally to a conception of societal evolution.

The first societal typologies were organized in terms of a series of evolutionary

---

[1] The most basic classificatory systems of all are the vocabularies of languages.

stages which linked the level of societal development with a specific historical period. A good example of this is found in the work of Auguste Comte, the pioneer French sociologist. Building on the work of earlier scholars, Comte proposed a three-stage division of human history: a "theological" stage which lasted until approximately A.D. 1300; a "metaphysical" (i.e., philosophical) stage which lasted until 1800; and finally, a "positivistic" (i.e., scientific) stage. Though his labels referred to basic ideological orientations, Comte maintained that all phases of a society's life are linked together in such a way that the shift from one stage to the next affected virtually every aspect of human life.

Over the years, various criteria have been proposed as bases for societal typologies. Some, like Comte, have suggested ideological criteria, others social organizational criteria, still others technological criteria.[2] We shall be chiefly concerned with the latter, since they classify societies in terms of what appears to be the basic determinant of most major evolutionary change.

Some of the most important efforts to classify societies on the basis of technology stem from the work of a Danish contemporary of Comte. While Comte was developing his grand theory of human history, Christian Jurgensen Thomsen, curator of the National Museum in Copenhagen, was wrestling with the more mundane problem of organizing his growing collection of prehistoric artifacts. Eventually, he hit upon the idea of organizing them according to the type of material from which they were made—stone, bronze, or iron. Archaeological research in Denmark had already made it clear that these were not just three alternative materials which men had used contemporaneously, but rather, that each had been the dominant material during a different period. In the earliest period, stone had been the basic material. Gradually it had been displaced by bronze, and bronze in turn by iron. This led Thomsen to formulate a three-stage scheme involving a Stone Age, a Bronze Age, and an Iron Age.

For a long time archaeologists found this extremely useful for classifying societies and locating them in history. With advances in the field, they gradually introduced a number of refinements into Thomsen's basic scheme. Thus the Stone Age was subdivided into the Paleolithic, Mesolithic, and Neolithic (i.e., Old, Middle, and New Stone Ages), and the Bronze Age into the Chalcolithic (i.e., mixed Copper and Stone) and true Bronze Ages.

Anthropologists, whose work brought them into contact with primitive men of the modern period, also recognized the importance of technological differences, but they developed a somewhat different mode of classification. The most influential anthropological typology was one devised by Lewis Henry Morgan, an early student of the Iroquois Indians. He believed that societies could be divided into three basic

---

[2] For examples of the use of ideological criteria, see the work of Pitirim Sorokin or Howard Becker. For examples of the use of social organizational criteria, see the work of Sir Henry Maine, Karl Marx, Ferdinand Toennies, Robert Redfield, Julian Steward, and Elman Service. The use of technological criteria will be discussed in the text above.

types—savage, barbarian, and civilized—and that these could be broken down further to form seven subtypes, differentiated by their level of technological development. In his opinion, pottery was the crucial innovation which set barbarian societies apart from savage, while the invention of the alphabet and the use of writing were the key developments distinguishing civilized societies from barbarian.[3]

On the basis of his field work among the Indians and his knowledge of history and archaeology, Morgan argued that modern primitive tribes, such as the Iroquois, are the equivalents, from an analytical and evolutionary standpoint, of primitive groups of the prehistoric past. He believed that the basic sociocultural patterns of tribes on the same level of evolutionary development are so similar that we observe the prehistoric patterns from which ancient agrarian societies evolved when we study modern primitives.[4]

Later generations of anthropologists have not always agreed with Morgan. In the early part of the present century, a vigorous attack was directed against his basic assumption that modern primitive groups can be equated with prehistoric groups. Under the leadership of Franz Boas, the most influential anthropologist of this period, it was argued that modern primitive societies are the end product of an adaptive process just as lengthy as that which produced modern industrial societies. Boas and his disciples ridiculed the notion that one could learn about the prehistoric ancestors of the ancient Greeks and Romans by studying the sociocultural patterns of the Australian aborigines or the Indians of the New World.

At this same time, the archaeological scheme of classification also came under attack. To begin with, researchers found that the terms they were using did not refer to the same time periods in every part of the world. For example, the Bronze Age occurred much earlier in the Middle East than in Denmark, and much earlier in Denmark than in Peru. Furthermore, there was apparently no necessary series of stages through which each society must pass. In much of Africa, for instance, there was no evidence of a Bronze Age: societies there had passed directly from the Stone Age to the Iron Age as a result of diffusion from the Middle East.

Such criticisms eventually undermined scholarly confidence in the effort to build a societal typology, and in evolutionary theory generally. Thus, from about 1920 until quite recently, interest in these subjects almost disappeared in both anthropology and sociology.

One notable exception to the trend was V. Gordon Childe, a distinguished British archaeologist. He continued to work within an evolutionary framework and significantly advanced our understanding of the evolutionary process. One of his major contributions was to lay the foundation for a shift in the basis of societal classification. Since Thomsen's day, archaeologists had been obsessed with the details of technology, i.e., the materials from which tools were made and the details

---

[3] Lewis Henry Morgan, *Ancient Society* (Cambridge, Mass.: The Belknap Press, 1964, first published 1877), pp. 16–18.

[4] *Ibid.*, pp. 22–23.

of their construction. Childe, directing attention to something far more fundamental, developed the thesis that the transition from the Mesolithic to the Neolithic was not simply a change in tool-making techniques. It was instead, he argued, the first great social revolution in human history. He showed that this minor shift in tool-making was usually linked with a radical shift in the basic subsistence technology of large numbers of societies and that this in turn generated major changes in social organization, and probably in ideology as well.[5] In the Neolithic, men became food *producers* for the first time in history and thereby freed themselves from the many restrictions incumbent on a people who depend on the luck of the hunt and on the search for edible plants. With the discovery of the techniques of plant cultivation and animal domestication, men laid the foundation for a radically new way of life.[6]

Childe's second major contribution to evolutionary theory was his thesis that the various archaelogical categories developed by Thomsen and others must be thought of as *technological,* not chronological, stages.[7] Thus he helped free archaeology from the notion that such categories as "Paleolithic" and "Neolithic" refer to distinctive time periods in the same way that the various geologic eras do.

For the most part, Childe's proposals have met with a favorable response from archaeologists, and their recent work increasingly reflects his influence. There is today general acceptance of his identification of the Neolithic with the beginnings of food production, as well as a growing appreciation of the importance of subsistence technology.[8] One also finds general acceptance of his thesis that archaeological categories are essentially technological stages.

A decade ago, Walter Goldschmidt, the American anthropologist whose work we noted earlier (see page 101), devised a new typology that was a definite improvement over earlier efforts.[9] His system of classification involved six basic societal types, shown in Fig. 6/1. The arrows in the diagram show the hypothesized developmental and chronological sequence of their appearance; their vertical position on the chart indicates their degree of technological development.

As Goldschmidt explained, his typology was built on the foundation laid by Morgan a century earlier.[10] His first two categories, the hunting and food-gathering

---

[5] For various statements of Childe's views, see *Man Makes Himself* (New York: Mentor, 1951, first published 1936); *What Happened in History* (Baltimore: Penguin, 1964, first published 1942 and revised 1954); *Social Evolution* (London: Watts, 1951); and "Archaeological Ages as Technological Stages," *Journal of the Royal Anthropological Institute,* 44 (1944), pp. 7–24.

[6] See this chapter and chap. 7.

[7] See especially his paper "Archaeological Ages as Technological Stages," *op. cit.*

[8] See, for example, Robert Braidwood and Gordon Willey (eds.), *Courses Toward Urban Life: Archaeological Considerations of Some Cultural Alternates* (Chicago: Aldine, 1962); Kwang-chih Chang, *The Archaeology of Ancient China* (New Haven, Conn.: Yale, 1963); or H. D. Sankalia, *Prehistory and Protohistory in India and Pakistan* (Bombay: University of Bombay, 1962).

[9] See *Man's Way: A Preface to the Understanding of Human Society* (New York: Holt, 1959), chap. 6.

[10] *Ibid.,* p. 183.

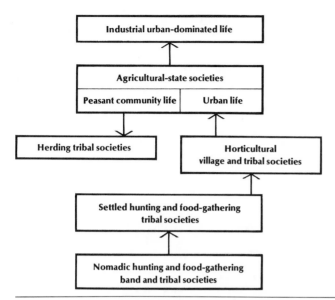

Fig. 6/1 Goldschmidt's societal typology

societies, are comparable to Morgan's savage societies; his herding and horticultural societies are roughly equivalent to Morgan's barbarian; and his agricultural-state and industrial societies are the same as Morgan's civilized. His typology is also closely linked to typologies in the archaeological tradition initiated by Thomsen. His hunting and gathering societies are the equivalent of Mesolithic and the more advanced Paleolithic societies; his herding and horticultural societies are the equivalent of Neolithic groups; and the agricultural-state and industrial are the equivalent of what Childe called the urban type. Thus, far from being a competing typology, Goldschmidt's work is simply one of the most recent efforts in a tradition that has been developing for more than a century.

The position of herding societies in Goldschmidt's scheme is especially interesting because it illustrates Childe's thesis that technological stages and chronological stages are not the same. As the diagram indicates, herding societies are less advanced technologically than agricultural-state societies but are, in Goldschmidt's judgement, evolutionary offshoots of them. The origin of herding societies, incidentally, has been a controversial issue for many years, and scholars are still divided on it. Though recent evidence does not support Goldschmidt's position, the issue is far from closed.[11]

A CURRENT TYPOLOGY

Though Goldschmidt's typology is a good one, it can be improved. Goldschmidt himself noted one weakness in his system of classification, observing that his

---

[11] Recent research indicates that animal domestication was discovered more than five thousand years before the plow was invented. It is difficult to believe that in all that time no group ever adopted herding as their basic mode of subsistence. The existence of such groups, however, has not yet been clearly documented.

horticultural category "is the broadest and internally the most varied of the lot, and closer examination may ultimately provide sensible and useful subdivisions."[12] The category of settled hunting and gathering societies also creates difficulties, since most of the societies in it rely heavily on fishing, and most are actually nomadic to some degree.[13] Such problems suggest the need for further refinements and modifications in the system of classification.

The typology used in this volume grew directly out of Goldschmidt's work and indirectly out of the work of Childe, Morgan, Thomsen, and the others who wrestled with this problem before him.[14] The chief differences between our system and Goldschmidt's are the subdivision of the horticultural and agrarian categories into simple and advanced types, the reorganization of the hunting and gathering categories, and the addition of several new categories, notably fishing, maritime, and hybrid societies. This enables us to deal more effectively with the problems we have already noted, as well as with others we will encounter shortly.

Figure 6/2 is a graphic summary of our system of classification. As in Goldschmidt's, societies are classified by their basic mode of subsistence (i.e., their basic method of obtaining the necessities of life). The vertical dimension indicates the degree of overall technological progress: the higher the societal type, the greater its capacity to mobilize energy and information. Simple hunting and gathering societies are the least advanced in this respect, industrial societies the most. As the diagram indicates, human societies may achieve comparable degrees of technological progress by following different evolutionary paths (i.e., by developing different, but equally advanced, subsistence technologies). Because of this, the categories cannot all be neatly ranked, one ahead of the other. Maritime and agrarian societies, for example, are roughly equal in terms of technological progress even though they employ very different subsistence technologies.

For a typology to be useful in theory and research, it must be as simple and unambiguous as the data permit. For this reason, the criteria used to classify societies have been held to a minimum. In most instances, *a single criterion* is used to differentiate between two "adjacent" categories (i.e., categories with a common boundary in Fig. 6/2). For the same reason, the criteria are the ones whose presence in a society can be easily ascertained (e.g., the use of plows).

A society is classified as "hunting and gathering" when this is its primary mode of subsistence. This does not mean that the group never employs other means to provide for its material necessities; most of the hunting and gathering societies studied in the last century have, in fact, relied on fishing or part-time horticulture

---

[12] Goldschmidt, *op. cit.*, p. 194.

[13] Goldschmidt specifically identifies thirteen societies with this category (*ibid.*, pp. 189–190). Twelve of these have been classified by Murdock in his Ethnographic Atlas, currently being published in *Ethnography*. Of these twelve, eight are coded as seminomadic or semisedentary, while the other four (the Haida, Kwakiutl, Hupa, and Yurok) are all reported to have derived half or more of their subsistence from fishing.

[14] For an earlier and somewhat less satisfactory version of this scheme, see Gerhard Lenski, *Power and Privilege: A Theory of Social Stratification* (New York: McGraw-Hill, 1966), pp. 91–93.

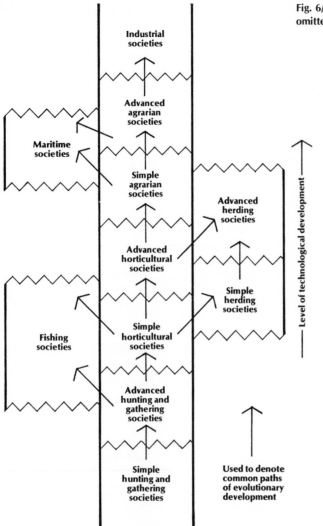

Fig. 6/2 **Societal typology for present analysis (hybrid types omitted)**

Used to denote common paths of evolutionary development

to some degree. But as long as hunting and gathering remains the primary mode of subsistence, we so classify them.

Simple hunting and gathering societies are those ancient prehistoric societies of the Lower and Middle Palaeolithic, the period prior to the last 35,000 years. These societies had only the most rudimentary technology. Their best weapon, for example, seems to have been nothing but a wooden spear.

The category of *advanced* hunting and gathering societies is reserved for the more advanced groups of the Upper Paleolithic and Mesolithic, together with the hunters and gatherers that have survived into the modern era. The key developments setting these groups apart are the spear-thrower and the bow and arrow. Both weapons appreciably increased the food-getting capability of a group.

Table 6/1 Minimal criteria for classification of horticultural and agrarian societies

Type of society	Plant cultivation*	Metallurgy*	Plow*	Iron*
Simple horticultural	+	−	−	−
Advanced horticultural	+	+	−	−
Simple agrarian	+	+	+	−
Advanced agrarian	+	+	+	+

* The symbol + means that the trait is present in the type of society indicated; the symbol − means it is absent.

The four categories of horticultural and agrarian societies constitute an evolutionary sequence of societies which depend on plant cultivation as their primary means of subsistence. We could lump them all together, but in doing so we would lose many valuable insights into the nature of the evolutionary process. The best way to describe the relationship among these four types of societies is to list *the minimal criteria* for each. As Table 6/1 indicates, if plant cultivation is the primary means of subsistence, but the society has neither metallurgy nor the plow, it is a *simple horticultural* society. If, however, the society possesses metal tools and weapons, it is *advanced horticultural*. If in addition, a group uses the plow in cultivation, it is a *simple agrarian* society. Finally, if it has all of these attributes and also manufactures *iron* tools and weapons, it is *advanced agrarian*.[15]

Fishing, herding, and maritime societies differ from the others in that they are *environmentally specialized types*. They are distinguished from other societies at comparable levels of development not so much in terms of the technology they *possess*, but rather in terms of the technology they *use*. Unlike other societal types, they rely disproportionately on those elements in their technology that are especially suited to the distinctive features of their environment. Thus a fishing society relies disproportionately on that part of its technology which is useful to it by virtue of its location on a body of water. A herding society relies disporportionately on those elements of its technology which enable it to subsist on open grasslands. Maritime societies, like fishing societies, utilized their proximity to water, though in a different way. Being technologically more advanced, they adapted their technology to the use of water for trade and commerce in an era in which the movement of bulky goods was much cheaper by water than by land.

With respect to level of technological development, herding societies are more varied than either of the other specialized societal types. For this reason, the category

---

[15] In Africa, south of the Sahara, most societies have long manufactured iron tools and weapons but have had a horticultural base. This has been due to the diffusion of the techniques of iron-making without a corresponding diffusion of the plow and agriculture. For purposes of analysis these societies must be classified as advanced horticultural, since they fail to meet the minimal criterion for agrarian societies (i.e., the presence of the plow).

is divided into simple and advanced types. The most important difference between them is that the latter employ horses or camels for transportation in work and warfare, while the former lack this important resource.

Industrial societies were the most recent to appear. The key development marking their emergence was the harnessing of new energy sources. Previously, the major sources were human and animal power, water, wind, and wood. Beginning in the eighteenth century, first coal, then petroleum, natural gas, hydroelectric power, and most recently atomic power have revolutionized subsistence activities. When these sources are dominant and industry replaces agriculture as the chief source of a society's income, societies are classified as industrial.

The jagged lines along the upper and lower boundaries of the various societal types in Fig. 6/2 indicate that a few of the most advanced groups within a societal type are able to mobilize a bit more energy and information than the least advanced societies in the next higher type. This apparent contradiction exists because of our decision to base the system of classification on the fewest possible criteria. As a result, a society that lacks a key differentiating element (e.g., the plow) may possess enough other technological elements to make it somewhat more advanced *overall* than a few of the least advanced societies that have the key element. Despite occasional incongruities of this kind, the benefits of this method of classification far outweigh the drawbacks.[16]

Finally, a word about *hybrid* societies. These are omitted from Fig. 6/2 because their inclusion would make the diagram cluttered and confusing. Hybrid societies are ones in which two or more modes of subsistence are intermingled. In some cases these societies are on the boundary between adjacent societal types. For example, a society might rely as much on fishing as on hunting and gathering. In another society, at a certain point in its history, a basic innovation like the plow may have spread to the point where roughly half the population used it while the other half still relies on an older tool or technique, such as the hoe. In neither case is it possible to place the society in a single category, and we have to classify it as a hybrid.

In other instances, the pattern of hybridization is more complex. This is particularly true when highly advanced societies come in contact with substantially less developed groups and crucial elements of technology diffuse from the former to the latter. Most African societies south of the Sahara today are good examples of this. They can only be described as industrializing horticultural societies (see Chapter 15).

SOCIETAL TYPES THROUGH HISTORY

As we have seen, men lived in simple hunting and gathering societies throughout most of human history. Approximately 35,000 years ago, advanced hunting and

---

[16] The chief advantages are: (1) the information needed to classify a society is most likely to be available when few criteria are used; (2) with fewer criteria, fewer categories are required and fewer societies will be unclassifiable because of contradictory characteristics (i.e., some characteristics pointing to one classification, others to another).

gathering societies began to replace these most primitive societal types. For the next 25,000 years, or until about 10,000 B.C., these two remained the only types of human society. Though there were many differences among societies as a result of environmental influences, men everywhere depended on hunting and gathering for their basic subsistence.

It is still not known just when this period of relative technological uniformity ended, but it seems to have been sometime during the Mesolithic era (from 10,000 to 7000 B.C.). The first new kind of society to emerge was probably the fishing type. Evidence of the practice of fishing can be traced back into the Upper Paleolithic, but the primitive nature of the equipment used at that time pretty well rules out the possibility that any group was yet relying primarily on fishing as a substitute for

Fig. 6/3   Hybrid societies employ elements of technology from two or more basic societal types. India, an industrializing agrarian society, employs basic elements of both agrarian and industrial origins as shown below

hunting.[17] With the invention of true fish hooks, nets, traps, boats, and paddles in the Mesolithic, however, the stage was set for some favorably situated group to make the shift from hunting and gathering to fishing and gathering.

Simple horticultural societies probably came next. The first of these societies appeared in the Middle East around 7000 B.C.[18] Though men began to use copper within the next 1,500 years,[19] it was not until nearly 4000 B.C. that metal tools and weapons became common enough to permit us to call any of these societies *advanced* horticultural.[20]

The plow seems to have been invented late in the fourth millennium, this innovation, too, occurring in the Middle East.[21] By 3000 B.C. it had become so widely adopted by societies in Mesopotamia and Egypt that we are justified in calling them simple agrarian.

Iron was discovered early in the second millenium but, like copper, did not become the dominant material in tools and weapons for a long time.[22] Thus, the first *advanced* agrarian societies did not appear until the early years of the first millennium B.C.

The origin of herding societies, as we noted, remains something of a mystery. The first evidence of animal domestication dates from about 9000 B.C., but the findings from this early site suggest a mixed economy.[23] Although we cannot say when men first relied on herding as their chief means of subsistence, it was probably some time after the first horticultural societies appeared.

Maritime societies date from the end of the third millennium B.C. The Minoans on the island of Crete seem to have been the first to rely on overseas commerce as their primary economic activity.[24] Unlike other major societal types, maritime societies have not had a *continuous* history. After flourishing in the Mediterranean world for two thousand years, they were wiped out by the growth of Roman power.

---

[17] See Jacquetta Hawkes, *Prehistory* (New York: Mentor, 1965), chap. 6, for a good summary of archaeological finds relating to fishing. See also Grahame Clarke and Stuart Piggott, *Prehistoric Societies* (New York: Knopf, 1965), chap. 7.

[18] For a good short summary of findings at these sites, see E. A. Hoebel, *Anthropology*, 3d ed. (New York: McGraw-Hill, 1966), pp. 188–193. See also James Mellaart, *Earliest Civilizations in the Near East* (London: Thames and Hudson, 1965) for a more detailed review of recent findings from this period and area.

[19] Mellaart, *op. cit.*, p. 105.

[20] See, for example, Leslie Aitchison, *A History of Metals* (London: Macdonald and Evans, 1960), vol. I, p. 41.

[21] E. Cecil Curwen and Gudmund Hatt, *Plough and Pasture: The Early History of Farming* (New York: Collier Books, 1961), p. 64.

[22] Aitchison, *op. cit.*, pp. 102 and 111–113.

[23] Mellaart, *op. cit.*, p. 20.

[24] William H. McNeill, *The Rise of the West: A History of the Human Community* (New York: Mentor, 1965), p. 150.

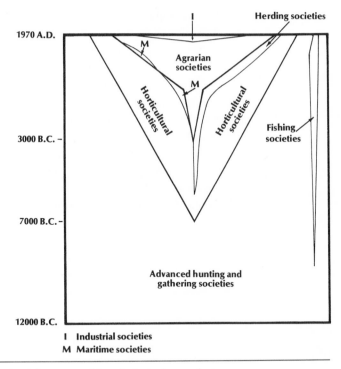

Fig. 6/4   Societal types from 12,000 B.C. to the present

During the Middle Ages, they enjoyed a revival for a number of centuries, only to disappear once more.

The last major societal type is the industrial. Although the basic inventions that mark the beginning of the modern technological revolution occurred in the eighteenth century, it was not until the nineteenth that Britain, pioneer in the Industrial Revolution, reached the point where it could be classified as a truly industrial society. Since then numerous other societies have followed Britain's lead.

CORRELATES OF SOCIETAL TYPE: SOME BASIC PATTERNS

In subsequent chapters, we shall examine each of the major societal types. First, however, we should check the validity of our basic theory by a comparative statistical analysis of the largest possible number and variety of human societies. If our theory is sound, we will find that differences in technology are linked with significant, predictable differences in social organization and ideology. Above all, we should find the kinds of relationships hypothesized by Goldschmidt. Differences in technology should be linked with

Differences in the size of groups
Differences in the permanence of their settlements
Differences in the extent of their division of labor and their organizational complexity
Differences in the amount of "leisure" enjoyed by their members

If these differences are not evident, we will be forced to reconsider our entire approach, but if they are, we will have good reason to believe that ecological-evolutionary theory and the typology derived from it are valuable tools in the study of human societies.

The richest source of systematic information on human societies is the Ethnographic Atlas published in each issue of *Ethnology*. This journal, edited by George Peter Murdock, provides a wealth of systematically coded data on hundreds of societies in all parts of the world. The data pertain to matters ranging from the subsistence technology of societies to the types of games their members play.

Though the journal has not classified these societies by societal type, most of the data needed to do so are in the codes, and where this is lacking, the original ethnographic reports usually provide it. Thus it is possible to apply our typology to this rich source of data, providing a more systematic survey of evolutionary patterns than has been possible before.[25]

As of April, 1966, the Ethnographic Atlas had reported data on 915 societies. These were distributed as follows among the basic societal types:[26]

Hunting and gathering	151
Simple horticultural	76
Advanced horticultural	267
Agrarian (both simple and advanced)	96
Fishing	44
Herding	60
Hybrids, maritime, industrial, and unclassifiable	221

In our analysis, we shall omit hybrid societies in order to concentrate on the more basic types. We shall also omit maritime and industrial societies because they are too few in number to be reliable, and in the latter case the sources of data were often questionable.[27]

---

[25] Pioneering efforts in this direction include the work of Leonard T. Hobhouse, G. C. Wheeler, and M. Ginsberg, *The Material Culture and Social Institutions of the Simpler Peoples* (London: Chapman & Hall, 1915). Unfortunately, because of the eclipse of evolutionary theory after World War I, this outstanding piece of work did not have the impact it might otherwise have had. In recent years there have been a number of efforts to analyze systematically coded bodies of data using various samples of societies, but these have seldom employed an adequate societal typology. Important recent work includes Raoul Naroll, "A Preliminary Index of Social Development," *American Anthropologist*, 58 (1956), pp. 687–715; Robert L. Carneiro, "Scale Analysis: Evolutionary Sequences and the Rating of Cultures," in Raoul Naroll and Ronald Cohen (eds.), *Handbook of Method in Anthropology*, forthcoming; and Alvin Gouldner and Richard Peterson, *Notes on Technology and the Moral Order* (Indianapolis, Ind.: Bobbs-Merrill, 1962).

[26] See the Appendix on pp. 503–507 for details on the classification of societies.

[27] Specifically, the codes on industrial societies were often based on the study of a single community that could in no sense be regarded as representative.

Societal type and population size

Goldschmidt's first hypothesis concerned the population of societies: the more advanced a society technologically, the greater its potential for population growth. There are two reasons for this. First, as a result of technological advance, higher densities can be sustained in a given area, making possible larger communities. Second, technological advance makes it possible for more communities to be united within a single political system.

Table 6/2 reveals both of these patterns. In hunting and gathering societies, communities are extremely small, averaging only about forty people each. Since these local groups are nearly always autonomous, and hence independent societies in their own right, the average hunting and gathering *society* actually contains only about forty people. In simple horticultural societies, communities average nearly a hundred, but again local groups are usually autonomous, so that community and society are the same. At the level of advanced horticultural societies, however, there are important changes. Not only are communities larger, but multicommunity societies are the rule. Thus, though the average advanced horticultural *community*

Table 6/2 Median size of communities and societies, by societal type

Type of society	Median size of communities	Median size of societies	No. of societies*
Hunting and gathering†	40	40	93–62
Simple horticultural	95	95	48–45
Advanced horticultural	280	5,800	107–84
Agrarian	‡	Over 100,000	58–48
Fishing	60	60	20–22
Herding	55	2,000	17–22

* Data are seldom available on a given subject for all 915 societies. This column indicates the number of societies for which data were available and on which the statistics are based. The first of the two figures indicates the number of cases on which the median size of communities is based, the second for the median size of societies.

† In this table and subsequent tables, all the hunting and gathering societies referred to are *advanced* ones.

‡ Murdock's method of coding community size does not permit one to give a precise figure for the median size of communities in agrarian societies since 57 per cent fall in a category labeled "one or more indigenous cities with more than 50,000 inhabitants." In other words, the content of the code shifts from a measure of central tendency to a measure of the upper limit of the range. It should also be noted that averages are much less meaningful in agrarian societies than in simpler societies owing to the greater range in size.

is only three times larger than the simple horticultural, the average advanced horticultural *society* is roughly sixty times larger than its simple horticultural counterpart. This trend continues in agrarian societies, where urban populations become common and the state covers even wider areas. Since 60 per cent of the agrarian societies for which we have data fall into Murdock's top category of "100,000 or more," it is not possible to give an exact figure for them. But it is obvious that they are substantially larger than their nearest rivals among the less advanced types.[28]

Table 6/2 is also relevant to our earlier discussion of the relative technological level of fishing, herding, and horticultural societies. The data show that fishing societies fall between hunting and gathering and simple horticultural societies in size. The figures for communities show the same for herding groups, but the more important figures for societal size place them between the simple and advanced horticultural. It may seem strange that although herding *communities* are no larger than fishing, herding *societies* are more than thirty times larger. The explanation seems to be that fishing communities generally occupy unusually favorable (in terms of food) environmental niches, enabling them to build up local population densities higher than normal for communities at their level of technological development, while herding peoples live in environments where exactly the opposite is true. At the societal level, however, the technological advances of herding societies permit them to expand geographically and develop politically to an extent not possible for the less advanced fishing groups. Moreover, political expansion is relatively easy in the steppe and prairie environments of herders, since there are so

---

[28] This particular code was not reported in the Ethnographic Atlas in *Ethnology* but in an earlier paper of Murdock's entitled "World Ethnographic Sample," *American Anthropologist*, 59 (1957), pp. 664–687. This paper provided data on a sample of 565 societies and offered a more limited range of information. The computations reported in Tables 6/2 to 6/13 are my own.

Fig. 6/5   The level of organizational development in a society is a function of the society's level of technological development: aerial view of Manhattan and artist's reconstruction of a Cherokee Indian village

few natural barriers. By contrast, the coastal and river territories of fishing peoples present many natural barriers which inhibit political expansion.

These data call attention to an important qualification concerning the relationship between a society's technological development and its organizational development. The latter tends to be a function of the former, but only to the extent that environmental conditions are held constant. To put it in slightly different terms, *the level of organizational development in a society is a function both of its level of technological development and of the abundance of resources in its environment.*

Societal type and permanence of settlements

According to Goldschmidt, technological progress also leads to an increase in the permanence of settlements. Hunting and gathering peoples are generally nomadic, whereas more advanced groups (except for herding peoples) are more settled. This is because hunting and gathering quickly depletes the supply of plants and animals in a small area and it becomes impossible to feed even a few dozen people. Murdock's data show this pattern clearly. Of the 147 hunting and gathering societies for which he obtained data, 90 per cent were nomadic in contrast to only 4 per cent of the 377 horticultural and agrarian societies.[29]

Societal type and division of labor

Goldschmidt cites the increased division of labor as another result of technological progress, and Murdock's data again provide support. Table 6/3 shows the frequency with which certain tasks are performed by specialists in each of the major

---

[29] Fourteen per cent were classified as fully migratory, 61 per cent as seminomadic, and 15 per cent as semisedentary.

Table 6/3 Frequency of craft specialization,* by societal type (in percentages)

Type of society	Metal working	Weaving	Leather working	Pottery	Boat building	House building	Average
Hunting and gathering	†	0	0	0	0	0	0
Simple horticultural	†	0	3	2	4	2	2
Advanced horticultural	100	6	24	24	9	4	28
Agrarian	100	32	42	29	5	18	38
Industrial‡	100	100	100	100	100	100	100
Fishing	†	0	0	0	9	4	2
Herding	95	11	22	†	†	0	21

* The term "craft specialization" as used here includes Murdock's category of industrial specialization.

† The activity in question is seldom found in this type of society.

‡ The figures for industrial societies are not from Murdock's data but are added simply for comparative purposes.

types of societies. Craft specialization of the kinds indicated is virtually unknown in hunting and gathering and simple horticultural societies. With advanced horticultural societies, such specialization occurs with some frequency, and the pattern becomes more prominent still in agrarian societies. Fishing societies closely resemble simple horticultural societies, while herding societies again occupy a position between the simple and advanced horticultural types.

Societal type and religious beliefs

Goldschmidt's other presumed correlates of technological progress—an increased supply of goods and services and increased "leisure"—cannot be tested with Murdock's data. But there are a variety of other things that are linked with progress, including cultural patterns in areas with no obvious dependence on technology. A good example of this is religion, where one might suppose technological variations are completely irrelevant. As Table 6/4 indicates, very few hunting and gathering or simple horticultural societies share the underlying Jewish and Christian belief in a God who not only created the universe but remains actively interested in it and in the moral aspects of human life. The majority of these societies, in fact, seem to lack even a belief in a Supreme Creator, and when such a belief *is* present, they usually assume him to be indifferent to man. In advanced horticultural societies, the pattern changes notably, with a majority of societies believing in an otiose (i.e., inactive) creator god. Belief in a Supreme Creator who is actively interested in his creation and who lends support to moral conduct is a common pattern only in agrarian and herding societies.[30]

---

[30] This way of classifying religious beliefs is based on a method originally developed by G. E. Swanson in *The Birth of the Gods: The Origin of Primitive Beliefs* (Ann Arbor, Mich: University of Michigan Press, 1960), chap. 3.

Table 6/4   Beliefs concerning God,* by societal type (in percentages)

Type of society	A	B	C	D	Total	No. of societies
Hunting and gathering	60	29	8	2	99	85
Simple horticultural	60	35	2	2	99	43
Advanced horticultural	21	51	12	16	100	131
Agrarian	23	6	5	67	101	66
Fishing	69	14	7	10	100	29
Herding	4	10	6	80	100	50

* A—no conception of Supreme Creator; B—belief in a Supreme Creator who is inactive or not concerned with human affairs; C—belief in a Supreme Creator who is active in human affairs but does not offer positive support to human morality; D—belief in a Supreme Creator who is active and supports human morality.

Table 6/5   Types of games, by societal type (in percentages)

Type of society	Games of physical skill	Games of chance	Games of strategy	No. of societies
Hunting and gathering	96	83	0	117
Simple horticultural	83	33	7	30
Advanced horticultural	90	37	68	41
Agrarian	92	60	60	25
Fishing	93	63	3	30
Herding	89	44	56	9

Societal type and games

Another feature of life that one would not expect to be closely related to technology and societal type is recreation. How men entertain themselves in their leisure moments seems more a matter of chance or whim. Yet even this proves to be linked to societal type (see Table 6/5). Games of physical skill are common in almost every society, but games of chance and games of strategy are not.[31] Games of strategy are normally found only in the more advanced societal types—advanced horticultural, agrarian, and herding—and are quite rare in simpler societies. Games of chance, on the other hand, are most common in hunting and gathering societies, then decline in frequency, only to become common again in agrarian societies, the most advanced of our series.

The reasons for these variations are not obvious, but the magnitude of the differences indicates that the patterns are real and not due to any inadequacies in the sample of societies. The most plausible explanation is that these games reflect people's experience in the more serious affairs of life. In societies where men have little control over, or understanding of, the forces that shape their lives, the games they invent are usually games of chance. On the other hand, where men have developed a measure of control over these forces and where their success more often depends on rational decision-making skills, games of strategy are more likely to be devised and enjoyed. In these more advanced societies, however, everyone does not share equally in opportunities for rational decision making. Usually there are sharply defined class systems, and life for members of the lower classes tends to be almost as primitive, almost as much beyond the individual's rational control, as life in more primitive societies. As a result, there seems to be a place for both types of games in these societies.

---

[31] This way of classifying games was developed by J. M. Roberts, M. J. Arth, and R. R. Bush in "Games in Culture," *American Anthropologist*, 61 (1959), pp. 597–605. Their explanation of differences in the occurrence of games of strategy is similar to mine; they attribute differences in the occurrence of games of chance to religious beliefs, finding such games linked with the belief that the gods or spirits are usually benevolent in their treatment of men.

Table 6/6 Marriage transactions, by societal type (in percentages)

Type of society	Bride service or bride price	Dowry	Other kinds of transactions	No. of significant transactions	Total	No. of societies
Hunting and gathering	37	0	11	51	99	148
Simple horticultural	45	0	16	39	100	74
Advanced horticultural	86	0	12	3	101	265
Agrarian	64	15	10	11	100	96
Fishing	59	0	18	23	100	44
Herding	93	2	4	2	101	60

Societal type and marriage practices

Societal type is also linked with variations in marriage practices and family life. Murdock's data show that these variations begin with premarital relations between the sexes, the more advanced societies tending to maintain stricter codes of conduct for girls. Other differences occur at the time of marriage. The more advanced a society technologically—at least up to the agrarian level—the greater the probability a strong economic component is present. In the more advanced societies, a man usually has to purchase his wife or render some form of service to the bride's father (see Table 6/6). Sometimes the pattern is reversed: the bride's parents then bear the burden of economic responsibility and have to provide their daughter with a dowry if they wish to marry her off. In this system, the marriageability of a girl tends to be proportional to the size of her dowry.

Following marriage, the decision as to where the couple will reside also reflects the influence of societal type. In the more advanced types, patrilocal residence (i.e., the couple resides with or near the husband's kinsmen) tends to be the rule. Whether the couple becomes a part of some extended family, whether they are a part of a sib or clan, and whether the marriage is monogamous or polygynous are all related, to a greater or lesser degree, to the basic system of subsistence.

Societal type and social inequality

Finally, Murdock's data show that societal type is related to the kind and degree of social inequality. Slavery, for example, is quite rare among hunting and gathering and simple horticultural peoples, but it is very widespread in advanced horticultural and herding societies (see Table 6/7). The existence of classes is also much more common in advanced societies (see Table 6/8).

Table 6/7   Presence of slavery in societies, by societal type (in percentages)

Type of society	Percentage having slavery	No. of societies
Hunting and gathering	10	142
Simple horticultural	14	66
Advanced horticultural	83	243
Agrarian	54	84
Fishing	51	43
Herding	84	50

Table 6/8   Presence of class systems, by societal type (in percentages)

Type of society	Percentage having a class system*	No. of societies
Hunting and gathering	2	143
Simple horticultural	17	69
Advanced horticultural	54	224
Agrarian	71	89
Fishing	32	41
Herding	51	49

* This includes those societies which Murdock codes as having "complex class systems," "dual stratification" and "elite stratification."

Another data source

Though Murdock's Ethnographic Atlas is the single richest source of systematically coded data on preindustrial societies, there are a number of others. Next to Murdock's codes, the best is probably one assembled a generation ago by Leo Simmons, a sociologist. As the basis for a study of the role of older people in primitive societies, Simmons coded data on seventy-one such groups.[32] Though his data cannot compare with Murdock's in terms of the number of societies examined, it is far superior with respect to the range of topics covered and thus it is a useful supplement.

[32] Leo Simmons, *The Role of the Aged in Primitive Society* (New Haven, Conn.: Yale, 1945).

Only three of our basic types are represented by enough cases in Simmons' codes to warrant review here. These three, and the number of cases in each, are:

Hunting and gathering	12
Simple horticultural	9
Advanced horticultural	17

Societal type and government

One subject which Murdock has largely ignored thus far is government. Fortunately, Simmons has not. To begin with, he coded information on the degree of power vested in chiefs. An analysis of these data show that with technological advance, the authority of chiefs increases substantially (Table 6/9). Similarly, technological advance is accompanied by the development and elaboration of systems of law (Table 6/10), as well as by an increase in the frequency of warfare (Table 6/11). In short, technological progress is associated with a general elaboration and development of political institutions and activities.

Table 6/9   Degree of power vested in chief, by societal type (in percentages)

Type of society	Substantial	Moderate	Slight	Total	No. of societies
Hunting and gathering	0	36	64	100	11
Simple horticultural	38	50	13	101	8
Advanced horticultural	63	25	13	101	16

Table 6/10   Degree of development of legal system, by societal type (in percentages)

Type of society	Substantial	Moderate	Slight	Total	No. of societies
Hunting and gathering	0	22	78	100	9
Simple horticultural	25	38	38	101	8
Advanced horticultural	69	15	15	99	13

Table 6/11   Incidence of warfare, by societal type (in percentages)

Type of society	Frequent	Intermediate	Rare or never	Total	No. of societies
Hunting and gathering	8	50	42	100	12
Simple horticultural	44	56	0	100	9
Advanced horticultural	82	12	6	100	17

Table 6/12 Private property rights in land, by societal type (in percentages)

Type of society	General	Frequent	Rare	Absent	Total	No. of societies
Hunting and gathering	0	11	11	78	100	9
Simple horticultural	14	57	14	14	99	7
Advanced horticultural	47	13	27	13	100	15

Societal type and cruelty

Simmons' data also afford an insight into certain of the grimmer concomitants of technological progress among primitive societies. The advance from hunting and gathering to advanced horticultural societies seems to be accompanied by a marked increase in the incidence of scalp taking, cannibalism, and human sacrifice. Unfortunately, Simmons was not able to obtain reliable information on these subjects for all his societies, so these generalizations cannot be accepted with complete confidence.[33] Nevertheless, the patterns are so strong and regular, and conform so closely to unsystematic observations, that one cannot ignore them.[34]

Societal type and property

A final subject on which Simmons provides valuable evidence is the development of private property rights in land. Land has always been one of the most basic of all human resources and hence the object of many struggles both within and between societies. Simmons' data support the long-held thesis that technological advance encourages the development of private property rights. These rights are rare in his small sample of hunting and gathering societies but common in both simple and advanced horticultural societies (see Table 6/12).

TECHNOLOGICAL DETERMINISM?

In the past, and even today, efforts to understand the role of technology in human affairs have been hindered by the tendency of many social scientists to think in categorical terms. Discussions of this subject often degenerate into futile arguments over unrealistically extreme positions. Over the years, a small number of scholars

---

[33] The number of societies for which information was lacking ranged from 23 per cent on cannibalism to 46 per cent on human sacrifice.

[34] To illustrate the strength and regularity of the patterns, scalp taking was a regular occurrence in one of seven hunting and gathering societies, four of six simple horticultural, and five of six advanced horticultural. Cannibalism was a regular occurrence in none of nine hunting and gathering societies, one of eight simple horticultural, and three of ten advanced horticultural.

have argued the case for a technological determinism that explains almost every sociocultural pattern in terms of technology.[35] Their opponents, eager to combat this exaggerated view and wanting to defend the importance of ideological factors, have minimized or denied the importance of technological forces.[36] The unreasonableness of *both* positions has apparently escaped many social scientists, with the result that both sociology and anthropology have been extremely slow in coming to a realistic assessment of technology's role in the evolutionary process.

Much of the confusion is due to the failure to think in *probabilistic* and *variable* terms.[37] Few, if any, significant social patterns are determined by one factor alone. Where human societies are concerned, one can rarely say that A, and A alone, causes B. Usually B is due to the combined effect of a number of factors and, while A may be the most important, it alone is not likely to be strong enough to determine the outcome. The most we can say, as a rule, is that if A is operative, B is likely to be present *with some degree of probability.*

The problem is further complicated because so many of the Bs we deal with exist in variable form. For example, when we talk about the population of a society, we are not interested in whether or not it exists, but in its relative size. This is true of most of the phenomena we are concerned with—the *degree* of occupational specialization, the *frequency* of warfare, the *extent* of the authority vested in chiefs, and so forth. To think in categorical terms about such things is at best misleading.

Clearly, then, the traditional controversy over technological determinism was a false issue. Technological factors are obviously incapable of explaining *all* social phenomena. On the other hand, the evidence indicates that they explain a great deal. How much they explain varies from subject to subject. We can see this in Table 6/13, which provides a measure of the explanatory power of the sixfold societal typology used in the analysis of Murdock's data.

To understand this table, first compare the values it shows for games of strategy, games of chance, and games of physical skill. These are 68, 50, and 13 respectively. Turning back to Table 6/5 (see page 135), we find that in the column dealing with games of strategy, the highest value is 68 and the lowest 0. This is a spread of 68 percentage points, which is the value assigned it in Table 6/13. Similarly, for games

---

[35] Leslie White, an anthropologist at the University of Michigan, has been the leading proponent of this point of view for many years. See, for example, his stimulating but extreme essay, "Energy and the Evolution of Culture," in *The Science of Culture* (New York: Grove Press, 1949), pp. 363–393.

[36] Talcott Parsons is one of many who have consistently minimized the role of technology in the process of social change. Though not as extreme as some in his views, he has been very influential. See *Societies: Evolutionary and Comparative Perspectives* (Englewood Cliffs, N.J.: Prentice Hall, 1966), especially pp. 113–114, for a recent statement of his views.

[37] The failure of many sociologists and anthropologists to think in probabilistic and variable terms is linked with the inadequate training many have received in statistics and with their failure to employ quantitative data. Correcting these deficiencies would, more than anything else, check the natural tendency to oversimplify problems and think in categoric terms. The rise in the level of statistical sophistication in the social sciences in recent years is a hopeful sign for the future but, unfortunately, many still receive degrees with only the most limited understanding of statistical theory and method.

Table 6/13 Maximum range of percentage differences between six basic societal types* for selected variables†

Variable	Maximum range
Specialization in metal working	100
Milking: practiced when possible	96
Leather working: wholly or largely a female activity	96‡
Boat building practiced	91
Nomadic communities	87
Local communities politically autonomous	83
Median size of communities 100 or more	80
Belief in God as active and moral force	78
Slavery practiced	74
Leather working practiced	71
Two or more levels of government above the local community	71
Pottery made	71
Class stratification	69
Games of strategy	68
Patrilocal residence	68
Urban communities of 5,000 or more	67
Bride price or bride service required	56
Weaving practiced	56
House construction: predominantly male activity	51
Patrilineal clans	51
Games of chance	50
Premarital virginity enforced for women	49
Weaving: predominantly male activity	46‡
Specialization in leather working	42
Extended family system	33
Specialization in weaving	32
Gathering: predominantly female activity	31
Specialization in pottery making	29
Pottery making: predominantly male activity	29§
Specialization in fishing	29
Fishing: predominantly male activity	22‡
Matrilineal clans	18
Specialization in house construction	18
Dowry system	15

* The societal types are those shown in Table 6/2 (page 131).

† Using Murdock's data.

‡ Percentage difference based on those societies in which the specified activity is carried on and for which data on sex specialization are available.

§ Herding societies omitted because too few practice pottery making. If included, the figure would rise to 46.

Table 6/13 continued

Variable	Maximum range
Games of physical skill	13
Specialization in boat building	9
Boat building: predominantly male activity	8‡
Specialization in hunting	7
Polyandry	1
Hunting: predominantly male activity	0‡

of chance the highest value in Table 6/5 is 83 and the lowest is 33, a difference of 50, and this is the figure shown in Table 6/13. Finally, for games of physical skill the extremes are 96 and 83, producing a difference of 13.

The differences between societal types shown in Table 6/13 cover the entire range of possibilities from 0 to 100 per cent. At the lower level, variations in technology are obviously irrelevant or of minor importance. In nearly every case this is because the activity in question is almost universally present or absent; hunting, for example, is predominantly a male activity in *every* society in Murdock's sample, while polyandry occurs in less than 1 per cent of them. At the upper level, however, variations in technology appear to be of real significance. To ignore these differences and attempt to make a blanket statement about the importance of technology would obviously be nonsense.

In summary, modern evolutionary theory takes a probabilistic, not a deterministic, view of the role of technology in social change. It views a society's basic subsistence technology as but one force in a field of forces that, together, determine its various characteristics. More precisely, it regards basic subsistence technology as *the most powerful single force in the field, not with respect to the determination of every single characteristic, but rather with respect to the total constellation of characteristics.*

This means that the first step in analyzing any society must be the determination of its position in a systematic typology based on subsistence technology. In this way, we are obliged to take account of the most powerful single force shaping human societies *at the start of our analysis.*

Our basic task for most of the remainder of this volume will be to apply these principles in a broadly comparative study of human societies. We will examine each of the major societal types that has emerged in the course of history, seeing how technological innovations have influenced developments in social organization and ideology and how developments in these areas have fed back upon technology and influenced *its* development. Our ultimate goal is to increase our understanding of the basic forces responsible for sociocultural evolution, in the hope that this will enable us to understand, and even control to some degree, the process of change which is such a striking, and at times threatening, feature of the contemporary world.

Part II
Preindustrial
Societies

*H*unting and Gathering Societies

Chapter 7

Hunting and gathering societies are unique, for they alone span the whole course of human history. From the emergence of the first men down to the present, there have always been societies obtaining their livelihood in this way. As we have said before, the probabilities are that none will survive into the twenty-first century because of the pressures generated by industrialization. Sociologists and anthropologists, while sorry to see them vanish, are thankful that some survived into the present century and thus could be studied by trained social scientists.

The survival of these groups has led, as we have seen, to a major controversy among social scientists. Some scholars, such as Lewis Henry Morgan, have seen in the hunting and gathering peoples of the modern era the living counterparts of prehistoric man. Others, such as Franz Boas, have denied the legitimacy of such a comparison, arguing that these modern groups are products of an evolutionary process as extended as that of any modern industrial society.

Though the latter view prevailed for a time, there are signs of a reversal. Many archaeologists now refer to the hunting and gathering peoples of prehistoric and modern times as "analogous peoples," and acknowledge the benefits to their discipline of inferences drawn from ethnographic studies.[1] A leading British archaeologist summed up the current view when he wrote that the archaeologist learns from the ethnographer

---

[1] For an example of the usage of the term "analogous peoples," see Grahame Clark and Stuart Piggott, *Prehistoric Societies* (New York: Knopf, 1965), p. 133. On the value of inferences from ethnography, see Frank Hole and Robert Heizer, *An Introduction to Prehistoric Archeology* (New York: Holt, 1965), especially pp. 211–214 and chap. 16, or Grahame Clark, *Archaeology and Society: Reconstructing the Historic Past*, 3d ed. (London: Methuen, 1957), pp. 172–174.

how particular peoples adapt themselves to their environments, and shape their resources to the ways of life demanded by their own cultures: he thus gains a knowledge of alternative methods of solving problems and often of alternative ways of explaining artifacts resembling those he recovers from antiquity. Study of ethnography will not as a rule . . . give him straight answers to his queries. What it will do is to provide him with hypotheses in the light of which he can resume his attack on the raw materials of his study. In fact, the great values of ethnography to the prehistorian is that it will often suggest to him what to look for. . . . By constant reference to the culture of living or recently living societies, the prehistorian should be able to enrich and fortify his inter- pretation of the past, as well as bring into the open problems calling for further research.[2]

In our analysis we will follow the conservative procedure of presenting the findings of archaeology and ethnography separately. Only after we have done this will we explore the question of whether they provide consistent or contradictory images of hunting and gathering societies.

THE ARCHAEOLOGICAL EVIDENCE

Archaeologists divide the history of mankind prior to the horticultural revolution into four basic eras. Starting with the earliest, these are:

Lower Paleolithic
Middle Paleolithic
Upper Paleolithic
Mesolithic

The Lower Paleolithic was, by far, the longest in duration. Beginning roughly 2 million years ago and lasting until about 150,000 years ago, it covered more than 90 per cent of human history. The approximate dates for the other three eras are shown in Table 7/1. That each era has been substantially shorter than the one preceding it is a matter of considerable importance, as we shall see.

---

[2] Clark, *op. cit.,* pp. 172–173. Quoted by permission of Methuen & Co., Ltd.

Table 7/1 Approximate dates of the Lower, Middle, and Upper Paleolithic and Mesolithic eras

| | Years before the present | | |
Era	Beginning date*	Ending date*	Approximate duration
Mesolithic	10,000	9,000	1,000
Upper Paleolithic	35,000	10,000	25,000
Middle Paleolithic	150,000	35,000	115,000
Lower Paleolithic	2,000,000	150,000	1,850,000

* Since the eras began and ended at different dates in various parts of the world, only the figures for the earliest beginning and ending dates are shown here.

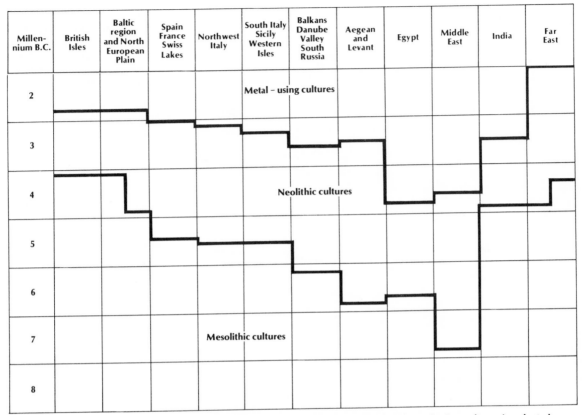

Fig. 7/1   Estimated dates for Mesolithic, Neolithic, and metal-using cultures in selected areas

During the early years of archaeological research, when investigations were still limited to Europe, it was generally supposed that the dates for the various eras were the same in all parts of the world. Today, as a result of research in other continents, we know better. For example, though the Lower Paleolithic ended in Europe about 150,000 years ago, it continued in eastern and central Africa for another 100,000 years.[3] Similarly, the Mesolithic survived for varying periods of time, as Fig. 7/1 indicates. Though it ended in parts of the Middle East about 7000 B.C., it survived in Britain and other parts of northern Europe until 3000 B.C. The figures in Table 7/1, therefore, oversimplify the picture to some extent.

Simple hunting and gathering societies of the Lower Paleolithic

As we have already noted (see page 96), there is good reason to doubt that the hominids[4] of the Lower Paleolithic were men in anything like the usual sense of

---

[3] See, for example, Sonia Cole, *The Prehistory of East Africa* (New York: Mentor, 1965), pp. 44 and 164.

[4] This is a generic term anthropologists have developed to refer to both modern man and his apelike prehistoric ancestors.

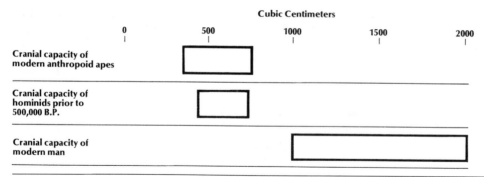

Fig. 7/2 Ranges of cranial capacity of modern anthropoid apes, hominids prior to 500,000 B.P., and modern man

the term. If by "man" we mean a creature whose mode of adaptation is primarily cultural and if we equate culture with the ability to use symbols, then it is very unlikely that the hominids that lived during most of that era were true humans. Students of the prehistoric past have often commented upon the painful slowness of technological progress during the Lower Paleolithic, and many have concluded that "this almost unimaginable slowness of change demonstrates a lack of inventiveness that could only survive among societies without fully articulate speech."[5]

Biological evidence points in the same direction. The cranial capacity of modern man ranges from 1,000 to 2,000 cubic centimeters, with an average of close to 1,500 cc.[6] By contrast, the cranial capacity of the hominids that lived throughout most of the Lower Paleolithic, or until about 500,000 years ago, ranged from 435 to 725 cc.[7] This is not unlike the 350- to 750-cc range of modern anthropoid apes. Though cranial capacity is not related to mental ability in modern man except in pathological cases of microcephaly and macrocephaly, the difference between the modern human range and that of the early hominids, together with the similarity between the latter's range and that of modern primates, reinforces the conclusion indicated by the slow rate of technological progress. As one authority has stated, "It is extremely unlikely that [these early hominids] could speak."[8] Thus, those who seek to extend the history of man to the dawn of the Paleolithic are stretching the definition of man almost beyond recognition.

[5] Jacquetta Hawkes, *Prehistory*, vol. I, part 1, of the UNESCO *History of Mankind* (New York: Mentor, 1965), p. 172. See also Grahame Clark, *The Stone Age Hunters* (London: Thames and Hudson, 1967), p. 25; Clark and Piggott, *op. cit.*, p. 45; and Cole, *op. cit.*, pp. 120 and 123, who refers to the "astonishing slowness in cultural development" in this era.

[6] These and the following figures are based on Carleton S. Coon, *The Origin of Races* (New York: Knopf, 1962), pp. 258–260; E. Adamson Hoebel, *Anthropology*, 3d ed. (New York: McGraw-Hill, 1966), chaps. 9 and 10; John Honigmann, *The World of Man* (New York: Harper, 1959), pp. 815 and 847–849; Cole, *op. cit.*, pp. 100–101; Bertram Kraus, *The Basis of Human Evolution* (New York: Harper, 1964), p. 224.

[7] In the latter part of the Lower Paleolithic, a new type of hominid appeared which modern anthropologists refer to as the Pithecanthropines (in contrast to the earlier Australopithecines). Their cranial capacity ranged from 750 to 1,300 cc, averaging about 1,000. Clearly, these creatures were much more likely to have been capable of speech than their predecessors.

[8] Coon, *op. cit.*, p. 259.

Fig. 7/3 Artist's reconstruction of the life of Peking man. This drawing from the British Museum follows closely available archaeological evidence

Our picture of life in the Lower Paleolithic is still extremely sketchy. Apart from skeletal remains, the evidence consists largely of thousands of simple stone tools apparently used to skin animals and cut off chunks of meat. For other tasks, such as digging out edible roots, a pointed stick would have sufficed.[9] How the earliest hominids obtained meat is debatable. Quite possibly they scavenged the remains left by carnivores.[10] Before the Lower Paleolithic ended, however, the hominids had become skilled hunters. The cave containing the bones of Peking man (c. 500,000 B.P.) was filled with thousands of animal bones. The fact that most of them had been split open indicates that the occupants of the cave had eaten the animals, opening the bones to get at the marrow. Most of the animals were large ones, indicating more than minor hunting skills.

Peking man was also a user of fire. Whether he was able to generate it is not known, but most scholars believe that he merely preserved fires started by lightning or other natural causes. Fire was undoubtedly used for warmth and, from a fairly early date, probably for cooking as well. Remains from an English contemporary of Peking man reveal another important use of fire—to harden the point of a wooden spear. This type of spear was apparently man's most advanced weapon until the Upper Paleolithic.

In the Lower Paleolithic the hominids or early men probably lived either in the open or in caves. There is no evidence of man-made dwellings until the Upper Paleolithic. Living in the open was more feasible than it might at first appear because the range of territory occupied during this period was largely restricted to the warmer regions (see Fig. 7/4).

Finally, archaeological evidence indicates that at least some groups practiced

---

[9] Cole, *op. cit.*, p. 122.

[10] *Ibid.*, p. 116.

Fig. 7/4 Approximate areas of tool-making hominid or human habitation in the Lower Paleolithic

cannibalism. In the cave where the remains of Peking man were found, several of the skulls were broken in a way that strongly indicates the brains were removed, presumably for food.

Beyond this, there is nothing we can say about life in the Lower Paleolithic except by way of inference based on our observations of modern primates and modern hunting and gathering societies. Since this will take us into the realm of ethnography and ethology, we will first complete our survey of the archaeological evidence.

Simple hunting and gathering societies of the Middle Paleolithic

With the beginning of the Middle Paleolithic approximately 150,000 years ago, the human character of the tool-makers is no longer a matter of debate. This is the era dominated by Neanderthal man. Biologically, Neanderthal man was much more like modern man (i.e., Homo sapiens sapiens) than were the hominids of the Lower Paleolithic. With respect to the important matter of cranial capacity, he closely resembled Homo sapiens sapiens, with a range from 1,300 to 1,600 cc and an average of nearly 1,500.

Culturally the resemblance is not nearly so strong. But one thing, at least, strongly suggests that Neanderthal man used symbols: he buried his dead and placed in the grave with them artifacts that strongly suggest a belief in some kind of life after death. These artifacts included food, implements, and red ochre, which some scholars suspect was believed to have the life-giving properties of blood. In at least one instance, animal bones and cinders were found in a grave, suggesting either burnt offerings or the remains of a funeral feast.[11] This evidence of abstract thought is indicative of speech and the use of symbols.

---

[11] For a good brief summary of Neanderthal burial remains, see Hawkes, *op. cit.*, pp. 289–290.

Fig. 7/5 **Excavating a Paleolithic site in Dordogne, France**

In other respects, however, the culture of Neanderthal man was closer to the Lower Paleolithic than to later periods. Apart from the burial of the dead, there seem to have been only two noteworthy innovations in the Middle Paleolithic. The first of these was the probable development of clothing. Though there is no direct evidence that Neanderthal man wore clothing, many archaeologists think it would have been essential because of the cold climates to which he was exposed during much of his history.[12] The abundance of flint scrapers found at Neanderthal sites reinforces this hypothesis, since they were probably used, among other things, to dress animal skins.

The other noteworthy innovation of Neanderthal man was his discovery of the usefulness of handles on tools. A handle usually multiplies the efficiency of a tool several times. In a striking tool, it increases the force of the blow by increasing the radius of the swing; in a cutting tool, it increases the force by bringing the more powerful muscles of the hand and arm to bear.[13] As far as we know, Neanderthal man did not reach the point of adding wooden handles to his tools, but he did discover the advantages inherent in using the long bone of an animal as a kind of ready-made handle, with the end of the bone serving as the head of the tool.[14]

---

[12] See, for example, Clark and Piggott, *op. cit.*, p. 59.

[13] S. A. Semenov, *Prehistoric Technology*, trans. by M. W. Thompson (New York: Barnes & Noble, 1964), p. 173.

[14] *Ibid.*

Advanced hunting and gathering societies of the Upper Paleolithic

With the appearance of modern man (Homo sapiens sapiens) approximately 35,000 years ago, the rate of technological innovation increased greatly. New kinds of tools and weapons appeared in such numbers (see Fig. 7/6) that we are forced to recognize the emergence of a new type of society, one appreciably higher on the scale of technological progress than any of its known predecessors in the Lower and Middle Paleolithic. We shall refer to these as *advanced* hunting and gathering societies to distinguish them from the more primitive groups of the earlier eras. Since the innovations were made over a 25,000-year period, the transition from simple to advanced hunting and gathering societies was gradual, and the latter term is far more applicable to societies late in the era than to those at the beginning.

Some of the most important innovations were in the manufacture of weapons. Though men had used the spear since Lower Paleolithic times, there were no significant improvements until the Upper Paleolithic, when several important ones appeared. One of the first was the spear-thrower. Using the principle of the lever, it doubled the distance a spear could be thrown.[15] At the other end of the spear, the men of the Upper Paleolithic placed sharpened bone points, and later, barbs as well.[16]

The most important innovation in weapons, however, was the bow and arrow. Utilizing the principle of the concentration of energy, Upper Paleolithic man

---

[15] *Ibid.*, pp. 202–203.

[16] Hoebel, *op. cit.*, pp. 176–177, and Hawkes, *op. cit.*, pp. 212–213.

Fig. 7/6 Assorted Paleolithic tools. The large chopper or hand ax in the center of the figure dates from the Lower Paleolithic. Since no other types of tools or weapons dating from this era have been found, it is assumed that these were all-purpose implements. By contrast, men in the Upper Paleolithic used a much wider variety of tools and weapons, a few examples of which are shown on either side of the Lower Paleolithic chopper

Fig. 7/7 Two comparisons of the spear and the bow and arrow

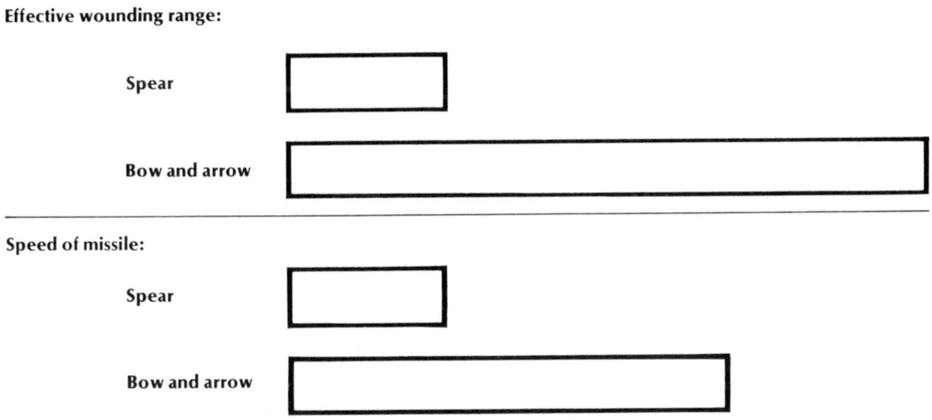

Effective wounding range:

Spear

Bow and arrow

Speed of missile:

Spear

Bow and arrow

created a weapon of great usefulness and versatility. Its effective wounding range is roughly four times that of the spear, and twice that of the spear thrown with the aid of a spear-thrower.[17] Furthermore, an arrow travels two and a half to three times faster than a spear. This is important not only because of the time advantage it affords the hunter, but also because the force of the blow is a function of the speed of the missile. Finally, in contrast with the spear, the bow and arrow permit the hunter to sight the missile at eye level, thus greatly increasing the accuracy of his aim.

Though less dramatic, the development of tools was no less important. As one writer has put it, "In the Upper Paleolithic Age man began to make the tool fit the task with an altogether new precision."[18] These innovations included such diverse tools as pins or awls, needles with eyes, spoons, graving tools, axes, stone saws, antler hammers, shovels or scoops, pestles and grinding slabs (used in grinding minerals to obtain coloring materials), and mattocks.

This era also provides us with the first definite evidence of man-made dwellings. These have been found in sites scattered from Czechoslovakia to Siberia and were left by mammoth hunters whose highly specialized way of life forced them to live in caveless country even during the winter. Figure 7/8 shows a modern reconstruction of one of these settlements. Not all were tentlike structures of the type shown, however; some were true earth houses.[19]

The discovery of these settlements is important, among other reasons, because they provide us with information on the size of human communities in this era. In general, they were quite small, many having as few as 6 to 30 persons. The largest settlement found would hold no more than 60.[20]

[17] This and the following statements concerning the bow and arrow are based on Semenov, *op. cit.*, pp. 202–204.

[18] Hawkes, *op. cit.*, p. 212.

[19] J. G. D. Clark, *Prehistoric Europe: The Economic Basis* (London: Methuen, 1952), pp. 132–133.

[20] Hawkes, *op. cit.*, pp. 184–188.

Fig. 7/8 Reconstruction of an Upper Paleolithic settlement in Czechoslovakia

Another significant innovation was the lamp, the oldest of which have been found in caves in Western Europe. These first lamps were simply shallow stone saucers, though some had a broad tongue extending from the rim to form a handle. Modern Eskimos use similar lamps today, with seal or walrus blubber for fuel and moss for a wick. Europeans of the Upper Paleolithic may have done the same, though they probably used ordinary fats.[21]

The best-known innovation of Upper Paleolithic man is his art. The drawings on the walls of caves in Western Europe (see Fig. 7/9) are world famous, but they are only one of the art forms developed in that era. There was sculpture of various kinds (Fig. 7/10) as well as bone and ivory carvings, often on the handles of weapons and tools (Fig. 7/11).

It would be hard to exaggerate the importance of these artistic remains, for they provide us with many insights into Upper Paleolithic life. Drawings of men dressed to resemble animals strongly suggest magical or religious practice, especially a belief in sympathetic magic. This belief—that anything done to an image, or a part, of a person or animal will affect that person or animal—is further evidenced by the fact that a great number of the drawings have spears or darts drawn or scratched into the animals' flanks.[22]

Sympathetic magic was apparently also used to produce fertility, in both humans and animals. At least this is the most likely explanation for the numerous female figures with exaggerated evidences of pregnancy (see Fig. 7/10). Most scholars think it is no coincidence that the artist ignored the facial features and devoted all of his attention to the symbols of fertility.

Many examples of Upper Paleolithic art indicate the development of ceremonies or rituals. This is suggested by the drawings of men dancing in animal disguises as well as by engravings of processions of men standing before animals, with their heads bowed and their weapons resting on their shoulders in a nonthreatening position. It has been suggested that these men are following the practice of some modern hunters and are asking the forgiveness of the animals they plan to kill.[23] In

---

[21] *Ibid.*, pp. 229–230.

[22] Clark and Piggott, *op. cit.*, pp. 93–95.

[23] Hawkes, *op. cit.*, pp. 293–294, including Fig. 35*b*.

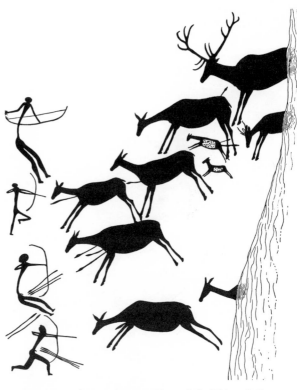

Fig. 7/9   The stag hunt, an Upper Paleolithic painting
from the wall of a cave in Spain

Fig. 7/10   The Venus of Willendorf,
an Upper Paleolithic sculpture

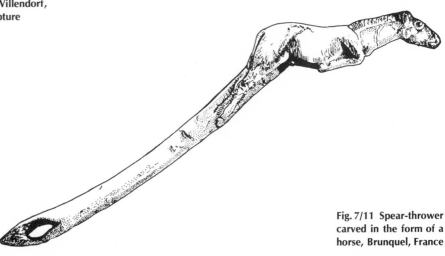

Fig. 7/11 Spear-thrower
carved in the form of a
horse, Brunquel, France

Fig. 7/12 Cave drawings like that of the "sorcerer" strongly suggest magical or religious practice, especially a belief in sympathetic magic

short, Upper Paleolithic art reveals the growth of human consciousness and man's efforts to understand and control his environment, and attests to the gulf developing between him and the rest of the animal world.

Upper Paleolithic art also provides the first hints of the beginnings of occupational specialization. Some have felt that several of the drawings are our earliest records of shamans or medicine men, though they may simply depict ordinary hunters engaged in common ritual activities. A stronger indication of specialization comes from a settlement site in Czechoslovakia. One of its three huts is still only partially excavated and little can be said about it as yet, while the second appears to have been a communal longhouse occupied by five family groups. But the third was a small circular hut that was evidently used for the manufacture of clay statuettes of animals and women, indicating the workshop of a shaman or medicine man.[24]

---

[24] See Bohuslav Klema, "The First Ground-plan of an Upper Palaeolithic Loess Settlement in Middle Europe and Its Meaning," in Robert Braidwood and Gordon Willey (eds.), *Courses toward Urban Life: Archeological Considerations of Some Cultural Alternatives* (Chicago: Aldine, 1962), pp. 199ff.

A final development in the Upper Paleolithic was man's migration to three new continents, North and South America and Australia.[25] The movement to the New World was made possible by the lowering of the sea level during the last Ice Age, when vast quantities of water were held in glaciers. This created a land bridge in the Bering Straits, providing direct access from Siberia to North America.[26] There may have been a similar link with Australia, though present evidence indicates that Upper Paleolithic man had to travel a part of the way by water.[27] If so, we must assume another major technical achievement, the invention of boats. The oldest boats found thus far date from the Mesolithic, but it is possible that future research will provide evidence of earlier ones.

Advanced hunting and gathering societies of the Mesolithic

With the Mesolithic, we come to the final era in which hunting and gathering were man's most efficient means of subsistence. Later, this simple way of life would be increasingly on the defensive, struggling to survive in the face of growing challenges from groups with more advanced and more efficient systems of production. In the Mesolithic, however, if hunting and gathering societies had any competition, it was only from fishing societies, and these were confined to limited areas. As we noted earlier, it is impossible to say just when the first fishing societies appeared, but archaeological evidence suggests that it was during the Mesolithic. The oldest remains of boats and boat equipment date from this period, as do the first true fish hooks, fish nets, and fish traps.[28] From the widespread distribution of these artifacts, it seems likely that fishing was practiced not just by true fishing societies, but also by many societies that continued to rely on hunting and gathering as their primary means of subsistence.

In Europe, many of the innovations in the Mesolithic reflect men's responses to changing climatic conditions. After the glaciers retreated, what had once been an open plain inhabited by vast herds of reindeer became forested. New flora and fauna appeared, necessitating substantial changes in the patterns of human life. The increased reliance on fishing was but one of these adjustments.

---

[25] For a summary of recent results of carbon dating in Australia, see Frederick McCarthy, "The Aboriginal Past: Archaeological and Material Equipment," in Ronald and Catherine Berndt (eds.), *Aboriginal Man in Australia: Essays in Honour of Emeritus Professor A. P. Elkin* (Sydney: Angus and Robertson, 1965), pp. 83–84. On the Americas, see R. F. Spencer, J. D. Jennings et al., *The Native Americans* (New York: Harper, 1965), chap. 1.

[26] Despite its latitude, much of this area was free from glaciers at this time. See Clark and Piggott, *op. cit.*, chap. 5, for a discussion of this movement and the relevant evidence. New findings are still coming in on this subject, however, and all conclusions, especially about the timing of the migration, are very tentative.

[27] See N. W. G. Macintosh, "The Physical Aspect of Man in Australia," in Berndt and Berndt, *op. cit.*, especially pp. 36–41.

[28] Hawkes, *op. cit.*, pp. 156–158, 213, and 266–228.

Another important response to the changed environment was the growth of wood-working tools and skills. Axes with handles became common, and the adze was introduced. As noted previously, the oldest known boat, a crudely dug out log found in Holland, dates from this period—approximately 6400 B.C. A wooden paddle found in an English site is about a thousand years older.

At this time the Middle East, unlike Europe, seems to have been largely open grassland. Here men first turned to the cereal grasses as a major source of food. Throughout most of this period they seem merely to have harvested wild grains as they ripened. But before the end of the Mesolithic they discovered that the same grains that were eaten could be planted and would become the source of a new crop.[29] Evidence of this is found in the many stone sickles unearthed at Mesolithic sites. They still show the distinctive sheen produced by the abrasive effects of thousands of stems of grass on the cutting surface of the blades. These sites also yielded pestles and mortars, apparently used for grinding grain, as well as clay-lined pits for storing it.[30] A second major innovation in subsistence technology was the domestication of sheep.[31] These two developments laid the foundation for the first major social revolution in human history.

Even during the Mesolithic, however, the effects of these advances were apparent. These Middle Eastern communities were able to support larger populations and a more settled mode of living. One cemetery, for example, contains the remains of eighty-seven individuals, another forty-five, and some of the graves reveal an elaborateness of construction not previously encountered.[32]

Despite its brevity, the Mesolithic era produced a variety of other innovations. These include the domestication of the dog, the invention of the sledge and the ice pick (the latter used to open holes for winter fishing), both the development of basketry and leather working and the invention of tools used in them. In addition, there were numerous advances in the manufacture of traditional tools and weapons. Recent research shows that by various devices, such as changes in the angle of the blade, men were able to strengthen stone tools and reduce their tendency to break under pressure.[33] As a result, the stone tools of the Mesolithic were considerably better than those of the Upper Paleolithic.

By the end of the Mesolithic, human societies had achieved an amazing

---

[29] There is no direct evidence that this discovery was made during the Mesolithic, but we define horti-cultural societies as those that obtain more than half of their food supply from the cultivation of plants, and obviously this did not happen overnight. The discovery of plant cultivation must have occurred many years, and perhaps some centuries, before true horticultural societies appeared.

[30] Hawkes, *op. cit.*, p. 255, and James Mellaart, *Earliest Civilizations of the Near East* (London: Thames and Hudson, 1965), chap. 2.

[31] Mellaart, *op. cit.*, p. 20.

[32] Clark and Piggott, *op. cit.*, p. 151; or Mellaart, *op. cit.*, pp. 26–27.

[33] Semenov, *op. cit.*, p. 203.

diversity. They had adapted to tropical conditions, to Arctic conditions, and to everything in between. Men were living in forests, in open grasslands, and even in deserts. Though some groups still relied entirely on hunting and gathering, an increasing number were getting a part of their food from fishing, horticulture, or herding. The Upper Paleolithic and the Mesolithic were in the fullest sense of the term, a time of "adaptive radiation," an explosive period of rapid change and increasing variability. In this case, however, the process was sociocultural in nature, rather than genetic.

The changing rate of change in the Paleolithic and Mesolithic

Just as many have commented on the "unimaginable slowness of change" in the Lower Paleolithic, so many have remarked on the quickening pace of change in the Upper Paleolithic. At one time, some scholars thought that the Mesolithic was a period of cultural decay and degeneration, but this view is now rejected and the Mesolithic is also seen as a period of rapid innovation, which laid the foundation for the Neolithic, or horticultural, revolution.[34]

This recalls our earlier hypothesis that the long-term evolutionary trend involves an acceleration of the rate of innovation. Before turning to the ethnographic evidence on modern hunting and gathering societies, we will take a close look at this matter to see to what extent archaeological data support or contradict it.

To explore this problem as systematically as possible, Table 7/2 lists all known innovations of importance from Lower Paleolithic through Mesolithic times.[35] If this table errs, it is probably in its omission of certain innovations of the later periods that were essentially refinements of earlier innovations. For example, Mesolithic man's important change in the blade angle of stone tools is not included. If all such innovations were recorded, the list for the Upper Paleolithic and Meso-lithic would be considerably longer.

To complete the analysis, Table 7/3 shows the duration of each period, the number of major technological innovations in it (excluding the nontechnical items bracketed in Table 7/2), and, based on this information, the rate of innovation. Because of the difficulty of measuring the duration of the Lower Paleolithic and Mesolithic eras, alternative calculations are provided. In the case of the Lower Paleolithic, one estimate is based on the assumption that human history began nearly 2 million years ago, a second on the older assumption of 1 million years

---

[34] The earlier misunderstanding of the Mesolithic was due in large measure to the impact of the discovery of the marvelous cave paintings of the Upper Paleolithic and the lack of anything similar in the Meso-lithic. Since then, scholars have realized that most of the art work of the latter period was probably lost because men moved out of caves and into more advanced, but less durable, dwellings. Moreover, art is probably not one of the better indicators for measuring technological advance (in an earlier era, as we have seen, scholars often failed to differentiate between different kinds of progress).

[35] This table is based largely on Clark and Piggott, *op. cit.*; Semenov, *op. cit.*; and Hawkes, *op. cit.*

Table 7/2   Technological and other innovations during the Lower, Middle, and
Upper Paleolithic and Mesolithic eras

Era	Innovations*	
Lower Paleolithic	Stone chopping, cutting, and scraping tools†	
	Wooden spear	Use of fire
	Fire-hardened spear point	[Cannibalism]
Middle Paleolithic	Use of bone for tools	[Ceremonial burial]
	Skin clothing (probable)	[Religion (probable)]
	Built-in handle for tools (i.e., long bone)	
Upper Paleolithic	Spear-thrower	Bow and arrow
	Man-made dwellings	Lamps
	Harpoon head	Fish gorgets
	Pins and/or awls	Needles with eye
	Antler hammers	Shovels or scoops
	Mattocks	Stone ax with hafted handle
	Stone saws	Graving tools
	Spoons	Pestles and grinding slabs
	Separate handles	Boats (very possible)
	[Painting]	[Sculpture]
	[Magic (probable)]	[Ornaments]
Mesolithic	Boats (?)	Fish hooks
	Fish nets	Fish traps
	Adze	Sickles
	Plant cultivation	Domestication of sheep
	Basketry	Leather-working tools
	Grinding equipment	Paving
	Sledge	Ice pick
	Comb	Domestication of the dog

* Items in brackets are nontechnological and are not counted in Table 7/3.
† These are multipurpose tools usually referred to by archaeologists as chopping tools or hand
axes. For purposes of Table 7/3 they will be considered a single innovation, since refinements of
tools are not otherwise listed or counted.

ago, and a third on the assumption that the early hominids were not truly human
and that history began only 500,000 years ago. In the case of the Mesolithic, one
estimate is based on the finding that the Mesolithic averaged about 3,000 years in
Europe and Asia, the other on the finding that it lasted only 1,200 years in the crucial
Middle Eastern area. Though these alternatives yield different values for the rate of
change, they do not have any significant effect on the basic pattern. The calculations
show a sharply rising rate of innovation. In fact, the lower estimate for the Mesolithic

Table 7/3 Rate of change during the Lower, Middle, and Upper Paleolithic and Mesolithic eras

Era	(A) Duration (in 1,000-year intervals)	(B) Number of major technological innovations	(B/A) Rate of innovation
Lower Paleolithic	1,850*	4	0.002
Lower Paleolithic	850†	3	0.004
Lower Paleolithic	350‡	3	0.009
Middle Paleolithic	120	3	0.025
Upper Paleolithic	25	17.5§	0.700
Mesolithic	3|	16.5§	5.500
Mesolithic	1.2¶	16.5§	13.750

* This estimate assumes that the Lower Paleolithic began 2 million years ago.
† This estimate assumes that the Lower Paleolithic began 1 million years ago.
‡ This estimate assumes that the Lower Paleolithic began 500,000 years ago.
§ Because of the great uncertainty concerning the era in which boats were invented, they are counted as half a unit in both the Upper Paleolithic and Mesolithic eras.
| This estimate assumes that the Mesolithic lasted approximately 3,000 years on the average.
¶ This estimate assumes that the Mesolithic lasted only 1,200 years in the area of minimum duration (i.e., the Middle East).

is more than 500 times the highest estimate for the Lower Paleolithic. The magnitude of the differences is so great that it is difficult to imagine that any new findings, or any more precise listing of major innovations, could possibly alter the picture.[36]

THE ETHNOGRAPHIC EVIDENCE

Fortunately for the student of human societies, hunting and gathering societies did not disappear with the emergence of new kinds of societies. In remote areas, especially in the New World and Australia, they continued to flourish. Though the settlement of these areas by Europeans and the spreading influence of industrialization are finally destroying them, we now have detailed descriptions of many of these groups. Thus their loss is not the great tragedy it would have been had it occurred several hundred years earlier, when the civilized world possessed almost no firsthand knowledge of them.

---

[36] For a similar conclusion, based on a less systematic survey, see Hawkes, *op. cit.*, pp. 172–173.

A hundred years ago, there were still large numbers of hunting and gathering societies in both the New World and Australia, and smaller numbers in southwest Africa, parts of the rain forest in central Africa, certain remote areas in southeast Asia and neighboring islands, and in arctic Asia. As recently as 1788 there were probably 5,000 hunting and gathering societies in Australia alone, and almost certainly as many more in North America.[37]

In our review of these societies, we shall concentrate on those whose way of life has been least affected by contact with agrarian and industrial societies. Our primary concern will be with the more remote and isolated groups and with groups that were studied before social contacts and cultural diffusion transformed or destroyed their traditional social patterns.

Even with these limitations, the societies we shall examine are by no means homogeneous. This can be seen quite clearly in the 151 hunting and gathering societies in Murdock's sample (see pages 503–504). At one extreme, 13 per cent of these societies relied entirely on hunting and gathering for their subsistence; at the other extreme, nearly 11 per cent relied on these techniques for only about half of it. The rest fell somewhere in between. Most of the groups (80 per cent) depended on fishing to some extent, with a few (15 per cent) obtaining nearly half from this source. A minority (23 per cent) derived a part of their subsistence from horticulture, and a few (less than 5 per cent) got nearly half this way. In short, some were pure hunting and gathering societies, but most of them incorporated limited elements of a fishing or horticultural technology, or both.[38] In this respect they resembled those hunting and gathering societies of the Upper Paleolithic and Mesolithic that supplemented their food supply by fishing.

Demographic patterns: Group density and size

Despite these variations, modern hunting and gathering societies[39] have much in common. To begin with, none is capable of supporting a large or dense population. Even in the most favorable environment, as in north central and northern California prior to white settlement, the population density for small localities rarely reaches 10 persons per square mile and, over larger areas, seldom exceeds 3 per square

---

[37] This figure is based on Elkin's estimate that there were approximately 300,000 aborigines in Australia at the time of the first white settlement. This estimate was divided by 60, a very generous estimate for the average size of these societies. See A. P. Elkin, *The Australian Aborigines*, 3d ed. (Sydney: Angus and Robertson, 1954), p. 10.

[38] Slightly over 3 per cent also kept pigs.

[39] When referring to "modern" hunting and gathering societies, I mean both those now in existence and those that survived into the modern era (i.e., the last several hundred years). In writing about these societies, the present tense is usually used for convenience.

Fig. 7/13 Members of a band of hunters and gatherers meeting with members of the Power Expedition (1871–1875) on the Kaibab Plateau near the Grand Canyon

mile.[40] In less favorable environments like Australia, much of which is desert, population density drops well below 1 person per square mile.[41]

All communities, then, are necessarily small. The largest contain only a few hundred persons, and these occur only in very favorable environments or in groups that rely on horticulture or fishing to a considerable degree. The Ethnographic Atlas provides information on the size of local communities in 93 of the 151 hunting and gathering societies. Nearly two-thirds have fewer than 50 persons per community, and only two have more than 200.

[40] See Martin Baumhoff, *Ecological Determinants of Aboriginal California Populations*, University of California Publications in American Archaeology and Ethnology, 49 (1963), especially pp. 227 and 231.

[41] See Elkin, *op. cit.*, and his estimate of an aboriginal population of 300,000 prior to white settlement. Since Australia contains nearly 3,000,000 square miles, this means an average density of only 1 person per 10 square miles. In Alaska, there was only 1 per 25 square miles at the time of its purchase by the United States (Hawkes, *op. cit.*, p. 183).

These two "exceptions" are quite interesting, incidentally, because far from disproving the importance of subsistence technology, they serve to underline it. In both instances, the societies obtain nearly half their food from horticultural activities and fishing.[42] In other words, they very nearly qualify as more advanced societal types.

The importance of this can be seen when we divide the hunting and gathering category into two subcategories: (1) those that obtain 85 per cent or more of their food supply from hunting and gathering and (2) those that obtain only 50 to 85 per cent in this way.[43] As Table 7/4 shows, the purer hunting and gathering communities are smaller, on the average, than those that depend on either fishing or horticulture to any great degree.

Societies, too, are small at this level of technological development. In more than 90 per cent of the groups in the Ethnographic Atlas each local band or community is politically autonomous and hence constitutes a separate society. Of the fourteen exceptions, all but one are societies in which horticulture or fishing provides an important secondary source of subsistence.[44]

Nomadism

Modern hunting and gathering communities also tend to be nomadic. Some groups are reported to remain in an area for periods as short as a week.[45] On the other hand, a few communities (approximately 10 per cent in Murdock's sample) occupy permanent settlements. Again, all of these either rely on fishing or horticulture as important secondary sources of subsistence or are located in unusually favorable environments.[46]

---

[42] The first of these groups was the Miami Indians; the second, the Carrier Indians.

[43] These figures of Murdock's are, of course, only estimates made by him and his associates, and are based on qualitative statements found in ethnographic reports.

[44] The one local group which was not autonomous and yet got most of its food from hunting and gathering was the Chamacoco, a South American Indian group that lived in an area of almost constant warfare and slave raiding following Spanish settlement. This is probably the explanation for this group's "abnormal" organization, since warfare sometimes causes groups at this level of development to establish temporary alliances with neighboring communities, and continuous warfare might well lead to a more permanent relationship. For other instances of temporary alliances during wars, see I. Schapera, *The Khoisan Peoples of South Africa* (London: Routledge, 1930), p. 156; or Antonia Serrano, "The Charrua," in Julian Steward (ed.), *Handbook of South American Indians*, Smithsonian Institution, Bureau of American Ethnology, Bulletin 143 (1946), vol. 1, p. 194.

[45] See, for example, John Garvan, *The Negritos of the Philippines* (Vienna: Ferdinand Berger, 1964), p. 27; or Edwin Loeb, *Sumatra: Its History and People* (Vienna: Institut für Volkerkunde, 1935), p. 283, on the Kubu.

[46] Only one of the 15 nonnomadic hunting and gathering societies in the Murdock sample depended on hunting and gathering for as much as three-quarters of its subsistence, whereas more than half of the 136 nomadic hunting and gathering societies were in this category. The one exception among the nonnomadic societies (the Nomlaki) was located in the Sacramento Valley of northern California, a territory as favorable for a hunting and gathering people as any in the world (see Baumhoff, *op. cit.*, pp. 205–231).

Table 7/4 Hunting and gathering societies classified by percentage of food supply obtained from hunting and gathering

Percentage of food supply obtained from hunting and gathering	Percentage of societies with average community size less than 50	Estimated median size	Number of societies
86–100 per cent*	88	29	32
50–85 per cent*	54	48	61

* These figures are not precise measurements, but rather rough estimates made by Murdock and his associates, based on qualitative statements in ethnographic reports.

The nomadic character of most hunting and gathering communities is an inevitable result of their subsistence technology. One anthropologist described the basic problem confronting nearly all these peoples when he wrote of a group of African pygmies that "after about a month, as a rule, the fruits of the forest have been gathered all around the vicinity of the camp, and the game has been scared away to a greater distance than is comfortable for daily hunting."[47] He went on to say that since "the economy relies on day-to-day quest, the simplest thing is for the camp to move." Except for variations in the frequency of moves this description fits most hunting and gathering peoples.

Economic conditions

Given the combination of a primitive technology and a nomadic way of life, it is impossible for most hunting and gathering peoples to accumulate many possessions. In describing the Negritos of the Philippines, one observer reports that "the possessions of a whole settlement would not be a good load for a sturdy carrier."[48] A student of the Siriono of Bolivia reports that "apart from the hammocks they sleep in and the weapons and tools they hunt and gather with, they rarely carry anything with them."[49] As he explains, "being seminomadic, they do not burden themselves with material objects that might hamper mobility." The few other things they use can be fashioned quickly from materials that are readily available throughout the whole area. The situation is virtually the same among the Bushmen of southwest Africa:

---

[47] Colin Turnbull, "The Mbuti Pygmies of the Congo," in James Gibbs (ed.), *Peoples of Africa* (New York: Holt, 1965), pp. 286–287.

[48] Garvan, *op. cit.*, p. 29.

[49] Allan Holmberg, *Nomads of the Long Bow: The Siriono of Eastern Bolivia*, Smithsonian Institution: Institute of Social Anthropology, 10 (1950), p. 11. See also Loeb, *op. cit.*, p. 300, who writes of the Orang Benua of Sumatra that "they carried all their possessions in a bamboo a foot long. These possessions consisted of blow-gun darts, a piece of poisoned wood on which they rubbed them, wood for making a fire [tinder?] and perhaps a small knife."

Fig. 7/14 Home and possessions of Paiute hunter in southern Utah in the 1870s

> It is not advantageous to multiply and accumulate in this society. Any man can make what he needs when he wants to. Most of the materials he uses are abundant and free for anyone to take. Furthermore, in their nomadic lives, without beasts of burden, the fact that the people themselves must carry everything puts a sharp limit on the quantity of objects they want to possess.[50]

The few hunting and gathering groups that have been able to establish permanent settlements naturally accumulate more possessions, but even they are greatly limited by the primitive nature of their society's technology.[51]

---

[50] Lorna Marshall, "The Kung Bushmen of the Kalahari Desert," in Gibbs, *op. cit.*, pp. 257–258. Quoted by permission of Holt, Rinehart and Winston, Inc. See also Charles Hose and William McDougall, *The Pagan Tribes of Borneo* (London: Macmillan, 1912), pp. 190–191, on the Punan.

[51] See, for example, Walter Goldschmidt, *Nomlaki Ethnography*, University of California Publications in American Archaeology and Ethnology, 42 (1951), pp. 333–335 and 417–428.

Fig. 7/15 Home and possessions of a Bushman family,
southwest Africa. See also
Fig. 5/3

Fig. 7/16 The daily quest for
food is a dominant concern in
the lives of most hunting and
gathering peoples: Bushmen
boys gathering nuts

The daily quest for food is a dominant concern in the lives of most hunting and gathering peoples. Together with such related activities as the manufacture of weapons and the preparation of food, it is their most time-consuming activity.[52] One writer has described the life of the Bushmen as "one long struggle for food."[53] The search for food also looms large in the thinking of such peoples. In describing the Sakai of Sumatra, the writer reports that "when they talk at night [around the camp-fire] it is mostly about food."[54] Another observer reports that among the Siriono of eastern Bolivia the two most frequent expressions are, "My stomach is very empty," and "Give me something."[55] He also states that food and the search for food are the most common subjects of dreams, leading him to conclude that an analysis of the dream life of this group "might support the theory that hunger is the most intense motivating force in that society."[56] This has not been true of all hunting and gathering peoples. Some, such as the Indians of northern California, have had the good fortune to live in areas where food was usually abundant and were not normally as pre-occupied with the subject. Yet even these groups occasionally had such acute food shortages that some of their members starved to death.[57]

Because of the time absorbed by the food quest and the primitive nature of the technology, the division of labor in hunting and gathering societies is largely limited to distinctions in terms of age and sex. In these societies, as in all others, there are basic differences between men's and women's work. Hunting and military activity fall to the male, as do political, religious, ceremonial, and artistic activities. The collection and preparation of vegetable products and the care of children are women's responsibilities.[58] Some activities, such as the construction of a shelter, may be defined as either men's or women's work, depending on the society.[59]

---

[52] For a valuable systematic analysis of the use of time by two small bands of Australian aborigines, see Frederick McCarthy and Margaret McArthur, "The Food Quest and the Time Factor in Aboriginal Economic Life," in Charles Mountford (ed.), *Records of the American-Australian Scientific Expedition to Arnhem Land: Anthropology and Nutrition* (Melbourne: Melbourne University Press, 1960), pp. 190–191.

[53] Schapera, *The Khoisan Peoples*, p. 91. See also the marvelous film on the Bushmen, "The Hunters."

[54] Loeb, *op. cit.*, p. 294. See also Frank Speck, *Penobscot Man* (Philadelphia: University of Pennsylvania Press, 1940), p. 34, who writes, "The hunt had an inconceivably prominent place" in the lives of the Penobscot Indians of Maine.

[55] Holmberg, *op. cit.*, p. 30.

[56] *Ibid.*, p. 91. See also Marshall, *op. cit.*, p. 255 who writes of the food quest among the Bushmen as "engaging powerful emotions."

[57] See, for example, Goldschmidt, *op. cit.*, p. 417. For an example of a group in which food shortages seem almost totally absent, see the Negritos of the Philippines (Garvan, *op. cit.*, pp. 50–51).

[58] In the sample of hunting and gathering societies in the Ethnographic Atlas, hunting was entirely a male activity in 97 per cent of the cases, and predominantly a male activity in the rest. On the other hand, gathering was wholly or largely a female activity in 91 per cent of the societies, and predominantly a male activity in only 2 per cent (in the remainder the activity was shared by both sexes).

[59] Of the hunting and gathering societies in the Ethnographic Atlas, 57 per cent defined this as a male responsibility, 25 per cent as a female, and only 18 per cent regarded it as appropriate to both sexes.

Fig. 7/17   Bushman hunter, southwest Africa

Still other activities may be defined as appropriate for members of either sex. Table 7/5 shows the division of labor between the sexes in one society. Though some of the details are peculiar to this group, the overall pattern is fairly typical. Division of labor along age lines is also inevitable, since both the very young and the aged are limited in their capabilities.

In hunting and gathering societies there is no division of labor into full-time occupational specialties, as in industrial societies. Some part-time specialization is usual however. For example, most of these societies have at least a headman and a shaman or medicine man. When their services are required, they function in these specialized capacities but, as one writer says of the headmen of the Bergdama and Bushmen, "when not engaged on public business they follow the same occupations as all other people."[60] He adds that this is most of the time. Other kinds of specialists are much less common. They include part-time workers in certain arts and crafts and occasionally an assistant to the headman. Such individuals are most likely to

[60] I. Schapera, *Government and Politics in Tribal Societies* (London: Watts, 1956), p. 93. See also Holmberg's description of the Siriono headman or chief quoted on p. 176, and Hose and McDougall, *op. cit.*, p. 190, on the Punan shaman.

Table 7/5 Division of labor between the sexes in Siriono society

Activity	Normally male	Normally female	Both sexes
Hunting	X		
Fishing	X		
Extracting honey	X		
Weapon-making	X		
Tool-making	X		
House-building	X		
Preparing utensils	X		
Cooking		X	
Caring for children		X	
Twining string		X	
Twining hammocks		X	
Carrying water		X	
Collecting firewood		X	
Pot making		X	
Weaving		X	
Preparing feather ornaments		X	
Stringing necklaces		X	
Collecting			X
Dressing game			X
Burden-carrying			X

Source: Adapted from Allan Holmberg, *Nomads of the Long Bow: The Siriono of Eastern Bolivia* Smithsonian Institution: Institute of Social Anthropology, 10 (1950), Table 2, p. 41.

be found in settled communities that are less dependent on hunting and gathering or in communities with an especially favorable environment.[61]

Within hunting and gathering groups, the family (either nuclear or extended[62]) is normally the only significant form of economic organization. Sometimes, when the practice of sharing is widespread and hunting and gathering are carried on as communal activities, even the family group ceases to be economically important.

With respect to subsistence, each local band is virtually self-sufficient. Some trade does occur, but except where contacts have been established with more advanced societies, the bartered items tend to be nonessentials, especially objects with a status or aesthetic value. Trade between two hunting and gathering communities usually involves things that are scarce or nonexistent in one group's territory but available in some abundance in the other's (e.g., certain kinds of shells, stones, feathers, etc.).

---

[61] See, for example, Goldschmidt, *op. cit.*, pp. 331–332, and Elkin, *op. cit.*, pp. 254ff.

[62] See p. 175 for a discussion of the extended family.

Fig. 7/18 Bushman shaman in trance

Trade with advanced societies is more likely to involve essential items. For example, many groups obtain metal tools and weapons in this way.[63] In the past, these imports were seldom important enough to alter seriously the basic character of these societies.[64] In recent years, however, as contacts with industrialized and industrializing societies have increased, the volume and importance of the imports have transformed most hunting and gathering groups into hybrid types.

---

[63] See, for example, Turnbull, *op. cit.*, pp. 287–288; Ivor Evans, *The Negritos of Malaya* (Cambridge: Cambridge University Press, 1937), pp. 57 and 112–113; Garvan, *op. cit.*, p. 66; or Hose and McDougall, *op. cit.*, p. 191. Turnbull warns, however, that many scholars exaggerate the dependence of the Pygmies on the neighboring horticultural villagers. He maintains that they turn to the villagers only for luxuries and diversion. See *Wayward Servants: The Two Worlds of the African Pygmies* (Garden City, N.Y.: Natural History Press, 1965), pp. 33–37.

[64] The introduction of the horse and gun among the Plains Indians of this country was an exception to the usual pattern.

Kinship

Ties of kinship are vitally important in most hunting and gathering groups. Members of modern industrial societies have difficulty appreciating the tremendous importance these ties assume among simpler peoples, since so much of our own social interaction is organized in terms of *non*kinship roles (as in relations between lawyer and client, teacher and student, or clerk and customer). Even our self-images are largely molded by our involvement in such roles.

By contrast, social interaction in hunting and gathering societies is usually organized around kinship roles, and self-images are formed by involvement in them. One student of the Australian aborigines reports that "in a typical Australian tribe it is found that a man can define his relations to every person with whom he has any social dealings whatever, whether of his own or of another tribe, by means of the terms of relationship."[65] Another writer goes so far as to say of these people that "every one with whom a person comes in contact is regarded as related to him, and the kind of relationship *must be* ascertained so that the two persons concerned will know what their mutual behavior should be."[66] He adds that kinship ties are the anatomy and physiology of aboriginal society and "must be understood if the behavior of the aborigines as social beings is to be understood."[67] Though there are exceptions to this, kinship is usually of great importance in hunting and gathering societies.[68]

Viewed in evolutionary perspective, the family has often been described as the matrix, or womb, from which all the other more complex and more specialized forms of social organization have evolved. While this may be an exaggeration,[69] it points to a basic truth: In hunting and gathering societies, kin groups perform many of the functions that are performed by schools, business firms, governmental agencies, and other specialized organizations in larger, more advanced, and more differentiated societies.

The kin groups in hunting and gathering societies are of two types, nuclear and extended families. A nuclear family includes a man, his wife or wives, and their unmarried children. Polygyny is widespread in hunting and gathering societies; only 12 per cent of the groups in Murdock's Ethnographic Atlas are classified as monogamous. It does not follow, of course, that 88 per cent of *families* are polygynous: this would be impossible given the roughly equal numbers of men and women. Usually only one or two of the most influential men have more than one wife, and they seldom have more than two or three. This limited polygyny is possible for several reasons: (1) girls usually marry earlier than boys, (2) men are more likely to be

---

[65] A. R. Radcliffe-Brown, "The Social Organization of Australian Tribes," *Oceania*, 1 (1930), pp. 44–45.

[66] Elkin, *op. cit.*, p. 56 (Doubleday Anchor edition); emphasis added.

[67] See also Service, *The Hunters*, p. 33.

[68] For some exceptions, see Turnbull, *Wayward Servants, op. cit.*, pp. 109–112.

[69] The community may be at least as old as the family as a form of social organization in the human line, in which case some or all of the other forms of social organization would have evolved from it.

killed, and (3) some men are forced to remain bachelors. Multiple wives appear to be an economic asset in these societies and, to some extent, a status symbol as well.

Divorce is permitted in virtually all hunting and gathering societies and is fairly common in some.[70] In others, however, it is made relatively difficult.[71] On the whole, there is great variability in this respect.

The nuclear family is usually part of a larger, more inclusive, and more important kin group known as the extended family.[72] This typically includes a group of brothers and their families or a father and his married sons with their families; in any event, it is usually organized around kinship ties among *males*.[73] The reasons for this practice are not definitely known, but it probably developed in response to the group's concern for safety. From this standpoint, the loss of a daughter through marriage would be much less threatening to a small group than the loss of a son.[74]

The extended family is also important economically, since the ties of kinship among its members encourage the practice of sharing. When the daily acquisition of food is as uncertain as it is in most hunting and gathering societies, a nuclear family could easily starve if it had to depend exclusively on its own efforts. A family might be surfeited with food for a time and than suddenly have nothing. Or all the adult members of the family could be ill or injured at the same time. In either case, the family would be dependent on the generosity of others. While sharing can, and does, take place between unrelated persons, kinship ties reinforce the tendency. In this connection, it is noteworthy that many hunting and gathering peoples create what we would call fictional ties of kinship when there is no "real" relationship by blood or marriage. These ties are just as meaningful to them as "true" kinship ties and serve to tighten bonds within the group.

By marrying outside the local group (a practice known as exogamy), a society gradually establishes a web of kinship ties with neighboring groups. According to one anthropologist, "One of the important functions of exogamy is that of opening territories so that peaceful movements can take place among them, and particularly so that any large temporary variations in food resources can be taken advantage of by related groups."[75]

---

[70] See, for example, Elkin, *op. cit.*, p. 50; Evans, *op. cit.*, p. 254.

[71] See, for example, Garvan, *op. cit.*, p. 82.

[72] Service, *op. cit.*, p. 42.

[73] See Elman Service, *Primitive Social Organization: An Evolutionary Perspective* (New York: Random House, 1962), chap. 3, especially p. 61. As Service points out, patrilocal organization appears to be the usual pattern in hunting and gathering bands when observed in "isolated aboriginal conditions." Other patterns occur chiefly in such groups only at the point of "breakdown and readaptation under the influence of civilization." See also Julian Steward, *Theory of Culture Change: The Methodology of Multi-linear Evolution* (Urbana, Ill.: University of Illinois Press, 1955), chaps. 7 and 8. For a more skeptical view, see Colin Turnbull, "Hunting and Gathering: Contemporary Societies," in *International Encyclopedia of the Social Sciences* (New York: Macmillan and Free Press, 1968), vol. 7, p. 23.

[74] Service, *Primitive Social Organization*, p. 49.

[75] *Ibid.*, p. 71.

Political patterns

Politically, modern hunting and gathering societies are extremely primitive. As we have seen, most local communities are autonomous and independent entities even though they have an average population of less than 50, including babes in arms. The primitive nature of their political systems is also evidenced by the limited development of specialized political roles and the very limited authority vested in their incumbents. The most common pattern is for a single headman to provide minimal leadership for the group.[76] The late Allan Holmberg, an anthropologist who lived among the Siriono of eastern Bolivia, wrote a description of their headmen that is close to being a portrait of the "average" headman in a hunting and gathering society.

> Presiding over every band of Siriono is a [headman], who is at least nominally the highest official of the group. Although his authority theoretically extends throughout the band, in actual practice its exercise depends almost entirely upon his personal qualities as a leader. In any case, there is no obligation to obey the orders of a [headman], no punishment for nonfulfillment. Indeed, little attention is paid to what is said by a [headman] unless he is a member of one's immediate family. To maintain his prestige a [headman] must fulfill, in a superior fashion, those obligations required of everyone else.
>
> The prerogatives of [a headman] are few. . . . The principal privilege . . . if it could be called such, is that it is his right to occupy, with his immediate family, the center of the [communal] house. Like any other man he must make his bows and arrows, his tools; he must hunt, fish, collect, and plant gardens. He makes suggestions as to migrations, hunting trips, etc., but these are not always followed by his [people]. As a mark of status, however, a [headman] always possesses more than one wife.
>
> While [headmen] complain a great deal that other members of the band do not satisfy their obligations to them, little heed is paid to their requests. . . .
>
> In general, however [headmen] fare better than other members of the band. Their requests more frequently bear fruit than those of others because [headmen] are the best hunters and are thus in a better position than most to reciprocate for any favors done them.[77]

There are similar reports on most other hunting and gathering societies.[78] In a number of instances it is said that the headman "held his place only so long as he gave satisfaction."[79]

---

[76] Occasionally there might be a second official. See, for example, Kaj Birket-Smith, *The Eskimos*, rev. ed. (London: Methuen, 1959), p. 145; Goldschmidt, *op. cit.*, pp. 324–325; and Speck, *op. cit.*, pp. 239–240.

[77] Holmberg, *op. cit.*, pp. 59–60. Quoted by permission of the Smithsonian Institution Press. Following an older usage, Holmberg refers to the leaders of Siriono bands as "chiefs." In current usage, such persons are usually referred to as "headmen," and the term "chief" is reserved for the leaders of tribes or other multicommunity societies. For this reason, the term "headman" has been substituted.

[78] See, for example, John Cooper, "The Ona," in Steward, *Handbook*, vol. 1, p. 117; A. R. Radcliffe-Brown, *The Andaman Islanders* (Glencoe, Ill.: Free Press, 1948), p. 47; Hose and McDougall, *op. cit.*, p. 182, on the Punan of Borneo; Speck, *op. cit.*, p. 239, on the Penobscot of Maine; and Schapera, *The Khoisan Peoples*, p. 151.

[79] Roland Dixon, "The Northern Maidu," in Carleton S. Coon (ed.), *A Reader in General Anthropology* (New York: Holt, 1948), p. 272.

Occasionally the headman enjoys a bit more power and privilege. For example, in the case of the Arunta of Australia the headman ". . . has, *ex officio*, a position which, if he be a man of personal ability, but only in that case, enables him to wield considerable power . . ."[80] Among the Bergdama of southwest Africa the headman "is treated with universal respect, being specified as a 'great man' by adults and 'grandfather' by children; he usually has the most wives (sometimes three or more); he has the pick of all wild animal skins for clothing himself and his family, and only his wives wear necklaces or girdles of ostrich eggshell beads; and he receives portions of all game killed in the chase, and tribute from men finding honey on growing tobacco."[81]

At the opposite extreme are a number of groups that do not even have a headman. This is true of 12 per cent of the hunting and gathering societies in the Ethnographic Atlas sample. In such cases, decisions which affect the entire group are arrived at through informal discussions among the more respected and influential members, typically the heads of families.[82]

The limited development of political institutions in hunting and gathering societies is due to several factors, all of which stem from the primitive nature of the group's subsistence technology. To begin with, their small size and relative isolation make it possible for them to handle their political problems very informally. Consensus is achieved much more readily in a small, homogeneous group of a few dozen people (of whom only the adults, and often only the adult males, have a voice) than in a larger, more heterogeneous community of hundreds or thousands. In the smaller group, a headman is valuable only if he has special knowledge, insight, or skills to contribute. This is why we so often read in ethnographic reports that the headman of a hunting and gathering band "held his place only so long as he gave satisfaction" and that his influence "depends almost entirely upon his personal qualities as a leader."

Even if the members of a hunting and gathering band desired a more complex and powerful political system, their economy could not support it. Most of these groups need all the manpower they possess just to provide food and shelter. At most, they can spare the headman from subsistence activities, but even this is beyond the capacity of most bands.

Finally, the primitive nature of the productive system prevents the growth of government through the usurpation of power by would-be tyrants. As we shall observe in later chapters, the growth of government in societies as they move up

---

[80] Baldwin Spencer and F. J. Gillen, *The Arunta: A Study of a Stone Age People* (London: Macmillan, 1927), vol. I, p. 10.

[81] Schapera, *Government and Politics*, p. 117. Quoted by permission of C. A. Watts & Co., Ltd. See also A. H. Gayton, *Yokuts-Mono Chiefs and Shamans*, University of California Publications in American Archaeology and Ethnology, 24 (1930), pp. 374–376.

[82] See, for example, Colin Turnbull, *Wayward Servants*, chaps. 11 and 12; or *The Forest People* (New York: Simon & Schuster, 1961), on the Mbuti Pygmies. As he indicates, the office of headman is sometimes found among these people, but it has been more or less forced on them by the Bantu villagers and is of little significance except in their contacts with these villagers.

the evolutionary ladder is a response not only to the needs and wishes of the group as a whole, but also to the ambitions of a predatory minority that sees in government an instrument that can be made to serve its own special interests.[83] In hunting and gathering societies, however, minority control and exploitation is impossible. All men are trained in the use of weapons, and the same weapons are available to all. The only differences are those inherent in the physical constitutions and personalities of the individuals themselves, and while a man who is unusually well endowed by nature may be the equal, or even the master, of two less favorably endowed men, it is not likely that he could coerce three or more who join forces against him. Furthermore, dissatisfied followers can desert their leader and join another band.[84] In short, opportunities for self-aggrandizement by political means are minimal in these societies.

Given the rudimentary nature of political institutions in hunting and gathering societies, one might suppose that there are few restrictions on the actions of individuals. In one sense this is true; there are few imposed by political authorities—no courts, no police, no prisons. The individual is hardly free, however, to do as he wishes. To begin with, his freedom of action is greatly limited by the very primitive nature of his society's technology. Compared with members of more advanced societies, hunting and gathering peoples are very restricted in where they go and what they do.

There are also restraints of a social origin. No human society can afford to be indifferent to the actions of its members. Even in the absence of a formal political authority, the group acts to control human conduct. Though there are minor variations from one hunting and gathering society to another, we can see the basic pattern of social control in groups as far apart as the Kaska Indians of the Canadian Northwest, the Andaman Islanders of southeast Asia, the Bushmen of southwest Africa, and the Punan of Borneo.[85] In each of these groups there are three basic types of social restraints. First, there is the system of blood-revenge, whereby the injured person, aided, perhaps, by his kinsmen, punishes the offender himself. As one student of the Bushmen put it, "when disputes arise between the members of the band . . . there is no appeal to any supreme authority, [since] . . . there is no such authority. . . . The only remedy is self-help."[86] Usually this mode of social control is invoked only when the victim of the offense is a single individual or family. When an entire band suffers because of the actions of an individual, a second method of control is likely to be employed. For example, should a man refuse to do

---

[83] For a more detailed discussion of this, see Gerhard Lenski, *Power and Privilege: A Theory of Social Stratification* (New York: McGraw-Hill, 1966), especially chaps. 5–8.

[84] See, for example, Schapera, *Government and Politics,* p. 193, on the Bergdama; or Turnbull, *Wayward Servants*, pp. 100–109, on the Mbuti Pygmies.

[85] See John Honigmann, *The Kaska Indians: An Ethnographic Reconstruction,* Yale University Publications in Anthropology, 51 (1954), pp. 90–92 and 96–97; Radcliffe-Brown, *op. cit.,* pp. 48–52; Schapera, *The Khoisan Peoples,* pp. 151–155; and Hose and McDougall, *op. cit.,* p. 182.

[86] Schapera, *op. cit.,* p. 152.

his fair share in providing food, he is punished by losing the respect of others.[87] In the case of more serious offenses, the penalty may be ostracism, or even banishment. The third method of control applies primarily to violations of ritual prescriptions; in such cases, spontaneous supernatural sanctions are thought to operate, and this is usually an effective deterrent. For example, the Andaman Islanders believe that killing a cicada causes bad weather, and the Bushmen believe that girls who do not observe the restrictions imposed on them at puberty change into frogs.[88] All three methods are very informal, a practice that is feasible only in a small group with intimate and continuous contact among its members.

Equality and inequality

The rudimentary nature of the political system and the primitive nature of the technological system contribute to yet another distinctive characteristic of modern hunting and gathering societies: minimal inequality in power and privilege. Differences between individuals are so slight, in fact, that a number of observers have spoken of a kind of "primitive communism." To some extent this is justified. As we have seen, effective political authority with the power to coerce is virtually nonexistent. Differences in *influence* exist, but only to the degree that those who are influenced permit, and only as a result of their respect for another individual's skills or wisdom. Should he lose this respect, he also loses his influence.

The chief exceptions to the near equality in wealth and economic privilege occur among the handful of nonnomadic groups, where some modest inequalities are reported.[89] In most societies, differences in wealth are very minor. Many factors are responsible for this. For one thing, the nomadic way of life prevents any substantial accumulation of possessions. Moreover, the ready availability of most essential resources (e.g., wood for bows, flint for stone tools, etc.) precludes the need to amass them, and technical primitivism severely limits the variety of things which can be produced. The absence of any coercive political authority is also a factor. Finally, there is the widespread practice of reciprocity or sharing in most of these groups.

As a general rule, the concept of private property has only limited development among hunting and gathering peoples. Things that an individual uses constantly, such as his tools and weapons, are always recognized as his, but fields and forests are the common property of the band. The territorial rights of bands, however, are taken quite seriously, and outsiders are usually obliged to ask permission to enter another group's territory to seek food.[90] Animals and plants are normally considered

---

[87] Radcliffe-Brown, *op. cit.,* p. 50.

[88] *Ibid.,* p. 51; and Schapera, *The Khoisan Peoples,* p. 152.

[89] See, for example, Goldschmidt, *op. cit.,* pp. 330–341.

[90] See, for example, Evans, *op. cit.,* p. 21; Marshall, *op. cit.,* p. 248; or Radcliffe-Brown, *op. cit.,* p. 29. For an exception, see Birket-Smith, *op. cit.,* pp. 145–146. For intermediate cases, see Honigmann, *The Kaska Indians,* pp. 84, 88, and 96; Elkin, *op. cit.,* p. 45; and H. Ling Roth, *The Aborigines of Tasmania* (London: Kegan Paul, Trench, Trubner, 1890), p. 71.

the common property of the band until they are killed or harvested. Then they become the property of the individual responsible, though his use of them is hedged about by the rule of sharing.[91]

A successful hunter usually does not keep his kill for himself alone or even, in most cases, for his family, but shares it with others.[92] The reason for this is the same as that which underlies the popularity of insurance in industrial societies: *it is an effective method of spreading risks.* As we have seen, neither an individual nor a nuclear family can be sure of obtaining its basic needs at all times. Poor hunting conditions, ill health, or just a streak of bad luck can render any individual or family incapable of providing for itself, and sharing food greatly enhances the entire group's chances of survival. Most of the societies that failed to develop this practice have probably been eliminated by the process of sociocultural selection.

Despite the near equality of power and wealth, there is a fair degree of inequality in prestige in most hunting and gathering societies. The interesting thing about this, from the viewpoint of a member of a modern industrial society, is the degree to which prestige depends on the *personal* qualities of individuals, rather than on such impersonal criteria as the offices or roles they occupy or the possessions they control. This is, of course, a natural consequence of the limited development of specialized offices and roles and the limited opportunities for the accumulation of possessions and wealth. But it sharply differentiates these societies from our own.

Writing of the Andaman Islanders, Radcliffe-Brown reports that they accord honor and respect to three kinds of people: (1) older people, (2) people endowed with supernatural powers, and (3) people with certain valued personal qualities, notably "skill in hunting and warfare, generosity and kindness, and freedom from bad temper."[93] Though he does not say so explicitly, men are apparently more likely than women to become honored members of the group. For the most part, these same criteria are employed by other hunting and gathering peoples. Skill in oratory is still another attribute that is honored in many of these groups.[94]

Because personal criteria are so important, the systems of stratification in these groups have an openness about them not found in more advanced societies. Almost no organizational or institutional barriers block the rise of talented individuals. For example, even where the office of headman is inherited, as it is in approximately half the societies,[95] it is clear not only that others can surpass him in achieving honor

[91] Sometimes certain trees become the private property of an individual who stakes a special claim to them, but this is uncommon and the number of trees involved is generally small. See, for example, Radcliffe-Brown, *op. cit.*, p. 41; or Goldschmidt, *op. cit.*, p. 333.

[92] See, for example, McCarthy and McArthur, *op. cit.*, pp. 179–180; Schapera, *The Khoisan Peoples,* pp. 100–101; Radcliffe-Brown, *op. cit.*, p. 43; Hose and McDougall, *op. cit.*, p. 187; or Speck, *op. cit.*, p. 47.

[93] Radcliffe-Brown, *op. cit.*, pp. 44–48.

[94] See, for example, Goldschmidt, *op. cit.*, pp. 324–326.

[95] Among the sample of hunting and gathering societies in the Ethnographic Atlas, 54 per cent had provision for the hereditary transmission of the office, usually to a son of the previous headman.

but that he himself may fail to win even a modest measure of it. The study of the Siriono Indians, quoted earlier, reports the case of one such headman, an individual who was a very poor hunter and whose status, as a result, was low.[96] The importance attached to age also contributes to the openness of the system. Almost any individual who survives to the later years is likely to attain a fair degree of honor and respect.

Tribal ties

As we have noted a number of times, local hunting and gathering groups are usually autonomous. Rarely are two or more communities brought together under a single leader, and when it happens it is usually in groups no longer completely dependent on hunting and gathering.

Despite the general absence of formal organizations beyond the local level, there are frequently *informal* structures. The most inclusive of these, and the most nearly universal as well, is the tribe—a group of people who speak a distinctive language or dialect, possess a common culture that distinguishes them from other peoples, and know themselves, or are known, by a definite name.[97] Unlike a society, a tribe is not necessarily organized politically. On the contrary, most are not, at least not among hunting and gathering peoples.

Though there is no direct evidence, it appears that most tribes were formed through a process of social fission. When the population of a hunting and gathering band grows too large for the resources of the immediate area, it splits into two groups. Division may also occur because of conflict within the band.[98] In either case, a new group is formed. Its members share, however, a common language and culture with the parent group. Normally the new group locates somewhere near the old one, if for no other reason than because their technology and accumulated experience become less relevant the further they move and the more their new environment differs from the one they have been used to. If this process of fission occurs often enough, a whole cluster of autonomous bands with the same language and a similar culture will emerge, forming a new tribe. Because of their common cultural heritage, these people will probably have some sense of group identification, and tribal members are likely to differentiate between those who share this heritage and outsiders who do not.

As this suggests, among hunting and gathering peoples the tribe is more important as a cultural unit than as a social unit. One writer, describing the tribal groupings among the Bushmen, reports that the tribe

> has no social solidarity, and is of very little, if any, importance in regulating social life. There appears to be no tribal organization among the Bushmen, nothing in the nature of a

---

[96] Holmberg, *op. cit.*, p. 58.

[97] This definition is based on Hoebel, *op. cit.*, p. 572, and Elkin, *op. cit.*, p. 25.

[98] Examples are the Punan of Borneo (Hose and McDougall, *op. cit.*, p. 183) or the Mbuti Pygmies of Africa (Turnbull, *Wayward Servants*, pp. 100–109).

central authority whose decisions are binding on all the members of the tribe, nor is collective action ever taken in the interests of the tribe as a whole. The tribe in fact is merely a loose aggregate of hunting bands which have a common language and name.[99]

This also applies to most other tribes of hunters and gatherers. Occasionally, as in Australia, an entire tribe comes together for some important event, but this is not typical.

From the organizational standpoint, the chief significance of tribal groupings in hunting and gathering societies lies not in the existing reality but in their evolutionary potential. With technological advance, these largely cultural groupings sometimes become important social units. Even among societies still on the hunting and gathering level, there is some evidence of movement in this direction. In a few of the more favorably situated sedentary groups, for example, several villages have been brought together under the leadership of a single individual.[100] This step was undoubtedly facilitated by the common cultural heritage of the groups involved.

Religion

Few facets of primitive man's life have received as much attention in the last hundred years as his religion. Yet, paradoxically, there are few areas where our understanding is less satisfactory. One reason is that too many writers have been tempted to twist the facts to fit their preconceived theories.[101] As a result, we have many very plausible, but mutually contradictory, theories—and a minimum of systematic analysis.

Another difficulty is the great diversity of beliefs and practices among hunting and gathering peoples. Primitive technological systems restrict men's freedom less in the realm of religious ideas than in most other areas.[102]

At a minimum, however, we can say that religion in some form is a part of all the more carefully studied hunting and gathering societies of the modern era. In all of these groups there is evidence that men have grappled with the problems of ultimate causation and meaning.[103] In myths and legends, they have developed

---

[99] Schapera, *The Khoisan Peoples*, p. 76. Quoted by permission of Routledge & Kegan Paul, Ltd.

[100] See, for example, Goldschmidt, *op. cit.*, p. 324.

[101] For a more detailed discussion of this point as it applies to the religion of the Australian aborigines, see W. E. H. Stanner, "Religion, Totemism and Symbolism," in Berndt and Berndt, *op. cit.*, pp. 207–237.

[102] In part, the diversity of religious beliefs and practices is due to cultural diffusion from more advanced societies. Apparently the diffusion of religious ideas occurs more easily than other types of diffusion (e.g., the diffusion of complex organization systems). See, for example, Loeb's comments on the religious ideas of various hunting and gathering peoples on Sumatra (*op. cit.*, pp. 216–217, 286–289, etc.). See also Hose and McDougall, *op. cit.*, p. 186.

[103] See, for example, W. E. H. Stanner's comments on this as it applies to the Australian aborigines, in "The Dreaming," in William Lessa and Evon Vogt (eds.), *Reader in Comparative Religion*, 2d ed. (New York: Harper & Row, 1965), p. 162. See also Evans, *op. cit.*, chaps. 14–18 and 24; Garvan, *op. cit.*, chap. 14; Turnbull, *The Forest People, op. cit.*, and others.

explanations for most of the recurring features of life and the world around them. Typically these explanations seem crude, irrational, and unscientific to members of industrial societies, at least on first inspection. But many of the scholars who have studied the matter carefully insist that they often contain profound insights that we usually associate only with the religions of more advanced societies.[104] Above all, these religions assert that the world is far more complex than it appears on the surface.[105]

Within modern hunting and gathering societies, religious differentiation is minimal, and religious conflict almost absent. There are none of the sectarian differences found in more advanced societies, unless they have been introduced by missionary efforts or other contacts with advanced societies. This does not mean that all members of a society share identical beliefs and practices. Rather, such differences as do exist are considered either complementary in nature or unimportant.[106]

The one really important religious distinction found in most hunting and gathering societies is associated with the role of shaman or medicine man. The shaman is essentially an individual who enjoys special powers as a result of his distinctive relationship with the spirit world. He uses these powers in various ways, one of the most common being to heal illness.[107] He may also use them to insure the success of hunting expeditions, to protect the group against evil spirits and other threats, and generally to insure the group's well-being.[108] Shamans do not always use their special power for the benefit of others, however. Often they employ their power to punish those who have offended them.[109]

Because of their role, shamans usually command respect and are often more influential than the headmen.[110] Sometimes, as with the Northern Maidu in California, the headman "was chosen largely through the aid of the shaman who was supposed to reveal to the old men the choice of the spirits."[111] The role of shaman tends to be profitable, since others are usually happy to offer gifts in exchange for his help or to maintain his goodwill. One early observer of the Indians of Lower

---

[104] See, for example, Stanner, "Religion, Totemism and Symbolism," *op. cit.*, especially pp. 215–216.

[105] See, for example, the Australian aboriginal concept of "The Eternal Dream Time," which one scholar has recently suggested might best be translated as "everywhen" (Stanner, "The Dreaming," *op. cit.*, p. 159).

[106] The religious distinctions between men and women among the Australian aborigines are a good example of complementary differences (see Elkin, *op. cit.*, chap. 7).

[107] See Service, *The Hunters*, p. 70.

[108] For descriptions of shamans and their practices, see Evans, *op. cit.*, chaps. 19–20; Honigmann, *op. cit.*, pp. 104–108; Schapera, *The Khoisan Peoples*, pp. 195–201; Radcliffe-Brown, *op. cit.*, pp. 175–179; Elkin, *op. cit.*, chap. 11.

[109] See, for example, Gayton *op. cit.*, pp. 392–398.

[110] See, for example, Dixon, *op. cit.*, p. 282.

[111] *Ibid.*, p. 272.

Fig. 7/19 A Siberian shaman of the eighteenth century, as seen by a Dutch traveler. Note the antler headdress and compare with the "sorcerer," Fig. 7/12, p. 158

California in Mexico wrote that successful shamans were able "to obtain their food without the trouble of gathering it . . . for the silly people provided them with the best they could find, in order to keep them in good humor and to enjoy their favor."[112] Though the shaman is normally a man, a woman might become one if she had the requisite experiences and if, like other shamans, she could prove her power through the healings and other feats.

The arts

Modern hunting and gathering peoples in widely scattered parts of the world have produced a variety of artistic works. Some are strikingly similar to the cave drawings and carvings of the prehistoric hunters and gatherers of the Upper Paleolithic. The motivations behind these efforts are not always clear, but in some cases it is plainly religious, in others magical.[113] And sometimes it appears to be simply aesthetic.

Music, too, plays a part in the lives of at least some hunting and gathering peoples. Colin Turnbull, who lived among the Pygmies of central Africa and came to know them better than any outsider, has written in detail of their *molimo* festivals, in which songs and the music of a primitive wooden trumpet play a central role.[114]

---

[112] Jacob Baegert, S.J., *Account of the Aboriginal Inhabitants of the California Peninsula*, in Coon *op. cit.*, p. 79. See also Radcliffe-Brown, *op. cit.*, p. 177.

[113] Some of the best evidence of religious motivation comes from Australia (see Elkin, *op. cit.*, pp. 191–192 or 232–234). For an example of art employed as an instrument in sympathetic magic, see Evans, *op. cit.*, pp. 130ff.

[114] Turnbull, "The Mbuti Pygmies," *op. cit.*, pp. 308–312; *The Forest People*, chap. 4; and *Wayward Servants*, pp. 259–267.

Fig. 7/20 Australian aborgine painting a design on a piece of bark. The design is based on a tribal legend

These festivals are of great religious significance and express the people's devotion to, and trust in, the forest. As with art, music is sometimes purely for entertainment.[115] Dancing is another valued feature of life in many hunting and gathering societies, and the motives for it are as varied as for art and music.

Demographic patterns: birth rates and death rates

Earlier in this section we noted the small size and low population densities of hunting and gathering groups. Before concluding this review of the ethnographic evidence, we need to consider briefly two of the basic determinants of population size, birth and death rates. These, together with the rates of in- and out-migration, are the only immediate determinants of population change in a society. All other factors (e.g., famines, wars, etc.) make their influence felt through one of these four. Hence, the size of a population at any given time can be stated algebraically as follows:

$$\text{Population}_{t2} = \text{Population}_{t1} + \text{Births}_{t1-t-2} + \text{In-migration}_{t1-t2}$$
$$- \text{Deaths}_{t1-t2} - \text{Out-migration}_{t1-t2},$$

where $t1$ and $t2$ refer to an earlier and a later point in time, and $t1-t2$ to the interval between.

---

[115] See, for example, Hose and McDougall, *op. cit.*, p. 192, and Speck, *op. cit.*, p. 270f.

It is usually difficult to determine these rates in most hunting and gathering societies. Ethnographers, unfortunately, have generally been more interested in such things as the details of rituals related to childbirth and the intricacies of marriage restrictions than with the birthrate or normal family size of societies. Such evidence as we have, however, indicates that birth and death rates are usually quite high. In Greenland, from 1922 to 1930, the average annual birthrate among the Eskimos was 42.3 per thousand inhabitants, or more than twice that of modern industrial societies.[116] In one Canadian Eskimo group that had minimal contact with the outside world, the average number of births per married woman was 5, and among women who had reached the age of forty-five, the average was over 10.[117] In the case of the Bushmen it is reported that since they know of no method of preventing pregnancy, pregnancies "follow in rapid succession during the course of married life, and it often happens that another child, or even two, may be born while the first is still at the breast."[118] The Negritos of Malaya have apparently been somewhat less prolific, if we may judge from one small study. According to this report, one group of thirty-two men aged forty and over had 151 children, or an average of nearly 5 apiece, with the prospect of more to come.[119] Finally, among the Punan of Borneo "large families are the rule; a family with as many as eight or nine children is no rarity."[120]

Despite appearances, most hunting and gathering societies make some effort to control their numbers. A recent survey of marriage practices in a sample of fifteen of these groups found that all but two practiced abortion, at least occasionally.[121]

One should not assume that because birthrates are high in these societies, communities are swarming with children. To begin with, the rate of infant mortality is also quite high. The study of the Negritos of Malaya reports that slightly over 40 per cent of the 150 children born to the thirty-two fathers were already dead at the time of the study. The study of the Bushmen specifically refers to the "high infant mortality caused by the natural hardships and strenuous conditions of Bushmen life." Similarly, the study of the Eskimos of Greenland speaks of "the very high mortality

---

[116] Birket-Smith, *op. cit.*, p. 44; compare with Table 12/1, page 347, which shows the rates for industrial societies.

[117] *Ibid.*

[118] Schapera, *The Khoisan Peoples*, p. 116.

[119] Evans, *op. cit.*, p. 16.

[120] Hose and McDougall, *op. cit.*, p. 183.

[121] See John Whiting, "Effects of Climate on Certain Cultural Practices," in Ward Goodenough (ed.), *Explorations in Cultural Anthropology: Essays in Honor of George Peter Murdock* (New York: McGraw-Hill, 1964). The calculations are my own and are based on Whiting's table 9, pp. 528–533. The hunting and gathering societies for which data on abortion were available were the Ainu, Semang, Aranda, Murngin, Tolowa, Tubatulabal, Yokuts, Ute, Walapai, Siriono, Ona, Abipon, Gaduveo, Nambicuara, and Timbira.

among infants."[122] Added to this, infanticide is practiced with some frequency in most hunting and gathering societies. The survey of marriage practices cited above found that infanticide occurred in all but three of the groups.[123] Its frequency is not reported, but among the Bushmen, at least, it is extremely common. Their children are not weaned until they are three or even four years old, and those born in the meantime are, as the Bushmen put it, "thrown away."[124] Because of the high birthrate, more than half of their children apparently die in this way. As a result of this and the high rate of infant mortality from natural causes, relatively few children survive and families are usually small. On the average, Bushmen women rear only two or three children.

Infant mortality and infanticide are but parts of a larger pattern producing high death rates. Accidents, illness, and starvation all take their toll. A student of the Eskimos of Greenland, for example, refers to "the very disproportionate mortality among men between the ages of twenty and thirty-five."[125] He cites statistics showing death rates at the end of the last century four to six times higher for these young men than for their counterparts in Denmark. As he points out, this was due to their dangerous occupations. But Eskimo men have no monopoly on danger, as accounts of elephant hunting among the Pygmies make clear. Men armed only with wooden spears are forced to come up beside one of these giant animals and stab it repeatedly in the belly in the hope of hitting the bladder. Or, as an alternative, they sneak up behind it and cut the tendons in its rear heel. Not surprisingly, fatal accidents are common.[126]

An ethnographer who lived among the Siriono of Bolivia estimates that the average life-span of those who survive infancy is only thirty-five to forty years.[127] By this age, the wear and tear of life under hunting and gathering conditions has left the human organism aged and decrepit. "Women who have passed through the menopause are assigned to the category of anility," and their male contemporaries fare no better. When the individual becomes too feeble to keep up with the rest in their migrations, or when serious illness overtakes him, he is abandoned and left to die.[128] This practice is quite common among hunting and gathering peoples, since the aged and infirm are a dangerous burden on the rest.

---

[122] Birket-Smith, *op. cit.*, p. 46.

[123] Again the calculations are my own. The societies involved are the Kung, Ainu, Andamanese, Vedda, Aranda, Murngin, Yokuts, Walapai, Warrau, Siriono, Ona, Abipon, Caduveo, and Timbira.

[124] Schapera, *The Khoisan Peoples*, p. 116.

[125] Birket-Smith, *op. cit.*, p. 46.

[126] See Patrick Putnam, "The Pygmies of the Ituri Forest," in Coon, *op. cit.*, p. 331; or Turnbull, *Wayward Servants*, p. 164.

[127] Holmberg, *op. cit.*, p. 85.

[128] Holmberg provides a vivid and moving eyewitness account of such an event.

A number of other reports support the hypothesis that physical aging begins much earlier in these societies than in our own. Summing up the evidence, one writer recently concluded that "in very primitive societies the average life expectancy at birth is only twenty-two years and individuals who live as long as fifty years are rare."[129] High birthrates, therefore, are essential for the survival of these societies.

ARCHAEOLOGICAL AND ETHNOGRAPHIC EVIDENCE COMPARED

Having completed our review of both the archaeological and ethnographic evidence on hunting and gathering societies, we are now in a better position to consider the relationship between prehistoric man and modern primitives, a problem that has divided students of human societies for years. Though indiscriminate comparisons of the two populations could be misleading, our evidence indicates that careful comparisons are not only valid but extremely valuable. To avoid confusion, however, we must recognize at the outset that modern hunters and gatherers can in no sense be equated with the hunters and gatherers of the *Lower* and *Middle* Paleolithic. If there is comparability, it is between these modern groups and the hunters and gatherers of the late Upper Paleolithic and Mesolithic. In other words, if we accept V. Gordon Childe's thesis that the various archaeological categories are really *technological* stages in the development of human societies (and not *chronological*), we will recognize that the Mesolithic, and probably the Upper Paleolithic as well, did not end everywhere in the world ten thousand years ago but survived in some areas down to the nineteenth and twentieth centuries.[130] As we noted at the beginning of this chapter, this view has gained increasing acceptance among archaeologists in recent years.[131]

We can see why, now that we are familiar with both sets of evidence. The similarities between modern hunters and gatherers and those of the late Upper Paleolithic and Mesolithic are numerous and basic; the differences are relatively few and much less important.[132] Similarities involve such crucial matters as technology and mode of subsistence, size of local groups, relative equality in wealth,[133]

---

[129] Gertrude Dole, "The Development of Patterns of Kinship Nomenclature," unpublished Ph.D. dissertation, p. 26; cited by Service, *op. cit.*, p. 80.

[130] See V. Gordon Childe, "Archaeological Ages as Technological Stages," *Journal of the Royal Anthropological Institute*, 44 (1944), pp. 7–24. See also the archaeologist Mellaart, *op. cit.*, p. 15, who writes: "Even today certain communities in the world preserve a paleolithic or mesolithic economy."

[131] See fn. 1, p. 147.

[132] I am excluding here those modern hunting and gathering peoples who have been socially and culturally overwhelmed in recent years by contact with more advanced societies. This is becoming increasingly common, and we must therefore rely heavily on older (especially pre-World War II) studies of such peoples.

[133] This is indicated by the absence of differentiation in burial remains from the Upper Paleolithic and Mesolithic. By contrast, in later eras one finds clear evidence of distinctions between rich and poor, the former having many rare and obviously costly objects buried with them.

and minimal occupational specialization. Similarities in art are also evident, suggesting further similarities in religious belief and practice.

The differences are largely of three types. First, in many modern hunting and gathering societies there are certain elements that originated in more advanced societies (e.g., certain metal tools and some religious ideas); this could not happen, of course, in the Upper Paleolithic and Mesolithic.[134] Second, modern hunting and gathering societies, unlike their prehistoric predecessors, are often crowded into the least desirable territories.[135] Finally, in the modern era, hunters and gatherers have no opportunities for territorial expansion, and thus are in a position where population growth is impossible and where the number of deaths must, of necessity, equal the number of births. Prehistoric hunters and gatherers, happily, were not always subject to this harsh restriction.

As we have seen, the archaeological record is much less complete than the ethnographic, being silent on many subjects where the latter provides a wealth of information. Therefore, when the ethnographic record shows patterns that are consistent for all or most modern groups and when these patterns do not depend on conditions peculiar to the modern era, scholars now generally regard them as applicable also to the advanced hunting and gathering societies of the late Upper Paleolithic and Mesolithic. This is a result of the growing awareness of the *limiting* nature of a hunting and gathering technology and economy.[136] Given a primitive technology and economy, large settlements, highly developed governments, literacy, schools, a high degree of occupational specialization, a market economy, a complex class system, and a host of other things are utterly impossible.

What *is* possible are small communities, usually autonomous, usually nomadic, led by headmen who have almost no authority and govern by persuasion. These groups are likely to be composed of a number of nuclear families linked together by ties of kinship, thus forming an extended family group. These kinship ties will probably be of great importance to both the individual and the community. The division of labor is likely to be almost entirely in terms of age and sex specialization, with very limited occupational specialization also a possibility. Possessions are certain to be few and near equality in wealth the rule. Finally, birth and death rates will be high, at least by the standards of modern industrial societies.

There may be limited variation in these matters, reflecting differences in environmental conditions or in the societies' level of technological development. Societies in very favorable locations and those with a somewhat more advanced technology (e.g., those able to supplement their food supply by fishing or horticulture) will probably be a bit larger, somewhat less nomadic, a little more developed

---

[134] Until recently, the effects of diffusion were most common in Africa and southeast Asia, where hunting and gathering peoples lived for centuries in close proximity to more advanced societies.

[135] Though not always, by any means. Many of the areas they occupied in Australia and the New World were highly desirable.

[136] See, for example, Clark and Piggott, *op. cit.*, pp. 130ff., or Hole and Heizer, *op. cit.*, pp. 225–226.

politically and specialized occupationally, and a bit wealthier and less egalitarian. These differences, however, would not be great.

At the same time, there are certain aspects of life where the hunting and gathering technology seems completely irrelevant. Observations of modern hunters and gatherers indicate that this is true of divorce. Every possibility, ranging from the complete absence of divorce to the most casual practice of it, has been observed.

Between the extremes, there are a number of areas where a hunting and gathering technology neither determines the pattern nor is irrelevant. Rather, it seems to predispose the group to adopt a particular alternative without completely precluding any of the others. Some marriage practices are a case in point: a minority of modern hunting and gathering societies (12 per cent of those in the Ethnographic Atlas sample) are monogamous even though the great majority permit polygyny. Apparently a hunting and gathering technology and the characteristics that accompany it are not strong enough to preclude either of these possibilities, but neither are they irrelevant. In statistical terms one would say that the characteristics of hunting and gathering societies act to increase the probability of polygyny and reduce the probability of monogamy. Since there is no reason to think that relevant conditions were different in late Upper Paleolithic or Mesolithic times, it is reasonable to suppose that roughly comparable probabilities prevailed then. In short, except where there is no distinctive pattern among modern hunting and gathering societies (e.g., as in the case of divorce) or where relevant conditions have changed (e.g., as in the case of death rates, which are influenced by the availability of new territories), we can assume substantial similarity between the advanced hunting and gathering societies of the late prehistoric era and those of recent centuries.

Appendix: Hints from ethology

One of the important new sciences is ethology, the study of animal behavior. Some of the most exciting work in this field has been done by a group of researchers who, for the first time, have systematically studied the behavior of primates living in their natural habitats.[137] Though their work has no direct bearing on the study of human societies, it is suggestive. It provides us with one more basis for making educated guesses about the life of our remote prehistoric ancestors, the hominids of the early Lower Paleolithic.

From this standpoint, the most important contribution of primate ethology is the finding that "all species of monkeys and apes live in social groups."[138] This tends to support the hypothesis that the societal mode of living is something man inherited from his primate ancestors, not something he invented.

It is also interesting to note how much the basic subsistence techniques of modern monkeys and apes have in common with those of both prehistoric and modern man at the hunting and gathering level:

---

[137] For an excellent introduction to the new field of primate behavior, see Irven Devore (ed.), *Primate Behavior: Field Studies of Monkeys and Apes* (New York: Holt, 1965).

[138] *Ibid.*, p. 612.

Fig. 7/21 All species of monkeys and apes live in groups: a group of baboons in Kenya

modern primates forage for fruits and vegetables, and some also hunt small game.[139] Even the use of simple tools is reported with some frequency.[140] Finally, there are similarities with respect to group size. Modern primate groups have from ten to fifty members, a range that is strikingly similar to that of human bands of hunters and gatherers in the Upper Paleolithic (see page 155 above).[141]

While it is possible that men and modern primates developed these patterns independently, it is more likely that they inherited them from remote common ancestors. If this is true, then in appears that the tool-making hominids of the Lower Paleolithic added precious little to their ancestral heritage. The chief innovations were some increased skill in hunting, the beginning of tool-*making*, and the discovery of a few of the uses of fire. Hardly an impressive record considering the vast time involved! But it reinforces our earlier judgment that cultural progress and the use of symbols were minimal throughout most of the Lower Paleolithic.

---

[139] The diet of modern anthropoids is largely frugivorous and herbivorous, but there is evidence that a number of species eat eggs and nestling birds, and chimpanzees, at least, eat bushpigs, smaller monkeys, the young of bushbucks, and even human babies (*ibid.*, pp. 443–445 and 477).

[140] *Ibid.*, pp. 380 and 440–443.

[141] *Ibid.*, p. 612.

*H*orticultural Societies

Chapter 8

Ten thousand years ago some long-forgotten inhabitants of the Middle East discovered that plants grow from seeds and applied this new insight to man's perennial problem of obtaining food. Little did they dream how greatly this discovery would change the conditions of human life! Little did they dream that they were laying the foundation for the growth of cities, the rise of empires, and the emergence of civilization!

We shall probably never know the exact circumstances that led to this important step, since writing was not yet invented and archaeological excavations are unlikely to tell us. Enough is now known, however, that some scholars are willing to make educated guesses.[1] It appears that for a long time many hunting and gathering societies in the Middle East had been harvesting the wild grasses from which our modern cereals evolved.[2] These people apparently learned that the grains these grasses produced, unlike most other kinds of foods available to them, could be stored—an important discovery in itself. Once in a while some grain was probably left in a storage pit long enough for it to sprout, and occasionally a few shoots must have survived long enough to become recognizable as young plants of the parent species. Perhaps someone, motivated by curiosity or necessity, transplanted a few of these young shoots and discovered that grains planted in this way would yield

---

[1] See, for example, E. Cecil Curwen and Gudmund Hatt, *Plough and Pasture: The Early History of Farming* (New York: Collier, 1961), chap. 10.

[2] *Ibid.*, p. 27. See also Robert Braidwood and Bruce Howe, "Southwestern Asia Beyond the Lands of the Mediterranean Littoral," and Jean Perrot, "Palestine-Syria-Cilicia," in Robert Braidwood and Gordon Willey (eds.), *Courses Toward Urban Life: Archaeological Considerations of Some Cultural Alternatives* (Chicago: Aldine, 1962), pp. 137 and 150; or James Mellaart, *Earliest Civilizations of the Near East* (London: Thames and Hudson, 1965), p. 23.

many times their number. There were probably many failures first, however, because no one yet understood even the rudiments of plant cultivation.

Regardless of how the discovery was made, our knowledge of the division of labor in primitive societies suggests that it was the work of women, not men.[3] Women are the ones most likely to have gathered the wild cereals and to have taken the grain from the storage pits to prepare it for eating. And, as we shall see shortly, in modern horticultural societies they are the ones most likely to perform the tasks of planting, cultivating, and harvesting.

In any case, the discovery was made and the foundation laid for a significantly new kind of society, one that could raise its own food, or the major part of it, and no longer be dependent on hunting and gathering. This same foundation would later serve as the basis for even more advanced types of societies, including our own.

SIMPLE HORTICULTURAL SOCIETIES IN PREHISTORIC ASIA AND EUROPE

We may never know precisely where and when the first horticultural society came into being, but recent archaeological research has established the general area and approximate date. Apparently it happened somewhere in the Middle East about 7000 B.C. There are currently three chief contenders for the honor: Asia Minor, Palestine, and the hill country to the east of the Tigris River. In each of these areas, ancient settlements dating from that period have been found in which horticulture was apparently the primary means of subsistence.[4]

From this area of initial development, horticultural techniques spread both east and west until eventually horticultural societies were established at points as distant as Britain and China. By the time they became established in these areas, however, the horticultural societies of the Middle East were already evolving into agrarian societies.

During recent years our knowledge of these early horticultural societies has been advanced substantially by new developments in the field of archaeology, including the excavation of new sites and the more extensive exploration of older ones. Increasing utilization of the skills of biologists and geologists has contributed greatly to our understanding of environmental conditions of that era. Most important of all, however, was the development, following World War II, of a new technique for dating archaeological remains. This technique, known as radiocarbon dating, made possible for the first time fairly accurate dating of prehistoric materials up to about 50,000 years of age.[5] Many formerly unanswerable questions can now be answered with an accuracy undreamed of twenty-five years ago.

---

[3] V. Gordon Childe, *What Happened in History*, rev. ed. (Baltimore: Penguin, 1964), pp. 65–66.

[4] See, for example, Braidwood and Howe, *op. cit.*, pp. 137, 152–153, and 346; or Mellaart, *op. cit.*, pp. 12, 32–38, 47–50, and 81.

[5] The technique is so named because it measures the amount of radioactive carbon remaining in dead material. For a good description of the technique, see Frank Hole and Robert Heizer, *An Introduction to Prehistoric Archaeology* (New York: Holt, 1965), pp. 145–150.

Characteristics of the societies

In traditional archaeological usage, the period in which simple horticultural societies were dominant in a region was known as the Neolithic, or New Stone, Age. This name was chosen because in early excavations in Europe and the Middle East, certain strata in some sites yielded new kinds of stone axes, adzes, and hammers, smoothed by grinding or polishing. Prior to the discovery of radiocarbon dating, these tools were one of the best indicators of the relative age of the stratum and its place in evolutionary history.

As research progressed, however, it became increasingly clear that these tools were neither the most distinctive feature of Neolithic societies nor their greatest technological achievement. As more and more sites were excavated, it became apparent that the really important innovations were in the area of subsistence technology. For the first time in history, men were *producing* their food, and hunting and gathering were relegated to a secondary role.

In this connection, it is important to recognize that these early horticultural societies had a mixed economy. Horticulture was their basic means of subsistence, but it was supplemented by herding, hunting, or gathering in various combinations.[6] The presence of livestock in many of these early societies was especially important, as we shall soon see.

Modern archaeologists now recognize that the term "Neolithic" focuses attention on the wrong thing. Recently a number of them have begun referring to the period in which these societies were dominant as "the era of effective food production."[7] We will call it simply "the horticultural era."

Following V. Gordon Childe, many archaeologists now refer to the emergence of horticultural societies as the first great social revolution in human history. From a long-term evolutionary standpoint, in which centuries are the smallest unit of time and most measurements are in millennia, Childe's view is certainly justified. It would be wrong to assume, however, that the rate of change seemed revolutionary to those affected by it. As far as we can judge today, the process was so gradual that the changes occurring in the lifetime of a single individual were not likely to have been either very numerous or very overwhelming.

One of the best indications we have of this slow rate of change is the evidence that in the Middle East men were already relying on cereal grains during much of the Mesolithic. Techniques of harvesting, storing, grinding, and cooking grains were apparently well established long before techniques of cultivation were developed. Furthermore, as we have noted, hunting, and to some extent gathering, continued to

---

[6] Braidwood and Howe, *op. cit.*, p. 140; Curwen and Hatt, *op. cit.*, p. 33; Mellaart, *op. cit.*, chaps. 3ff.; V. Gordon Childe, "The New Stone Age," in Harry Shapiro (ed.), *Man, Culture, and Society* (New York: Oxford Galaxy, 1960), p. 103.

[7] See Braidwood and Willey, *op. cit.*; or Robert Braidwood, "Domestication: The Food-producing Revolution," in *International Encyclopedia of the Social Sciences* (New York: Macmillan and Free Press, 1968), vol. 4, pp. 245–247.

play an important part in the lives of the early horticulturalists.[8] We may also assume that there was considerable continuity in other areas of life, especially kinship, religion, and politics. The survival of fertility cults, indicated by the widespread presence of female figurines in Neolithic remains, is but one indication.[9]

Our use of the term "revolutionary" in connection with the rise of horticultural societies, then, is based primarily on our awareness of the long-term implications of the change, and from this standpoint the label is surely correct. To begin with, the emergence of simple horticultural societies meant more permanent settlements. No longer were men obliged to move about constantly in search of game and other food. On the contrary, the practice of horticulture forced them to remain in one place for extended periods. In the Middle East and southeastern Europe, truly permanent settlements seem to have been established. Elsewhere, simple horticulturalists have usually had to move their settlements every few years, since their primitive methods of cultivation depleted the soil to the point where it could not sustain the population.[10] Why this was not necessary in the Middle East and southeastern Europe is still a mystery, since modern research indicates that only fertilization (by alluvial deposits or by man), irrigation, the use of the plow, or crop rotation permits land to be kept under continuous cultivation,[11] and thus far there is no evidence of any of these practices. We know, however, that these early horticulturalists kept livestock, and it is possible that the value of manure was discovered at an early date.[12] The failure of the practice to spread to other areas may have been due to the greater availability of arable land elsewhere.

In any case, the shift from hunting and gathering to horticulture substantially increased the permanence of human settlements, enabling people to accumulate many more possessions than they ever had before. This is very evident in the archaeological remains left by horticulturalists of the Neolithic era. Tools and weapons are much more numerous and varied than in Paleolithic and Mesolithic sites. Particularly noticeable is the appearance for the first time of large, bulky objects such as stone cups and bowls and, later, pottery.[13] Dwellings also became much more substantial. Some buildings contained several rooms and a small courtyard (see Fig. 8/1) and were made of materials like sun-dried clay blocks, capable of lasting for as long as two generations.[14] Even more noteworthy is the appearance

---

[8] See fn. 6.

[9] Jacquetta Hawkes, *Prehistory*, vol. I, part 1, of the UNESCO *History of Mankind* (New York: Mentor, 1965), pp. 442–452; Mellaart, *op. cit.*, p. 42; Childe, "The New Stone Age," *op. cit.*, p. 107.

[10] Childe, *op. cit.* pp. 100–101.

[11] See, for example, B. H. Farmer, "Agriculture: Comparative Technology," in *International Encyclopedia of the Social Sciences, op. cit.*, vol. 1, pp. 204–205; or Curwen and Hatt, *op. cit.*, p. 68 and chap. 16.

[12] Childe, *What Happened in History*, pp. 64–65.

[13] Mellaart, *op. cit.*, pp. 50–51; or Perrot, *op. cit.*, pp. 156–157.

[14] Hawkes, *op. cit.*, pp. 384–395; Childe, "New Stone Age," *op. cit.*, pp. 104–105; or Perrot, *op. cit.*, pp. 154–155.

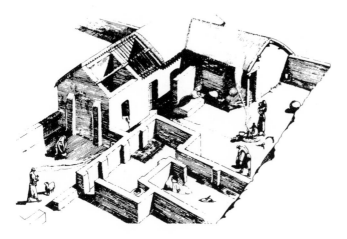

Fig. 8/1 Reconstruction of Neolithic farmhouse, Hassuna, Iraq (c. 5000–5500 B.C.)

of such things as religious shrines or ceremonial centers, village walls, and even occasional paved or timbered (corduroy style) roadways or alleys.[15] Though none of the latter are typical of Neolithic—or prehistoric simple horticultural—communities, neither are they rare or exceptional.

The change from a hunting and gathering to a horticultural economy also resulted in larger settlements and denser populations. Jarmo, one of the oldest horticultural villages yet discovered, contained twenty to twenty-five houses and an estimated population of 150,[16] nearly four times that of the average hunting and gathering band. Neolithic villages in Europe had from eight to fifty houses, suggesting populations ranging up to at least 200.[17] In several cases there were even more striking concentrations of population. One of the most famous is the village or town located on the site of Jericho nearly six thousand years before the days of Joshua. Recent excavations there uncovered a community that apparently housed 2,000 to 3,000 inhabitants.[18] Still more recent excavations of Çatal Hüyük in Asia Minor have revealed a community with an even larger area and, presumably, a larger population.[19]

These two communities, though obviously exceptional, illustrate another important development associated with the rise of horticultural societies—the rapid expansion and growing importance of trade and commerce.[20] Modern scholars feel that the "great" size of Jericho and Çatal Hüyük was not due simply to the

---

[15] Hawkes, *op. cit.*, pp. 395–401, and Mellaart, *op. cit.*, pp. 40–42.

[16] Mellaart, *op. cit.*, p. 47.

[17] Childe, "New Stone Age," *op. cit.*, p. 105. Elsewhere Childe speaks of twenty-five to thirty-five households as "a not uncommon number" in central Europe and southern Russia. See *What Happened in History, op. cit.*, p. 66.

[18] Mellaart, *op. cit.*, p. 36; or Hawkes, *op. cit.*, p. 310.

[19] Mellaart, *op. cit.*, pp. 81–101.

[20] See, for example, Childe, "New Stone Age," *op. cit.*, p. 106; or *What Happened in History, op. cit.*, pp. 67–68. See also Braidwood and Howe, *op. cit.*, p. 138.

practice of horticulture. As one writer has put it, "It is . . . most unlikely that agriculture should have flourished more at Jericho, 200 metres below sea-level, than elsewhere in Palestine. Some other resource must have existed, and this was probably
trade."[21] As he points out, Jericho commanded the resources of the Dead Sea, notably
salt, bitumen,[22] and sulphur, all useful materials in simple horticultural societies and
not readily available everywhere. This view of Jericho as an early center of trade is
supported by the discovery there of products such as obsidian from Asia Minor and
cowrie shells from the Red Sea. In the case of Çatal Hüyük, obsidian (i.e., volcanic
glass, a material much sought after for use in weapons and other things) seems to
have been the key local resource on which its growth depended. Even in small
villages far removed from such centers as Jericho and Çatal Hüyük, there is evidence
of trade. For example, shells from the Mediterranean were found in the sites of
Neolithic villages and graves throughout the Danube basin and far down the Oder,
Elbe, and Rhine river valleys in northern Europe.[23]

The growth of trade and commerce suggests an increase in occupational
specialization as well, at least in the chief commercial centers. Direct evidence
of this has been found in a number of sites. For example, a community south of
Jericho yielded a number of small workshops where such specialized craftsmen
as a butcher, a beadmaker, and a maker of bone tools worked.[24] This kind of specialization, however, was apparently limited to the emerging trade centers.[25]

Despite the increase in trade and occupational specialization, most communities
remained largely self-sufficient and most families still produced nearly all of the
things they used.[26] Thus it is not surprising to find important innovations continuing
to appear in the domestic arts. The two most notable were the invention of pottery
and of weaving.[27] Pottery is so common in Neolithic sites that for a long time no
site was considered truly Neolithic unless pottery was present. Recent research has
shown, however, that pottery did not appear until some time after the emergence of
the first horticultural societies.[28]

There is little evidence of warfare during the early Neolithic. Graves rarely
contained weapons and most communities had no walls or other defenses.[29] Some,
it is true, had ditches and fences, but these were on a scale more suitable for pro-

---

[21] Mellaart, *op. cit.,* p. 36. See also p. 84 for his views on Çatal Hüyük.

[22] Bitumen was used to fix blades in their handles, mend pottery, etc. (*ibid.,* pp. 20–21).

[23] Childe, "New Stone Age," *op. cit.,* p. 106.

[24] Mellaart, *op. cit.,* pp. 43–44.

[25] See Childe, *What Happened in History,* p. 67.

[26] Childe, "New Stone Age," *op. cit.,* p. 106, and *What Happened in History,* p. 67.

[27] For a good review of these developments, see Hawkes, *op. cit.,* pp. 401–410 and 414–417; or V. Gordon Childe, *Man Makes Himself* (New York: Mentor, 1953), pp. 76–80.

[28] See, for example, Mellaart, *op. cit.,* chap. 8.

[29] Childe, "New Stone Age," *op. cit.,* p. 107, or *What Happened in History,* p. 74.

tection against marauding animals than against human enemies. The walls surrounding Jericho are something else, and were obviously defenses against human foes.[30] But who they were is still a mystery. Later in the Neolithic the picture changed drastically and warfare became increasingly common. In this period "battleaxes, daggers and other arms appear in the grave of every adult male." The reason for this change is not clear, but some scholars think it was linked with the growth of population and the resulting scarcity of new land suitable for horticulture. It may also have been related to declining opportunities for hunting, a traditional male activity. Warfare, with its demands for bravery and skill in the use of arms, would be a natural substitute among men with more free time on their hands than ever before, and the frictions created by the growing pressure for land would provide a ready-made justification. Finally, some experts suspect that the increase in warfare was linked with the increase in wealth, especially in the form of cattle which could be moved so easily.[31]

Diffusion

From its origins in the Middle East, the new way of life spread slowly east and west. Simple horticultural societies were eventually established throughout almost all of Europe and North Africa. In Asia, their spread was more irregular, and they never did develop in large areas because the land was unsuited to plant cultivation.[32]

From the long-term evolutionary standpoint, this new way of life spread quite rapidly, but again, from the perspective of an individual lifetime, the pace was extremely slow. The distance from the Middle East to China is approximately 5,000 miles, and it took the new technology at least three thousand years, possibly more, to cover it. The movement westward was even slower: four thousand years were required to reach Britain, 3,000 miles away. In other words, the new way of life spread at the rate of only a mile or two per year on the average.

Various factors contributed to the spread of horticulture, but one of the more important was the growth of population. Given the tendency for human populations to increase until checked by the limitation of resources, population pressures would naturally build up in the original area of horticultural practice, leading to the formation of new settlements on the outer fringes whenever possible. This would mean either the movement of the horticultural population into previously unoccupied territory or the invasion of territory occupied by hunting and gathering peoples. In the latter case, the advantage would clearly lie with the horticulturalists, since both technology and group size are important in determining the outcome of

[30] Hawkes, *op. cit.*, p. 358; or Mellaart, *op. cit.*, pp. 33–36.

[31] Childe, "New Stone Age," *op. cit.*, p. 107.

[32] See, for example, H. D. Sankalia, *Prehistory and Protohistory in India and Pakistan* (Bombay: Bombay University Press, 1962), pp. 152–155; or Sir Mortimer Wheeler, *Early India and Pakistan* (London: Thames and Hudson, 1959), pp. 80ff.

struggles between societies. According to both archaeological and ethnographic evidence, simple horticultural societies are, on the average, at least twice the size of hunting and gathering societies.[33] Technologically they would have an advantage, too, since their new mode of production would provide the men with far more "leisure" that could be used in military pursuits (see page 224 below).

In the process of diffusion, there was a definite tendency for the whole cluster of horticultural traits to spread together, but there were exceptions. Weaving, for example, apparently never reached horticultural Britain, and large trading centers like Jericho and Çatal Hüyük were limited to the Middle East.[34] On the other hand, certain elements of the horticultural way of life were adopted by some groups that still relied primarily on hunting and gathering. In parts of northeastern Europe and northern Asia, for example, pottery and polished stone axes, both basic horticultural or Neolithic innovations, were widely used by hunting and fishing peoples.[35] Developments like these demonstrate the need for those irregular boundaries between societal types shown in Fig. 6/2 (page 124).

The spread of horticulture to China is especially interesting because it provides us with one of the first points of contact between prehistory and history. Horticulture reached China late enough, and writing developed there early enough, that some memory of the early horticultural era was preserved in legends that were eventually written down. For a long time scholars believed that this material was entirely fictional, but modern archaeological research has substantiated enough of it that it is now taken much more seriously.[36] Though fact and fiction are obviously intermingled, the factual element is strong enough to be intriguing.

According to legend, China's earliest inhabitants were hunters, but the increase of population eventually forced a shift to horticulture. As one source recounts, "The ancient people ate meat of animals and birds. At the time of Shen-nung [an early legendary ruler and culture hero] there were so many people that the animals and birds became inadequate for people's wants and therefore Shen-nung taught the people to cultivate."[37] Another source relates that Shen-nung introduced pottery, while others describe the era of Shen-nung as a period of peace and self-sufficiency: "During the Age of Shen-nung people rested at ease and acted with vigor. They cared for their mothers, but not for their fathers. They lived among deer. They ate what they cultivated and wore what they wove. They did not think of harming one another."[38] This preference for mothers is especially interesting because it is so

---

[33] For the ethnographic evidence, see Table 6/2, p. 131.

[34] On the absence of weaving in Britain, see Hawkes, *op. cit.*, p. 326.

[35] *Ibid.*

[36] See Kwang-chih Chang, *The Archaeology of Ancient China* (New Haven, Conn.: Yale, 1963), pp. 130–131. See also Curwen and Hatt, *op. cit.*, pp. 16–18, on truths contained in ancient traditions.

[37] Chang, *op. cit.*, p. 132. Quoted by permission of Yale University Press.

[38] *Ibid.*, pp. 131–132. Quoted by permission of Yale University Press.

Fig. 8/2 The Emperor Shen-nung, according to an artist of the seventeenth century B.C.

contrary to the later Chinese tradition of respect for the father; yet it fits in with one of the distinctive characteristics of horticultural societies (see page 219 below). Finally, one other legend described the Age of Shen-nung as the last era in which men were free from coercive political authority: "People were administered without a criminal law and prestige was built without the use of force. After Shen-nung, however, the strong began to rule over the weak and the many over the few."[39]

Progress

During the horticultural era, technological progress was almost continuous, especially in the Middle East. In addition to pottery making and weaving, metals were discovered and the basic principles of working them developed. Thus it is not surprising to find that the simple horticultural societies of the latter part of the era were generally more advanced than their predecessors three thousand years earlier. The societies that flourished throughout Mesopotamia around 4000 B.C. are a good example of this. These groups apparently shared a common culture, called the Ubaid culture after one of the sites where its remains are found.

---

[39] *Ibid.*, p. 133. Quoted by permission of Yale University Press.

Ubaid culture was notable in many ways. To begin with, large settlements were relatively common. This is indicated by the size of cemeteries, one of which contained more than a thousand graves, as well as by the large temples that dominated these communities.[40] Technical skills of many kinds were highly developed. Some copper tools and weapons were used, at least in the northern area, while in the south, sickles and other tools were made from clay fired at high temperatures, a process that produced a remarkably efficient substitute for the stone that was lacking in the area.[41] Trade seems to have been extensive throughout Mesopotamia at this time (facilitated by the simple sailboats that plied the myriad waterways[42]) and may have been responsible for the wide diffusion of Ubaid culture. As one writer has said, "Never before had a single culture been able to influence such a vast area, if only superficially."[43] Compared with these societies, the first horticultural societies of the seventh millennium appear primitive indeed. The difference between them is a measure of the tremendous progress achieved by the simple horticulturalists of the Middle East during the first part of the horticultural era.

---

[40] Mellaart, *op. cit.*, pp. 130–131, and V. Gordon Childe, *New Light on the Most Ancient East* (London: Routledge, 1952), pp. 118ff.

[41] Childe, *New Light*, p. 115, and Hawkes, *op. cit.*, p. 425.

[42] Childe, *New Light*, ibid.

[43] Mellaart, *op. cit.*, p. 130.

Fig. 8/3 Artist's reconstruction of the Ubaid Temple at Tepe Gawa

ADVANCED HORTICULTURAL SOCIETIES IN PREHISTORIC ASIA AND EUROPE

Each of the many inventions and discoveries of the horticultural era increased man's control over his environment to some degree. None, however, had such far-reaching effects as the discovery of the principles of metallurgy. This is why archaeologists continue to use it as the basic criterion for marking the end of the Stone Age.

Middle Eastern beginnings

To the nontechnically inclined, the shift from stone to metal may suggest a radical break with the past and an innovation without roots in earlier practice. Actually, however, the use of metals evolved by a series of small steps from the earlier use of stone.

Since the Upper Paleolithic, and perhaps before that, men had been keenly aware of the differences between various kinds of stone. Certain types, because of their hardness, were recognized as much more suitable than others for tools and weapons. Men were also attentive to differences in color, and this led them to select some rocks for ornamental purposes and others as sources of pigments for use in painting. This interest in unusual rocks undoubtedly attracted men to copper. In its native form, copper appears as purplish-green or greenish-black nuggets which, when scratched or rubbed, show a yellowish-red kernel of pure copper.

At first, copper was simply hammered cold into small tools and ornaments like awls, pins, and hooks. A few articles made by this method have been found in sites dating to the middle of the sixth millennium B.C.[44] Sometime shortly after 5000 B.C., men discovered the technique of annealing.[45] By alternately heating and hammering the metal, they rendered it less brittle and thus could use it for a wider variety of objects. The heat from a simple wood fire was sufficient for this process. Subsequently (late in the fifth millennium B.C.), men discovered techniques for extracting copper from various kinds of ores by means of smelting, as well as ways to melt "pure" copper and cast it in molds.[46]

These discoveries illustrate again the cumulative character of technological progress. Recent studies show that both smelting and melting copper require higher temperatures than a simple wood fire can produce. This strongly suggests that these important discoveries presupposed the invention of pottery and the pottery kiln.[47] And this, in turn, presupposed the existence of settled communities.

So far as we can judge, the use of copper tools and weapons increased rather

---

[44] Mellaart, *op. cit.*, p. 105.

[45] R. J. Forbes, *Studies in Ancient Technology* (Leiden: Brill, 1964), vol. 9, p. 30; or Leslie Aitchison, *A History of Metals* (London: MacDonald and Evans, 1960), vol. I, p. 21.

[46] Aitchison, *op. cit.*, p. 40.

[47] *Ibid.*; or Forbes, *op. cit.*, vol. 8, p. 26.

slowly for 1,500 or 2,000 years.[48] Various factors were responsible for this. For one thing, until smelting techniques were discovered, the supply of copper was extremely limited. Even when it was available, it often had to be carried some distance to the potential users, and the primitive methods of transportation then in use made this costly. Second, because metal working (particularly smelting and casting) was probably mastered by only a few specialists, these men may have treated their skills as a kind of magic, as smiths in modern horticultural societies often do, in order to protect their lucrative monopoly. Finally, since any man could make his own tools and weapons out of stone, most people were undoubtedly reluctant to switch to the more costly product.[49] Thus, though copper was discovered as early as the middle of the sixth millennium B.C., no truly advanced horticultural society (i.e., one in which metal tools and weapons were widespread) seems to have developed before the end of the fifth millennium or the early part of the fourth (i.e., around 4000 B.C.).

If this is true (there is still some uncertainty about it[50]), then the period when advanced horticultural societies flourished in the Middle East was relatively brief. As we shall see in the next chapter, agrarian societies may have begun to appear as early as the latter part of the fourth millennium. The pattern was similar in most of Europe and in India. In fact, China is the only major area in the Old World where advanced horticultural societies flourished for any extended period of time.

Because of this and because of the limitations of the archaeological record, it is difficult to describe the advanced horticultural societies of most of prehistoric Europe and Asia as accurately as we would like. Other sources of information on societies of this type, notably the modern ethnographic record, are much more rewarding. Except in the case of China, the most we can presently say with assurance about these early societies is that during the period in which they flourished (in the Middle East, the so-called Ubaid period) there was continued growth in the size and density of populations, continued progress in technology, further increases in occupational specialization and trade, greater urbanization of the population (i.e., more people freed from the task of raising their own food), marked development of specialized religious and political institutions, and increasing social inequality. In short, societies were becoming larger, more productive, and more differentiated.

We might also attribute writing to advanced horticultural societies. It all depends on where we draw the line dividing them from agrarian societies, and what we assume about the origins of writing (e.g., whether it was invented by the Sumerians or by an earlier people whose remains have not yet been found). Though the weight of evidence is currently against the view that writing was invented by advanced horticulturalists, it is clear that the inventors were not far from that level of development.

---

[48] Childe, *Man Makes Himself*, p. 99.

[49] V. Gordon Childe, *The Bronze Age* (Cambridge: Cambridge University Press, 1930), p. 11.

[50] See, for example, Childe, *New Light*, p. 116.

The Chinese experience

China was something of an exception to the usual evolutionary pattern at the advanced horticultural level. For reasons that are not clear, the advanced horticultural era lasted longer in China than in most other areas. On the basis of modern research, it appears that it began in the early part of the second millenium B.C. and lasted until the middle of the first.[51]

Because the plow was so long delayed in coming to China, the overall level of technological development achieved there during the advanced horticultural era seems to have surpassed what was achieved in advanced horticultural societies elsewhere. One indication of this is the fact that the dominant metal during most of the era in China was bronze, while in the Middle East and Europe it was copper. This difference is significant because the manufacture of bronze represents an important advance in metallurgy, involving, as it does, the principle of alloying. In the Middle East, the technique of making bronze was not really understood until the early part of the third millennium B.C., some time *after* the first agrarian societies had made their appearance.[52] These variations in the sequencing of major innovations (i.e., bronze

---

[51] On the emergence of advanced horticultural societies and the early use of metals, see Te-k'un Cheng, *Archaeology in China: Shang China* (Cambridge, England: Heffer, 1960), chap. 10; Chang, *op. cit.*, chap. 6; William Watson, *China: Before the Han Dynasty* (New York: Praeger, 1961), chap. 2. On the emergence of agrarian societies, see Chang, *op. cit.*, pp. 197–198; or Cho-yun Hsu, *Ancient China in Transition* (Stanford, Calif.: Stanford University Press, 1965), pp. 130–132.

[52] Some bronze seems to have been manufactured accidentally a few centuries earlier as a result of using copper derived from ores containing tin; but the deliberate and conscious alloying of metals did not begin until after 3000 B.C. See Forbes, *op. cit.*, vol. 9, pp. 151–152.

Fig. 8/4   Bronze ritual axe of the kind used for beheading human victims. Shang dynasty, twelfth or eleventh century B.C.

and the plow) remind us again of the inadequacy of *unilinear* theories of evolution, which assume that all societies follow exactly the same evolutionary path. Some variation is the rule, not the exception.

When the advanced horticultural era in China (i.e., China of the Shang and most of the Chou dynasties) is compared with the simple horticultural, the differences are striking. During the earlier era, northern China was covered with numerous small, largely self-sufficient, autonomous villages. In the later period, the villages were no longer autonomous, and a few of them had grown into urban centers of some size and substance.

The emergence of towns was due to the military successes of their leaders, and these, in turn, were due to their possession of bronze weapons. As one scholar summarized this period, "In the course of a few centuries the villages of the plain fell under the domination of walled cities on whose rulers the possession of bronze weapons, chariots, and slaves conferred a measure of superiority to which no Neolithic community could aspire, however populous and well fed."[53]

The importance of this development can hardly be exaggerated. For the first time in Chinese history, men found the conquest of their fellow men a profitable alternative to the conquest of nature. Much the same thing happened in other parts of the world during this stage in societal development. Thus, beginning in advanced horticultural societies and continuing in agrarian, we find as much, or more, energy expended in war as in the age-old struggle for subsistence. One might almost say that bronze was to man's conquest of his fellow man what plant cultivation was to his conquest of nature. Both made major breakthroughs possible.

From the military standpoint, China's advanced horticulturalists enjoyed a great advantage over the simple horticulturalists. Recently excavated burial remains show that they wore elaborate armor, including helmets; carried shields; and were equipped with spears, dagger-axes, knives, hatchets, and reflex bows capable of a pull of 160 pounds.[54] In addition, they employed horse-drawn chariots carrying teams of three men.

These peoples also enjoyed a numerical superiority: every victory brought more people under their control, enabling them to enlarge their armies still further.[55] This would not have been possible in a hunting and gathering society, where the primitive nature of the technology made it impossible to incorporate a defeated people into the conquering group. At that level of development the economic surplus (i.e., production in excess of what is needed to keep producers productive) was too small and irregular to permit this. But with the introduction of horticulture, the situation changed dramatically. For the first time in history the conquest, control,

---

[53] Watson, *op. cit.*, p. 57.

[54] Cheng, *op. cit.*, pp. 206–207.

[55] Shang kings, for example, mounted "many military expeditions with an army of between 3,000 and 5,000 men." *Ibid.*, p. 210, and Hsu, *op. cit.*, p. 67.

and exploitation of other groups became possible—*and profitable*. All that remained to transform this possibility into a reality was some advance in military technology that would give one society a definite advantage over its neighbors. This bronze did. It tipped the balance of military power decisively in favor of the advanced horticulturalists.

The earliest advanced horticultural society in China of which we have any archaeological knowledge was that established by the Shang people in either the eighteenth or sixteenth century B.C.[56] Though Shang society was ruled by a single dynasty for at least five hundred years, its structure was basically feudalistic. In most regions, especially those remote from the capital, effective power was in the hands of feudal lords who paid tribute to the king and supported him militarily but otherwise enjoyed great autonomy.[57] They were so independent, in fact, that they often waged war among themselves. The same was true in the Chou dynasty that followed.

During the Shang and Chou periods, marked social inequality was the rule. These societies were divided into two basic classes, a small warrior-nobility and the great mass of common people.[58] The warrior-nobility formed the governing class and lived in the walled cities, which served as their fortresses. It was they who enjoyed most of the benefits of the new technology and the new social system. The chief use of bronze was in the manufacture of weapons and artistic and ceremonial objects for the benefit of this class. Almost none of this relatively scarce material was made available to the common people for farm tools.[59] Much the same situation existed in the Middle East and Europe during the Bronze Age. As one writer has put it, this was a world in which metals played a major role in the military and cultural spheres but not in the economic.[60]

Kinship ties were extremely important in the political systems of advanced horticultural China. Membership in the governing class was largely hereditary, and as far as possible leading officials assigned the major offices under their control to kinsmen.[61] The origins of these noble families is unknown, but it seems likely that

---

[56] According to ancient Chinese legends, the Shang dynasty was preceded by a Hsia dynasty. For a time, both were thought to have been fictional, but archaeological research has proven the existence of the Shang dynasty, and most scholars now assume there was an earlier Hsia dynasty and that it could have ruled over an advanced horticultural society. See Chang, *op. cit.*, pp. 130–131; or Cheng, *op. cit.*, pp. xix-xxii.

[57] Cheng, *op. cit.*, pp. 200–206.

[58] *Ibid.*, pp. 200–215 and 248. For a more detailed picture of the system of stratification in the Chou era, see Hsu, *op. cit.* In reading this book one must keep in mind that the Chan Kuo period, the period of the Warring States, is included, and by then, north central China seems to have reached the agrarian level of development.

[59] Watson, *op. cit.*, p. 141, and Chang, *op. cit.*, pp. 195ff.

[60] Aitchison, *op. cit.*, p. 97.

[61] Hsu, *op. cit.*, pp. 3–7, and chap. 4.

Fig. 8/5   Bronze ritual vessels from late eleventh or early tenth century B.C., found in tomb in Shensi province. Each vessel had its prescribed and specific use

they were descended from the village headmen of the Neolithic era and from the close associates of early conquerors.

The walled towns where the aristocracy lived were small by modern standards but nonetheless represented an important innovation in China. One recently excavated town, probably an early capital of the Shang state, was surrounded by a wall enclosing an area of slightly over one square mile.[62] The size of the walled area, however, does not tell the full story of these towns, especially in the earlier period. Many of the common people had their homes and workshops outside the protected area and cultivated nearby fields.

The walled area, while basically a fortress, was also a political and religious center, as well as the residential area for the governing class. Religious activities were quite important and were tied closely to the political system—so closely, in fact, that one writer described the Shang state as "a kind of theocracy."[63] Though this is something of an overstatement, it is clear from ancient inscriptions that the ruler did perform major religious functions and was what we would describe today as head of both church and state.

The physical structure of these early urban centers was impressive and reflects

[62] Chang, *op. cit.*, p. 150.

[63] Watson, *op. cit.*, p. 106. See also Hsu, *op. cit.*, pp. 15ff., on the interrelations between religion and politics in Chou China.

the evolution of the state and its newly achieved ability to mobilize labor on a large scale. One indication of the state's capacity for this is the wall around Cheng-chou, an early Shang capital: one scholar estimates that it required the labor of 10,000 men working eighteen years.[64] Such massive undertakings apparently utilized large numbers of captives taken in war, many of them later used as human sacrifices.[65]

Not much is known about the daily life of the common people, but their chief functions in society were obviously to produce the economic surplus on which the governing class depended and to provide the manpower for their various projects and military campaigns. Not all the labor was of the brute, physical type, however. Some men were employed in occupational specialties that provided the new and unusual luxury goods which the governing class demanded for display and for ceremonial purposes; others produced military equipment.[66] We do not know to what extent these were full-time jobs, but many of these specialists were probably part-time farmers. This growth of occupational specialization was undoubtedly accompanied by some growth in trade.

Despite their increasingly exploitative character, the advanced horticultural societies of China made important progress in a number of areas. The more important innovations included the use of writing, the use of currency, the use of the horse, probably the practice of irrigation, and possibly the manufacture of iron just prior to the emergence of the first agrarian society. In addition, there were scores of lesser innovations too numerous to mention. Some of these were probably independent inventions or discoveries by the Chinese, others the result of diffusion. In most cases, it is still impossible to determine which are which.

HORTICULTURAL SOCIETIES IN PREHISTORIC AMERICA

Scholars have long debated whether knowledge of the principles of plant cultivation spread throughout the Old World from a single source or whether they were discovered independently more than once. Proof of multiple, independent discoveries would be very difficult to come by, and we may never know for certain. Currently the majority of scholars seem inclined to the view that the knowledge originated in a single place and spread from there, but their arguments are hardly compelling.[67]

---

[64] Chang, *op. cit.,* p. 150.

[65] *Ibid.,* p. 159.

[66] *Ibid.,* p. 171.

[67] While the diffusion hypothesis seems likely in the case of the various cereal grains, it is less convincing in the case of the various root crops, such as taro, yams, and manioc, which are of such importance in many of the islands of the South Pacific and which are grown chiefly in tropical and semitropical areas. The area in which root crops have been cultivated is so different from that in which the cereals have been grown, and the techniques of cultivation so different, that it is difficult to believe that knowledge of cereal cultivation served as the basis for the cultivation of root crops. Unfortunately, this problem has been ignored in most discussions of the question.

Fortunately, we do not need to solve that problem in order to prove that human progress beyond the hunting and gathering level did not depend on a single lucky accident or one stroke of genius. The sociocultural isolation of the New World during most of the last nine thousand years provides the basis for this assertion. Recent archaeological research in Mexico shows that plant cultivation began there no later than 3700 B.C., and possibly as early as 7000.[68] Since horticulture did not reach eastern Asia until at least 4000 B.C., and probably much later, it is impossible to explain plant cultivation in the New World by diffusion from Asia. Diffusion from Europe or North Africa is even less likely. Finally, the slow and gradual increase in the practice of horticulture in the New World suggests an indigenous development rather than an established way of life imported from abroad.[69]

This independent development is important because it gives us an opportunity to test the hypothesis that technology limits the forms of social organization which can develop and predisposes a society to adopt certain patterns rather than others. If subsistence technology is as important as ecological-evolutionary theory asserts, the basic patterns of social organization in the horticultural societies of the New World should not be too different from those in Europe and Asia.

Simple horticultural societies

Though plant cultivation in the New World began by at least the first half of the fourth millennium B.C., there were no true horticultural societies (i.e., ones that obtained at least half of their subsistence by this method) until the middle or latter half of the second millennium.[70] These appeared first in Mexico and spread from there both north and south. By the time of European exploration and settlement, they covered much, though by no means all, of the New World. The rate of diffusion seems to have been very similar to that in the Old World. For example, it took approximately 2,200 years for simple horticultural societies to spread from their point of origin near Mexico City to the head of the Ohio River near Pittsburgh, a distance of about 2,000 miles.[71]

In the main, the similarities between the simple horticultural societies of the prehistoric past in the two hemispheres are striking. In both areas the shift from hunting and gathering to horticulture was associated with increasing population size and density, a more settled pattern of village life, increased wealth or possessions, more substantial dwellings and other buildings, the beginnings of craft specialization, the appearance of markets, increased trade, the establishment of relatively

---

[68] Gordon Willey, "Mesoamerica," in Braidwood and Willey, *op. cit.*, p. 88.

[69] *Ibid.*, p. 100.

[70] *Ibid.*, pp. 91ff.; and Robert Braidwood and Gordon Willey, "Conclusions and Afterthoughts," in Braidwood and Willey, *op. cit.*, pp. 335 and 344ff.

[71] Braidwood and Willey, *op. cit.*, p. 347.

permanent religious centers, and even such specifics as the manufacture of ground stone implements and pottery and the discovery of the principles of metallurgy.[72] There is also evidence in both areas that militarism increased after horticultural societies had become well established.

At the same time, however, there are certain differences between the two hemispheres that warn against an overly deterministic view. In Mexico and Guatemala many of the simple horticultural societies of the prehistoric era evolved, in certain areas, to a degree normally associated only with more advanced societies. During the first millennium A.D., they developed numerous settlements that are remarkable not only for their size, but also for their material and intellectual achievements. The most famous of these were developed by the Mayas of Yucatan.

From the standpoint of size, Mayan communities seem to have been much larger than simple horticultural settlements in the Old World. In some cases, populations reached 10,000 or more.[73] The most impressive of their material accomplish-

---

[72] For developments in the New World, see Willey, *op. cit.*, pp. 91–101; Donald Collier, "The Central Andes," in Braidwood and Willey, *op. cit.*, pp. 169–174; Gerardo Reichel-Dolmatoff, *Colombia* (New York: Praeger, 1965), chap. 5.

[73] The size and nature of some of these centers is a subject of much debate. Some claim they housed as many as 200,000 residents; others argue that they were merely religious centers with relatively small residential populations that served the surrounding peoples. For the two views, see Sylvanus Morley, *The Ancient Maya* (Stanford, Calif.: Stanford University Press, 1946), p. 315, and J. E. S. Thompson, "A Survey of the Northern Mayan Area," *American Antiquity*, 2 (1945), pp. 2–24. Even if the early Mayan centers were not residential, however, it appears that later Mexican settlements were.

Fig. 8/6 Artist's reconstruction of the Mayan ceremonial center at Copan, Honduras

ments were the massive temple complexes, some of which have survived for more than a thousand years. Their intellectual achievements are no less remarkable and include the invention of a primitive, ideographic system of writing, a numeral system that included the concept of zero centuries before this was invented in the Old World, and a calendar that was amazingly accurate.[74]

In any comparison of simple horticultural societies, the Mayas stand out as unique.[75] Despite their lack of metal, they achieved a level of societal development comparable in many respects to advanced horticultural societies. This raises the interesting question of how they did it, a question with important implications for our understanding of societal development.

Part of the explanation of their unusual attainments lies in the nature of horticultural systems in general and of theirs in particular. Research has shown that a modern Mayan farmer, using largely the same techniques his ancestors used in pre-European times, can raise in 190 days enough corn to supply the basic needs of several families for a year.[76] Even making allowance for the labor required for other subsistence needs and making adjustments for technological advances (e.g., the introduction of metal tools), it is clear that the native economy was capable of supporting large numbers of people who were wholly or partially freed from the task of providing their own food—at least as long as the supply of good land lasted. Those who did not have to farm could devote themselves to a variety of specialized activities, ranging from the cultivation of the arts and sciences to the construction of massive temple complexes. There may well have been a similar potential in the simple horticultural systems of the Old World but, if so, it was not utilized until the advent of metal.

A second key to the puzzle is apparently found in the role of religion in Mayan societies. A striking feature of all the major settlements is the centrality and dominance of the complex of temple buildings. The priests who directed the construction of these massive buildings obviously had great authority or influence. We may never know how they acquired their power, but it seems more than coincidence that this large-scale temple construction began about the same time as the development of the calendar, writing, and the numerical system.[77] Since these innovations were all made by the priestly class, or soon became their special monopoly, and since this knowledge was essential in determining the timing of crucial events in the annual horticultural cycle (planting, harvesting, etc.), it is not surprising that the common

---

[74] On the Maya, see Morley, *op. cit.,* chap. 12. On the more general distribution of these intellectual skills, see Willey, *op. cit.,* pp. 91ff., or Victor von Hagen, *The Ancient Sun Kingdoms of the Americas* (Cleveland: World Publishing, 1961), pp. 47–58.

[75] This statement and many of the ones that follow apply not only to the Mayas but also to a number of other less well known groups nearby.

[76] Morley, *op. cit.,* pp. 154–158. For figures from other parts of the horticultural world, see R. F. Watters, "The Nature of Shifting Cultivation," *Pacific Viewpoint,* 1 (1960), p. 93.

[77] Morley, *op. cit.,* p. 209, and Willey, *op. cit.,* pp. 94–96.

Fig. 8/7   Mayan temple at Tikal

people accorded the priests high status and readily followed their leadership.[78] The influence of the priests was further enhanced by practices such as prophecy, divination, and healing, all of which increased the people's dependence on them, and by the fact that they worked in close alliance with the governing nobility.

Finally, these societies occupied an area rich in a fortunate combination of soft and hard rock. The hard rocks, basalt and diorite, were admirably suited to cutting the softer rocks, limestone and sandstone. Furthermore, the softer stones were kinds that tend to harden after exposure to the elements, which greatly enhanced their value.[79] Few other simple horticulturalists have been so favorably situated.

[78] Morley, *op. cit.*, pp. 144–147.

[79] *Ibid.*, chap. 14.

The Mayan case is yet another reminder that there are alternative evolutionary paths for societies. Some, of course, have been followed much more often than others. The usual pattern at the simple horticultural level has been the formation of many small, relatively undifferentiated, autonomous farming villages. Because of the productivity of the horticultural economy, however, the formation of occasional trading centers similar to early Jericho has been one alternative. Another has been the development of larger and more complex "theocratic" communities like those created by the Mayas and their neighbors.

No one can say with certainty why one, rather than another, of these alternatives was adopted, but nontechnological factors were undoubtedly important, especially in the case of the temple builders of the New World. Prior to the beginnings of temple construction, the technology of that area was apparently unexceptional. Thus we are led to look elsewhere for an explanation.

As we have seen, the environment provided these people with certain essential building materials. But obviously these materials did not provide the stimulus for temple building. This could have come only from their religious system. Apparently out of appreciation to the gods for their blessings, and especially for their help in certain crucial horticultural activities, the Mayas voluntarily offered them a portion of both their harvest and their labor. Under the direction of the priests, these contributions provided the material base for the development of an elaborate temple cult. Thus, the surplus of which the horticultural economy was capable was protected against the perennial threat of uncontrolled population growth. Instead of permitting the number of farmers to multiply until the surplus was "destroyed" (i.e., consumed by more farmers at the subsistence level), these societies embarked on a course that checked population growth and promoted social inequality, but preserved the economic surplus. This was accomplished by using the surplus to support the activities of the priests and a wide variety of other temple-related specialists.

In many ways this pattern of development is remarkably similar to the one that developed in a number of the most advanced horticultural societies of the Middle East in the fourth millennium B.C. In those groups, too, religion played an essential role in the preservation of the surplus and the creation of a more differentiated social system. They, too, had an intellectual elite of priests who introduced writing and counting, devised calendars, and developed the science of astronomy. Here, too, these skills apparently enhanced the priests' status, giving them the necessary power to develop an elaborate temple cult. The similarities extend even to the construction of massive temples.[80] The chief difference between the early theocracies of the Middle East and of Mexico is that the former did not emerge until *after* the discovery of the basic principles of metallurgy.

---

[80] For discussions of these developments, see, among others, Childe, *Man Makes Himself*, chap. 7; or Henri Frankfort, *The Birth of Civilization in the Near East* (Bloomington: Indiana University Press, 1959), pp. 58ff.

Fig. 8/8 Human sacrifice, from carving on the Mayan Temple of the Jaquars, Chichen Itza, Mexico

Before leaving the Maya, we must take at least brief note of the dark side of their religious heritage, the practice of human sacrifice (see Fig. 8/8). By modern standards, this practice was chillingly barbaric. One writer describes the ceremony this way:

> The victim was presented in the nude, his body painted blue, his head decorated with a pointed headdress. The place of execution was either the precinct of the temple, or the summit of the pyramid where the altar was erected; the altar of sacrifice was a heavy stone with a convex surface. Four assistants or *chaces*, also painted blue, took hold of the four limbs of the victim and laid him on his back on the stone so that his thorax projected. The sacrificer or *nacom*, equipped with a flint dagger, opened the lower left part of the breast, put his hand into the incision, tore out the beating heart, placed it on a plate and gave it to the priest or *chilán*. The *chilán* quickly smeared with blood the image of the god in whose honor the ceremony had been celebrated. The *chaces* threw the still warm body to the bottom of the pyramid where the priests of lower rank stripped it of all its skin, except for the hands and feet. The *chilán* dressed himself in this bloody skin and danced in company with the spectators. When the victim had been a particularly valiant soldier, the scene was accompanied by ritual cannibalism. The hands and feet were reserved for the *chilán*.[81]

Practices of this kind have been relatively common in horticultural and simple agrarian societies, in both the Old World and the New.

Advanced horticultural societies

The earliest use of metal in this hemisphere was in central Peru around 1000 B.C.[82] At first, as in the Old World, relatively pure pieces of metal were simply hammered into ornaments of various kinds. In the New World, however, gold, not copper, was the most common metal in the early period. Later, techniques for melting, alloying, casting, smelting, and refining were developed. Not long after the time of Christ, copper began to be used in tools and weapons with considerable frequency, and the first advanced horticultural societies apparently date from the first half of the

[81] From Paul Rivet, *Maya Cities*, trans. by M. and L. Kochin (New York: Putnam, 1960), p. 78. Quoted by permission of G. P. Putnam's Sons.

[82] Victor von Hagen, *The Desert Kingdoms of Peru* (London: Weidenfeld and Nicolson, 1965), p. 82; or Collier, *op. cit.*, p. 169.

first millennium.[83] From Peru, knowledge of metallurgy spread northward and eventually reached Mexico early in the second millennium A.D.[84]

In most respects, the *advanced* horticultural societies of Peru resembled the *simple* horticultural societies of Mexico (the use of metal tools and weapons never became widespread enough in Mexico to justify calling any of the Mexican societies *advanced* horticultural). Both had numerous semiurban settlements with populations sometimes in excess of 10,000. Both also had architectural structures of massive

[83] Collier, *op. cit.,* p. 170; or Julian Steward and Louis Faron, *Native Peoples of South America* (New York: McGraw-Hill, 1959), p. 99.

[84] See von Hagen, *Ancient Sun Kingdoms,* p. 62; or Forbes, *op. cit.,* vol. 8, p. 14. Some of the Indians in what is now the United States cold-hammered pure copper prior to contact with Europeans. It is not known whether this represents an independent discovery on their part or was the result of diffusion from Mexico. See Forbes, *op. cit.,* vol. 9, pp. 2–5.

Fig. 8/9   Ruins of Incan fortress. Note the careful masonry; no mortar was used by the Incas

proportions. These were usually of a religious nature in both instances, though religion seems to have been somewhat less central to societal life in Peru. Crafts of many kinds were highly developed in both areas, and social inequality was pronounced. And in both cases there was a small privileged elite of nobles and priests, set apart from the masses of common people whose labors supported them and their activities.

There were also a number of differences, most of them minor. Two deserve special attention, however. First, the intellectual achievements of the Peruvians were somewhat inferior to those of the Mexicans. In particular, they lacked a system of writing—though they did have a primitive system of record keeping which was based on an intricate technique of knotting ropes.

The second important difference was in the political realm. Small, independent city-states were the rule in Mexico until a relatively late date.[85] In Peru, by contrast, empire building began simultaneously with the use of metals for weapons.[86] During the first millennium A.D., conquests were on a very modest scale; the largest Peruvian state controlled a territory of only 20,000 square miles.[87] But in the centuries that followed, empires steadily grew in size, culminating in the Incan Empire. This was the largest empire created by any native people in the New World and one of the largest ever created by any horticultural people. In the short space of a century, a series of Incan rulers built an empire covering 350,000 square miles and containing several million inhabitants.[88]

HORTICULTURAL SOCIETIES IN THE MODERN ERA

In recent centuries, horticultural societies have been found in four parts of the world—the islands of the Pacific, southern Asia, Africa below the Sahara, and the New World. Most of those in the Pacific and the New World were simple horticultural societies; those in Africa and Asia were all advanced. Before European expansion and colonialism in the sixteenth century, horticultural societies occupied about as much of the earth's surface as any societal type. Since then, however, they have declined greatly because of conquest and absorption by more advanced societies and also because of hybridization resulting from cultural diffusion. Except in hybrid form (i.e., as industrializing horticultural societies), it is doubtful that they can survive much longer.

Simple horticultural societies

Simple horticultural societies are found today in only three parts of the world: the remote interior of the Amazon River basin; certain islands of the Pacific, especially

---

[85] Morley, *op. cit.*, pp. 159–161.

[86] Collier, *op. cit.*, pp. 170–173; Steward and Faron, *op. cit.*, pp. 86–100.

[87] Von Hagen, *The Desert Kingdoms*, p. 31.

[88] Steward and Faron, *op. cit.*, pp. 115 and 121.

Fig. 8/10   Sketch of village of simple horticulturalists near coast of North Carolina, by John White (c. 1585)

New Guinea; and parts of the hill country of southeast Asia. In recent centuries, they also occupied much of North and South America.

In most matters where comparisons are possible, the simple horticultural societies of modern times are strikingly similar to the modal type of prehistoric times. In other words, they are usually small, largely self-sufficient, politically autonomous villages with populations ranging from a few dozen to a few hundred.[89] Compared with modern hunting and gathering societies, their settlements are much more permanent in nature; most groups move only every few years, when forced to by the exhaustion of the soil.[90]

---

[89] As noted earlier, the average size of those in Murdock's Ethnographic Atlas sample was 95. In 79 per cent of these societies, communities were politically autonomous under aboriginal conditions.

[90] Only 10 per cent of the hunting and gathering societies in the Ethnographic Atlas sample maintained fairly permanent settlements, and virtually all of these relied on either fishing or horticulture as a secondary source of subsistence. By contrast, 87 per cent of the simple horticultural societies maintained such settlements.

As in prehistoric times, the greater permanence of modern horticultural settlements results in a greater accumulation of goods and the construction of more substantial buildings.[91] These developments are associated with a more diversified production of goods and services and an increase in trade.[92] Finally, as in the simple horticultural societies of the later Neolithic, warfare is fairly common.[93]

A careful comparison of societies in the two eras also reveals some differences. In particular, there are a number of indications that simple horticultural societies of the modern era are not, *on the average*, quite as advanced technologically as their prehistoric counterparts. For example, of those in Murdock's Ethnographic Atlas sample, more than a third did not make pottery and more than half did not practice weaving, both common practices in simple horticultural societies of prehistoric times. Also, nearly half keep no livestock.[94] These differences are at least partly due to environmental factors (e.g., the New World has few native animals suitable for domestication). As a result of these differences in technology, the modern groups have also been, on the average, a bit less developed in most other respects (e.g., size, division of labor, etc.).

As with hunting and gathering societies, the ethnographic record not only supports the view provided by archaeology, but broadens and enriches it. For example, modern studies show that ties of kinship are extremely important in simple horticultural societies. In many instances, especially in the less advanced, these ties provide the basic framework of the social system.[95] This is hardly surprising in view of the small size of these groups: the average individual is related in some way to many, perhaps most, of those with whom he comes in contact, and therefore he must take his kinship obligations into account in dealing with them. The absence of most types of competing social systems (e.g., craft guilds, political parties, etc.) further enhances the importance of kinship.

Kinship systems in these societies are sometimes very complex, with intricate systems of rules governing relations between many categories of kin. Extended family groups are quite common and usually very important, since they perform a number of essential functions for their members.[96] Above all, they function as *mutual aid*

---

[91] A number of instances are reported in which simple horticulturalists have built structures 50 or more feet long. The Kiwai Papuans probably hold the record among modern simple horticulturalists, having constructed one building 519 feet long. See Gunnar Landtman, *The Kiwai Papuans of British New Guinea* (London: Macmillan, 1927), p. 5. For other examples, see Gerhard Lenski, *Power and Privilege* (New York: McGraw-Hill, 1966), p. 121.

[92] Lenski, *op. cit.*, pp. 124–125.

[93] *Ibid.*, p. 122.

[94] These are my own calculations from Murdock's sample of 915 societies.

[95] See, for example, Steward and Faron's statement (*op. cit.*, p. 300), with reference to the villagers who occupied most of the northern half of South America, that "kinship was the basis of society throughout most of this area." Many similar statements could be cited.

[96] See E. Adamson Hoebel, *Anthropology* (New York: McGraw-Hill, 1966), pp. 374–376, for a good brief summary of these functions.

Fig. 8/11 Aerial view of Yana-mamö village, Brazil. The village is built in the shape of a bandshell; the structure is about 70 feet in diameter and 30 feet high (see Fig. 8/12 for an interior view). The village contains about sixty people Gardens are shown in the fore-ground, the chief crops being plantains and manioc

associations, providing the individual with protection against his enemies and with economic support when needed. While both of these functions are very important, the former is crucial because the political system in these societies is still much too primitive to provide effective police services. Extended families also perform important regulatory functions in the area of marriage, and they sometimes have important religious functions as well. Finally, the most powerful or most respected extended family often assumes leadership functions for the entire community with its head serving as headman for the village.

One interesting and significant feature of the kinship system in these societies is the emphasis many of them give to ties with the mother's relatives. In this respect, horticultural societies, both simple and advanced, are unique. This can be seen clearly in the Ethnographic Atlas sample, where the percentage of societies of various kinds having matrilineal kin groups (i.e., extended family groups organized on the basis of common descent through the female line) were as follows:[97]

Hunting and gathering societies	10%
Simple horticultural societies	26%
Advanced horticultural societies	27%
Agrarian societies	4%

Another indication of the importance attached to kinship ties on the female side is the frequency with which married couples live with or near the wife's female

[97] For similar findings based on Murdock's earlier sample of 565 societies, see David Aberle, ''Matrilineal Descent in Cross-cultural Perspective,'' in David Schneider and Kathleen Gough (eds.), *Matrilineal Kinship* (Berkeley: University of California Press, 1961), table 17-4, p. 677.

Fig. 8/12 Yanamamö woman harvesting plantains, a type of banana that is usually cooked before eating. Plantains and manioc (a starchy tuber) provide about 70 per cent of their caloric intake

matrilineal relatives (i.e., the practice known as matrilocality). Using the Ethnographic Atlas sample again, the frequency in different societal types was as follows:

Hunting and gathering societies	3%
Simple horticultural societies	15%
Advanced horticultural societies	5%
Agrarian societies	1%

These unusual patterns seem to be linked with the women's contribution to subsistence in horticultural societies: in many of these groups, they do most of the work of cultivation (see Table 8/1). Where men engage in other activities that make a substantial contribution to the subsistence needs of the group (i.e., by hunting or

Table 8/1   The division of labor between the sexes in horticultural and agrarian societies

	Percentage distribution:				
Type of society	Farming primarily a female responsibility	Both sexes share equally	Farming primarily a male responsibility	Total	Number of societies
Simple horticultural	37	49	14	100	51
Advanced horticultural	50	27	23	100	142
Agrarian	7	37	56	100	43

Source: Murdock's Ethnographic Atlas sample of 915 societies.

Table 8/2   Matrilineality and matrilocality among simple horticultural societies, by percentage of subsistence obtained by hunting and herding

Percentage of subsistence obtained by hunting and herding*	Percentage of societies matrilineal	Percentage of societies matrilocal	Number of cases
26 per cent or more	13	6	16
16 to 25 per cent	25	17	28–29†
Less than 15 per cent	39	22	23

* These figures are estimates (see footnote, Table 7/4).
† Information was available on matrilineality for 28 societies, and on matrilocality for 29.
Source: Murdock's Ethnographic Atlas sample of 915 societies.

herding), matrilineal and matrilocal patterns are not so likely to develop. But where such contributions are lacking, or are of minor importance, these patterns are much more common (see Table 8/2).[98]

Though village autonomy is still the rule in simple horticultural societies, as in hunting and gathering, the frequency of multicommunity societies is much

---

[98] Aberle reached a similar conclusion (*op. cit.*, p. 725). He states that "in general, matriliny is associated with horticulture, in the absence of major activities carried on and coordinated by males . . ."

greater.[99] These groups usually contain only a handful of villages, seldom more than ten.[100] Usually they have been formed by a process of confederation involving villages that belong to a single tribe.[101] In most instances, military considerations of either an offensive or defensive nature provide the motivation to confederate.

Despite the formation of these larger, more inclusive societies, the power of political leaders remains quite limited in nearly all simple horticultural societies. Except in matters of war and relations with other societies, local villages enjoy virtual autonomy. Both the village headman and the tribal chief depend more on persuasion than coercion to achieve their goals. In part this is a result of the limited development of the governmental system (i.e., a leader has few subordinates so dependent on him that they are obliged to carry out his instructions). In part it is due to the absence of the kinds of weapons that could be monopolized by a governing class to give it the power to control the rest of the population (bronze weapons, for example, are expensive and can be made only by specialists and therefore their production can be monopolized by a wealthy minority).

In some simple horticultural societies, shamans also serve as headmen or chiefs because of the awe or respect in which they are held.[102] In other societies, secular leaders assume important religious functions and become quasi-religious figures. As one writer notes, a "chief's influence is definitely enhanced when he combines religious with secular functions."[103] In short, in many simple horticultural societies of the modern era, just as in the prehistoric past, church and state are closely linked and sometimes almost become one.

The only other important basis of political power in these societies is membership in a large and prosperous kin group. As we noted previously, the senior member and leader of the largest, most powerful, or most respected lineage group often becomes the village headman or tribal chief.[104] At a minimum, he can usually count

---

[99] Multicommunity societies constitute only 2 per cent of all pure hunting and gathering societies (i.e., those in which fishing and horticulture are not important secondary sources of subsistence), but 23 per cent of all simple horticultural societies.

[100] Lenski, *op. cit.*, pp. 119–120.

[101] For an early statement of this, see Lewis Henry Morgan, *Ancient Society* (Cambridge, Mass.: Belknap Press, 1964, first published 1877), pp. 109ff.

[102] This seems to have been quite common in South America. See Steward and Faron, *op. cit.*, p. 301, on the Indians of eastern Brazil and the Amazon basin; or Julian Steward, "The Tribes of the Montaña and Bolivian East Andes," in Julian Steward (ed.), *Handbook of South American Indians*, Smithsonian Institution, Bureau of American Ethnology, Bulletin 143 (1946–50) vol. III, p. 528. For a slightly different pattern in North America, see Irving Goldman, "The Zuni Indians of New Mexico," in Margaret Mead (ed.), *Cooperation and Competition Among Primitive Peoples*, rev. ed. (Boston: Beacon Press, 1961), p. 313.

[103] Robert Lowie, "Social and Political Organization," in Steward, *Handbook*, vol. V, p. 345. For examples of this, see the *Handbook*, vol. III, pp. 85, 355, 419, and 478. See also Steward and Faron, *op. cit.*, p. 244.

[104] See, for example, Alfred Metraux, *Native Tribes of Eastern Bolivia and Western Matto Grosso*, Smithsonian Institution, Bureau of American Ethnology, Bulletin 134 (1942), p. 39, on the Araona; or Leopold Pospisil, "Kaupauku Papuan Political Structure," in F. Ray (ed.), *Systems of Political Control and Bureaucracy in Human Societies*, Proceedings of the 1958 Meetings of the American Ethnological Society, p. 18.

on the support of his kinsmen, and, in a society with such limited political development, this is a substantial political resource.

Social inequality is generally rather limited, though societies differ in this. While extremes of wealth and political power are absent, substantial differences in prestige are not uncommon. Political and religious leaders usually enjoy high status, but this depends far more on their achievements than on mere occupancy of the office. There are few sinecures in these societies. Other bases of status include military prowess (which is highly honored in nearly all societies), skill in oratory, age,

Fig. 8/13 Women planting taro in a simple horticultural society in New Guinea. Note the stumps which remain in the field, a practice which is common among horticulturists. They do not clear fields as completely as agriculturalists, who use the plow

lineage, and in some cases the possession of wealth in the form of wives, pigs, and ornaments.[105] Each society tends to have its own peculiar combination of these criteria.

The more advanced the technology and economy of a simple horticultural society, the greater tends to be the degree of social inequality in it. Societies that practice irrigation, own domesticated animals, or practice metallurgy for ornamental and ceremonial purposes are usually less egalitarian than groups that have not taken these steps. We can see this quite clearly when we compare the villagers of eastern Brazil and the Amazon river basin with their more advanced neighbors to the north and west who, in pre-Spanish days, practiced irrigation and metallurgy (the metal they used was gold, which is too soft for use in tools and weapons, and therefore they cannot be considered advanced horticulturalists). Hereditary class differences were absent in the former groups but quite common in the latter, where a hereditary governing class of chiefs and nobles was set apart from the larger class of commoners.[106]

As we saw in Chapter 6, warfare is much more common among simple horticulturalists than among hunters and gatherers. This is probably a by-product of the increased "leisure" for men which the new economy made possible. In most hunting and gathering societies men spend most of their waking hours in subsistence activities; the inability to store and accumulate food makes it impossible for them to devote sustained periods to other activities. With the change to horticulture, most of the burden of providing subsistence shifts to the women. A common pattern in these societies is for the men to perform the occasional heavy work of clearing new fields, leaving the lighter but more time-consuming work of planting, cultivating, and harvesting to the women. Though the men still hunt, this is no longer such an essential activity and they can use their new freedom for other things. A number of possibilities are open to them. Some spend more time on the arts and crafts. Others devote more time to religious and ceremonial activities.[107] The most popular use of the new freedom, however, is making war.[108]

There are several reasons for this. Warfare, as we have seen, is a natural substitute for hunting. Like hunting, it provides a testing ground for masculine skills and therefore is an appropriate basis for status competition. Furthermore, skill in warfare is essential to the welfare of these societies in a way that hunting no longer is.

As warfare grows in importance in a society, several new patterns develop.

---

[105] For a more detailed discussion of these bases of status, see Lenski, *op. cit.*, pp. 126–131.

[106] See Steward and Faron, *op. cit.*, pp. 302–303, on the former, and pp. 213–214, 243, 248–249, etc., on the latter.

[107] This was the chief use of the new freedom by the Pueblo Indians of the American southwest.

[108] For an excellent description of the role of warfare in the life of one South American tribe, see Napoleon Chagnon, "Yanamamö Social Organization and Warfare," *Natural History*, 76 (December, 1967), pp. 44–48.

Fig. 8/14 Yanamamö men, intoxicated on ebene, a hallucinogenic drug, prepare for a "friendly" duel with a neighboring village with which they are allied. Such duels often turn violent and lead to warfare. This is an interior view of the village shown in Fig. 8/11

First and foremost is the cult of the warrior, which heaps honors on successful fighters. Record keeping and publicity are no less important to these warrior-heroes than to modern athlete-heroes, and in the absence of statisticians and sports writers, they invent techniques of their own—especially trophy taking. Some of the more popular trophies are scalps, skulls, and shrunken heads, all of which are preserved and displayed like modern athletic trophies.

Ceremonial cannibalism, a surprisingly widespread practice among simple horticultural societies, may have developed as a by-product of trophy collecting. Utilitarian cannibalism (i.e., eating other humans to satisfy serious hunger) is an ancient practice, traceable to distant prehistoric times, but ceremonial cannibalism seems a more recent invention. The basic idea underlying it is the belief that one can appropriate for himself the valued qualities of a conquered enemy by eating his body.[109] Ceremonial cannibalism is usually surrounded by a complex, and often prolonged, set of rituals, as the following account from South America indicates:

---

[109] Lest this idea appear utterly fanciful, it should be noted that in recent years experimental psychologists have shown that when earthworms that have learned certain simple responses are ground up and fed to other earthworms, the latter show these same responses without training. See especially the work of James McConnell as reported in *The Wormrunner's Digest*.

Fig. 8/15 Three Jivaro tsantsas. The Jivaro Indians of western South America collected heads as trophies of their prowess. They developed a special technique for shrinking and preserving the heads of their victims. The skin was removed from the skull and hot sand poured in repeatedly to dry and shrink it, after which the lips were sewed together

The prisoners taken by a Tupinamba war party were received with manifestations of anger, scorn, and derision, but after the first hostile outburst, they were not hampered in their movements nor were they unkindly treated. Their captors, whose quarters they shared, treated them as relatives. The prisoners generally married village girls, very often the sisters or daughters of their masters, or, in certain cases, the widow of a dead warrior whose hammock and ornaments they used. They received fields for their maintenance, they were free to hunt and fish, and they were reminded of their servile condition by few restrictions and humiliations.

The period of captivity lasted from a few months to several years. When, finally, the date for the execution had been set by the village council, invitations were sent to nearby villages to join in the celebration. The ritual for the slaughter of a captive was worked out to the most minute detail. The club and cord which figured prominently in the ceremony were carefully painted and decorated in accordance with strict rules. For three days before the event, the village women danced, sang, and tormented the victim with descriptions of his impending fate. On the eve of his execution a mock repetition of his capture took place, during which the prisoner was allowed to escape but was immediately retaken; the man who overpowered him in a wrestling match adopted a new name, as did the ceremonial executioner.

The prisoner spent his last night dancing, pelting his tormentors, and singing songs which foretold their ruin and proclaimed his pride at dying as a warrior. In the morning he was dragged to the plaza by old women amidst shouts, songs, and music. The ceremonial rope was removed from his neck and tied around his waist, and it was held at both ends by two or more men. The victim was once more permitted to give vent to his feelings by throwing fruit or potsherds at his enemies. The executioner, who appeared painted and dressed in a long feather cloak, derided the victim, who boasted of his past deeds and predicted that his relatives would avenge him.

The actual execution was a cruel game. The prisoner was allowed sufficient freedom of movement to dodge the blows aimed at him; sometimes a club was put in his hands so that he could parry the blows without being able to strike back. When at last he fell, his skull shattered, everyone shouted and whistled. Old women rushed in to drink the warm blood, children were invited to dip their hands in it, and mothers smeared their nipples so that even infants could have a taste. While the quartered body was being roasted on a babracot the old women, who were the most eager to taste human flesh, licked the grease running from the sticks. Certain delicate or sacred portions, such as the fingers and the grease around the liver, were given to distinguished guests.[110]

The high incidence of warfare in simple horticultural societies serves to keep open the channels of vertical mobility. Almost every boy becomes a warrior and thus has a chance to win high honors and great influence. At the same time, however, a comparison of hunting and gathering and simple horticultural societies reveals a strengthening of those elements in the social system that make it possible for favored members of one generation to transmit their advantages to their children. To begin

---

[110] Alfred Métraux, "Warfare-Cannibalism-Trophies," in Julian Steward (ed.), *Handbook of South American Indians*, Smithsonian Institution, Bureau of American Ethnology, Bulletin 143 (1948), vol. V, pp. 400–401. Quoted by permission of the Bureau of American Ethnology.

with, the general organizational development associated with horticultural societies contributes to that end. The occupants of key positions, such as headmen, are somewhat less dependent on their personal skills than are their counterparts in hunting and gathering groups. The institutional structure of many of these societies seems to have evolved to the point where a leader no longer needs to prove that he is the best man in the group, but only that he is competent to fill the position. In large part this is possible because a headman or chief in a simple horticultural society often has assistants to help him, as well as other resources besides his own personal abilities to draw on. Another factor with a similar effect is the greater amount of private property (e.g., pigs and valued ornaments) that can be transmitted from one generation to the next. Finally, the greater strength of extended family groups, and the greater inequality among them, contribute to this end. On balance, therefore, the accident of birth—being born into one family rather than another—counts for more in simple horticultural societies than in hunting and gathering.

Advanced horticultural societies

For several centuries, advanced horticultural societies have been limited to two parts of the world, sub-Saharan Africa and southeast Asia. In sub-Saharan Africa they occupied almost all of the land until recently; other types of societies—hunters and gatherers, herders, and fishers—were relatively few in number. In southeast Asia, on the other hand, *agrarian* societies occupied most of the land.

These advanced horticulturalists of modern times differ in one important respect from their prehistoric predecessors: the dominant metal in their societies has been iron, not copper or bronze. This fact is important because iron ores are much more plentiful than copper and tin, and iron is therefore available in sufficient quantity to permit its use in ordinary tools as well as in weapons.

The history of Africa proves once again that the evolutionary process does not compel societies to follow exactly the same pattern of development. Most of sub-Saharan Africa never experienced a Bronze Age. During the period when bronze was dominant in the Middle East, cultural contacts between Egypt and the territories to the south were minimal.[111] By the time there was sufficient contact to permit diffusion of specialized skills like metallurgy, iron had become dominant.

Compared with hunting and gathering or simple horticultural societies, advanced horticultural are usually larger and more complex. Table 6/2 (page 131) summarizes the evidence from Murdock's sample. *Communities* in advanced horticultural societies are three times larger than those in simple horticultural societies, and seven times larger than those in hunting and gathering. A comparison of the size of *societies* is even more striking: on the average, advanced horticultural

---

[111] Sonia Cole, *The Prehistory of East Africa* (New York: Mentor, 1965), p. 299.

Fig. 8/16 Partial view of village of advanced horticulturalists, Dahomey

societies are 60 times the size of simple horticultural and 140 times the size of hunting and gathering.[112]

As one would expect, advanced horticultural societies are also organizationally more complex. Of those in Murdock's sample, some have as many as *four* layers of government above the local community; no simple horticultural society in the sample has more than *two* layers. These data also show that village autonomy is the rule in simple horticultural societies but the exception in advanced horticultural. In 79 per cent of the former, villages are autonomous; in 71 per cent of the latter they are *not*.

Another evidence of organizational complexity is the extent of occupational specialization. Table 6/3 shows that craft specialization is much more common

---

[112] If one uses the arithmetic mean rather than the median, which is used in Table 6/2, and if one assumes that the means for Murdock's three categories of states are 5,000, 50,000, and 500,000, then the differential between simple and advanced horticultural drops to 30—still a substantial figure. The differential between advanced horticultural and hunting and gathering societies remains the same.

Fig. 8/17   Basket weaver at work beside his home, Guinea

in advanced horticultural societies than in simple. In six basic areas of production, craft specialization was present only 2 per cent of the time in simple horticultural societies, but 28 per cent in advanced.

Murdock's data also show that a marked increase in social inequality is associated with the emergence of advanced horticultural societies. Class stratification was reported in only 17 per cent of the simple horticultural societies, as opposed to 54 per cent of the advanced (see Table 6/8). In addition, the class systems of the latter are generally more complex, involve greater degrees of inequality, and are more often hereditary.[113] The presence of slavery in 83 per cent of the advanced horticultural societies, but only 14 per cent of the simple, is a striking illustration of this (see Table 6/7).

This growth in social inequality is closely linked with the growth of government. A generation ago, Meyer Fortes, one of the pioneer students of African political systems, argued that most African societies fell into one of two basic categories: those "which have centralized authority, administrative machinery, and judicial

---

[113] Of the simple horticultural societies, 15 per cent had hereditary systems of stratification, compared to 47 per cent of the advanced horticultural societies. None of the simple had complex systems of stratification (i.e., three or more classes apart from slaves), compared with 7 per cent of the advanced.

institutions—in short, a government—and in which cleavages of wealth, privilege, and status correspond to the distribution of authority"; and those that had none of these attributes.[114] Though recent studies suggest that this twofold division is something of an oversimplification, they confirm that African societies differ in the ways described by Fortes and that there is a strong relationship between the development of the state and the growth of social inequality.[115]

The differences in African political systems afford a valuable opportunity for studying the processes that promote the development of the state. One student of east Africa, a region with marked differences in political development, suggests one important factor there has been the emergence of groups of retainers, men who are dependent for their safety and livelihood on the leaders of powerful extended family groups.[116] Individuals are forced into this situation when they lose the support of their own extended family and are thrown on their own. This can happen because of misconduct, leading to expulsion from the group, or it can result from the destruction or disintegration of their kin group because of war, famine, or other disaster. An isolated individual cannot survive for long in east Africa; his only hope is to attach himself to some kin group on whatever terms he can get. Usually the price is acceptance of the authority of the group's leader.

Since there is a natural tendency for these "kinless" men to attach themselves to the most powerful leaders, power tends to pyramid and the powerful become more powerful. This tendency is reinforced by the practice of polygyny. Strong kin groups tend to be wealthy, and wealthy groups can purchase more wives, who bear more sons and fighting men. Finally, the position of successful family groups and their leaders is strengthened by the development of myths that attribute special qualities to these leaders (e.g., the power to control rain). In these ways, marked imbalances gradually develop in size, wealth, and power of kin groups.

The final link in this chain is forged when less powerful extended families, or even whole communities, are brought under the control of a more powerful family. Many times this is the result of conquest, but more often than one might imagine it comes about by the voluntary action of the weaker group, which wishes to avail itself of the resources of the stronger group (e.g., its military strength for protection against enemies, its leader's magical powers, or its ability to maintain law and order and end a destructive cycle of blood revenge and family feuds).

The subordinate group in these cases is usually allowed to retain its land, and its leader usually keeps his authority within the group. The subordinate group must

---

[114] Meyer Fortes in Fortes and E. E. Pritchard (eds.), *African Political Systems* (London: Oxford, 1940), p. 5.

[115] In one recent study of twenty-two African horticultural societies, a correlation of .67 (Kendall's tau) was found between level of political development and level of social inequality (see Lenski, *op. cit.*, p. 163). See also Basil Davidson with F. K. Buah, *A History of West Africa: To the Nineteenth Century* (Garden City, N.Y.: Doubleday Anchor, 1966), p. 174.

[116] See Lucy Mair, *Primitive Government* (Baltimore: Penguin, 1962), especially chap. 4. The discussion that follows is based largely on her work.

Fig. 8/18   Woman spreading rice to dry in the sun, Liberia

pay tribute to the leader of the dominant group, however, thus insuring the creation of an economic surplus. The leader of the dominant group uses this surplus to support his kinsmen and retainers, which increases their dependence on him, and—it is hoped—their loyalty as well.

One might suppose that these processes, once set in motion, would continue until eventually all of Africa was brought under a single authority. Actually, however, powerful countervailing forces prevent this from happening. Chief among these are the limitations of technology, especially in the area of transportation. Advanced horticulturalists in Africa, as in the New World, had no knowledge of the wheel and used no draft animals until contact with Europeans. As a result, the further a ruler's power extended into outlying areas, the weaker it became. These areas were vulnerable to attack by foreign enemies, but even more serious, they were vulnerable to revolt. From the territorial standpoint, the largest kingdom ever to develop in sub-Saharan Africa was probably the kingdom (or empire) of Mali. In the early fourteenth century, it controlled approximately 500,000 square miles in the western Sudan.[117] Most African kingdoms were much smaller.

By the standards of modern industrial societies, the governments of Africa's advanced horticultural societies were extremely unstable. Revolts were a common occurrence, not only in outlying provinces but even in the capitals. These were seldom, if ever, popular risings. Rather, they were instigated by powerful members of the nobility, often the king's own brothers.[118] This pattern was so common that the Zulus developed the proverb that "the king should not eat with his brothers lest they poison him."[119]

In virtually all of the politically advanced societies of horticultural Africa there was a sharply defined cleavage between an hereditary nobility and the mass of common people. Historically, this distinction grew out of the state-building process.[120] The nobles were usually the descendants of past rulers and their chief

---

[117] Estimated from the map in Davidson, *op. cit.*, p. 56.

[118] See, for example, I. Schapera, *Government and Politics in Tribal Societies* (London: Watts, 1956), pp. 153ff.

[119] *Ibid.*, p. 169. See also the Swazi proverb that "nobles are the chief's murderers."

[120] See, for example, Davidson, *op. cit.*, chaps. 14.

Fig. 8/19   Early bronze casting of Dahomean chief and his entourage of relatives and retainers. Note the fine workmanship, a native art form in West Africa predating European contact

lieutenants or hereditary leaders of groups that had been subordinated. The nobles were a warrior aristocracy that was supported by the labors of the common people. Below the commoners there was often a class of slaves, many of them captives taken in war. As in other horticultural societies, they were frequently slaughtered as human sacrifices.

In the advanced horticultural societies of Africa, as in the New World and elsewhere, religion and politics were intimately related. In many instances the king was viewed as divine, or as having personal access to divine powers.[121] This undoubtedly served to legitimize their many tyrannical and exploitative practices. And it helps explain why no efforts were made to establish other kinds of political systems: given the ideological heritage of these societies, such a thing was inconceivable. This ideology did not protect a ruler against attacks from his kinsmen, however, since they shared his special religious status and hence were qualified to assume the duties and privileges of the royal office—if only they could seize it.

A comparison of the politically advanced societies of sub-Saharan Africa with those that remained autonomous villages shows that the former are more developed in other ways as well. For example, they are far likelier to have full-time craft specialization.[122] Also, they are more likely to have urban or semiurban settlements—a few with populations of 20,000 or more.[123]

Before concluding this discussion of advanced horticultural societies in the modern era, a brief comment on those in southeast Asia is necessary. The striking feature of these societies is their relative backwardness, especially from the standpoint of political development. In most instances they remain on the level of village autonomy, and when multicommunity societies do develop, they are invariably small.[124] Urban or semiurban settlements are absent. The reason for this appears to be ecological. Centuries ago this region came under the domination of more powerful agrarian societies. Horticultural societies usually survived only in hill country, where transportation was difficult and the land unsuitable for the plow and permanent cultivation. This combination of more powerful neighbors and the deficiencies of their own territories apparently prevented anything but the most limited kind of development.

---

[121] See, for example, George Peter Murdock, *Africa: Its Peoples and Their Culture History* (New York: McGraw-Hill, 1959), p. 37.

[122] In an earlier volume, I reported finding a correlation of .63 between level of craft specialization and political development in a sample of twenty-two African horticultural societies (see Lenski, *op. cit.*, p. 162). At that time I viewed this relation as indicating the influence of technology on political development. On further reflection I am inclined to think this is a two-way relationship, and that the primary causal flow is from political development to craft specialization rather than the reverse.

[123] See, for example, P. C. Lloyd, "The Yoruba of Nigeria," in James Gibbs (ed.), *Peoples of Africa* (New York: Holt, 1965), pp. 554–556.

[124] For an example of a multicommunity society, see P. R. T. Gurdon, *The Khasis* (London: Macmillan, 1914). This author reports that these people were divided into fifteen small states averaging 15,000 in population and controlling about 400 square miles apiece (pp. 1 and 66).

In this connection it should be noted that ecological factors of a different type had a similar effect in certain parts of Africa. Recent research indicates that political development was quite limited in the tropical rain forests. Apparently the lush growth of vegetation and other hindrances to the movement of armies and goods in such areas made it impossible to build and maintain extensive kingdoms.[125]

HORTICULTURAL SOCIETIES IN EVOLUTIONARY PERSPECTIVE

Few events in human history can match in importance the discovery of the principles of plant cultivation. It is no exaggeration to say that the discovery of horticulture in the realm of technology was comparable to the invention of symbols in the realm of communication. Each was a decisive break with the animal world. Hunting and gathering, like the use of signals, are techniques that man inherited from his pre-human ancestors. Horticulture and symbols, by contrast, are uniquely human.

Among the many changes brought about by the adoption of horticulture, three stand out for their tremendous importance: (1) the growth of the human population, (2) the greater permanence of their settlements, and (3) the possibility of establishing a stable economic surplus. More people meant more minds at work trying to improve the conditions of human life, with all that implies for the rate of technological advance. More permanent settlements meant more opportunity for people to accumulate possessions; hence a greater incentive for them to exercise inventiveness and creativity in the productive realm. A stable economic surplus meant new organizational opportunities, particularly opportunities for occupational and institutional specialization. Collectively, these developments added up to a revolutionary change in the conditions of human life.

Not all horticultural peoples took full advantage of the new opportunities. Some remained on the level of the relatively undifferentiated, autonomous farm village. This suggests that horticulture is a necessary condition, but not a sufficient cause, for the emergence of more complex social systems. The formation of such systems requires some kind of specialized institution that will appropriate part of what is produced before the growth of population consumes all of it. Sometimes religious institutions perform this function, motivating men to offer up their surplus to the gods and to the priests who serve them. In other instances political institutions collect the surplus by means of taxes and tribute. In either case, a segment of the population is freed from the task of providing its own food supply and permitted to engage in specialized activities of various kinds.

Before concluding this summary, a brief comment on the ethical consequences of the horticultural revolution is needed, lest anyone suppose that the technological and social organizational progress achieved by horticultural societies implies ethical progress as well. As numerous scholars have noted, it is one of the great

---

[125] Lenski, *op. cit.*, pp. 160–162. See also Davidson, *op. cit.*, pp. 76–77.

ironies of evolution that progress in the technological and social organizational spheres is often linked with ethical regress. The emergence of horticultural societies provides several striking examples. Some of the most shocking, by the standards of modern industrial societies, are the increased head hunting, scalp taking, cannibalism, human sacrifice, and slavery, all of which are much more common in the technologically and organizationally progressive horticultural societies than in the more backward hunting and gathering groups.

Another development that can be regarded as ethical regression is the decline in the practice of sharing and the growing acceptance of economic and other kinds of inequality. This is not as simple a matter as it seems on the surface, however, As we have seen, the growth of inequality appears to be an inevitable consequence of the formation of an economic surplus in societies at this stage of development. And the formation of an economic surplus seems to be a prerequisite for the development of civilization, with all that that implies—and for the improvement of the standard of living. In other words, without an economic surplus, all the benefits of technological advance would be swallowed up by population growth, and the result would simply be more people living at the subsistence level. Our view of the ethics of this growth in inequality, therefore, depends largely on whether we take a short-term or long-term view. If we judge it from the standpoint of the several generations most immediately involved, we will probably conclude that it was ethically regressive. But if we judge it from the standpoint of all subsequent generations, we might very well take the opposite view. This is a problem to which we will want to return in the final chapter.

Chapter 9
Agrarian Societies

During the horticultural era there were many important advances in farming: scores of new plants were brought under cultivation; a number of new animals were domesticated; and the principles of orchard husbandry, irrigation, and fermentation were discovered. Each of these had a significant effect on human societies, but none had the impact of the plow, which some have called "the prerequisite of civilization."[1]

To appreciate the importance of the plow, we need to keep in mind two basic problems that confront farmers everywhere: controlling weeds and maintaining the fertility of the soil.[2] With traditional horticultural tools and techniques, both of these problems grow more severe the longer a plot is cultivated. Weeds multiply faster than horticulturalists with their hoes can root them out. At the same time, the soil's nutrients seep into the ground, below the reach of plants and too deep to be returned to the surface with hoes or other simple tools. Within a few years, the yield usually becomes so small that the cultivator abandons the plot and moves elsewhere.[3]

The plow, if it did not eliminate these problems, at least reduced them to manageable proportions and made the permanent cultivation of fields a common practice for the first time in history. Because it turns the soil over to a greater depth than the hoe, the plow buries weeds, not only killing them but adding humus to the soil. Deeper cultivation also brings back to the surface the nutrients that have seeped below root level.

---

[1] Gudmund Hatt, "Farming of Non-European Peoples," in E. Cecil Curwen and Gudmund Hatt, *Plough and Pasture: The Early History of Farming* (New York: Collier, 1961), p. 218.

[2] This paragraph and the one which follows are based on B. H. Farmer, "Agriculture: Comparative Technology," in *International Encyclopedia of the Social Sciences* (New York: Macmillan and Free Press, 1968), vol. 1, pp. 204–205.

[3] In a few instances, horticulturalists have been able to maintain continual cultivation because of irrigation (natural or artificial) or fertilization. See, for example, *ibid.,* p. 204.

The invention of the plow paved the way for another crucial innovation, the harnessing of animal energy.[4] As long as the digging stick and hoe were the basic tools of cultivation, men and women had to supply the energy. But the plow could be pulled, and it did not take long for people to discover that oxen could do the job, and do it more efficiently. The importance of this discovery can hardly be exaggerated, since it established a principle with broad applicability. As V. Gordon Childe has stated, "The ox was the first step to the steam engine and the [gasoline] motor."[5]

More immediately, however, the harnessing of animal energy relieved man of one of the more exhausting forms of labor required by the new mode of food production and led to greatly increased productivity. With a plow and a pair of oxen, a man could cultivate a far larger area than he could with a hoe.[6] In addition, the use of oxen led, in many societies, to stall-feeding, and this in turn led to the use of manure, a practice which contributed further to soil fertility.[7] In short, the shift from the hoe to the plow meant fields kept permanently under cultivation, larger crops, and the potentiality of a much larger economic surplus and more complex forms of social organization.[8]

SIMPLE AGRARIAN SOCIETIES

The earliest evidence of the plow comes from Mesopotamian cylinder seals and Egyptian paintings dating from a little before 3000 B.C.[9] Modern research indicates that the plow, like so many other innovations since the Paleolithic, presupposed certain earlier inventions and discoveries—underlining again the cumulative nature

---

[4] See Hatt, *op. cit.*, pp. 217–218.

[5] V. Gordon Childe, *What Happened in History* (Baltimore: Penguin, 1964), p. 89.

[6] Childe, *Man Makes Himself* (New York: Mentor, 1951), p. 100.

[7] Farmer, *op. cit.*, p. 205.

[8] See Childe, *Man Makes Himself*, p. 100. In recent years, some have argued that agriculture is not really a more efficient system of food production than horticulture, but that horticulture is more efficient in the tropics, agriculture in temperate regions. To support their views, they cite a number of instances in which farmers familiar with both methods chose horticulture and, in a few instances, reverted from agriculture to horticulture because the latter was more productive.

Though there are undoubtedly some areas in the world where horticultural techniques are more efficient than agricultural, these are certainly atypical (a 1957 study by the Food and Agriculture Organization of the United Nations showed that only 7 per cent of the world's population were using horticultural techniques, and many of these people were using them because of ignorance of the alternative). Furthermore, horticultural societies have clearly not achieved the efficiency in other areas of technology or the complexity of social organization and ideology that agrarian societies have. At best, the most advanced of the former can be compared with the least advanced of the latter. In short, the overall evolutionary potential of a horticultural technology is greatly inferior to that of an agricultural.

Though I know of no single paper that provides a comprehensive, balanced analysis of this important problem, a good understanding of it may be gained from R. F. Watters' excellent paper, "The Nature of Shifting Cultivation: A Review of Recent Research," *Pacific Viewpoint*, 1 (1960), pp. 59–99, especially pp. 77–95.

[9] E. Cecil Curwen, "Prehistoric Farming of Europe and the Near East," in Curwen and Hatt, *op. cit.*, pp. 64–65; or C. W. Bishop, "The Origin and Early Diffusion of the Traction Plow," *Antiquity*, 10 (1936), p. 261.

Fig. 9/1 Early Egyptian ox-drawn plow (c. 2700 B.C.). Note the primitive method of harnessing the animals—a simple bar attached to their horns

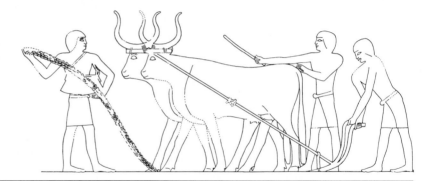

of technological change. The first plows of the Mesopotamians and Egyptians were simply modified versions of the hoe, the basic farm implement of all advanced horticultural societies. In the earliest period, the plow was probably pulled by men, but before long, cattle and oxen began to be used for pulling, greatly increasing the efficiency of the operation.

As in the case of horticulture, the techniques of agriculture spread by diffusion until agrarian societies were eventually established throughout most of Europe and much of North Africa and Asia. For reasons that remain obscure, use of the plow never spread to sub-Saharan Africa until the period of European colonialism. In the New World, too, it was unknown until introduced by Europeans.

The full impact of the new technology was not felt immediately in either Mesopotamia or Egypt. Nevertheless, the shift from horticulture to agriculture was quickly followed by several important developments, notably, the invention of writing, the rise of urban communities, and the beginnings of empire building (e.g., in Egypt, this led to the unification of the entire country under a single ruler for the first time in history).[10]

As we have seen, similar developments occurred (though at later dates) in horticultural societies in China and Mexico, proving that an agrarian economy was not a *necessary* precondition for literacy, urbanism, and imperialism. But the rarity of these phenomena in horticultural societies and their frequency in agrarian societies indicate that the shift to agriculture, by increasing productivity, greatly increased the probability of their occurrence.[11]

---

[10] Historians have long spoken of this period as "the dawn of civilization," treating either the invention of writing or the rise of cities as the basic characteristic of a civilized society. Recently some scholars have argued that Egypt developed a civilization without cities. See, for example, John A. Wilson, "Civilization Without Cities," in Carl Kraeling and Robert Adams (eds.), *City Invincible: A Symposium on Urbanization and Cultural Development in the Ancient Near East* (Chicago: University of Chicago Press, 1960), pp. 124–136; or William McNeill, *The Rise of the West: A History of the Human Community* (New York: Mentor, 1963), pp. 87–88. While there were surely differences between Egyptian and Mesopotamian cities, it seems to be semantic gamesmanship to deny the existence of Egypt's. Several of the commentators on Wilson's paper make just this point (see Kraeling and Adams, *op. cit.*, pp. 136–162). Especially telling was the comment of one Mesopotamian specialist who noted that when the Assyrians came to Egypt, they spoke of "hundreds of cities" (*ibid.*, p. 140).

[11] See the earlier discussion of deterministic versus probabilistic theories, p. 59.

The role of religion in the formation of the surplus

In early Mesopotamia and Egypt, religion was an extremely powerful force in the life of society. Mesopotamian theology held that "man was . . . created for one purpose only: to serve the gods by supplying them with food, drink, and shelter so that they might have full leisure for their divine activities."[12] Each temple was believed to be, quite literally, the house of a particular god, and each community had its own special deity. Priests and other attendants constituted the god's court or household, and their chief task was to minister to his needs. A secondary responsibility was to mediate between the god and the community, seeking to discover his will and appease his anger. In order for them to perform these tasks, temples and their staffs had to be supported by a steady flow of goods. Over the years, they were continually enlarged and became increasingly costly. In fact, the temple became, in many respects, a substantial business enterprise, a development that apparently provided the stimulus for the invention of writing, which was originally a means of recording the temple's business activities.[13] Many scholars have described these early Mesopotamian city-states as theocracies, since the local deity was regarded as the real ruler and the king merely as his "tenant farmer."[14]

---

[12] Samuel Noah Kramer, *The Sumerians: Their History, Culture, and Character* (Chicago: University of Chicago Press, 1963), p. 123.

[13] Childe, *Man Makes Himself*, pp. 143–144.

[14] See, for example, Sir Leonard Woolley, *The Beginnings of Civilization*, vol. I, part 2, of the UNESCO *History of Mankind* (New York: Mentor, 1965), pp. 116, 119, 198, 449ff., etc.

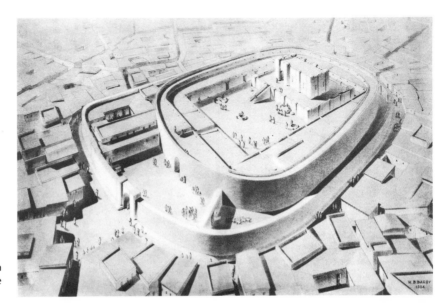

Fig. 9/2 Early Mesopotamian temple and its environs: temple oval at Khafaja

Egypt was also a theocracy, but of a different type. One scholar has compared the Egyptian and Mesopotamian patterns in this way:

> Egypt's theocracy was of a totally different kind from that of Sumer; instead of the earthly ruler being but the chosen representative and the "tenant farmer" of the sovereign deity, Pharaoh was himself a god, and his government was divine simply because it was Pharaoh's. The other gods did not and could not dispute his authority. To whatever deity of the Egyptian pantheon the local temple might be dedicated, yet Pharaoh's statues adorned it and, likely as not, the reliefs on the walls celebrated Pharaoh's exploits.[15]

Furthermore to his subjects Pharaoh "was the incarnation, the living embodiment, of the god of any district he happened to be visiting; he was their actual God in living form, whom they could see, speak to, and adore."[16] Like the gods of the Mesopotamian city-states, he was theoretically the owner of the land and hence entitled to a portion of all that was produced, and, as in Mesopotamia, he used his revenues to support a small army of specialists (e.g., officials, craftsman, soldiers, etc.).

In later years, there was a secularizing trend, especially in Mesopotamia.[17] By then, however, societies had developed other institutional arrangements—notably political ones—to insure the continued transfer of the economic surplus from the peasant producers to the governing class. Nevertheless, religion continued to play an important role as a legitimizing agency: it provided a rationale to justify otherwise intolerable transfers of the fruits of men's labors.

The experience of Mesopotamia and Egypt thus supports our earlier impressions (based on the experience of Mexico and China) concerning the role of religion in the formation of the economic surplus. Technological advance creates the possibility of a surplus; religion can transform this possibility into a reality. Technological advance makes it *possible* for farmers to produce more than they need to stay alive and productive; religion can provide them with a motivation to *do* it and with a rationale for transferring the surplus to others. While other possibilities exist (e.g., the political system can also provide the necessary motivation and rationale), it is significant that in at least four cases—Mesopotamia, Egypt, Mexico, and China— religion apparently played this role. This is an aspect of the evolutionary process which our own highly secularized generation is apt to overlook.

---

[15] Quotation from p. 127, *Prehistory*, vol. I, part 2, by Sir Leonard Woolley (Harper & Row, 1963).

[16] Margaret Murray, *The Splendour That Was Egypt* (London: Sidgwick & Jackson, 1949), p. 174.

[17] On Mesopotamia, see Woolley, *op. cit.*, p. 356; or A. Leo Oppenheim, *Ancient Mesopotamia: Portrait of a Dead Civilization* (Chicago: University of Chicago Press, 1964), pp. 84–85. On Egypt, see Ralph Turner, *The Great Cultural Traditions: The Foundations of Civilization* (New York: McGraw-Hill, 1941), vol. I, p. 187; or George Steindorff and Keith Seele, *When Egypt Ruled the East*, rev. ed. (Chicago: Phoenix Books, 1963), p. 83.

Scale of organization

In the first few centuries after the shift to agriculture, there was striking growth in the size of a number of communities, especially in Mesopotamia.[18] These became the first full-fledged cities in history. The largest of them were invariably the capitals of the largest and most prosperous societies. It is impossible to obtain accurate figures on the size of the cities and towns of the third and second millennia B.C., and scholars disagree on the interpretation of the evidence. Some believe, however, that one or more of these cities passed the 100,000 mark.[19]

Egypt was the largest of the simple agrarian societies of ancient times, and politically it was the most stable. She enjoyed the unique distinction of surviving as a united and independent nation throughout most of the third and second millennia B.C. This achievement was due to Egypt's unique ecological situation: no other society enjoyed such excellent natural defenses and was so little threatened by powerful neighbors.

In the second half of the second millennium, Egypt embarked on a program of expansion and brought under her control what is now Israel, Lebanon, Syria, and part of Jordan to the northeast, and part of the Sudan and Eritrea to the south. There were also other important empires in this era, including those established by the Babylonians in the eighteenth century B.C. and the Hittites in the thirteenth century. Babylonia succeeded briefly in uniting most of Mesopotamia, while the Hittites conquered much of what is now Turkey and Syria.

Organizational developments

These conquests posed serious organizational problems for the rulers of early agrarian societies. Traditional modes of government organized around an extended family proved completely incapable of administering the affairs of societies whose populations now sometimes numbered in the millions. Though rulers continued to rely on relatives to help them perform the most essential tasks of government, they were forced to turn increasingly to others. One expedient was to incorporate a conquered group as a subdivision of the state, leaving its former ruler in charge in a subordinate capacity. Eventually, however, all of the more successful rulers found it necessary to create new kinds of organizational structures, ones not based on ties of kinship.

We can see these newer patterns developing in both military and civil affairs. The earliest armies, for example, were simply organizations of all the able-bodied

---

[18] Robert Adams, "Factors Influencing the Rise of Civilization in the Alluvium: Illustrated by Mesopotamia," in Kraeling and Adams, *op. cit.*, p. 33.

[19] See, for example, Kramer, *op. cit.*, pp. 88–89; Woolley, *op. cit.*, p. 125; or Kingsley Davis, "The Origin and Growth of World Urbanism," *American Journal of Sociology*, 60 (1955), p. 431. See also Oppenheim, *op. cit.*, p. 140, who, though declining to estimate size, reports the area of Ninevah to have been larger than Ur (generally thought to have been over 100,000) and Uruk nearly as large.

Fig. 9/3 Egyptian soldiers attacking a fortress (c. 1940 B.C.)

men in the society.[20] During this period, wars were of short duration and fought only after the harvest was in. As a result, the period following the harvest came to be known as the "season when kings go forth to war." This limitation was essential because, with the shift to agriculture, the responsibilities of men in farming were greatly increased.

As long as wars were brief and limited to skirmishes with neighboring peoples, this arrangement was adequate. But once rulers became interested in empire building, the traditional system proved impossible. As early as the middle of the third millennium in Mesopotamia, would-be empire builders established small, but highly trained, professional armies. For example, Sargon, the famous Akkadian king, had a standing army of 5,400 men who "ate daily before him."[21] As far as possible, recruits were sons of old soldiers, and thus a military caste was gradually created. The Egyptians followed a similar policy except that they relied chiefly on foreign mercenaries.[22] These new armies soon came to be *royal,* rather than national, armies.[23] Their expenses were paid by the king out of his enormous revenues, and the profits resulting from their activities were his also. Not only were these armies useful in dealing with foreign enemies, they also served as a defense against internal threats.[24]

In civil affairs, too, the casual and informal practices of simpler societies proved inadequate. As states expanded and the problems of administration multiplied, new kinds of governmental positions were created and a governmental bureaucracy began to take shape.[25] In addition to the many officials who comprised the royal

[20] Woolley, *op. cit.,* pp. 185ff., or Steindorff and Seele, *op. cit.,* p. 89.

[21] Woolley, *op. cit.,* p. 188. Later armies were even larger.

[22] *Ibid.,* p. 187; or Steindorff and Seele, *op. cit.,* p. 90.

[23] Woolley, *ibid.*

[24] Turner, *op. cit.,* p. 312.

[25] McNeill, *op. cit.,* p. 68; Turner, *op. cit.,* pp. 310–311; Steindorff and Seele, *op. cit.,* chap. 9; Pierre Montet, *Everyday Life in Egypt: In the Days of Ramesses the Great,* trans. by A. R. Maxwell-Hyslop and Margaret Drower (London: E. Arnold, 1958), chap. 10; Oppenheim, *op. cit.,* pp. 70ff., 230f., and 276–277.

court and were responsible for administering the king's complex household affairs, there were officials scattered throughout the countryside to administer the affairs of units ranging from small districts to provinces with hundreds of villages and towns. Each official had a staff of scribes and other lesser officials to assist him, and written records became increasingly important as the administrative problems grew more complex.[26]

Throughout most of the history of the simple agrarian societies of antiquity, writing was a specialized art mastered by only a few individuals after long apprenticeships.[27] This is easily understandable, considering the complex, prealphabetic systems of writing then in use. Even after a process of simplification that lasted over two thousand years, cuneiform script still had between 600 and 1,000 distinct characters. Before one could learn to read or write, he had to memorize this formidable array of symbols and learn the complex rules for their combination. The Egyptian hieroglyphic and hieratic scripts were equally complicated. Thus, those

---

[26] Oppenheim, *op. cit.*, p. 276. As one writer reports, "Sumerian bureaucracy has left us a staggering number of texts; we are unable to venture a guess as to how many tablets beyond the far more than 100,000 now in museums may be buried in southern Mesopotamia."

[27] Childe, *Man Makes Himself,* pp. 148–149, or *What Happened in History,* p. 144.

Fig. 9/4 Model of a royal granary (c. 2000 B.C.) found in tomb of Meket-Re. Note the scribes and other officials recording the deliveries of grain

Fig. 9/5 Two sides of a limestone tablet found at Kish, Mesopotamia, showing examples of the oldest known picture writing (c. 3500 B.C.). Included are the signs for a head, hand, foot, threshing sledge, and numerals

who could write formed a specialized occupational group in society—the scribes—and their services were much in demand. For the most part this occupation was filled by the sons of the rich and powerful, since only they could afford the costs of the necessary education.[28] Because of the political importance of their skill and the limited supply of qualified personnel, most scribes were at least marginal members of the governing class.

One consequence of the growth of empires and the development of bureaucracy was the establishment of the first formal legal systems. Over the centuries every society had developed certain conceptions of justice as well as informal techniques for implementing them. In most cases, the latter consisted of the practice of blood revenge, whereby the injured party and his relatives exacted vengence themselves. Recognizing the anarchic tendencies inherent in this system, men apparently sought settlement by arbitration. For this purpose, they naturally turned to the most respected and most powerful members of the community. In this way, headmen and other political leaders gradually acquired judicial powers.

Then, as empires grew, peoples of diverse cultures were brought within the framework of a single political system. In many instances, the official appointed to rule over an area would not be a native of it and would therefore be unfamiliar with local conceptions of justice (which varied considerably from place to place). As a result, pressures were generated to clarify and standardize judicial practice. This led, in time, to the promulgation of formal codes of law, the most famous being the Code of Hammurabi, the great Babylonian empire builder of the early second millennium.

The development of monetary systems

Money as we think of it was absent in the first simple agrarian societies. There were, nevertheless, certain standardized media of exchange.[29] Barley served this function

---

[28] See especially Kramer, *op. cit.,* p. 231.

[29] At present, it is impossible to say whether such media were developed in horticultural or in agrarian societies. Their presence from the very beginning of the simple agrarian era suggests that they were in existence previously. The same conclusion is suggested by the use of cattle, shells, and other media in modern horticultural societies, but in the absence of archaeological evidence this remains conjecture.

in ancient Mesopotamia, wheat in Egypt. Wages, rents, taxes, and various other obligations could be paid off in specified quantities of these grains.[30]

As media of exchange, grains were less than ideal, since they were both perishable and bulky. So, from a fairly early date, various metals, particularly silver and copper, were used as alternatives.[31] Initially, they were circulated in the form of crude bars of irregular size and weight and their use was restricted to large transactions, since metal was still relatively scarce. Later, as metals were easier to obtain, smaller units were manufactured to facilitate local trade, and their size and weight were gradually standardized. As the last stage in the process, governments assumed the responsibility for manufacturing metallic currencies, and full-fledged monetary systems appeared. This did not occur, however, until the very end of the simple agrarian era.

The growth of monetary systems was tremendously important for the subsequent development of societies. Money has acted as a lubricant, facilitating the movement, exchange, and, ultimately, the production of goods and services of every kind. Where a money economy prevails, the market for the things each individual produces is greatly enlarged because his products can be sold even to persons who produce nothing he wants. Thus the effective demand for goods and services is maximized.

One immediate consequence of the emergence of a money economy is the growth of opportunities for merchants, or middlemen, who purchase goods which they do not want for themselves but which they know are wanted by people who lack easy access to the producers. Once a class of merchants has come into being, they serve not only to satisfy existing demands, but to create new ones. By displaying new and uncommon articles, they generate needs and desires that did not exist before and thereby stimulate economic activity.

In the long run, the growth of a money economy subverts many of the values of simpler societies, especially the cooperative tendencies and traditionalism inherent in extended family systems. In their place it fosters a more individualistic, rationalistic, and competitive orientation and lays a foundation for many of the attitudes and values which are basic to modern industrial societies.

For the most part, these developments were very limited in the simple agrarian societies of the ancient Middle East. The newly emerging monetary economies barely penetrated the rural villages where most of the people lived. Even in the cities and towns, the role of money was very limited compared to what we are accustomed to. In short, the major impact of money still lay in the future.

Sociocultural cleavages

In the simple agrarian societies of the ancient world, there were several very important lines of cleavage. First, there was the cleavage between the small governing

---

[30] See Turner, *op. cit.*, vol. I, p. 263; or Childe, *What Happened in History*, p. 118.

[31] Childe, *op. cit.*, pp. 118–119.

Fig. 9/6   Cleavages within simple agrarian societies

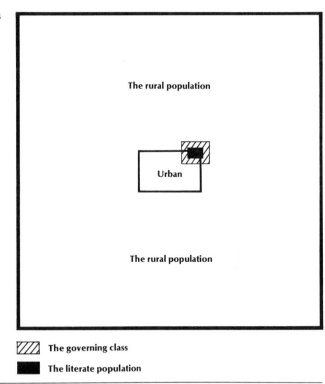

class and the much larger class of individuals who, having no voice in political decisions, had to turn over all or most of their surplus to the governing class. Second, there was the division between the small urban minority and the vast majority of peasant villagers. Finally, there was the cleavage between the small literate minority and the illiterate masses.

As Fig. 9/6 indicates, these three lines of cleavage tended to converge. As a result, the small governing class lived in a very different world from that of the illiterate, rural peasant majority—despite the fact that both were members of the same society. As one historian has pointed out, the invention of writing, when linked with the great social cleavage between the governing class and the governed, led to the formation of two increasingly distinct subcultures.[32] The subculture of the common people was a mixture of primitive superstition and the kinds of practical knowledge they needed in their daily lives. It was extremely parochial in outlook and knew little of the larger world beyond the village. The subculture of the governing class, by contrast, incorporated many of the refinements we would identify with "civilization." It included elements of philosophy, art, literature, history, science, administrative techniques, and above all a contempt for physical labor of any kind (except warfare) and for those who engage in it. In short, the governing classes not only possessed a different body of information, they also had a different set of values.

[32] See Turner's excellent treatment of this topic, *op. cit.*, pp. 317–323.

In many respects the differences *within* simple agrarian societies were greater than those *between* them. An Egyptian peasant in the latter half of the second millennium B.C. could have adapted far more easily to the life of a Babylonian peasant than to the life of a member of the governing class of his own society. As this gulf widened, members of the governing class found it increasingly difficult to recognize the ignorant, downtrodden peasants as fellow human beings. The scribes of ancient Egypt were fond of saying that the lower classes were "without heart" (meaning that they lacked intelligence) and therefore had to be driven with a stick like cattle.[33]

Slowdown in rate of technological innovation

Another crucial development in these societies was the marked slowdown in the rate of technological innovation and progress that began within a few centuries after the shift from horticulture to agriculture. Childe described the change this way:

> Before the [agrarian] revolution comparatively poor and illiterate communities had made an impressive series of contributions to man's progress. The two millennia immediately preceding 3,000 B.C. had witnessed discoveries in applied science that directly or indirectly affected the prosperity of millions of men and demonstrably furthered the biological welfare of our species by facilitating its multiplication. We have mentioned the following applications of science: artificial irrigation using canals and ditches; the plow; the harnessing of animal motive-power; the sailboat; wheeled vehicles; orchard husbandry; fermentation; the production and use of copper; bricks; the arch; glazing; the seal; and—in the earliest stages of the revolution—a solar calendar, writing, numerical notation, and bronze.
>
> The two thousand years after the revolution—say from 2,600 to 600 B.C.—produced few contributions of anything like comparable importance to human progress. Perhaps only four achievements deserve to be put in the same category as the fifteen just enumerated. They are: the "decimal notation" of Babylonia (about 2,000 B.C.); an economical method for smelting iron on an industrial scale (1,400 B.C.); a truly alphabetic script (1,300 B.C.); aqueducts for supplying water to cities (700 B.C.).[34]

Childe went on to note that two of these four innovations (the smelting of iron and the development of the alphabet) "cannot be credited to the societies that had initiated and reaped the fruits of the urban revolution," but rather were the products of somewhat less advanced neighboring societies.[35]

On first consideration, this slowing of the rate of technological advance seems an unlikely development. Larger populations, improved communications, and the

---

[33] Adolf Erman, *Life in Ancient Egypt*, trans. by H. M. Tirard (London: Macmillan, 1894), p. 128.

[34] Childe, *Man Makes Himself*, p. 180, quoted by permission of C. A. Watts & Co., Ltd. See also McNeill, *op. cit.*, p. 53; or Childe, *What Happened in History*, pp. 183ff.

[35] *Man Makes Himself*, p. 181. Elsewhere, Childe adds a third innovation (or a fifth to the total list), the invention of glass in Egypt. See *What Happened in History*, p. 183.

greater store of knowledge available to potential innovators should have produced still higher rates of innovation. The fact that they did not poses an important problem.

As scholars like Childe have seen, the explanation lies in the transformation of the social organization and ideology of societies.[36] Specifically, the development of the state and the growth of social inequality that followed the shift from horticulture to agriculture created a situation in which those who were engaged in the daily tasks of production were gradually reduced to the barest subsistence level, and kept there, by their more powerful superiors. Thus these peasant producers lost the normal incentive for creativity; any benefits that might result from an invention or discovery would simply be appropriated by the governing class. At the same time, the governing class, though motivated to create a more productive economy, no longer had the necessary knowledge of, and experience with, subsistence technology, and thus were in no position to make creative innovations. In short, expertise and incentive were inadvertently divorced, with disastrous results from the standpoint of technological progress.

Under the circumstances, it is hardly surprising that the governing class turned increasingly to warfare and conquest as the most promising means of increasing their wealth. Warfare was something they understood; furthermore, in their system of values it was one of the few occupations considered appropriate for members of their class. Thus, the energies of this powerful and influential class were turned from the conquest of nature to the conquest of man.[37] Thanks to the new agrarian technology, this could be a highly profitable enterprise. With the peasants producing much more than they needed, there was a steady flow of taxes, tithes, and rents to support the host of specialists that catered to the whims of the governing class, as well as the army of soldiers and officials that implemented their wishes.[38]

These developments help explain the advances in social organization made during this period. Having cut themselves off from the sweaty world of technology and directed their efforts instead to the conquest of man, the members of the governing class found a new challenge for their creative talents in the problems of social organization.[39] The exercise of power and the manipulation of others were activities in keeping with their dignity. Furthermore, they were rewarding: other things being equal, the better a group of men is organized, the greater their chances of success in struggles with other groups.[40]

---

[36] See Childe, *Man Makes Himself*, chap. 9, for a classic discussion of this subject. The analysis that follows is heavily indebted to Childe's provocative discussion, but varies from it in some details and emphases.

[37] See Childe, *What Happened in History*, p. 184.

[38] One is reminded of the ancient tale of the goose that laid the golden eggs. This was not simply a story for children: the peasantry was the goose.

[39] McNeill, *op. cit.*, p. 53, hints at this briefly.

[40] For a classic statement of this principle, see Gaetano Mosca, *The Ruling Class*, trans. by Hannah Kahn (New York: McGraw-Hill, 1939), p. 53.

There is some reason to believe that the great influence of organized religion in these societies also contributed to the technological slowdown. The religions of the simple agrarian societies of the ancient Middle East inculcated an inordinate respect for the powers of magic, which undoubtedly discouraged interest in technological innovation.

ADVANCED AGRARIAN SOCIETIES

During the period in which simple agrarian societies dominated the Middle East, the most important technological advance was the discovery of the technique of smelting iron. Prior to this, bronze was the most important metal. But the supply was always limited, and since the demands of the governing class always took precedence over the needs of peasants, the metal was used primarily for military and ornamental purposes. Bronze never really replaced stone and wood in ordinary tools, particularly agricultural tools, and so the impact of bronze on the economy was somewhat limited.

Men knew of iron at least as early as the first half of the third millennium B.C., but apparently only in its meteoric form, which is very scarce.[41] Sometime during the second millennium, perhaps as early as 1800 B.C., the Hittites of Asia Minor discovered iron ores and invented a technique for smelting them. For centuries they kept this a closely guarded secret, which brought them both economic and military advantage. During the thirteenth century, however, they came under attack from the Egyptians and Assyrians, as well as from barbarians from southeastern Europe, and their nation was destroyed about 1200 B.C. This led to the dispersal of the Hittites and the rapid spread of the technique of iron smelting.

As one would expect, in view of the nature of the class structure of simple agrarian societies, the initial use of iron was limited largely to the governing class. Some of the earliest iron objects recovered from Egypt were a dagger, a bracelet, and a headrest found in the tomb of the pharaoh Tutankhamen. Prior to the military collapse of the Hittites, iron was five times more expensive than gold, forty times more than silver. Only later, perhaps during the eighth century B.C., was it commonly used for ordinary tools. Thus, not until this period were there true advanced agrarian societies—though the Middle Eastern societies of the previous three or four centuries were certainly transitional types.

During this transitional period two further discoveries greatly enhanced the value of iron.[42] First it was found that if the outer layers of the iron absorbed some carbon from the fire during the forging process, the metal was somewhat hardened. Later it was discovered that this carburized iron could be hardened still further by quenching the hot metal in water, thus producing steel. With these developments,

---

[41] For a good summary of the early history of iron, see Leslie Aitchison, *A History of Metals* (London: Macdonald & Evans, 1960), vol. I, pp. 97–110. The discussion that follows is based largely on Aitchison.

[42] See Aitchison, *op. cit.*, pp. 111–113.

iron became not only more common, and hence cheaper, than bronze, but also more useful for both military and economic purposes. As one writer has said, "After the discovery of quench-hardening, iron gradually passed into the position from which it has never subsequently been ousted; it became the supremely useful material for making all the tools and weapons that are intended for cutting, chopping, piercing or slashing."[43]

From its point of origin in the Middle East, iron-making spread until eventually it was practiced throughout most of the Old World (even in many horticultural societies). By the time of Christ, advanced agrarian societies were firmly established in the Middle East, throughout most of the Mediterranean world, and in much of India and China. Within the next thousand years the advanced agrarian pattern spread over most of Europe and much of southeast Asia and expanded further in India and China. Still later it was transplanted to the European colonies in the New World. Advanced agrarian societies still survive in hybridized form in much of Asia, the Middle East, and Latin America, where they constitute the majority of the problem-ridden, underdeveloped nations of our day. We shall examine these partially industrialized agrarian societies in Chapter 15.

Technology

Compared with simpler societies, advanced agrarian societies enjoyed a very productive technology. Unfortunately, however, the same conditions that slowed the rate of technological advance in simple agrarian societies continued to operate. As a result, their progress was not nearly what one would expect on the basis of their size, the degree of communication among them, and, above all, their store of accumulated knowledge.[44]

Nevertheless, over the centuries quite a number of important innovations were made. A partial list would include the catapult, the crossbow, gunpowder, horseshoes, a workable harness for horses, the stirrup, the wood-turning lathe, the auger, the screw, the wheelbarrow, the rotary fan for ventilation, the clock, the spinning wheel, porcelain, printing, iron casting, the magnet, water-powered mills, windmills, and, in the period just preceding the emergence of the first industrial societies, the workable steam engine, the fly shuttle, the spinning jenny, the spinning machine, and a number of other power-driven tools. As a result of these and other innovations, the level of technological efficiency gradually rose until the most advanced agrarian societies of the eighteenth century A.D. were considerably superior, from the technological standpoint, to their predecessors of 2,500 years before.

---

[43] *Ibid.*, p. 113.

[44] See, for example, Charles Singer's comparison of the level of technology in the ancient empires of Egypt and Mesopotamia prior to 1000 B.C. and later in Greece and Rome, in "Epilogue: East and West in Retrospect," in Singer (ed.), *A History of Technology* (Oxford: Clarendon Press, 1956), vol. II, pp. 754–755.

Fig. 9/7   Medieval town of Montepeyroux, France, now almost deserted

This rise in the level of technological efficiency was not uniform throughout the agrarian world, despite diffusion. Knowledge still spread slowly in most cases, and some areas were considerably more advanced than others. During much of the advanced agrarian era, especially from 500 to 1500 A.D., the Middle East, China, and perhaps India were technologically more advanced than Europe.[45] In part, this was simply a continuation of older patterns (i.e., the Middle East was the center of innovation for more than five thousand years following the horticultural revolution). Even more important, however, were the effects of the collapse of the Roman Empire. For centuries afterwards, Europe was divided into scores of petty kingdoms and principalities that had only enough resources to maintain the smallest urban settlements and the most limited number of occupational specialists. Therefore, Europeans were inactive on many of the most promising and challenging technological frontiers of the time. While they made relative gains during the later Middle Ages—thanks largely to the diffusion of knowledge from the east—Europeans did not really catch up until the sixteenth century and did not take the lead until even later.

---

[45] *Ibid.*, pp. 754–772.

Scale of organization

In any comparison with simple agrarian societies, the greater organizational development of the advanced is very evident on both the societal and communal levels. On the societal level, there is roughly a tenfold differential between the largest society in each of the two categories. The largest simple agrarian society was probably Egypt in the latter half of the second millennium, at which time it controlled roughly 800,000 square miles.[46] By contrast, the Russian Empire in the mid-nineteenth century covered nearly 8 million square miles; even as early as the reign of Peter the Great (1689–1725) it covered nearly 6 million.[47] Several other advanced agrarian societies built empires that far surpassed the ancient Egyptians. These

---

[46] See, for example, Turner's map, *op. cit.*, p. 232.

[47] Jerome Blum, *Lord and Peasant in Russia from the Ninth to the Nineteenth Century* (Princeton, N.J.: Princeton University Press, 1961), p. 278. One might object that much of the Russian Empire was sparsely settled, but the same was true of the Egyptian.

Fig. 9/8 Medieval town of Ribe, Denmark. This town has changed little since the Middle Ages

include the Spanish Empire in the eighteenth century (5 million square miles), the Chinese Empire at various times since the first century B.C. (up to 4 million square miles), the Umayyad Empire in the eighth century (3 million square miles), and the Roman Empire in the second century (2 million square miles).[48]

Populations, too, were much larger. The largest simple agrarian society probably had fewer than 15 million members.[49] By contrast, the largest advanced agrarian society, mid-nineteenth century China, had approximately 400 million.[50] Though that was exceptional, India reached 175 million in the middle of the nineteenth century, and both the Roman and Russian empires had at least 70 million.[51]

Similar differences are found at the communal level. The populations of the largest cities in simple agrarian societies probably were not much over 100,000. By contrast, the upper limit for cities in advanced agrarian societies appears to have been about 1,000,000—although, as with all population figures from earlier times, there is considerable uncertainty.[52] Only the capitals of great empires ever attained such a size, and they maintained it but briefly. Cities of 100,000 were much more numerous than in simple agrarian societies, though still quite rare.[53]

Differentiation of parts

Growth in the scale of organization was accompanied by an increasing differentiation of the parts. For the first time, there was significant economic specialization by regions and by communities, and it was accompanied by increased occupational specialization.

---

[48] See, for example, the reference maps in T. W. Wallbank et al., *Civilization*, 5th ed. (Chicago: Scott, Foresman, 1965), vol. I., pp. 658–671.

[49] This estimate was based on the known boundaries of these societies and on the fact that the Roman Empire, which was much larger and contained a much smaller percentage of uninhabitable land, had a maximum population of only about 70 million. See *The Cambridge Ancient History* (London: Cambridge, 1939), vol. XII, pp. 267–268. It is also noteworthy that in Roman times Egypt had a population of only 6 to 7 million. Even if allowance is made for the greater size of the Egyptian Empire in the days of Egypt's independence, it is difficult to imagine a total population much in excess of 15 million. See Charles Issawi, *Egypt in Revolution: An Economic Analysis* (New York: Oxford, 1963), p. 20.

[50] Chung-li Chang, *The Chinese Gentry: Studies on Their Role in Nineteenth-Century Chinese Society* (Seattle: University of Washington Press, 1955), p. 102.

[51] On India, see Kingsley Davis, *The Population of India and Pakistan* (Princeton, N.J.: Princeton University Press, 1951), pp. 24–25; on Rome, see *The Cambridge Ancient History, op. cit.*, pp. 267–268; on Russia, see Blum, *op. cit.*, p. 278.

[52] See, for example, Gideon Sjoberg, *The Preindustrial City: Past and Present* (Glencoe: Free Press, 1960), pp. 80ff; Jerome Carcopino, *Daily Life in Ancient Rome: The People and the City at the Height of the Empire* (New Haven, Conn: Yale, 1940), pp. 16–21; A. Andreades, "De la population de Constantinople sous les empereurs byzantins," *Metron*, 1 (1920), p. 101; George Sansom, *A History of Japan* (Stanford, Calif.: Stanford University Press, 1963), vol. III, p. 114; and Irene Taeuber, *The Population of Japan* (Princeton, N.J.: Princeton University Press, 1958), p. 27.

[53] Davis reports that there were "less than 50" in 1800 (*op. cit.*, p. 434). At this time no society could be classified as an industrial society, though the new industrial techniques were certainly beginning to have some effect.

The Roman Empire provides a good illustration of both regional and communal specialization. North Africa and Spain were noted as suppliers of dried figs and olive oil; Gaul, Dalmatia, Asia Minor, and Syria for their wine; Spain and Egypt for salted meats; Egypt, North Africa, Sicily, and the Black Sea region for grain; and the latter for salted fish as well.[54] The tendency toward specialization at the community level is illustrated by a passage from a manual for wealthy farmers, written in the second century B.C., which advised:

> Tunics, togas, blankets, smocks and shoes should be bought at Rome; caps, iron tools, scythes, spades, mattocks, axes, harness, ornaments and small chains at Cales and Minturnae; spades at Venafrum, carts and sledges at Suessa and in Lucania, jars and pots at Alba and at Rome; tiles at Venafrum, oil mills at Pompeii and at Rufrius's yard at Nola; nails and bars at Rome; pails, oil urns, water pitchers, wine urns, other copper vessels at Capua and at Nola; Campanian baskets, pulley-ropes and all sorts of cordage at Capua, Roman baskets at Suessa and Casium.[55]

[54] Turner, *op. cit.*, p. 911.

[55] F. R. Cowell, *Cicero and the Roman Republic* (London: Penguin, 1956), p. 79. Quoted by permission of Penguin Books.

Fig. 9/9   Occupational specialization in an advanced agrarian society: silversmith in his shop, Manama Babrun Island, Persian Gulf

Fig. 9/10 Occupational specialization in an advanced agrarian society: baker spreading dough, Saudi Arabia

Similar patterns are reported in other agrarian societies.[56] Even at the village level a measure of specialization was not uncommon. In the agricultural off-season, peasants often turned to handicrafts to make ends meet, and certain villages gradually developed a reputation for superior skill in the production of a particular commodity.

In the larger urban centers, occupational specialization reached a level that surpassed anything achieved in simpler societies. For example, a tax roll for Paris from the year 1313 lists 157 different trades.[57] The clothing industry alone contained such specialized occupations as wool combers, wool spinners, silk spinners (two kinds), weavers (seven kinds), dyers, fullers, calenderers, shearmen, tailors (four kinds), headdress makers (seven kinds, including specialists in felt, fur, wool and cotton, flowers, peacock feathers, gold embroidery and pearls, and silk), and girdle makers. Though such specialization could be found only in the larger cities, smaller cities often had forty or fifty different kinds of craftsmen, and even small towns had ten or twenty.[58] In addition to craft specialists, urban centers contained specialists in

---

[56] See, for example, Blum, *op. cit.*, pp. 126 and 394–395, on Russia; or Ralph Linton, *The Tree of Culture* (New York: Vintage Books, Random House, 1959), p. 231, on China.

[57] S. B. Clough and C. W. Cole, *Economic History of Europe* (Boston: Heath, 1941), p. 25.

[58] *Ibid.* See also Blum, *op. cit.*, pp. 16 and 126.

government, commerce, religion, education, the armed forces, and domestic service. The list should also include specialists engaged in illegal occupations, since these were a normal component of every advanced agrarian society.

The polity

In nearly all of these societies, the state was the basic integrative force. This was inevitable in societies created by conquest and maintained for the benefit of a tiny governing class. The state's coercive powers were necessary to hold the natural antagonisms of its subject peoples in check. In their exercise of these powers, the governing classes created new societies (i.e., they produced sociocultural unity among formerly disparate groups).

At the head of nearly every advanced agrarian state was a single individual, the king or emperor. Monarchy was the rule, republican government an infrequent exception limited almost entirely to the least powerful and least developed societies and to those on the margins of the agrarian world.[59] The prevalence of monarchical government seems to have been due to the militaristic and exploitative character of these societies. Governments were constantly threatening, or being threatened by, their neighbors, and all the while they were in danger from internal enemies. The latter included dissatisfied and ambitious members of the governing class, eager to seize control for themselves, and also restless, hostile members of the numerically dominant lower classes. Under such conditions, republican government was nearly impossible.[60]

Because of a tendency to romanticize the past, many people today are unaware of the frequency of both internal and external conflict in the great agrarian empires. In Rome, for example, 31 of the 79 emperors from Augustus to Romulus Augustulus were murdered, six were driven to suicide, four were forcibly deposed, and several more met unknown fates at the hands of internal enemies.[61] Though Rome's record was worse than most, internal struggles occurred in all advanced agrarian societies.[62] Peasant risings were another source of internal stress. One expert states that "there were peasant rebellions almost every year in China," and an authority on Russia reports that in the short period from 1801 to 1861 there were no less than 1,467

---

[59] Gerhard Lenski, *Power and Privilege: A Theory of Social Stratification* (New York: McGraw-Hill, 1966), pp. 197–198.

[60] For the effect of war on the forms of government, see Herbert Spencer, *The Principles of Sociology* (New York: Appleton, 1897), vol. II, part 5, chap. 17; Pitirim Sorokin, *Social and Cultural Dynamics* (New York: Bedminister Press, 1962), vol. III, pp. 196–198; or Stanislaw Andrzejewski, *Military Organization and Society* (London: Routledge, 1954), pp. 92–95.

[61] These figures were calculated from A. E. R. Boak, *A History of Rome to 565 A.D.*, 3d ed. (New York: Macmillan, 1943), and Harold Mattingly, *Roman Imperial Civilization* (New York: Doubleday Anchor, 1959), using Mattingly's list of emperors, pp. 351–355.

[62] For figures on several other societies, see Lenski, *op. cit.*, p. 235.

peasant risings in various parts of that country.[63] Though most of these risings remained local actions, it was only because authorities acted swiftly and ruthlessly. Had they not, many would have spread as widely as the famous English revolt of 1381 or the German Peasants' War of 1524–1525.[64]

External threats were no less frequent or serious: warfare was a chronic condition. A survey of the incidence of war in eleven European countries in the preindustrial period found that, on the average, these countries were involved in war nearly every second year.[65] Such conditions obviously required strong centralized authority. Societies without it were weeded out in the selective process, unless they happened to occupy a particularly remote and inaccessible territory.

Most members of the governing class considered political power a prize to be sought for the rewards it offered, rather than an opportunity for public service, and the office of king or emperor was the *supreme* prize. This is the only interpretation one can put on the perennial struggle for power within agrarian states, or the use made of it after it was won. Efforts to raise the living standards of the common people were rare, efforts at self-aggrandizement typical.[66] In many of these societies, government offices were bought and sold like pieces of property which the purchasers used to obtain the greatest possible profit. Office holders typically demanded payment before they would act, and justice was commonly sold to the highest bidder.[67] No wonder the common people of China developed the saying, ''To enter a court of justice is to enter a tiger's mouth.''[68]

These practices reflected what is known as the proprietary theory of the state, according to which the state is a piece of property that its owners may use, within rather broad and ill-defined limits, for their personal advantage.[69] Guided by this theory, agrarian rulers and governing classes saw nothing immoral in the use of what we (not they) would call ''public office'' for private gain. To them, it was simply the legitimate use of what they commonly regarded as their ''patrimony.'' It is said of the Ptolemies of Egypt, for example, that they showed the first emperors of Rome ''how a country might be run on the lines of a profitable estate.''[70] In the case of medieval Europe we read:

---

[63] Wolfram Eberhard, *Conquerors and Rulers: Social Forces in Medieval China* (Leiden: Brill, 1952), p. 52, and Blum, *op. cit.*, p. 558.

[64] For an interesting popular account of the former, see Philip Lindsay and Reg Groves, *The Peasants' Revolt, 1381* (London: Hutchinson, n.d.).

[65] Sorokin, *op. cit.*, vol. III, chap. 10, especially p. 352.

[66] See, among others, Lenski, *op. cit.*, pp. 210–242 and 266–284, for more detailed documentation.

[67] *Ibid.*, pp. 222–225.

[68] Robert K. Douglas, *Society in China* (London: Innes, 1894), p. 104.

[69] See Max Weber, *The Theory of Social and Economic Organization*, trans. by A. M. Henderson and Talcott Parsons (New York: Free Press, 1947), pp. 341–348; and *Wirtschaft und Gesellschaft*, 2d ed. (Tübingen: Mohr, 1925), vol. II, p. 679–723.

[70] Mattingly, *op. cit.*, p. 137. See also Turner, *op. cit.*, vol. II, p. 620; or Michael Rostovtzeff, *The Social and Economic History of the Roman Empire*, rev. ed. (Oxford: Clarendon Press, 1957), p. 54.

The proprietary conception of rulership created an inextricable confusion of public and private affairs. Rights of government were a form of private ownership. "Crown lands" and "the king's estate" were synonymous. There was no differentiation between the king in his private and public capacities. A kingdom, like any estate endowed with elements of governmental authority, was the private concern of its owner. Since "state" and "estate" were identical, "the State" was indistinguishable from the prince and his personal "patrimony."[71]

The proprietary theory of the state can be traced back to horticultural societies and, in a sense, even to hunting and gathering groups. In those simpler societies, the private and public aspects of political leadership were hopelessly confused. When a surplus first began to be produced, at least part of it was turned over to the leader, who held it as trustee for the group. As long as the surplus was small and in the form of perishable commodities, there was little the leader could do with it except redistribute it, thereby winning status for his generosity. Eventually, however, as we saw in Chapter 8, it grew large enough to permit him to create a staff of dependent re-

---

[71] Hans Rosenberg, *Bureaucracy, Aristocracy, and Autocracy: The Prussian Experience 1660–1815* (Cambridge, Mass.: Harvard, 1958), p. 506. Quoted by permission of Harvard University Press.

Fig. 9/11 Courtyard of Kronberg Castle, Elsinore, Denmark, built by Frederick II in the sixteenth century. Note the elaborate and costly artwork

tainers who could be used to enforce his wishes. At this point, the proprietary theory of the state was born. Later rulers merely applied it on an ever-expanding scale, as productivity and the economic surplus steadily increased.

Recent research provides a good picture of the extremes to which rulers and governing classes have carried the proprietary principle. In late nineteenth century China, for example, the average income for families not in the governing class was approximately 20 to 25 taels per year. By contrast, the governing class averaged 450 taels per year, with some receiving as much as 200,000.[72] The emperor's income, of course, was considerably larger than even this. To cite another example, the English nobility at the end of the twelfth century and early in the thirteenth had an average income roughly 200 times that of ordinary field hands, and the king's equaled that of 24,000 field hands.[73] Putting together the evidence from many sources, it appears that the combined income of the ruler and the governing class in most advanced agrarian societies equaled *not less than half of the total national income*, even though they numbered 2 per cent or less of the population.[74]

Despite their many similarities, the political systems of advanced agrarian societies varied in a number of ways. The most important was in the degree of political centralization. In some societies the central government was very strong, in others its powers were severely limited. These differences largely reflected the current state of the perennial struggle between the ruler and the other members of the governing class. A king or emperor naturally wanted the greatest possible control over his subordinates, and the latter just as naturally wanted to minimize it. When the ruler was dominant, the political system was despotic, autocratic, or absolutist; when the governing class was relatively free from monarchical control, the system tended to be feudalistic or oligarchic.

Since land (including the peasants who worked it) and political office were the most valuable resources in agrarian societies, struggles between rulers and the governing class usually revolved about the issue of their control. In a few instances, powerful rulers like the Ottoman emperor Suleiman and the Mughal emperor Akbar managed to gain almost complete control over these resources. During their reigns, both land and offices were held at the ruler's pleasure and were subject to instant confiscation should the services of the holder be judged unsatisfactory.[75] A Dutch

---

[72] Chung-li Chang, *The Income of the Chinese Gentry* (Seattle: University of Washington Press, 1962), Summary Remarks, supplement 2, and chap. 1.

[73] On the King's income, see Sir James H. Ramsay, *A History of the Revenues of the Kings of England: 1066–1399* (Oxford: Clarendon Press, 1925), vol. I, pp. 227 and 261. For the income of the nobility, see Sidney Painter, *Studies in the History of the English Feudal Barony* (Baltimore: Johns Hopkins, 1943), pp. 170–171. For the income of field hands, see H. S. Bennett, *Life on the English Manor: A Study of Peasant Conditions, 1150–1400* (London: Cambridge, 1960), p. 121.

[74] Lenski, *op. cit.*, pp. 219 and 228.

[75] See, for example, Albert Lybyer, *The Government of the Ottoman Empire in the Time of Suleiman the Magnificent* (Cambridge: Harvard, 1913); or W. H. Moreland, *The Agrarian System of Moslem India* (Allahabad: Central Book Depot, n.d.).

traveler writing in the early seventeenth century left a vivid picture of the situation in the Mughal Empire at that time:

> Immediately on the death of a lord who has enjoyed the King's *jagir*, be he great or small, without any exception—sometimes even before the breath is out of the body—the King's officers are ready on the spot and make an inventory of the entire estate, recording everything down to the value of a single piece, even to the dresses and jewels of the ladies, provided they have not concealed them. The King takes back the whole estate absolutely for himself, except in a case where the deceased has done good service in his lifetime, when the women and children are given enough to live on, but no more.[76]

In Turkey under Suleiman, the chief officers of state were recruited from the ranks of specially trained slaves over whom the sultan held life and death power.[77] At the other extreme, during much of the medieval period Europe's feudal lords were virtually autonomous. Though their lands were typically acquired by royal grants given in exchange for pledges of service, the rulers usually lacked the power to enforce them.[78]

While examples of both extremes can be found, the usual pattern was something in between. Typically, the powers of the ruler and the governing class were fairly evenly balanced. Various factors influenced the balance and determined the precise location of a society on what might be called the autocracy-oligarchy scale. In general, the larger a state and the poorer its transportation and communication facilities, the greater the opportunities for members of the governing class to infringe on royal prerogatives.[79] A great deal also depended on the personal qualities of the ruler. Ruthless, energetic, and intelligent men were usually able to improve their position, while those without such qualities were apt to see it weakened. A ruler who was successful in foreign wars was especially likely to dominate his governing class, since conquests provided him with new resources to distribute and this always strengthened the bonds of "loyalty." The case of William the Conqueror was a classic example.

Patterns of inheritance and succession also greatly influenced the balance of power. A system of primogeniture in the governing class tended to prevent the

---

[76] F. Pelsaert, *Jahangir's India*, trans. by W. H. Moreland and P. Geyl and quoted by B. B. Misra, *The Indian Middle Classes* (London: Oxford, 1961), p. 47. Quoted by permission of W. Heffer and Sons, Ltd.

[77] Lybyer, *op. cit.*, pp. 47–58 and 115–117.

[78] See, for example, James Westfall Thompson's statement that "the medieval state was a loose agglomeration of territories with rights of property and sovereignty everywhere shading into one another," in *Economic and Social History of the Middle Ages* (New York: Appleton-Century-Crofts, 1928), p. 699. See also Marc Bloch, *Feudal Society*, trans. by L. A. Manyon (Chicago: University of Chicago Press, 1962), especially chaps. 14–24; Blum, *op. cit.*, chap. 2; or Sidney Painter, *The Rise of the Feudal Monarchies* (Ithaca, N.Y.: Cornell, 1951), and *Studies in the History of the English Feudal Barony*.

[79] For a more detailed discussion of the factors influencing this balance, see Lenski, *op. cit.*, pp. 234–240.

Fig. 9/12 Working equipment for member of the governing class in sixteenth-century Germany

Fig. 9/13 Armor of a Japanese nobleman of the sixteenth century

breakup of large estates, keeping intact this important base of power.[80] Rules governing succession to the throne were also very important. Where there was a principle of automatic succession, as in most European countries, children and other weak individuals could become rulers. This provided the governing class an excellent

[80] See, for example, Karl Wittfogel, *Oriental Despotism: A Comparative Study of Total Power* (New Haven, Conn.: Yale, 1957), pp. 79ff.; Alan Simpson, *The Wealth of the Gentry, 1540–1660* (London: Cambridge, 1961), pp. 107–108; Blum, *op. cit.*, pp. 82 and 378; Misra, *op. cit.*, pp. 44 and 50; and Jean Hippolyte Mariéjol, *The Spain of Ferdinand and Isabella*, trans. by Benjamin Keen (New Brunswick, N.J.: Rutgers University Press, 1961), pp. 276–277.

opportunity to increase its powers.[81] By contrast, where there was an open contest, there were few weak rulers. To become ruler of the Mughal Empire, for example, a prince had to kill his own brothers. This system produced a succession of strong emperors who held to the barest minimum the rights of the governing class.[82]

Finally, the balance of power depended on the unity of the governing class. When it presented a united front, it could bring far more pressure to bear than when it was torn by internal conflicts. Skillful rulers recognized this and typically sought to exploit differences in rank, wealth, ethnicity, region, and religion for their own advantage.[83]

The economy: an overview

Because politics and economics were always tightly intertwined in advanced agrarian societies, those who dominated the political system also dominated the economic. The leading office holders in government were usually the chief landholders as well, and in these societies land was the most important economic resource. As one economic historian expressed it, "In pre-market societies [among which he includes agrarian], wealth tends to follow power; not until the market society [does] power tend to follow wealth."[84]

As this statement suggests, the economies of agrarian societies operated on a very different basis from those of most modern industrial societies. In determining the central economic questions of how resources should be used, what should be produced and in what quantities, and how the product should be distributed, the basic market forces of supply and demand were much less important than the arbitrary decisions of the political elite. In Heilbroner's terminology, these were *command* economies rather than market economies.[85]

The economy of an advanced agrarian society consisted of two distinct parts: its agricultural economy, and the commercial and industrial economy of its urban centers. These were not of equal importance, however: a leading student of ancient history recently estimated that the Roman state derived approximately twenty times more tax revenue from agriculture than from trade and industry. He went on to say that "this apportionment of the burden of taxation probably corresponded roughly to the economic structure of the empire. All the evidence goes to show that its

---

[81] See, for example, Painter, *The Rise of the Feudal Monarchies*, pp. 127–129.

[82] Moreland, *op. cit.*, pp. 92–100.

[83] For examples of the application of the policy of "divide and rule," see Mariéjol, *op. cit.*, pp. 264ff., or Rosenberg, *op. cit.*, pp. 152ff.

[84] Robert Heilbroner, *The Making of Economic Society* (Englewood Cliffs, N.J.: Prentice-Hall, 1962), p. 27. See also H. R. Trevor-Roper, "The Gentry 1540–1640," *The Economic History Review Supplements*, No. 1 (n.d.); or Bloch, *op. cit.*, who wrote of "that age when true wealth consisted in being the master." (p. 192.)

[85] Heilbroner, *op. cit.*, pp. 9–44.

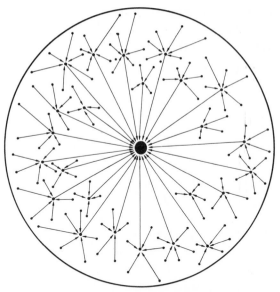

Fig. 9/14 Graphic representation of the flow of goods in advanced agrarian societies

wealth was derived almost entirely from agriculture, and to a very small extent from industry and trade."[86] The same could be said of every other agrarian society. It does not follow, however, that the urban economy was of little interest to the governing class. On the contrary, it was of tremendous interest because it provided them with the luxuries they valued so highly. The urban economy, however, depended on the rural economy and on its ability to produce a surplus that could support the urban population.

In many respects the economies of agrarian societies of the past remind one of trees with root systems spreading out in every direction, constantly drawing in new resources. Graphically, the pattern was that shown in Fig. 9/14. At the center of the society was the national capital, controlled by the king or emperor and the leading members of the governing class. Surrounding it were various provincial or regional capitals controlled by royal governors and other members of the governing class. Each of these, in turn, was surrounded by smaller county seats and market towns controlled by the lower-ranking members of the governing class. Finally, each of these towns was surrounded by scores of small villages. In the larger empires, there was often another layer interposed between the county seats and the regional capitals.

In this system, there was a steady flow of goods from the smaller units to the larger, or from the villages to the county seats and from there to the regional and national capitals. Basically this flow was induced by taxation, but it was supplemented by rents, interest on debts, tithes, and profits, all of which helped effect the transfer of the economic surplus from the peasant villagers to the urban-based governing class and their allies and dependents.

---

[86] A. H. M. Jones, *The Later Roman Empire 284–602: A Social Economic and Administrative Survey* (Oxford: Blackwell, 1964), vol. I, p. 465.

Some scholars have argued that this was actually a symbiotic exchange relationship in which the villagers freely traded the goods they produced for goods and services produced in the urban centers. While there was an element of this, the historical record shows that basically it was a one-sided, coercive relationship in which the peasants were forced to give far more than they received. The peasants recognized this, even if some modern scholars do not, and they resented it, as shown by the frequency of their protests and hopeless revolts.[87]

In exchange for their surplus, the peasants could buy in the urban centers commodities that were not available in their villages (e.g., certain metal tools, salt, etc.). The towns and cities were also religious centers in many cases, and the peasants often availed themselves of these facilities. Finally, the peasants benefited to some degree from the maintenance of law and order provided by urban-based governments, even though the law was used disproportionately to protect the rights

---

[87] See pp. 257–258 above on peasant revolts. See also G. G. Coulton, *The Medieval Village* (Cambridge: Cambridge University Press, 1926), chaps. 11 and 24–25.

Fig. 9/15   The city as a religious center. Hindu temple in Nepal

of the governing class and keep the peasants in their place. The maintenance of order is especially important in an agrarian society where so much depends on the success of each harvest, and where each harvest depends on months of effort. Disruption at *any* point in the agriculture cycle can be disastrous for everyone.

The rural economy

In most advanced agrarian societies, the ruler and the governing class (including the religious leaders) owned a grossly disproportionate share of the land. Though there are no precise figures for earlier times, the traditional pattern can still be seen in many parts of Latin America, the Middle East, and southeast Asia. As Table 9/1 indicates, even now a minority of 1 to 3 per cent of the population owns from one-third to two-thirds of the arable land in these countries.

Table 9/1 Landholdings of the governing class in selected nations in the mid-twentieth century

Nation	Percentage of population	Percentage of arable land owned
Chile	1.4	63
Northeast Brazil	2	48
Egypt	0.4	34
	3	56
Jordan	3.5	37
Lebanon	0.2	50
	1.4	65
Iraq	3	67
Northcentral India	1.5	39
	3.3	54
South Vietnam	2.5	50

Sources: Chile—Frederico Gil, *The Political System of Chile* (Boston: Houghton Mifflin, 1966), p. 148; Northeast Brazil—Josué de Castro, *Death in the Northeast* (New York: Random House, 1966), p. 154; the Middle Eastern nations—Morroe Berger, *The Arab World Today* (Garden City, N.Y.: Doubleday Anchor, 1964), pp. 196–199; North-central India—Baljit Singh and Shridhar Misra, *Land Reforms in Uttar Pradesh* (Honolulu: East-West Center Press, 1964), p. 28; South Vietnam—*The Washington Post*, October 17, 1965, p. A 8.

Not only has the governing class usually owned the major share of the land, it has often owned most of the peasants who worked it. Systems of slavery and serfdom have been common in agrarian societies, with large landholdings and large numbers of slaves or serfs normally going hand in hand. Thus it was only natural that a large landholder like Count Sheremetev, a mid-nineteenth century Russian nobleman who owned 2 million acres of land, should also own nearly 300,000 serfs.[88] Rulers, understandably, had the largest holdings. Prior to the emancipation of the serfs, the czar owned 27.4 million of them.[89]

But even when the peasant owned his own land and was legally free, he usually found it difficult to make ends meet. A bad crop one year, and he had to borrow money at usurious rates, sometimes as high as 120 per cent a year.[90] In any event, there were always taxes, and these usually fell more heavily on the peasant landowner than on his wealthier neighbor, either because of special exemptions granted the latter or simply because of his greater ability to evade such obligations.[91] If a

[88] Blum, *op. cit.*, pp. 369–370.

[89] *Ibid.*, pp. 356–357.

[90] Sjoberg, *op. cit.*, p. 215.

[91] See, for example, Chang, *op. cit.*, pp. 37–51.

Fig. 9/16   Peasant plowing with traditional wooden plow, Iran

Fig. 9/17   Peasants transplant-ing rice, Indonesia

peasant did not own his land, he had to pay rent, which was always set high. In addition, he was often subject to compulsory labor service, tithes, fines, and obligatory "gifts" to the governing class.[92]

Because the number and variety of obligations was so great, it is difficult to determine just how large the total was, but in most societies it appears to have been not less than *half* the total value of the goods that the peasants produced.[93] The basic philosophy of the governing class seems to have been to "tax" the peasants to the limit of their ability to pay.[94] This philosophy is illustrated by a story told of a leading Japanese official of the seventeenth century who, returning to one of his estates after an absence of ten years and finding the villagers in well-built houses instead of the hovels he remembered, exclaimed, "These people are too comfortable. They must be more heavily taxed."[95]

Living conditions for most peasants were very primitive, and it is doubtful that they were better off in most respects than most hunters and gatherers. For example, the diet of the average peasant in medieval England consisted of little more than

---

[92] For a survey of these obligations, see Lenski, *op. cit.*, pp. 267–270.

[93] *Ibid.*, p. 228.

[94] See, for example, Blum, *op. cit.*, p. 232; or Moreland, *op. cit.*, p. 207.

[95] Sansom, *op. cit.*, vol. III, p. 29.

the following: a hunk of bread and a mug of ale in the morning; a lump of cheese and bread with perhaps an onion or two to flavor it, and more ale at noon; a thick soup or pottage followed by bread and cheese at the main meal in the evening.[96] Meat was rare, and the ale usually thin. Household furniture consisted of a few stools, a table, and a chest to hold the best clothes and any other treasured possessions.[97] Beds were uncommon; most peasants simply slept on earthen floors covered with straw. Other household possessions were apparently limited to cooking utensils.

In some cases, the lot of the peasant was not even this good. Frequently conditions became so oppressive that it was impossible to eke out a livelihood and the peasants were forced to abandon their farms.[98] In China, conditions were so wretched that female infanticide was widely practiced. One nineteenth-century scholar reported records indicated that as many as a quarter of the female infants born in some districts were killed at birth.[99] Sometimes signs were posted in these areas, "Girls may not be drowned here." Though obviously an extreme case, the conditions that gave rise to it were by no means limited to China.

---

[96] Bennett, *op. cit.*, p. 236.

[97] *Ibid.*, pp. 232–236.

[98] See, for example, Moreland, *op. cit.*, p. 147, on India; or Blum, *op. cit.*, pp. 163, 266–268, 309–310, and 552ff., on Russia.

[99] Douglas, *op. cit.*, p. 354.

Fig. 9/18 Peasant village, Colombia

Fig. 9/19 Country home of member of the governing class, Colombia. Compare with peasant homes in Fig. 9/18. The owner of the hacienda above seldom stays here, preferring his other home in the city of Cali

To compound the misery created by their economic situation, peasants were often subjected to cruel treatment. Families were sometimes split up if it served their master's economic interests.[100] Peasants often found it difficult to defend their wives and daughters from the amorous attentions of the governing class, and in some areas the lord of the manor maintained the notorious *jus primae noctis*.[101] Finally, peasants were subject at all times to the whims and tempers of their superiors, who might invoke severe punishments even for minor offenses. Petty thievery was often punished by death, frequently by cruel and frightful means.[102]

To the governing class, all this seemed only natural since most of them, like their predecessors in simple agrarian societies, viewed the peasants as essentially subhuman. In legal documents in medieval England, a peasant's children were not

[100] Blum, *op. cit.*, pp. 424 and 428, on Russia; and Gunnar Myrdal, *An American Dilemma* (New York: McGraw-Hill, 1964), p. 931, on the American South.

[101] Literally, the right of the first night (i.e., the right to deflower brides on their wedding night). See Coulton, *op. cit.*, pp. 80 and 464–469; Blum, *op. cit.*, pp. 426–427 and 437; G. M. Carstairs, "A Village in Rajasthan," in M. N. Srinivas (ed.), *India's Villages* (Calcutta: West Bengal Government Press, 1955), pp. 37–38.

[102] Bennett, *op. cit.*, 196; Coulton, *op. cit.*, pp. 190–191, 248–250, and 437–440.

his *familia*, but his *sequela*, meaning "brood" or "litter."[103] Estate records in Europe, Asia, and America often listed the peasants with the livestock.[104] It is hardly surprising, therefore, that so civilized a man as Cato the Elder should have argued that slaves, like livestock, should be disposed of when no longer productive.[105]

As shocking as these views seem today, they were not completely unreasonable. So divergent were the ways of life of the governing class and the peasantry, and so limited their contacts (normally a class of officials and retainers stood between them[106]), that it is surprising that some members of the privileged class recognized the fact of their common humanity, not that the majority failed to do so.

Despite the heavy burdens laid on them, not all peasants were reduced to the subsistence level. By various devices, many contrived to hide a part of their harvest

---

[103] G. G. Coulton, *Medieval Panorama* (New York: Meridian Books, 1955), p. 77; or Thompson, *op. cit.*, p. 708.

[104] William Stubbs, *The Constitutional History of England* (Oxford: Clarendon Press, 1891), vol. I, p. 454n.; Wolfram Eberhard, *A History of China*, 2d ed. (Berkeley: University of California Press, 1960); p. 32; and Yosoburo Takekoshi, *The Economic Aspects of the History of the Civilization of Japan* (New York: Macmillan, 1930), vol. I, pp. 60–63.

[105] See Boak, *op. cit.*, p. 127; or Cowell, *op. cit.*, p. 64. For an example of the application of Cato's principle in medieval Europe, see Bennett, *op. cit.*, p. 283.

[106] See, for example, Bloch, *op. cit.*, p. 337; or George Homans, *English Villagers of the 13th Century* (Cambridge, Mass.: Harvard, 1942), p. 229.

Fig. 9/20 Peasants carrying their produce to market, Java. Note the absence of animals and wagons

and otherwise evade their obligations.[107] A small minority even managed, by rendering special services to the governing class or by other means, to rise a bit above their fellows, operating larger farms and generally living a bit more comfortably.[108]

For the majority, however, the one real hope for a substantial improvement in their lot lay, ironically, in disasters such as plagues, famines, and devasting wars. For when death reduced their numbers to the point where good workers were in short supply, the governing class was forced to bid competitively for the peasants' services, raising their income above the subsistence level.[109] Normally, however, high birthrates kept this from happening or, when it did, soon brought about a return to the former situation.

The urban economy

In thinking of the great civilizations of the past, most of us conjure up images of Rome, Constantinople, Alexandria, Jerusalem, Damascus, Baghdad, Babylon, and the other great cities that loom so large in the historical record. Thus it is with a sense of shock that we discover that all the urban communities, large and small together, rarely if ever held more than 10 per cent of the population of any of these societies, and often much less.[110]

How can this be? The explanation is that we have been victims of an illusion. Because history was recorded by literate men—men who nearly always lived in cities and towns and regarded the life of the rural villages as unworthy of their attentions—their chronicles are primarily of city life, particularly the life of the governing class.

The most striking feature of the cities and towns of these societies was the great diversity of people who lived in them. Urban residents ranged from the most illustrious members of the governing class to beggars and other destitute people who barely managed to stay alive. Unlike so many of the cities and towns of modern industrial societies, these were not primarily industrial centers. Though considerable

---

[107] See, for example, Morton Fried, *The Fabric of Chinese Society: Study of the Social Life of a Chinese County Seat* (New York: Praeger, 1953), pp. 104–105; Moreland, *op. cit.*, pp. 168 and 207; and Bennett, *op. cit.*, pp. 100–101, 112–113, and 131ff.

[108] See, for example, the franklins in thirteenth-century England (Homans, *op. cit.*, pp. 248–250).

[109] May McKisack, *The Fourteenth Century* (Oxford: Clarendon Press, 1959), pp. 331–340; Lindsay and Groves, *op. cit.*, pp. 30, 34, and 63; Charles Langlois, "History," in Arthur Tilley (ed.), *Medieval France* (London: Cambridge, 1922), pp. 150–151; and Paul Murray Kendall, *The Yorkist Age* (Garden City, N.Y.: Doubleday, 1962), pp. 171ff.

[110] Sjoberg, *op. cit.*, p. 83; Lynn White, *Medieval Technology and Social Change* (Oxford: Clarendon Press, 1962), p. 39; Henri Pirenne, *Economic and Social History of Medieval Europe* (New York: Harvest Books, n.d., first published 1933), p. 58; J. C. Russell, *British Medieval Population* (Albuquerque: University of New Mexico Press, 1948), p. 305; Blum, *op. cit.*, pp. 268 and 281.

industrial activity was carried on in them, their political and commercial functions, and frequently their religious ones, were more important.

Since the cities and towns were the centers of government, most members of the governing class preferred to live in them.[111] As a result, urban populations included not only the necessary complement of civil and military officials, but the extensive households of the governing class as well. Servants were far more numerous in these societies than in ours, both because of the absence of labor-saving devices and because the governing class viewed manual work of any kind as degrading. Furthermore, one of their chief forms of status competition was to see who could maintain the most luxurious households. The household staff of the head of one small kingdom, Edward IV of England, numbered 400.[112] A more important ruler, such as the Roman emperor at the height of the empire, had thousands. As one historian put it, one "is dumbfounded by the extraordinary degree of specialization [and] the insensate luxury."[113] One group of servants was responsible only for the emperor's palace clothes, another for his city clothes, another for those he wore to the theater, yet another for his military uniforms. Other servants attended strictly to the eating vessels, a different group to those for drinking, another to silver vessels, and still others to gold ones and those set with jewels. For entertainment, the emperor had his own choristers, an orchestra, dancing women, clowns, and dwarfs. Lesser members of the governing class obviously could not maintain household staffs as elaborate as this, but many had staffs of hundreds, and some had a thousand or more.[114] All this was made possible by the labors of the peasantry.

Part of the peasants' surplus also went to support two important groups that were allied with the governing class, yet separate from it. The first of these was the clergy, of whom more will be said shortly. The second was the merchant class. Merchants were a peculiar group in the structure of agrarian societies. Though some of them were extremely wealthy, they were rarely accepted as equals by members of the governing class—even by those less wealthy than they. Merchants worked to obtain their wealth, and by the values of the governing class this was unpardonable.[115] Nevertheless, the latter avidly sought the goods that the merchants sold and coveted their wealth, acquiring it whenever they could by taxes, marriage, or

---

[111] They were also attracted to them because they were the social and cultural centers of their societies. See Sjoberg, *op. cit.*, pp. 108–116. This pattern also prevailed in the American South. See Samuel G. Stoney, *Plantations of the Carolina Low Country* (Charleston: Carolina Art Association, 1938), p. 36.

[112] Kendall, *op. cit.*, p. 157.

[113] Carcopino, *op. cit.*, p. 70.

[114] *Ibid.*, and Kendall, *op. cit.*, pp. 202 and 206.

[115] See, for example, Sjoberg, *op. cit.*, pp. 183ff. For an interesting illustration of the persistence of this pattern into the latter part of the nineteenth century in England, see W. Somerset Maugham, *Cakes and Ale* (New York: Pocket Books, 1944), p. 29.

outright confiscation.[116] The attitude of the merchants toward the governing class was equally ambivalent: they both feared and envied them but, when given the chance, emulated their way of life and sought to be accepted by them.

Like modern advertising men, the merchants of agrarian societies often created a demand for their goods, thereby spurring productivity. And like modern advertisers, they created demands chiefly for luxuries. One reason for this was the high cost of moving goods. With the primitive transportation available, only lightweight luxury items, such as silks, spices, and fine swords, could be moved very far without the costs becoming prohibitive. A report on China shortly after World War II indicates

---

[116] On acquisition by marriage, see Elinor Barber, *The Bourgeoisie in 18th Century France* (Princeton University Press, 1955., p. 89; or Sansom, *op. cit.,* vol. III, pp. 128–129. On confiscation, see Misra, *op. cit.,* pp. 25–27; Takekoshi, *op. cit.,* vol. II, pp. 251ff.; Kendall, *op. cit.,* p. 181; or Ramsay, *op. cit.,* vol. I, p. 58.

Fig. 9/21   Like modern advertising men, merchants often created a demand for their goods, especially luxuries: market scene, Morocco

Fig. 9/22   The cost of moving goods was extremely high in agrarian societies because of the primitive methods of transportation: market scene, Saudi Arabia

the enormous differential between traditional and modern methods of transportation there. To ship one ton of goods one mile, the costs were as follows (measured in U.S. cents):[117]

Steamboat	2.4
Rail	2.7
Junk	12.0
Animal-drawn cart	13.0
Pack mule	17.0
Wheelbarrow	20.0
Pack donkey	24.0
Pack horse	30.0
Carrying by pole	48.0

[117] John Lossing Buck, *Secretariat Paper No. 1: Tenth Conference of the Institute of Pacific Relations*, Stratford on Avon, 1947, reprinted in Irwin T. Sanders et al., *Societies Around the World* (New York: Dryden Press, 1953), p. 65.

Figures from Europe are strikingly similar: in 1900, for example, it cost *ten times* more to move goods by horse-drawn wagon than by rail.[118] In short, modern methods of transportation have slashed this expense by 80 to 95 per cent.

The prosperity of the merchant class was due in no small measure to the labors of a humbler class with which they were closely affiliated—the artisans, who numbered approximately 3 to 5 per cent of the total population.[119] Except for the peasantry, this class was the most important productive element in the economy. Most artisans lived in the urban centers and, like the rest of the urban population, were dependent on the surplus produced by the peasants. Craft specialization was rather highly developed in the larger urban centers, as we have seen.

The shops in which the artisans worked were small by modern standards. There was no factory type production of the kind with which we are familiar. In Rome in the first century B.C., a shop employing fifty men was considered very large.[120] A pewter business employing eighteen men was the largest mentioned in any of

---

[118] Clough and Cole, *op. cit.*, p. 445.

[119] See, for example, John Nef, *The Conquest of the Material World* (Chicago: University of Chicago Press, 1964), p. 69.

[120] Cowell, *op. cit.*, p. 80. See also William Woodruff, *Impact of Western Man: A Study of Europe's Role in the World Economy* (New York: St. Martin's, 1966), p. 254.

Fig. 9/23   Butcher shop, Saudi Arabia

Fig. 9/24   Craft specialization was highly developed in agrarian societies: Indian potter at work

London's medieval craft records, and even this modest size was not attained until the middle of the fifteenth century.[121] Typically the shop was also the place of residence; work was carried on either in the living quarters or in an adjoining room.[122]

The economic situation of the artisans, like that of the merchants, was variable. In Peking at the time of World War I, wages ranged from $2.50 a month for members of the Incense and Cosmetic Workers Guild to $36 a month for members of the Gold Foil Beaters Guild.[123] In general, those in highly skilled trades and some of the self-employed fared moderately well by agrarian standards. Apprentices and journeymen in less skilled trades, however, worked long hours for bare subsistence

---

[121] Sylvia Thrupp, *The Merchant Class of Medieval London* (Ann Arbor, Mich.: Ann Arbor Paperbacks, University of Michigan Press, 1962), p. 9.

[122] See, for example, Nef, *op. cit.*, p. 78.

[123] Sidney Gamble, *Peking: A Social Survey* (New York: Doran, 1921), p. 183.

wages. In Peking, for example, a seven-day workweek and ten-hour workday was typical, and many artisans remained too poor to marry.[124]

Merchants and artisans in the same trade were commonly organized into guilds. These organizations were an attempt to create, in an urban setting within agrarian societies, a functional approximation of the extended family group in horticultural societies. Many guilds spoke of their members as brothers, for example, and functioned as mutual aid associations, restricting entry into the field, forbidding price cutting, and otherwise striving to protect the interests of the membership.[125] Because a guild included merchant employers as well as artisan employees, the former were dominant, controlling key offices and adopting policies that benefited themselves more than the artisans.[126]

Beneath the artisans in the social structure of the cities were a variety ot other kinds of people. These included the unskilled laborers who supplied much of the animal energy required by the system. Working conditions for these men were usually terrible, and injuries common. As a result, their work life tended to be short. For example, early in the present century, the average Peking rickshaw man was able to work only five years, according to one authority.[127] The class of unskilled laborers shaded off into still more deprived groups—the unemployed, the beggars, and the criminals. The high birthrates of agrarian societies resulted in an oversupply of unskilled labor, and such people usually drifted to the cities, hoping to find some kind of employment. As long as they were young and healthy, they could usually find work as day laborers. But after they were injured or lost their youth and strength, they were quickly replaced by fresh labor and left to fend for themselves, usually as beggars or thieves. No agrarian society found a solution to this problem. But then, the leading classes were not especially interested in finding one. The system served their needs quite well just the way it was.

Many of the sisters of the men who made up the urban lower classes found their livelihood as prostitutes. Moralists have often condemned these women as though they elected this career in preference to a more honorable one. The record indicates, however, that most of them had little choice: the only alternative that most could hope for was a life of unrelieved drudgery and poverty as servants or unskilled laborers.[128] The men they might have married were too poor to afford wives, and the system of prostitution was often, in effect, a substitute for marriage

---

[124] *Ibid.*, p. 185.

[125] Thrupp, *op. cit.*, pp. 19, 30, etc.

[126] *Ibid.*, pp. 23 and 29–31; James Westfall Thompson, *Economic and Social History of Europe in the Later Middle Ages, 1300–1530* (New York: Century, 1931), p. 398.

[127] After that, he was good for little except begging. See Gamble, *op. cit.*, p. 283.

[128] In Asia many were sold into prostitution by their parents. See Gamble, *op. cit.*, p. 253. Many more, in every part of the world, were ignorant country girls seeking work in the city who were trapped by hired procurers, while still others were driven to it by unemployment and lack of funds. See M. Dorothy George, *London Life in the XVIIIth Century* (London: Kegan Paul, Trench, Trubner, 1925), pp. 112–113.

forced on many men and women by society. To be sure, the poor were not the only ones to avail themselves to the services of prostitutes, nor were all girls forced into the "profession" by poverty. But economic problems were clearly the chief cause of its high incidence.

Demographic patterns

As we have noted, the population potential of advanced agrarian societies far surpassed that of simpler societies. This potential slowly rose over the centuries as a result of technological advances in food production. Thus China's population gradually increased from about 50 million in the middle of the second century A.D., to around 240 million in the late eighteenth century, and then, more rapidly, to 400 million by the middle of the next century.[129] In Japan it grew from about 10 million in the thirteenth century to 35 million in 1875, and in Britain from one million in the eleventh century to 6 million in the early eighteenth.[130]

Birthrates have always been high in advanced agrarian societies, averaging about 40 births per year per thousand population, or more than double that of modern industrial societies.[131] In general there seems to have been little interest in limiting the size of families, since large families, especially ones with many sons, were valued for both economic and religious reasons. From the economic standpoint, children were viewed by peasants as an important asset, a valuable source of cheap labor.[132] In modern industrial societies, it is easy to forget how much work was required on a peasant farm. Religion added an extra incentive for large families either by encouraging cults of ancestor worship in which the perpetuation of the family line was essential, or simply by declaring large families to be the will of God.[133] The chief deterrent to large families was probably the reaction of women to the strains and risks of repeated pregnancies; but since they were subordinate to their husbands, who favored large families, their views counted for little.[134]

---

[129] Eberhard, *op. cit.,* pp. 108 and 274; and Chang, *op. cit.,* p. 102.

[130] Taeuber, *op. cit.,* pp. 20 and 41, on Japan; Russell, *op. cit.,* p. 235, and D. V. Glass and D. E. C. Eversley, *Population in History* (Chicago: Aldine, 1965), p. 240, on England.

[131] Warren Thompson and David Lewis, *Population Problems,* 5th ed. (New York: McGraw-Hill, 1965), p. 386; O. Andrew Collver, *Birth Rates in Latin America: New Estimates of Historical Trends and Fluctuations* (Berkeley, Calif.: Institute of International Studies, 1965), pp. 26–30; Glass and Eversley, *op. cit.,* pp. 467, 532, 555, and 614. One of the lowest rates for an agrarian society prior to the twentieth century was for eighteenth-century Sweden, and it was nearly 36 per thousand (*ibid.,* p. 532).

[132] See, for example, Horace Miner, *St. Denis: A French-Canadian Parish* (Chicago: Phoenix Books, The University of Chicago Press, 1963), p. 65; Berger, *op. cit.,* p. 116; Coulton, *The Medieval Village,* p. 322; Manning Nash, *The Golden Road to Modernity: Village Life in Contemporary Burma* (New York: Wiley, 1965), pp. 265–266.

[133] See, for example, John Noss, *Man's Religions,* rev. ed. (New York: Macmillan, 1956), pp. 227, 304ff., and 420–421; Miner, *op. cit.,* pp. 65–66.

[134] Miner, *op. cit.,* p. 170.

Despite high birthrates, advanced agrarian societies grew slowly. Sometimes they failed to grow at all or even declined in size. The reason, of course, was the death rates, which were usually almost as high as the birthrates, and sometimes higher. Wars, disease, accidents, and starvation all took their toll. Infant mortality was especially high before the development of modern sanitation and medicine. Recent studies show that the average child born in Rome two thousand years ago could not expect to live more than 20 years.[135] Even as recently as the seventeenth century, the children of British queens and dutchesses had a life expectancy of only 30 years, with nearly a third dead before their fifth birthday. Those youngsters of the elite who survived the dangerous infant years still had a total life expectancy of only a little more than 40 years.[136] For the common people, conditions were even worse. With death rates averaging nearly 40 per thousand per year, life expectancy could not have been much over 25 years.

The larger cities were notoriously unhealthy places, especially for the common people. The citizens of Rome, for example, had a shorter life expectancy than those in the provinces.[137] This was also true in England in the early eighteenth century. During the first half of that century, there were an estimated 500,000 more deaths

---

[135] Harrison Brown, *The Challenge of Man's Future* (New York: Viking Compass, 1956), p. 75.

[136] T. H. Hollingsworth, "A Demographic Study of the British Ducal Families," in Glass and Eversley, *op. cit.*, tables 2 and 5, pp. 358 and 360.

[137] Brown, *op. cit.*, p. 75.

Fig. 9/25 The streets of medieval towns were generally little more than narrow alleys effectively excluding all but a minimum of light and air: street scene, France

Fig. 9/26 Street scene, Peru: note the overhanging upper story

than births in London.[138] Some of the reasons for this become clear when we read descriptions of sanitary conditions in medieval cities. As one historian depicts them:

> The streets of medieval towns were generally little more than narrow alleys, the over-hanging upper stories of the houses nearly meeting, and thus effectually excluding all but a minimum of light and air . . . In most continental towns and some English ones, a high city wall further impeded the free circulation of air . . . Rich citizens might possess a courtyard in which garbage was collected and occasionally removed to the suburbs, but the usual practice was to throw everything into the streets including the garbage of slaughter houses and other offensive trades . . . Filth of every imaginable description accumulated indefinitely in the unpaved streets and in all available space and was trodden into the ground. The water supply would be obtained either from wells or springs, polluted by the gradual percolation through the soil of the accumulated filth, or else from an equally polluted river. In some towns, notably London, small streams running down a central gutter served at once as sewers and as water supply . . . In seventeenth century London, which before the Fire largely remained a medieval city, the poorer class house had only a covering of weatherboards, a little black pitch forming the only waterproofing, and these houses were generally built back to back. Thousands of Londoners dwelt in cellars or horribly overcrowded tenements. A small house in Dowgate accommodated 11 married couples and 15 single persons . . . Another source of unhealthiness were the church vaults and graveyards, so filled with corpses

---

[138] Warren Thompson, *Population Problems,* 3d ed. (New York: McGraw-Hill, 1942), p. 73.

that the level of the latter was generally raised above that of the surrounding ground. In years of pestilence, recourse had to be made to plague pits in order to dispose of the harvest of death.[139]

This account calls attention to one of the striking demographic characteristics of advanced agrarian societies: the disasters that periodically overtook them and produced sharp peaks in the death rates.[140] The most devastating of all, the Black Plague that hit Europe in the middle of the fourteenth century, is said to have killed a third of the population of France and England, half that of Italy, and to have left the island of Cyprus almost depopulated.[141] Crop failures and famines seldom affected such large areas, but they were much more frequent and could be just as deadly where they struck. One Finnish province lost a third of its population during the famine of 1696–1697, and many parts of France suffered comparable losses a few years earlier.[142] Even allowing for a considerable margin of error in the reports of such disasters, it is clear from other kinds of evidence—the severe labor shortages that followed plagues and famines, and the abandonment of farms—that the number of deaths was huge. Because of these disasters, the growth of advanced agrarian populations was anything but continuous.

Religion

During the era in which advanced agrarian societies were dominant, a number of important changes occurred in the religious sphere. The most important by far was the emergence and spread of three new religions. Buddhism, Christianity, and Islam each proclaimed a supranational or universal faith, and each succeeded in creating a community of believers that transcended national boundaries. In all of the older faiths, religious belief and affiliation were determined by the accident of birth and residence. Where one lived determined the god or gods he worshipped. The prevailing view was that there were many gods and, like kings, each had his own people and his own territory.

The ancient Israelites were perhaps the first to reject this view and move toward a more universalistic outlook. Centuries before the birth of Christ, the prophets proclaimed that there was only one God and that He ruled over the entire world. For a time, Judaism was a missionary religion and won converts in many parts of the Roman world.[143] This phase ended, however, when the early Christian missionaries won most of these gentile converts over to their faith. After this, the

---

[139] M. C. Buer, *Health, Wealth, and Population in the Early Days of the Industrial Revolution, 1760–1815* (London: Routledge, 1926), pp. 77–78. Quoted by permission of Routledge & Kegan Paul Ltd.

[140] D. E. C. Eversley, "Population, Economy, and Society," in Glass and Eversley, *op. cit.*, p. 52.

[141] Warren Thompson, *op. cit.*, p. 58. See also Brown, *op. cit.*, p. 32.

[142] K. F. Helleiner, "The Vital Revolution Reconsidered," in Glass and Eversley, *op. cit.*, p. 79.

[143] See Kenneth Scott Latourette, *A History of Christianity* (New York: Harper, 1953), pp. 15–16.

Jewish people left the implementation of their universalistic vision to Christians and Muslims, who eventually converted, at least nominally, most of the population of Europe, North Africa, the Middle East, and some of the people of India, central Asia, China, and southeast Asia.

Buddhism, the other great universalistic faith, began in India as an heretical offshoot of Hinduism and spread through most of southeast Asia, China, Korea, and Japan, though it later died out in the land of its origin. Older ethnic faiths like Hinduism, Confucianism, and Shintoism continued to survive in much of Asia, but even they incorporated some elements of universalism in their thought.

The emergence and spread of the new universalistic faiths reflected the broader social and intellectual horizons opened up by the improved means of transportation and the spreading web of trade relations. Empire building also helped to weaken parochial or "tribal" views. As men's knowledge of other societies increased, and with it their awareness of the essential unity of mankind, the basic postulate of the older ethnic faiths was gradually undermined.

Another important development was the increasing separation of religious and political institutions.[144] Compared with advanced horticultural and simple agrarian

---

[144] See Robert Bellah, "Religious Evolution," *American Sociological Review*, 29 (1964), pp. 367–368.

Fig. 9/27   The Badhshahi, royal mosque in Lahore, Pakistan, built by Aurangzeb, a Moghul emperor

societies, the state had become a much more secular institution. Kings and emperors were still said to rule "by the grace of God," the divine right of kings was generally accepted, and occasionally a ruler claimed to be a god. But few rulers functioned as their nation's high priest, and theocracies (i.e., states in which a priesthood rules in the name of God) were almost unknown. This separation was part of the much more general trend toward institutional specialization that is so basic in the evolutionary process from the horticultural era on.

Despite the growing *organizational* separation of politics and religion, the two systems continued to work closely together, and political and religious leaders were normally allied. This was especially evident in struggles between the governing class and the common people. When rebellious voices challenged the right of the governing class to control the economic surplus produced by the peasants, the clergy usually defended the elite, asserting that their power had been given them by God and any challenge to it was a challenge to His authority.[145] By legitimizing the actions of the governing class in this way, the clergy reduced the need for costly coercive efforts.

---

[145] See, for example, Lenski, *op. cit.*, pp. 4 and 7–9. See also Kendall, *op. cit.*, pp. 232ff.

Fig. 9/28 Religious procession in the village of Marin, Venezuela

In appreciation for this, and also because of their own religious beliefs, agrarian rulers were often extremely generous with religious groups, giving them large grants of land and special tax exemptions. In effect, a symbiotic relationship was established, with religious groups legitimizing the actions of the governing class in return for generous financial support. Modern research indicates that religious groups frequently owned as much as a quarter or a third of a nation's land.[146]

Despite such profitable alliances, most religions fostered some concern for distributive justice. This is especially evident in Judaism and Christianity.[147] One historian captured the contradictory nature of the medieval church in this insightful characterization: "Democratic, yet aristocratic; charitable, yet exploitative; generous, yet mercenary; humanitarian, yet cruel; indulgent, yet severely repressive of some things; progressive, yet reactionary; radical, yet conservative—all these are qualities of the Church in the Middle Ages."[148]

Magic and fatalism

Before we leave the subject of ideology, there are two other aspects of the world view of agrarian societies that deserve comment: (1) the widespread belief in the efficacy of magic, and (2) the equally widespread attitude of fatalism.[149] Logically, these are contradictory. If magic really works, men do not need to be fatalistic, and if men are true fatalists, they should have no confidence in magic. But men are seldom completely logical in their view of life. In their more optimistic moments they often hope for things they know are impossible. Considering the tremendous pressures operating on the masses of common people in agrarian societies and the limited sources of information available to them, it is hardly surprising that so many of them held these mutually contradictory views. At least they offered a ray of hope.

The prevalence of these beliefs, however, was another factor that contributed to the slow rate of technological advance in agrarian societies. Neither belief was likely to motivate men to try to devise better tools and techniques. On the contrary, one encouraged them to look to magic for the solutions to their problems; the other convinced them that success was, after all, simply a matter of fate.

Kinship

Kinship ties continued to be important for the individual in advanced agrarian societies. For society, however, their importance was greatly diminished compared

---

[146] Lenski, *op. cit.,* pp. 257–258.

[147] *Ibid.,* pp. 262–266, for a more detailed treatment of this aspect of religion.

[148] Thompson, *Economic and Social History of the Middle Ages,* p. 684.

[149] See, for example, Carlo Levi, *Christ Stopped at Eboli* (New York: Farrar, Straus, 1947), chaps. 11ff., for a good description of the role of magic in one agrarian community. On fatalism, see, for example, Edward Banfield, *The Moral Basis of a Backward Society* (New York: Free Press, 1967), pp. 36–37, 41, 107ff., etc.

with hunting and gathering or horticultural societies. The explanation for this lies in the growth in the scale of organization. As long as communities and societies were small, the kinship system could serve as an integrative force helping to unite the entire population. Later, when the growth of population made this impossible, the largest and most powerful extended family in a society, supplemented perhaps by its dependent retainers, could still provide enough men to staff the political system. By the time the level of advanced agrarian societies was reached, however, even this became impossible. Civil and military offices were so numerous that not even the largest extended family could fill them all. Thus the kinship system could no longer provide the structural basis for the political system.

Family ties could still be extremely important for the individual, however. Many civil and military offices in agrarian societies were a family's patrimony and were handed down from father to son like any other family possession. The classic case of this was the royal office itself in most societies, but the pattern was much more widespread than that. When offices were not privately owned, they were often closed to anyone who was not a member of the nobility or whose family did not qualify by less formal criteria as one of "the right families." Even when these criteria were not invoked in the allocation of offices, family ties were still important. Family funds might be needed to purchase an office, and those who had it in their power to assign an office were, of course, influenced by their own family connections. While similar practices still occur in modern industrial societies, they are usually a violation of the law and lack general public approval. But in advanced agrarian societies, these practices were usually an accepted part of the way of life, and there was little criticism, and still less punishment, of those who engaged in them.

In the economic realm, the family was usually the basic unit of organization. This was equally true in urban and rural areas. Businesses were almost always family enterprises; the corporate form of enterprise, owned jointly by unrelated persons, was virtually unheard of, even in the largest cities. And in rural areas the basic work unit was the family.

It is not unfair to say that in these societies the family was largely an economic and/or political organization. While this can be demonstrated in many ways, some of the best examples are associated with marriage. For instance, because of its economic implications, marriage was considered much too important to be decided by young people, and marriages were usually arranged by the parents, often with the aid of marriage brokers.[150] Sometimes the young couple did not even meet until the ceremony itself. In selecting spouses for their children, parents were usually concerned most with the economic and status implications of the match, and only secondarily with other matters. Marriage arrangements often involved an outright economic transaction, either the payment of a bride-price (i.e., payment for the bride) or a dowry.[151] Among members of the governing class, marriages were

---

[150] Sjoberg, *op. cit.*, pp. 146ff.

[151] *Ibid.*, p. 155.

usually arranged with an eye to their political implications; by skillful management of the marriages of its children, a family could do a great deal to improve its political position.

As one would suppose, marriages contracted in this way did not always produce psychological or sexual compatibility between the spouses, but then, this was not necessarily expected. For those pleasures, wealthier men often turned to mistresses and concubines. Despite this, marriage ties were usually quite durable because of their strong economic or political bonds.

Within the family, male dominance was the rule. Obedience was generally held to be the highest ideal for women and children.[152] This was but part of the general authoritarian pattern that characterized so much of the life of agrarian societies.

Cleavages and conflicts

The sociocultural cleavages that divided advanced agrarian societies were similar to the ones in simple agrarian. Most important of all was the division along class lines. In advanced agrarian societies, however, this could no longer be described simply as a cleavage between the governing class and the rest of the population. The class structure had become more complex. Some merchants were now wealthier than some members of the governing class, for example, and between these privileged classes and the mass of common people was a growing middle class of self-employed artisans, small merchants, minor officials, lesser members of the clergy, and well-to-do peasants. In conflicts with the poor, the wealthy merchants and middle class usually aligned themselves with the governing class, but at other times they did their best to advance their own interests at the expense of the governing class.

Second, the cleavage between city people and country folk was still there, intensified, if anything, by increasing urbanization. Less and less was it possible to describe towns and cities as overgrown villages. More and more they were taking on their own distinctive way of life, one that seemed completely alien to the visiting peasant or the migrant from a rural area. And because of the concentration of the literate and privileged classes in the urban centers, the villages seemed to city dwellers social and cultural backwaters, their residents culturally backward and stupid. There was a great deal of barbed humor by city people at the expense of country "yokels," and by country people at the expense of city "slickers" who were not quite as smart as they thought they were when confronted with some of the problems of rural life.

Third, the cleavage between literate and illiterate continued, the chief difference being that in advanced agrarian societies most of the privileged class were literate:

---

[152] *Ibid.*, pp. 163ff.; Henry Orenstein, *Gaon: Conflict and Cohesion in an Indian Village* (Princeton, N.J.: Princeton University Press, 1965), pp. 53–57; Kendall, *op. cit.*, chaps. 11 and 12; L. F. Salzman, *English Life in the Middle Ages* (London: Oxford, 1927), pp. 254–256.

writing was no longer a craft specialty. In most societies, this spread of literacy was greatly facilitated by the invention of the alphabet, though Chinese experience shows this was not essential.

Religion was the basis of an important new cleavage in many advanced agrarian societies. Although religious conflicts existed in simple agrarian societies, they were largely power struggles within the governing class. The majority of the population had little interest in their outcome. With the rise of the new universalistic faiths, however, the common people were often drawn into these struggles. In many areas, especially in the Middle East and India, this led to the formation of largely endogamous (i.e., forbidding marriage outside the group), culturally differentiated, and hostile religious groups. Each group sought control of the machinery of government in order to protect and further its own special interests. Members of religious minorities were often discriminated against politically, economically, and legally.

On the whole, the divisions within advanced agrarian societies were more serious than those within simple agrarian. In particular, they were much more likely to lead to violence. Earlier we noted the frequency of peasant risings. Though most of these were local incidents involving small numbers of people, some spread and became large-scale insurrections. In either case, they represented something new in history. Nor was it only the peasants who revolted against the governing class. The artisans followed suit on a number of occasions, as did the merchants.[153] And these groups, unlike the peasants, sometimes emerged victorious. In Europe, the merchants were so successful in their challenges to the governing class that eventually *they* became the governing class in many cities and towns. Ultimately, this proved to be a very important development.

Sociocultural variations

In surveying societies at the same level of development, it is natural to emphasize those characteristics which are common to them all, or at least widespread among them, and to slight the differences, thus giving an impression of greater uniformity than really exists. Obviously there are variations in every area of societal life, and we have noted many of them in passing, or hinted at them in qualifying phrases, saying that a particular pattern was found in "most" or "many" societies.

Technologically, for example, the first advanced agrarian societies were much more like their simple agrarian predecessors than like the advanced agrarian societies of Europe on the eve of the Industrial Revolution. The size of societies in this category ranged all the way from tiny principalities to great empires. Most were monarchies, but a few were republics. Similar variations occurred in almost every area of life.

Clearly, then, variation is a normal condition in societies at the advanced

---

[153] See, for example, H. van Werveke, "The Rise of the Towns," in *The Cambridge Economic History of Europe* (Cambridge: Cambridge University Press, 1963), vol. 3, pp. 34–37; L. Halphen, "Industry and Commerce," in Tilley, *op. cit.*, pp. 190–192; or Pirenne, *op. cit.*, pp. 187–206.

agrarian level—indeed, at *every* level of societal development. There is, however, one important difference: In the simplest societal types (i.e., hunting and gathering and simple horticultural societies), intratype variation was largely the result of differences in the physical environment. We see this clearly when we compare the Eskimos with the Australian aborigines, or the Indians of the rich northern California area with the Bushmen of the Kalahari Desert. By contrast, differences in the physical environment of advanced agrarian societies have played a much smaller role. This decline is exactly what evolutionary theory would lead us to expect, since the further a society advances on the evolutionary scale, the greater is its ability to overcome the limitations of its environment.

Chapter 10
Specialized Societal Types

Up to this point in our survey of human societies, we have concentrated on those types that are in the mainstream of evolutionary history, those that developed their technologies around the resources of fields and forests. The societies to which we now turn have adapted to more specialized, less typical environments—two to aquatic conditions, the third to semidesert grasslands and other marginal environments. Though these specialized societies have contributed to sociocultural evolution in numerous ways, their overall contribution has been more limited than that of the mainstream societies. This is due to their smaller numbers and the specialized nature of the problems with which they have dealt in their subsistence activities. Because of their more limited contribution, we shall not examine them in the same detail as the others.

FISHING SOCIETIES

Actually it is something of a misnomer to call any group a "fishing" society, for none ever depended exclusively on fishing for its food supply.[1] Except in the arctic, nearly all fishing peoples obtain fruits and vegetables by foraging or cultivation. Many of them also supplement their diet by hunting or, occasionally, by raising

---

[1] According to Murdock's Ethnographic Atlas, the Manus of New Guinea come as close to this as any people in the world (see *Ethnology*, vol. 6, no. 2 (April, 1967), pp. 170–230. Yet, as Margaret Mead indicates in her report, these people depend heavily for their subsistence on garden products which they obtain through trade from neighboring peoples, and to a lesser degree on pigs which they raise and obtain through trade. See Margaret Mead, *Growing Up in New Guinea* (New York: Mentor, 1953, first published 1930), especially pp. 173–174.

livestock. To call a society a fishing society, then, simply indicates that fishing and foraging are its most important subsistence activities.

In recent centuries, fishing societies have been found in many parts of the world, but they have been most common in the northwestern part of North America—Oregon, Washington, British Columbia, Alaska, and the arctic regions of Canada. They have occurred less frequently in northern Asia and among the islands of the Pacific (most of the Pacific peoples have been simple horticulturalists) and in scattered parts of Africa, South America, and elsewhere.

Historically, fishing societies are probably the second oldest type, emerging in the Mesolithic era, or about a thousand years before the first horticultural societies. The actual practice of fishing is, of course, even older and more widespread and has provided a supplementary source of subsistence in most societies since at least Upper Paleolithic times.

In some ways fishing societies might be regarded simply as specialized hunting and gathering societies, but adapted to aquatic environments rather than terrestrial.

Fig. 10/1 African fishing village, Dahomey: in terms of organizational development, fishing societies stand midway between hunting and gathering and horticultural societies. Compare this picture with Figs. 7/8, 7/14, 7/15, 8/10, and 8/16

One might argue that the chief difference is simply that fish, rather than land animals, are the object of the chase and that the technology of the group is modified accordingly. But this ignores a crucial fact: Fishing economies usually have a potential for supporting larger, more sedentary populations than hunting and gathering economies. There are two reasons for this. First, fish have much higher reproductive rates than most land animals, especially the larger animals on which hunters depend. This means that primitive fishing peoples are less likely to deplete the food resources of their territory than hunters are. As a result, it is easier for fishing peoples to establish permanent settlements, with all that this implies for the accumulation of wealth and the growth of social inequality. Moreover, fishing groups are often able to obtain their food in less time than hunting and gathering groups because they waste less time working territories with half depleted resources. Fishermen, therefore, usually have more time to devote to nonsubsistence activities.

A second basic difference between them is that fishermen usually work only a small fraction of the food-producing territory. When primitive peoples fish a large body of water, like an ocean, a sea, or a large lake, the kinds of boats they use prevent them from going beyond a certain limit. As a result, even if they catch all the fish in the territory they work, the supply is quickly replenished by the great surplus spawned in adjacent areas. Nothing like this can happen on land, at least not after hunting and gathering bands occupy all of the habitable territory in an area. This second difference, therefore, reinforces the effects of the first.

Thus, even though fishing societies are technologically as primitive as hunting and gathering societies, we would expect them to be somewhat larger, more sedentary, and in other ways a bit more advanced.[2] This is, in fact, precisely what we find. With respect to size, they are half again as large: Murdock's sample shows that the average size of fishing communities is approximately 60, the average size of hunting and gathering groups only 40.[3] With respect to sedentariness, only 9 per cent of the hunting and gathering societies live in permanent settlements as compared with 49 per cent of the fishing societies.

A comparison of political systems also indicates the greater potential inherent in a fishing economy. Less than 10 per cent of hunters and gatherers are organized into multicommunity societies in contrast to nearly a quarter of the fishing societies. Social inequality, too, is more pronounced and more common. Slavery is reported in only 10 per cent of the hunting and gathering societies, but in slightly over half of the fishing. The difference is even greater for hereditary slavery, a more extreme form; it is practiced by less than 3 per cent of the hunting and gathering groups and by 37 per cent of the fishing. A system of hereditary nobility is also much more common in the latter (32 per cent versus 2 per cent). Finally, as another indication

---

[2] For an earlier discussion of this, see Gordon Hewes' excellent paper, "The Rubric 'Fishing and Fisheries,'" *American Anthropologist*, 50 (1948), pp. 241–242.

[3] See Table 6/2, p. 131 above.

Fig. 10/2   Indian fishing village, British Columbia (c. 1880)

of the growth of their economy and their greater wealth, fishing peoples are much more likely to link marriage with some economic transaction. This happens in 77 per cent of these groups, but in only 48 per cent of the hunting and gathering.

In terms of organizational development, fishing societies have about as much in common with simple horticultural societies as with advanced hunting and gathering.[4] Depending on the criterion, they sometimes lean more toward one, sometimes the other. For example, in average size of community they more closely approximate advanced hunting and gathering societies.[5] In permanence of settlements, they are midway between the other two.[6] Finally, in frequency of multi-community societies, fishing societies are almost indistinguishable from simple horticultural.[7]

From an evolutionary standpoint, the line of development represented by fishing societies has been something of a blind alley. Unlike the mainstream types, these societies did not evolve into more advanced ones.[8] The reasons for this are

---

[4] For a good illustration of this, see Philip Drucker's excellent description of the Indians of the Pacific Northwest in *Cultures of the North Pacific Coast* (San Francisco: Chandler, 1965).

[5] The averages are hunting and gathering, 40; fishing, 60; simple horticultural, 95.

[6] The percentage of permanent settlements are hunting and gathering, 10; fishing, 49; simple horticultural, 87.

[7] The percentages are hunting and gathering, 10; fishing, 23; simple horticultural, 21.

[8] Unless, perhaps, some evolved into maritime societies. To date, however, there is no real evidence that this ever happened. Maritime societies seem to have evolved out of advanced horticultural or agrarian societies.

quite simple. To begin with, the areas suited to a predominantly fishing economy are not only very limited but are scattered and strung out along thin coastal strips so that opportunities for consolidation into large political entities are negligible.[9] Instead, when neighboring horticultural societies develop larger and more powerful states, fishing societies are usually conquered and absorbed. Then, although fishing continues in the area, it is but a minor part of the economy of the larger society, and the leaders of the fishing settlements are reduced to the status of minor officials,

[9] See Hewes, *op. cit.*, pp. 240–241.

Fig. 10/3 The Shui-jen, or water people of south China, are descended from fishing peoples of an earlier time. They still depend on fishing for their livelihood and remain separate from the mainland population

too weak to hold into the local surplus for local use. As a result, fishing communities in agrarian societies have often been socially and culturally less advanced (except in subsistence technology) than fishing communities in more primitive fishing societies. Typically, their situation is no better than that of peasant villages, and for the same reason—their surplus is confiscated by the more powerful elements in the society.[10]

Though fishing societies did not give rise to more advanced societal types, they should not be thought of as evolutionary blind alleys. For example, they cannot be compared to animals like the dinosaurs, whose entire line was wiped out and who therefore made no lasting genetic contribution. The technological advances made by fishing societies have not been lost but rather have become a part of the cultural heritage of most modern societies. This reminds us again of the differences between sociocultural and organic evolution.

HERDING SOCIETIES

Herding societies, like fishing societies, represent an adaptation to specialized environmental conditions. Other than that, the two have little in common. Their environments are very different, and their technologies, while overlapping some-what, are basically on different levels.

Technologically, herding groups cover the same range of development as horticultural and simple agrarian societies. Animals were first domesticated about the same time plants were first cultivated, and the two practices typically went hand in hand in the horticultural and agrarian societies of the Old World.[11] In some areas, however, crops could not be cultivated because of insufficient rainfall, the shortness of the growing season (in northern latitudes), or the mountainous character of the terrain. This was true of much of central Asia, the Arabian peninsula, and North Africa, and parts of Europe and sub-Saharan Africa. Though horticulture and agriculture were not feasible, it was often possible to raise livestock.[12] Thus a new and different type of society gradually came into being.

A pastoral economy necessarily promotes a distinctive way of life.[13] To begin with, it usually necessitates a nomadic or seminomadic way of life.[14] In fact, in early Greek, the word from which the English word "nomad" derives meant a herder

---

[10] For an interesting account of one such group, see Wilmond Menard, "The Sea Gypsies of China," *Natural History*, 64 (January, 1965), pp. 13–21.

[11] This was not true in most of the New World, where there were almost no domesticated animals.

[12] Usually these societies have also had some secondary means of subsistence, frequently horticulture or agriculture on a small scale.

[13] For a brief general introduction to some of these societies, see Carleton Coon, "The Nomads," in Sydney Fisher (ed.), *Social Forces in the Middle East* (Ithaca, N.Y.: Cornell, 1955), pp. 23–42.

[14] See, for example, Lawrence Krader, "Pastoralism," in *International Encyclopedia of the Social Sciences* (New York: Macmillan and Free Press, 1968), vol. II, pp. 456–457.

Fig. 10/4   Bedouin family camped in ruins of a deserted town, Saudi Arabia

of cattle.[15] In the sample of herding societies in the Ethnographic Atlas, more than 90 per cent are wholly or partially nomadic. In this respect they closely resemble hunters and gatherers.

Herders are also like hunters and gatherers in the size of their communities. On the average, they are a bit smaller than fishing communities and much smaller than simple horticultural, as the following figures show:

Hunting and gathering societies	40
Herding societies	55
Fishing societies	60
Simple horticultural societies	95

The explanation for this is primarily environmental. Given the limited resources of their territories, large and dense settlements are impossible.[16]

Despite the small size of their communities, herding *societies* are usually fairly large. Whereas the typical hunting and gathering, fishing, or simple horticultural society contains but a single community, the average herding society contains several dozen.[17] Thus the median size of herding societies far surpasses that of the other three types:

Hunting and gathering societies	40
Fishing societies	60
Simple horticultural societies	95
Herding societies	2,000

---

[15] John L. Myres, "Nomadism," *Journal of the Royal Anthropological Institute,* 71 (1941), p. 20.

[16] Krader reports the average density of population in Mongolia was less than one per square mile, and among the Tuareg of Africa it was even lower (*op. cit.,* pp. 458–459).

[17] The percentages of single-community societies were 90, 78, 77 and 13, respectively, in Murdock's Ethnographic Atlas sample.

The size of herding societies results from the combined influence of environment and technology. Open grasslands, where the majority of herders live, present few natural barriers to movement. Furthermore, since early in the second millennium B.C., many of the herding peoples have mastered the art of horseback (or camel) riding, which facilitates political integration.

The basic resource in these societies is livestock, and the size of the herd is the measure of the man. Large herds signify not only wealth but power, for only a strong man or the head of a strong family can defend such vulnerable property against rivals and enemies. Hence, in most of these societies, and especially in the more advanced (i.e., those with horses and herds of larger animals such as cattle), marked social inequality is the rule. Hereditary slavery, for example, is far more common in herding societies than in any other type (62 per cent as against 3 to 37 per cent in the rest). Other kinds of inequality are also very common, especially inequality of wealth.[18]

With respect to kinship, herding societies are noteworthy on at least two counts. First, they are more likely than any other type of society to require the payment of a bride price or bride service (93 per cent compared with 37 to 86 per cent in other types). Second, they are the most likely to require newly married couples to

---

[18] As shown in Table 6/8, p. 137, class stratification, by Murdock's definition, is present in 51 per cent of these societies.

Fig. 10/5   Bedouins drawing water for their herds, Saudi Arabia

Table 10/1 Religious beliefs of agrarian
societies, by percentage of subsistence derived
from herding

Percentage of subsistence from herding	Percentage believing in active, moral creator God	Number of societies
36–45	92	13
26–35	82	28
16–25	40	20
6–15	20	5

live with the husband's kinsmen. This occurs in 97 per cent of herding societies compared with only 49 to 79 per cent in other types.

These strong patriarchal tendencies have several sources. To begin with, they reflect the mobile and often militant character of pastoral life. Raiding and warfare are frequent activities and, as we have noted before, this stimulates the growth of political authority. Moreover, the basic economic activity in these societies is man's work. In this respect they stand in sharp contrast to horticultural societies, where women so often play the important role in subsistence activities. It is hardly coincidence that horticultural societies are noted for their frequent female-oriented kinship patterns (e.g., matrilineality), while herding societies are noted for the opposite.

Herding societies are extremely interesting from the religious standpoint. No other societal type so closely resembles Judaism and Christianity in its conception of God. In 40 of the 50 herding groups for which the Ethnographic Atlas has data, there is a belief in a Supreme Deity who created the world and remains actively concerned with its affairs, especially with man's moral conduct. This combination of beliefs is rare in other societies except agrarian, where it occurs in two-thirds of the cases.[19] But even there, as Table 10/1 makes clear, its occurrence varies directly with the importance of herding activities to the particular group.

For those familiar with religious history, this relationship is not surprising. The Hebrews, who played such an important role in the rise and spread of monotheism, were originally a herding people. And Islam, one of the most uncompromisingly monotheistic faiths, enjoyed most of its earliest successes among the herding peoples of the Arabian peninsula.

Why this relationship developed is far from clear, but the fact is undeniable. One can find repeated evidence of the affinity between the pastoral way of life and these religious concepts in Biblical texts which describe God as a shepherd and His

---

[19] Among the rest, it is most common in advanced horticultural societies, but even there occurs in only 16 per cent of the cases; in the other types, the frequency ranges from 2 to 10 per cent.

people as sheep. The shepherd's pastoral relationship with his flock apparently suggested answers to the perennial questions concerning man's nature and destiny and the power which ultimately controls them. These answers have not been obvious to all herding peoples, however, since a number of pastoral groups in Asia and Africa have come up with very different ones. The most we can say is that pastoral life increases the probabilities that men will arrive at this kind of answer.

One of the most important technical advances made by herding peoples was harnessing the energy of horses (and later camels) for purposes of transportation. This practice originated in the eighteenth century B.C., when herding groups in the Middle East began to harness horses to chariots.[20] This gave them an important military advantage over their less mobile agrarian neighbors and enabled such groups as the Hyksos, Kassites, and Mitanni to win control of much of the Middle East—at least until their techniques spread to the more numerous agrarian peoples. Herders later learned to *ride* their horses, which led to a new wave of conquests beginning in the ninth century.[21] During the next 2,500 years, a succession of advanced herding groups attacked agrarian societies from China to Europe and frequently conquered them. The empires and dynasties they established include some of the most famous in history—the great Mongol Empire, for example, founded by Genghis Kahn early in the thirteenth century A.D. and expanded by his successors. At the peak of its power, the Mongol Empire stretched from eastern Europe to the shores of the Pacific and launched attacks against places as far apart as Austria and Japan. Other famous empires and dynasties founded by herding peoples include the Mughal Empire, established in India by one branch of the Mongols, the Manchu dynasty in China, the Ottoman Empire in the Middle East, and the early Islamic Empire established by Muhammad and his followers.

Despite their frequent military victories, herding peoples were never able to destroy the agrarian social order. In the end, it was always they, not the agrarian peoples, who changed their mode of life. There were a number of reasons for this, but it was primarily because the herders were motivated chiefly by greed. They saw agrarian societies as rich prizes and coveted the luxuries which the governing classes of these societies enjoyed. After a few early conquerors attempted to turn fields into pastures, they soon found how costly this was and abandoned the effort. Why kill the goose that lays the golden eggs? Thus, despite many impressive victories, the limits of the herding world were never enlarged.

Though herding continued to be an important secondary source of subsistence in the agrarian world, it was the primary source only in areas not suited to cultivation. In recent centuries, even these areas have, in most cases, been brought under the control of agrarian or industrial societies, and herding societies are vanishing like other preindustrial types.

---

[20] See William McNeill, *The Rise of the West: A History of the Human Community* (New York: Mentor, 1965), pp. 126f.; or Ralph Turner, *The Great Cultural Traditions* (New York: McGraw-Hill, 1941), p. 259.

[21] For a good discussion of this important subject, see McNeill, *op. cit.*, pp. 256ff.

MARITIME SOCIETIES

Maritime societies have been the rarest of all the basic societal types. Not one survives today. Yet they once played an important role in the civilized world.

Technologically, maritime societies had a lot in common with agrarian societies. What set them apart was the way they used their technology to take advantage of the opportunities afforded by their environmental situation. Located on large bodies of water in an era when it was cheaper to move goods by water than by land, these peoples peoples found trade and commerce far more profitable than either fishing or the cultivation of their limited land resources, and gradually created societies in which overseas trade was the chief economic activity.

The first maritime society in history was probably developed by the Minoans on the island of Crete, late in the third millennium B.C. The wealth and power of the Minoan rulers probably "depended more upon foreign trade and religious prerogative than upon land rents and forced services."[22] The island location of Minoan society was important, not only because it afforded access to the sea, but because it provided protection against more powerful agrarian societies. Maritime societies were always dependent on the absence of powerful neighboring societies and usually developed on islands or peninsulas that were difficult to attack by land (see Fig. 10/6). Their only military advantage was in naval warfare.

---

[22] *Ibid.,* p. 111.

Fig. 10/6 Maritime societies usually developed on islands or peninsulas: aerial view of Tyre, an important maritime society of the ancient world. When Tyre was a leading Phoenecian city, there was no land bridge connecting it to the mainland

In the next 1,500 years a number of other maritime societies were established in the Mediterranean world. These included the Mycenaeans, or pre-Hellenic Greeks of the second millennium B.C., the Phoenicians, the Carthaginians, the Athenians, and the Corinthians.[23] The spread of the maritime pattern was due largely, perhaps wholly, to diffusion and the migration of maritime peoples. The Mycenaeans adopted it from the Minoans, whom they conquered and ruled for a hundred years beginning about 1500 B.C. Some of the Mycenaeans later settled in the coastal cities of the eastern Mediterranean, the area subsequently known as Phoenicia. The Phoenicians in turn established colonies in various parts of the Mediterranean, Carthage being the most famous. Finally, toward the end of the second millennium, Mycenae was conquered by invaders and many of its inhabitants migrated to Athens, which had not yet become an important commercial center.

Eventually, all of these groups were conquered by societies of other types and either destroyed or absorbed as subunits. This was not the end of overseas trade and commerce, of course, since these remained important activities in advanced agrarian societies. It did mean, however, a temporary end to societies in which overseas trade and commerce were the dominant economic activity. Then, more than a thousand years later, there was a revival of maritime societies during the Middle Ages. In the Mediterranean, Venice and Genoa were the prime examples; in the Baltic, Hamburg, Luebeck, Danzig, and other north German towns in the Hanseatic League. The last important maritime society was Holland, which in the seventeenth and eighteenth centuries apparently derived the major part of its income from overseas trade.[24]

In many ways maritime societies resembled advanced agrarian societies, particularly their urban centers. But there were also a number of important differences. To begin with, most maritime societies were very small—at least by comparison with agrarian societies. They usually contained no more than a single city and its immediate rural hinterland. Athens was probably typical in this respect; at its height it covered only about 1,000 square miles.[25] Only two of the maritime societies developed empires worthy of the name and, significantly, both of these (the Carthaginian and Dutch) were *overseas* empires.[26] In each case the empire seems to have been created more as an adjunct of commercial activity than as a militaristic venture.

---

[23] In the case of Athens, for example, it is estimated that by the fourth century B.C., only 20 per cent of the cereals consumed were grown in Attica and the rest were imported. See V. Gordon Childe, *What Happened in History* (Baltimore: Penguin, 1964), p. 207.

[24] England moved far in this direction in the seventeenth, eighteenth, nineteenth, and early twentieth centuries but probably never quite reached the point where her dependence on overseas commerce exceeded her dependence on, first, agriculture and, later, industry.

[25] Alvin Gouldner, *Enter Plato: Classical Greece and the Origins of Social Theory* (New York: Basic Books, 1965), p. 6.

[26] On the less familiar Carthaginian empire, see Donald Harden, *The Phoenicians* (New York: Praeger, 1963), chaps. 5 and 6.

This curious feature is linked with other, more basic peculiarities of maritime societies. In a largely agrarian world in which monarchy was the normal—almost universal—form of government, maritime societies stand out for their republicanism. Athens is the most familiar example, but many less famous Greek city-states were also maritime societies and republican. Republican government also flourished among the Phoenicians, the Carthaginians, the Venetians, the city-states of the Hanseatic League, and the Dutch. While monarchies were not unheard of, they were most common in the earlier periods, suggesting that they were a carryover from an earlier, premaritime tradition.

Fig. 10/7 A sixth-century B.C. warship and merchantman depicted on Athenian cup. The warship seems to be a pirate vessel overhauling an unsuspecting cargo ship that is moving under shortened sail. Athens was a leading maritime society in this period

The explanation for the republican tendency in maritime societies seems to be that commerce, rather than warfare and the exploitation of peasant masses, was the chief concern of the governing class. Being less involved in military activities than the typical agrarian state, these nations had less need for a strong, centralized, hierarchical government. An oligarchy of wealthy merchants could do the job. Its chief tasks would be to lay down rules regulating commercial competition and to provide naval forces capable of defending the merchants' access to foreign ports. The fact that navies rather than armies were the chief military arm of maritime states was also important, because this greatly reduced the risk of military coups. Unlike armies, navies are usually busy in places far removed from the seat of government, and this affords a considerable measure of protection for civilian leaders.

Another peculiarity of maritime societies was their unusual system of values and incentives. As we saw in the last chapter, the governing class in agrarian societies typically viewed work of any kind as degrading. Since this was the class that all others emulated, their view of economic activity rubbed off on the rest. This was especially evident in the case of merchants, who, when they became wealthy, usually gave up their commercial activities. As we noted, this antiwork ethic undoubtedly contributed to the slowdown in the rate of technological innovation

Fig. 10/8   Venetian room showing the wealth which commercial activities brought to merchants and officials of maritime societies

and progress. In maritime societies, by contrast, the merchants were the dominant class, and a very different view of economic activity prevailed. Though much more research is needed on the subject, there is reason to believe that the rate of technological advance was greater in maritime societies than in agrarian and that maritime societies made disproportionate technological and economic contributions to the emergence of modern industrial societies. It also appears that the rate of technological advance in *agrarian* societies was correlated with the sociopolitical strength of the merchant class. In other words, the greater the social status and political influence of the merchants, the greater tended to be the rate of technological and economic innovation.[27]

---

[27] Compare, for example, the relative status of merchants and the relative rates of innovation in Europe and India in the sixteenth, seventeenth, and eighteenth centuries. Both status of merchants and the rate of innovation were higher in Europe. While this could have been mere coincidence, a careful examination of the evidence suggests a causal link.

Preliminary Recapitulation

Having completed our survey of the various types of preindustrial societies, we are ready to consider the three that are most important today—industrial, industrializing agrarian, and industrializing horticultural societies. Before we turn to them, however, it may be well to pause and look back over the long evolutionary span and see how some of the more crucial developments in human history relate to our basic theoretical framework.

BEGINNINGS

Man as we know him is the product of a tremendously long evolutionary process. The first significant step was apparently taken about two million years ago, when our early ancestors began to manufacture tools (the *use* of tools, as we noted, is not a distinctively human practice). The next major step was the use of symbols and the accompanying emergence of culture. The first definite indications of this are found in the burial practices of Neanderthal man, approximately 150,000 years ago. Finally, in the Upper Paleolithic, no more than 35,000 to 40,000 years ago, the last major step was taken: sociocultural evolution replaced organic evolution as the dominant mode of human adaptation.

Man and his subhuman ancestors always lived in societies. While the basic elements of societal life are therefore attributable to our genetic heritage, this is not the whole story: the more complex societal patterns that have developed rest on cultural foundations. Were the key elements of the cultural heritage of modern societies somehow lost, organizations of their complexity could not survive; there would be a rapid regression to a far more primitive level of organization. Though this is unlikely, it is possible, since cultural information is seldom shared by all members of a society. Thus, a large number of people might survive a disaster and yet not possess, among them, enough technological information to maintain more than a rudimentary social system.

Throughout most of the prehistoric period, technological progress was painfully slow. There were fewer advances during all the hundreds of thousands of years of the Lower Paleolithic than in the last century alone. This was due to the very small numbers of people, the paucity of information they had to work with, and the difficulties of communication between societies. Later, as population and information increased, the rate of technological advance gradually accelerated. Even so, progress was infinitely slower than it is today.

DIVERSIFICATION AND PROGRESS

Until about ten thousand years ago, every human group was a hunting and gathering society. They were hardly carbon copies of one another, however. Because of man's gradual spread over the earth, societies were forced to adapt to many kinds of environments, ranging from the arctic to the tropical. There were probably also many differences in their marriage patterns, religious practices, and other aspects of life; but the archaeological record is silent on this. There is considerable variation in these areas among modern hunters and gatherers, however, and there is no reason to suppose it was any different then.

The emergence of the first fishing societies during the Mesolithic was an important new development. Man had at last devised techniques and tools that enabled him to take advantage of the resources of a radically different kind of environment, one that made possible population growth, more permanent settle-

ments, the formation of multicommunity societies, and increased "leisure." These, in turn, made possible the production of new kinds of goods and services, the accumulation of property, and the elaboration of ritual and ceremony—in short, a significant enrichment of human life.

About a thousand years later, an even more revolutionary development occurred when men discovered the basic techniques of plant cultivation and animal domestication. For the first time relatively permanent settlements could be maintained in almost any environment. Previously this had been possible only in coastal areas where fishing was carried on, and in a few unusual areas like northern California. The larger populations and increased "leisure" that fishing groups enjoyed became available to other societies, and to an even greater degree. But from the evolutionary standpoint, the most important development was the formation of an economic surplus, since this opened up so many organizational and ideological possibilities.

The formation of a surplus was not an automatic by-product of the adoption of horticulture; many horticultural societies, and even a few agrarian ones, did not take this step (see Fig. 10/9). This techno-

Fig. 10/9 Estimated percentage of societies with an economic surplus, by level of technological development

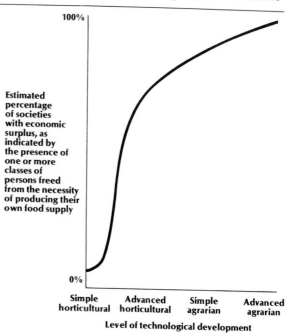

100%

Estimated percentage of societies with economic surplus, as indicated by the presence of one or more classes of persons freed from the necessity of producing their own food supply

0%

Simple horticultural   Advanced horticultural   Simple agrarian   Advanced agrarian

Level of technological development

logical advance, while *necessary* for the formation of a surplus, apparently was not enough. The horticultural revolution made it *possible* for a farmer to produce more than his family required, but there had to be something to make him want to *do* it. Political authorities were still too weak to compel him, so whatever he did had to be voluntary. In a considerable number of societies, religion provided the necessary incentive.

Once an economic surplus was established, some people could forget about subsistence activities and devote all of their time and energy to other things. While some specialization may occur without it, an economic surplus is essential for any real increase in the division of labor.

The surplus also led to increased status and class differentiation. Those who were powerful enough to control the surplus became the governing class in a society. They were supported by the mass of common people, whose duty it was to produce all they could.

As the productive capacity of societies increased, there gradually emerged an intermediate class of specialists who catered to the governing class and helped them procure, and dispose of, the surplus. Servants, retainers, officials, merchants, craftsmen, soldiers, and much of the clergy formed the bulk of the new class. As a rule, they lived near the governing class, often in the same households, and these clusters of people became the nucleus of the gradually emerging urban communities.

With the creation of stable surpluses, warfare became increasingly profitable. No longer were powerful and aggressive groups limited to hit-and-run raids and plundering expeditions. Now they could establish permanent control over weaker groups and take their surplus, in the form of tribute or taxes, on a regular basis. In short, conquest and empire building became feasible for the first time in history, thereby opening up a road to wealth that was to prove far more attractive to rulers and governing classes than the more pedestrian route of technological innovation.

These developments made the process of inter-societal selection even more important than it had been before. Since military advantage lay with the larger, technologically more advanced, and organizationally more efficient societies, these tended to survive at the expense of their opposites. Similarly,

militaristic and exploitative societies had an advantage over more peaceful and humane ones.

Meanwhile, despite many developments that should have stimulated technological advance, the rate of innovation actually began to *slow* after the rise of the first agrarian societies. This appears to have been the first major break in the long process of acceleration that started far back in the Paleolithic. The new ideologies and exploitative forms of social organization generated by the agrarian revolution were primarily responsible for this retardation.

As societies grew in size and complexity, ties of kinship proved less and less satisfactory as the basis of social organization and had to be supplemented and replaced by more formal ties. From the standpoint of societal cohesion, political ties between rulers and their subjects were the most significant. These were supplemented by an expanding network of commercial ties generated by economic institutions and by ideological and communal ties created by religious institutions. These newer integrative forces, however, could no more prevent the development of intrasocietal antagonisms and conflict than could kinship bonds. If anything, antagonisms became more serious, since they now involved groups and classes of men, not just individuals.

This points up a basic irony of sociocultural evolution: In the process of solving one set of problems, men usually create others. Sociocultural evolution is thus not only a problem-solving process, it is also a problem-producing one. Sometimes it almost seems to be a process whereby men trade old problems for new ones.

Why, then, have men tried so hard to achieve progress if its fruits are not sweeter? To begin with, we must remember that much of man's progress has not been a matter of choice. Some hunting and gathering groups may have preferred to continue their traditional way of life, but their lands were confiscated by more powerful groups with a more advanced technology. Other less advanced groups have had the same experience. The process of intersocietal selection, then, has not been a voluntary one.

But this is not the whole answer. Many individuals and many societies have voluntarily adopted more efficient tools and techniques and new ways of doing things because of a belief that the gains would outweigh the costs. And they were right—up to a point. Technological advance has often meant more food, better health, longer life, less exhausting labor, and a little leisure for many individuals of the generation that initially adopted the advance—and even for their children and grandchildren. Those who took this step had no way of knowing that an increase in population would eventually result from the technological advance and wipe out all of the gains in just a few generations, leaving their descendants little or no better off than men had been before the innovation. And even had they known, they would not have chosen differently.

Until recently, the members of advanced societies (i.e., agrarian and maritime) had found only one way to halt this frustrating chain of events: a system of social organization which ruthlessly appropriated anything the common people could spare and gave it to the governing class.[28] No dramatic increase in population was likely to ensue under this system;

death rates and birthrates remained about equal. In this way, some of the benefits of technological advance were preserved, if only for a tiny minority of the population. For the masses, however, conditions seldom improved.

Once this system was firmly established in a society, it was virtually impossible to turn back to a less sophisticated technology. For one thing, because the population was larger and denser than it had been before, such a reversal would mean starvation and death for large numbers of the common people. Nor would the governing class have allowed it; from their viewpoint, technological advance was a fine thing. The elites in agrarian societies have almost always been better off than their counterparts in less advanced groups. Most agrarian societies thus found themselves virtually "locked into" the technological status quo. They could not afford to turn back, and they could move forward only very slowly. This, then, was the situation that prevailed on the eve of the Industrial Revolution.

---

[28] One other alternative was to control population growth by abortion, infanticide, monasticism, prostitution, and the like; but these techniques never were adopted widely enough to solve the problem.

Part III
Industrial and Industrializing Societies

*T*he Industrial Revolution
Chapter 11

During the past nine thousand years, human societies have undergone several revolutionary transformations. The only one that is fully documented, however, is the Industrial Revolution. Thus it affords a unique opportunity to study a sociocultural revolution and its underlying causes. We shall begin by clarifying what we mean by the term "Industrial Revolution" and then briefly review its history.

THE CONCEPT OF THE INDUSTRIAL REVOLUTION

Toward the end of the nineteenth century, economic historians began using the term "Industrial Revolution" to refer to the series of dramatic technological and economic innovations made in England during the period from about 1760 to 1830.[1] In their view, the mechanization of the textile industry, the technical advances in, and expansion of, the iron industry, the harnessing of steam power, the establishment of the factory system, and other related developments of that period revolutionized the English economy. What had still been essentially an agrarian system in the middle of the eighteenth century had become an industrial system by the middle of the nineteenth.

In more recent years, many scholars have attacked the time limits assigned the Industrial Revolution by earlier writers. Some of them feel it is a mistake to put any terminal date on a revolution which, they maintain, is still continuing.[2] Other

---

[1] See, especially, the lectures of Arnold Toynbee (uncle of the contemporary historian), delivered at Oxford in 1880–81 and recently republished under the title *The Industrial Revolution* (Boston: Beacon Press 1956). Though not the first to use the term, Toynbee did much to give it currency in scholarly circles.

[2] See, for example, Robert Heilbroner, *The Making of Economic Society* (Englewood Cliffs, N.J.: Prentice-Hall, 1962), pp. 101–102.

critics argue that the starting date is much too late and assert that the acceleration in industrial activity began not in the middle of the eighteenth century, but in the middle of the sixteenth.[3]

Both of these criticisms have some merit. The rate of technological advance did, in fact, begin to accelerate at least two hundred years before 1760. But it does not follow that we are justified in treating these earlier developments as part of the Industrial Revolution. If it is to be meaningful, the term must be reserved for *those developments that brought about a substantial increase in the economic importance of industrial activity.* Refinements and improvements of older techniques do not qualify unless they significantly increased the proportion of the population dependent on industrial activity or the percentage of the gross national product obtained from this source.[4] Using these criteria, we cannot put the start of the Industrial Revolution much, if any, before the middle of the eighteenth century.[5] The earlier events, however, obviously contributed to the later ones.

The other criticism of the dates originally assigned the Industrial Revolution is sounder: the Industrial Revolution definitely was not over by 1830. Only its first phase ended at that time. Subsequently, there have been at least three other phases, and each has contributed substantially to the importance of industrial activity in the societies involved, as well as to the general transformation of the societies themselves.

We cannot assign precise dates to these phases, since they are rather arbitrary divisions in what is essentially a continuous process of development. However, we can assign approximate dates to help us see more clearly the progression of events. In the initial phase, which began in the middle of the eighteenth century when England was still an agrarian society, the revolution was centered in the textile, iron, and coal industries, and the invention of the first true steam engine was probably the most important innovation. The second phase got its start in the middle decades of the nineteenth century and was characterized by the rapid growth of the railroad industry, the invention of techniques for the mass production of steel, the replacement of sailing ships by steamships, and the application of the new technology to agriculture. Around the turn of the century, the Industrial Revolu-

---

[3] See, for example, John Nef, *The Conquest of the Material World* (Chicago: University of Chicago Press, 1964), especially part 2.

[4] If such refinements and improvements were included, it would be hard to avoid dating the beginning of Industrial Revolution in the Mesolithic, since technological progress of some kind, however slow, has been virtually continuous since then. One cannot use the criteria stated in the text above to date the *end* of the Industrial Revolution, since many societies have already reached the point where there is virtually no room for increase in the proportion of the population dependent on industrial activity or in the percentage of the GNP obtained from this source, yet the revolution in the techniques and tools of production is obviously continuing. The only standard we can use to mark the end of the Industrial Revolution would be a drastic slowing in the rate of growth of technological innovation—or the beginning of a new era.

[5] See especially Phyllis Deane and W. A. Cole, *British Economic Growth 1688–1959: Trends and Structure* (Cambridge: Cambridge University Press, 1962), chap. 2.

tion entered a third phase, whose areas of rapid growth were the automobile, electrical, telephone, and petroleum industries. World War II marked the beginning of the fourth phase, distinguished by remarkable development in aviation, aluminum, electronics, and plastics. Today, we are on the threshold of a fifth phase, in which the utilization of nuclear power, rocket engines, computers, and automation promise to be some of the most important technological advances.

Our review will deal with the Revolution as it has developed in the world as a whole, not as it has developed in individual societies. The phases are not stages that every society must pass through to become industrialized. On the contrary, late-comers are likely to skip over certain phases, or at least parts of them. Furthermore, they will probably combine elements from different phases. For example, an underdeveloped nation today will often develop simultaneously its railways, high-ways, and airways.

First phase

The first phase of the Industrial Revolution, as we just noted, began in the middle of the eighteenth century and lasted about a hundred years. Geographically, it was centered in England, where there was a great burst of technological innovation. Many of the best-known innovations occurred in the textile industry and were of two kinds—machines that increased the efficiency of human labor and machines that harnessed new sources of power. John Kay's flying shuttle is a good example of the former. This machine, invented in 1733, made it possible for one weaver to do the work formerly done by two. Because it upset the traditional balance between spinning and weaving, the flying shuttle triggered a succession of additional inventions. With flying shuttles operating, spinners could not keep up with the

Fig. 11/1 Replica of James Hargreaves' spinning jenny

increased demand for yarn until James Hargreaves replaced the traditional spinning wheel with his spinning jenny. This enabled a worker to spin 4 threads simultaneously and, after a number of modifications, *120* threads! Though the spinning jenny was a big improvement from the standpoint of speed, it had one serious defect: the yarn was so coarse and loose that flax had to be mixed with the cotton to produce a satisfactory fiber. This was remedied when Richard Arkwright invented the water frame, a machine that was able to spin pure cotton. Then, in 1779 Samuel Crompton invented the spinning mule, which produced cotton threads that were both strong and fine. All these advances in spinning reversed the earlier situation and created a demand for improvements in weaving techniques, which had now become the bottleneck in the industry. Edmund Cartwright's invention of a primitive power loom in 1785—the first of a series of advances in weaving machines—helped to restore the earlier balance.

By the end of the eighteenth century, the new machines were so large and heavy that they were almost impossible to operate. Cartwright's power loom, for example, required two powerful men to work it at a slow rate—and they had to be spelled after a short time.[6] One solution was water power, which had already been used for a variety of purposes for many centuries. Unfortunately, England was poorly supplied with suitable streams and rivers; furthermore, the wheels and troughs used in water systems were inefficient and wasted a lot of power.[7] Eventually James Watt invented the first true steam engine, a source of power that could be employed

---

[6] Paul Mantoux, *The Industrial Revolution in the Eighteenth Century*, rev. ed. (London: Cape, 1961), pp. 243–244.

[7] *Ibid.*, p. 312.

Fig. 11/2   Replica of James Watts' lap engine

anywhere.[8] By the end of the century, it had been adapted for use in the textile industry.

The net effect of these innovations was a rapid expansion of the British textile industry, especially in the manufacture of cotton goods. Between 1770 and 1845, the value added to the national income by the cotton industry increased fortyfold; by the rest of the textile industry, more than threefold; and by the industry as a whole, more than fivefold.[9] Though unspectacular by contemporary standards, this was a striking rate of growth by traditional agrarian standards. In evaluating it, we should also remember that the actual increase in production was even larger than these figures indicate, since the per unit costs of production dropped considerably during this period.

Another industry that expanded greatly during the first phase of the Industrial Revolution was iron manufacturing. Despite increasing demand for iron products, technical difficulties held it back until late in the eighteenth century. One problem was the growing shortage of wood, needed to provide charcoal for smelting and refining. This was partially solved early in the century when Abraham Darby discovered that coke could be substituted in the smelting process. But a serious bottleneck remained. Because it is hard and brittle, pig iron cannot stand up under pounding or rapid movement. Before it can be used for most purposes, it must be converted into wrought, or malleable, iron. This had always been done by open hearth refining, but only a small quantity could be produced at a time and charcoal was still required. These problems were finally solved in the 1780s when Henry Cort developed the double process of puddling and rolling. These innovations opened the way for rapid expansion of the iron industry: in 1788, England produced only 68,000 tons of iron; by 1845, 1,600,000.[10]

Between them, the iron industry and the steam engine substantially increased the demand for coal. The steam engine also helped alleviate the ancient problem of flooding in the mines by pumping out the water that constantly seeped into the shafts and tunnels. Though not quite so dramatic as the growth of the iron industry, the figures for coal are still impressive. In 1760, the British produced barely 5 million tons; by 1845 this had risen to 46 million tons.[11]

No discussion of developments in this period would be complete without mention of the machine tool industry. Although it never achieved the size or financial importance of the textile, iron, and coal industries, it was essential to technological progress because it produced the increasingly complex industrial

---

[8] Earlier in the century, Thomas Savery and Thomas Newcomen invented the atmospheric engine, which provided the foundation for Watt's work. Its only practical use, however, was to pump water out of mines.

[9] Deane and Cole, op. cit., p. 212.

[10] For 1788, see Clive Day, Economic Development in Europe (New York: Macmillan, 1942), p. 134; for 1840, see Deane and Cole, op. cit., p. 225.

[11] Deane and Cole, op. cit., pp. 55 and 216.

machinery. The foundations for this industry were laid in the middle of the eighteenth century with the invention of the first practical lathe. Further advances over the next several decades resulted in a lathe capable of precision work to the thousandth of an inch.[12] For many years, the same tool was used for drilling, boring, grinding, and milling, but eventually special tools were designed for the various operations.

Another basic advance in the eighteenth century was the production of machines with interchangeable parts. This greatly facilitated industrial growth, since damage to one part of a complex machine no longer meant that the entire machine had to be discarded or a new part specially manufactured. Spare parts could now be kept on hand and replacements made by mechanics with fewer skills and equipment than those required by machinists in the machine tool industry.

During this initial phase of the Industrial Revolution, Britain became the first nation in which industry replaced agriculture as the most important form of economic activity. It was probably sometime during the second decade of the nineteenth century that Britain's industrial activity first began contributing more to the national income than her agriculture.[13] The United States would not reach this point until the early 1880s.[14]

Second phase

The second phase of the Industrial Revolution began in the middle decades of the nineteenth century. Expansion continued at a rapid pace in the textile, iron, and coal industries, but there were now breakthroughs in a number of others as well. By the end of the century industrialization had occurred in most parts of the British economy. Meanwhile, the Industrial Revolution began to play a significant role in some of the other countries of northwestern Europe and in the United States.

One of the most important developments during this phase was the application of the steam engine to transportation. Attempts to use the steam engine in this way began as early as 1769, but a satisfactory method was not found until 1825. Although progress was slow at first, by 1850 nearly all of England was linked together by the new railroad network.[15] This was tremendously important because the lower cost of moving goods by rail (see page 275) contributed to a reduction in the price of many heavy, bulk commodities and thus led to increased demand. In addition, railroads helped break down local monopolies and oligopolies (i.e., markets with only a few sellers), which added to the competition and further lowered prices.

---

[12] W. S. Woytinsky and E. S. Woytinsky, *World Population and Production: Trends and Outlook* (New York: Twentieth Century Fund, 1953), p. 1147.

[13] *Ibid.*, tables 30 and 37.

[14] U.S. Department of Commerce, *Historical Statistics of the United States, Colonial Times to 1957* (Washington: Government Printing Office, 1960), p. 139.

[15] J. H. Clapham, *An Economic History of Modern Britain*, 2d ed. (Cambridge: Cambridge University Press, 1930), vol. I, pp. 391–392.

Thus, England gradually became a single giant market for an increasing number of commodities, a development destined to have far-reaching consequences.

Even before the steam engine was adapted to land transportation, it was being used on water. For many years, however, it was limited to coastal and river shipping because inefficient engines made it impossible to bunker enough wood or coal for long voyages. Furthermore, paddle wheels did not work well in high seas. As late as 1850 Europe had only 186,000 net tons of steamships, compared with more than 5 million net tons of sailing ships.[16] In the next several decades, many advances were made in steamship construction. Efficient compound engines, developed in the 1860s, solved the problem of bunkering fuel. Iron and steel began to replace wood, making possible longer and larger ships with greater carrying capacity (the upper limit in length for wooden vessels was only about 300 feet). Finally, the screw propeller replaced the cumbersome and easily damaged paddle wheel. After this, the number of steamships increased rapidly and by 1893 world steam tonnage exceeded sailing tonnage.

This was also a period of advance and expansion in the iron industry. A way was finally found to produce steel cheaply and in large quantities. Thanks to a series of inventions beginning with the Bessemer process in 1856, the price of steel was cut in half by 1870, thus making it available for many new purposes.[17] Between 1845 and the early 1880s, the production of iron and steel in Britain increased more than fivefold.[18] This meant that in less than a century and a half, the increase had

---

[16] These and the following figures are from S. B. Clough and C. W. Cole, *Economic History of Europe* (Boston: Heath, 1941), pp. 594–595.

[17] *Ibid.,* pp. 535–537.

[18] Deane and Cole, *op. cit.,* p. 225.

Fig. 11/3   Model of the DeWitt Clinton, built in New York City in 1831. On its first run between Albany and Schenectady, it covered a 12-mile stretch in less than an hour

been 500-fold (from 17,000 tons per year to approximately 8,500,000). What is more, the quality of the product was vastly superior.

The tremendous growth in railroads and steamships and the expansion of the iron industry all combined to increase the demand for coal. Though there were numerous advances in mining techniques during this period, there were no major breakthroughs. Nevertheless, inventions of the earlier period, together with the improved engines and other products of the steel industry, enabled British production to increase fivefold, and the contribution of the coal industry to the national income rose from 2 per cent to 7.5 per cent.[19]

During this second phase, a number of new industries emerged in addition to the railroads. None of them was as important during the nineteenth century, but some were destined to surpass the railroads in the twentieth. One of the first of these newer industries developed as a result of Charles Goodyear's discovery of the technique of vulcanization. Prior to this, rubber goods became sticky in hot weather, stiff and brittle in cold. Vulcanizing took care of this and laid the foundation for the modern rubber industry. About the same time, Samuel Morse and several others invented the telegraph, and this too quickly became the basis of a new industry. Before long, a method was found for making dyes from coal tar, and by then the importance of the chemical industry was firmly established. During the 1860s, Werner Siemens invented the electric dynamo, making the industrial use of electricity practical for the first time. A second crucial development in this field was the invention of the transformer in the 1880s. This overcame one of the greatest impediments to the use of electricity, the loss of energy during long-distance transmission. Though no great technical breakthroughs were involved, the petroleum industry also got a start in these years, chiefly by providing a substitute for whale oil in lighting homes.

The Industrial Revolution began to make itself felt even in the area of agriculture, through improved equipment (e.g., sturdier steel plows), new kinds of machines (e.g., threshing machines, mowers, reapers, steam plows, etc.), and synthetic fertilizers from the growing chemical industry. The result was a substantial increase in productivity. In Germany, for example, production per acre rose 50 per cent between the late 1870s and the early 1900s.

All during this period, industrialization was spreading rapidly across Europe, especially the western part, and to North America. Before the century closed, the British lost their position of economic and technological leadership. The situation in the iron and steel industry illustrates the trend. Although Britain nearly doubled her production of pig iron between 1865 and 1900, her share of the world market dropped from 54 to 23 per cent.[20] Her chief rivals were the United States and Germany, and their production of pig iron increased more than sixteenfold and

---

[19] Production figures are from Deane and Cole, *op. cit.*, p. 216; figures on the national income are based on tables 37 and 54 of the same volume.

[20] Clough and Cole, *op. cit.*, p. 538.

THE INDUSTRIAL REVOLUTION: ANOTHER VIEW

The Industrial Revolution has been a technological triumph without parallel in human history. Morally, however, its fruits have not always been so sweet as the poet Thomas Hood made clear in his early description (1843) of factory life in "The Song of the Shirt."

With fingers weary and worn,
  With eyelids heavy and red,
A woman sat in unwomanly rags,
  Plying her needle and thread,—
    Stitch—stitch—stitch!
In poverty, hunger, and dirt;
  And still with a dolorous pitch
She sang the "Song of the Shirt!"

"Work—work—work
  While the cock is crowing aloof!
And work—work—work
  Till the stars shine through the roof!
It's Oh! to be a slave
  Along with the barbarous Turk
Where woman has never a soul to save
  If this be Christian work!

"Work—work—work
  Till the brain begins to swim!
Work—work—work
  Till the eyelids are heavy and dim!
Seam, and gusset, and band,
  Band, and gusset, and seam,—
Till over the buttons I fall asleep,
  And sew them on in a dream!

"O men with sisters dear!
  O men with mothers and wives!
It is not linen you're wearing out,
  But human creatures lives!
    Stitch—stitch—stitch,
  In poverty, hunger, and dirt,—
Sewing at once with a double thread,
  A shroud as well as a shirt! . . .

eightfold respectively. The American share of the market jumped dramatically from 9 to 35 per cent, while the German share rose from 10 to 19 per cent.

As these figures indicate, though industrialization was spreading, it was still largely limited to a few countries. The United States, Britain, Germany, and France together produced 84 per cent of the world's iron in 1900. A similar picture emerges when the value of *all manufacturing activity* is examined. In 1888, the percentages are estimated to have been as follows:[21]

United States	32%
Britain	18%
Germany	13%
France	11%
All other countries	26%

The fact that "all other countries" contributed more to *all* types of manufacturing then they did to iron production alone (and at an earlier date) indicates that the new technology spread more rapidly in light industries, such as textiles, than in heavy industries. This was because the former required less capital and the pace of technological advance in these industries had already slowed considerably, reducing the need for highly skilled and innovative personnel.

That last factor points up a final characteristic of this phase of the Industrial Revolution: the growing dependence on science and engineering. Prior to 1850 most of the major advances were made by simple craftsmen or gentlemen amateurs. After that, most of the key inventions came from people with formal technical or scientific training. This was especially true in the new chemical industry, but it was also evident in the older iron industry. Considerable training was needed to conceive and build such complex devices as the Bessemer converter and the Siemens-Martin open-hearth furnace.

Third phase

Around the turn of the century, the Industrial Revolution entered a phase which lasted to the beginning of World War II. One of the most dramatic and significant developments in this period was the expansion of the automobile industry. Not only was its own rate of growth remarkable but, equally important, it generated a tremendous demand for the products of a number of other industries: in 1937, the American automobile industry consumed 20 per cent of the nation's steel, 54 per cent of its malleable iron, 73 per cent of its plate glass, 80 per cent of its rubber, and 90 per cent of its gasoline.[22] The average car in this period required 3,385 pounds of steel, 697 pounds of iron, 171 pounds of rubber, 106 pounds of glass, 66 pounds

---

[21] Calculated from Woytinsky and Woytinsky, *op. cit.*, p. 1003.

[22] *Ibid.*, p. 1164.

Fig. 11/4 Fiat automobile plant, Turin, Italy

of cotton, 61 pounds of paper products, 54 pounds of copper, as well as other material.

The key inventions that gave rise to the industry were made in the latter half of the nineteenth century, the most important being the gasoline engine. Only in the final years of the century, however, did commercial production begin. In 1900 no more than 20,000 automobiles were produced in the entire world, with France the largest single producer.[23] By 1913 world production had risen to 600,000, with the United States producing more than 80 per cent; by 1929 world production passed the 6 million mark, and America produced 85 per cent of the total.[24] During the next decade, production slumped, owing to the worldwide depression.

The electrical industry was another that grew fantastically during the third phase of the Industrial Revolution. In 1900 the capacity of all the generating plants in the world was less than 2.5 million kilowatts; by 1940 it had increased 200-fold to more than 480 million kilowatts.[25] Even the depression of the 1930s failed to halt this industry's surge. Again the United States led the way, producing 40 to 45 per cent of the world's electrical power.

The proportional growth of the petroleum industry was somewhat less dramatic,

---

[23] This figure is an estimate based on Clough and Cole's report of French production in 1902 (*op. cit.*, p. 773) and the Woytinskys' report of American production in 1900 and 1902 (*op. cit.*, p. 1168).

[24] Woytinsky and Woytinsky, *op. cit.*, pp. 1165–1166, including fig. 328.

[25] *Ibid.*, p. 966.

because it had already enjoyed substantial growth before 1900. Even so, between 1900 and 1940 production increased from 150 million barrels annually to over 2,000 million.[26] Though this 13-fold increase may seem small compared with the 200-fold increase in the electrical industry, it really is not, since ratio comparisons are misleading when they are so large. We get a more meaningful comparison when we ask what percentage of the 1940 production figure reflected growth since the turn of the century. Viewed this way, the difference turns out to be minor: 92 per cent for the petroleum industry, 99.5 per cent for the electrical.

The telephone industry was another which experienced rapid growth in this period. Between 1900 and 1940, the number of telephones in this country increased from 1.4 million to 20.8 million.[27] By the latter date, the industry had investments valued at $5 billion and an annual revenue of more than $1.2 billion.[28]

During the third phase, as during the second, the Industrial Revolution was felt not only in new sectors of the economy, but in new parts of the world as well. This meant some change in the relative ranking of nations. While the United States continued to be the leading industrial nation, Britain, Germany, and France all lost ground in *relative* terms (see Table 11/1), despite substantial increases in *absolute* terms. Relative gains were registered by many nations that had just begun to feel

---

[26] The 1900 figure is estimated from information provided by the Woytinskys, *op. cit.*, pp. 897–900; the 1940 figure is from fig. 257, p. 897.

[27] J. Frederic Dewhurst and Associates, *America's Needs and Resources* (New York: Twentieth Century Fund, 1955), p. 317.

[28] *Statistical Abstract of the United States, 1963* (Washington: Government Printing Office, 1963), p. 516.

Table 11/1 **Percentage distribution of world industrial output (excluding handicrafts), by nation, in 1888 and 1937**

Nation	1888	1937
United States	32	34
United Kingdom	18	10
Germany	13	10.5
France	11	5
Russia	8	10
Japan	No data	4
All others	18	26.5

Source: Calculated from W. S. Woytinsky and E. S. Woytinsky, *World Population and Production: Trends and Outlook* (New York: Twentieth Century Fund, 1953), pp. 1003–1004.

the full impact of the Industrial Revolution. The gains by Russia and Japan were especially noteworthy as they moved up into the ranks of the leaders in industrial output.

Fourth phase

No previous war was as dependent on industrial activity as World War II. Every major nation made tremendous efforts to increase its output of military supplies. One of the more important long-term consequences of this was the great stimulus given the aviation industry. In the United States, the production of aircraft increased from 3,600 in 1938 to more than 96,000 in 1944.[29] Though this rate could not be sustained once the war ended and military needs were reduced, the air transport industry expanded rapidly. From 1940 to 1950, the number of passenger-miles flown by scheduled airlines rose from 1.2 billion to 10 billion, and by 1968 this had increased to more than 100 billion.[30] The use of airlines to haul freight and mail grew even faster: between 1940 and 1968 the number of ton-miles rose from 15 million to nearly 4 billion.[31] The annual income of the airlines is approximately $5 billion and rising steadily.[32] Though Europe's growth was somewhat slower, European airlines (not counting the U.S.S.R.) flew nearly 60 billion passenger-miles in 1966.[33] The year 1958 marked a significant shift in transportation patterns: for the first time, more passenger-miles in America were covered by planes than by trains, and planes replaced steamships as the major carriers of trans-Atlantic travelers!

Just as automobiles spurred the petroleum industry, so aviation spurred the aluminum industry. Though it was first manufactured in the nineteenth century, production of aluminum was quite limited until Germany and Italy started building their air forces in the 1930s. In the three decades from 1938 to 1966, world production increased more than tenfold from 458,000 tons to 5 million, and is still increasing as new uses continue to be found.[34] As in most of the rapidly expanding industries of the third and fourth phases, American production represented a major share: since World War II, the United States has produced about half of the world's output.

Electronics is another industry with roots in earlier periods that came into its own in the fourth phase. Its products fall into two chief categories: (1) component

---

[29] Woytinsky and Woytinsky, *op. cit.*, p. 1171.

[30] *Statistical Abstract, 1963*, p. 586; and *World Almanac, 1969*, p. 250. The 1968 figure is estimated from returns for the first 6 months of that year.

[31] *World Almanac, 1969, ibid.* The 1968 figure is estimated from returns for the first 6 months of that year.

[32] This figure is a projection for 1970 and is based on the *World Almanac, 1969*, p. 134.

[33] Calculated from the United Nations, *Statistical Yearbook, 1967*, pp. 445 and 455.

[34] The 1938 figure is calculated from J. Frederic Dewhurst and Associates, *Europe's Needs and Resources* (New York: Twentieth Century Fund, 1961), p. 627; the 1966 figure is from the United Nations, *Statistical Yearbook, 1967*, p. 301, but translated into short tons for comparability.

materials, such as transistors, diodes, electron tubes, resistors, and capacitors; and (2) end products, such as computers, testing and measuring equipment, industrial control equipment, microwave communications systems, television and radio equipment, phonographs, tape recorders, and high-fidelity systems. The military needs of World War II stimulated rapid development in electronics and led to a number of spectacular technological breakthroughs. Radar, the most important, gave impetus to the invention of transmitters and detectors capable of using wave lengths far shorter than those used previously in radio. The war also accelerated the development of "miniaturization," as well as servomotors—small power units that respond instantly to signals—and it contributed to the perfection of feedback systems, in which machines not only act but react. These innovations laid the foundation for automated equipment and computers. Unfortunately, it is almost impossible to obtain statistics on the tremendous growth of this industry, because government records still divide its productivity under a number of older, traditional headings.

The plastics industry is another that has come into its own during the current phase of the Industrial Revolution. Its origins go back to 1861 and the work of Alexander Parkes, who plasticized nitrocellulose with camphor to produce artificial ivory and a substitute for horn to use for spectacle frames. Thanks to many subsequent developments, plastics have become the most versatile of modern materials: they can now be manufactured to almost any set of specifications. Not surprisingly, the industry has mushroomed. As recently as the late 1930s, world output was less than 200,000 tons; by 1966 it was nearly 15 million and still growing.[35] In the latter year, American production was half of the total.

During this period, several of the rapid growth industries of the third phase continued to maintain a high rate of growth. Between 1940 and 1966, world output of electricity increased sevenfold and world production of motor vehicles and petroleum sixfold.[36] In these, as in other rapid growth industries, American production was a major component, its contribution in 1966 ranging from 25 per cent of the world total in petroleum to 42 per cent in motor vehicles.

From the standpoint of the geographical distribution of industrial activity, the most striking feature in the fourth phase has been the rise of the Soviet Union (see Table 11/2). The continued decline in relative terms of England, France, and Germany is also significant. The United States, however, has continued to hold the lead it gained in the second half of the nineteenth century. Table 11/2 provides two different measures of industrialization, since it is not clear which index is the more accurate. If, as seems likely, the energy consumption index is the better one, Soviet

---

[35] The figure for the late 1930s is based on the Woytinskys' statement about output in the U.S. and other countries in that period (*op. cit.*, p. 1201); the 1966 figure is from the United Nations, *Statistical Yearbook, 1967*, p. 281, but translated into short tons.

[36] 1940 production figures may be found in Woytinsky and Woytinsky, *op. cit.*, pp. 897, 966, and 1167; the 1966 figures are from the United Nations, *Statistical Yearbook, 1967*, pp. 201, 312, and 356.

Table 11/2 Percentage distribution of world industrial output, by nation, 1961

Nation	Share of world industrial output as measured by:	
	Value added by industrial activity	Consumption of energy
United States	31	34
Soviet Union	19	16
Germany (East, West, and Berlin)	10	7*
United Kingdom	7	6
Japan	4	3
France	3	3
All others	26	31

Sources: For value added figures, United Nations, Department of Economic and Social Affairs, *The Growth of World Industry, 1938–1961* (New York: United Nations, 1965), tables 12, 13, and 26; for energy consumption, *Statistical Abstract of the United States, 1967*, table 1274.
* The component of energy consumption for Berlin was estimated.

Table 11/3 Per capita energy consumption, by nation, 1964*

Nation	Energy	Nation	Energy	Nation	Energy
United States	9595	Ireland	2453	Algeria	371
Canada	7878	Israel	2248	Syria	367
United Kingdom	5139	Roumania	2072	Albania	331
Sweden	5080	Italy	1961	Egypt	314
Australia	4931	Japan	1954	Bolivia	228
Belgium	4636	Argentina	1378	Thailand	183
Denmark	4515	Yugoslavia	1202	India	171
West Germany	4267	Chile	1113	Kenya	124
Norway	3963	Spain	1104	Congo	90
Soviet Union	3789	Mexico	997	Pakistan	87
Poland	3608	Greece	831	Indonesia	85
Netherlands	3508	Lebanon	654	Tanzania	62
France	3019	Peru	625	Burma	54
Finland	2838	Portugal	532	Nigeria	52
Hungary	2825	South Korea	510	Haiti	33
Switzerland	2698	China	493	Afghanistan	26
South Africa	2665	Turkey	393	Ethiopia	16
New Zealand	2644	Brazil	389	Nepal	9

Source: United Nations *Statistical Yearbook*, 1967, table 141.
* Measured in kilograms of coal equivalent consumed per year.

growth has not been quite as great as indicated by the "value added" index while more growth has been achieved by nations other than the six leaders.

Tables 11/1 and 11/2 are measures of the total industrial output of nations, not of the relative degree of their industrialization. To find that, we must use a per capita measure of their industrial activity. As Table 11/3 shows, this changes the picture. The lead of the United States and the Soviet Union is reduced considerably, and the relative position of the smaller nations improves. For example, little Denmark passes the Soviet Union.

As Table 11/3 makes clear, there is currently tremendous variation in degree of industrialization. *For purposes of classification, we shall regard as industrial societies those nations that consume at least 1,000 kilograms of coal equivalent per person per year.* Obviously, however, this is no more than an arbitrary cutoff point on what is essentially a *continuum of development.*

Fifth phase

Recent developments indicate that the Industrial Revolution will soon be entering (or is entering) a fifth phase, one that will be characterized by a rapid increase in the utilization of nuclear power, rocket engines, computers, automation, and cybernation. The trends are already in motion. For example, in 1955 the first nuclear installation began operating in the Soviet Union with a capacity of 5,000 kilowatts.[37] By 1966, eleven nations had such installations and produced more than 32 billion kilowatt-hours.[38]

---

[37] United Nations, *Statistical Yearbook, 1965*, p. 353.

[38] United Nations, *Statistical Yearbook, 1967*, p. 364.

Fig. 11/5 The emerging fifth phase of the Industrial Revolution is characterized by increasing reliance on nuclear power: artist's rendering of Con Edison's Indian Point nuclear power plant in Buchanan, New York, on the Hudson River. Scheduled for operation in 1973, the plant will have a capacity of more than 2.1 million kilowatts

CAUSES OF THE INDUSTRIAL REVOLUTION

For more than a century, scholars have debated the causes of the modern economic and social revolution, particularly the question of why it occurred where and when it did. As we noted earlier (see pages 64 and 101), the basic disagreement has been over the importance of technological and economic factors relative to others. One group of scholars, following the lead of Max Weber, has argued the importance of ideological factors; others have denied or minimized them.

Although this controversy continues, there is growing agreement that no single factor can account for the emergence of modern industrial societies. Rather, they resulted from an unusual combination of events. Had not all or most of them occurred at the time they did, and in conjunction with one another, agrarian societies might still be the dominant societal type today and for many centuries to come.

Historical perspective

Before we begin to look for the causes of the Industrial Revolution, it may be well to note again how the structure of agrarian societies impeded technological progress. In these societies, a tiny governing class typically controlled the economic surplus and used it largely for their own advantage. This elite had every reason to be interested in more efficient methods of production, but because they looked with disdain on manual labor they were in no position to make technological contributions. Furthermore, they regarded war and the conquest of other societies as a surer way of gaining wealth. The common people, on the other hand, though technically knowledgeable, lacked incentive. If a peasant built a better mousetrap, he could be sure that the benefits would go to someone else. In short, technological expertise and economic incentive were divorced. And to make matters worse, the religions of agrarian societies usually encouraged an inordinate respect for tradition and an unprofitable confidence in magic.

These conditions prevailed not only in the simple agrarian societies of the ancient Middle East, but in virtually all agrarian societies through all of history. Forces that might otherwise have generated technological advance were largely canceled out by the system of social organization. This does not mean there were *no* advances in agrarian societies, but simply that the rate of advance was much slower than one would expect on the basis of the size of their populations, the extent of their contact with other societies, and the amount of information available.

Another point to keep in mind in considering the causes of the Industrial Revolution is the fact that this was the first important technological and economic revolution to originate in northwestern Europe. All the other crucial technological breakthroughs of the last ten thousand years had occurred in or near the Middle East—plant cultivation, animal domestication, the metallurgical discoveries, the invention of the plow, and the invention of the sailing ship. During most of this time, northwestern Europe was a remote and underdeveloped cultural backwater. What progress it made was chiefly the result of diffusion from more advanced centers.

The first indications that northwestern Europe might become something more than a second-rate outpost of civilization came in the thirteenth, fourteenth, and fifteenth centuries, when it began catching up to some extent through its own inventions and discoveries. For the most part, however, Europe remained dependent on diffusion until the beginning of the sixteenth century.[39]

These facts are easy to forget at a time when we take for granted the technological superiority of northwestern Europe and its overseas settlements. But if we are to understand the Industrial Revolution, it is essential that we keep in mind just how recent the current pattern really is. For this will lead us to ask, What happened at that point in history to shift the locus of technological innovation to an area which had previously been one of the more backward regions of Eurasia?

Conquest of the new world

When we state the problem this way, our attention is inevitably drawn to two unique events: (1) the discovery and conquest of the New World, and (2) the Protestant Reformation. By almost any criterion, these were the two most significant developments in Western Europe in the fifteenth and sixteenth centuries.

Every schoolboy knows that Columbus "discovered" the New World in 1492. What is sometimes forgotten is how quickly the task of exploration and conquest was accomplished. By 1533 the two leading empires of the New World, the Aztec and Incan, had already been subjugated. These victories, and others that followed, brought immense new resources under the control of Western Europeans.

The impact of this on Europe was tremendous. From a very early date colonial governments began shipping back vast quantities of gold and silver, with the result that the continent's supply tripled between 1500 and 1650.[40] One important consequence of this was to hasten the spread of a cash economy and the demise of the old barter system. Though money had been a medium of exchange for more than two thousand years, the supply of precious metals was so limited that many payments were still made in kind rather than in cash. This was especially true in rural areas, but by no means only there.

This situation seriously hindered both economic and technological advance because an economy that operates on the basis of barter lacks flexibility and the flow of resources from areas of oversupply to areas of short supply tends to be sluggish. Furthermore, the rational calculation of economic advantage is quite difficult under a barter system. The more widely money is used in exchange, however, the easier it becomes for men to calculate their costs and income and determine which of the alternatives open to them is likely to yield the greatest profit. This is

---

[39] See, for example, Charles Singer, "Epilogue: East and West in Retrospect," in Singer (ed.) *A History of Technology* (Oxford: Clarendon Press, 1956), vol. II, p. 755ff.

[40] Clough and Cole, *op. cit.*, pp. 127–128.

extremely important in breaking down the barriers to technological innovation. In a society whose technological progress has been halting and uncertain for centuries and which lacks an efficient system of accounting, men with money to invest are likely to conclude that traditional forms of investment are wisest. Moreover, where money is scarce, men tend to state obligations (e.g., wages, rents, etc.) in relatively inflexible and traditional terms, which makes the economy less responsive to changing conditions and new opportunities. All this began to change in Western Europe during the sixteenth and seventeenth centuries because of the inflow of precious metals from the New World.

The gold and silver from the New World had a second important effect: it produced inflation. This was a natural consequence of the greatly increased supply of money together with the much more limited increase in the supply of goods. Prices doubled, tripled, even quadrupled within a century. As is always the case under such conditions, some prospered and others were hurt. In general, those with fixed incomes, notably the landed aristocracy and wage earners, were hurt; entrepreneurs of all sorts tended to benefit. This meant a marked improvement in the position of the merchants relative to the governing class. More of the economic resources of European societies were winding up in the hands of a class of men who had some knowledge of, and interest in, both economics and technology. More than that, these were men who were oriented to rational profit making (a far from typical orientation in agrarian societies) and were therefore motivated to provide financial support for technological innovations that would increase the efficiency of men or machines. The rise in prices in the sixteenth century was "at once a stimulant to feverish enterprise and an acid dissolving all customary relationships."[41]

The benefits to Europe that resulted from the discovery and conquest of the New World were not limited to the sixteenth and seventeenth centuries. Though the flow of gold and silver began to decline within a century, other commodities of a more utilitarian nature started flowing back, and the colonies in the New World provided new and growing markets for European products. For example, in the period from 1698 to 1775, Britain's trade with its colonies increased more than fivefold.[42] All this strengthened the position of European merchants and provided new sources of capital that they could divert into industrial development as opportunities arose.

The Protestant Reformation

A quarter of a century after Columbus discovered the New World, Martin Luther took the first decisive steps in what came to be known as the Protestant Reformation. For more than half a century, scholars have debated the nature of the relationship

---

[41] R. H. Tawney, *Religion and the Rise of Capitalism* (New York: Mentor, 1947), p. 117.

[42] *Ibid.*, p. 257.

Table 11/4   Median per capita income for groups of nations classified by dominant religious tradition, 1957

Type of nation (i.e., dominant religious tradition)	Median income	No. of Nations
Protestant	$1,130	11
Mixed Protestant-Catholic	881	6
Eastern Orthodox	365	5
Roman Catholic	329	33
Moslem	137	20
Primitive religions	88	15
Eastern religions (Hinduism, Buddhism, etc.)	75	16
Others (including mixed types)	362	7
All nations	224	113

Source: Compiled from data presented in Bruce Russett et al., *World Handbook of Political and Social Indicators* (New Haven, Conn.: Yale, 1964), tables 44 and 73–75. Nations with Communist governments are classified on the basis of their traditionally dominant faith.

between this epoch-making religious revolution and subsequent developments in economics and technology. On one point, however, there is no room for argument: Protestant nations are unique in the modern world by virtue of their high level of economic development. As Table 11/4 indicates, the median per capita income of predominantly Protestant nations is five times the median for all the nations in the world, and nearly six times the median for all *non*-Protestant nations. Compared with Roman Catholic and Eastern Orthodox nations, there is more than a threefold advantage. Added to this is the fact that the Industrial Revolution got its start in a predominantly Protestant nation which remained the leader in industrialization until another predominantly Protestant nation took over.

The modern controversy over the relationship between Protestantism and economic development stems largely from the work of Max Weber. Reacting against what he regarded as Marx's excessively economic interpretation of history, Weber sought to show that the most important economic development of modern times, the rise of capitalism, owed much to the new religious outlook promoted by the reformers, the Calvinists and Puritans in particular.[43] Although the reformers did not intend to produce an economic revolution, Weber believed that this was an unintended by-product of their labors and that various aspects of the new Protestant teachings contributed to this. In the first place, the reformers laid great stress on the

[43] For the basic statements of Weber's views, see *The Protestant Ethic and the Spirit of Capitalism*, trans. by Talcott Parsons (New York: Schribner, 1958); *The Sociology of Religion*, trans. by Ephraim Fischoff (Boston: Beacon Press 1963); and *From Max Weber: Essays in Sociology*, trans. by H. H. Gerth and C. W. Mills (New York: Oxford, 1946), pp. 302–322. For a good summary of his views, see Reinhard Bendix, *Max Weber: An Intellectual Portrait* (Garden City, N.Y.: Doubleday, 1960), chaps. 3–8.

Fig. 11/6 Max Weber (1864–1920), famed German sociologist of the early twentieth century and proponent of the thesis that the Protestant Reformation was one of the important forces giving rise to modern capitalism

importance of work as a form of service to God. Luther, for example, insisted that all honest forms of work are Christian callings just as truly as the ministry or priest-hood. This challenged both the medieval Catholic view of work as basically a penalty for sin and the traditional aristocratic view of work as degrading and beneath the dignity of a gentlemen. At the same time, it supported the merchants and craftsmen in their efforts to legitimize their way of life. Second, the new Prot-estant faiths encouraged the growth of rationality and undermined traditionalism and magic. Though the reformers dealt with this only in the area of religion—and even there only imperfectly—they stimulated a trend that ultimately had broad ramifications. Some branches of Protestantism encouraged their adherents to plan their lives in rational terms rather than simply live from day to day (e.g., Methodism, as its name implies). Finally, many of the newer Protestant faiths encouraged believers to deny themselves the pleasures of this world and live frugally, a practice which led to capital accumulation by those who were economically successful. To the extent that they followed these teachings, Weber argued, men developed a new outlook on life: they worked harder and more rationally and lived more thriftily. In short, men's personalities were remolded by the Reformation in ways that helped undermine the traditional agrarian economy and stimulate economic and technological innovation. In his later years, Weber modified his views to the extent of recognizing the roots of what he called the Protestant Ethic (i.e., the new view of work) in *pre*-Reformation Christianity and ancient Judaism. Thus he would not have been surprised by the differences shown in Table 11/4 between the Eastern Orthodox and Roman Catholic countries on the one hand and the Moslem and Oriental faiths on the other.

Weber's work has been subjected to attack from many quarters.[44] The most persistent and weighty criticism has stressed the interaction between developments in religion and economics. Though Weber recognized this, in some of his best-known writings he tended to neglect the impact of economic forces on religion.

Probably none of Weber's critics has been as influential and insightful as the English economic historian R. H. Tawney, who pointed out that Calvinism and Puritanism were influenced at the start by the urban background of their leaders and by the heavy representation of merchants and craftsmen in their membership. He wrote:

> As was to be expected in the exponents of a faith which had its headquarters at Geneva, and later its most influential adherents in great business centers, like Antwerp with its industrial hinterland, London, and Amsterdam, its leaders addressed their teachings, not of course exclusively, but none the less primarily, to the classes engaged in trade and industry, who formed the most modern and progressive elements in the life of the age. In doing so they naturally started from a frank recognition of the necessity of capital, credit and banking, large-scale commerce and finance, and the other practical facts of business life. They thus broke with the tradition which, regarding a preoccupation with economic interests "beyond what is necessary for subsistence" as reprehensible, had stigmatized the middleman as a parasite and the usurer as a thief. They set the profits of trade and finance, which to the medieval writer, as to Luther, only with difficulty escaped censure as *turpe lucrum*, on the same level of respectability as the earnings of the laborer and the rents of the landlord. "What reason is there," wrote Calvin to a correspondent, "why the income from business should not be larger than that from land-owning? Whence do the merchant's profits come, except from his own diligence and industry?"[45]

Calvinism and Puritanism did not, of course, condone all forms of business activity. Far from it. But they did accord it a measure of legitimacy and respectability denied it by nearly all earlier ideologies. Wherever Calvinist thought became dominant, profit seeking was viewed not as a necessary evil or as a means of upward mobility, but as a legitimate and useful activity in its own right.

Tawney also pointed out that Calvinism gradually changed after its founder's

---

[44] For an introduction to the critics, see Robert W. Green (ed.), *Protestantism and Capitalism: The Weber Thesis and Its Critics* (Boston: Heath, 1959). This volume gives brief excerpts from a number of the leading critics and provides a useful bibliography on pp. 115–116.

[45] Tawney, *op. cit.*, pp. 92–93. Quoted by permission of Harcourt, Brace & World, Inc.

death. Later Calvinists neglected some of his teachings and emphasized others that were more congenial with the needs and aspirations of the commercial class, by then an important part of the membership of the group. For example, the corporate elements in Calvinism were weakened and the individualistic elements strengthened. Thus the group abandoned the practice of excommunication, which had been an important means of discipline in the earlier years, and left discipline more and more to the conscience of the individual—enlightened, presumably, by Calvinist teaching. This in turn led to a gradual withdrawal of the church from the realm of economics and the elimination of even those restraints on economic activity that Calvin had retained. In Tawney's view, the social teachings of the Puritans and other later Calvinists were a complex mixture "derived partly from the obvious interests of the commercial classes, partly from [their] conception of the nature of God."[46]

On many points, Tawney agreed with Weber. He shared the latter's view of the importance of Luther's doctrine of the calling—the doctrine that all who do honest work have Christian vocations and therefore serve God. He, too, appreciated the importance of the Calvinist and Puritan condemnation of self-indulgence. In short, like Weber he saw the Protestant Reformation as establishing a new system of values and creating a new type of personality, both more conducive than their older counterparts to economic and technological progress. Tawney put it this way:

> [Calvinist] teaching, whatever its theological merits or defects, was admirably designed to liberate economic energies, and to weld into a disciplined social force the rising bourgeoisie, conscious of the contrast between its own standards and those of a laxer world, proud of its vocation as the standard-bearer of the economic virtues . . . Calvinism stood, in short, not only for a new doctrine of theology and ecclesiastical government, but for a new scale of moral values and a new ideal of social conduct.[47]

The agricultural revolution

A third development that contributed to the Industrial Revolution was the agricultural revolution in eighteenth century England. This earlier revolution has been largely forgotten because of the more dramatic events that followed on its heels. Nevertheless, at the time it was recognized to be of great importance, and it clearly contributed to the rise of industry.

The agricultural revolution, like the industrial, was stimulated in part by the economic disturbances generated by the discovery of the New World. The rise in prices worked a hardship on the landowning class. After many of them had suffered severe losses, they realized something would have to change if they were ever to regain their prosperity. Fortunately, the more rational and experimental outlook stimulated by the growth of the money economy and the rise of Protestantism began

---

[46] *Ibid.*, p. 192.

[47] *Ibid.*, p. 98. Quoted by permission of Harcourt, Brace & World, Inc.

to permeate even the rural landowning class, everywhere noted for its conservatism and traditionalism.

During the eighteenth century, a number of wealthy landowners began a serious search for ways to increase the yields of their estates. This led to several important innovations. Early in the century, Charles, Viscount Townshend, brother-in-law of the prime minister, discovered a system of crop rotation that enabled English farmers to avoid leaving a quarter of their land fallow each year; by rotating barley, clover, wheat, and turnips, land could be kept in continuous production without depleting its resources. As the word spread, farm yields increased considerably. Later in the century, Robert Bakewell, another wealthy landowner, discovered the principle of selective breeding. Bakewell made a small fortune from the stud farm he established and at the same time contributed to an increase in the size and quality of British livestock. Finally, Jethro Tull, another innovator from the land-owning class, was one of several who developed machines to help mechanize farming and increase the efficiency of farm labor. He was also the author of an early textbook designed to rationalize farming practices and make farming more profitable. Tull claimed that his methods had enabled him to increase the annual profits on a twenty-acre farm from £131 to £334 over a ten-year period. Though later investigations cast doubt on the magnitude of his claim, the book was extremely popular and helped to increase the efficiency of English farming.

Another important development in the eighteenth and early nineteenth centuries was the passage of the famous enclosure acts, whereby wealthy landowners gained control of several million acres of common pasture land, woodland, and scattered strip holdings of small yeoman farmers. This worked a terrible hardship on the common people. As Oliver Goldsmith described in his poem "The Deserted Village," many poor farmers were forced to abandon what was left of their small holdings and migrate to the developing industrial centers. These ruthless seizures were clearly stimulated by the shift to a money economy and the spread of the commercial spirit. Its ultimate effect was to destroy the traditional system of agricul-

---

EXCERPT FROM "THE DESERTED VILLAGE" BY OLIVER GOLDSMITH

Ill fares the land, to hast'ning ills a prey,
Where wealth accumulates, and men decay:
Princes and lords may flourish, or may fade;
A breath can make them, as a breath has made;
But a bold peasantry, their country's pride,
When once destroy'd, can never be supplied.

ture with all its built-in inefficiencies and replace it with a new large-scale, capitalistic, and rationalistic system of enterprise. From this time on, English farming began to take on the character of a modern business.

From the standpoint of the Industrial Revolution, all of these developments were very important. In the first place, the agricultural innovations resulted in a more ample supply of food and increased the efficiency of its production. This, in turn, released a considerable portion of the population from the necessity of working on the land. Although the basic limitation on the growth of urban populations is always the level of productivity of the rural economy, increased agricultural efficiency cannot, *by itself*, insure urban growth; the additional food is too easily consumed by an increase in the rural population. The enclosure acts, therefore, as harsh and immoral as they were, served to insure that this did not happen. The excess rural population was forced to migrate to the new industrial towns, thus providing the manpower needed by the expanding industries. Without these changes in England's agriculture, it is doubtful that the Industrial Revolution would have developed nearly as rapidly as it did, and it might have stalled completely at some early point because of insufficient manpower, insufficient agricultural resources, or both.

The benefits of cumulation

The Industrial Revolution also owed much to the simple cumulation of technological knowledge that had occurred over the centuries of the agrarian era. While the rise of agrarian societies was associated with a marked slowing of the *rate* of technological advance, this was not the same as a complete halt in the innovative process. New inventions and discoveries were made, and the store of useful information did increase, if slowly.

Because sociocultural innovation is cumulative and because the number and type of inventions are a function of the already existing store of technical knowledge, the chances for some kind of a major technological breakthrough were bound to be greater in the eighteenth century than in the fifteenth, and greater in the fifteenth than in the first century A.D. or the tenth century B.C. This does not mean that the Industrial Revolution was *inevitable* by the eighteenth century, or even by the twentieth. On the contrary, if the developments we have enumerated had not occurred, agrarian societies would probably still be the most advanced in the world.

Concluding note

As our analysis indicates, the causes of the Industrial Revolution were more complex than the causes of earlier technological revolutions. Unlike its predecessors, this one required the disruption, or at least the weakening, of a well-established system of social organization and the rejection of a deeply rooted ideology.

The discovery of the New World and the Protestant Reformation seem to have been the chief catalytic agents that triggered the essential changes. They undermined the organizational and ideological foundations of the agrarian way of life and thereby freed creative forces which had been severely curbed for a long time. Then, with a relatively broad base of accumulated information to build on, it was only a matter of time until men would make the inventions and discoveries that were at the heart of the Industrial Revolution. And, as subsequent events proved, it did not take long at all!

CAUSES OF THE CONTINUING INDUSTRIAL REVOLUTION

As Max Weber noted more than half a century ago, any explanation of the economic and social revolution of modern times must address itself to two problems. After we have dealt with *its origin*, we still must explain *its continuation*.

While the origin has easily been the more controversial of the two, we cannot simply take the fact of the continuing revolution for granted, as though it were inevitable or its causes self-evident. On the contrary, because we live in the era of the continuing revolution, we have a special interest in the forces that are changing our societies and our lives.

Destruction of the old social order

The old social order was not destroyed overnight. In fact, many elements of it still persist even in the most advanced industrial societies. In Europe, for example, it is evident in the aristocratic and elitist character of the educational systems, particularly at the university level. In this country, racial patterns are among the more important survivals of the agrarian order. As these attitudes and practices are gradually eliminated and as educational and other opportunities become available to more of the population, new energies and new talents are released to make their contribution to the technical and social revolution. Eventually, of course, this contribution will cease. But it seems safe to say that we have not yet reached that point. Many of the old practices and prejudices that have so long inhibited innovation and change continue to hang on, and some show considerable vitality.

The institutionalization of innovation

Modern industrial societies have not been content merely to remove impediments to technological innovation, but have consciously tried to stimulate it. One of the most important steps has been the democratization of the educational system and the extension of educational opportunities to citizens of every class. Another has been the redefinition of the nature of educational institutions. Whereas their sole function once was to transmit the cultural heritage of the past, in the last century institutions of higher education have become research centers as well. This trend is still continuing.

More recently, business groups and government agencies have also discovered the importance of research and have set up research units within their own organizations. According to one source, expenditures for scientific research and development in this country rose from $166 *million* in 1930 to nearly $19 *billion* in 1964.[48] Today, for the first time in history, human societies are systematically searching for new and better solutions to their problems.

Thanks to increasingly sophisticated methods of observation and measurement, which run the gamut from the electron microscope to public opinion polling, modern research becomes more fruitful year by year. These techniques permit far more precise comparisons between the performance of proposed innovations and the older tools and techniques they are designed to replace, while the newer methods of cost accounting provide more accurate comparisons of relative costs and profits.[49] This naturally speeds the acceptance of useful innovations and thus contributes to the continuing revolution in modern technology.

The changing nature of warfare

While there are many reasons for the growing emphasis on research, the most important (at least insofar as importance is gauged by financial support) is the changing nature of warfare. Prior to the Industrial Revolution, military technology changed slowly. Among nations on the same level of societal development, victory was usually determined by the size of the armies and the organizational and tactical skills of their commanders.

Today, all this is changed. Military technology becomes obsolete in a few years. The size of armies and the skills of their commanders are becoming—perhaps already are—less important than the productive capacity of a nation's economy and the technological skill of its engineers and scientists. To maintain their relative military status, the leading nations are forced to invest increasing amounts in military research. This now involves biological, chemical, and space research, as well as the more traditional kinds. At the present time, it is hard to see how this costly acceleration of military research can be halted without either the formation of a single world state to end military rivalries or an atomic war that would so cripple these societies that they could not continue research activities of *any* kind.

---

[48] U.S. Department of Commerce, *Long-term Economic Growth: 1860–1965* (Washington: Government Printing Office, 1966), p. 198.

[49] Critics have noted, however, that these modern methods of accounting completely fail to take account of human values that are not monetized. For example, they make no allowance for the high value many people place on the preservation of rare or beautiful species of birds and animals that are threatened by the use of commercially profitable pesticides like DDT. They only show that farmers will buy such products and that businessmen can make a profit producing them. This is a serious (perhaps tragic) flaw, but it does not slow the pace of technological innovation.

Fig. 11/7 The birthrate in modern industrial societies has been substantially reduced and the growth in productivity now, for the first time in history, far outruns the growth in population in many societies

Population control

Another enormously important factor in the continuing revolution is man's newly achieved ability to control the birthrate. By now it should be clear that population growth can easily offset any gains in productivity that result from technological advance. Unless this is prevented, most men are doomed to live at, or near, the subsistence level—and life at that level is not conducive to innovation and progress.

In past centuries, various techniques of population control were tried, but none was really successful. With the Industrial Revolution, the problem became more serious than ever, as advances in medicine and sanitation drastically cut the death rate. Infant mortality, long a deadly killer, was greatly reduced, with the result that many more people survived into the child-bearing years.

Fortunately, the Industrial Revolution also brought advances in chemistry and related fields that led to new and better methods of birth control. As a result, the birthrate in modern industrial societies has been substantially reduced and the growth in productivity has, for the first time in history, far outrun the growth in population. This in turn has meant that it is possible—also for the first time—for all segments of the population to share in the benefits of technological advance and that the historic necessity of keeping millions of people at the subsistence level has been eliminated. The slower rate of growth also makes it feasible to educate more of the population. All of these factors combine to produce more people who are physically and intellectually equipped, and psychologically motivated, to participate in the search for new and useful information.

Increased information and improved communications facilities

The continuing technological revolution is, in part, a natural consequence of the increased store of information and the improved facilities for transmitting it within and between societies. Since inventions are recombinations of existing elements of information, the larger the store of such elements, the greater the potential for further innovation. Thus, the advances in the early stages of the Industrial Revolution laid the foundation for further advances, now and in the future.

Today, millions of books and technical publications disseminate information widely and quickly, and the growing use of computers promises to accelerate the process even more. Telephones and modern transportation are also important, since they facilitate contacts between people working on related problems.

The new ideology

Not surprisingly, the changes of recent centuries have resulted in a radical shift in men's values. In the past, people generally looked on innovation and change as dangerous and undesirable. Departures from tradition were usually judged guilty until proven innocent. This attitude has almost been reversed in industrial societies. In the arts, for example, innovation is often praised simply for its own sake. Many people are prepared to applaud the artist who does something—anything—no one has done before, without regard to aesthetic criteria. In education too, a higher value is now placed on innovation. Rote learning is scorned by many educators, and "creativity" has come to be the quality most sought in students, particularly in leading colleges and universities. Even in business and religion, there is a tendency to value the new above the old, regardless of its relative merits by other standards.

Whatever else its consequences, this shift in values makes it easier for technological innovators to gain a hearing for their ideas. Ideology, which once slowed the rate of innovation, has become a stimulant.

Future prospects

Since the middle of the eighteenth century, the Western world has been caught up in a technological revolution that has radically transformed the conditions of human life. Any thoughtful person, after surveying this period of history, is bound to wonder "What next?"

Before we tackle this question, however, we should take a careful look at contemporary industrial and industrializing societies, since they are the products of the revolution thus far. They will be our chief concern in the next four chapters. Then, after we have examined them, we will be in a better position to consider that most difficult question of all—the question of the future.

$\mathcal{I}$ Chapter 12
ndustrial Societies:
Part 1

In the century and a half since England became the first industrial society, she has been joined by more than a score of other nations, including most of those in Europe, the English-speaking democracies overseas, several Latin American states, Japan, South Africa, and Israel. Some of these nations have barely crossed the threshold dividing agrarian from industrial societies (see page 326), while others have moved well beyond this point. It is with the latter that we shall be chiefly concerned, since they provide us with our clearest picture of what industrial societies are like when the agrarian elements are largely eliminated.

If we were to carry this logic to its extreme, we would focus exclusively on American society, since it is currently the most advanced of all the industrialized nations. This would be a mistake, however, for no single society can be regarded as the prototype of all the others. While industrial societies have much in common, they are not carbon copies of one another anymore than agrarian societies are. The differences between them are as important as their similarities, because they provide us with some idea of the range of alternatives that are possible for industrializing nations. For this reason alone, we cannot afford to limit our analysis to a single society.

THE TECHNOLOGICAL BASE

In the early stages of the Industrial Revolution, many elements of the agrarian way of life survived relatively unchanged. Today, however, in societies that are well into the fourth phase of the revolution, the old order has largely vanished. Nowhere is this truer than in the realm of technology.

One of the best indications of the dramatic nature of the change is the shift away from the sources of energy on which agrarian societies so long relied. Traditionally, men and animals were the chief sources used in "work" (i.e., activities such as pushing, pulling, lifting, cutting, and digging, which have been, or theoretically could be, performed by the muscle power of men, but *not* activities such as cooking, smelting metals, or providing heat, light, or refrigeration).[1] To some extent muscle power was supplemented by water (harnessed by water wheels) and wind (harnessed by sailing ships and windmills). As recently as 1850, these traditional sources supplied more than 87 per cent of the energy used in work in the United States. *Today they account for less than 1 per cent.*[2] In their stead, we rely on coal, petroleum, natural gas, hydroelectric power, and nuclear power. These sources, except for coal, were still untapped in 1850, and even coal was not used in the performance of work until the invention of the steam engine.

---

[1] This definition of "work" is based on J. Frederic Dewhurst and Associates, *America's Needs and Resources* (New York: Twentieth Century Fund, 1955), pp. 905–906.

[2] For 1850, see *ibid.*, p. 1116; for 1950, Dewhurst shows that traditional sources supplied 1.6 per cent of the energy, by the early 1960s this had apparently dropped below 1 per cent, according to reports on the increase in the newer energy sources. See, for example, *Statistical Abstract of the United States, 1963,* table 716, and compare with Dewhurst, tables 25/3 and 25/4.

Fig. 12/1 Diesel engine works, Denmark

Not only have energy *sources* changed, but the *quantities* produced have multiplied enormously. In 1850, all prime movers (i.e., steam engines in factories, sailing vessels, work animals, etc.) had a capacity of 8.5 *million* horsepower; by 1967 this had risen to 17 *billion*, a 200-fold increase in per capita terms.[3]

This remarkable jump in the production and consumption of energy was closely linked with comparable increases in the production and consumption of a wide variety of raw materials. Consider iron and steel, for example: American production rose from 20 *thousand* tons in 1820 to 218 *million* in 1967,[4] Britain's from 7 *thousand* tons in 1750 to 36 *million* in 1964.[5] In each case, the increase was more than 5,000-fold.

Equally dramatic growth is evidenced by the production and consumption of many other raw materials. In one recent year, the United States produced 4.5 tons of sand and gravel for every man, woman, and child in the population, 4 tons of stone, 2.7 tons of coal, 2.1 tons of crude petroleum, 0.5 tons of iron ore, 740 pounds of cement, 560 pounds of clay, 350 pounds of salt, 300 pounds of phosphate rock, 170 pounds of lime, 110 pounds of sulpher, 100 pounds of gypsum, and 45 pounds of uranium ore, to cite but a few items.[6] Altogether, mineral production is in excess of 15 tons per person per year.

The more advanced industrial societies clearly stand in a radically new relation to the physical world. They have already overcome many of the historic limitations set by the natural environment, and there is little doubt that further advances will be made in the next century. In short, these societies have achieved over their environments a degree of control undreamed of only a few centuries ago. As conservationists constantly remind us, industrial societies are radically changing the face of the globe. Some species of animals have been wiped out and many more are in danger of extinction, forests have been cleared, mountains leveled, rivers converted into giant sewers, and the atmosphere polluted. Even the effects of climate have been minimized, thanks to modern systems of heating, air conditioning, and irrigation. With the recent advent of space exploration, yet another historic limitation has been overcome.

So far, we have no completely satisfactory measure of a society's technological progress, but one of the better ones is per capita income. This is highly correlated with most other measures of technical development, and it has the added virtue of being available in extended time-series for a number of countries.

---

[3] U.S. Department of Commerce, *Historical Statistics of the United States: Colonial Times to 1957* (Washington: Government Printing Office, 1960), series S 1-14, and U.S. Department of Commerce, *Statistical Abstract of the United States, 1968* (Washington: Government Printing Office, 1966), table 753.

[4] The 1820 figure is from W. S. Woytinsky and E. S. Woytinsky, *World Population and Production: Trends and Outlook* (New York: Twentieth Century Fund, 1953), p. 1101; the 1967 figure is from *The World Almanac, 1969*, p. 129.

[5] The 1750 figure is from the Woytinskys, *op. cit.* p. 1100; the 1963 figure is from the United Nations, *Statistical Yearbook, 1967*, tables 126 and 127, and converted to short tons.

[6] Production figures are from *The World Almanac, 1967*, p. 815. Per capita calculations are my own.

Fig. 12/2   Steel mills, Pittsburgh, Pennsylvania

Studies of per capita income in the United States show a dramatic increase from approximately $345 per person per year in 1871 to approximately $3,200 in 1967 (the 1871 figure has been adjusted to take account of inflation in the intervening years).[7] As striking as this ninefold increase is, it understates the magnitude of the difference between a typical advanced agrarian society of the past and American society today. The United States in 1871 was already well on the road toward industrialization; in fact, as we noted in the last chapter, the value of its industrial production surpassed its agricultural production as early as the 1880s. Therefore, to get an accurate idea of the productive level of traditional agrarian societies, we must look elsewhere. There are two possible sources for this: the records of European nations during much earlier stages of industrialization, and the records of under-developed nations in more recent years.

Two of the best sources in the first category are Britain and Sweden. In Britain, per capita income in 1801 seems to have been somewhere near $135 per year

---

[7] The 1871 figure is estimated from data provided in *Historical Statistics of the United States*, series F 1-5 and 6-9. It was assumed that the ratio of national income to gross national product was the same in 1869–73 as in 1897–1901. The 1967 figure is calculated from *The World Almanac, 1969*, p. 133. Price adjustments were based on data in *ibid.*, p. 141, and on data in *Historical Statistics*.

(measured in 1965 dollars).[8] In Sweden in 1861, it was approximately $150 per year (in 1965 dollars).[9]

Data from predominantly agrarian societies in the twentieth century are remarkably similar. In 1938, the earliest year for which reliable estimates are available for most of these societies, per capita income (again in 1965 dollars) was estimated to have been as follows:[10]

Greece	$172
Colombia	161
Egypt	141
Peru	138
Turkey	134
Mexico	130
Brazil	112
India	76
China	38

Like Britain in 1801 and Sweden in 1861, these societies had already experienced some degree of industrialization, which suggests that if this influence could be stripped away, the average figure would not be much in excess of $100 per person per year. Even if we double this to allow for the likelihood of underreporting of production in rural areas, the current American figure represents more than a fourteen-fold increase.

This is probably the best estimate we can currently make of the relative technical efficiency of agrarian societies of the past and the leading industrial society of the 1960s. While most industrial societies have not yet reached this point, many soon will, and the trend for all of them is upward.

DEMOGRAPHIC PATTERNS

Growth in numbers

On the eve of the Industrial Revolution, during the early years of the eighteenth century, the population of the world was approximately 600 million.[11] Today, less

---

[8] This figure was calculated by the author and is based on data presented by Phillip Deane and W. A. Cole, *British Economic Growth, 1688–1959* (Cambridge: Cambridge University Press, 1962), tables 72 and 90, with adjustments for the changing value of the dollar and pound.

[9] This figure was calculated by the author and is based chiefly on data presented by Woytinsky and Woytinsky, *op. cit.*, p. 387, with adjustments for the changing value of the dollar and krone.

[10] These figures are based on those in *ibid.*, pp. 389–390, multiplied by 2.23 to take account of the effects of inflation between 1938 and 1965.

[11] This estimate is based on A. M. Carr-Saunders, *World Population* (Fair Lawn, N.J.: Oxford, 1936), p. 42, and Walter F. Willcox, *Studies in American Demography* (Ithaca, N.Y.: Cornell, 1940), p. 45.

than three centuries later, it is more than 3.6 billion.[12] To many people, there is nothing surprising about a five- or sixfold increase in a 250- to 300-year period; but to demographers this rate of change is revolutionary. Throughout most of the agrarian era, world population apparently grew about 0.1 per cent per year.[13] Today, it is averaging 1.9 per cent, almost a twentyfold increase.[14]

While the rate of increase has been greatest in industrial societies, the hybrid societies of Asia, Africa, and Latin America have also undergone substantial growth, as modern sanitary and medical technology has eliminated many of the historic scourges that previously checked their population growth. Unfortunately, other aspects of the new technology, notably techniques of production and contraception, have not spread so readily, and as a result many of these nations are now facing a demographic catastrophe (see Chapter 15).

In Europe, the birthplace of the Industrial Revolution, population has increased "only" about fivefold since 1700. In part this is because of the heavy migration of Europeans to the New World and Oceania. If we take the whole area of European settlement into account, the rate of increase is nearly ninefold (from about 135 million to 1,200 million). And were it not for the newer methods of birth control, the population of Europe, the Americas, and Oceania alone would almost certainly be 3 billion, possibly more. The rate of growth of industrial societies is clearly no measure of their *potential for sustaining numbers*. If Europeans were willing to live at the subsistence level, as millions do in Asia, Europe alone could support a population of several billion.

Fertility and mortality

To understand the modern demographic revolution, we have to look beyond the figures on total population to those on fertility and mortality. They reveal the striking fact that the great increase in population during recent centuries has been achieved without any increase in the birthrate. In fact, it has occurred in spite of a substantial *decline* in many parts of the world.

Throughout most of history, human societies maintained a demographic equilibrium, with their birthrates and death rates roughly equaling one another. Over the long run the birthrate was usually a little higher than the death rate, with the result that there was a slow increase in population.[15] This modest growth was made

---

[12] This is my own estimate for 1970 based on the United Nations estimate for 1966 with allowance made for a nearly 2 per cent annual increase till 1970. See United Nations, *Demographic Yearbook, 1967,* table 1.

[13] Warren Thompson and David Lewis, *Population Problems,* 5th ed. (Fair Lawn, N.J.: Oxford, 1965), pp. 383–385.

[14] United Nations, *Demographic Yearbook,* 1967, table 1.

[15] Occasionally, however, there were long-run declines. For example, Egypt is estimated to have had a population of 6 to 7 million in Roman times, but only 2.5 million in 1798. See Charles Issawi, *Egypt in Revolution: An Economic Analysis* (New York: Oxford, 1963), p. 20.

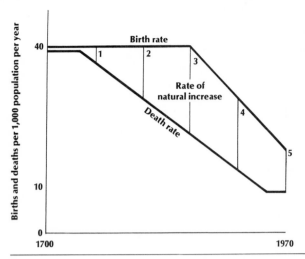

Fig. 12/3 Generalized long-term trends in fertility, mortality, and natural increase in industrialized societies. The vertical lines measure the rate of natural increase at five different periods of time

possible by technological advance. In the short run, the death rate often exceeded the birthrate because of wars, famines, and plagues. Most societies apparently established an equilibrium at about 40 births and deaths per thousand population per year.

Then, during the eighteenth century, the death rate began to drop in some societies as a result of their increased productivity, improved transportation (which eliminated localized famines resulting from crop failures, formerly an important cause of death), and advances in sanitation and medicine. Today, the death rate in the more advanced industrial societies is under 10 per thousand per year.

The decline in the birthrate was much slower, however. In most of the new industrial societies, there was no permanent decrease until the end of the nineteenth century. This combination of a birthrate at the traditional level and a steadily declining death rate naturally resulted in a sharply rising rate of natural increase, as shown by the growing length of the first three vertical lines in Fig. 12/3.

So far, not a single industrial society has achieved an equilibrium, but sooner or later, every one of them must. Their only choice will be the level at which it occurs. It could be at the traditional level of 40 per thousand per year; but this would mean a very short life expectancy for most people. It could also occur in the neighborhood of 12 to 14 per thousand per year; this would mean a life expectancy of 70 to 80 years for the average person. An equilibrium could hardly be established at 10 or less per year in the near future, since that presupposes an average life expectancy of 100 years or more in a population in equilibrium, and mortality tables show that medical science has made only limited progress in raising the life expectancy of older people.[16] It is quite possible, however, that there will continue to be some

---

[16] Death rates of 10 or less are possible in societies that are growing fairly rapidly even when average life expectancy is 70 years or less. But in a stationary population, death rates this low can occur only if the average life expectancy is 100 years or more.

population growth in most industrial societies for several more generations, with the death rate remaining around 10 and the birthrate somewhat higher, perhaps 15.

Almost no one wants to return to the traditional situation in which nature held sway and man had virtually no control over this vital aspect of his life. As a result, the birthrate is already below 20 in most industrial societies (see Table 12/1). The only exceptions are nations recently settled by Europeans and still underpopulated, such as New Zealand, and marginal industrial societies, such as Spain, Ireland, and Argentina.

Table 12/1 Crude birth rates for selected industrial societies in 1967

Nation	Crude birthrate*
Hungary	14.5
Belgium	15.2
Sweden	15.5
Czechoslovakia (1966)	15.6
Poland	16.3
Finland	16.5
France	16.8
Germany, West	17.3
Austria	17.4
United Kingdom	17.4
U.S.S.R.	17.5
Switzerland	17.7
United States	17.9
Norway	18.0
Canada	18.0
Italy	18.1
Denmark	18.4
Netherlands	18.9
Japan	19.3
Australia	19.5
Yugoslavia	19.5
Ireland	21.1
Spain	21.1
New Zealand	22.4
Argentina	22.5

* The term "crude birthrate" refers to the number of live births per year per 1,000 population.
Source: United Nations, *Demographic Yearbook, 1967*, table 7.

THE SYSTEM OF SOCIAL ORGANIZATION: INTRODUCTION AND OVERVIEW

Scale of organization

Despite their great technological achievements, or actually because of them, industrial societies have not set any spectacular records for size. From the demographic standpoint, China, only an industrializing agrarian society, remains the largest ever formed by man. Its present population, which is believed to be approaching 800 million, puts it far ahead of the largest industrial society, the Soviet Union, with approximately 240 million. India, another hybrid society, also far surpasses the Soviet Union; its present population is over 500 million.

Industrial societies are not especially impressive from the geographical standpoint, either. As we noted in Chapter 9, Czarist Russia built an empire covering nearly 8 million square miles. Under Communist leadership, the boundaries have been enlarged to embrace 8.6 million square miles, hardly a remarkable increase.

But comparisons like these are misleading. Industrial societies have a *capacity* for expansion, both demographic and geographic, that far exceeds the potential of agrarian societies. Inventions like the airplane and radio have made the entire planet smaller today than England was just a few centuries ago. One can now communicate with people on the other side of the world in a matter of minutes, and meet them in a matter of hours. From the technical standpoint, it would be easier to govern the entire world today than it was to govern most small kingdoms in the past. Within the next century or two, therefore, a substantial expansion in societal size is likely, and a single global society well within the realm of possibility.

So far, however, industrial societies have been extremely zealous in guarding their national sovereignty. Moreover, the new military technology has made war a costly and unreliable road to expansion. Judging from events of the twentieth century, nations now stand to gain much more by peaceful economic development than by wars of conquest. In this respect, industrialization has reversed a relationship that existed since at least the beginning of the agrarian era.

If societal expansion does come, then, it will probably result from pressures generated by economic competition. In the modern world, the low cost of moving goods has forced firms in every country into competition with their foreign counterparts. In this situation, firms based in the small countries are usually at a serious disadvantage: having a smaller volume of sales to begin with, they cannot spread their fixed costs over as many units and as a result they wind up with higher prices. (In the auto industry, for example, the design costs for a new model are fixed costs: they remain the same regardless of whether the model is a great success and sells millions, or flops and sells only a few hundred thousand. By contrast, the costs of the materials that go into the cars are variable costs: the more cars sold, the greater the expenditures for these items.) Since the price of any commodity is a

Table 12/2   Relationship of sales volume to per unit costs of production

Firm	No. of units sold	Variable costs*	Fixed costs†	Total costs	Cost per unit‡
A	10,000	$10,000	$5,000	$15,000	$1.50
B	8,000	8,000	5,000	13,000	1.63
C	5,000	5,000	5,000	10,000	2.00

* Variable costs need not be exactly proportional to sales, but they have been shown this way to simplify the illustration.
† Normally, fixed costs would not be exactly the same for the several firms, but they have been shown this way to simplify the illustration.
‡ Cost per unit equals total costs divided by sales volume.

function of both fixed and variable costs, the producer with the largest volume of sales enjoys an advantage over his competitors, especially in an industry where fixed costs are a significant part of the total (see Table 12/2). In this situation, the largest producer usually increases his share of the market at the expense of smaller firms, because he can consistently underprice them. In the end, he will probably drive them into bankruptcy unless they have some offsetting advantage, such as greater organizational efficiency, tariff protection, or the like.

In response to this problem, a number of small countries have formed customs unions, which eliminate tariffs on goods shipped between member nations. This was tried first by Belgium, the Netherlands, and Luxembourg (the Benelux Union); later, by these same countries with France, West Germany, and Italy (the European Economic Community). These new arrangements have helped Western European firms to compete with American firms in world markets. But this has not been achieved without some loss of national sovereignty, and arrangements like these may prove to be the first step toward political unification.

The most striking development with respect to the scale of organization in the modern world has been the formation of global political entities—first the League of Nations, then the United Nations. Though their powers have been minimal, the very fact of their existence is indicative of the changes wrought by the Industrial Revolution. A few centuries ago, organizations like these could not have functioned. Today, despite the limitations imposed upon the United Nations, there is a real possibility that it may yet evolve into a more inclusive kind of political system than the world has ever seen.

Industrialization also means growth in the size of organizations at the community level. In agrarian societies, the largest communities never had much over a million inhabitants. Prior to the Industrial Revolution this figure was attained only a few times, and then only by the capitals of empires that controlled the resources of vast territories. Today, by contrast, approximately 120 cities have populations of a

Fig. 12/4   New York City: view south from the top of the RCA Building, showing the Empire State Building and lower Manhattan

million or more, and only a minority of them are national capitals.[17] Ten cities have more than 5 million; and Greater New York and Tokyo have already passed the 10 million mark and are still growing. By the end of the century, some students of urbanism expect to see the cities on the east coast of the United States linked up in a giant megalopolis stretching from Boston to Washington. While this is by no means a certainty, much of the technology needed to maintain such a community is already available. If these hopes (or fears) of the experts are not realized, it will probably be because men *choose* not to live that way—not because they are unable to do it.

Differentiation of parts

From the structural standpoint, industrial societies are by far the most complex that have ever existed. No other type of society has contained such a variety of differentiated subunits. This is true both of the roles individuals fill and of the groups of which these roles are a part.

Nowhere is this more evident than with respect to occupational roles: the United States Department of Labor has identified more than 20,000 different kinds of jobs in this country.[18] The meat-packing industry nicely illustrates the extremes

---

[17] *The World Almanac, 1969*, pp. 578–579 and 652–654.

[18] See *Dictionary of Occupational Titles* (Washington: Government Printing Office, 1965), vol. I, p. xv.

to which occupational specialization has been carried. Here are a few of the more specialized jobs in that industry, each a full-time, 40-hour-a-week job:

aitchbone breaker	jowl trimmer
belly opener	leg skinner
bladder trimmer	lung splitter
brain picker	rump sawyer
gland man	side splitter
gut puller	skull grinder
gut sorter	snout puller
head splitter	toe puller
jawbone breaker	

("What does your daddy do?" "Oh, he's a snout puller over at the packinghouse.")

In recent years, automated machinery has been substituted for human labor in many highly specialized blue-collar jobs, but this has been more than offset by the growing number of highly specialized white-collar jobs. In the medical profession, for example, the general practitioner is rapidly being replaced by a growing variety of specialists.[19] The same is happening in the academic world: the general historian

---

[19] The percentage of physicians in general practice in the United States dropped from 48 to 23 per cent between 1950 and 1966. See *Statistical Abstract of the United States, 1968*, table 86.

Fig. 12/5 Extreme occupational specialization is characteristic of industrial societies: IBM assembly line

is being replaced by the specialist in eighteenth-century German history or nine-teenth-century French history. This pattern is repeated in most other professional and managerial occupations.

Specialization is also evident in the wide variety of associations found in every industrial society. Here is but a small sample of nationwide groups in the United States today:

Aaron Burr Association
Acoustical Society of America
Actors Equity Association
Administrative Management Society
Adult Education Association of the U.S.A.
Advertising Federation of America
Aerospace Industries Association of America
Aerospace Medical Association
Agricultural History Society
Air Force Association
Air Force Sergeants Association
Air Lines Pilots Association
Air Pollution Control Association
Aircraft Owners and Pilots Association
Alcoholics Anonymous
Altrusa International
Aluminum Association
American Amputation Foundation
American Anthropological Association
American Federation of Labor and Congress of Industrial Organizations
American Latvian Association
American Legion Auxiliary
American Medical Association

A recent issue of *The World Almanac* listed over a thousand such groups, even while omitting most religious groups, labor unions, and political parties.[20]

Community specialization is also common in industrial societies, with the production of autos, textiles, tobacco, recreation, education, government, and other things often concentrated in a single city or group of cities. We find specialization even at the national level. In a world dominated by advanced industrial nations, some countries concentrate on oil, others on rubber, coffee, sugar, or manufactured goods. Were the world not still divided into autonomous nation-states that are concerned with maintaining balanced economies, this tendency would be even more

---

[20] *The World Almanac, 1967*, pp. 497–512.

pronounced. For greater national specialization is technically feasible and, from an international standpoint, would certainly be more profitable.

Increased social interaction

The amount of social interaction in a modern industrial society would stagger the imagination of the members of simpler societies. Never before have people had so much contact with so many other people. To a large extent, this is the natural result of increasing urbanization: communities are larger, people live closer together, and increased contact is inevitable. Industrialization also has an effect: the home is no longer the workplace except for a small minority of men; children spend half their days in crowded schools; and women are increasingly drawn outside the home by a variety of responsibilities and opportunities.

The revolutionary advances in communication and transportation have played a major role in breaking down former barriers to social contact. Political leaders and others often travel in excess of 100,000 miles in a single year. Ordinary citizens, too, travel more than ever before: Americans have recently been averaging *at least* 7,000 to 10,000 miles every year.[21] In addition to the contacts resulting from all this movement, hundreds of millions of additional ones are made daily by telephone and mail. In the United States, there are currently over 400 million telephone conversations daily and 200 million exchanges by mail.[22]

The mass media have opened up still another avenue of interaction. Moreover, they reach even those individuals whose other contacts are limited by lack of transportation, poor health, or geographical isolation. Although the flow of communication is in only one direction, and the image at best only two-dimensional, their impact is tremendous. A striking illustration of this came at the time of President Kennedy's assassination: millions of people all over the world watched the events which followed it on television, many weeping openly and later reporting that their feelings of involvement and loss were comparable to what they had experienced upon a death in their own family.

One consequence of the growth of social interaction has been the steady erosion of *localism* and *local subcultures*. Everything has been affected, from local dialects and customs (quite marked in agrarian societies) to local loyalties. National norms and national loyalties are replacing them. From the standpoint of cultural diversity, this is a great loss, as evidenced by the tiresome similarity of most American cities and towns. On the other hand, from the standpoint of social and political harmony, this development has probably been an important step forward.

---

[21] This estimate is based on reports of automobile and air transportation. These show that *intercity* traffic alone averaged nearly 5,000 miles per person per year. See *Statistical Abstract of the U.S., 1968*, table 802.

[22] *Ibid.*, tables 721 and 727.

THE POLITY

The democratic trend

One of the most striking changes associated with the emergence of industrial societies has been the rise of democratic government. The agrarian societies from which most democratic nations evolved were, as we have seen, largely monarchical. Maritime societies, although republican, were oligarchic. The kind of democracy that prevails in most industrial societies today was unknown in civilized societies before the Industrial Revolution.

Not all industrial societies have been democratic, of course. Fascist and Communist dictatorships have flourished in a number of these societies in the past, and still exist, though in modified form, in Eastern Europe, Spain, and Argentina.[23] In addition, Britain, the Scandinavian countries, the Low Countries, and Japan retain certain monarchical trappings. But even these countries reflect the democratic drift that is linked with the industrialization process. In the case of the constitutional monarchies, the real power lies in the hands of democratically elected officials; kings and emperors are little more than ceremonial heads of state. As for dictatorships, some of them have been eliminated (e.g., Germany and Italy), while others have been liberalized, so that a larger proportion of the population has some influence in the political process (e.g., Yugoslavia, Hungary, and even, to some degree, the Soviet Union).[24] Though the level of democratic participation achieved in these nations falls far short of what exists elsewhere, the *trend* is important. In recent years, the only industrial societies in which significant reversals have occurred are Poland, Czechoslovakia, and Argentina, and even in these cases the prospects of an eventual resumption of the earlier trend are fairly good. Furthermore, in two of these nations the reversal was due to foreign influences, while the third is a rather marginal industrial society; such reversals have not occurred in advanced industrial societies as a result of internal developments except in Germany in the 1930s, a country struggling with a most unusual combination of problems.

In discussions of political systems, democracy is often treated in categorical, rather than variable, terms. Too often we simply say that nations are, or are not, democracies, ignoring variations in the degree of citizen participation in the political process. This is a serious mistake, for no large society has ever enjoyed pure democracy. This would mean, in effect, the participation of every citizen in every deci-

---

[23] Dictatorships also exist in Greece, Brazil, and a number of other countries that cannot yet be considered industrial societies.

[24] For example, in the 1967 parliamentary elections, Hungarians were permitted to choose between rival candidates for the first time since the Communist seizure of power. According to press reports, there were lively contests in many cases. Similar steps had been taken previously in Yugoslavia, and in the Soviet Union some competition is permitted at the nomination stage. For a slightly dated summary of Soviet citizen participation, see Zbigniew Brzezinski and Samuel Huntington, *Political Power: USA/USSR* (New York: Viking, 1965), pp. 90–104.

sion—a practice that would result in utter chaos and the abandonment of every other useful activity. Even the most democratic nations achieve no more than representative democracy, a system in which most of the adult population are permitted, at infrequent intervals, to cast ballots for a limited number of candidates for public office and, between elections, to voice their support or criticism of the actions of the elected officials. Without denying the democratic elements present in such a system, it is clear that everyone does *not* have an equal voice in political decisions. Professional politicians and party functionaries always have disproportionate influence, and so, as a rule, do the wealthy who finance election campaigns and otherwise subsidize and influence elected officials.[25]

Once we recognize the impossibility of pure democracy in large organizations, it is easier to distinguish the varying degree of democracy attained by different societies, or by a particular society at different times. The United States, for example, enjoys a much greater degree of democracy today than at the beginning of the nineteenth century. The elimination of property restrictions on the franchise, the direct election of senators, women's suffrage, the voting provisions in recent civil rights legislation, and the "one man, one vote" decisions of the Supreme Court have all increased the percentage of Americans allowed to participate in the electoral process or increased the effectiveness of their participation. Similar trends can be observed in the recent history of other highly democratic nations, such as Britain and Sweden.[26]

Causes of the democratic trend

The democratic trend resulted primarily from the Industrial Revolution and the forces that gave rise to it. We have already seen how the discovery of the New World weakened the power of the traditional governing class in Western Europe and strengthened the position of the merchant class. This class had long been noted for its republican tendencies, both in maritime societies and in the urban centers of agrarian societies. Then, during the seventeenth and eighteenth centuries, it made its bid for a major share of political power in Britain, France, and the United States. To achieve this legitimately, however, the merchants and those allied with them had to have the support of an ideology that could justify the transfer of power and take the place of the ancient belief in the divine right of rulers. This was developed by a host of philosophers and pamphleteers who maintained that the powers of

---

[25] See, for example, Henry Ehrmann, *Organized Business in France* (Princeton, N.J.: Princeton University Press, 1957), pp. 224ff.; V. O. Key, Jr., *Politics, Parties, and Pressure Groups*, 3d ed. (New York: Thomas Y. Crowell, 1952), especially chap. 18; or Drew Pearson and Jack Anderson, *The Case Against Congress* (New York: Simon & Schuster, 1968), especially parts II and IV.

[26] In Sweden, for example, property restrictions on the franchise were not finally eliminated until after World War I. See Dankwort Rustow, *The Politics of Compromise: A Study of Parties and Cabinet Government in Sweden* (Princeton, N.J.: Princeton University Press, 1955), pp. 84–85.

Fig. 12/6 Luther's doctrine of the priesthood of all believers had political implications of a revolutionary nature; though Luther did not recognize this, others soon did

government are derived from the consent of the governed, and it proved to be invaluable in the political struggles of that era. Above all, it convinced the merchant class and its allies that what they were doing was right and just. Without this impetus, they might have failed completely.

Among the various factors that contributed to the rise and spread of the new democratic ideology, Protestantism looms large. Whatever else the Reformation accomplished, it proved that established authority *could* be challenged and overthrown. But beyond that, the Protestant doctrine of the priesthood of all believers had political implications of a revolutionary nature; and though Luther and Calvin did not recognize that fact, others soon did. Both the bitter German Peasants' Revolt of 1525 and the Leveller movement a century later in England were stimulated by it. That doctrine also led to the adoption of democratic or semidemocratic polities in many of the more radical Protestant groups, such as the Anabaptists, Mennonites, Baptists, Quakers, Puritans, and Presbyterians. It is no coincidence that the democratization of ecclesiastical governments began some generations before the democratization of civil governments, and that when the latter did begin, its early successes were chiefly in countries where ecclesiastical democratization had already made considerable headway. The first major and enduring victory of the democratic movement was in the United States, a country which since colonial days had been a refuge for the more radical and more democratic Protestant groups.

The discovery of the New World also contributed to the rise of the new democratic ideology. From an early date Europeans were fascinated by stories of the Indians, and many believed that their way of life revealed the condition of man in a state of nature. A myth, or mystique, quickly developed about "the noble savage" who, free from the fetters of autocratic government, achieved true nobility of character.[27] The monarchical form of government was increasingly depicted by intellectuals as a corrupting and unnatural institution. Building on this view of primitive man, political theorists like Locke and Rousseau propounded the social contract theory of government, which maintained that government is the creation of the people and therefore answerable to them. These ideas, together with the democratic outlook stimulated by Protestantism, successfully mobilized popular sentiment against monarchical governments and hastened their decline.

As important as these influences were, it is doubtful that the democratic movement would have succeeded without the technological contribution of the Industrial Revolution. To begin with, industrialization eliminated the traditional need for large numbers of unskilled and uneducated workers living at or near the subsistence level. As new sources of energy were tapped and machines were built to perform the more routine tasks, societies had to start producing more skilled and educated workers. People like these, however, are much less likely to be politically apathetic and servile. On the contrary, they tend to be self-assertive, jealous of their rights, and politically demanding.[28] Such characteristics are essential in a democracy, for they counterbalance and hold in check the powerful oligarchical tendencies present in any large and complex organization.

Industrialization also made possible the remarkable development of the mass media. To a great extent, this has been a response to the spread of literacy and to the increased demand for information generated by the rising level of education. Through newspapers, magazines, radio, and television, the average citizen of a modern industrial society stays in far closer touch with political events than his

---

[27] See, for example, *The Conquest of Granada* by the seventeenth-century poet Dryden, in which he wrote:

I am as free as Nature first made man,
Ere the base laws of servitude began,
When wild in woods the noble savage ran.
(Part I, act I, scene I)

[28] Many recent studies have documented the relationship between high rates of literacy and education on the one hand and democratic government on the other. See, for example, Daniel Lerner, *The Passing of Traditional Society: Modernizing the Middle East* (New York: Free Press, 1958), especially pp. 63–64 and 86–89; or S. M. Lipset, *Political Man* (Garden City, N.Y.: Doubleday, 1960), pp. 53–58.

counterpart in agrarian societies could possibly be. While much of the information he receives is extremely superficial and distorted, nevertheless it generates interest and concern. Thus the media not only satisfy a need, they also stimulate it.[29]

Finally, industrialization stimulated the growth of urban communities and this, too, strengthened democratic tendencies. Isolated rural communities have long been noted for their lack of political sophistication and for their patriarchal and paternalistic political patterns. Urban populations, by contrast, have always been better informed and more willing to challenge established authority. Thus, merely by increasing the size of urban populations, industrialization contributed to the democratic trend.

Political parties

The growth of democracy and the rise of industrial societies have produced a totally new kind of political organization, the mass political party, which serves to mobilize public opinion in support of political programs and candidates. Wherever there are more candidates than offices, there is a process of selection, and candidates supported by organizations are usually the ones that survive.

At the present time, party organizations differ in several respects. Some, including the Republican and Democratic parties in this country, are largely pragmatic, brokerage-type parties. They have no strong ideological commitments and no definite political programs. Their chief goal is to gain control of public offices and then to trade favors with special-interest groups, giving preferential legislative treatment in exchange for electoral and financial support. This cannot be said publicly, of course, and so party rhetoric takes the form of glittering generalities about service to the nation. In this type of party, discipline is weak or nonexistent, since each elected official is a free agent, permitted to work out his own "deals." Some degree of party unity is maintained because individual interest groups often establish relations with the officials of one party and prefer to continue working with them. This unity is reinforced by the tendency of the more ideologically inclined to separate into opposing camps, liberals gravitating toward one party, conservatives toward the other. Sometimes the more ideologically inclined win control of the party machinery, as the Goldwaterites did in 1964, but these periods are usually short-lived.

In contrast to the brokerage-type parties, most of those formed in the latter part of the nineteenth century and the first half of the twentieth had strong ideological commitments. Such parties, including both the Fascist parties of the right and the Socialist and Communist parties of the left, usually had well-developed programs for what they regarded as the rehabilitation of society and, in most instances, were willing to be defeated again and again rather than compromise with principles they held sacred.

---

[29] On the relationship between democracy and the development of the mass media, see Lerner, *op. cit.*, and Lipset, *op. cit.*, pp. 51–52.

Since World War II, however, many of these parties have become more flexible and pragmatic. The Communists of Yugoslavia and the Socialists of Britain are two examples of the newer trend. This reversal seems to be rooted in the high rate of technological and social change characteristic of industrial societies. Political programs devised in the last century, or even in the early decades of this one, have become obsolete in many respects, especially in their more specific prescriptions. Modern Socialists and Communists, therefore, increasingly find themselves obliged to innovate, both politically and economically. Western European Socialist parties, for example, have largely abandoned their former objective of nationalizing all basic industries, and Eastern European Communist parties have introduced the

Fig. 12/7   The growth of democracy and the rise of industrial societies have produced a totally new kind of political organization, the mass political party: the British Labour Party assembled in convention

profit mechanism into their economies, and elections between competing candidates into their polities.[30]

In addition to pragmatic, brokerage-type parties and ideological parties, there are two other types that deserve mention. The first are those based on subgroup loyalties, sometimes ethnic, more often religious. The Catholic parties of Western Europe are the best example of this. The other major type of party is the nationalistic, of which the German National Socialist, or Nazi, Party is a classic example. Nationalist parties are quite common today in underdeveloped countries, especially in those recently freed from colonial rule; but they are very rare in industrial societies. It is not hard to see why this is so: nationalist parties require some fairly deep-seated and continuing national grievance if they are to prosper. Germany developed such a grievance as a result of the Versailles Treaty following World War I, and the National Socialists capitalized on it. This pattern was not repeated after World War II despite Germany's second loss, perhaps because of the revelation of the many Nazi atrocities. Widespread feelings of national guilt and the postwar economic boom apparently blunted any sense of grievance that might otherwise have developed.

While nationalistic parties are rare in industrial societies today, nationalistic elements occur, in varying degrees, within other parties. This is especially true of the more conservative parties, most of which have a long tradition of patriotic and nationalistic concerns.[31] These nationalistic tendencies will undoubtedly continue as long as international tensions and conflicts remain.

Political conflict and stability

Every social system generates internal conflict, and industrial societies are no exception. Nevertheless, they are remarkable for their success in channeling such conflict into nonviolent forms. Compared with agrarian societies, particularly, they are far less prone to revolution and serious political upheavals. This is especially true of those societies that are past the transitional or early phase of industrialization. In fact, a recent study of 62 nations found a correlation of .965 between level of political stability and level of socioeconomic development.[32]

---

[30] See, for example, Kurt Shell, *The Transformation of Austrian Socialism* (New York: University Publishers, 1962), especially chaps. 6 and 7; Rustow, *op. cit.*, chap. 8; Albert Parry, *The New Class Divided: Science and Technology vs. Communism* (New York: Macmillan, 1966), chap. 7; or Brzezinski and Huntington, *op. cit.*, p. 231. See also fn. 24 above.

[31] This is due to the dominant role of the upper classes in these parties. Members of this class find it easy to identify their own private interests with the national interest, since they benefit disproportionately from national prosperity.

[32] Ivo Feierabend and Rosalind Feierabend, "Aggressive Behaviors Within Polities, 1948–1962: A Cross-National Study, "*Journal of Conflict Resolution*, 10 (1966), table 3. The measure used is Yule's Q. Results of this study suggest that rates of political instability are greatest in societies making the transition from agrarian to industrial, though results were not statistically significant. See the term "correlation" in the Glossary for an explanation of the meaning of the coefficient, .965.

There are a number of reasons for this. The greater productivity of these societies and the more equitable distribution of goods and services[33] give the majority of the population a vested interest in political stability. Revolution and anarchy are costly for most members of advanced industrial societies. In addition, the democratic ideology strengthens the allegiance of most segments of the population to the government and weakens support for revolutionary movements. Especially noteworthy in this connection is the loyalty shown the government by the military and the absence of military coups in the more advanced industrial societies.[34] Finally, the very complexity of the structure of industrial societies seems to generate a readiness to compromise controversial issues. This is partly because there are so many people in intermediate positions between the contending groups (e.g., people with modest property holdings standing between those with great wealth and those with little or none). These people are likely to benefit most from peaceful compromise and to shy away from extreme or violent solutions. Moreover, since the complexity of industrial societies means that each individual simultaneously fills a number of roles and often belongs to a variety of groups, people who are opponents in one controversy are likely to be allies in the next. For example, middle- and working-class Catholics who are divided over labor-management controversies may very well find themselves allies on church-state issues. This, too, has a moderating effect.

Although political conflicts are restrained in industrial societies, they are still present in a variety of forms involving a wide range of issues. The most common type of conflict is between the "haves" and the "have-nots" and, in most democratic, multiparty nations, is the most important single factor defining the basic framework for partisan politics. Typically, one or more parties openly appeal to the working class and other disadvantaged elements in the population, promising improved conditions if they are elected. Opposing parties rely for support on the more privileged elements in the population, though they usually avoid stressing these ties in their campaign rhetoric. Nevertheless, the relationship is recognized by most people.

Britain provides a good example of the typical relationship between economic class and party preference. As Table 12/3 shows, support for the Labour Party has been more than twice as strong among members of the working class as among members of the middle and upper classes. The strength of this relationship between party preference and economic class is quite variable in industrial societies, and Britain's position is intermediate. Class differences are most pronounced in the Scandinavian countries, least pronounced in the North American, as Table 12/4 shows. The limited relation between class and party preference in the latter is probably due to the absence of working-class parties with strong ideological commit-

---

[33] See Gerhard Lenski, *Power and Privilege: A Theory of Social Stratification* (New York: McGraw-Hill, 1966), pp. 308–313.

[34] Though military coups have been common in many parts of the world in recent decades, it is impossible to find a pure case in a truly advanced industrial society.

Table 12/3   Party preferences of the British population by economic class (average of three samples from 1943 to 1962)

| | Percentage favoring: | | |
| | Labour | Liberals and Conservatives | Total |
Class			
Upper and middle classes	28	72	100
Working class	61	39	100

Source: Adapted from Robert Alford, *Party and Society* (Chicago: Rand McNally, 1963), p. 136.

Table 12/4   Relationship between economic class and party preference in nine industrial societies as measured by percentage difference in support of liberal and/or leftist parties between (a) the upper and middle classes and (b) the working class

Nation and date	Percentage point difference
Norway, 1957	58
Finland, 1958	49
Italy, 1953 (males only)	37
Australia, average of 7 surveys, 1951–61	35
Britain, average of 3 surveys, 1943–62	33
West Germany, 1955	31
France, 1956	28
U.S., average of 7 surveys, 1944–60	18
Canada, average of 10 surveys, 1945–61	7

Sources: Adapted from Erik Allardt and Yrjö Littunen (eds.), *Cleavages, Ideologies and Party Systems: Contributions to Comparative Political Sociology,* in *Transactions of the Westermarck Society,* vol. X (Helsinki: The Academic Bookstore, 1964), pp. 102 and 212; Robert Alford, *Party and Society* (Chicago: Rand McNally, 1963), pp. 136, 202–203, 234–235, and 274–275; S. M. Lipset, *Political Man* (Garden City, N.Y.: Doubleday, 1960), pp. 225 and 227; and Morris Janowitz, "Social Stratification and Mobility in West Germany," *American Journal of Sociology,* 64, (1958), p. 22.

ments. All the major parties in the United States and Canada are pragmatic, brokerage types, which tend to play down class-related issues rather than emphasize them.

Another factor that influences the relation between class and party preference is the presence of important ethnic and religious divisions within the population. It is probably no coincidence that the three countries in Table 12/4 with the strongest relation between class and party preference are also the three most homogeneous from an ethnic and religious standpoint. By contrast, Canada has for years been torn

Fig. 12/8 French Canadian separatists demonstrating in Montreal, Quebec, October 10, 1964. Canada has been torn for years by struggles between an English-speaking Protestant majority and a large French Catholic minority

by struggles between an English-speaking Protestant majority and a very large French Catholic minority. In both Canada and the United States, religion and ethnicity are at least as powerful as class in determining party preference. In a number of other countries, religious groups even sponsor their own political parties. The most powerful of these are the predominantly Catholic parties in Italy, Germany, Austria, Belgium, and the Netherlands. In the Netherlands, three of the four major parties are organized along religious lines: one Catholic, one conservative Calvinist, and one liberal Calvinist.

Modern industrial societies differ dramatically from traditional agrarian societies by virtue of their willingness to permit ethnic and religious minorities and the economically disadvantaged to participate in the political process. In agrarian societies, such groups had almost no political power. In industrial societies, by contrast, these groups have sometimes won control of the machinery of government, or at least a share in it, as the socialists have done in Scandinavia and Britain, the French Catholics in Canada, and the Catholics in the Netherlands.

The growth of government

Apart from the rise of democracy, the most important political change associated with industrialization is the great growth of government. The governments of modern industrial societies are engaged in a far wider range of activities and perform a much more diversified set of functions than governments in any other type of society. In a traditional agrarian society, the government's chief functions were the preservation

Table 12/5 Annual per capita expenditures by governments in 5 industrial and 5 industrializing agrarian societies

Society	Per capita expenditures
Industrial societies:	
United States	$592
Sweden	386
Australia	193
Argentina	62
Spain	35
Industrializing agrarian societies:	
Greece	68
Ceylon	25
Brazil	21
Peru	20
Burma	9

Source: Calculated from United Nations, *Statistical Yearbook, 1964*, tables 2, 171, and 176.

of law and order, defense, taxation, and the support of religion. In modern industrial societies, there are dozens of new ones. Governments now educate youth; regulate and direct the economy; provide welfare, job training, and housing; administer social security programs; support scientific and technological innovation; maintain and improve transportation and communication facilities; and create recreational facilities, to name some of the more important functions.

Table 12/5 compares the per capita expenditures by governments of a few industrial and industrializing agrarian societies. As this table indicates, while there is some overlap between the two groups, the ranges are quite different. Expenditures average almost nine times greater in the industrial nations. If data were available for Communist-bloc nations and if the influence of industrialization could be eliminated from the other group, the difference would be even larger.

This difference results primarily from the greater productivity of industrial societies: they produce more, therefore they can afford to do more. Not only are their per capita expenditures larger, but a much higher proportion of their gross national product goes for government activities. In one recent year, government expenditures in 22 industrial societies averaged 24.1 per cent of their gross national products. By contrast, government expenditures in 17 industrializing agrarian societies averaged only 15.2 per cent, or about three-fifths as much.[35]

[35] These figures are arithmetic means; medians equaled 24.5 and 15.0 per cent respectively. These figures were calculated from the United Nations, *Yearbook of National Account Statistics, 1964*, part C. The figures reported are for all levels of government from local to national.

The greater activity of government is closely linked with its increasing democratization. As the masses of common people gain a voice in government, they demand services seldom provided them in agrarian societies. They want, among other things, educational opportunities, recreational facilities, assistance when they are old or sick or unemployed, protection against dishonest merchants, and many other things. As the government expands to provide these services, democratic tendencies are further strengthened. An educated and economically secure population usually participates more intelligently and effectively in the democratic process, and is much less likely to be attracted to totalitarian programs, than an illiterate and economically insecure population.[36]

Another factor contributing to the growth of government in an industrial society is the greater interdependence of its population. We have seen how occupational specialization has progressed to the point where virtually everyone is engaged in specialized work. Everyone, therefore, is dependent on the labors of others and on the maintenance of the complex system of exchange by which goods and services reach the ultimate consumer. In a society like this, any disruption of the economy is bound to have serious consequences for everyone.

Similarly, in a society geared to a high degree of interaction between its members, dependable systems of transportation and communication are essential. And in its urban centers, where people live cheek by jowl, well-organized fire, police, and health services are imperative. Private individuals and organizations are incapable of assuming these responsibilities alone: only government can commandeer the resources and exercise the authority needed to deal with such fundamental problems.

The growth and transformation of the government bureaucracies

One of the best measures of the growth of government activity is provided by statistics on the size of its bureaucracy. In the United States, for example, the number of employees of the federal government has shown a steady upward trend for the last century and a half:[37]

1816	5,000
1861	37,000
1901	239,000
1931	610,000
1961	2,436,000

This increase has far outdistanced the growth of the population as a whole. The latter increased slightly over 20-fold in this period, whereas the number of federal employees increased nearly 500-fold. Contrary to the opinion of some, it is not

---

[36] See, for example, Lipset, *op. cit.*, chaps. 2 and 4.

[37] *Statistical Abstract of the United States, 1963*, table 535, and *Historical Statistics*, series Y 241–250.

only the federal bureaucracy that has been growing. From 1940 (the earliest year for which national totals are available) to 1966, the number of employees of state and local governments rose more than 150 per cent, while the general population grew only about 50 per cent.[38]

The great growth in the powers of government and in the size of its bureaucracy has made top administrative officials (i.e., civil servants, not elected officials) powerful figures in every industrial society. While this might be interpreted as merely a continuation of the old agrarian pattern with its dominance by an hereditary governing class, actually it is not. Government offices are no longer regarded as private property to be bought and sold and transferred to one's children. Rather, they are usually assigned on the basis of competitions in which technical competence, training, and experience are the chief criteria. Furthermore, in the exercise of office, officials are expected to act on the basis of the public interest rather than private advantage. While this ideal is not fully achieved, there is a marked contrast between the practices of the officials in a modern industrial society and those in a traditional agrarian society. The United States has discovered this, to its regret, in trying to deal with the officials of many of the governments of southeast Asia, the Middle East, and Latin America.

In large measure, the explanation for this change lies in the rise of the new democratic ideology, which asserts that the powers of government are derived from the people and that governments are supposed to be instruments of the people. This is in sharp contrast to the traditional proprietary ideology of agrarian societies, which defined the state as the property of the ruler. When modern officials use public office for private advantage, they are subject to severe censure, and in some cases to guilt feelings as well. These kinds of restraints were largely absent in agrarian societies.

Despite the less venal behavior of public officials in modern industrial societies, the great power they exercise is a matter of concern, since their conception of what constitutes a wise and responsible use of this power is not always shared by others. Like everyone else, they have biases. The fact that most high officials are recruited from the more prosperous segments of society creates one kind of bias.[39] The fact that they are exposed, with increasing frequency, to specialized professional training creates another (e.g., a common criticism of American city managers is their preoccupation with technical efficiency, which they often promote at the expense of democratic values).[40]

So far the critics of official power have not come up with any feasible alternative. The sheer size and complexity of government in a modern industrial society renders

---

[38] *Statistical Abstract, 1968*, table 605, and *Historical Statistics*, series Y 205–222.

[39] On the social origins of federal officials, see W. L. Warner et al., *The American Federal Executive* (New Haven, Conn.: Yale, 1963), table 33B.

[40] See, for example, Edward Banfield and James Wilson, *City Politics*, (Cambridge, Mass.: Harvard, and the M.I.T. Press, 1963), chap. 13 and conclusion.

mass participation in the decision-making process impossible. A substantial delegation of power, therefore, is inevitable, and those to whom the power is delegated will generally do what they deem appropriate. In short, there are decided limitations to the applicability of democratic principles in any large-scale organization.

Warfare

Sometimes, in our more pessimistic moments, it seems as if war were one of the permanent features of human life. Yet when we examine the record carefully, we find that under some conditions, war has been rather infrequent or absent altogether. Historically, wars have usually been most common when (1) population pressures forced societies to compete for limited space, (2) technological advance was slow and conquest was a more promising route to riches than economic development, and (3) a small governing class controlled the political life of societies.

Because these conditions were maximized during the long agrarian era that preceded the Industrial Revolution, it is easy to suppose that the patterns of that era—which constitutes most of recorded history—reflected a basic element in man's nature. A broader view of history, however, shows that the incidence of warfare has varied and, like most social patterns, has responded to changing social conditions.[41] This suggests that we would be foolish to assume its inevitability.

In several respects, the developments associated with the Industrial Revolution indicate that warfare may be less common in the future than it was in the past, or at least in the agrarian era. Though world population is still growing very rapidly, there are effective and acceptable techniques for controlling it. Such techniques have, in fact, already reduced the rate of population growth in industrial societies to a point well below the rate of growth of the gross national product. There is no reason this cannot happen in every country and bring improvements in the standard of living for all of mankind. Another development, the democratic revolution, has destroyed the political monopoly of the governing class in a large number of societies. Although wars of aggression may sometimes be profitable for a small governing class, they are seldom profitable for the majority of citizens. As a result, in most democratic nations, there is a deep-seated resistance to war that cannot be overcome except by the most determined propaganda campaigns or by fears for national survival. This resistance has been greatly increased by advances in modern military technology, which have now reached the point where all of mankind's gains of the last several hundred years could be erased in a few hours of all-out warfare between the major powers.

These developments do not insure the end of war, of course, but they increase the probability of peaceful coexistence and competition between the major powers. When wars occur, they are much more likely to involve nonindustrialized societies. Even though one or more industrial societies may be brought into these conflicts,

---

[41] See Table 6/11, p. 138.

as in Korea and Vietnam, war between the major powers will be avoided if at all possible. If it does occur, however, it is not likely to come about, as in agrarian societies of the past, simply because the ruler of a nation sees an opportunity for economic and political self-aggrandizement. Rather, it would probably result from an escalation of emotions on both sides that finally destroyed inhibitions rooted in reason. Happily, this possibility has become less likely as it has come to be recognized.

*C*hapter 13
*I*ndustrial Societies: Part 2

THE ECONOMY

Urbanization of production

In agrarian societies, productive activities were centered in the rural villages. Agriculture was the dominant industry, and farmers were a substantial majority of the labor force. In addition to farming, the rural population often engaged in a variety of crafts during the off-season, welcoming the chance to supplement their meager incomes. Urban populations were small, and many of their residents were not gainfully employed (i.e., the leisured members of the governing class). Moreover, those who were employed were often producing nonessential or luxury goods and services for the upper classes.

The Industrial Revolution changed all this. From an early date, the new technology required an urban location. The costly power-driven machines invented during the first phase of the revolution were most profitable when operated in factories, and factories required large concentrations of people living nearby. When they were built in rural areas, as sometimes happened, their owners found it impossible to hire enough workers unless they built adjoining tenements, which simply created new urban settlements. While the new industries generated a growing demand for workers in the cities and towns, advances in agriculture reduced the need for farm workers. And so, before the end of the eighteenth century, there began a massive migration which only now shows signs of having run its course.

Today, in the more advanced industrial societies, the historic distribution of population is reversed. Whereas 90 per cent or more of the people in agrarian societies lived in rural areas and 10 per cent or less in urban, 90 per cent or more now live in urban centers and no more than 10 per cent in rural areas. In 1967 the

Fig. 13/1 New York City: view southwest from the top of the RCA Building

U.S. Bureau of the Census reported the farm population as 10.8 million, or 5.5 per cent of the total, but this was really a polite fiction.[1] Nearly half of this group earned most of its income from sources other than farming.[2] Families that derived at least half of their income from farming made up less than 3 per cent of the population. And many of these were older people who were clinging to small, inefficient farms, and who would be replaced by machines as soon as they retired.

[1] U.S. Department of Commerce, *Current Population Reports*, Series P-27, No. 38 (April, 1968).

[2] Edward Higbee, *Farms and Farmers in an Urban Age* (New York: Twentieth Century Fund, 1963), pp. 45–46.

As the farm population has declined, the urban population has soared. Nearly two-thirds of the U.S. population now live in communities of 50,000 or more and over one-third in communities of 1,000,000 or more.[3] The rapidity of this growth is one reason for many of the problems plaguing urban communities today.

The rise of market economies

In a recent book entitled *The Making of Economic Society*, Robert Heilbroner writes:

> Looking not only over the diversity of contemporary societies, but back over the sweep of all history, [the economist] sees that man has succeeded in solving the production and distribution problems in but three ways. That is, within the enormous diversity of actual social institutions which guide and shape the economic process, the economist divines but three overarching *types* of systems which separately or in combination enable humankind to solve its economic challenge. These three great systemic types can be called economies run by Tradition, economies run by Command, and economies run by the Market.[4]

In a traditional economy, the basic questions of production and distribution—what shall be produced? in what quantities? and for whose benefit?—are answered by repeating the society's past practices. In a command economy, the opinions and values of those who control the government provide the answers. In a market economy, the basic economic decisions are made through a complex interaction of the forces of supply and demand, reflecting the opinions and values of all the individuals and organizations in the society in proportion to their wealth.

The economies of most societies are actually a complex blend of all three of these elements, but modern industrial societies are unique by virtue of the strength and importance of the market element. Prior to the Industrial Revolution there was no society with what could properly be called a *market economy*—that is, an economy in which the basic problems of production and distribution are settled primarily by the free play of market forces.[5]

Several things are necessary to produce a true market economy.[6] To begin with,

---

[3] Calculated from *Current Population Reports,* Series P-25, No. 371 (August, 1967), table A; and *Statistical Abstract of the United States, 1967,* tables 2 and 15.

[4] Robert Heilbroner, *The Making of Economic Society* (Englewood Cliffs, N.J.: Prentice-Hall, 1962), p. 9. Quoted by permission of Prentice-Hall.

[5] See, for example, Karl Polanyi's statement that "previously to our own time no economy has ever existed that, even in principle, was controlled by markets . . . Though the institution of the market was fairly common since the later Stone Age, its role was no more than incidental to economic life." From *The Great Transformation: The Political and Economic Origins of Our Time* (Boston: Beacon Press, 1957), p. 43. Maritime societies may have been an exception to this assertion, but unfortunately we lack the data to test this.

[6] Heilbroner, *op. cit.,* pp. 42–44 and 64–65.

the economy must be monetized: money must become a pervasive element in the daily life of every member of society, and most of the things men value, including labor, must be available for a price. In addition, land, labor, and capital must be mobile; traditional restraints on their use or transfer have to be eliminated. Men should be free to sell their ancestral land if that is profitable; workers should be free to leave their present jobs and take new ones if they can get higher wages; and businessmen should be free to use their capital however they wish. Restraints on economic activity based on family sentiments, religious taboos, social customs, or organizational restrictions (guild restrictions on output, for example, or legal restrictions on the migration of serfs and slaves) should be minimal. In short, individual economic advantage, as measured in monetary terms, must become the decisive determinant of economic action.

As we have seen, the discovery of the New World gave a powerful impetus to the first requirement: the great flow of bullion from the Spanish colonies increased the supply of precious metals in Western Europe severalfold. At the same time, the Protestant Reformation and the ideological changes that followed it, such as eighteenth-century Deism and the Enlightenment movement, weakened the traditional social bonds that immobilized men and property. These same factors also sparked the Industrial Revolution. Once it was underway and the economy had begun to change, the effect tended to be cumulative. Each change stimulated further changes; the more resources that came under the control of Western Europe's entrepreneurial class, for example, the better they were able to promote further changes.

By the end of the nineteenth century, it looked as if every industrial society would soon have an almost pure market economy. These societies were coming increasingly under the control of political parties dominated by businessmen committed to the philosophy of laissez-faire capitalism or free enterprise. Following in the main the teachings of Adam Smith, the pioneer economist, this new governing class argued that the most productive economy, and the most beneficial, was one that was entirely free of governmental restrictions. The only role government should play in society's economic life, according to these men, was the role of policeman to insure the faithful fulfillment of contracts. They were firm believers in the principle that "that government governs best which governs least."

Movement toward the mixed economy

It was not long, however, before it became evident that the new market economy was not the unmitigated blessing its enthusiasts made it out to be. In the pursuit of profits, businessmen were adopting practices that were obviously harmful to others. For example, in an attempt to cut labor costs, many employers were firing adult workers and replacing them with children, simultaneously creating unemployment and endangering the health and safety of children. In other instances, efforts to reduce costs resulted in dangerous working conditions and the production of shoddy, even unsafe, merchandise.

Fig. 13/2   The Mines Act of 1842 prohibited the employment of boys under the age of ten in mines

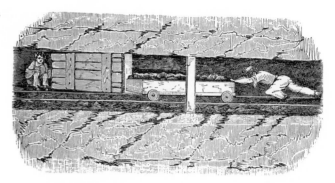

Protests soon began to be raised, sometimes by social reformers like Robert Owen, sometimes by poets and novelists like Thomas Hood and Upton Sinclair. Even before the middle of the last century, the British Parliament started enacting legislation to protect society against the extremes of free enterprise. The Factory Acts of 1833 and 1844, the Mines Act of 1842, and the Ten Hour Law of 1847 prohibited the employment of children under the age of nine in textile factories, restricted children under thirteen to 6½ hours work per day in factories, forbade the employment of boys under ten and women in the mines, limited women and young people aged thirteen to eighteen to ten working hours per day, and provided for inspectors to enforce these laws.[7] By 1901, the minimum age for child labor in England was raised to twelve, and in 1908 limitations were finally imposed on the working hours of men. Other legislation forced employers to provide for the safety of their employees in dangerous industries and established the first minimum wage. In Germany under Bismarck, new laws provided for sick leave and for workmen's compensation in the case of injuries sustained on the job. The crowning achievement of German legislation in this period was the Old Age and Security Law of 1889.

Although the United States was generally slower in adopting regulatory legislation, it pioneered in several areas, especially in the protection of consumers. By the latter part of the nineteenth century, it was becoming evident that a market system has an inherent tendency to lose its competitive character and evolve in the direction of monopolistic enterprise—at least in fields where fixed costs are a significant percentage of total costs. To protect the public against monopolies and to preserve the element of competition in the economy, Congress passed the Sherman Antitrust Act in 1890. Another important piece of American legislation in this period was the Pure Food and Drug Act of 1906. Again, the purpose was to protect consumers against the abuses of an unregulated free enterprise system.

Despite such legislation, however, market forces remained dominant in industrial societies until the great depression of the 1930s. The terrible dislocations which developed in this decade finally forced political leaders to adopt a series of new laws that provided for greatly increased governmental involvement in economic

---

[7] S. B. Clough and C. W. Cole, *Economic History of Europe* (Boston: Heath, 1941), pp. 693–698.

affairs. Failure to act might easily have resulted in revolution and the complete destruction of the market system. What happened instead, in most countries, was a substantial curtailment of the power of market forces and a corresponding increase in the element of command (i.e., governmental regulation).

Since the 1930s, the economies of most industrial societies have continued to move in the direction of a mixed market-command economy. This trend reflects a growing understanding of the defects or limitations which are inherent in a pure market economy. In the first place, there is a definite tendency for the rich to get richer and the poor poorer. This is because of the influence of fixed costs which, as we have noted, provide a built-in advantage for the producer with the largest volume of sales. There is a spiraling effect, too, so that the larger his volume of sales becomes, the greater his competitive advantage, leading to an ever greater share of sales and an ever greater advantage until the smaller producers are finally driven into bankruptcy. Except for its antitrust legislation, the United States would long ago have had monopolies in most fields of production. It is one of the great ironies of history, seldom recognized by opponents of governmental regulation, that the survival of the market system increasingly depends on governmental regulation.

The second great defect of a pure market economy is its inability to provide adequately for the corporate needs of the society, as contrasted with the individual needs of its members. This defect has forced most nations with this kind of economy to strengthen the element of command at the expense of the market when threatened with war. To meet the requirements of national security, they have to limit the production of nonessentials. The situation is basically the same when a nation is faced with any serious problem: decisions as to what is to be produced and how it is to be used cannot be left entirely to individuals. When they are, the results are like those John Kenneth Galbraith describes in *The Affluent Society*, where in one especially caustic paragraph he writes of the typical American family

> which takes its mauve and cerise, air-conditioned, power-steered, and power-braked automobile out for a tour [passing] through cities that are badly paved, made hideous by litter, blighted buildings, billboards, and posts for wires that should long since have been put underground. They pass on into a countryside that has been rendered largely invisible by commercial art. . . . They picnic on exquisitely packaged food from a portable icebox by a polluted stream and go on to spend the night at a park which is a menace to public health and morals. Just before dozing off on an air mattress, beneath a nylon tent, amid the stench of decaying refuse, they may reflect vaguely on the curious unevenness of their blessings.[8]

This neglect of the corporate interests of society is not due merely to popular indifference, as some claim. Rather, the mechanism of a market economy does not lend itself to solving problems of this kind. They can be solved only by political

---

[8] (Boston: Houghton Mifflin, 1958), p. 253. Quoted by permission of Houghton Mifflin.

means. As a result, there has been, by popular demand, a steady transfer of responsibility from the private to the public sector in nearly all industrial societies. This has meant more of a balance between the elements of the market and command in the economies of these societies.

Economic trends in totalitarian states

In societies controlled by Fascist or Communist regimes, market forces have been relegated to a very secondary position.[9] This is only what we would expect, given the strong ideological and programmatic commitments of these parties. Guided by a vision of a "better" society, their leaders have sought to utilize all their nation's resources to achieve their goals. Since they could never persuade everyone to accept their program voluntarily, they have had to rely on the techniques of command. This has meant, in effect, a planned economy. The succession of five-year plans adopted by the Soviet Union is a classic example of this.

In recent years Communist leaders have become increasingly aware of the limitations inherent in this type of economic system. First in Yugoslavia, then in the Soviet Union, and later throughout all of Eastern Europe, elements of the market system were reintroduced into areas of the economy from which they had been excluded for years.[10] The reason for this seems to have been the inefficiencies of centralized planning. To be really effective, economic planning must take account not only of all the thousands of commodities produced, but also of all the interrelations among them, since the production of one commodity is always contingent on the availability of many others. One Soviet economist is reported to have argued that a sound plan for the Soviet machine industry alone would require provision for more than 15 billion interrelations.[11] Because it is impossible to coordinate successfully such a fantastic number of relationships, shortages have repeatedly developed in some commodities and surpluses in others.

The great virtue of the market system is its *automatic* mechanism for balancing supply and demand. When the demand for a product goes up, the price goes up, too, which gives producers an incentive to turn out more of it. Conversely, a slump in the demand for something causes prices to go down and reduces incentives. All this is accomplished without costly centralized planning.

Until recently, the market system was generally equated with capitalism and for this reason was unthinkable to Soviet leaders. In the last decade, however, Soviet economists have shown that the market mechanism is not necessarily linked with private enterprise and that its reintroduction into Communist economies would not

---

[9] For a good discussion of the economy in Nazi Germany, see Franz Neumann, *Behemoth: The Structure and Practice of National Socialism* (New York: Oxford, 1942), part II.

[10] See, for example, Alec Nove, *The Soviet Economy*, rev. ed. (New York: Praeger, 1966), especially chap. 9.

[11] See Joseph Alsop, "Matter of Fact," *The Washington Post*, January 13, 1964.

bring about a return to capitalism. With this point clarified and with the more pragmatic orientation of the new generation of Soviet leaders, the way was cleared for experimentation. This has been so successful that nearly all of the Communist nations in Europe are now employing market mechanisms to some degree.

This suggests that in the future there will probably be less variation in this important aspect of industrial societies than there has been in the past. Both Communist and non-Communist societies are moving toward a more balanced type of economy, in which both market and command will play important roles. Market forces will be used to achieve greater efficiency, while command will be used to protect the corporate interests of society and to limit the growth of social inequality. This is not to say, of course, that differences between economic systems will be eliminated (Communist governments seem determined to prevent the reestablishment of privately owned enterprises, for one thing), but they will probably be reduced.[12]

New types of economic organizations

The economies of agrarian and maritime societies were usually organized around three types of units—family enterprises, guilds, and state enterprises. Of these, only state enterprises play a major role in modern industrial societies. Guilds have vanished entirely and family enterprises have declined to the point where they play at best a secondary role, and in some nations not even that. In their stead, a number of new kinds of organizations have emerged, among them corporations, cooperatives, labor unions, and professional and industrial associations. These, together with state enterprises, constitute the major economic units in industrial societies.

Corporations   The modern corporation easily ranks as one of the most important inventions of modern times and, like many major innovations, evolved over a period of time. Its origins go back to the middle of the sixteenth century when English and Dutch merchants, trading with remote areas, banded together in what came to be known as joint stock companies.[13] This form of organization had several advantages over family enterprises and partnerships. Above all, it permitted the pooling of large amounts of capital and the spreading of risks. This was extremely important in ventures where risks were great and large investments essential. In addition, a joint stock company, unlike a family enterprise or a partnership, was not disrupted by the death of one of the owners. Either his heirs inherited his stock, or, if they wanted to get the money out of the enterprise, they could sell the stock to someone else. This was not possible in a partnership, since the law required (as it

---

[12] Many Soviet scholars feel that American social scientists try to blur the differences. For a good statement of their view, see Alex Simirenko (ed.), *Soviet Sociology: Historical Antecedents and Current Appraisals* (Chicago: Quadrangle, 1966), pp. 327–339.

[13] See, for example, Clough and Cole, *op. cit.*, pp. 148ff.

still does) that if one of the partners died or wished to withdraw, the partnership be dissolved and the assets distributed.

During the next several centuries, the joint stock company gradually spread to new fields of enterprise. More important, a series of changes made the corporate form of organization safer and more attractive to investors. For one thing, the development of preferred stock (i.e., shares that had first claim on profits and on assets in the case of bankruptcy) and organized stock markets facilitated the exchange of stock. Most important of all, however, was the adoption of the principle of limited liability. Prior to the nineteenth century, stockholders in most corporations, like owners of family businesses and members of partnerships, had unlimited liability in case of bankruptcy. This meant that they stood to lose not only their investment in the company, but all their other possessions if they were needed to satisfy the claims of creditors. This naturally made investors extremely cautious; unless they had firsthand knowledge of the business and those running it, they were taking a great risk. The passage of laws limiting the liability of stockholders to the investment itself greatly stimulated the flow of capital into this new form of enterprise.

In today's industrial societies, nearly all of the largest and most powerful private enterprises are organized as corporations. In the United States in 1960, for example, 75 per cent of all business was done by corporations, and among larger concerns (i.e., those with annual receipts of $100,000 or more), they accounted for 87 per cent of the total.[14] The very largest concerns, those with annual profits in the hundreds of millions or billions of dollars, are all corporations. At the present time, privately owned corporate assets constitute more than 63 per cent of the national wealth of this country.[15] A single firm, American Telephone and Telegraph, has assets totaling over $30 billion, and General Motors recently had receipts totaling over $20 billion in a single year. American Telephone and Telegraph has more than 3.0 million shareholders, General Motors more than 1.4 million.

As corporations have grown, their character has changed substantially. Most important, control of the largest ones has been slipping from the owners to the top managers.[16] As one observer recently put it, "Almost everyone now agrees . . . that, typically, control is in the hands of management; and that management normally selects its own replacements."[17] The cause of this shift is the fragmentation of stock ownership, an almost inevitable by-product of the growth of corporations. In

---

[14] Calculated from the *Statistical Abstract of the United States, 1963*, p. 489.

[15] *Ibid.*, calculations based on data for 1958, pp. 346 and 494.

[16] See A. A. Berle, Jr., and Gardner Means, *The Modern Corporation and Private Property* (New York: Macmillan, 1932), especially book 1; or Robert A. Gordon, *Business Leadership in the Large Corporation* (Berkeley: University of California Press, 1961) on American corporations. For the trend in Europe, see P. Sargant Florence, *Ownership, Control, and Success of Large Companies: An Analysis of English Industrial Structure and Policy, 1936–1951* (London: Street and Maxwell, 1961); or David Granick, *The European Executive* (Garden City, N.Y.: Doubleday Anchor, 1964).

[17] E. S. Mason (ed.), *The Corporation and Modern Society* (Cambridge, Mass.: Harvard, 1959), p. 4.

Fig. 13/3 New York headquarters of American Telephone and Telegraph. In this giant corporation no individual owns as much as 1 per cent of the stock

American Telephone and Telegraph, for example, no person owns as much as 1 per cent of the stock, and most own only a minute fraction of 1 per cent. Furthermore, the stockholders are scattered throughout the world. Mobilizing a majority of the voting stock to wrest control from the managers would be virtually impossible.

The growing power of managers in industry is part of a larger trend evident in many facets of life in modern industrial societies. In government, industry, education, religion, labor, and other areas, organizations have grown so large, and administrative problems so complex, that those who constitutionally hold ultimate power (e.g., the voters, stockholders, trustees, or members) cannot possibly exercise more than the most limited control over administrators and managers.[18] Under the circumstances, most of the responsibility for day-to-day decisions gravitates into the hands

---

[18] For a classic statement of the problem, see Robert Michels, *Political Parties: A Sociological Study of the Oligarchical Tendencies of Modern Democracy*, trans. by Eden and Cedar Paul (New York: Dover, 1959, first published in 1915). Michels' study is of special interest because he focused on the Socialist parties of Western Europe, which had an intense commitment to democratic principles; yet, as he demonstrates, even they could not avoid the development of an administrative oligarchy in their own organizations.

of administrators and managers. This process is now virtually complete in nearly all of the larger corporations, and managers exercise most of the powers that in theory belong to the stockholders.

Labor unions   One of the most striking differences between agrarian and industrial societies is the development of organizations designed to advance the interests of the common people. The two most obvious examples are working-class political parties and labor unions.

The origins of modern labor unions can be traced back to the latter part of the eighteenth century, when small groups of workingmen in both England and the United States banded together to negotiate with their employers on wages, hours, and working conditions. During the nineteenth century the movement had many ups and downs, but over the long run the gains far outweighed the losses. Laws forbidding union organization and strikes were gradually repealed and more stable organizations established. By 1900 there were 2 million union members in Britain and nearly a million each in the United States and Germany.

Today, labor unions claim approximately 18 million members in the United States; and union-backed political parties hold office, or have held or shared office, in Britain, Scandinavia, the Low Countries, France, Italy, Austria, the United States, and Australia. In English-speaking nations the unions have been the dominant force in the workingmen's movement, and the labor parties derivatives of them; on the Continent the reverse has been true.

As corporations have grown in size, so have unions: for example, the United Auto Workers Union currently has about 1.3 million members. Size has proven essential in bargaining with corporate giants like General Motors, which in one recent year reported profits of more than $2 billion.

With their growth in size and power, and with their increasing respectability, labor unions have lost much of their former idealistic and reformist fervor. Under the leadership of often elderly administrators and bureaucrats, they play an ever more cautious and conservative role, both economically and politically. Even in Britain and Scandinavia, where the power of the unions is particularly marked, union leaders have largely abandoned their former goal of nationalizing the economy. Today they see their chief task as simply maximizing the wages of their own members, thus assuring them a larger share of the benefits of an affluent society. Some labor leaders refuse to accept this view, but they seem to be losing ground.

In totalitarian societies, the function of labor unions has been quite different from what it is in democratic nations.[19] In both Communist and Fascist nations, unions have been used by the dominant party as an instrument of social control. In theory, the unions are instruments of the workers; in practice, they have been instruments of the Party. Recently there have been some indications that the unions

---

[19] See, for example, Emily Clark Brown, *Soviet Trade Unions and Labor Relations* (Cambridge, Mass.: Harvard, 1966).

may play a more independent role in the future, but so far this is more promise than reality.

Professional associations   Another new form of economic organization is the professional association. With increasing frequency, professional people (e.g., doctors, lawyers, teachers, chemists, accountants, architects, etc.) have organized into associations ostensibly designed to insure high standards of performance in their field but, in practice, functioning largely to advance their economic and other interests. The most publicized, and most controversial, of these organizations in the United States has been the American Medical Association. As a result of its aggressive efforts, the medical profession has become the most lucrative single occupation in the country (see Table 13/2, page 385). In totalitarian nations, professional associations, like labor unions, are primarily instruments of the Party, though the superior education and greater social importance of professional workers have made their organizations somewhat more difficult for the Party to control and manipulate.

Cooperatives   A fourth important organizational innovation is the cooperative. Its history is closely linked with the two other important working-class movements of modern times; socialism and trade unionism. Like them, it grew out of the efforts of workingmen to improve their situation.

In the earliest stages, leaders of the cooperative movement attempted to establish cooperative communities, such as the one Robert Owen founded in New Harmony, Indiana, in the 1820s. Very soon, however, the energies of the movement were channeled into consumers' and producers' cooperatives. The first were retail

Fig. 13/4 The threshing and sacking machine shown here is owned by a Danish farmers' cooperative and is used by members on a rotating basis

Fig. 13/5   Cooperative housing development, Sweden

stores owned by groups of consumers, with the profits either shared by the members or turned back into the movement to help establish other cooperative ventures. Producers' cooperatives were associations of craftsmen or farmers who banded together and formed their own businesses, competing with privately owned enterprises. As in consumers' cooperatives, profits were shared by the members or turned over to the movement.

In many industrial societies, including the United States, the cooperative movement has met with only limited success, with cooperatives accounting for no more than a small per cent of the total volume of business in any industry except agriculture. This is not the situation everywhere, however. In Scandinavia in particular, cooperatives are an important element in the economy: at least a third of the wage-earners in these countries belong to a cooperative, with the ratio highest in Denmark.[20] Farmers' cooperatives have been an important element in the Danish economy since the latter half of the nineteenth century, and by 1939 nine-tenths of the farm population were organized into one large cooperative. In Sweden, too, the cooperative movement enjoyed great success, and in recent years much of agricultural production and urban housing have been controlled by cooperatives, as have a third of its retail trade and a tenth of its wholesale trade and nonfarm production.

In general, cooperatives have been most successful in agriculture, housing, and retail and wholesale trade—industries in which capital requirements are not too great and small enterprises are not at a serious competitive disadvantage. The pattern is highly variable from industry to industry, and as Table 13/1 indicates, from country to country as well.

---

[20] J. Frederic Dewhurst et al., *Europe's Needs and Resources: Trends and Prospects in Eighteen Countries* (New York: Twentieth Century Fund, 1961), p. 754. See also Marquis W. Childs, *Sweden: The Middle Way*, rev. ed. (New Haven, Conn.: Yale, 1947).

Table 13/1 Percentage of housing units constructed by cooperatives, 1957

Country	Percentage constructed by cooperatives
Finland	56
Denmark	49
Germany	30
Norway	28
Sweden	27
Netherlands	26
Austria	18
Switzerland	10
Britain	0
France	0
Italy	0
Ireland	0

Source: Economic Commission for Europe, *Annual Bulletin of Housing and Building Statistics for Europe, 1957*, table 8, in J. Frederic Dewhurst, et al., *Europe's Needs and Resources: Trends and Prospects in Eighteen Countries* (New York: Twentieth Century Fund, 1961), p. 237.

Cooperatives have also found a place in the economies of Eastern European nations. In the Soviet Union they have functioned primarily as a transitional form in the shift from private to state enterprise.[21] This has been particularly true in agriculture, where collective farms, a form of cooperative, have played a major role for a long time and, as recently as 1962, still farmed 53 per cent of the cultivated land. Over the years, state enterprises have grown at the expense of cooperatives and one might well predict their eventual elimination. This may be premature, however, in view of the recent efforts of Communist regimes to decentralize their economies and move toward a mixed market-command system. Cooperatives could prove to be a valuable kind of organization under these circumstances. We should add that the experiments of the Yugoslavs, the economic as well as political pioneers of the Communist world, also point in this direction. By allowing workers a voice in plant policy and a share in plant profits, they have adopted the principle, if not the name, of the cooperative mode of organization.

Continuing forms of organization

Along with these newer kinds of economic organizations, certain older ones have continued to operate and, in some cases, to flourish. These include the family-owned

---

[21] Nove, *op. cit.*, pp. 41–45.

enterprise, which survives in most industrial societies and even in some of the Communist bloc nations. In Poland and Yugoslavia, for example, there are still privately owned farms and small businesses, though they are hedged about with many restrictions, particularly on their growth. In non-Communist societies, family businesses thrive in a wide variety of fields, but in many areas they are being crowded out by newer forms of organization, especially the corporation. Farming is the last major industry to remain predominantly under family control, but even there corporations and cooperatives are making major inroads in a number of countries.[22] This is an inevitable consequence of the capital required to operate a farm in a technologically advanced society, where a single lettuce-picking machine can cost over $20,000, a diesel tractor as much as $32,000.[23]

---

[22] For an excellent description and analysis of trends in American agriculture, see Higbee, *op. cit.* For a similar volume on Europe, see P. Lamartine Yates, *Food, Land and Manpower in Western Europe* (London: Macmillan, 1960).

[23] Higbee, *op. cit.*, pp. 10 and 54.

Fig. 13/6   Harvesting wheat on a family farm in North Dakota

An older form of organization that has fared better is the state-operated enter-prise, which flourished for thousands of years in agrarian societies and even in some advanced horticultural. In modern industrial societies, the role of state enterprises varies considerably. In some, notably the Communist bloc nations, they are domi-nant. For example, state enterprises in the U.S.S.R. account for 98 or 99 per cent of nonagricultural production and nearly half of agricultural.[24] Their role is much smaller in the United States; yet even here they operate the postal system, many electric and water companies, some bus companies, some hospitals and other health facilities, many insurance programs, most educational institutions, some housing facilities, many recreational facilities, most transportation facilities (e.g., highways, ports, etc.), and many banking services.

Most European nations stand somewhere between the United States and the Soviet Union with respect to the scope of state enterprises. Railroads there, for example, are 90 to 100 per cent government-owned.[25] Of the scheduled airlines in Western Europe, only Swissair is less than half government-owned, and radio and television broadcasting are government enterprises in every country but the United Kingdom and Luxembourg. The state also plays a major role in Europe's electric, gas, insurance, banking, mining, iron, and steel industries and, in some countries, in the automobile, chemical, and machine tool industries as well.

SOCIAL STRATIFICATION

As we have seen in earlier chapters, the production of goods and services always gives rise to problems of distribution and to the phenomenon of social stratification. In modern industrial societies, systems of stratification are tremendously complex. A person's chances of obtaining the good things of life depend upon his—or the head of his family's—occupation and education, and often on his wealth, political status, race, ethnicity, and religion as well. Age and sex are also bases of stratifica-tion. One cannot hope to answer the question, *Who gets what, and why?*, without taking each of these systems of stratification into account.

Occupational stratification

For the great majority of people the most important determinant of their share of society's product is their position in the occupational system of stratification. A few hold positions that pay a million dollars or more per year in salaries, bonuses, and other forms of compensation. At the other extreme, some cannot even find employ-ment. Between these extremes, the vast majority work in jobs that provide anything

---

[24] Nove, *op. cit.*, pp. 28–29.

[25] This and the following statements are based on Dewhurst et al., *Europe's Needs and Resources*, pp. 436–440.

Table 13/2 Mean incomes of males, aged 25–64, by occupation, United States, 1959

Occupation	Mean*	Occupation	Mean*
Physicians and surgeons	$19,493	Electricians	$6,244
Dentists	16,057	Plumbers and pipefitters	5,857
Lawyers and judges	15,793	Firemen	5,729
Economists	10,225	Machinists	5,690
Physicists	9,621	Office machine operators	5,545
Real estate agents and brokers	9,219	Policemen	5,474
Electrical engineers	9,092	Mail carriers	5,265
Buyers and dept. heads (stores)	8,616	Bricklayers and stone masons	5,192
Psychologists	8,449	Plasterers	5,152
Editors and reporters	8,430	Bookkeepers	5,091
Civil engineers	8,423	Mechanics and repairmen	5,033
Insurance agents and brokers	7,994	Bank tellers	4,891
Chemists	7,973	Radio and TV repairmen	4,769
Accountants and auditors	7,825	Auto mechanics	4,682
Locomotive engineers	7,581	Truck and tractor drivers	4,635
Officials and public administrators	7,358	Shipping and receiving clerks	4,532
Foremen	7,053	Carpenters	4,531
Tool and die makers	6,802	Bus drivers	4,392
Salesmen and sales clerks	6,666	Barbers	4,388
Secondary school teachers	6,290	Painters	4,128

* The purchasing power of the dollar was approximately one-fourth higher in 1959 than in 1970, and the figures in this column should be increased by that amount to make them meaningful in today's terms.
Source: *U.S. Census of Population, 1960; Occupation by Earnings and Education*, table 1.

from bare subsistence wages to ample comforts. Table 13/2 shows the *mean* incomes for a sample of occupations as reported in the 1960 Census of the United States.[26]

The two basic divisions in the occupational structure of a modern industrial society are the one separating rural and urban workers and, within the urban group, the one separating manual and nonmanual workers. With increasing industrialization, the first distinction is declining in importance. The second, however, continues to be a major one. It is, in fact, the basis of the popular distinction between the working and middle classes: people are usually regarded as members of the working class if their family is headed by a manual worker, and middle class if their family is headed by a nonmanual worker (i.e., someone whose work is primarily mental). This is also the basis of the distinction between "blue-collar" work and "white-collar" work. From the standpoint of income, prestige, and working conditions, white-collar jobs are usually more rewarding than blue-collar jobs. This is

[26] The mean equals the sum of their incomes, divided by the number of persons in the occupation. It is nearly always somewhat higher than the median, which is the income of the middle person in a ranked series (i.e., half have higher incomes, and half have lower).

Fig. 13/7 One of the basic divisions in the occupational structure of a modern industrial society is that which separates manual from nonmanual workers

true even in Communist countries, although the area of overlap between the two categories is greater there.[27]

The simple threefold classification of farmers, manual workers, and nonmanual workers is often too crude to be useful; yet it is not practical to consider individually each of the thousands of different occupations. As a result, somewhat more detailed methods of classification have been devised, the most important of which is one used by the U.S. Bureau of the Census. This divides occupations into the ten categories shown in Table 13/3. For some purposes, however, even this is too crude. In particular, students of stratification often find the need to separate self-employed proprietors from salaried managers and officials, since the characteristics of these groups are quite different in many respects.

---

[27] See, for example, Stefan Nowak, "Changes in Social Structure and Social Consciousness," *Polish Sociological Bulletin*, No. 2:10 (1964), table 3; and Adam Sarapata, "Social Mobility," *Polish Perspectives*, 9 (January, 1966), pp. 18–27.

Table 13/3   Relative size of occupational categories and median earnings of year-round, full-time male workers, United States

Occupational category	Percentage of males in category (1965)	Median earnings* (1966)
Urban occupations:		
Professional, technical, and kindred workers	11.9	$9,205
Managers, officials, and proprietors	13.2	8,826
Sales workers	6.0	7,553
Clerical and kindred workers	7.0	6,542
Craftsmen, foremen, and kindred workers	19.0	7,161
Operatives and kindred workers	20.5	6,135
Service workers	7.0	5,117
Laborers, except farm and mine	8.0	5,133
Rural occupations:		
Farmers and farm managers	4.5	3,547†
Farm laborers and foremen	2.9	2,576
Total	100.0	$6,856

* Earnings do not include rents, interest, and other forms of income not derived from occupation.
† Median earnings figures for these occupations are underreported, since a large part of the earnings are in kind, not cash, and are often not reported.
Source: Bureau of Labor Statistics estimate reprinted in *World Almanac, 1967*, p. 323; and U.S. Bureau of the Census, *Current Population Reports*, Series P-60, No. 53, table 25.

Another popular scheme of classification divides the blue-collar and white-collar categories into upper and lower halves. Sometimes this is done on the basis of income; sometimes the census categories are used, with the first two categories in Table 13/3 defined as upper white collar; the next two as lower white collar; craftsmen, foremen, and kindred workers as upper blue collar; and the rest of the urban occupations as lower blue collar.

The method of classification one uses depends largely on the kind of problem he is studying and the kinds of data he has. As a rule, the more specific categories are preferable, but frequently they cannot be used with cross-national or historical data because the detailed information they require is not available for every country or time period.

With increasing industrialization, the percentage of men in farming has declined rapidly. The categories of farmers and farm laborers currently contain a high percentage of older men whose sons have migrated to cities. As these men die or retire, their farms are usually bought up by farmers or agricultural corporations operating on a large scale, and as a consequence, these categories will probably soon drop to no more than 2 or 3 per cent of the male labor force in the United States.

Table 13/4   Frequency distribution of adult male
population among occupational classes, United States,
1900 and 1965

Occupational class	1900	1965	Ratio 1965/1900
Upper white collar*	10	25	2.50
Lower white collar†	7	13	1.86
Upper blue collar‡	13	19	1.46
Lower blue collar§	28	36	1.29
Farmer and farm laborer	42	7	0.17
Total	100	100	1.00

* This includes managers, officials, and proprietors, and pro-
fessionals, technical, and kindred workers.
† This includes sales and clerical and kindred workers.
‡ This includes craftsmen, foremen, and kindred workers.
§ This includes operatives and kindred workers, service workers,
and laborers, except farm and mine.
Sources: *Historical Statistics of the United States: Colonial
Times to 1957*, series D 72-122; and Bureau of Labor Statistics
estimate reprinted in *World Almanac, 1967*, p. 323.

In the early stages of industrialization, blue-collar occupations increase faster than the rest of the labor force. Before long, however, the rate of growth of white-collar occupations catches up and overtakes them. As Table 13/4 illustrates, one of the striking features of the industrialization process is the way the rate of growth of an occupational class tends to be directly proportional to its status level: the higher the class, the faster it grows. We would expect this, of course, knowing that industrialization means the replacement of human energy and manual skills with other energy sources and with machines.[28]

The rapid growth of higher-level occupations has not occurred in every subclass, however. The growth of entrepreneurial or proprietary occupations, for example, has not even kept up with the growth of the labor force as a whole. In fact, in recent years, there has actually been a decline in the number of proprietors in the fields of construction, manufacturing, transportation, communications, utilities, wholesale, and retail trade, banking and finance, insurance and real estate, and several lesser areas. Between 1950 and 1960, the number of self-employed people in these fields dropped from 2.2 to 1.7 million, while salaried managers increased from 1.6 to 2.3 million.[29]

[28] Similar trends are evident in nearly all industrial societies. For example, in the Soviet Union the proportion of professionals in the labor force rose from 2 per cent in 1928 to approximately 7 per cent in 1965, and the proportion of trained specialists rose from 5 to 17 per cent. See Nicholas DeWitt, *Education and Professional Employment in the USSR* (Washington, D.C.: National Science Foundation, 1961), p. 463.

[29] *U.S. Census of Population, 1960: Occupational Characteristics*, table 25.

Property stratification

Linked with the occupational system of stratification in most industrial societies is a system of stratification based on the ownership of property. They are so closely related (see Table 13/5) that it is easy to overlook the latter. This tendency has been encouraged by the schools and mass media, which frequently treat the ownership of property simply as a by-product of occupational success. While this is true to some extent, it obscures the fact that the great fortunes in modern industrial societies are usually inherited and are not the result of their owners' occupational activities. Any correlation between the wealth and occupational status of such people reflects the influence of wealth on occupational success, not the reverse.

Data on wealth are extremely difficult to obtain because most people, especially the wealthy, are reluctant to discuss the subject. Furthermore, the property holdings of the wealthy are often so numerous and their values subject to so much fluctuation (e.g., day-to-day changes in the stock market) that exact calculations are difficult to make. It appears that J. Paul Getty is presently the wealthiest American and that he owns property worth one to two billion dollars.[30] Several dozen others have holdings valued at a hundred million or more. The lower one goes in the property system, the more people there are, with the largest number concentrated at or near the bottom. Tables 13/6 and 13/7 show the patterns in Britain and the United States some years ago; unfortunately, reliable figures for more recent years are not available. As these

---

[30] See Philip Stern, *The Great Treasury Raid* (New York: Random House, 1964), p. 21; *Newsweek*, July 15, 1963, p. 48; or Ferdinand Lundberg, *The Rich and the Super-Rich* (New York: Stuart, 1968), p. 42.

Table 13/5   Net worth, by occupational categories, United States, 1953

Occupational category	Median net worth*
Self-employed proprietors	$17,000
Managers	8,500
Professional and semiprofessional	6,300
Clerical and sales	2,900
Skilled and semiskilled workers	2,700
Unskilled and service workers	400
All occupational categories	4,100

* The purchasing power of the dollar was approximately one-third higher in 1953 than in 1970, and the figures in this column should be increased by that amount to make them meaningful in today's terms.
Source: Federal Reserve Bulletin, "1953 Survey of Consumer Finances: Part IV. Net Worth of Consumers, Early 1953," September, 1953, Supplementary Table 6.

Table 13/6   Estimated distribution of wealth in Britain, 1946–1947

Assets in pounds	Percentage of population	Percentage of wealth
Less than 100	60.6	4.2
100 to 999	27.8	11.6
1,000 to 4,999	8.9	21.0
5,000 to 9,999	1.4	11.4
10,000 to 24,999	0.9	16.4
25,000 to 99,999	0.4	19.2
100,000 and over	0.06	16.3
Total	100.00	100.0

Source: Kathleen M. Langley, "The Distribution of Capital in Private Hands in 1936–38 and 1946–47 (part 2)," *Bulletin of the Oxford University Institute of Statistics* (February, 1951), table XVB, p. 46.

Table 13/7   Estimated distribution of wealth in the United States, 1953

Assets	Percentage of population	Percentage of wealth
Less than $3,500	50.0	8.3
$3,500 to $10,000	18.4	10.2
$10,000 to $20,000	21.2	29.3
$20,000 to $30,000	5.8	13.4
$30,000 to $50,000	2.7	9.5
$50,000 to $100,000	1.0	6.2
$100,000 to $1,000,000	0.9	16.6
$1,000,000 to $10,000,000	0.04	5.2
$10,000,000 and over	0.0006	1.3
Total	100.0	100.0

Source: Calculated from Robert Lampman, *The Share of Top Wealth-holders in National Wealth: 1922–1956* (Princeton, N.J.: Princeton University Press, 1962), tables 34 and 99.

figures indicate, the concentration of wealth was much greater in Britain than in the United States at that time (in Britain the top 1.36 per cent of the population owned 51.9 per cent of the wealth), which may explain why the socialist movement was more successful there.

In many industrial societies, especially those with brokerage-type political parties, the very wealthy are also extremely powerful politically. Their power derives from the great imbalance between the costs of obtaining public office and the salaries these offices pay.[31] Campaign expenses for important offices often run into the hundreds of thousands, or even millions, of dollars, while their salaries are seldom more than $50,000 a year, and often much less. Since the great majority of voters are unwilling to help underwrite these costs (recent surveys show that only 4 to 10 per cent even claim they make a financial contribution[32]), only three kinds of men can hope to win important public offices: (1) men of wealth; (2) men financed by men of wealth; and (3) men financed by labor unions or other politically active organizations of the nonwealthy.[33]

Not all wealthy politicians are extreme conservatives, as the careers of Edward Kennedy and Nelson Rockefeller demonstrate. Such men are often moderately liberal, perhaps because of ideological commitments, perhaps because this is necessary to win high public office—one of the few things they cannot buy for themselves directly in the open market. The most vigorous promoters of the rights of property, on the other hand, are often men of modest means whose political careers depend on the support of wealthy patrons.

The clearest indication of the political power of the wealthy is the tax legislation written on their behalf. During the 1950s, for example, a special section of the Internal Revenue Code was passed for the exclusive benefit of Louis B. Mayer, former head of M-G-M studios, exempting him from $2 million in taxes; another special section was written for the benefit of Mrs. Gerard Swope, widow of the former president of General Electric, saving her $4 million.[34] These are but two of many such instances over the years. Even more generously, Congress has written into the tax laws special provisions that benefit large numbers of the wealthy, as in the case of the mineral depletion allowances. Such provisions have been so generous that in 1967 there were twenty-one people in this country with annual incomes of $1,000,000 or more who incurred *no federal income tax at all.*[35] One with an income

[31] For a good analysis of the role of money in American politics, see either V. O. Key, Jr., *Politics, Parties, and Pressure Groups*, 3d ed. (New York: Thomas Y. Crowell, 1952), chap. 18, or Drew Pearson and Jack Anderson, *The Case Against Congress* (New York: Simon & Schuster, 1968).

[32] Angus Campbell, Philip Converse, Warren Miller, and Donald Stokes, *The American Voter* (New York: Wiley, 1960), p. 91; or Maurice Duverger, *Political Parties: Their Organization and Activity in the Modern State*, trans. by Barbara North and Robert North (London: Methuen, 1959), p. 95. As Duverger notes, the percentage of contributors is higher in Sweden and Britain, but only because of automatic enrollment of many union members in the Socialist parties.

[33] Recent studies show that only 3 per cent of the members of the U.S. House of Representatives come from the working class, and not more than 10 per cent of the Senate were even raised in working-class or poor farm families. In the Canadian House of Commons, in one recent session, only 1 per cent of the membership was from the working class. In Australia and Britain, however, because of large, well-organized Labor parties, 19 per cent were from the working class. See Robert Alford, *Party and Society: The Anglo-American Democracies* (Chicago: Rand McNally, 1963), p. 98; and Donald Matthews, *U.S. Senators and Their World* (Chapel Hill, N.C.: University of North Carolina Press, 1960), pp. 21 and 27.

[34] See Stern, *op. cit.,* chap. 3, for these and other examples.

[35] *Newsweek*, February 24, 1969, p. 65. There were a total of 155 people with incomes of $200,000 or more who incurred no federal tax.

of nearly $20 million, in fact, owed not a penny, and another multimillionaire incurred no tax obligation for more than a dozen years in a row. All of this while people with less than $5,000 a year were being taxed an average of 9 per cent of their income!

The United States is not unique in this. The Italian government has long been notorious for its unwillingness to tax the wealthy; and in France, Canada, Japan, Spain, and a number of other industrial societies, the wealthy have great political power.[36]

But the propertied elite have not been so fortunate in all industrial societies. In the Scandinavian democracies and Britain, for example, well-organized working-class parties have wrested political power from the wealthy, shifting more of the financial burden of government from the poor to the rich and more of its benefits from the rich to the poor. In the Communist nations of Eastern Europe, the private ownership of most forms of income-producing property has been completely eliminated and differences in wealth substantially reduced. The position once occupied by the propertied elite in those countries has been taken over by the new political elite.

Political stratification

In agrarian societies of the past, the system of political stratification was the most important, especially for those who aspired to the top in power, privilege, and prestige. It was inevitable in societies with monarchical polities and largely command economies that those with political power would enjoy wealth and honor. Those with wealth and honor, on the other hand, were not necessarily assured of power; in fact, without political power they could not count on keeping what they had. The ruler or members of the governing class could easily seize a man's possessions; and freedom, even life itself, was by no means secure for one who lacked political power.

In most industrial societies, however, the situation is quite different. Where there is a democratic polity and a market economy, the system of political stratification has lost its former dominance. This is not to say that political power cannot be used to gain wealth and honor; obviously it can. Political officeholders, however, are no longer in a position to appropriate the majority of the economic surplus. In fact, they now control far less than the propertied elite.[37]

There have been, and still are, some exceptions to this. In industrial societies with dictatorial polities and command economies, the political system of stratifica-

---

[36] On Canada, see John Porter, *The Vertical Mosaic: An Analysis of Social Class and Power in Canada* (Toronto: University of Toronto Press, 1965), part II, especially chaps. 7–9 and 12–13; on France, see Henry Ehrmann, *Organized Business in France* (Princeton, N.J.: Princeton University Press, 1957), chap. 5; or Philip Williams, *Politics in Post-War France* (London: Longmans, 1954), especially part 4.

[37] See, again, Robert Heilbroner's statement, *op. cit.*, p. 27, that "in pre-market societies, wealth tends to follow power; not until the market society will power tend to follow wealth."

tion is still dominant. This is especially true of the Communist nations of Eastern Europe, where, ironically, something resembling the agrarian pattern of political stratification has been preserved. More recently, however, signs of a liberalizing and democratizing trend in the polity and the reintroduction of market forces in some segments of the economy suggest that the dominance of the political system of stratification may not continue indefinitely.

The dominant class in the political system in totalitarian nations—and hence the dominant class in these societies—consists of the fulltime party workers or functionaries. In the Soviet Union, these have long been known as the *apparatchiki*,

Fig. 13/8 Leonid Brezhnev, the chief of the <u>apparatchiki</u> in the Soviet Union in the late 1960s

the group that Milovan Djilas, Communism's famous heretic, denounced as "the new class."[38] He chose this hated label to emphasize the striking similarity between this class and the power-wielding, privilege-seeking, exploitative classes of other societies. This class is not large, probably numbering only about one per cent of the population;[39] but its near monopoly of political and economic power, combined with the growth of the modern state, makes it extremely powerful. In the early stages of its history, following its rise to power, idealists and political zealots usually dominate the class; but after its power has been consolidated, careerists infiltrate, giving rise to the privilege-seeking tendencies of the class.

Beneath the party functionaries is the much larger class of ordinary party members. In the Soviet Union, it includes about 8 per cent of the adult population. A minority of these members are volunteer activists who provide leadership in the lower echelons of party affairs; the majority play a much more limited role, like most church members in this country.

Still lower in the political class system of a totalitarian state are those people who, though outside the party, are not regarded as hostile to it. This includes some who would like to join the party but lack relevant qualifications; others who are covertly hostile to the party and stay outside as a matter of principle; and still others who are politically apathetic. This class normally includes the vast majority of the population.

Finally, at the bottom of the system are people who are officially designated as enemies of the party. The size of this class varies considerably from time to time and from country to country, and the circumstances of its members vary from minor restrictions on their movements to imprisonment, torture, and execution.

Democratic multiparty societies also have political class systems, but they lack the extremes of reward and punishment and they are not as important in the life of the nation. In their general structure, they resemble the political class system in one-party, totalitarian states. At the top is a class of people for whom politics is a vocation. Most of these professionals depend on politics for their livelihood, but some, like the Kennedys, are men of wealth who are involved for other reasons. In a number of countries, like the United States, party activity can be extremely lucrative. For example, in 1964 President Johnson's family had a fortune valued at $9 to $14 million, "amassed almost entirely while Mr. Johnson was in public office; mainly since he entered the Senate and began his rise to national power in 1948."[40]

---

[38] See Milovan Djilas, *The New Class: An Analysis of the Communist System* (New York: Praeger, 1959), especially pp. 37–69.

[39] Recent estimates of the number of *apparatchiki* range from 150,000 to 750,000 (with allowance for their families, this would bring the size of the class to 500,000 to 3,000,000). For the lower estimate, see Merle Fainsod, *How Russia is Ruled* (Cambridge, Mass.: Harvard, 1963), pp. 206–207; for the higher, see Klaus Mehnert, *Soviet Man and His World*, trans. by Maurice Rosenbaum (New York: Praeger, 1961), p. 21.

[40] *New York Times*, June 10, 1964, p. 25.

His is not an isolated case, at least not among politicians in brokerage-type parties. Typically, these men seem to feel they are entitled to use their public office for private gain and regard the income as a kind of "broker's fee" paid by the public and the special interests they serve.[41] Though the ethics of such practices are extremely dubious, most political leaders stay carefully within the law (as interpreted by fellow members of the political class).

In ideologically oriented democratic parties, the leaders are much less likely to use their position for private financial advantage. Their rewards are chiefly power, fame, and the satisfaction of implementing their beliefs.

A second important class in most multiparty nations is composed of wealthy individuals and business leaders who take an active interest in politics but do not make it their vocation. These men (known to professionals as "fat cats") provide political organizations with one of their most essential ingredients—money. Some of them seem to want only the excitement of political participation and other psychic benefits, but most of them are interested in more substantial rewards (e.g., oil depletion allowances, special tax advantages, lucrative government contracts, etc.).

Beneath the professional politicians and wealthy contributors is a class of volunteer workers. This is a very mixed group and includes people motivated by political ideals, by private ambition (i.e., the hope of joining the ranks of the professionals), or by a combination of both. This class is always small, seldom more than a small per cent of the population, and it has a high rate of turnover.[42]

The lowest rung in the political system in multiparty states is occupied by the great majority of citizens whose political activity is limited to voting and a vague identification with one or another of the parties. As voting records show, many people do not take even this much interest in the political process.

In the political class system, as in some of the others, the benefits to the individual tend to be proportional to his investment of time and money. For this reason, a disproportionate share of the benefits accrue to the professional politicians and their wealthy allies. Their opportunities for self-aggrandizement are at least somewhat limited, however, by the widespread right of suffrage, which serves as a check on their self-seeking tendencies: they know that if they push their private advantage too far, they may be voted out of office.

Educational stratification

The roots of educational stratification go far back in history. Even in hunting and gathering societies, shamans enjoyed greater power and prestige because of their

---

[41] See, for example, Senator Russell Long's comments on the hearings of Senator Dodd. He stated that at least half of the senators who were on the committee investigating Dodd could not stand a similar investigation. For an earlier study of the use of political power for private gain, see Harold Zink, *City Bosses in the United States* (Durham, N.C.: Duke, 1930), pp. 37–38.

[42] See, for example, Duverger, *op. cit.* p. 114; or Campbell et al., *op. cit.*, pp. 90–93.

Fig. 13/9 The lowest level in the political system in multiparty states is occupied by the great majority of citizens whose political activity is limited to voting and a vague identification with one or another of the parties

special knowledge. After the invention of writing and the formation of schools early in the agrarian era, educational stratification became increasingly important. As we saw in Chapter 9, only a minority learned to read and write because the costs of education were prohibitive for peasants. Most of those who became literate were children of the middle and upper classes, and this skill insured that they could stay there when their schooling was completed. For the top positions in society, education was seldom of crucial importance; at most, literacy was required, sometimes not even that. Because these positions were usually filled by inheritance, the best-educated men tended to occupy the middle levels of the governmental and religious establishments and used their skill in the service of the elite.

Certain elements of this older system have carried over into modern industrial societies. An individual's educational opportunities and attainments are still linked with the class position of his parents. Children of the wealthy and powerful stand a far better chance of obtaining a university education, especially at the best institutions, than the children of the poor.

It is easy, however, to exaggerate the similarity between the agrarian and the industrial systems. There definitely have been changes, many of them in response to the rise and spread of the new democratic ideology. For one thing, an effective democratic polity requires a literate electorate. Furthermore, the new ideology demands equality of opportunity and, since education has become the key to opportunity,[43] free public education has become a basic right. Another factor promoting change has been the modern information revolution; because the value of information is proportional to its dissemination, societal leaders are obliged to promote its spread through education.

As a result of these developments, there is no longer a division between a literate minority and an illiterate majority.[44] Illiteracy has, in fact, almost disappeared in advanced industrial societies. At the same time, other educational distinctions have become important, particularly those based on amount of education. In the United States an individual is usually categorized according to whether he has less than a high school education, a high school diploma, a college diploma, or an advanced degree. As a result of the bureaucratization of government and industry, the great majority of jobs in the United States, and increasingly in other industrial societies as well, have educational prerequisites, and the individual who lacks them is automatically ineligible. This affects not only his chances of being hired, but his chances for promotion. In this respect, modern bureaucratic personnel practices have created a civilian counterpart of the military caste system, with its sharp cleavage between officers and enlisted men. Just as the ceiling for the promotion of privates is normally the rank of sergeant, so the ceiling for production workers tends to be the rank of foreman, or possibly plant superintendent. Higher ranks are reserved for people with more education, and they are recruited outside the organization. Figure 13/10 illustrates this pattern.

---

[43] See Peter Blau and O. Dudley Duncan, *The American Occupational Structure* (New York: Wiley, 1967), p. 403.

[44] In the United States, however, there are a large number of persons who, though technically literate (i.e., they can sign their names and read or write a few simple words), cannot read and write well enough to use these skills in their work. Such persons are often referred to as "functional illiterates."

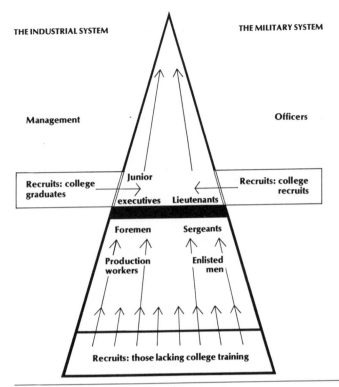

THE INDUSTRIAL SYSTEM

THE MILITARY SYSTEM

Fig. 13/10 Recruitment and promotional patterns in modern industry and the military compared

Management

Officers

Recruits: college graduates

Junior executives

Lieutenants

Recruits: college recruits

Foremen

Sergeants

Production workers

Enlisted men

Recruits: those lacking college training

This best single measure of the importance of education today is found in recent census data on the relationship between education and income. In 1966 these were the median annual incomes of American males in the peak earning years (i.e., 45 to 54):[45]

0–7 years of education	$ 3,941
8 years of education	5,774
1–3 years of high school	6,675
4 years of high school	7,557
1–3 years of college	8,886
4 years of college	11,646
5 years or more of college	12,946

Comparing agrarian and industrial societies, it appears that the educational elite of the latter have more influence on national policy. This is not to say that they have become politically dominant or that advanced academic degrees are necessary for top political office. However, college or university training is becoming almost a prerequisite for top office, and top political leaders are increasingly forced to rely on the educational elite for help in making major decisions. The role of physical

[45] *Current Population Reports*, Series P-60, No. 53 (December, 1967), table 22.

scientists in planning military and space programs, and of social scientists in economic and social policies, is taken for granted today. This pattern is by no means limited to the United States. In the Soviet Union, for example, the startling reintroduction of market mechanisms was due in no small measure to the efforts of economists, and physical and medical scientists have had comparable influence in other areas of public policy.[46] Although the political elite are interested only in the information these experts can provide, it is seldom possible to get it in pure form; almost invariably, the personal values of the experts intrude, but often so subtly as to be unrecognized even by the experts themselves. As a result, today's educational elite have a much larger voice in high-level decision making than their predecessors in agrarian societies ever had.

Racial, ethnic, and religious stratification

Most industrial societies have racial, ethnic, or religious cleavages. Canada, for example, has a serious cleavage between its French and English groups, Belgium between Flemings and Walloons, Germany between Protestants and Catholics, and the United States between whites and blacks—to name but a few of the more important ones. As long as groups like these have no effect on how goods and services and other benefits are distributed, they stand outside the system of social stratification. However, when membership in them has an appreciable influence on people's access to those things, these groups become a part of the system. In that case, the groups are, in effect, classes: they are aggregations of people who stand in a similar position with respect to some resource that influences their access to power, privilege, or prestige. They are obviously classes of a special kind, however. For one thing, the resource involved is the individual's *membership in a group*, rather than his personal wealth, occupation, etc. For another thing, these classes have a greater degree of group or class consciousness than most others do and it is more difficult to move into or out of them. Because of these differences, some sociologists call them *status groups*, and in instances where movement into or out of the group is virtually impossible the label *caste* is often used.

The most striking example of this type of stratification in the United States involves the two major racial groups. Since early in this country's history, blacks have been a subordinated group. Before the Civil War this was underlined by the legal position of the majority of blacks, who were slaves and the property of members of the white group. Even before the Emancipation Act, some blacks achieved considerable success in the occupational, educational, and property systems of stratification, but despite this they continued to suffer from handicaps imposed on them because of their identification with the black group. Their access to clubs, churches,

---

[46] For a popular account of the role of the educational elite in Soviet society and its intrusion into politics, see Albert Parry, *The New Class Divided: Science and Technology vs. Communism* (New York: Macmillan, 1966).

housing, and services of almost every kind was much more limited than that of whites with comparable status in other systems of stratification.

Today, many of the limitations of the past have been removed. Recent civil rights legislation insures blacks equal treatment in stores, hotels, restaurants, and other business establishments, at least in most sections of the country. But racial discrimination continues in housing, club membership, and some other areas. Even more important, the general cultural deprivation of recent centuries has left many blacks unable to take full advantage of the new opportunities. So much basic learning occurs while a child is small that large numbers of black children with poorly educated parents are already badly handicapped when they begin school. These youngsters generally make slow progress and leave school poorly equipped to compete in the occupational system. It is hardly surprising, therefore, that the median income of black men has not been much more than half that of white men in recent years ($3,665 vs. $6,390 in 1966).[47]

While the white population is sometimes thought of as a unit, it is, of course, actually divided along both ethnic and religious lines. From the ethnic standpoint, people of British extraction enjoy the highest status, then those of other northwestern European ancestry, followed by those of southern and eastern European ancestry.[48] Among religious groups, Protestants rank first, followed by Catholics, then by Jews. These rankings simply reflect the historic dominance of the Protestants of British ancestry who first settled this country.[49] Until about 1830, most whites shared these characteristics, and they naturally occupied the dominant positions in all the major institutions. Since most of the later immigrants were poor, had little education, and were unable to speak English, they tended to fill the more menial positions. The more they had in common with the older stock, the more readily they were accepted in marriage and in the better jobs, clubs, and neighborhoods. Northwestern European Protestants were thus accepted more readily than southern and eastern European Catholics and Jews. Religious differences, it may be added, have proved much more resistant to assimilation than ethnic differences, most of which are rapidly being eliminated. In fact, some scholars see the religious cleavage as a relatively "permanent" feature of American life.[50]

Ever since the Civil War, the Democratic Party has been the political instrument

---

[47] *Current Population Reports,* Series P-60, No. 53, table 21.

[48] Members of minority groups usually adopt the dominant group's prestige evaluations for groups other than their own. Sometimes they even adopt its evaluation of their own group. See, for example, Emory Bogardus, *Social Distance* (Yellow Springs, Ohio.: Antioch Press, 1959), pp. 26–29.

[49] See Tamotsu Shibutani and Kian Kwan, *Ethnic Stratification: A Comparative Approach* (New York: Macmillan, 1965), chap. 9.

[50] For one of the first statements of this point of view, see Ruby Jo Reeves Kennedy, "Single or Triple Melting Pot? Intermarriage Trends in New Haven, 1870–1940," *American Journal of Sociology,* 49 (1944), pp. 331–339. For more recent statements, see Will Herberg, *Protestant-Catholic-Jew* (Garden City, N.Y.: Doubleday, 1956), and Milton Gordon, *Assimilation in American Life: The Role of Race, Religion, and National Origins* (Fair Lawn, N.J.: Oxford, 1964).

for groups that felt themselves discriminated against by the nation's political, economic, and social elite (i.e., wealthy northern Protestant families of British origin). This is the reason why the Democratic Party has attracted such diverse groups as southern whites, Negroes, Catholics, Jews, and the working class. Through political action, these groups have eliminated many discriminatory practices. By contrast, the Republican Party has tended to be the political instrument for the historically dominant groups and has sought to protect their advantages.

In contrast with the United States, Canada has no serious racial division, but it is more sharply divided along religious and ethnic lines. The most serious cleavage is between French-speaking Catholics and English-speaking Protestants. Although the French Catholics settled the country first, they were conquered by the British, who dominated the political system from the eighteenth century on. The problem was further aggravated because the English-speaking Protestants industrialized while the French Catholics hung on to the agrarian way of life. As a consequence, the English Protestants dominated the economy, too, even in Quebec, the home province of the French Catholics.[51] In recent years, although the French have succeeded in eliminating many discriminatory practices through political action, a minority still favor secession.[52]

Despite the current importance of racial, ethnic, and religious stratification in a number of industrial societies, there is reason to believe their importance will decline in the years ahead. With the spread of the democratic-egalitarian ideology, the more powerful and privileged classes have been forced to make concessions. On the whole, they have preferred to give ground in the racial-ethnic-religious area, rather than in the political and economic, because it entails less sacrifice. For example, when Negroes are given equal opportunities in the job world, it is not the jobs of the managerial and professional classes that are threatened, but the jobs of white workingmen. Similarly, when social facilities are integrated, the clubs of the wealthy are the last to be affected. As an old Latin proverb put it, "It is easy to be generous with other people's property," and as embattled elites have discovered in the modern world, it is easy to give away other people's privileges. Those who have wealth and occupational status do not need to depend on racial, ethnic, or religious status; therefore, if there are pressures for change toward a more democratic and egalitarian social order, this is the area in which they are most willing to make concessions. They are likely to be supported in this by the educational elite, since they, too, find this is a painless form of change. And those intellectuals who are themselves members of minority racial, ethnic, and religious groups have everything to gain and nothing to lose.

---

[51] See, for example, Everett C. Hughes, *French Canada in Transition* (Chicago: University of Chicago Press, 1943), especially chap. 7. See also Porter, *op. cit.*, chap. 3.

[52] One survey showed that an eighth of all French Canadians favored this, and one-quarter of all the college educated, who are the leaders and molders of public opinion. See *Maclean's*, 76 (November 2, 1963), p. 14.

Age and sex stratification

Age and sex have been bases of social differentiation in every society throughout history. The social roles of men and women have differed, as have the roles of children, adults, and the aged. In almost every case, these role differences have involved differences in power, privilege, and prestige.

The ultimate basis of these distinctions lies in human biology.[53] Children are both physically and intellectually less developed than adults. Having had fewer chances to acquire experience and information, they are at a competitive disadvantage. For women, the primary handicap has been of a different nature. Throughout most of human history, the limitations imposed by frequent pregnancy and nursing prevented most women from competing with men in political and military activities, which were usually the basic determinants of power and prestige. Nevertheless, through the institution of the family, women insured for themselves many basic rights and a substantial share in the goods and services produced by societies.

There are elements of both continuity and change in the systems of age and sex stratification in industrial societies. Middle-aged and older people continue to be dominant in the political, property, and occupational systems. In recent years, for example, the median age of United States Senators has been 56 years and, with the Senate's system of seniority, committee chairmen have been even older.[54] One national study of business leaders indicated a median age of 54; another, limited to the managerial elite showed a median of 61.[55] A study of American military leaders found their average age was 54.4 years; and a study of the very wealthy showed that the average age of men with estates valued at $5 million or more was 69.[56] The situation is similar in other advanced industrial societies, including the Soviet Union.[57] On the other hand, younger people are now challenging the authority of their elders to a degree that was unthinkable in agrarian societies.

As far as sex stratification is concerned, men continue dominant both politically and occupationally, but women have made substantial gains in the property and educational systems. Laws that restricted their right to own property have been eliminated in most industrial societies, and in the United States women now own

---

[53] This is not to deny the important influence of sociocultural systems on status relations between the sexes and between different age categories.

[54] Calculated from Matthews, *op. cit.*, fig. 1.

[55] W. Lloyd Warner and James Abegglen, *Occupational Mobility in American Business and Industry, 1928–1952* (Minneapolis: University of Minnesota Press, 1955), p. 30, and Mabel Newcomer, *The Big Business Executive* (New York: Columbia, 1955), p. 112.

[56] Calculated from Morris Janowitz, *The Professional Soldier* (New York: Free Press, 1960), p. 63, and Robert Lampman, *The Share of Top Wealth-Holders in National Wealth: 1922–1956* (Princeton, N.J.: Princeton University Press, 1962), tables 48 and 49.

[57] See, for example, Gerhard Lenski, *Power and Privilege: A Theory of Social Stratification* (New York: McGraw-Hill, 1966), p. 407.

much of the wealth.[58] In the same way, former barriers to higher education have been largely eliminated. American women, for example, now constitute 38 per cent of the students enrolled in colleges and universities.[59] Even in the political arena, women have made substantial gains. As recently as 1900, women were permitted to vote only in New Zealand and four states in this country.[60] Today they enjoy this right in every advanced industrial society except Switzerland.

In the occupational world, the historic distinction between men's work and women's work has also begun to blur. This has been made possible by the great

---

[58] Lampman, *op. cit.*, p. 96. This study shows that among the rich, women now own about 40 per cent of the wealth.

[59] *Statistical Abstract of the United States, 1966*, table 149.

[60] William J. Goode, *World Revolution and Family Patterns* (New York: Free Press, 1963), p. 55.

Fig. 13/11 Locomotive engineer, U.S.S.R.

reduction in the birthrate and by the development of labor saving devices which greatly shorten the time that women must spend on basic household responsibilities. In some societies women now enter the labor force in almost the same numbers as men. In one recent year, women constituted 46.7 per cent of the labor force in the Soviet Union.[61] This figure was inflated somewhat as a result of the heavy death toll among Soviet men in World War II; but even if there had been equal numbers of the sexes in the population, women would still have made up 42.5 per cent of the labor force.[62] In the United States, too, the percentage of women gainfully employed has steadily risen. In 1890 only 19 per cent of women 14 or older were employed outside the home. Today this figure is nearly 37 per cent, with women constituting more than 36 per cent of the labor force.[63]

Despite these increases, women are still far from achieving occupational equality and are concentrated in the less remunerative occupations. In 1966, only 5 per cent of Americans earning $10,000 or more per year were women.[64] A similar situation prevails in other industrial societies.[65] To some extent this is because women are handicapped during the early, and often critical, years of employment, when child-bearing and child-rearing interrupt their careers. But it also seems to be a matter of choice, since many women prefer marriage and homemaking. These factors naturally cause most employers to favor men for the more responsible and demanding positions, which further reduces women's chances in the job world and increases their preference for homemaking.

Consequences of social stratification

The unequal distribution of power, privilege, and prestige divides the members of industrial societies as surely as it did the members of agrarian societies. Those who have similar resources tend to associate with one another and to stand apart from the rest. This inevitably leads to the formation of class-based subcultures and class-based communities.

The differences that divide the classes are partly economic. The poor obviously cannot afford many of the things that are an integral part of the middle class way of life, and the middle classes cannot afford many of the things that are essential to the upper class way of life. But it is not material differences alone that are divisive.

---

[61] Bruce Russett, et al., *World Handbook of Political and Social Indicators* (New Haven, Conn.: Yale, 1964), table 4.

[62] This adjustment is based on data on the sex composition of the Soviet population as reported in the United Nations *Demographic Yearbook, 1963*, p. 226.

[63] Calculations based on *The World Almanac, 1969*, pp. 143 and 596.

[64] Calculated from *Current Population Reports*, Series P-60, No. 53 (December 28, 1967), table 18.

[65] Though much has been made of the fact that women constitute three-quarters of the doctors in the Soviet Union, this occupation is not especially lucrative there, and the leading physicians continue to be men. The same seems true in most other fields.

Fig. 13/12 George Bernard Shaw's play <u>Pygmalion</u> and <u>My Fair Lady,</u> the American musical comedy based on it, revolve around class differences in speech and etiquette and their role as a barrier to upward mobility

Differences in values and world views, in experience and information, in social norms (especially the etiquette of daily life), and even in speech, are equally important.

It would be impossible to describe here all of the differences that sociologists have found between the classes in modern industrial societies. The subject fills volumes.[66] Suffice it to say that hardly any aspect of life is untouched. Even one's chances for survival are influenced by his class membership: white babies born in the United States today can expect to live seven years longer than nonwhite.[67] Class

---

[66] For a good summary of much of this, see Harold M. Hodges, *Social Stratification: Class in America* (Cambridge, Mass.: Schenkman, 1964), especially chaps. 6–11.

[67] *The World Almanac, 1969*, p. 763.

also affects many basic personality traits, since its influences begin to operate immediately after birth. To a large degree, a person's needs and desires, his goals and ambitions, and even his self-image are molded by the system of stratification. And not least of all, class affects his chance of success in school and in the world of work. Sometimes these influences are extremely subtle, as in the case of protein deficiency in infancy. It was only recently discovered that many children of the poor suffer permanent mental impairment because their families cannot provide them with a proper diet in their early years.

Despite our physical proximity to people of other classes, most of us never have the opportunity to see their life "from the inside." At best, we are spectators who watch from a distance—and often misunderstand what we see. (This is what black militants are saying when they insist that whites are unable to "think black.") In the past, talented novelists have bridged this gap, often by sharing their own experiences with readers of other classes. Today, sociologists and anthropologists are adding to our appreciation of what it means to live in other classes.[68] But it is important to remember that vicarious experiences are no substitute for direct, personal experience.

From the standpoint of society, one of the most important consequences of stratification is the dissension it generates between individuals and between classes. Where there is opportunity for upward mobility, competition is inevitable: this is a natural consequence of the maximizing tendency in human nature. Where status is primarily ascribed, however, class conflict often ensues. People born into classes to which fewer of the good things of life are assigned are likely to join with others in the same situation and try to force society to make more rewards available to them, while those in the favored classes usually resist their efforts. We see this continually in struggles between workers and employers, in racial conflicts, and in student efforts to get more power in the affairs of universities and colleges and in the larger society.

The stakes in struggles like these can be extremely high. In industrial societies, the outcome, more often than not, has favored the *less* advantaged class, resulting in a fairly steady, if slow, reduction in social, economic, and political inequality. While this is not always evident in short-run comparisons, it becomes clear as soon as we compare the more advanced industrial societies of the modern world with agrarian societies of the past (see "The Egalitarian Trend," opposite page).

Vertical mobility

Compared with agrarian societies, industrial societies afford far more opportunities for individuals to better themselves. In the agrarian era, high birthrates ensured an oversupply of labor in almost every generation. At every social level, a certain per-

---

[68] See, for example, A. B. Hollingshead, *Elmtown's Youth* (New York: Wiley, 1949); St. Clair Drake and Horace Cayton, *Black Metropolis* (New York: Harcourt, Brace & World, 1945); Elliot Liebow, *Tally's Corner* (Boston: Little, Brown, 1967).

centage of the children were forced to take employment in an occupation less rewarding than their fathers', or join the ranks of the beggars, outlaws, prostitutes, and vagabonds. Though some improved their situation even under these conditions, the downwardly mobile were much more numerous.[69]

In industrial societies, conditions are strikingly different. While birthrates have been falling, technological innovation has been increasing the proportion of high-status occupations (see page 388). As a result, the traditional excess of downward mobility has been replaced by an excess of upward mobility. A recent survey by the U.S. Bureau of the Census compared the occupations of men today with those of their fathers and found that those who had risen from blue-collar occupations to white collar were 2.5 times as numerous as those who had dropped from white-collar to blue-collar.[70] Even if we divide the urban occupational hierarchy into three or four levels, the ratio of upward to downward mobility is about the same. This ratio is higher than in most other countries (owing, apparently, to the more rapid expansion of higher-status occupations here); but nearly every industrial society has eliminated the excess of downward mobility.[71]

This has undoubtedly been a factor in reducing the threat of the working-class revolution which was predicted by Marx and Engels. If, in every generation, a quarter or more of the sons of working men are able to rise into the ranks of the middle class, resentment against the system is almost certain to be less than if only a few per cent move up the ladder (as Marx and Engels expected). Furthermore, when those who rise are generally the more talented and ambitious members of their generation, a lot of the potential leadership for protest movements is permanently lost to the working class.

It is probably no coincidence that a great deal of the leadership and support for protest movements in the more advanced industrial societies has come from individuals who are members of racial, ethnic, or religious minorities. Upward mobility for people in these groups is difficult, and for many, virtually impossible. Unable to escape the limitations society imposes on them, the more talented and ambitious are apt to turn their energies to social protest, especially programs designed to eliminate the differential between their own group and more favored ones.

The egalitarian trend

Throughout most of human history, technological progress has been linked with increasing social inequality. Industrial societies, however, have apparently reversed

---

[69] For a more detailed discussion of this, see Lenski, *op. cit.*, pp. 289–291.

[70] Calculated from *Current Population Reports*, Series P-23, No. 11, table 1.

[71] A few surveys indicate an excess of downward mobility, but there is reason to believe that these results are sometimes due to the failure to ensure that respondents report their father's occupation when he was *their age.* This is important because mobility also occurs within careers, and here, too, upward mobility is more common than downward.

Fig. 13/13 Public housing project for low-income families, Denmark. Compare this with American public housing projects

the trend. In agrarian societies the ruler and governing class usually received not less than half of the national income, and in some instances as much as two-thirds.[72] Since they numbered only about 2 per cent of the population, this meant that the other 98 per cent got only half or less of the total.

In modern industrial societies, the top 2 per cent of the population does not receive anything like the share of their agrarian counterparts. Depending on the country involved, on how one estimates the extent and distribution of unreported income (e.g., capital gains, half of which do not need to be declared as income in the United States), and on how one assumes the benefits of government are distributed among various classes, the most favored 2 per cent of the population receives anywhere from 10 to 25 per cent of the national income.[73] Though far more than their proportionate share, it is still a great deal less than agrarian elites enjoyed.

Politically too, as we have seen, there is a trend toward greater equality. Though no society has anything approaching a pure democracy, a much larger percentage of the population has some voice in political decisions in industrial societies than in agrarian. Furthermore, there is a much closer approximation of the principle of equal justice before the law. There are no separate legal codes and separate courts

[72] Lenski, *op. cit.,* p. 228.

[73] *Ibid.,* pp. 308–313.

for different classes, nor do the laws of most industrial societies even recognize different classes (such as slaves, nobles, serfs, etc.), as was common in agrarian societies.[74]

A number of factors have been responsible for the recent egalitarian trend.[75] For the most part, they are the same ones that led to the democratic trend (see page 355), for it is simply part of the more general trend toward equality.

There is one other factor that must be mentioned, however—the speed and magnitude of the increase in productivity in industrial societies. When national income is rising rapidly and promises to continue to rise as long as political and economic stability are maintained, the dominant classes find it to their interest to make some concessions to the lower classes to prevent costly strikes, riots, and revolutions. Even though they give ground in *relative* terms, they come out far ahead in *absolute* terms in an expanding economy. For example, an elite would enjoy a substantially greater income if it settled for "just" 25 per cent of the gross national product in a $900 billion economy than if it stubbornly fought to preserve a 50 per cent share and, in the process, provoked so much internal strife that the economy stalled at the $100 billion level. In short, the new technology has provided the elites of modern industrial societies with an option undreamed of in agrarian societies; and judging by the results, it has proved highly attractive.

---

[74] As Edwin Sutherland has pointed out, however, the crimes that businessmen are likely to commit as a part of their normal business activity (e.g., fraudulent advertising, price fixing, etc.) are handled in the United States by a special set of courts (civil rather than criminal) and the penalties are usually fines rather than imprisonment, all of which adds up to preferential treatment. See *White Collar Crime* (New York: Holt, 1949). Moreover, current tax laws permit businesses to deduct many of these fines as legitimate business expenses—thus transferring most of the cost to the public!

[75] For a more thorough discussion of this subject, see Lenski, *op. cit.*, pp. 313–318.

Chapter 14
Industrial Societies:
Part 3

KNOWLEDGE AND BELIEFS

Knowledge

During the last five centuries, the bounds of human knowledge have expanded tremendously. The voyages of exploration that began in the fifteenth century gave man, for the first time, an accurate picture of the earth. The work of the astronomers in the sixteenth and seventeenth centuries laid the foundation for a realistic view of our solar system. More recently, physicists, chemists, biologists, geologists, and astronomers have given us a vision of a universe of infinite complexity, whose age must be measured in billions of years and whose distances involve hundreds of millions of light-years. Finally, in the last hundred years, the social sciences have begun the task of demythologizing the social order, challenging ancient theories about the nature of man and society, and subjecting virtually every aspect of human life to systematic scrutiny.

Until the nineteenth century, the search for new knowledge was carried on largely outside the universities, because they perceived their function as the transmission of the wisdom of the past—especially the cultural traditions of the governing class. Their curricula included classical literature, philosophy, theology, history, mathematics, and a smattering of traditional science (e.g., Ptolemaic astronomy, Aristotelian biology, etc.).

By the middle of the nineteenth century, the physical and biological sciences had advanced to the point where the universities found it difficult, even embarrassing, to ignore them, and departments and faculties of chemistry, physics, astronomy, geology, and biology were gradually established. Later, the social sciences were introduced into the curriculum, though the process is still far from complete, especially in European universities. The new sciences were frequently opposed by the older disciplines, which rejected the view that knowledge is acquired chiefly by experimentation and controlled observation rather than by mediation, inspiration, or the study of ancient authorities.

As the various sciences became established in the universities, the concept of the university's purpose gradually changed. Whereas teaching had once been central, just as in elementary and secondary schools, the search for new knowledge became an equally important responsibility. In fact, in the leading universities today it takes precedence. As we noted earlier, this is due not only to the interests and ambitions of scientists, but even more to the demands of political and economic leaders who have discovered that science is the best source of the information essential to their various enterprises. Hence, they pour increasing sums of money into scientific activity in the universities and frequently set up research centers in government and industry to work on more applied problems.

Man's elaborate search for information about his environment has produced such fantastic results that there has literally been a revolution in his view of the world. While much of the new information is understood only by a small scientific elite, particularly in the more technical fields, public education and the mass media have carried at least a general understanding of the crucial findings to most members of industrial societies.

Because the practical application of this vast store of information has proved so rewarding, people have largely abandoned their former reliance on magic. Now even the least educated members of industrial societies are disinclined to take it seriously in most areas of life. There has also been a substantial decline in fatalism: modern men are usually confident that something can be done about most of their problems, particularly the technical ones.

Religion

The spread of the new scientific knowledge has shaken and unsettled many traditional beliefs, as well as the institutional systems based upon them. Nowhere is this more evident than in the area of religion. The thought forms of all the great historic faiths—Judaism, Christianity, Islam, Hinduism, and Buddhism—bear the imprint of the agrarian era during which they evolved, and this poses serious problems for men who live in industrial societies. Many beliefs about the physical world and the social order that were "self-evident" to people in agrarian societies appear alien and primitive to contemporary man. This has generated an acute theological crisis for all the major faiths, especially for those in industrial societies. The intellectual leaders of these groups must continually translate the valid elements of their traditions into modern terms, and this is not always easy. Somehow they must steer a course between irrelevant orthodoxy and heretical innovation.[1] The turmoil

---

[1] See, for example, the writings of recent theologians and theological popularizers, such as Bultmann, Tillich, Bonhoeffer, Robinson, Pike, and Cox.

within the Roman Catholic Church since Vatican Council II is but one in a series of intellectual crises experienced by religious groups in recent centuries.

Beginning as early as the eighteenth century, new religious movements were established with the aim of reconciling men's beliefs with the new knowledge and thought forms. In eighteenth-century England and America this took the form of Deism, a forerunner of later Unitarianism. In France at the time of the Revolution, the new authorities created the Cult of Reason and the Cult of the Supreme Being, while the common people established the Cult of the Martyrs of Liberty. In the nineteenth century, efforts of this kind were even more frequent. For example, in his later years, Auguste Comte, the founder of sociology, established a humanistic cult that survived on a small scale until World War II.

The most successful of the new prophets and messiahs, however, has proved to be Karl Marx, the founder of modern Communism. He propounded a faith that became a highly popular movement among working people and peasants in societies struggling to make the difficult transition from the agrarian way of life to the industrial. Moreover, his followers succeeded in seizing control of societies that contain a third of the world's population, and have turned their educational systems and mass media into instruments of propaganda for the faith.

From a functional standpoint, Marxism is remarkably similar to the great historic faiths. Like them, it provides answers to the ultimate questions of human existence, and guidance for the individual perplexed by the problems of life. Friedrich Engels, Marx's lifelong collaborator, commented on this when he wrote:

> The history of early Christianity has notable points of resemblance with the modern working class movement. Like the latter, Christianity was originally a movement of oppressed people: it first appeared as the religion of slaves and emancipated slaves, of poor people deprived of all rights, of peoples subjugated or dispersed by Rome. Both Christianity and the workers' socialism preach forthcoming salvation from bondage and misery; Christianity places this salvation in a life beyond, after death, in heaven; socialism places it in this world, in a transformation of society. Both are persecuted and baited, their adherents are despised and made the objects of exclusive laws, the former as enemies of the human race, the latter as enemies of the state, enemies of religion, the family, social order. And in spite of all persecution, nay, even spurred on by it, they forge victoriously, irresistibly ahead. Three hundred years after its appearance Christianity was the recognized state religion in the Roman world empire, and in barely sixty years socialism has won itself a position which makes its victory absolutely certain.[2]

This was written in 1894, twenty-three years before the Russian Revolution. More recently, the Soviet poet Evgeny Evtushenko, in his autobiography written for Western readers, referred to Communism as "my religion." And Svetlana Alliluyeva (or Stalina) spoke of her conversion to belief in God as marking the end of her

---

[2] From *Marx and Engels: Basic Writings on Politics and Philosophy*, pp. 168–169, edited by Lewis Feuer. Copyright in 1959 by Lewis S. Feuer. Reprinted by permission of Doubleday & Company, Inc.

belief in Communism, indicating the functional equivalence of the two competing world views in her life.[3] Finally, countless non-Communist scholars have observed the striking functional similarities between Communism and the great historic faiths. Maurice Duverger, the French political scientist, is typical of these. He writes:

> The party not only provides [the militant Communist] with organization for all his material activities, more important still it gives him a general organization of ideas, a systematic explanation of the universe. Marxism is not only a political doctrine, but a complete philosophy, a way of thinking, a spiritual cosmogony. All isolated facts in all spheres find their place in it and the reason for all their existence. It explains equally well the structure and evolution of the state, the changes in living creatures, the appearance of man on the earth, religious feelings, sexual behavior, and the development of the arts and sciences. And the explanation can be brought within the reach of the masses as well as being understood by the learned and by educated people. This philosophy can easily be made into a catechism without too serious a deformation. In this way the human spirit's need for fundamental unity can be satisfied.[4]

Because of its basic functional similarity to religions such as Christianity, Judaism, and Islam, many scholars refer to Communism as a secular, or nontheistic, religion. This designation is largely a matter of taste and depends on whether the term "religion" is restricted to a belief in God or a supernatural realm, or applied to any basic system of beliefs about the force or forces that ultimately shape the nature and destiny of man and the world. (The more inclusive definition would embrace not only Communism and other modern nontheistic faiths as religions, but classical Buddhism and the parts of Hinduism that also fall outside the more restricted definition.)

In addition to Marxism, a host of other secular religions have sprung up in the last hundred years. Some, like Marxism and the historic faiths, have been formally organized (for example, Nazism, Ethical Culture, or the cult formed by Ayn Rand). But many have remained highly amorphous, as in the case of the various brands of humanism preached by John Dewey, Bernard Shaw, Sigmund Freud, and Bertrand Russell. Instead of forming congregations or organizations of believers—a necessity in the agrarian era—these leaders have relied on books, magazines, and other mass media to spread their gospels. They have also enjoyed support in universities, many of whose faculty members have served as missionaries for these faiths.

These techniques have proved quite successful. While it is difficult to estimate the number of followers of these newer faiths, they are at least a substantial minority

---

[3] See Evgeny Evtushenko, *A Precocious Autobiography* (New York: Dutton, 1963), p. 42. See also the newspaper accounts of Svetlana Alliluyeva's statement to the press on her arrival in New York, April, 1967.

[4] Maurice Duverger, *Political Parties: Their Organization and Activity in the Modern State*, trans. by Barbara North and Robert North (London: Methuen, 1959), pp. 118–119. Quoted by permission of Methuen & Company, Ltd.

Fig. 14/1 Three recent religious leaders: Karl Marx, founder of Marxism; Paul Tillich, Protestant theologian; Bertrand Russell, humanist spokesman

in every industrial society, and a majority in some. They include large numbers of people who still call themselves Christians or Jews, but whose beliefs and practices bear little relation to the historic tenets of these faiths.

The rise of these new secular religions directs attention to one of the most striking changes in the realm of ideology: the shift in man's conception of the force or forces that ultimately shape his destiny and the world's. In the agrarian era, these forces were largely (though not entirely) conceived of in *personal* terms. God (or the gods) was the ultimate power and, like man, was thought of as a reasoning Being with emotions. While some religious leaders rejected crude anthropomorphic conceptions of God, they still emphasized the spiritual qualities he shares with man. Today, by contrast, people are more inclined to think of the ultimate power or powers in *impersonal* terms. This is true not only in the secular religions, but in the historic faiths as well. It can be seen, for example, in the writings of Christian theologians like the late Paul Tillich, who preferred to describe God as "the ground of all being," a phrase repeated over and over again in contemporary theological writing.[5]

The nature of the ultimate power to which religious symbols refer has certainly not changed! What *has* changed is man's information and experience—and it is from these sources that he draws his conclusions about the nature of ultimate reality. Because his senses are so limited, man has no choice but to rely on analogies and inferences in his efforts to comprehend something as complex as "ultimate power."

During the agrarian era, man's experience of power in both society and nature pointed to a world controlled by spiritual or personal forces. In society, the actions of governments clearly reflected the whims and eccentricities of their rulers: as the Founding Fathers of this country observed, those were governments of men, not of laws. In the natural world, a similar situation appeared to prevail: nature was often unpredictable and, like government, seemed to be responding to the whims and wishes of an arbitrary ruler.

Today, man's observation and experience suggest a different conclusion. The world of nature revealed by modern physics, chemistry, and astronomy often appears to be a world of machinelike regularity and predictability. While it is true that elements of irregularity and unpredictability do occasionally appear (e.g., the Heisenberg principle in physics or mutations in genetics), most people simply accept them as a part of a pattern not yet fully understood or, perhaps, as unimportant exceptions to the rule.[6] In the social world, too, power is much more impersonal. The forces of the market system are a classic example: a man may be ruined financially without anyone having willed it. In the political realm, the growth of bureaucracies and their increasing impersonality have transformed the character of government. Modern bureaucracies are usually no respecters of persons; as Kafka and other writers have pointed out, they follow rules and procedures with an often mindless impersonality.

Because men must draw inferences about ultimate power from what they experience and observe of power in society and nature, it would be surprising if they had not moved toward a more impersonal conception since the Industrial Revolution. We cannot say, of course, whether this view is more valid than the older one. This is a question science is incapable of answering.[7] Today, as in the past, men's most basic beliefs rest ultimately on the foundation of faith.

There is one other important development in the religious area that requires comment. Whereas in agrarian societies church and state were normally close allies,

---

[5] For a good popular account of the newer developments by an advocate of the impersonal view, see Bishop John A. T. Robinson, *Honest to God* (Philadelphia: Westminster Press, 1963).

[6] If these elements continue to appear, the trend could be reversed, but for the present that seems unlikely.

[7] See, for example, Peter Berger, *The Sacred Canopy* (Garden City, N.Y.: Doubleday, 1967), p. 100; or William J. Goode, *Religion Among the Primitives* (New York: Free Press, 1964), p. 23.

this is not the case in most industrial nations. The Communist nations of Eastern Europe are the chief exceptions. There, state and "church" (in the form of The Party) are closely allied, though in Yugoslavia there is a loosening of this tie. Formal ties are also maintained in a number of other countries (as in Scandinavia and Britain), but functionally they have lost most of their importance. Ties with the state in those nations are often a hindrance to the church because government approval is required for so many of its actions; and the state, for its part, now depends but little on the support of the church and therefore tends to be unresponsive to its needs.

The causes of this shift are varied, but one of the more important is the rise of democratic government and the resulting decline in social and economic inequality. When a society is governed by a tiny minority that exploits and oppresses the masses of common people, political control is a tenuous thing. The rulers and governing classes of agrarian societies knew this, and they depended on the clergy to legitimize their rule by preaching that their power was ordained of God and that to rebel against it was to rebel against God. In exchange, the government helped the clergy stamp out heresy and rival faiths and provided financial support.

As governments have become more democratic, the legitimizing function of the clergy has become less necessary to the elite (it is probably no coincidence that "church"-state ties are still strongest in Communist countries where democratic tendencies are weakest). Furthermore, with the growing belief that the world is controlled by impersonal forces that are unresponsive to human petitions, political leaders are less likely to trust in the ability of the clergy to help them when they are in a tight spot.

KINSHIP

Declining functions of kin groups

Historically, kin groups have been the matrix from which every other form of social organization evolved. In the simplest societies, almost every aspect of life was centered within the family. Kin groups were all-purpose organizations that provided for their members' political, economic, educational, religious, and recreational needs.

This could not last. In order for societies to grow in size and complexity, relationships had to be established between individuals who were not related to one another. And people who were related had to become involved in relationships that violated the norms of the kinship system—for example, an individual of inferior rank in an extended family put in a position where he exercised political authority over relatives of higher rank in the kin group.

While the functions of kin groups began to change thousands of years ago, no type of society has ever gone as far in altering their role as modern industrial societies. In agrarian societies, the family was still the basic unit of production and the state was normally the property of the royal family. Education, too, was still predominantly a family responsibility; most boys learned the male role by assisting their fathers, and girls the female role by assisting their mothers. Even when a boy was apprenticed to a master craftsman, he lived in his household in a kind of pseudo-familial relation.

By contrast, in advanced industrial societies ties of kinship are greatly reduced. The extended family is often so scattered that meaningful relations among its members are nearly impossible.[8] Furthermore, the nuclear family is no longer the basic unit of production, as it was in agrarian societies. With few exceptions, productive activities have been transferred to corporations, state enterprises, and other such organizations. In politics, family ownership of the state has been eliminated; and nepotism, while it still occurs occasionally, is no longer accepted as normal or legitimate. Finally, the schools have assumed many of the family's responsibilities of training and supervising children.

Today the family's basic function is to order the private and personal aspects of the lives of its members. This means continued responsibility for some of its historic functions—reproduction, child-rearing, and the channeling of sexual behavior—as well as new or enlarged responsibilities with respect to personality development, affective relationships, and the consumption of goods and services.

One of the clearest indications of the change is in the area of courtship and marriage. In most horticultural, herding, agrarian, and maritime societies, marriage was thought of largely in economic terms (and in the case of members of the governing class, in political terms as well). This was reflected in the practice of arranged marriages, in which the parents took the major responsibility for deciding whom their son or daughter would marry, and in the requirement of a bride price or a dowry. For companionship, men looked to other men; for love and sexual satisfaction, the more prosperous often kept mistresses or concubines, whom, unlike their wives, they were able to choose.

By contrast, people in industrial socities view marriage largely in romantic terms. As our movies, magazines, and music testify, it is the union of a man and a woman who are attracted to one another physically and psychologically and who expect to find continuing pleasure in one another's company. Parents may offer advice, but as likely as not it will be ignored. Bride price and dowry are irrelevant and mistresses have lost their former respectability. On the other hand, if the marriage fails to live up to expectations, there are relatively few economic, moral, or legal impediments to its dissolution.

The fact that the divorce rate is not higher than it is, however, suggests that it is easy to underrate the actual functional importance of the nuclear family. In societies where people move so frequently and are involved in such a variety of organizations, they find abundant opportunities to develop superficial relationships. Yet their very mobility makes it harder for them to achieve sustained, intimate relations of the

---

[8] Recent research shows that the extended family is not dead by any means, especially in the working class. Its importance, however, has definitely declined since the Industrial Revolution.

kind which involve all aspects of an individual's personality—including the memory of shared experiences. If sustained primary group ties are essential for the development of emotionally mature and stable personalities, as social psychologists believe, then this function of the family is actually growing in importance.

The family also plays an increasingly important role in the consumption of goods and services. With such a great diversity of products available in contemporary societies, intelligent purchasing has become much more difficult. This can have serious consequences because, to a considerable degree, our purchasing practices create the immediate environment in which we live. In most families this responsibility falls largely on the housewife, and if she is skillful, the result is a happier, more favorable environment for her family.

Fig. 14/2 Chaperoning, arranged marriages, and dowry or bride price have largely ended since the Industrial Revolution. Members of industrial societies view marriage more in romantic than in economic terms

Changing composition of the nuclear family

The Industrial Revolution has changed not only the family's functions, but its composition as well. Above all, there has been a drastic reduction in the number of children as Table 14/1 indicates. British marriages contracted around 1860 produced an average (median) of 6 children. Two generations later, the median had dropped to 2! Families with 8 or more children declined from 33 per cent of the total to only 2 per cent.

Though the decline was more rapid in Britain than in most industrial societies, the general pattern has been similar. In the United States, for example, the average number of children ever born to women who were between the ages of 45 and 49—in other words, those who had most recently reached the end of their child-bearing years—dropped as follows:[9]

1880	5.4
1920	3.7
1960	2.4

---

[9] Warren Thompson and David Lewis, *Population Problems*, 5th ed. (New York: McGraw-Hill, 1965), table 9/6. These figures are only for women who had ever married.

Table 14/1   Distribution of British families of various sizes for marriages contracted around 1860 and 1925

Number of children born	Percentage of families with specified number of children:	
	Marriages around 1860	Marriages around 1925
None	9	17
One	5	25
Two	6	25
Three	8	14
Four	9	8
Five	10	5
Six	10	3
Seven	10	2
Eight	9	1
Nine	8	0.6
Ten	6	0.4
Over ten	10	0.3
Total	100	101

Source: Royal Commission on Population, *Report* (London: H. M. Stationery Office, 1949), p. 26.

For British women married around 1925, the comparable figure was approximately 2.3.

In industrial societies today, families with more than four children are unusual; the majority have one to three. The United States has been something of an exception, but even here the pattern is changing. After World War II, its birthrate shot up to 26.6 per thousand, and until the early 1960s it never went below 23.0. Beginning in 1958, however, it started to decline rather rapidly and by the middle of 1968 had dropped to 17.4, a fairly typical figure for industrial societies (see Table 12/1).[10] So, while there are currently more families with four or five children in the United States than in most other industrial societies, this distinction will probably not continue much longer.

Comparisons like the one in Table 14/1 are misleading if we assume that they reflect differences in the number of children living within a family at the same time. For one thing, in the earlier period the death rate among children was much higher than it is today. Table 14/2 shows how the rate for Swedish children has declined since the eighteenth century (these figures are used because Sweden has some of the oldest reliable statistics in this area). In the middle of the eighteenth century, 43 per cent of Swedish children died before they reached the age of five.[11] Of those who survived, 14 per cent died before they were twenty. In other words, half of the children died before their twentieth birthday. By contrast, in the middle of the twentieth century, 97 per cent of the Swedish children lived at least that long. Obviously, with so many deaths in the first years of life, the number of children *living* in an agrarian family was considerably lower than the number of children *born* into it.

Another factor that reduced the number of children living with their parents at

---

[10] *The World Almanac, 1969*, p. 757

[11] The figure of 43 per cent is arrived at by taking the average annual death rate of 86.6 shown in table 14/2 and multiplying by 5 (for the first five years of life) and dividing by 1,000 (the base against which the annual death rate was calculated).

Table 14/2 **Average annual death rates, by age, Sweden, 1751–1959 (rate per 1,000 population)**

Age	1751–1780	1881–1910	1955–1959
0–4	86.6	36.3	4.2
5–9	13.8	5.9	0.5
10–14	7.2	3.6	0.4
15–19	7.0	4.6	0.7

Source: From *Statistical Abstract of Sweden* as cited in Warren Thompson and David Lewis, *Population Problems*, 5th ed. (New York: McGraw-Hill, 1965), p. 374.

any given time was the long duration of the child-bearing period. Women who had eight, ten, or more children often bore them over a twenty-year period or longer. By the time the youngest child was five or ten, many of his older brothers and sisters had left home. Thus, while nuclear families were certainly larger in agrarian societies, the number actually living together at one time was not so very different. At the time of the first United States census in 1790, the average household (i.e., a group of two or more persons related by blood, marriage, or adoption, and residing together) numbered 5.7; in the 1960s it was 3.7.[12]

A second noteworthy change in the composition of the family is the elimination of the last vestiges of polygyny. Industrial societies are the only major type in which it has never been socially approved. Among preliterate societies, only 13 per cent insist on monogamy;[13] in agrarian societies, monogamy is more common, though still far from universal (until recently, polygyny was practiced throughout the whole of the Muslim world extending from the East Indies to Morocco). The shift in industrial societies reflects the changing character of the family, especially the growing importance of affective ties between husband and wife and the declining importance of economic functions.

Finally, the modern family includes fewer relatives outside the nuclear group; households today seldom accommodate aged grandparents, unmarried aunts and uncles, or even grown children. This is no longer necessary in most families because modern urban communities provide many alternative facilities, such as apartments, nursing homes, restaurants, laundries, and so on. Moreover, as these facilities have developed, changes have occurred in societal values: most members of industrial societies are extremely jealous of their privacy and apparently regard it more highly than they do the advantages afforded by more inclusive households.

Divorce

During the last century, the divorce rate in the United States has risen substantially. In 1890 it stood at 0.5 per thousand population per year. By 1967 it had risen more than fivefold to 2.7[14] Many people have concluded from this that a high divorce rate is an inevitable result of industrialization.

Recently, however, as the problem has been studied more carefully in comparative cross-national terms, doubts have been cast on that view.[15] Statistics assembled by the United Nations show great variation among societies at similar stages of industrialization, and remarkable similarities among those with very different

---

[12] *Current Population Reports*, P-20, No. 122, p. 3.

[13] This is my own calculation based on 603 hunting and gathering, horticultural, fishing, and herding societies in Murdock's sample of 915 societies (see p. 130 above). I have omitted 104 hybrid societies, most of which are preliterate. If these were included, the figure would rise to 15 per cent.

[14] *World Almanac, 1969*, p. 757.

[15] See especially William J. Goode, *World Revolution and Family Patterns* (New York: Free Press, 1963).

Table 14/3 Number of divorces per thousand population for a sample of industrial and industrializing agrarian societies, 1965

Nation	Rate
Industrial societies:	
United States	2.5
Hungary	2.0
U.S.S.R.	1.6
Austria	1.2
England (1964)	0.7
Canada	0.5
Italy	0.0
Industrializing agrarian societies:	
Morocco (1955)	2.9
United Arab Republic	2.2
Iran	1.0
Syria	0.6
Iraq (1962)	0.2
Ceylon (1962)	0.2
Thailand (1962)	0.1

Sources: United Nations, *Demographic Yearbook, 1966*, table 26; United Nations, *Demographic Yearbook, 1963*, table 29; and *Statistical Abstract of the United States, 1967*, table 48.

economies (see Table 14-3). This makes it difficult to claim that industrialization is the major cause of high divorce rates. Rather, it appears that this is an area where technology allows great latitude. Divorce rates actually seem to depend far more on the beliefs and values of those who control the political systems of nations. For example, while Stalin ruled Russia, divorce laws became extremely strict and the divorce rate was very low.[16] Since his death, his successors have relaxed the laws and the rate has risen considerably.[17]

In general, Muslim, Communist, and Protestant societies have been more permissive in this respect, and Buddhist and Catholic societies more strict. But there are exceptions to this. For example, as Table 14/3 shows, Muslim Iraq currently has a divorce rate only a sixth that of Catholic Austria as a result of recent restrictive legislation.

---

[16] See, for example, Vladimir Gsovski, "Family and Inheritance in Soviet Law," in Alex Inkeles and Kent Geiger (eds.), *Soviet Society* (Boston: Houghton Mifflin, 1961), pp. 533–535.

[17] Between 1956 and 1962, the rate nearly doubled. See United Nations, *Demographic Yearbook, 1963*, p. 655.

Industrialization is not totally irrelevant to divorce patterns, however. Smaller families, the development of nursery facilities, and above all, more job opportunities for women make it much easier for divorcees to establish and maintain their own households. Thus divorce in an industrial society does not usually force a woman to return to her father's household or become dependent on a brother or uncle, as it would in an agrarian society.

Widowhood and remarriage

In agrarian societies, a very high proportion of families were broken during the child-bearing and child-rearing years by the death of one or both parents. The chances of this were at least 50-50, and in some societies even higher. For example, in mid-eighteenth century Sweden the probability was about 0.51 (i.e., 51 chances per 100 marriages); in late eighteenth century France around 0.61; and earlier in our own century, about 0.71 in India.[18]

In most countries this pattern resulted in frequent remarriages. Hardy individuals who survived to old age had often had two or three spouses. Marriages between widows and widowers were common and led to merged families with complicated combinations of half-brothers and half-sisters. Fairy tales about cruel stepmothers continue to bear witness to the unhappy situations which often resulted.

In modern industrial societies, widowhood before middle age is relatively infrequent. In the United States the probability of either husband or wife dying between the ages of 20 and 45 is only 0.10.[19] This means that the likelihood of the nuclear family's disruption was actually considerably greater in agrarian societies despite the rise in the divorce rate in many industrial nations.

Loosening of ties

Another basic change in family life is the loosening of ties among the members. The agrarian family, as we have seen, tended to be a work group. This was almost invariably the case among peasants, who were the majority of the population, but it was typical of artisans, too. The place of work and the place of residence were normally the same, and all the members of the family, including children, shared in the work.

In industrial societies the pendulum has swung to the opposite pole. Very few men work at home and most work too far away to return even for the midday meal. The same is increasingly true of married women, and the schools now draw children out of the family for a major part of their waking hours.

---

[18] Calculated from Thompson and Lewis, *op. cit.,* p. 374; J. Bourgeois-Pichat, "The General Development of the Population of France Since the Eighteenth Century," in D. V. Glass and D. E. C. Eversley (eds.), *Population in History* (Chicago: Aldine, 1965), p. 498; and W. S. Woytinsky and E. S. Woytinsky, *World Population and Production: Trends and Outlook* (New York: Twentieth Century Fund, 1953), p. 181.

[19] Calculated from *Statistical Abstract of the United States, 1966,* p. 53.

Fig. 14/3   Prior to industrialization, a very high proportion of families were broken during the child-bearing, child-rearing years by the death of one or both parents

As a result, family members spend much less time with one another than they did in agrarian societies. A child in the lower grades may be with his teacher more than with his mother. Similarly, a teen-ager may spend more time with his friends than with his parents, and a businessman see more of his secretary than his wife. This is bound to have its effects on family ties.

A classic illustration of the problem is the familiar dinner table dialogue in which the parents ask the children, "What happened at school today?" or the wife asks her husband, "What happened at the office?" The standard answer is, "Oh, nothing." This does not mean that nothing really happened, but rather that nothing happened that could be easily explained or that would be meaningful to people unfamiliar with the setting. The frequency with which this response is given is a good measure of the loosening of ties within the family group.

This is not necessarily bad, however, even from the standpoint of its effect on family solidarity. Family ties were frequently *too close* in the past and as likely to generate resentment and hate as their opposites. (There is a good illustration of this in the next chapter, page 466). The unity of the family group in a modern industrial society rests more on a foundation of common interests and mutual attraction than it did when social and economic necessity offered people very few choices. Despite its negative aspects, therefore, the new situation seems about as conducive to harmonious solidary relations within the family as those which prevailed in the past.

STUDENT COMMUNITIES AND THEIR SUBCULTURES

One of the most striking organizational developments in industrial societies has been the emergence of student[20] communities with their highly distinctive subcultures. In simpler societies, children are incorporated into the adult world of work at the earliest possible age. While still quite small, they are given a variety of chores appropriate to their abilities. As they grow older they are given more difficult and more responsible jobs until, in their early or middle teens, they assume almost full adult responsibilities—at least from an economic standpoint. Even in agrarian societies, only a tiny fraction would still be in school at this age.

Under such a system, young people were quickly absorbed into the adult community. To be sure, their youth limited their involvement; but the important point is that they were not cut off as they are in industrial societies. In these societies, opportunities for employment are severely restricted for teen-agers, and law and custom compel them to remain in school—a world made up almost exclusively of other young people. The only adults present are a handful of teachers, administrators, and janitors who, while important in the formal structure of the school, are very marginal in the informal social world of the students.

Not surprisingly, these new communities have developed distinctive cultures of their own. This happens whenever groups of people with common concerns are brought into frequent contact with one another. Although these subcultures vary a great deal from one student group to the next, they have several important characteristics in common. To begin with, they are characterized by a succession of fads and fashions. While their basic values remain fairly constant from year to year (e.g., resistance to adult authority, the desire for fun, etc.), the way they are expressed constantly changes, as styles in music, speech, and clothing illustrate. To some extent these changes are the result of manipulation and exploitation by businessmen. But they are also a device which student communities use to maintain the boundary between themselves and the adult community. The more rapidly fads and fashions change, the harder it is for adults to keep up with them. This forces adults to keep their distance and prevents them from moving in and dominating the student world. In addition, it provides a criterion by which the otherwise dominant adults can be

---

[20] The term "student," as used in this section, includes hippies and other young people who have dropped out of school but live on the fringes of the student world and have some thought of returning later to complete their education.

judged inferior. (This is a common pattern in lower-status groups: the poor, for example, have often made asceticism a virtue and hence a basis for condemning the rich.)

Another characteristic of student communities is their rejection of adult values and adult authority. Sometimes it almost seems that their values are simply inversions of adult values. And related to this is a third important characteristic: intolerance of nonconformity. This is so despite their own tendency to flaunt the standards of the adult community. Deviation from the student group's standards is often punished severely, frequently by ridicule and ostracism. This harsh treatment is apparently necessary because many students feel a great ambivalence; they are torn between a basic respect for the values of the adult community and the desire to be accepted by their peers. Without discipline, there would probably be so many defections from the group and its standards that it could not survive as anything but a small, deviant, patently inferior subgroup within society. As long as the majority of students can be held in line, however, the legitimacy of their subculture and its right to a measure of autonomy can be maintained. In many respects their situation is similar to that of workingmen when unions were first being formed. The majority of them, too, were ambivalent, and it took rigorous discipline to establish the right of the group to a measure of autonomy.

Unfortunately, the analogy breaks down at one point: workingmen did not usually become owners and managers of industry, but students do eventually become adults. As a result, the growing separation between adults and students is a source of serious difficulties; for so many of the decisions that are crucial to a person in his adult years are made while he is still in the student community and subject to its values. Given the conflict between the values of the two communities, many decisions that are made in the light of student values prove unsound later.

A classic example of this is the heavy investment some boys make in athletics at the expense of their studies. In the student community, where athletic success is often rewarded far more highly than academic success, this makes good sense. With rare exceptions, however, high school and college athletes find the demand for their skills in the adult world very disappointing. One in a hundred may have a brief career as a professional athlete, and only a minority of these find it really rewarding. Unfortunately, early decisions are largely irreversible: not many men can return to high school in their middle twenties and make up what they neglected years before.

A similar situation exists with respect to marriage. Decisions with life-long consequences are often made while the individual is still a member of the student community. But the qualities that make a person a desirable date frequently prove irrelevant to his or her desirability as a marriage partner.

Student communities and their distinctive subcultures have a number of far-reaching consequences for industrial societies. In the long run, however, the most important is likely to be their effect on the processes of social change. By opposing the values of the older generation, student communities develop in each new generation a predisposition to favor the new and the experimental. In this way, they have become an important force for social and cultural change.

INTRATYPE VARIATION: TRENDS AND PROSPECTS

In recent decades there has been a great deal of variation among industrial societies. The differences have been especially pronounced between totalitarian nations with their command economies, on the one hand, and democratic-capitalistic nations on the other. Twenty years ago it seemed that these were fundamentally different kinds of industrial societies, both stable and durable, both with excellent chances of surviving for the indefinite future.

Today the picture is changed. Signs of convergence have been increasingly evident for a number of years. Since Stalin's death in 1953, there has been a definite trend toward political liberalization in most industrial societies under Communist control (this is not true of China and Albania, but neither of these comes close to being an industrial society). This trend has gone further in some societies than others, and has suffered reversals in several instances. But the basic trend seems clear. Similarly, in the economic area there has been a definite relaxation of the former emphasis on centralized planning and a shift away from the other techniques of a command economy. For a number of years now, market forces have been permitted to play a much larger role.

Meanwhile, the democracies have taken steps to increase government regulation of their economies and restrict the play of market forces. For more than a generation, they have been moving toward an economy that contains substantial elements of both market and command. Politically, there is little evidence of any shift toward the totalitarian pattern, though some extreme critics profess to see this too.

Signs of convergence are occurring in other areas as well. The generational cleavage, for example, is common to both types of societies. In fact, the most alienated and revolutionary elements in both totalitarian and democratic nations are usually found among university students. The growing importance of science, the increasing influence of the educational elite, and the weakening position of professional politicians are other common trends.

Industrial societies are not, of course, moving toward a single uniform pattern. Differences will certainly remain; but they will probably be less marked than those that separated Hitler's Germany or Stalin's Russia from the Western democracies. The explanation for the convergence seems to be that some political and economic systems are more costly and less satisfactory than others. If they are considered essential for ideological reasons, such systems can be maintained for some time by a dictatorial regime willing to pay the price. But this presupposes a government run by a dedicated elite that is firmly committed to ideological principles. And such elites seldom remain in control for long. Though they can sometimes lead a success-ful revolution, once its success is assured they begin to be crowded out by pragmatic and self-seeking careerists who are more interested in promoting their private interests than in implementing some set of abstract ideals.

As far as we can judge from the experience of industrial societies thus far, extremely centralized polities and economies cost more to maintain than less centralized ones. Therefore they are less common than democratic polities and economies that mix the elements of market and command. However, events of the twentieth century prove that the costs are not impossible if a powerful minority of dedicated fanatics is determined to make the rest of society pay the price (see the Appendix following Chapter 3).

PROGRESS AND PROBLEMS

In many ways modern industrial societies can be regarded as the crowning achieve-ment in man's long struggle to build a better life. Never before has he had such a store of accumulated information. Never before has he been able to harness such powerful forces in his own behalf. Never has the human population been as large as it is today, or as secure from the threat of starvation.

Yet for all his achievements, man is not free from problems—not even from the threat of extinction. The problems he faces today, however, differ from his earlier ones in one respect at least: They are increasingly *problems of man's own making, by-products of the material progress of which he is so proud.* Today more than ever, we can appreciate the reversal of the old saying: Invention has, indeed, become the mother of necessity—and with a vengeance.

Examples of this are all around us. The drug thalidomide provides a classic case: it nicely solved the problem of sleeplessness for many people, but when taken by women early in pregnancy (usually before the fact of pregnancy was known), it frequently resulted in badly deformed babies. Though an extreme case, it is not atypical. The drug industry alone could furnish thousands of other examples. The side effects of drugs are often so subtle or so slow in manifesting themselves, however, that they can be detected only by the most careful research.

We are only now beginning to discover how many elements of the new tech-nology have these harmful "side effects." Cigarettes produce lung cancer, factories and automobiles pollute the air, sewage systems make cesspools of beautiful rivers and lakes, insecticides destroy valuable wildlife, and the new supersonic jets shatter nerves and windows alike.

But it is not only the new technology that creates problems. New, highly bureaucratized systems of social organization, with their impersonal—sometimes mindless—operations, are the source of other difficulties. People whose needs do not fall neatly into one of the prepackaged routines that these organizations are "programmed" to handle often wind up horribly frustrated. And even those who manage to avoid this are likely to be alienated by the organization's impersonality.

Yet for all the shortcomings of modern industrial societies, it is doubtful that many people would elect the older agrarian way of life with its widespread poverty, hunger, injustice, ignorance, exploitation, and disease. When people talk about the superiority of the great civilizations of the past, they reveal either an ignorance of the past or a commitment to an unusual set of values. Taken as a whole, the agrarian way of life was decidedly inferior to the industrial, and the best evidence of this is the eagerness with which most members of agrarian societies industrialize or migrate to industrial societies when they have the chance, and the reluctance of members of industrial societies to migrate to agrarian societies.

The inescapable conclusion, therefore, is that industrial societies, for all their defects, represent a significant advance over agrarian societies—and not only in technological terms. While a few individuals may not share this judgment, the vast majority clearly do.

Chapter 15
Industrializing Societies

Despite the rapid spread of industrialization during the last two centuries, less than a third of the world's population live in societies that can be called industrial as we have defined the term. The great majority, however, do live in societies that have been substantially influenced by the Industrial Revolution—either by the diffusion of modern industrial technology or by its products obtained through trade. These influences have produced a large number of societies that are best described as *industrializing agrarian* and *industrializing horticultural* societies—the ones we commonly refer to as the underdeveloped, or developing nations.

These nations are in a transitional phase, moving from the older agrarian or horticultural way of life to the modern industrial. Social scientists usually refer to this as the *modernization* process, a term that serves as a reminder that sociocultural progress involves *all* aspects of the life of society, not only the technological. Unfortunately, the transitional period is proving to be longer and more difficult than most scholars had expected. For both theoretical and practical reasons, then, these societies merit careful study.

In most analyses, industrializing agrarian and industrializing horticultural societies are lumped together indiscriminately. This is a serious mistake, since the two types differ in a number of important respects. In this chapter, therefore, we will deal with them separately.

First, however, a word concerning the place of other preindustrial types in the contemporary world. As we noted earlier, quite a number of hunting and gathering, fishing, and simple horticultural societies did survive into the modern era in isolated areas. But recent advances in transportation have opened up most of these areas and removed this once effective source of protection. As a result, most of these groups have either been destroyed or herded onto reservations where they live as wards of their conquerors, usually under conditions that make their traditional way of life impossible. Even the few groups which still preserve a high degree of autonomy (e.g., the Bushmen in Southwest Africa) have usually adopted some tools and other elements from more advanced societies and thus are no longer pure types. This does not make them *industrializing* societies, of course: that implies something utterly beyond their adaptive capacities. Groups with such a primitive subsistence base could not possibly evolve into anything so advanced in the little time that is still available to them. They are, at best, peculiar hybrids with a very limited future.

Maritime societies disappeared years ago, most of them absorbed by expanding agrarian societies. Herding societies have been more resistant, but in recent years they, too, have been largely absorbed into expanding industrial, industrializing agrarian, or industrializing horticultural societies. Though tribes of herdsmen remain distinct subgroups in many of them (Saudi Arabia, Iraq, Morocco, Kenya, etc.), because they are minority groups they do not set the tone for the society as a whole. There are a few societies in which herding peoples are dominant or nearly so—for example, Mongolia, Somalia, and Upper Volta—and others where herding is of major importance—including Jordan, Saudi Arabia, Mauritania, and Afghanistan. Research on these societies has been very limited, however, and they are not, as a group, very important on the world scene. Therefore we will not attempt to examine their special characteristics and problems here.

INDUSTRIALIZING AGRARIAN SOCIETIES

By one criterion, at least, industrializing agrarian societies are the most important type in the world today: more people live in them than in any other. But this is not the only reason for their importance. These societies have, for decades, been struggling with problems that constantly threaten to overwhelm them. Despite a measure of industrialization, the majority of their citizens are as poor as the common people ever were in traditional agrarian societies. At the same time, improved education and the mass media have raised their hopes and expectations and given them a sharp awareness of a better kind of life. This contradiction has created a revolutionary situation that threatens to involve the entire world.

Sometimes it is suggested that the basic problem of the underdeveloped countries is simply their technological and economic backwardness and stagnation. Actually, however, their problems are much more complex than that and involve every major social institution—polity, economy, family, religion, and education.

Technology and productivity

Technologically, an industrializing agrarian society is a bewildering mixture of the ancient and the modern. Peasant farmers using techniques and tools very much like those their forefathers used two thousand years ago work in sight of such marvels of modern technology as the Aswan dam in Egypt or the Tata iron and steel works in India.

Fig. 15/1   The old and the new: Indian farmer plowing with his bullocks under high-power electric transmission lines

Unfortunately from the developmental standpoint, the old technology is much more common, especially in the agricultural sector of these economies. In one recent year, an average of 62 per cent of the labor force of 32 industrializing agrarian nations was engaged in agriculture, and yet all these people produced only 36.5 per cent of the gross national product.[1] This differential would have been even greater if many of these countries did not have income from relatively modern plantations (tea, rubber, etc.) operated by foreigners from industrial societies.

There are marked differences in the level of technological and economic development among industrializing agrarian societies. With per capita energy consumption as a measure, levels range from only 9 kilograms of coal equivalent per year in Nepal to 831 in Greece. The average for all industrializing agrarian societies is actually closer to the former: in 1963 the median for 47 of them was only 234.

In general, the level of technological development is higher in the Middle East, North Africa, and Latin America than in south and east Asia. Median figures for per capita energy consumption in these areas in 1963 were as follows:

Middle East and North Africa	280
Latin America	243
South and East Asia	84

These figures do not include any of the industrial societies in those areas.

---

[1] These figures are medians; the means are almost identical. The calculations are based on Bruce Russett et al., *World Handbook of Political and Social Indicators* (New Haven, Conn.: Yale, 1964), tables 49 and 50.

Many discussions of the underdeveloped countries give the impression that they are technically and economically stagnant or, at the very least, developing less rapidly than industrial societies. But data assembled by the United Nations in recent years show that this is not the case. Between 1938 and 1961, the productivity of the underdeveloped countries increased at exactly the same rate as that of the industrial countries—3.6 per cent per year in each case.[2]

Unfortunately, the least developed of the developing nations are the very ones that are advancing at the slowest rate. Thus, in the period just mentioned, the industrializing nations of south and east Asia had an average annual growth rate of only 2.6 per cent, while those in Latin America had a rate of 4.5. Because the level of production in the Asiatic nations was already so low, and their birthrate so high that it consumed more than half of the productive increase, any improvement in the standard of living was bound to be very limited. From 1938 to 1961, real per capita income in the United States and Canada increased $991; in the industrializing societies of south and east Asia it increased only $15.[3] Because of the extreme social inequality that characterizes these societies, it is possible that the common people's standard of living did not improve at all in this quarter century. Yet Americans continue to be puzzled by the appeal of communism in that part of the world!

Demographic patterns

With the introduction of modern medicine and sanitation, death rates have been cut drastically in almost every industrializing agrarian society. But except in rare cases, birthrates have remained high, usually around 40 per thousand population per year. Year in, year out, the populations of the underdeveloped nations continue to swell, consuming a large part of their hard-won gains in productivity.

Table 15/1 shows in detail the cost of uncontrolled population growth for the industrializing nations of south and east Asia and Latin America. Had they been able to maintain a balance between births and deaths from 1938 to 1961, their per capita income would have grown at a faster rate than industrial societies experienced during that period. Instead, they fell further behind, even in Latin America where the average annual increase in gross domestic product[4] was greater than in industrial societies.

Uncontrolled population growth is a serious problem for industrializing societies not only because it means so many mouths to feed, but because it complicates

---

[2] United Nations, Department of Economic and Social Affairs, *The Growth of World Industry, 1938–1961* (New York, 1965), table 4. The figure cited is the average annual growth of the gross domestic product. The definition of industrial countries used in that study was slightly more restrictive than the one used in this volume (Argentina, Chile, Venezuela and Yugoslavia were treated as industrializing countries), and the industrializing horticultural are lumped together with the industrializing agrarian. These differences do not seem to have altered the picture very much.

[3] *Ibid.*, table 12. The figure for south and east Asia excludes Japan. Real income is a measure that eliminates the effects of inflation and deflation (i.e., the figures are in constant 1958 U.S. dollars).

[4] Gross domestic product equals gross national product minus net income from abroad.

Table 15/1   Average annual rate of growth of gross domestic product and population for countries outside the Communist bloc

Period	Average annual rate of growth		
	GDP	Population	Difference*
Industrial societies:†			
1938–1948	3.1	1.0	2.1
1948–1958	3.9	1.3	2.6
1958–1961	4.6	1.2	3.4
1938–1961	3.6	1.1	2.5
Latin America:‡			
1938–1948	4.4	1.9	2.5
1948–1958	4.6	2.6	2.0
1958–1961	5.0	2.9	2.1
1938–1961	4.5	2.4	2.1
South and East Asia, except Japan:			
1938–1948	2.0	1.2	0.8
1948–1958	3.0	1.9	1.1
1958–1961	3.4	2.4	1.0
1938–1961	2.6	1.6	1.0

* This equals *per capita* increase in gross domestic product.
† This does not include Argentina, Chile, Mexico, Venezuela, and Yugoslavia.
‡ This includes Argentina, Chile, Mexico, and Venezuela.
Source: United Nations, *The Growth of World Industry*, 1938–1961 (New York, 1965), table 4.

the entire process of societal development. For one thing, mass public education is prohibitively expensive in these nations, and yet without it the population is not equipped for most kinds of jobs in modern industry. This forces large numbers of people to find employment in traditional industries, which for most of them means farming. But they can be accommodated only by subdividing already small farms to the point where they are hopelessly inefficient and the introduction of modern machinery is impossible. In Egypt, for example, 70 per cent of the farm owners had less than half an acre in 1950.[5] As one writer observed, "Most of those who are working the land work not because the land requires their labor but because they require the work."[6] He went on to say that as early as 1939 it was estimated that 10 per cent of Egypt's farmers could supply all the necessary labor if Egypt's farms were

[5] Manfred Halpern, *The Politics of Social Change in the Middle East and North Africa* (Princeton, N.J.: Princeton University Press, 1963), p. 80.

[6] *Ibid.*

even half as mechanized as America's farms were at that time. The story is much the same in most industrializing agrarian societies.

Another complication results from the fact that the surplus population is too poor to generate a demand for the many kinds of industrial products that are an essential component of the economy of every industrial society. Poverty prevents these people from purchasing anything but the most basic traditional commodities. Finally, this surplus population compounds all the other problems by its own productive achievements: an abundance of children. The society is thus trapped in a vicious circle.

In view of all this, it is hardly surprising to learn that there is a correlation of −0.49 between the birthrate and the average annual growth of per capita productivity.[7] This indicates a rather strong relationship between high birthrates and low rates of economic progress.

In recent years the leaders of a few of these societies have finally begun to

---

[7] See the Glossary for an explanation of correlation coefficients. The study cited was Russett et al., *op. cit.*, p. 277, and was based on data from 55 nations.

Fig. 15/2   Peasant family, Colombia

grasp the seriousness of the population problem and its relation to economic growth. Tentative efforts have been made to encourage married couples to adopt modern methods of contraception, but these have not been very successful in most cases.[8] In view of the limited funds invested in these programs, one could hardly expect anything else. An increasing number of social scientists believe, however, that investments in birth control will accomplish far more in raising the standard of living than equal investments in industry—at least at this point in the developmental process.

The economy

The economies of industrializing societies can be divided into two basic parts. The traditional component differs little from the economies of agrarian societies of the last two thousand years. The tools and techniques are much the same and so, unhappily, is the level of productivity. In contrast, the modern—or at least modern-izing—component employs tools, techniques, and patterns of economic organiza-tion that have, for the most part, been borrowed from industrial societies.

This newer component, however, is not simply a scaled-down version of the economy of the average industrial society—a few small steel mills, a small auto plant or two, some textile mills, wholesale and retail distributors, and so forth. Compared with more advanced economies, the modern component in the average under-developed country is very one-sided or imbalanced and very highly specialized.

To understand why this is so, we have to recognize the tremendous difference between the circumstances under which these nations are industrializing and those under which Western Europe and the United States industrialized. Today's develop-ing nations have to make the transition in a world dominated politically and economically by *already* industrialized nations, nations that have well-established home markets with high volumes of sales, nations that have become the builders of industrial machinery for the rest of the world. Add to this the relatively low cost of moving goods today, and the industrializing countries are left without much of a competitive advantage *even in their home markets;* European and American firms can easily undersell Latin American and Asian manufacturers in a wide variety of fields, especially in the heavy industries.

As a result, many of the industrializing societies have been forced into a peculiar ecological niche; they have become producers of the world's raw materials. Furthermore, because of pressures generated by world markets and their own desire to maximize income, they often become dangerously specialized. For example, 74 per cent of Burma's foreign exchange comes solely from the sale of rice, 72 per

---

[8] Recent reports from Taiwan and South Korea are more encouraging. In Taiwan the birthrate has been reduced from 45 per 1,000 in 1955 to 32.4 per 1,000 in 1966. See the Report of the President (Frank W. Notestein) of the Population Council for 1966 in *Annual Report,* pp. 11–16.

cent of Egypt's from cotton.[9] Twenty industrializing agrarian countries rely on a single commodity for over half their foreign earnings, and fifteen others receive 50 per cent or more from only three commodities.

A nation in this situation is highly vulnerable to any shift in the world economy that affects its specialty. Technological innovations in particular—things like synthetic rubber and synthetic fibers—can permanently reduce, or even eliminate, the demand for it. This sensitivity to change naturally creates an unstable "boom or bust" atmosphere, hardly conducive to the development of rational economic planning and development by either native businessmen or governments. Instead, it encourages a speculative attitude whose goal is quick profits and an early transfer of capital to less risky ventures.

Despite their drawbacks, these specialized industries are an important source of income for developing nations and facilitate capital accumulation, which is so necessary in the modernization process. In addition, they increase the number of people with modern skills and a modern economic orientation. Modernization and industrialization are impossible without large numbers of such individuals.

It is still too early to say whether the benefits of specialized industries will, in the long run, outweigh their costs. A lot will depend on the attitude of the more advanced nations. If countries like the United States, Britain, and the Soviet Union regard industrializing nations simply as pawns to be manipulated and exploited for their own economic and political advantage, the long-term benefits for the developing nations are likely to be small. On the other hand, if the leading nations act responsibly, the benefits could be considerable. This is one area in which modern statesmen have a truly important choice confronting them.

The polity

One of the greatest hindrances to modernization and industrialization in these societies has been the kind of governing class they inherited from the past. This class had a good thing going for centuries, and its contemporary members have usually seen no need for change. The ideal society, for them, lies in the past, in the days before intellectuals and the common people ever heard of liberty, equality, democracy, socialism, and communism. From their perspective, change has been something to be feared and fought—or occasionally, as in the case of aid programs sponsored by industrial societies, exploited for their own benefit.

In the last hundred years, however, a growing number of voices have been raised against the old order and its backward-looking, exploitative character. Sometimes proponents of modernization have seized control of the government with the idea of using the power of the state as a force for political, economic, and social

---

[9] This and the following information on foreign trade is from Jagdish Bhagwati, *The Economics of Under-developed Countries* (New York: World Universal Library, 1966), pp. 56–59.

change. These modernizers have been a heterogeneous lot. Some have been military men with a strong spirit of nationalism, like Atatürk and Nasser; some, civilian nationalists like Nehru, Bourguiba, and Cárdenas. A number have been Communists, e.g., Lenin, Tito, Mao Tse-tung, and Castro; while in at least one case—Iran—the monarch himself played this role.

Would-be modernizers have usually found, however, that it is not enough simply to win control of the government. To implement their plans, they must have the support of thousands of lower- and middle-level officials who are both efficient and honest. Unfortunately, such men are hard to find in societies that for centuries have neglected education and viewed government office as a means for personal self-aggrandizement. As a result, the efforts of the top leaders are often frustrated by the incompetence and corruption of lesser officials.[10]

One of the most basic decisions confronting the leaders of industrializing societies today concerns the role of the state in the industrializing and modernizing process. In recent decades these leaders have had two radically different models of social organization to choose from: one provided by the Western democracies, especially Britain, France, and the United States; the other by the Communist nations, the Soviet Union and China in particular. In practical terms, the choice has been between a society in which the state plays a limited role in the economy and other areas of life and parliamentary rule and free elections prevail, and a society in which the state directs and controls the economy and other areas and a strong executive authority dominates the government without permitting free elections.

Until World War II, most would-be modernizers took the Western democracies for their model. Parliamentary government and free elections appeared to be the key to progress. Unhappily, however, the adoption of democratic forms by underdeveloped nations seldom produced the expected results. Democratic governments were often toppled by military juntas representing the old order. Even those that survived such threats rarely experienced the economic progress anticipated.

In recent decades, the rapid advances of the Soviet Union and the promises of Communist theory have offered an attractive alternative. The key to progress in this model has appeared to be the systematic, and if necessary ruthless, mobilization of a society's resources by a regime with a definite plan for the future.

For some years now, many leaders in underdeveloped countries have found the choice a difficult one. On the one hand, they have been attracted by the liberal, humane, and pragmatic principles of the democratic model. On the other hand, they have been impressed by the capacity of totalitarian systems to mobilize resources

---

[10] See, for example, A. H. Hanson, *The Process of Planning: A Study of India's Five-Year Plans, 1950–1964* (London: Oxford, 1966), part II, especially chap. 8; Peter Franck, "Economic Planners," in Sydney Fisher (ed.), *Social Forces in the Middle East* (Ithaca, N.Y.: Cornell, 1955), pp. 137–161; Louis Walinsky, *Economic Development in Burma, 1951–1960* (New York: Twentieth Century Fund, 1962), part V, especially chap. 29; or Lennox A. Mills, *Southeast Asia* (Minneapolis: University of Minnesota Press, 1964), chap. 11.

and by their promise of political stability and economic progress. With respect to the latter, many leaders have come to doubt that a full-fledged democratic system can be both stable and economically progressive in a society characterized by widespread poverty and illiteracy among the common people, exploitative traditions among the old upper class, and a critical shortage of technical skill and capital.

As a result, many leaders have begun to experiment with various hybrid forms of government, incorporating elements from both of the new models and usually from the traditional system as well. Some of these experiments have been disasters, like Sukarno's "guided democracy" in Indonesia. Others, such as Bourguiba's Tunisian republic, have enjoyed both economic growth and political stability without resort to terror or extreme coercion.

Egypt's Nasser has stated the goals and methods of these hybrid types as well as anyone. The six objectives of the Egyptian revolution, according to him, are "elimination of imperialism and its helpers, elimination of feudalism, elimination of monopoly and its domination of the government, the establishment of universal social justice, the formation of a strong, patriotic, national army, and the creation of sound democratic life."[11] In his view, however, democracy cannot be put first, for the effort to establish it would undermine the whole revolutionary effort. In an address to the nation in 1954, he said, "There will be democracy and freedom, but we must first be free from exploitation, despotism, and slavery. I cannot understand how there can be freedom if I am not free to find my bread and make a living, and free to find employment."[12]

In recent years, a growing number of Western social scientists have reluctantly concluded that truly democratic regimes *are* less well equipped to survive the terrible political stresses in these societies and at the same time provide the rate of economic growth essential for their future.[13] This is not to say that democracy is impossible in these countries: Ceylon, Costa Rica, India, Lebanon, the Philippines, and Uruguay prove otherwise.[14] These are the exceptions, however, not the rule. Of fifty-three industrializing agrarian societies in 1967, only these six were full-fledged democracies. Several others were moving that way and might be called semidemocratic

[11] Halpern, *op. cit.*, p. 244.

[12] *Ibid.*

[13] See, for example, David Apter, *The Politics of Modernization* (Chicago: University of Chicago Press, 1965); or S. M. Lipset, *The First New Nation* (New York: Basic Books, 1963), p. 11. For a good bibliography on the subject, see the footnotes to the article by Charles Moskos and Wendell Bell, "Emerging Nations and Ideologies of American Social Scientists," *The American Sociologist*, 2 (1967), pp. 67–72. Moskos and Bell challenge the view cited above, but while their article serves as a valuable criticism of deterministic tendencies in some of their opponents (i.e., tendencies to deny that the liberal democratic model can *ever* be made to work in industrializing societies), their basic argument is not convincing.

[14] Moskos and Bell, *op. cit.*, fn. 11, mention a number of other industrializing countries they regard as democratic, but many of these are either industrial or industrializing horticultural societies, or inappropriate for other reasons (e.g., Greece has since fallen to a military junta).

Fig. 15/3 Modernizers have been a heterogeneous lot. Some have been military men like Nasser, some civilian nationalists like Nehru, a number have been Communists like Castro, while in at least one case—Iran—the monarch himself played this role

(especially Colombia, Panama, and Peru). A number of others contained democratic elements, but these were generally subordinated to authoritarian elements, both traditional and modern.

Even more serious, however, is the apparent inability of democratic regimes to keep up with the nondemocratic and mixed types in the vital area of economic growth. Data on eight industrializing agrarian democracies for the years 1960 to 1964 show their average annual rate of growth in real domestic product, on a per capita basis, as follows (in percentages):[15]

Brazil	1.5
Ceylon	−0.4
Chile	1.0
Greece	7.9
India	0.7
Jamaica	2.3
Philippines	0.8
Uruguay	−1.3

This list includes two countries that were subsequently taken over by military juntas (Brazil and Greece) and two that have since crossed our arbitrary boundary between industrial and industrializing societies (Chile and Jamaica). Even with these included, the median growth rate for these countries was only 0.9 per cent per year. By contrast, the median for twenty-five nondemocratic and mixed nations was 2.3 per cent.[16]

In the previous decade, from 1950 to 1959, there was a similar difference, though not quite so large. The median growth rate for seven then-democratic nations (Chile, Brazil, Ceylon, India, Pakistan, the Philippines, and Uruguay) was 1.4 per cent; for nineteen nondemocratic and mixed types it was 2.4 per cent.

Though these differences may appear quite modest, they actually mean that it would take more than a generation longer for some nations to double their per capita income than for others to do so. With a growth rate of 2.3 or 2.4 per cent per year compounded annually, this could be accomplished in slightly over thirty years; at a rate of 1.2 per cent (which is the weighted average of the rates from 1950 to 1964 for democratic nations) it would take sixty years. For people who no longer accept poverty as inevitable, this is probably too slow.

One cannot be dogmatic about the future, since nations, like individuals, are free to choose uneconomical alternatives (i.e., alternatives supported by other values, especially ideological ones). In general, however, the poorer an individual or nation, the likelier it is to prefer the alternative that is economically most attractive. This

---

[15] These and the following figures are from the United Nations, *Statistical Yearbook, 1965,* tables 183 and 184.

[16] These countries were Bolivia, Burma, Cambodia, Colombia, Cyprus, Ecuador, Guatemala, Haiti, Honduras, Iran, South Korea, Malaysia, Morocco, Nicaragua, Pakistan, Paraguay, Peru, Portugal, Southern Rhodesia, Syria, Taiwan, Thailand, Tunisia, Turkey, and South Vietnam.

suggests that democracy's prospects in the underdeveloped countries of the world are not very favorable for the near future. The *long-term* prospects, however, are much brighter. In part, this is because rapid economic growth appears to be much more compatible with democratic government in a prosperous nation than in a poor one. And even if this is not true, a prosperous nation, like a prosperous individual, can more easily afford the luxury of adopting the alternative it prefers even if it is not the most economically advantageous one.

Social stratification

Systems of stratification in industrializing agrarian societies are as varied as the polities and economies with which they are linked. Some are still predominantly agrarian in character (see Chapter 9), with only minor admixtures of modern elements. Others are much more modern, but even they differ in degree of modernization and in the extent to which the polity inclines toward the liberal democratic or the totalitarian model.

The composition of the upper class clearly reflects these variations. The stronger the traditional element in the polity and the less developed the economy, the more the upper class tends to be an aristocracy of long-established, wealthy, landowning families that consider the control of government, army, church, and other basic social institutions their natural right. Regardless of whether the government is constitutionally a monarchy, a republic, or a democracy, in fact it is an oligarchy.

The middle class is usually very small, consisting chiefly of merchants, lesser officials, lesser members of the religious establishment, and a small number of prosperous peasants. Increasingly, however, it also includes business and professional men with modern skills, members of the civil service with modern educational qualifications, and teachers trained in the newer disciplines.

With political modernization and greater industrialization, the leading members of these new occupations begin to penetrate the upper class. Some of the most successful businessmen rival or surpass the old aristocracy in terms of wealth, while politically active individuals begin to challenge the old elite's control of the government. This does not mean that the aristocracy accepts these new groups as their social equals; on the contrary, they reject them for as long as possible. The result is that there are, for a time, two largely separate and parallel systems of stratification. The traditional system is strongest in the rural areas, the newer one in the cities. With increasing modernization, however, the newer elements gradually become dominant politically, economically, and even socially, though the process is usually not completed until some time after the society has become fully industrialized.

In societies that adopt the totalitarian pattern, or lean in that direction, the old upper class is destroyed more quickly. Sometimes this is accomplished by imprisonment and execution, sometimes by confiscation of property and denial of access to political office. In these societies, just as in industrial societies under Communist control, the new political elite is the dominant class. It is an ironic footnote to history, however, that a disproportionate number of this new elite come from the upper and middle classes of the old regime.

As the foregoing suggests, industrialization and political modernization drastically alter the value of social resources. Landownership and membership in old aristocratic families lose much of their value. By contrast, modern education and membership in the modernizing party or movement become extremely important. In societies modeled after the liberal democracies, where large-scale private enterprise is permitted, ownership of factories, banks, and other large businesses is also a very valuable resource.

The value of modern education, especially training in engineering and science, is substantial in both totalitarian states and democracies. This has had one interesting, though almost certainly temporary, consequence: it places the younger generation in a relatively advantageous position. This advantage is often reinforced by the effects of political revolutions. Because they are usually the work of younger men who distrust the older generation and prefer to surround themselves with their age peers, revolutions tend to be followed by a period in which youth is an asset and younger men are promoted much more rapidly than they otherwise would be.

Among the lower classes in these societies, the major differences are the result of differences in economic development. The less economic development, the higher the percentage of peasants and the smaller the urban working class, especially those in factories and other modern industries. Conversely, the more economic development, the fewer peasants and the more urban workers. At one extreme, 80 to 95 per cent of the labor force in Nepal, Laos, Afghanistan, Haiti, and Iraq are still engaged in

Fig. 15/4   Upper-class housing, Colombia

agriculture and only a small percentage in industry.[17] At the opposite extreme, countries like Guyana, Cyprus, Ecuador, Portugal, and Cuba have only half or less of their workers in agriculture and 12 to 17 per cent in industry.

Cleavages and conflict

Few societies in history have been as seriously divided as the majority of those now undergoing industrialization. Most of them are torn not only by the ancient cleavages that have always existed in agrarian societies, but by others peculiar to societies industrializing at the present time.

Most basic of the older cleavages is the one between the few who control the nation's resources and the vast majority who supply the labor and receive in return little more than the bare necessities. The traditional cleavages between urban and rural populations and between the literate minority and the illiterate majority are also present, though in some ways they are less pronounced now because advances in transportation and communication have reduced the isolation, and hence the ignorance, of the rural and illiterate.

As we have already seen, the struggle to industrialize and modernize creates its own cleavages and conflicts. The more favored classes are divided between those educated along traditional lines and those with modern scientific and technical training. These groups have difficulty understanding one another and are mutually prejudiced. Another new cleavage separates the landowning aristocracy and the new elite of industrial entrepreneurs, many of whom surpass the older group in wealth.

---

[17] Russett et al., *op. cit.*, tables 50 and 53.

Fig. 15/5 Lower-class housing, exterior view, Rio de Janeiro, Brazil

Fig. 15/6 Lower-class housing, interior view, Rio de Janeiro, Brazil

As the patrimonial, monarchical system found in most agrarian societies breaks down, many new groups become politically active and many new issues become politically relevant. This is true even in societies where democratic principles are observed more in the breach than in practice. For example, the political unrest and other changes associated with industrialization often exacerbate historic tensions between religious and ethnic groups. One can see this in such widely scattered countries as Vietnam, Indonesia, India, Lebanon, Iraq, and Guyana, to name but a few whose interethnic or interreligious conflicts have been especially serious. The breakdown of the older political system and attempts to establish a democratic regime can also produce serious tensions between civilian political leaders and the military. Struggles between these groups have caused crises in many Latin American, Middle Eastern, and Asian nations. In more democratic countries, mass political parties have introduced yet another cleavage. Though support for the various parties tends to follow other lines of cleavage, it is seldom a simple reflection of them, and therefore causes further differences within an already badly divided population.[18]

---

[18] See, for example, Myron Weiner, *Party Building in a New Nation: The Indian National Congress* (Chicago: University of Chicago Press, 1967).

Finally, the rapid rate of change characteristic of industrializing societies invariably creates a cleavage between the generations. Though there are no valid measures, it appears to be more serious than its counterpart in already industrialized societies. This conclusion is suggested both by the frequency and bitterness of the conflicts between students and political authorities in these nations and by the frequency of revolutionary activity by "young Turks" (the Kemalists in Turkey after World War I, Nasser's associates in Egypt, the Fidelistas in Cuba, Ben Bella in Algeria, the early Apristas in Peru, etc.). This is, of course, what we would expect given the rapid pace of change in these countries. The experiences of the different generations, and hence the information and values on which they base their action, are so dissimilar that conflict is almost inevitable. As in industrial societies, universities are often centers of discontent because they bring together large numbers of people who not only have very little power, but who have had maximum exposure to new ideas. The result, not surprisingly, has often been explosive.

Education and progress

The importance of education for economic growth is now abundantly clear: the most prosperous nations are those that have invested heavily in education. Recent research shows that in the United States, Japan, and the Soviet Union—three of the most striking examples of economic growth—"high levels of national expenditure on education preceded industrialization."[19] In Czarist Russia as early as the end of the last century, 44 per cent of the men between 30 and 39 were literate, and in urban areas the figure was as high as 69 per cent. In Japan, half the male population was literate a generation before that; and in the United States 90 per cent of white adults were literate as early as 1840.

Other studies of the relation between education and economic progress reinforce this conclusion. A recent survey of 68 nations found a correlation of 0.42 between the percentage of children aged 5 to 19 attending school and the rate of annual growth of per capita production, and a correlation of 0.49 between the literacy rate and growth in per capita production.[20]

Developments in a number of industrializing countries, however, suggest that it is not enough for them simply to provide more education regardless of what kind it is. A number of countries have seriously overemphasized the humanities and classical forms of higher education at the expense of the sciences and engineering.[21] In one recent year, 34 per cent of the university students in Western Europe were

---

[19] Neil Smelser and S. M. Lipset (eds.), *Social Structure and Mobility in Economic Development* (Chicago: Aldine, 1966), pp. 29ff. Statistics cited in this paragraph are from the same source.

[20] See the Glossary for an explanation of correlation coefficients. The study cited is Russett et al., *op. cit.,* p. 277.

[21] See, for example, Smelser and Lipset, *op. cit.,* pp. 36ff.

studying science or engineering, compared to only 23 per cent in Asia and 16 per cent in Latin America.[22]

These proportions are important not only because the technical skills of scientists and engineers are essential to industrializing societies, but because these societies have so much trouble absorbing the growing number of nontechnical professionals they turn out. In India, for example, 58 per cent of the students were recently enrolled in the humanities, fine arts, and law.[23] When they graduate, many of these young people cannot find jobs that utilize their skills and, unwilling to accept lesser employment (a reflection of the traditional value system of agrarian elites and would-be elites, who disdain most forms of work), they become a kind of intellectual proletariat with deep-seated hostilities toward the existing social order. Because such people are easily attracted to revolutionary movements, there is increased political instability, and this in turn hampers economic progress. In short, far from aiding economic growth, an oversupply of nontechnically trained students in a society can actually hinder it.

One might well ask why the leaders of these societies allow this kind of educational imbalance to develop. There are several reasons. First, in allowing the humanities to dominate their educational systems, they are copying the oldest and most prestigious educational institutions in the world—Oxford, Cambridge, and the famous continental universities—as well as their own native traditions. Second, it costs much more to provide technical education, and these nations have very limited resources. Finally, it has not been very long since the nature of this problem first became evident. It is to be hoped that with the information now available to them, these nations will begin to revise their educational programs.

Belief systems and ideologies

Most leaders of modernizing movements are convinced that social and economic progress requires more than increased capital and improved techniques of production. Equally important are new creeds and new gods to arouse and mobilize the common people, who for centuries, sunk in lethargy and apathy, have taken a fatalistic view of life. Ironically, even such a dogmatic and supposedly orthodox Marxist as Mao Tse-tung has come to place the spiritual struggle for men's minds and souls on a par with, or even ahead of, the struggle to transform the economy. Max Weber's thesis about the importance of beliefs in a nation's economic development seems to have found greater acceptance among the leaders of developing nations than it has among social scientists.

Today, in all but the most backward parts of the industrializing agrarian world, there is an intellectual ferment and clash of ideas between the advocates of tradi-

---

[22] *Ibid.*, p. 37. In the Soviet Union, the figure has been as high as 46 per cent.

[23] *Ibid.*

Fig. 15/7   Two faiths

tional belief systems and the proponents of newer ones. The situation is often extremely complicated because both traditionalists and modernizers are themselves each divided on many points, while still others favor various blends of the old and the new.

Much of the intellectual and ideological resistance to modernization has come from advocates of the traditional faiths. In south and east Asia, this means Buddhism, Hinduism, and sometimes Islam; in the Middle East, Islam or sometimes Eastern Orthodoxy; in Latin America and Portugal, Roman Catholicism. In all of these areas, religious leaders have often been leaders in conservative and traditionalist movements as well. This is hardly surprising, considering the historic role of these groups in agrarian societies and the nature of their beliefs. All of them tend to see man's quest for truth as essentially complete: what men need to know has already been revealed—in the Vedas, or in the Koran, or to the Sangha, or to the Church. True wisdom, therefore, lies in turning to the religious authorities for guidance and in following their directions. In describing the traditionalist approach to education in the Middle East today, one writer has said:

> Education, as far as it is under the control of the ulema [the spiritual leaders of the Muslim community], is still bound up with authoritarianism, rote learning, and a rigid devotion to ancient authorities—providing only already known solutions to already formulated problems.[24]

Much the same could be said of traditionalist education in Latin America and south and east Asia. Those who approach education this way see little need for change, unless it is to root out whatever modernizing influences have crept in.

---

[24] Halpern, *op. cit.*, p. 122.

In the late nineteenth and early twentieth centuries, many Western intellectuals thought these older faiths would simply die out as their adherents came to recognize the "obvious" superiority of Western creeds such as Protestantism, humanism, and communism. All three of these newer faiths were then winning converts, especially among the better educated, and it seemed to be only a matter of time until the older faiths would vanish altogether.

Since World War I, however, and even more since World War II, the situation has changed drastically in many areas, especially in North Africa, the Middle East, and south and east Asia. With the growth of nationalist movements and a growing resistance to colonialism of every kind, many of the traditional faiths have experienced a remarkable reinvigoration. After Ceylon won its independence, for example, a number of Christian converts there reconverted to Buddhism. In India, Hindu traditionalist forces have become strong enough to outlaw the entry of foreign missionaries. In Egypt, Nasser imprisoned or executed most of the leaders of the Communist Party.

In some instances, reinvigoration has come about because of reform movements within the religious group itself. Vatican Council II, for example, provided a powerful impetus to modernizers within the Roman Catholic Church in Latin America, giving the church renewed vigor in a number of countries, particularly in Chile.[25] Though professional religious leaders have been the most conspicuous proponents of traditionalism, they have usually had strong support from the old governing class, especially from the large landowners. In fact, the rural population as a whole has generally supported them; it has not taken much imagination for these people to see that industrialization would render most of their skills obsolete. For similar reasons, members of the old "professions"—for example, midwives, herbalists, and practitioners of traditional medicine—have been strong supporters of traditionalist ideologies and belief systems.

Ranged against people like these are individuals and groups who by virtue of educational, occupational, or other experience have been converted to the newer faiths. Early in a modernization movement, a disproportionate number of the leaders are people who have been converted through visits to industrialized societies, either as students or workers.[26] Later, however, most of the leaders are individuals who have been won over by experiences right in their own countries. Frequently they are children of members of the old governing class, gravitating, after conversion, to positions of leadership because of their superior training and other resources.

As noted earlier, there are usually competing movements within the camp of modernizers, some advocating Western-style democracy, others the socialist or

---

[25] See, for example, Ivan Vallier, "Religious Elites: Differentiations and Developments in Roman Catholicism," in S. M. Lipset and Aldo Solari, *Elites in Latin America* (New York: Oxford, 1967), pp. 190–232; or William V. D'Antonio and Frederick B. Pike (eds.), *Religion, Revolution, and Reform* (New York: Praeger, 1964).

[26] For Latin America, see Robert E. Scott, "Political Elites and Political Modernization: The Crisis of Transition," in Lipset and Solari, *op. cit.*, p. 133.

Communist model, still others some kind of hybrid system. The liberal Western model was the first to be advocated in most industrializing agrarian nations. It has won its greatest support from the more prosperous segments of the new middle class—professional men, managers in new industries, and others with modern education. Socialist and Communist movements were usually introduced next. Their support has been greatest among intellectuals and the economically insecure—landless peasants, underemployed or unemployed urban workers, etc.

The hybrid approach to modernization is the most recent and reflects the negative reactions of the current generation of leaders to both of the older models. This approach seeks to synthesize not only liberalism and totalitarianism, but modernism and traditionalism as well. The traditionalist component is clear in most of the nationalist ideologies that have flourished throughout the industrializing agrarian world since World War II. To some extent, nationalism is a natural reaction against colonialism, and crucial in the process of nation-building. This is especially true of countries that remained under foreign control until recently.

But there is more to modern nationalism than this. It is also an effort to reassert the importance of the cultural traditions of non-European peoples (or, in the case of Latin America, of peoples not in the Anglo-American tradition). This helps heal the breach between traditionalists and modernists by providing a middle position that is more or less acceptable to both. Moreover, it gives dignity to a nation's leaders in their relations with European (or Anglo-American) peoples. In this respect, the function of these nationalist movements is similar to that of the "black nationalist" movement in the United States, which seeks to increase the self-respect of black people by emphasizing the worth of the black cultural tradition.

Unfortunately, the deliberate cultivation of nationalist sentiments easily leads to the hatred of other nations. Even when this is not a spontaneous development, hard-pressed leaders of industrializing nations may encourage it solely to divert criticism from themselves and their policies. It is easy to blame "devilish neighbors" for all the defects and shortcomings, inevitable and otherwise, of one's own nation. A number of leaders in industrializing nations have succumbed to the temptation to do this; but as the experiences of Sukarno in Indonesia and certain Arab leaders in the Middle East demonstrate, this policy is not without risks of its own.

INDUSTRIALIZING HORTICULTURAL SOCIETIES

Prior to the modern era, advanced horticultural societies were found in several locations in the New World, most of Africa south of the Sahara, and some parts of southeast Asia. But during the last several centuries, more advanced societies conquered a number of these groups (as in the case of the Incas and Aztecs) and destroyed others by sociocultural assimilation (the fate of many backward hill tribes in India).[27]

---

[27] See, for example, F. G. Bailey, *Tribe, Caste, and Nation* (Manchester, England: Manchester University Press, 1960).

In Africa south of the Sahara, however, things have been different. There, much of the traditional horticultural way of life has survived into the second half of the twentieth century, apparently because the period of European colonial rule was so brief and its impact on most of the native societies relatively limited. We easily forget that the period of European rule in most of sub-Saharan Africa began only in the latter part of the nineteenth century and ended early in the second half of the twentieth. Hence the process of institutional disintegration and transformation in these societies was just beginning. By contrast, many of the horticultural societies in the New World and southeast Asia have been under alien control since the sixteenth century or longer. For this reason, the concept of industrializing horticultural societies is really applicable only in Africa south of the Sahara.

These societies and industrializing agrarian societies have problems that are similar in a number of respects. Both types are confronted with a variety of radically new social and cultural elements introduced by diffusion from technologically more advanced societies. Both find that these new elements throw their traditional relations out of kilter and create serious tensions. Furthermore, both experience an almost continuous state of crisis because things are changing so fast.

At the same time, there are a number of important differences between them that reflect their horticultural and agrarian backgrounds and that cause them to respond differently, in many instances, to the impact of industrialization. To avoid unnecessary repetition, we will focus chiefly on these differences, referring only briefly to the points of similarity. Unless this is kept in mind, it may appear in what follows that the differences between industrializing agrarian and industrializing horticultural societies are greater than they actually are.

Technology and productivity

Technologically, industrializing horticultural societies are much less advanced than industrializing agrarian, especially in their indigenous technology. This is revealed in a number of ways. For one thing, they are much less urbanized. In one year recently, industrializing agrarian societies had an average of 18 per cent of their populations in cities of 20,000 or more while industrializing horticultural had only 5 per cent.[28] This is important, because the size of the urban population is a good measure of the growth of specialized crafts and of trade and commerce. In the average industrializing horticultural society, therefore, many more people are engaged in producing the most rudimentary necessities, especially food and fibers: 85 to 90 per cent of the labor force, compared with about 65 per cent in an industrializing agrarian society.[29]

---

[28] Calculations based on Russett, *op. cit.*, table 9. The figures shown are medians.

[29] *Ibid.*, table 50, plus George Horner, "Selected Cultural Barriers to the Modernization of Labor," in William H. Lewis (ed.), *French-Speaking Africa: the Search for Identity* (New York: Walker, 1965), p. 171. The figures are medians.

Fig. 15/8 Harvesting in a cocoa grove, Ghana. Like many underdeveloped nations, Ghana is heavily dependent on a single crop; 62 per cent of its foreign exchange comes from cocoa

Another indication of the technological and economic lag of horticultural societies is their low level of productivity. Their backwardness in this respect is not evident in most of the standard measures of productivity, such as per capita income. Using this measure, countries like Ghana, Liberia, the Congo, or Kenya appear to be at least as productive as China, India, Burma, or most of the other industrializing agrarian societies of southeast Asia. However, per capita measures of productivity are simply inadequate for determining the level of technological development, because they fail to take into account the greater population density that agrarian technologies and economies sustain. With these measures, we unwittingly destroy some of the prime evidence of their technological superiority.

A much better measure of technological development in industrializing societies is *per area* income. The question then becomes: How much can the society produce per square mile of territory? There is some distortion even in this measure because of the influence of large deserts and other unproductive territories. But while this may appreciably affect the figures for a particular society, its effect on large groups of them is not great. Figures on gross national product show nearly a fivefold difference in the productivity of the two types of societies. In forty-nine industrializing agrarian nations, the median value of the gross national product was

$10,400 per square mile; in sixteen industrializing horticultural nations, it was only $2,200.[30]

Population and standards of living

Despite the greater technological efficiency of the average industrializing agrarian society, its standard of living is often no higher than in industrializing horticultural societies because, as we noted above, its population is so much larger. With an economy five times more productive than the typical industrializing horticultural society, its population is also about five times denser per cultivatable acre, thus effectively precluding any improvement in the standard of living. Before the invention of modern methods of contraception, this growth in population was, of course, almost inevitable.

Under present conditions, the low population densities of industrializing horticultural societies may well be one of their greatest assets. Unlike industrializing agrarian societies, they are not saddled with huge populations that must be put to work even though their employment reduces the level of productive efficiency (as in the case of peasants working excessively subdivided farms[31]). In the race to industrialize and modernize, while most of the advantages—literacy, skilled manpower, commercial experience, urbanization, and so on—lie with industrializing agrarian societies, this one, at least, belongs to industrializing horticultural societies. Considering how serious the population problem is and how easily it can erase the benefits of increased productivity, it is just possible that in the long run this single advantage may prove as important as all the advantages on the other side.

At present, the birthrates in most sub-Saharan societies appear to be close to the human maximum (i.e., 40 or more per thousand population). Death rates, meanwhile, have dropped considerably from the old equilibrium level; although there is little reliable data, they are currently estimated to be somewhere around 20 per thousand. The average annual rate of population increase, therefore, is about 2 per cent per year, a dangerously high rate, but still a little lower, apparently, than in Latin America and the Middle East.[32]

The economy

Because the urban sector of the economy in horticultural societies is much less developed than in agrarian societies, its population has had even less experience

---

[30] Calculations based on GNP data in Russett, *op. cit.*, table 43, and area data in U.S. Department of Commerce, *Statistical Abstract of the United States, 1966* (Washington: Government Printing Office, 1966), table 1287, and *The World Almanac, 1952*, pp. 289ff.

[31] See the statement on p. 434 above concerning Egypt's peasants. By contrast, see E. A. G. Robinson (ed.), *Economic Development for Africa South of the Sahara* (New York: St. Martin's, 1964), p. 123; or Guy Hunter, *The New Societies of Africa* (New York: Oxford, 1962), pp. 193ff.

[32] See United Nations, *Demographic Yearbook, 1963*, table 23, and United Nations, *Growth of World Industry*, chap. 4, table 4.

with such fundamentals of modern life as money, trade and commerce, markets, occupational specialization, literacy, and bureaucracy. This makes it very difficult for modernizing governments and businesses to find skilled personnel to staff their organizations. The problem is especially serious in an era of nationalism (and nationalism is just as strong in these societies as in industrializing agrarian societies), because national pride often demands that businesses and government be staffed with native personnel even at the expense of organizational efficiency.[33]

Data on literacy provide some idea of the magnitude of the difference between industrializing agrarian and horticultural societies in these matters. In the late 1950s, 44 per cent of the adult population in the average (median) industrializing agrarian society was literate; in industrializing horticultural societies the comparable figure was 7.5 per cent.[34] Assuming literacy as a minimum requirement for effective participation in modern economic life and assuming also that these nations will not be able to increase their rate of literacy any faster than other nations have done, it appears that it will take industrializing agrarian societies at least fifty years to develop a qualified labor force and industrializing horticultural societies at least ninety.[35]

The horticultural background of these societies creates still other problems for their economic development. The reasons become evident when we compare the nature and meaning of work in traditional horticultural and modern industrial

---

[33] See, for example, Gwendolen Carter (ed.), *African One-Party States* (Ithaca, N. Y.: Cornell, 1962), pp. 371ff. and 461ff.; Hunter, *op. cit.*, chap. 9, especially pp. 223 ff.; International Bank for Reconstruction and Development, *The Economic Development of Uganda* (Baltimore: Johns Hopkins Press, 1962), pp. 23–24; or Ken Post, *The New States of West Africa* (Baltimore: Penguin, 1964), chap. 6.

[34] Calculations based on Russett et al., *op. cit.*, table 64. The figures are based on 55 industrializing agrarian societies and 16 industrializing horticultural.

[35] Russett et al., *op. cit.*, table 65, provide data on the average annual increase in the rate of literacy for 43 countries since about 1920. The median increase is 0.7 per cent per year; only 9 countries of the 43 had a rate in excess of 1.0 per cent.

Fig. 15/9 Medical laboratory, Louvanium University, Leopoldville, Republic of the Congo

societies. Not long ago, the Inter-African Labour Institute characterized work traditions in horticultural Africa this way:

1. Work is viewed in its relation to the basic institution of family or clan; within the family, it is divided on the basis of age and sex.
2. Work is linked with religious rites.
3. Work activities are considered and evaluated in the light of a subsistence economy rather than a profit economy (i.e., one oriented to the production of the necessities of life rather than to the maximization of profits in a market economy).
4. Work requires neither foresight nor planning.
5. Time is largely irrelevant in work activities; no time-limits are set for most tasks.
6. There is little specialization.
7. For men, work is episodic; when a task has to be done, men often do it without a break, but intervals of inactivity are long and frequent.
8. Men hardly ever work alone; work activities (e.g., hunting parties and work parties) often resemble a collective leisure activity in modern industrial society.[36]

These traditions do little to prepare the members of these societies, especially the men, for the demands of work in a modern industrial society. A parallel list of the characteristics of work activities in industrial societies would, in fact, be an almost perfect contradiction.

One of the biggest problems is suggested by item 7 above. In analyzing horticultural societies, we saw how often farming is primarily women's work. Men's responsibility may be limited to the occasional clearing of new fields. Since women do the sustained, tedious chores—planting, cultivating, and harvesting crops—men are free to do more interesting and exciting things—hunting, fighting, politicking, socializing, and participating in ceremonial activities. The disciplined, routinized, and tedious forms of work encountered in an industrial economy are seldom encountered by men in these societies. In this respect, the peasant farmers of agrarian societies are far better prepared. Yet even they have found the transition difficult.[37]

There is tremendous economic and social variation in sub-Saharan Africa today. At one extreme there are still a few tribes and villages that have been virtually untouched by the influences of industrialization; at the other, cities like Dar es Salaam where the older patterns have been all but destroyed.[38] In between is every

---

[36] Based on Inter-African Labour Institute, *The Human Factors of Productivity in Africa*, as summarized in Lewis, *op. cit.*, p. 168. Many of these propositions were supported in papers presented to a recent conference on competing demands for labor in traditional African societies, cosponsored by the Joint Committee on African Studies of the Social Science Research Council, the American Council of Learned Societies, and the Agricultural Development Council. See William O. Jones, "Labor and Leisure in Traditional African Societies," *Social Science Research Council Items*, 22 (March, 1968), pp. 1–6.

[37] See, for example, J. L. Hammond and Barbara Hammond, *The Town Labourer, 1760–1832* (London: Guild Books, 1949, first published 1917), especially chap. 2.

[38] On the latter, see, for example, J. A. K. Leslie's fascinating study, *A Survey of Dar es Salaam* (New York: Oxford, 1963).

conceivable combination of the old and the new—such as the woman in Nairobi who practiced witchcraft in order to earn the down payment on a truck so she could go into the trucking business.[39] (A more common pattern is for a person to work part-time in a factory while continuing to practice traditional horticulture.)

One observer reports that there have been four basic economic patterns in Africa in recent years.[40] The first, which is now extremely rare, is the pure subsistence economy in which the local village consumes only what it produces or obtains through barter with its neighbors. The second pattern he calls "taxed subsistence," in which a cash crop is raised, or young men sent out to work for cash, to pay taxes levied by the government. The third might be called a mixed economy: villagers still rely on a subsistence economy for their basic necessities, but simultaneously work for cash—not only because of taxes, but so they can buy modern consumer goods. The fourth pattern is a predominantly cash economy in which even food is bought and laborers are hired to work on the farms.

These patterns, which typically follow one another in sequence, show how internal and external forces combine to transform a society's economy. On one side there are the preferences and desires of the local population; on the other, the demands and attractions introduced by alien groups and institutions. Outsiders sometimes underestimate the power of the internal forces and interpret economic development as a process forced on reluctant villagers who want nothing more than to be left alone to live as their fathers did for centuries. But the problem is far more complex than this romanticized view suggests. Given a choice, most horticultural peoples choose the industrial way of life—sometimes *in toto*, like the family that migrates to the city; sometimes in part, like the couple that stays in the village but earns all the cash they can to buy modern tools, cloth, soap, a sewing machine, a radio, a bicycle, and the other products of an industrial economy.

The polity

One of the striking features of sub-Saharan Africa is how young most of its societies are: almost without exception, they were established in the late nineteenth or the twentieth centuries. Most of them are the products of European colonialism, and their boundaries are the result of the rivalries of missions or colonial governments, the outcomes of battles, the location of rivers, and a variety of other things, most of which had little to do with the boundaries of the societies they replaced. Actually, the process was not too different from the one that produced most of the modern nations of Europe, Asia, and the New World.

Because of their newness, most African societies suffer from serious internal divisions that stem from traditional tribal loyalties. The colonial powers seldom destroyed the older tribal groups. On the contrary, they usually preserved them as

---

[39] Hunter, *op. cit.*, p. 85.

[40] *Ibid.*, p. 94.

instruments of administrative control, with tribal rulers serving as lower echelon officials in the new colonial societies. The fiction of their autonomy was often maintained in order to put the burden, and the onus, of social control on these leaders. Not infrequently, tribal rivalries were encouraged as an application of the ancient principle "Divide and rule." As a result, even after independence was won, there was a fundamental tension between tribal loyalties and national loyalties in most parts of Africa. This problem is one that few industrializing agrarian societies have had to contend with.

Fig. 15/10   Tribal chief on visit to Monrovia, capital of Liberia

The consequences have been serious for most sub-Saharan societies, however. In the Congo, tribal divisions nearly destroyed the new society in its first few years of independence. In the case of Nigeria the fuse burned more slowly, but the result was more serious. In most other countries, it remains an important divisive force, sometimes with the potential for civil war.[41] When they were still fighting for independence, many African leaders (as well as their friends in the Western academic world) ignored or minimized the importance of these tribal loyalties, thinking that their countrymen valued them as little as they did and that the ties were rapidly losing their vitality. Although this seems to be true in a few countries, it has proved a serious misjudgment in most.[42] Even in cities and towns, tribal loyalties are still meaningful to some degree.[43] In the light of American experience with ethnic loyalties, and considering the virtual absence of national institutions in Africa until recently, this is hardly surprising. However, with increasing urbanization, with the establishment of schools that indoctrinate children in a nationalistic outlook, and with the growth of the mass media to reinforce these early lessons, we can expect the eventual disappearance of tribal loyalties. But this will probably take decades and in the meantime these allegiances will probably produce many bitter conflicts.

In other respects, the polities of industrializing horticultural societies have a lot in common with those of industrializing agrarian. Attempts at planning, even basic administrative activities, are often hamstrung by the lack of trained personnel and by policies which require the rapid Africanization of the civil service. This is especially serious because most of these governments are committed to programs of economic planning and development.[44]

Another important similarity is the trend that one writer has referred to as "the erosion of democracy."[45] Prior to independence most political leaders in these countries professed to be democrats in the Western European sense (i.e., believers in parliamentary government, a multiparty system, free elections, etc.). Very soon, however, confronted by opposition which threatened to turn them out of office or by incipient chaos resulting from the tribalization of politics and the return to power of tribal chiefs and the other proponents of traditionalism, most of them retreated to an advocacy of a one-party state with control largely or wholly in the hands of a strong executive (i.e., themselves). In a number of countries, civilian government was terminated and leadership assumed by the military (though in some instances this

---

[41] See, for example, Aristide Zolberg, *One-Party Government in the Ivory Coast* (Princeton, N.J.: Princeton University Press, 1964), pp. 202ff. and 286f.; Hunter, *op. cit.*, pp. 286–298; or Lucy Mair, *New Nations* (Chicago: University of Chicago Press, 1963), pp. 114–122.

[42] See, for example, Brian Weinstein, *Gabon: Nation-Building on the Ogooue* (Cambridge, Mass.: M.I.T., 1966).

[43] See Leslie, *op. cit.*, p. 32; or Merran Fraenkel, *Tribe and Class in Monrovia* (London: Oxford, 1964), especially chap. 3.

[44] See Apter, *op. cit.*, pp. 130 and 328–330; or Hunter, *op. cit.*, p. 289.

[45] Mair, *op. cit.*, pp. 122ff.

may have been a step toward the restoration of democratic government, as in the case of Ghana).

Although many of the new governments have survived intact thus far, the pressures on them are growing more intense. One British observer has outlined the nature of the process:

> As a new African government first assumes power, there seems to be much in its favor. There is enthusiasm, there are congratulations and good wishes from the world; many promotions to make, ambassadorships to be filled, national development plans to occupy energies and give a sense of progress and achievement. Above all, it is an African government, it is "ours."
>
> But there is a debit side. Naturally, the age-old frustrations of being governed were turned against the colonial power over years of agitation and electioneering. The anti-colonial struggle had aroused much expectation of greater freedom from restraint which is not compatible with the other goals of the nationalist movement. Nervous [foreigners] had often quoted the wilder expectations of the uneducated ("We shall print more bank notes"; "The Bank will be nationalized and forced to give us loans") and as caricature these stories are not important. But there is a more serious side. In rural areas there could be great impatience with continuing agricultural reform; and in the modern sector much expectation of a quick inheritance of opportunities and profits of expatriate trade [i.e., businesses owned by foreigners]. And there are other reversals. The Trade Unions, once a weapon of anti-colonialism, may seem to be sabotaging the national effort.[46]

He goes on to describe the problems national leaders face in trying to control the self-seekers within their party organization: "The imposition of a standard of conduct and discipline is a trying task for a victorious party." But these are all secondary compared to the really serious problems forced on them. Though they take different forms in different countries, these are common to most: "tribalism; the conflict between traditional and modern—the old authority and the new democratic forms; the whole control and status of land; the whole system of local administration; and ultimately, the moral standards and social norms which are to be established in society."[47] With the elimination of the colonial regime, all the hostilities are now focused on the new national governments—and this is sometimes more than they can cope with.

Social stratification

Most of the new nations in sub-Saharan Africa profess socialist ideals. This does not mean, however, any real concern with the elimination of economic inequality. Rather, as one writer says, "quite often . . . the socialism of Africa is another name

---

[46] From *The New Societies of Africa*, pp. 286–287, by Guy Hunter, published by Oxford University Press under the auspices of the Institute of Race Relations, by permission of Oxford University Press.

[47] *Ibid.*, p. 288.

for nationalism. The common element of the various forms of [African] socialism . . . is the emphasis on development goals for which individuals must make sacrifices."[48] Another observer puts it even more strongly:

> There is . . . little or no emphasis on the moral aspects of socialism, the gap between rich and poor. In Tropical Africa as a whole . . . the salaries and perquisites of the ruling group and of the whole professional and educated class are at or near the old [colonial] level, the profits of contractors and politicians are enormous, while very large sections of the economy remain at the old levels. Despite constant inquiry, we could find little evidence of "socialist" thinking in this moral sense, save among a few of the younger intellectuals in Lagos and Accra. . . .[49]

As in industrializing agrarian societies, patterns of stratification vary according to the relative political strength of the modernizing forces and the older forces of traditionalism. Where the latter are dominant, as in northern Nigeria, the upper class is made up of the rulers of the old society: the chiefs, kings, or emirs, together with their ministers and retainers. Where the modernizers are in control (the more typical situation), the upper class is largely made up of the new political and intellectual elite and, in most countries, the new entrepreneurial elite. The intellectual elite is the tiny minority with higher education—professional men, higher civil servants, and the like.[50]

Beneath the economically and politically dominant class, there are two fairly distinct systems of stratification. In the rural areas, where the traditional patterns prevail, an individual's status is largely a function of his own or his family's relation to traditional authorities (the village headman, the tribal chief, etc.). In urban areas, where the modern system of stratification is centered, education, occupation, income, and connections with the new political authorities are usually crucial.[51]

Cleavages and conflict

By now it should be clear that few societies in history have been more badly divided than the industrializing horticultural societies of the latter part of the twentieth century. Like industrializing agrarian societies, they are heir to nearly all of the

---

[48] Apter, *op. cit.,* p. 329.

[49] From *The New Societies of Africa,* p. 289, by Guy Hunter, published by Oxford University Press under the auspices of the Institute of Race Relations, by permission of Oxford University Press. See also Daniel Bell, "Socialism," in *International Encyclopedia of the Social Sciences* (New York: Macmillan and Free Press, 1968), vol. 14, pp. 528–529.

[50] See, for example, C. C. Wrigley, "The Changing Economic Structure of Buganda," in L. A. Fallers (ed.), *The King's Men: Leadership and Status in Buganda on the Eve of Independence* (New York: Oxford, 1964), pp. 52–53; or Fraenkel, *op. cit.,* chap. 6.

[51] Just as in industrial societies, status inconsistencies often develop. See, especially, Fraenkel, *op. cit.,* pp. 203–211. Their effects remain to be studied.

Fig. 15/11 Where the modernizers are in control, the upper class is largely made up of the new political and intellectual elite: Jomo Kenyatta, first Prime Minister of Kenya and graduate of the London School of Economics

cleavages of traditional societies as well as being subject to those of modern industrial societies. In one respect, however, their situation is even worse than the agrarian: because they are such young nations, loyalties to the older, smaller units—the tribal groupings that until recently were autonomous societies—remain strong. This introduces a powerful divisive force involving deep emotional commitments, which are always difficult to control by rational, political procedures. But time is on the side of the advocates of national unity: with each passing year, the hold of the older loyalties weakens. Therefore, if civil war can be avoided for the next several decades, the problem will probably be resolved in most of these societies.

Religion and ideology

The traditional religions of sub-Saharan Africa were relatively undeveloped, both organizationally and intellectually. There were no complex organizations of priests or monks as in the major religions of the agrarian world, no body of sacred writings to serve as the core of a common faith, no tradition of religio-philosophical speculation, and, most important of all, no supranational faith uniting the members of different societies. As a result, the older native faiths could not easily defend themselves against the inroads of Islam and Christianity, especially when they were introduced by peoples who were politically and economically stronger and whose way of life, therefore, seemed so obviously worthy of emulation.

Africans who still cling to the older tribal faiths are usually the residents of the more isolated rural areas and the less educated residents of the towns. Since this describes the majority of the people in these societies, adherents of the older faiths are obviously still numerous. In the Congo, for example, only 36 per cent are Christians or Muslims, in Nigeria 45 per cent, and in Dahomey 20 per cent.[52] Among the modernizing elements of the urban population, however, the picture is very different. In Dar es Salaam, a city of 100,000 in Tanzania, a recent survey showed that 99.8 per cent of the population claim to be either Muslim or Christian—and this in a country still 60 per cent non-Muslim and non-Christian.[53] Similarly, on the other side of Africa, in Monrovia (the capital of Liberia), 72 per cent regard themselves as either Christians or Muslims, although in the country as a whole, only 9 per cent do so.[54]

Conversions to Islam and Christianity are frequently for nonreligious reasons. For many, it is simply a status symbol, a means to identify with modern ways and avoid being regarded as an ignorant, backward countryman. In Dar es Salaam, for example, many pagan tribesmen "on arrival in town call themselves Muslims—some few call themselves Christians—in order to conform, not to be conspicuous in a [community] where Islam is supreme and where to 'have no religion,' as people put it, is the mark of the uncivilized. Some go so far as to be circumcised and to be formally admitted to Islam: most merely use a Muslim name instead of a tribal one; some have two names, a Christian and a Muslim, to cover all eventualities."[55] Under the circumstances, it is hardly surprising to find that "the outward observances of religion are strikingly absent in Dar es Salaam: it is rare to see an African Muslim praying his daily prayers . . . in Ramadhan [the Muslim month of fasting] people may be seen anywhere eating and drinking publicly during the daily hours [a forbidden practice]," and the consumption of alcohol, also forbidden, is almost universal.[56] In Monrovia, where Christianity is dominant, the pattern is not quite so

---

[52] Figures based on Russett et al., *op. cit.*, tables 74 and 75.

[53] The figure for Dar es Salaam is from Leslie, *op. cit.*, p. 210; that for Tanzania from Russett et al., *op. cit.*, tables 74 and 75.

[54] Fraenkel, *op. cit.*, p. 154; and Russett et al., *op. cit.*, tables 74 and 75.

[55] From *A Survey of Dar es Salaam*, p. 211, by J. A. K. Leslie, published by Oxford University Press, by permission of Oxford University Press.

[56] *Ibid.*, pp. 210–211.

pronounced, but even here "the professing of Christianity remains a basic require-ment of 'civilized' status," and "for a great many of the civilized, church membership has become largely a question of social status, and has little more significance than membership [in] other types of associations."[57] In many areas, both urban and rural, even those who have adopted Christianity or Islam continue traditional pagan practices.[58]

In the early years of colonial rule, Christian missions were an important force for modernization. This was due primarily to the mission schools, which introduced literacy and elements of Western culture and, most important of all, opened up a channel of communication to the larger world. As a result, the areas that came under Christian influence advanced more rapidly than those where paganism or Islam prevailed. In discussing Tanzania, one writer asserts:

> Mission schools and mission hospitals have been very important factors in changing tribal society, although their influence has been felt much more strongly in some areas than others. Very nearly a one-to-one correlation exists between mission influence, the cash-crop economy, fertile land, education, and the general desire for progress.[59]

Similarly, many visitors to Africa have commented on the singular success of the Christian Ibo of southeastern Nigeria (or Biafra) compared to the Muslim and pagan tribes to the north.

With the rise of the independence movement after World War II, identification with Christianity became a more ambiguous social attribute. Christianity was linked with colonialism, and colonialism was, by definition, a force holding Africa back. The missionaries came under heavy attack for dominating the churches and refusing to allow native Christians to advance to positions of leadership. Furthermore, in an era of great social turmoil and insecurity, mission-brand Christianity often seemed too tame and too Western. In many areas, native leaders founded new sects, some basically Christian, others largely pagan, many a mixture of the two.[60] These sects usually have their greatest appeal for individuals who are in midpassage in the difficult transition from traditional culture to modern. Such people are subject to great insecurity, both economically and intellectually, and the sects often provide an element of reassurance. They are also popular because of their acceptance of polygyny and certain other traditional African practices that have been condemned by the missionaries.

---

[57] Fraenkel, *op. cit.*, pp. 158 and 162.

[58] Hunter, *op. cit.*, p. 74, provides numerous examples.

[59] Carter, *op. cit.*, pp. 433–434. © 1962 by Cornell University. Used by permission of Cornell University Press.

[60] See, for example, Vittorio Lanternari, *The Religions of the Oppressed: A Study of Modern Messianic Cults*, trans. by Lisa Sergio (New York: Knopf, 1963), chap. 1; or Mair, *op. cit.*, pp. 171ff.

In sub-Saharan Africa, as in other industrializing areas, nontheistic faiths also compete with the older faiths. The most important of these is nationalism. In many cases, nationalism does not demand supreme loyalty but functions simply as a secular ideology. Sometimes, however, it becomes a matter of ultimate loyalty and assumes a truly religious character. In Ghana, for example, Nkrumah assumed messianic titles while his party (the Convention People's party) took on quasi-religious functions.[61] This tendency is so marked that some students of the modernization process now speak of *political* religion in contrast to *church* religion.[62] Whether nationalism will survive in this extreme form no one can say. Its chances are probably closely linked with the fate of the new nation's efforts to modernize: the quicker and easier the modernization process, the poorer the chances for an extreme nationalism; the slower the change, and the more painful, the likelier it becomes.

Kinship and family

In the traditional horticultural societies of precolonial Africa, extended family groups were extremely important. As one writer put it, in Africa "the [extended family] was the basic building block of society."[63] More than that, it was psychologically the center of the individual's world, establishing his identity and defining most of his basic rights and responsibilities.

Now with industrialization and modernization, the historic bases of power of the extended family are being destroyed. In the modern sector of the economy, the extended family no longer controls the individual's access to the means of livelihood the way it did in the traditional economy by its control of land. Similarly, in the area of government, family ties lose much of their value in dealings with an increasingly impersonal government bureaucracy. Last but not least, the cult of the ancestors, centered in the extended family, declines in importance as Christianity and Islam grow.

Under the old system, most of the advantages of the extended family were enjoyed by the older generation, while the disadvantages fell disproportionately on the younger. Before the growth of cities and towns, young people had no choice but to accept the burdens and patiently wait the day when they would become the privileged elders. Industrialization changed all this: at the very least, it offered youth an escape from the authority of the elders; at best, a rise to fame and fortune beyond the wildest dreams of those who stayed behind in the villages.

We get some idea of how conditions have changed from the following excerpt from a document that an African townsman wrote, explaining to a European why

---

[61] The same has been true of Sekou Toure's Democratic party in Guinea. See, for example, Apter, *op. cit.*, p. 299, fn. 36.

[62] *Ibid.*, chap. 8.

[63] L. A. Fallers, "Social Stratification in Traditional Buganda," in Fallers, *op. cit.*, p. 99.

Africans leave the villages. In it, he describes a typical conversation between two young villagers, one of whom says:

> Lucas, old boy, we have a very hard life here in the country; the authorities—I don't know if it is the chief or his assistants—have their knives into us. And as for Father and even Mother . . . ! Listen, it was only the other day, you've seen the maize, cucumbers, and vegetables, all ripe? Well, this day hunger followed me around all day, I ran away from it but my feet wouldn't get me away, so I thought it best to go to our field and help myself to some cucumber. I admit I took one and swallowed it down without chewing. Then I got a mad desire to eat some maize and broke off three and went home to roast them. Presto, as the first was ready I began to eat it, then the second, when in come my parents from visiting. They see me and start straight in to abuse me, tell me never to darken their door again. That evening there was a big storm with lightning, one bolt of which struck a tree in that field and it fell and ruined a stretch of crops: then in the morning everyone said: Ah, yes, Juma ate unblessed food before we had sacrificed, that's why their field was destroyed. So the news spread and they sent me to expiate it, and when I got there the omens were against me and I was an outcast to the whole village. My father is an old man but he has no gratitude; since he was exempted from tax he has been to work for the chief only five times, every time it is his turn it's me that goes . . . .
>
> I hate it here, better get a change of air—town air—even if it kills me. I am lucky enough to have borrowed the fare down, though I haven't enough to come back. But every day they sit on me, and now there is nothing for it but to disappear and give myself a break; in the town there are many people and many jobs, but here what job can a chap get? It's just the messenger coming in the morning, early, with a little bit of paper summoning me to the court; you get there and they tell you, you are charged by the agricultural inspector for not having a cassava field; if you ask who the inspector himself is, you're told, "That child over there." If you ask who is prosecuting and where he is they'll say, "So you are one of these bush lawyers are you? Do you suppose a full agricultural inspector will tell lies?"
>
> Elders like this are not to be borne, in the end you may be had up for murder, better go to town where nobody knows me, and nobody will say what's that you're eating, what's that you're wearing, every man for himself and mind his own business: but here! You've only to cough and somebody ticks you off for getting your feet wet.
>
> Last week I returned from safari with the dresser, carrying his loads, and only a little later they volunteered me again to carry the D. C.'s [District Commissioner's] loads, nothing but work, any time there's loads to be carried it's always me. . . .Well now, the rains are starting and lorries won't pass, off I go again. Soon I'll develop wheels and be a public service vehicle. Go to town any day.[64]

Life in the extended family was obviously not the idyllic experience that those who romanticize simpler societies make it appear. For the thousands of young Jumas, the choice is clear.

---

[64] From *A Survey of Dar es Salaam*, pp. 27–29, by J. A. K. Leslie, published by Oxford University Press, by permission of Oxford University Press.

Fig. 15/12 The lure of the city; Lagos, capital of Nigeria

Actually, the break with the extended family is seldom as sharp as Juma's musings suggest. When they get to town, young men usually search out their kinsmen, who help them find employment and get settled. But in the long run the ties of the extended family are seriously weakened, and industrializing horticultural societies have not yet developed any real substitute for them.[65] This is a fairly serious source of social instability, but the experience of industrial societies suggests it is inevitable.

Another problem confronting these societies is the shift from polygyny to monogamy. Polygyny was practiced in almost all the traditional horticultural societies of sub-Saharan Africa, while monogamy, as we have seen, is the rule in all modern industrial societies. The Christian missions fought polygyny vigorously, but with only limited success. Their opposition to it is, in fact, reputed to be one of the major reasons many Africans have been reluctant to be baptized. In the long run, however, the same forces that led to the spread of monogamy in other industrial and industrializing societies will probably prevail here.

Considering the historic importance of kinship in horticultural Africa, such revolutionary changes are bound to be unsettling. Their effects will surely be felt at both the individual and societal levels for a long time to come.

Concluding note

From the evolutionary standpoint, the experiences of industrializing horticultural societies are extremely important, providing as they do a dramatic illustration of one of the most basic differences between sociocultural and organic evolution. In organic evolution, change is made one step at a time—and it is always slow. But sociocultural evolution does not have this limitation. By means of diffusion, five thousand years of slow and painful development can be compressed into a few short generations.

---

[65] *Ibid.*, pp. 60–61; or Fraenkel, *op. cit.*, pp. 127ff.

Chapter 16
Retrospect and Prospect

The study of societal evolution is much like the study of a giant mural. In both cases, we are almost overwhelmed by the many small details. If we are to grasp the picture as a whole and develop any feeling for it, we must stand back from time to time and view the picture in its entirety.

We began this volume with the larger view, but for the last nine chapters we have concentrated on different parts of the panorama. Now we must step back once more to view the basic outlines and overarching patterns in order to discover, if we can, any that eluded us before. In particular, we will try to determine the extent to which technological progress has been accompanied by progress toward man's other basic goals—freedom, justice, morality, and happiness.

We will also consider the fascinating and important question of what the future holds. If sociology is to help people understand the societies in which they live and on which they depend, it cannot limit its concern to those of the past and present. Because tomorrow's world promises to be so different from today's, predictions are necessarily risky. But that is not sufficient reason to avoid this vital subject.

LOOKING BACK: THE LONG VIEW

A million years ago, the ancestors of modern man gave little indication that they were anything more than another variety of primate. There was nothing to suggest that this species would one day evolve into the dominant form of life, a creature capable of overcoming most of the limitations imposed on him by his environment and able to alter even the environment itself in major respects.

Today, we take all this for granted. With the wisdom of hindsight, we see that man was destined for a unique role. We see, moreover, that the key to his accomplishments lay in his ability to use symbols—the building blocks of culture—to mobilize energy and information. We also understand how he gradually escaped from the restraints of the genetic mode of adaptation and how sociocultural evolution finally replaced organic evolution as the dominant mode of human adaptation about thirty-five thousand years ago.

The significance of this is hard to exaggerate. Sociocultural evolution, unlike organic evolution, has a natural tendency to "snowball." Despite occasional reversals of relatively short duration, this tendency has been manifest throughout man's entire history. As a result, we find ourselves today in the most revolutionary era of all. The rate of change is now so high that change has become the central fact of life.

The use of symbols, the building of cultures, the whole process of sociocultural evolution—these are, by their very nature, social phenomena and, as such, presuppose the existence of human societies. And long before there were men, primates lived in societies, which indicates that societies were prerequisite to the development of all the more distinctly human qualities. Thus, the study of cultures and the study of human societies are inextricably intertwined.

DISTORTIONS

In our survey of human societies, certain distortions were unavoidably introduced. For example, because so little nontechnical evidence survives from the prehistoric era, our description may well exaggerate the importance of subsistence activities in the daily life of Paleolithic societies. Similarly, because we took an evolutionary approach to the study of human societies and incorporated the whole span of human history into our analysis, we have necessarily concentrated on the more basic patterns and neglected the exceptional ones. Such a survey can never do justice to the human scene. However, we are all aware of the richness and complexity of human life, and of its amazing variety. Not only is this part of our daily experience, but all of history and literature remind us of this wonderful diversity. For most of us, then, an overemphasis on the basic patterns comes as a badly needed corrective.

PROGRESS RECONSIDERED

So far in our discussions of progress, we have carefully restricted its meaning to technological advance, specifically to the raising of the upper level of the capacity of societies to mobilize energy and information. It is clear that progress so defined has occurred at the global level throughout virtually the whole of human history. The capacity of modern industrial societies to mobilize energy and information far surpasses that of the most advanced agrarian societies a thousand years ago, and their capacity was far above that of their most advanced predecessors of earlier eras.

Progress in this limited sense, however, has never been man's ultimate goal; and today, more than ever before, he is concerned with progress in the ethical sense and in terms of human happiness and freedom. This growing concern with the less utilitarian aspects of progress is, itself, interpretable in evolutionary terms: modern theories of motivation recognize that people's interests and concerns change as their conditions change.[1] As long as basic needs like physical safety, food, and shelter are inadequately satisfied or their future satisfaction is uncertain, they tend to remain uppermost in men's minds. But once these needs have been satisfied and men are confident they will be able to provide for them in the future, then new needs and new concerns become dominant. Thus, the further a society advances technologically, the greater the number of its members who care about, and actively pursue, progress in terms of freedom, justice, morality, and happiness.

Freedom

That the affluent members of modern industrial societies put a high value on freedom is attested to by the growing challenge to all forms of authority, not only in the liberal democracies of the West but in totalitarian nations as well. Even those who are not in the forefront of the modern libertarian movement are likely to consider the degree of freedom accorded the individual one of the basic measures of the attractiveness, and hence of the progress, of a society, and they would deny that a technologically advanced, politically repressive dictatorship can be called progressive.

But human freedom is more than freedom from repressive social controls; it is also liberation from the limitations imposed by nature. Primitive hunters and gatherers who have to spend most of their waking hours in an exhausting search for food are not truly free. For freedom does not exist where there is no alternative; and freedom can be measured only by the range of choices that are available. The fewer viable choices, the less freedom—and it matters little, from the standpoint of freedom, whether the restrictions are imposed by nature or by one's fellow men.[2]

Once we recognize this, it becomes clear that man's long struggle to advance technologically is not irrelevant to his desire for freedom. Every one of his technological innovations has contributed, to a greater or lesser degree, to his ability to overcome natural limitations on his actions. Thanks to this long struggle, he is now free to talk across oceans or from a ship in space, free to travel faster than sound, free to live a longer life in better health while he enjoys a range of experiences far surpassing in richness and variety what was available to the greatest kings and emperors of the past.

---

[1] See especially A. H. Maslow, *Motivation and Personality* (New York: Harper, 1954), chap. 5, and p. 47 in this volume.

[2] Psychologically, it seems easier for men to accept restrictions imposed by impersonal physical forces than those imposed by other men, but this does not make the individual any more free.

There has been a price to pay, of course: technological progress has necessitated larger and more complex systems of social organization. If we want the option of flying to another part of the country instead of walking there, or of watching the day's events on a screen in our home instead of hearing about them weeks later, we have to accept the social controls that are implied. The goods and services essential for such options can be produced only when there are organizations with rules and with sanctions to enforce the rules, and individuals with authority to exercise the sanctions. And these organizations can function efficiently only within the context of a society with rules to govern the relationships between them and an authority system to enforce the rules. The only alternative is anarchy—and the loss of all the freedoms that modern technology affords.

Critics of modern society often say that the price has been too high, that the increased social restrictions outweigh the gains in freedom we derive from modern technology. They may be right—this is a matter each of us must decide for himself. In thinking about it, however, we need to beware of romanticizing the past. Before deciding that men are less free than they used to be, we should read the records of peasant life in agrarian societies and of the life of horticultural and hunting and gathering peoples. In doing this, we must avoid the temptation to abstract the attractive features and ignore the appalling ones. We must remember that slavery and serfdom were not accidental characteristics of agrarian societies but reflections of basic, inescapable conditions of that way of life, as were the high mortality rate and short life-span of hunting and gathering peoples.

Once we recognize how unreasonable it is to compare the harsh realities of modern industrial societies with some rosy version of life in less advanced societies, we are in a better position to consider whether freedom is a correlate of technological advance. First of all, we can say that technological progress has at least raised the *upper* level of freedom in human societies. The people with the greatest measure of freedom in modern nations—that is, members of the upper classes—have a far wider range of choice than people with the greatest measure of freedom in less advanced societies. This is true with respect to everything from the individual's use of a leisure hour to his use of a lifetime. We can state, therefore, that there is, in this limited sense, a high positive correlation between technological progress and gains in human freedom.

The relation between technical progress and freedom for the *average* member of society is more complicated. If we compare the typical peasant in an agrarian society with a typical hunter and gatherer, it is not at all clear that there were any gains. In fact, the peasant was hedged about with numerous new social controls, while gaining very little in freedom from natural controls. Thus, during much of the course of evolutionary history—especially after the formation of the state—the average person experienced a decline in freedom. With the rise of industrial societies, however, the pattern changed. Once the difficult period of transition is passed technological progress and gains in freedom for the average man *do* begin to be positively related, as Fig. 16/1 illustrates.

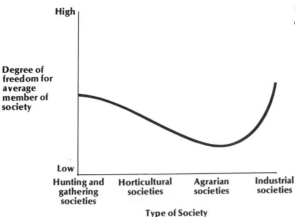

Fig. 16/1   Degree of technological development and degree of freedom for average member of society, by societal type

For the *least* free members of society, there appears to have been little change through the years. If we compare the least free members of modern societies (the inmates of many mental and penal institutions and the very poor) with the least free members of other societies, it is hard to see much difference: both are severely restricted. The chief difference is that in the more advanced societies the restrictions are usually imposed by society, in the simplest societies by nature.

Before leaving the subject of freedom, we should take note of the popular misconception, fostered by modern political polemics, that governmental activity necessarily results in a loss of freedom for the members of society. This is at best a half truth. A government's rules and regulations do, of course, place restrictions on some, but only in the process of creating freedom for others. For example, when the United States established a severe penalty for kidnapping in the 1930s to restrict the actions of a small predatory minority, it did so in order to increase the freedom of countless children and their parents. Similarly, the passage of the Pure Food and Drug Act restricted the freedom of a number of businessmen who were willing to sell spoiled food and dangerous drugs as long as there was profit in it, but it increased the freedom of the rest of the population. The same is true of virtually every government regulation: *it redistributes freedom, taking from some and giving to others.*

The crucial question, therefore, is whether the gains in freedom for the beneficiaries outweigh the losses for the rest. Naturally no one welcomes new limitations on his actions. Those who are threatened with them resist vigorously, since most individuals and most groups are concerned primarily with their own immediate interests and only secondarily with the common welfare. One of the most effective methods of fighting controls is propaganda, especially propaganda designed to convince the public that the proposed legislation is a threat to "freedom." A good case can easily be made for this if one presents only one side of the picture. In recent years, a number of highly favored groups in our society have followed this practice (e.g., many elements in the business community, the American Medical Association, certain labor unions, etc.). What they fail to mention is the fact that most of the newer legislation, such as Social Security or Medicare, has been adopted because the gains in freedom for those who benefit are more significant than the losses for others. This is, of course, only what we should expect in a democratic society. In short the great growth in the powers of government in modern democratic societies has generally increased freedom for the average person, not restricted it.[3]

Justice

Most of us would probably include justice in any definition of progress. To call an unjust society "progressive" appears a contradiction in terms. Yet even the most cursory view of history reveals that many societies have been advanced in techno-logical terms without being advanced in terms of justice.

Before asking how common this is, we must try to spell out what we mean by justice. Unfortunately, it is much easier to talk about justice than to define it— especially to define it in a way that satisfies everyone. Consider distributive justice: Is it more just for a society to reward on the basis of contribution to the common good or on the basis of need? Should the handicapped person, for example, be as well rewarded as those who outproduce him? And should the talented get more than those with less natural ability? Similar questions in the area of criminal justice demand an answer. Does the principle of an eye for an eye and a tooth for a tooth express an adequate standard of criminal justice? Or must a society seek to remove the conditions that stimulate criminal activity (e.g., extreme poverty) and strive to reform the criminal after he is caught? And what about the Biblical principle that much will be required of those to whom much is given, implying a severer standard for the more fortunate members of society?

Questions like these point up the difficulty of measuring progress with respect to justice. Where values are so different, it is nearly impossible to arrive at a common definition. Moreover, when we consider individual cases, we see how difficult it is to apply abstract, general standards of justice. So much depends on the circum-stances. Thus, an action that is just in one situation may be flagrantly unjust in another.

To deal adequately with this subject would require volumes. All we can do here is call attention to a few relatively uncontroversial, but important, trends. To begin with, there has clearly been a long-term trend toward a more formal and impersonal administration of criminal justice. In the simplest societies, everything was left to the injured individual and his kinsmen, who sought retribution by whatever means they judged appropriate. This commonly led to prolonged feuds and the multi-plication of injuries and damage to property. As more power was vested in rulers,[4]

---

[3] The situation is not necessarily the same in totalitarian states. On the contrary, until they begin to democratize, the increased powers of government are used primarily to control the actions of the average citizen and thus result in a substantial loss of freedom.

[4] In a number of cases, the growth in a ruler's power apparently resulted from the desire of people to escape the destructive cycle of blood vengeance. See, for example, A. W. Southall, *Alur Society* (Cam-bridge, England: Heffer, 1956), and Lucy Mair, *Primitive Government* (Baltimore: Penguin, 1962), chap. 4.

the practice of blood vengeance was gradually replaced by judgments rendered on the basis of a code of laws, in courts administered by chiefs or kings or by their ministers. This had several advantages. First, it introduced a greater element of rationality into the process; the decision no longer depended on the relative strength of the contending parties. Second, it transferred responsibility for making the decision to a more disinterested third party. Finally, it placed the burden of executing the decision on a third party that was stronger than either of the contending parties, thus breaking the endless and often escalating cycle of the feud.

Since the Industrial Revolution, there has been further progress in the administration of criminal justice. Most important, a substantial body of new legislation has been written, enlarging the rights of the less favored segments of the population. In addition, harsh punishments for minor offenses (e.g., hanging a man for stealing an egg) have been largely eliminated and serious efforts made to get rid of conditions that foster crime.

Whether there is more justice in industrial societies than in hunting and gathering societies is hard to evaluate, and one's answer is bound to reflect one's values. Those who value the orderly, businesslike administration of justice by modern courts will probably decide that substantial progress has been made. Those who are more concerned with distributive justice and who believe that men should be rewarded on the basis of their need or their contribution to society will not be so sure. They may well conclude that the long-term trend has been curvilinear, with a fairly steady decline from prehistoric times until the agrarian era, but since then a reversal.

Morality

Morality presents just as complex a problem as justice. Moral codes have varied tremendously, and the way one reads the evolutionary record depends largely on his own personal code. Almost every form of human behavior has been supported by some group at some time or other. Even killing and cruelty have been endorsed by the warrior codes of many societies, and ritual murder and human sacrifice encouraged as a sacred duty.

In the modern era, codes like these have little support. Most members of industrial societies believe that killing and deliberate cruelty are wrong and are justified only by extreme circumstances. The persistence of these activities simply attests to man's remarkable capacity for justifying and rationalizing his actions. Nevertheless, there is a growing acceptance, in principle, that these things are wrong and, for our purposes here, this is sufficient. It gives us a standard against which to measure trends in morality—at least with respect to this important dimension of it.

Judging from available evidence, the evolution of societies from the hunting and gathering to the horticultural level was marked by a serious moral decline. Hunting and gathering peoples, as we have seen, tend to be peaceful and not inclined to warfare. Perhaps the excitement of the chase gives men sufficient outlet for their combative and competitive tendencies, or perhaps hunting simply consumes too much of their time and energy. At any rate, after the introduction of horticulture, men had more free time than ever before. One outlet for this was warfare, another religion; and not infrequently the two were combined in barbaric cults that featured the display of human trophies or the sacrifice of captured enemies.

With the emergence of agrarian societies, the forms of human cruelty changed somewhat, but the incidence seems to have remained about the same. Warfare continued, but proportionately fewer people were involved because societies were larger and the new armies were made up of military specialists. But as the warrior cults declined, they were replaced by new forms of military savagery—plundering, burning, and raping of conquered communities, for example—and battles themselves became more deadly. In addition, as class differences within societies became more pronounced, immorality in intragroup relations increased. The history of every agrarian society is replete with instances of exploitative and brutal treatment of the lower classes. Nowhere is this more evident than in the punishments exacted for minor offenses.

In the last hundred years, many of the traditional forms of cruelty have been eliminated. On the other hand, new and more deadly practices have developed. Gas chambers, nuclear bombs, germ warefare, and napalm are but a few of the newer techniques for killing and maiming. Even so, it appears on balance that there has been some progress, primarily because of the growth of democratic government. The physical safety and well-being of the masses of common people are certainly much better protected in modern industrial societies than in agrarian. Not that the millennium is here—far from it. But there has been some progress.

Taking the long view, it is hard to detect any durable relationship between technological and moral advance. The former, as we know, has tended to follow a rising curve; morality, in the limited sense used here, has apparently taken a curvilinear course in which an initial period of decline was followed by a long period when moral standards remained at low ebb, and finally by some movement upward. Hardly grounds for believing that moral and technical progress go hand in hand!

Happiness

Of all the possible measures of progress, happiness is the most elusive, for it depends so much—perhaps primarily—on the quality of one's interpersonal relations, whether there is love, mutual respect, cooperation, and so forth. And these do not seem to depend upon the level of technological development. Studies of modern hunting and gathering groups indicate that very primitive people develop these qualities as often as members of modern industrial societies.[5]

---

[5] See, for example, Colin Turnbull, *The Forest People* (New York: Simon & Shuster, 1961); or John Garvan, *The Negritos of the Philippines* (Vienna: Ferdinand Berger, 1964).

There is one respect, however, in which technological progress is definitely relevant to this kind of happiness. Some of life's greatest tragedies involve the premature death of a loved one—a cherished child, the parent of small children, the partner in a happy conjugal relation. We saw how common this was in most societies prior to the Industrial Revolution and can therefore appreciate what the recently expanded life-span has meant in terms of human happiness.

There is no denying that happiness also seems to depend on the quantity of goods and services a person consumes. But this statement must be qualified. While such a relationship does apparently exist within every society at any given time, it is far from clear that it applies between societies, especially if they are not contemporary or are not in close touch. There is no reason to suppose, for example, that people in societies of the past, or even in certain remote societies today, have been unhappy because of the great discrepancy between their possessions and those that members of industrial societies take for granted.

The important thing is what a person has relative to those around him, not its absolute quantity or value. Thus, the headman in a simple horticultural society of the past was probably very happy with his few special privileges because they were more than his neighbors had and as good as anything of which he had knowledge. By contrast, a middle-class American, surrounded with goods and services that the headman never dreamed of, may feel terribly deprived when he compares himself with his more affluent neighbors or with the smiling people paraded before him in endless TV commercials. In short, insofar as happiness is based on material possessions, the degree of inequality is what is significant: the greater it is, the greater the resulting unhappiness will probably be. This suggests that the technological progress achieved up to and including the agrarian era lowered the level of human happiness, since inequality increased constantly during that time. Since then, industrial societies with their more egalitarian economies and polities have undoubtedly reversed the trend, although the level of inequality is still far higher than in hunting and gathering groups. To the extent that happiness depends on equality of possessions, therefore, we would expect to find less of it today than in prehistoric times. All things considered, it is hard to believe that technological advance is more strongly related to happiness than to justice or morality.

Concluding thoughts

In an earlier chapter we asked, in effect, why it is that men have invested so much of themselves in the struggle for technical advance if it has not been more consistent in producing happiness and justice. We answered that men have been more concerned with the immediate consequences of their choices and actions than with the long-term results and that the latter do not usually become evident until it is too late for society to reverse its course. We said, also, that men are rarely motivated by a desire for happiness and justice for mankind as a whole but concentrate their energies on achieving these things for themselves and those closest to them. Since what is advantageous for one group is often achieved at the expense of others, the costs of progress have often outweighed the benefits for mankind as a whole. Further, we noted the part played by intersocietal selection, which has favored the technically advanced. Thus, the more technologically oriented societies have usually survived, while those motivated more by a desire for happiness and justice have tended to disappear.

Idealists may well ask, therefore, whether technological progress has not, in fact, been a bitch goddess. Had human history come to an end a thousand years ago, one would have been forced to agree. But recent developments, especially those of the past hundred years, hold out the hope that technology may yet make a very positive contribution to the attainment of mankind's higher goals. There is nothing inevitable about this, of course, and it will surely not occur automatically; but it looks as if the new technology is at least bringing into the realm of *the possible* a social order with more freedom, justice, morality, and happiness than any society has yet known.

Whatever our judgment about the wisdom of man's pursuit of technological advance, one point is clear: It is only in this very limited sense, and in terms of the several correlates we noted on page 101, that mankind as a whole has achieved fairly continuous and substantial progress. In short, the limitation set on the meaning of progress in the early chapters of this volume is essential if we are to avoid a serious misinterpretation of human history.

LOOKING AHEAD

Of all the jobs a sociologist is asked to do, none causes him more uneasiness than making predictions about the future. With every passing year, as the rate of change accelerates, it becomes harder to base our predictions about the nature of tomorrow's world on the nature of today's. Yet as one social scientist said recently,

> All of us find it very hard to see where the future is going. But we must try to do it. It is an intellectually and morally intolerable state of affairs that we plan twenty and thirty years ahead when we take a mortgage on a house . . . but pretend that in the matters of war and peace, or in the matters of the life and death of mankind, we can't see further ahead than two years at most.[6]

Like it or not, individuals, groups, and nations must make decisions that affect the future—and make them on the basis of predictions about the nature of tomorrow's world. If these predictions are wrong, the decisions will also be wrong. Obviously, therefore, we have a vested interest in improving the accuracy of our predictions.

---

[6] From a statement by Karl Deutsch in a Yale Reports broadcast quoted in *Yale Alumni Magazine*, May, 1967, p. 15.

Determinism versus probabilism once again

Earlier in this volume, when we examined the issue raised by deterministic theories, we observed that most social scientists now avoid both extreme positions. They reject the determinists' thesis that the future course of events is inevitable or pre-determined, and hence completely predictable if one only has sufficient information on relevant sociological variables. Similarly, they reject the thesis that it is impossible to make any predictions at all. Rather, they take a position that has come to be known as probabilism, maintaining that all *possible* future developments are not equally *probable*. Some are unlikely because they would cost so much more than feasible alternatives. Others are unlikely because they presuppose certain prior developments and these have not yet occurred and are not likely to occur in time. Still others are unlikely because they presuppose value commitments that neither the nation's current leaders nor those apt to replace them show signs of making. By contrast, other developments are much more likely because they promise substantial benefits for a small investment; or because necessary prior developments have already taken place; or because they are consonant with the values of those who are likely to make the decisions.

Because it is in this sense and this sense only that sociological prediction is possible, its value is directly proportional to the care and skill that go into estimating the probabilities of the various alternatives and to the accuracy of the information on which they are based. In some ways, prediction is easier now than it used to be; we have far more information on human societies, and in far more precise form. On the other hand, as we have noted a number of times, the rate of change is such that it is extremely hazardous to base anything on the assumption of continuity. Furthermore, as the margin between a society's total productivity and what it requires for its basic material needs grows wider, the range of options available to the society increases. No longer can we simply predict that gains in productivity will be used to satisfy man's elemental needs. In the future, societies' resources will be increasingly directed to the satisfaction of needs and desires that did not even exist until recently, except perhaps in the minds of a few visionaries. The race between the United States and the Soviet Union to put a man on the moon was a good example of this. So despite the fact that we have more and better information, prediction is harder now than ever.

Technology

Benjamin Franklin once said that nothing is certain in this world but death and taxes. Were he alive today, he might wish to add technological progress. To predict continuing progress at an accelerating rate, one need not depend simply on an extrapolation of the current trend.[7] The basic factors responsible for the trend—the magni-

---

[7] Prediction based solely on extrapolations (i.e., projection of current trends) is one of the least reliable of the several techniques for predicting because it ignores the question of why the current trend exists and whether the forces responsible for it will continue to operate. Some of the more serious errors in sociological prediction have resulted from overreliance on extrapolation.

tude of the existing store of information, the great size of societal populations, and the amount of communication between societies—give every indication of providing even stronger impetus in the future than they do today. Moreover, advanced industrial societies are engaging, for the first time in history, in a systematic, large-scale pursuit of new knowledge. Investments in scientific and technological research and development are rising steadily, while computers and other devices that increase men's powers of acquiring and analyzing data add their own boost to the rate of change.

At present, only two things seem at all likely to change the picture in any significant way: a nuclear holocaust or a rate of change that proves psychologically or socially intolerable. Should a nuclear holocaust destroy the fabric of modern industrial societies, there would probably be a permanent reversion to the agrarian level. In a provocative volume entitled *The Challenge of Man's Future*, Harrison Brown notes that the rise of modern industrial societies was dependent on a combination of circumstances that have vanished, thus making a future rebirth of industrial societies an unlikely occurrence. He argues the case this way:

> Our ancestors had available large resources of high-grade ores and fuels that could be processed by the most primitive technology—crystals of copper and pieces of coal that lay on the surface of the earth, easily mined iron, and petroleum in generous pools reached by shallow drilling. Now we must dig huge caverns and follow seams ever further underground, drill oil wells thousands of feet deep, many of them under the bed of the ocean, and find ways of extracting elements from the leanest ores—procedures that are possible only because of our highly complex modern techniques, and practical only to an intricately mechanized culture which could not have been developed without the high-grade ore resources that are so rapidly vanishing.
>
> As our dependence shifts to such resources as low-grade ores, rock, seawater, and the sun, the conversion of energy into useful work will require ever more intricate technical activity, which would be impossible in the absence of a variety of complex machines and their products—all of which are the result of our intricate industrial civilization, and which would be impossible without it. Thus, if machine civilization were to stop functioning as the result of some catastrophe, it is difficult to see how man would again be able to start along the path of industrialization with the resources that would then be available to him . . .
>
> Our present industrialization, itself the result of a combination of no longer existent circumstances, is the only foundation on which it seems possible that a future civilization capable of utilizing the vast resources of energy now hidden in rocks and seawater, and unutilized in the sun, can be built. If this foundation is destroyed, in all probability the human race has "had it." Perhaps there is possible a sort of halfway station [agrarian society?] in which retrogression stops short of a complete extinction of civilization, but even this is not pleasant to contemplate. . . .[8]

The other threat to a rising rate of innovation—the attainment of a psychologically or socially intolerable rate of change—seems less likely in the near future

---

[8] From *The Challenge of Man's Future* by Harrison Brown, pp. 222–223. Copyright 1954 by Harrison Brown. Reprinted by permission of The Viking Press, Inc.

but very real over the long run. It is only logical to suppose that there is a limit to the rate at which individuals and society can adapt to change. For the individual, change implies learning, and frequently the simultaneous *unlearning* of established response patterns. At some point, the adaptive capacities of large numbers of individuals would surely begin to fall short of the demands put on them. Even before that point is reached, many people will find that the rewards of the new learning do not match the costs, and resistance to innovation will increase.

Societies have their limits, too. Because the parts of a complex society are tied together in so many ways, one change may necessitate dozens more. Industrial societies already have difficulty keeping up with all the ramifications of recent innovations. For example, the growing problems of air and water pollution are but two of the unintended consequences of the adoption of the new technology. We are currently trying to cope with these problems by means of further technological innovation. How long we can continue to meet the problems resulting from change in this way is an interesting question, since the complications that result from change multiply even faster than the changes that produced them.

Not all the complications are in the area of material technology; many involve basic social relations whose disruption could prove even more serious than problems like air pollution. For example, if the reluctance of many members of modern societies to respond to authority and the milder forms of coercion continues to grow in scope and intensity, it could force a choice between anarchy and despotism.

There is always the possibility, however, of a stabilizing of the rate of change in areas that affect the average person in his daily life, and a concentration of future innovation in areas with an immense number of problems but with minimal repercussions for the average person. Space exploration is one obvious example, organ transplants another. Much of the innovative potential of modern industrial societies could easily be consumed in the effort to overcome specialized technical problems in areas like these. The changes that resulted might require little adjustment from most of us, while contributing a great deal to knowledge and human happiness. Unfortunately, we cannot count on this; events of the last twenty-five years have shown that esoteric inventions in specialized fields can have enormous and unexpected implications for every member of society.

Content of change Turning from the *rate* of future technological innovation to its *content*, we encounter a subject so vast and so technical that we can do no more than call attention to a few of the highlights. The authors of a recent volume that looks ahead to the year 2,000 listed 100 areas in which, in their judgment, important technological innovations are "very likely" during the last third of this century. They also noted 25 developments they consider "less likely, but important possibilities," and another 10 "far-out possibilities."[9] Table 16/1 gives examples from all three categories.

---

[9] Herman Kahn and Anthony Wiener, *The Year 2000: A Framework for Speculation on the Next Thirty-Three Years* (New York: Macmillan, 1967), tables 18–20.

Table 16/1   Examples of possible and probable technological innovations in the last third of the twentieth century, according to Kahn and Wiener

Examples of innovations rated as "very likely"
1. Multiple applications of lasers and masers for sensing, measuring, cutting, heating, welding, power transmission, communication, illumination, destructive (defensive), and other purposes
2. New or improved materials for equipment and appliances (plastics, glasses, alloys, ceramics, intermetallics, and cermets)
3. New sources of power for ground transportation (storage battery, fuel cell, propulsion or support by electro-magnetic fields, jet engine, turbine, and the like)
4. Major reduction in hereditary and congenital defects
5. Extensive use of cyborg techniques (mechanical aids or substitutes for human organs, senses, limbs, or other components)
6. New or improved uses of the oceans (mining, extraction of minerals, controlled "farm-ing," source of energy, and the like)
7. Three-dimensional photography, illustrations, movies, and television
8. Automated or more mechanized housekeeping and home maintenance
9. Extensive and intensive centralization (or automatic interconnection) of current and past personal and business information in high-speed data processors
10. Other new and possibly pervasive techniques for surveillance, monitoring, and control of individuals and organizations
11. Capability to choose the sex of unborn children
12. More extensive use of transplantation of human organs
13. Chemical methods for improving memory and learning
14. Practical large-scale desalinization
15. Artificial moons and other methods for lighting large areas at night

Examples of innovations rated as "less likely but important possibilities"
1. "True" artificial intelligence [i.e., via computers]
2. Artificial growth of new limbs and organs (either in situ or for later transplantation)
3. Effective chemical or biological treatment for most mental illnesses
4. Chemical or biological control of character or intelligence
5. Conversion of mammals (humans?) to fluid breathers
6. Automated highways

Examples of "far-out possibilities"
1. Life expectancy extended to substantially more than 150 years
2. Major modification of human species (no longer Homo sapiens sapiens)
3. Interstellar travel
4. Lifetime immunization against practically all diseases
5. Laboratory creation of artificial live plants and animals

Source: Adapted from Herman Kahn and Anthony Wiener, *The Year 2000: A Framework for Speculation on the Next Thirty-Three Years* (New York: Macmillan, 1967), tables XVIII–XX.

To the layman, predictions like these may seem to be sheer guesswork. Actually they are not—at least not the first two categories. The 100 "very likely" developments are little more than an enumeration of fairly obvious applications of extant inventions and discoveries. The first item, for example, simply involves the application of recently invented lasers and masers to a variety of tasks. All the details have not yet been worked out, but the important point is that the fundamental innovations —the laser and maser—are accomplished facts. And as early as the beginning of 1967, almost every corporation and self-respecting university in the nation had already obtained a laser of some sort for research purposes.[10] That same year more than a hundred specific applications of lasers were being investigated, though only a handful had actually been adopted (e.g., "spotwelding" detached retinas).[11]

Several areas stand out because of their great promise in the next several decades. Some, like the use of lasers and masers, involve fundamental innovations so new that scientists and engineers have explored only a small fraction of their potential. Others are of special significance because major improvements are expected in the original innovation. Computers are a good example of this: in the fifteen years from the early 1950s to the middle 1960s, computer performance[12] increased at least tenfold every two or three years.[13] Though we cannot expect this pace to continue, computers will surely be capable, before the end of the century, of handling a number of problems that are far beyond their present capacity.[14]

The new knowledge about genetics and drugs deserves special mention if only because of its awesome potential. For the first time in history, men will soon be able to manipulate their biological nature and behavior on a large scale, in terms of both the number of people involved and the range of behaviors and physical characteristics affected. There is enormous potential for good in this field: genetic defects may be corrected, painful memories erased, mental retardation overcome, and so on. At the same time, there are frightening possibilities in drugs and genetic manipulation as means of social control. As one writer has said, "each major addition to our knowledge brings its corollary: power to control. In brain research, [increased] knowledge means increased power to control the mind of man . . ."[15]

So far we have been considering only those anticipated technological innovations that will be refinements and applications of existing ones. Clearly this is not

---

[10] *New York Times,* January 15, 1967.

[11] Kahn and Wiener, *op. cit.,* p. 98.

[12] The measure of computer performance used here is the size of the memory space divided by the basic "add time" of the computer (which measures roughly a computer's ability both to hold and to process information).

[13] Kahn and Wiener, *op. cit.,* p. 88.

[14] *Ibid.,* p. 89.

[15] David Krech, "Controlling the Mind Controllers," *Think,* July-August, 1966, pp. 3–7, quoted by Kahn and Wiener, *op. cit.,* p. 110.

the whole story. New fundamental innovations are virtually certain, but it is almost impossible to predict what they will be. Fundamental innovations resemble genetic mutations in a number of ways, including their unpredictability. We should not exaggerate this quality, however; some degree of prediction *is* possible. We know the areas in which societies are investing the most money and effort. We also know which areas have been "mined out," so to speak. If this information were properly analyzed, it could provide the basis for more effective long-range predictions. But for now, future fundamental innovations remain largely a matter of guesswork.

Gap between industrial and industrializing societies   Before we leave the subject of technology, we should consider one final question: What is going to happen to the present gap between industrial nations and those that are still industrializing? Will it be reduced, remain about as it is, or grow even wider? The ease with which technological knowledge has diffused in the past seems to suggest that industrializing societies will soon begin to narrow the gap. There are a number of factors in the current situation, however, that make this unlikely. First, the great complexity of the new technology presupposes a highly developed educational system, but industrializing nations, as we have seen, are so weak in this respect that their brightest young men usually have to go abroad to learn the new technology. Once in the more advanced countries, they are frequently reluctant to return home and "the brain-drain" becomes another major problem.[16] To complicate matters further, most developing nations suffer from a severe shortage of capital and the new technology is extremely expensive. Finally, because their markets are so small and the rate of technological innovation is so high, underdeveloped countries often find that new equipment becomes obsolete before its costs can be recovered. As a result, they are often forced to go on using tools and techniques years after they have been replaced in the more advanced nations. All things considered, therefore, it seems that the gap between the two kinds of societies will remain at least as wide as it is today, and it could even grow.

The physical and biological environment

Over the course of evolutionary history, man's relation to his biological environment has changed dramatically. Hunting and gathering societies simply had to adapt to environmental conditions; there was little they could do to alter them. Following the horticultural revolution, men gradually began to change the face of the earth, clearing forests and planting gardens in their place. Although the balance of nature was affected wherever this happened, the impact was still not great; for horticulturists usually had to move every few years, and their abandoned gardens reverted to wilderness. The agrarian revolution, however, ended all this. Now men cultivated permanent fields, and the land no longer reverted to forest.

---

[16] See, for example, Walter Adams (ed.), *The Brain Drain* (New York: Macmillan, 1968).

But all the changes of the past were nothing compared to the impact of modern industrial societies. Today, man puts his mark on every part of the globe, even on the remotest polar regions, the oceans, and the atmosphere. So much has been written in recent years about the destruction wrought by modern industrial societies that the specifics are well known to everyone.[17] Suffice it to note that the terrible pollution of rivers, lakes, and streams is now beginning to affect the oceans; that the pollution of the air has an alarming effect on the incidence of disease and death in the cities; and that the upsetting of the ecological balance has already resulted in the permanent loss of a number of plant and animal species.

As industrialization increases and the human population multiplies, there is every reason to expect these problems to become more severe. Yet in most industrial societies, mechanisms for protecting natural resources are very inadequate, particularly legislation that would make industries responsible for their use, or misuse, of them. The problem is urgent not only because the loss of unique varieties of animal and plant life is final and irreversible, but because the interrelation between all parts of the natural world means that damage to one species or one environment can have far-reaching implications for many others. Because of the rapidity and scope of change and the current lack of understanding of the problem by those in positions of power, many experts believe that events of the next fifty years could well determine the kind of environment in which man will live for centuries to come.

Population

If world population were to continue growing at its present fantastic rate, it would increase 8-fold in the next hundred years, 64-fold in the next two hundred, and over 500-fold in the next three hundred. Even if such numbers could somehow be supported, most people would probably find life in such a world very unattractive. Since cheap, efficient, and morally acceptable methods of birth control are now available,[18] the only question is when this rate of growth will begin to fall and how far it will drop.

Since industrial societies are currently growing at less than half the world rate (see Table 12/1), the problem obviously lies with the industrializing nations, in most of which the traditional level of 40 or more births per thousand population still prevails. There are several reasons for this. First, until recently most of the leaders of these societies were either unaware of, or indifferent to, the population problem and its consequences. Second, even where there was concern, there appeared to be no

---

[17] To cite but a single example, see Rachel Carson, *The Silent Spring* (Boston: Houghton Mifflin, 1962).

[18] Pope Paul VI, in his recent encyclical, "Humanae Vitae," reaffirmed the views of his predecessors Pius XI and XII that modern methods of birth control are sinful. Judging from reaction to his pronouncement, however, the number of Catholics who reject papal teaching on this subject is extremely large and influential, and it seems likely that Paul's successor will make significant changes in Catholic teaching in this area.

solution: contraceptives were either too expensive or required more education than most people in those countries had. Third, because of the economic value of sons in rural areas and because of the high death rates, most men resisted efforts to limit the number of their offspring. Finally, until quite recently the development programs sponsored by industrial societies focused almost exclusively on increasing production and ignored the economic implications of population growth. Now that too is changing and the prospect for lower birth-rates in these countries is improving.

Modest reductions in birthrates in the years immediately ahead will not suffice, however. Death rates in these countries are still fairly high (often 20 or more per thousand population), and improved sanitation and medicine are due to bring them down. Until they reach rock bottom (i.e., 9 or 10 per thousand), the decline in death rates will simply offset much of the decline in birthrates. One can only hope that the newer methods of contraception will produce a much faster drop in the birthrates of these nations than occurred in industrial nations.

It is probably premature to ask how far the world's birthrate will eventually fall, but it is interesting to speculate about it. At one point we suggested that a new equilibrium of births and deaths could be established somewhere in the neighborhood of 12 to 14 per thousand of each per year, with a resulting average life expectancy of 70 to 80 years *in a stable, or nonexpanding, population.* While this may occur in some, or even all, of the more advanced industrial societies in the next generation, it is much less likely in industrializing societies, whose members constitute the majority of the world's population. For the world as a whole, then, the next twenty-five to fifty years will probably see continued growth but at a declining rate, with the decline beginning in the very near future.

Looking further ahead, one can envision a day when men decide that the great population growth of recent centuries resulted in more people than are really desirable in a world that values the *quality* of human life above the *quantity.* They might then reduce their numbers through very stringent planning of births. This would be a dramatic departure in evolutionary history, but it is already technically possible. Considering the growing concern with the quality of human life, such a development may very well occur.

Scale of organization

So far, industrialization has meant larger societies, partly as a result of population growth within existing societies, partly as a result of their enlargement through merger and conquest. These trends have been evident in both industrial and industrializing societies, though conquest has been important primarily in Africa's industrializing horticultural societies.

With population growth almost certain to continue for some time, especially in the underdeveloped countries, and with merger and conquest also possible, if less certain, the small nation is rapidly becoming an economic and political anachronism. Economically, its home markets are too small to foster the growth of giant corporations or provide the benefits of mass production. Politically, it is incapable of self-defense and smaller than any nation needs to be in this age of rapid transportation and communication.

In consequence, a number of multistate organizations have already formed and, despite the resistance of many national leaders, there are almost certain to be more in the next several decades. This would probably be advantageous for the great majority of people in Europe, Latin America, sub-Saharan Africa, the Middle East, and southeast Asia. Pressures to move in this direction promise to be especially strong in Western Europe, which has suffered such a drastic erosion of political and economic power over the last half century and stands to lose still more if it continues in its present divided state.

Multistate organizations will not solve the problems of international competition and conflict. They might, in fact, intensify them by increasing the number of world powers of roughly equal strength. The best hope for eliminating the threat of war appears to lie in the formation of a single nation of global scope, but support for this is still extremely limited. Most political leaders continue to believe that peace can be preserved and their nation's interests protected within the framework of the present multination system. Probably nothing short of a near disaster—or something comparable, such as the invention of a cheap and terribly destructive weapon—could change enough minds to bring about global political unification. World unification could also result from conquest by some single nation, but this, too, seems unlikely. The strong nationalistic feelings evident in so many parts of the world today would make administration of a world empire extremely difficult, as would the widespread democratic and egalitarian tendencies of the modern era. In short, prospects for world unification, by merger or by conquest, are still remote.

Differentiation

Barring a disastrous war and a resulting technological regression, there will almost certainly be fewer societies a hundred years from now than there are today. Since each society is the bearer of a unique sociocultural tradition, this will also mean less sociocultural differentiation—*of this type.*

Other kinds of sociocultural differentiation, however, seem almost certain to increase. With machines doing more of the basic work, people will be able to devote more of their time and energy to the things they want to do. If our assumptions about the nature of man were correct (see Chapter 2), his "higher" needs are more varied than his basic ones. Therefore, as people increasingly turn their efforts to the satisfaction of these needs, their activities are likely to become more diversified.

This tendency is already evident in all of the more advanced industrial societies. Consider, for example, people's need for entertainment. Never before have there been so many different forms of it available, or such a variety of occupations in the field. The same diversity is found in most fields—even, in some cases, to the extent of rendering traditional job classifications obsolete. In a major university, for example, every faculty member fills a unique niche. When he resigns or retires, no one will be an exact replacement for him. Some of his responsibilities will be assumed by colleagues, some will be discontinued, while the man hired to replace him will take over only a part of his predecessor's duties and add others. The old position will, in effect, cease to exist and a new one will be created to fit the new appointee. Although universities are extreme in this respect, many other organizations are moving in the same direction, and this custom-tailoring of occupational roles is likely to become much more common in the years ahead.

Opportunities for differentiation and individuality are also growing outside the world of work. In highly productive societies, increased leisure and other resources allow people to develop and express their own distinctive abilities and personalities to an unprecedented degree. This growth in individuality seems almost certain to continue as technological advance provides ever greater leisure and higher standards of living.

Social interaction

In the last hundred years, vastly improved systems of transportation and communication have revolutionized patterns of social interaction. For example, they have all but destroyed the historic isolation of villages and towns. It is hard to find members of advanced industrial societies whose lives are still circumscribed by the boundaries of their local community; even those who never travel have the world brought to them by the mass media.

The same thing is happening in industrializing societies. As better roads are built and the mass media become more common, village isolation breaks down and national cultures become more prominent. In advanced industrial societies and in the upper classes of those still industrializing, even national differences are beginning to dissolve. This is evidenced by the internationalization of such things as popular music and dances, clothing styles, foods, words and phrases from a variety of languages, figures from the entertainment world, supermarkets, and other phenomena that were, not long ago, strictly national (or local) in character.

One of the most striking changes is the current spread of English, and to a lesser degree French, as a second language in many smaller nations. This trend (which is especially pronounced in the Scandinavian countries and Holland) may, if it continues, see a number of languages go the way of Gaelic. In language, as in the free enterprise system, there is a tendency for the rich to get richer and the poor poorer. The more numerous and powerful those who use a language, the greater the pressure on others to learn it. Conversely, the smaller and less powerful the population speaking it, the less likely others will choose it for a second language. The great power of the Soviet Union suggests that Russian, too, is destined for greater use in the future, though travel restrictions by the Russian government on its own people and on foreigners has done much to hinder this.

Someday in the distant future, mankind's linguistic diversity may be completely eliminated except for regional and class dialects. This would be a tremendous boon to communication and remove one source of international tension. On the other hand, it would make most of the great works of literature accessible only to trained specialists.[19] However, it could be argued that this is already true of all the older works in every language. Much of Chaucer and even Shakespeare, for example, are incomprehensible to most modern English-speaking people unless they have special aids or training.

The polity

The most striking trend in the political realm during the last two centuries has been the growth of democratic forms and practices and the decline of monarchical ones. While this has been especially marked in industrial societies, it has not been limited to them: democracy has also made some headway in many industrializing societies. The first question, therefore, is whether or not this trend will continue.

In discussing the prospects for further democratization, we will have to consider separately (1) industrial societies that are already democratic, (2) Communist-bloc nations, and (3) societies that are still industrializing. With respect to the first, we have already emphasized that even though we call them democracies, none has yet approached the democratic ideal of an equal voice for everyone. In most of these nations, the influence of the wealthy and the better educated is out of all proportion to their numbers, and the influence of the poor very limited despite their numbers. Even where this problem has been substantially overcome, as in the Scandinavian democracies, a minority of professional politicians and political activists still tend to dominate the political process. Those in positions of power prefer to ignore these facts, but they are facts nonetheless.

There is good reason to believe that large numbers of citizens in our present-day democracies are terribly frustrated by their inability to make their voices heard or their influence felt. This discontent is not limited to the poor and disenfranchised; it is shared by many in the middle class who, because of their education, have become vitally interested in the affairs of government and generate their own growing pressure for greater democratization. The McCarthy movement in the 1968 presidential election was one manifestation of this.

Those who control the machinery of government naturally resist such pressures. One of their most powerful arguments in defense of the status quo is the risk of chaos and anarchy if too many are involved in the decision-making process, especially ill-informed and poorly educated people. While there is considerable merit in this argument, it will carry less weight as educational levels rise and more of the

---

[19] Translations rarely do justice to the originals. While a few translations become notable literary achievements in their own right, they invariably differ from the original in many basic respects. This is especially true of poetry, for it is impossible to match rhyme, meter, sense, and imagery all at the same time.

population is equipped to voice intelligent opinions on major political issues. Television, too, may contribute to a better-qualified electorate—provided the commercial and entertainment elements are not allowed to monopolize that medium.

But what is most urgently needed at the present time is a way for the public to register its views on vital issues. Lobbying is notoriously unsatisfactory because of its unrepresentativeness; writing letters is little better. So far the most promising development along this line is the public opinion survey—the Gallup and Harris polls, for example. This is an important step, but surveys have not yet really been integrated into the political process, and their influence on legislation has been limited. If discontent with current democratic forms continues to increase during the next few decades, some movement toward greater democratization may result, but radical change in that direction is unlikely.

One may also ask about the prospects for change in the opposite direction. Democratic governments appear to be solidly entrenched in all of the more advanced industrial societies outside the Communist bloc. It is easy to forget that only once did an advanced industrial society abandon democratic government as a result of internal forces (Germany in the 1930s); all other nondemocratic regimes in these societies came about either because industrialization itself occurred under a nondemocratic regime (as in the Soviet Union) or as a result of foreign conquest or its equivalent (as in Czechoslovakia in 1948). Considering the stresses which most industrial nations have experienced—wars, depressions, racial and ethnic group struggles, and so on—this is no small accomplishment. For the next few decades, the chief threats to democracy in these societies will probably be war and internal subversion. If either of these threatens societal survival, or if propaganda makes them *appear* to be threats, citizens may be persuaded to give up their political rights and concentrate power in the hands of some charismatic leader or totalitarian party. Happily the chances of this do not appear great.

Perhaps the most striking testimony to the appeal of democracy is found in the Communist-bloc nations of Eastern Europe. Events since the death of Stalin prove that despite a long, ruthless suppression, the desire for democracy was never extinguished. First in Yugoslavia, later in Poland and Hungary, more recently in Czechoslovakia and the Soviet Union itself, East Europeans have clearly indicated their wish for a greater voice in their governments. And they have gotten results, too, despite tragic repressions in Poland, Hungary, Czechoslovakia, and the Soviet Union. Democratic elements are slowly being introduced into the political systems of most Eastern European nations. A number of them, for example, now allow people who are not members of the Communist Party to run for public office. Some also provide a way for the electorate to reject candidates put up by party officials, and this has actually been done on several occasions. Although democracy still exists in only rudimentary form outside of Yugoslavia, the trend is clear. However, the rate of change remains painfully slow.

Turning, finally, to the societies that are still industrializing, it looks as if they will experience a strengthening of democratic tendencies as their educational and economic standards rise. By the end of the century, the number of moderately democratic nations will probably be appreciably higher than it is today. At the same time, quite a number are likely to remain wholly or largely nondemocratic. This is almost inevitable considering the limited economic development of so many of them, and the tremendous strains to which they are subject.

In summary, we appear to be moving into an age of mass politics. Not since the rise of horticultural societies has such a large proportion of the world's population been politically active. If we have been at all accurate in assessing future probabilities, the proportion is destined to become even larger.

The economy and social stratification

There is little reason to expect radical departures from the status quo as far as the economy and social stratification are concerned. The most likely prospects are for present trends to continue in industrial societies, with the industrializing nations following pretty much in their wake. In other words, we can probably expect some strengthening of the element of command in the economies of the Western democracies and some strengthening of market forces in Communist nations, at least in those that are already industrialized. In matters of social stratification, the power, privilege, and prestige of the managerial and professional classes will probably continue to rise relative to other classes, though countervailing forces will almost certainly keep them from becoming anything comparable to the old agrarian elite. Above all, the strengthening of democratic tendencies in the polity should reinforce egalitarian tendencies in both the economy and the stratification system.

Another development that is interesting to speculate about is the growth of economic specialization on the national level. The forces favoring it, especially among industrializing nations, are powerful; but at the same time there are strong internal political pressures against it. From the economic standpoint of the world as a whole, this development would be both logical and highly advantageous: each country would produce the things it is best equipped, in terms of its natural resources, to produce. However, as long as the world is divided into a hundred or more independent nations, economic issues will probably continue to be settled by national leaders on the basis of what they consider best for themselves and for their nations.

Kinship

Historically, kin groups were the basic building blocks of societies. In addition to their role in reproduction and socialization, they played a vital part in political and economic life. In fact, in the simplest societies the kinship system was the basic force that held the group together.

Today things are different, especially in industrial societies. Kin groups have lost many, perhaps most, of their historic functions, particularly in the important areas of politics and economics. Although some new functions have been added and some old ones retained, they are concentrated in areas of personal, rather than societal, importance. As a result, the preservation and protection of the kinship system is no longer the urgent matter for society that it once was.

When we look to the future, the extended family appears almost certain to continue its decline, largely as a result of increasing geographic mobility. Under such conditions, it is extremely difficult to maintain ties with all of one's aunts, uncles, and cousins, to say nothing of second cousins once removed and great-aunts.

The future of the nuclear family is harder to predict. If the present trend continues, parents and children will see less of one another—especially in the early years, the one period when the traditional closeness is still usually preserved. The nursery school movement is almost certain to expand and to enroll more, and younger, children. While some people feel this is an unnatural practice, others counter that it is only an extension of an ancient practice. One writer reminds us that "in the past, whenever human beings have acquired sufficient resources and power, as among aristocracies, they have put the burden of child-rearing on other shoulders" (i.e., those of slaves and servants).[20] He also points out that child-rearing has traditionally been viewed as an arduous and even painful experience[21] and that life in modern industrial societies may strengthen these tendencies. If so, we can clearly expect further attenuation of the relation between parents and their offspring.

Ties between husband and wife will probably also be weakened, or at least strained, as a result of the increasing employment of married women. If women have fewer children and more education, their desire for careers, as opposed to mere jobs, is likely to increase. Counterbalancing this erosive influence, however, is the deeply rooted need of both men and women for the intimate, intense, comprehensive, and sustained relationship that only the family seems able to provide. In addition, there is good reason to believe that the family's present system of sexually complementary skills—men more knowledgeable about mechanics and women about cooking, for example—produces a happier pattern of living than any possible alternative.

It is these conflicting tendencies that make predictions so tenuous. Perhaps the most we can say is that the nuclear family seems certain to continue for the immediate future but that its survival will increasingly depend on individual choice rather than on economic and political necessity. Also, family patterns may become more varied, again reflecting the declining influence of necessity and the growing area of choice.

One important innovation that seems more likely all the time is the develop-

---

[20] Barrington Moore, Jr., "Thoughts on the Future of the Family," in *Political Power and Social Theory* (New York: Harper Torchbooks, 1965), pp. 172–173. See also Ralph Linton, *The Study of Man* (New York: Appleton-Century, 1936), p. 246.

[21] See, for example, the Biblical account of David and his son Absalom, or Jesus' parable of the prodigal son.

ment of societal reproductive policies. Traditionally, such decisions were left to husbands and wives, though large families have sometimes been encouraged by financial subsidies (as in Nazi Germany, where large families were encouraged because of their military value). Today, with the growing concern about overpopulation, governments will probably become more active in their efforts to control birthrates. At the very least they can be expected to subsidize research in methods of birth control and programs to diffuse information; many governments will probably make contraceptives, sterilization, and possibly even abortions available to those who cannot afford them. If these methods are not enough, tax incentives to encourage small families may be established.[22]

In the late nineteenth and early twentieth centuries, there was a great deal of agitation for government regulation of the *quality* of children brought into the world. Supporters of the eugenics movement argued that only the more intelligent and talented should be allowed to reproduce. (Many were concerned at that time because the poor—and seemingly less intelligent and talented—were having larger families than the well-to-do, and it was feared that this was causing a deterioration of the human genotype.) Thus far, however, attempts to distinguish between the influences of environment and heredity on these attributes have been unsuccessful, and there is still no way to identify superior genetic capacity. Moreover, recent work in genetics suggests that it could prove disastrous to breed the human population with respect to a limited set of criteria. As we saw earlier, the long-term ability of a population to survive and prosper seems to depend on its genetic *variability*, since individuals who are poorly adapted to one set of conditions may prove to be better adapted to those that emerge later on. While humans with inferior learning capacity would probably never be superior adaptors, they might carry other kinds of genes that would prove crucial at some future date. Thus, any lessening of man's genetic variability is very risky. All that is likely to happen in the next several decades is an effort to eliminate some of the most serious genetic defects through medical testing, marriage counseling, and possibly genetic manipulation.

Knowledge and beliefs

All the evidence indicates that man will continue to accumulate information at an accelerating rate. With an unprecedented base of knowledge on which to build his search for more, and with ever higher investments in the search, the pattern is not likely to be altered by anything short of a major world disaster or man's arrival at the upper limit of his capacity to tolerate rapid change.

It does not follow, of course, that man is going to find answers to all the questions he is asking. Some, like the causes of cancer, appear to be complex enough to elude him for a long time. Some seem to be inherently unanswerable—the problem underlying Heisenberg's principle of indeterminacy, for example, and many of

---

[22] In other words, couples with more than two or three children may be subject to special taxes.

the problems related to organic and sociocultural evolution (e.g., problems whose relevant data have been lost or destroyed, or generalizations that can be tested by only a single case).

Continuing advances in science are certain to have religious repercussions. We have already noted that the ultimate Power or powers responsible for man and his world are not amenable to direct observation and study and that answers to the basic questions posed by the major religions must be based on inferences drawn from what is observable. So far, developments in the natural sciences seem to be more compatible with belief in an impersonal power or powers, and recent social trends have encouraged this interpretation. One result has been the growth of various humanistic faiths—faiths whose supreme object of worship is man himself.

But these newer faiths rest on an eighteenth-century view of man, a view that is essentially uncritical and inordinately optimistic.[23] Though the issue has yet to be faced squarely, there is good reason to doubt that the findings of modern biology, psychology, and the social sciences provide much justification for it. Men seemingly have, as a part of their genetic heritage, a built-in tendency to seek their own or their group's advantage at the expense of other individuals and groups. Though this is modified by enlightened self-interest, and sometimes by strongly held religious convictions as well, few men appear to be capable of the day-in, day-out, self-sacrificing and noble way of life that the humanistic faiths presuppose. As a result, these newer faiths may be in for a crisis as severe as the older faiths experienced following the discoveries of Galileo and Darwin.[24]

Given all the contingencies and imponderables, efforts to predict anything in the area of religion are singularly unpromising. For the present, the wisest course of action would probably be to observe carefully the beliefs and practices of those members of the more advanced industrial societies who are most exposed to the newer patterns of life. Even so, it may not be easy to distinguish between meaningful trends and the increasingly common "fads and fashions" of belief which gain so much attention from the mass media.[25]

The higher goals

Our final question is perhaps the most important: what are the prospects for the higher goals of human action, freedom, justice, morality, and happiness? Though men have often sacrificed these goals for the sake of more mundane ones like power and technological advance, they have rarely been indifferent to them; and as their basic needs are more fully assured, their concern for the higher goals become more salient.

---

[23] See, for example, Franklin Baumer, *Religion and the Rise of Skepticism* (New York: Harcourt, Brace, 1960), chaps. 1–3.

[24] *Ibid.,* chap. 4.

[25] The extensive discussion of the odd "death of God" thesis is a good example.

The prospects for freedom look good. Technological advance promises us even further release from the restraints imposed by our physical environment. With respect to social constraints, of course, the possibility of restrictions like those envisioned by Orwell in *1984* are growing as technology advances: the mass media, new electronic devices, drugs, and a number of other innovations all have an obvious potential for being used this way. On the other hand, if current democratizing trends continue and the governments of industrial societies become more responsive to the majority of their citizens, the kind of controls envisioned by Orwell are most unlikely. As long as the members of these societies do not let themselves be stampeded into transferring power to political extremists, as the Germans did in the 1930s, the prospects for greater freedom for the average citizen are good.

With respect to justice, morality, and happiness, we can add little to our earlier discussion. In other words, there is good reason to hope that recent trends will continue. And yet, if the study of evolution teaches us anything at all, it teaches that man is often his own worst enemy. Possibly his greatest challenge is the social and moral one of learning to live in peace and brotherhood.

Happily, many of the forces that once generated war and injustice are being weakened by the new technology. Scarcity with respect to basic necessities, for example, could be something for the history books within the next fifty years if men really set their minds to the task. In short, we seem to be approaching a point in history where peace, justice, and brotherhood are viable alternatives for the first time since the forces of intersocietal selection began to make their deadly influence felt. One can only hope that enough people will have the vision to recognize this unique opportunity and the wisdom to seize it.

$\mathcal{G}$lossary

Achieved role A role which can legitimately be changed through the effort (or lack of effort) of the individual.

Adaptation The process of adjusting to, or adjusting, environmental conditions; hence, broadly, problem solving.

Aggregation A generic term referring to any collection of individuals; a population. The term includes populations which constitute groups as well as those that do not.

Agrarian era The period in history when there were no societies technologically more advanced than agrarian societies (c. 3000 B.C. to A.D. 1850).

Agrarian society A society in which agriculture is the primary means of subsistence. *Advanced* agrarian societies are differentiated from *simple* by the presence of iron tools and weapons.

Agriculture The cultivation of fields using the plow.

Alteration An innovation that involves a change in the form of some aspect of culture, but no new information or new combination of existing information.

Analogue Something which is similar to something else; especially something which is *functionally* similar.

Anthropoid The suborder of primates including man and the families most closely related to man.

Artisan A craftsman; usually applied to craftsmen in agrarian or maritime societies.

Ascribed role A role which cannot legitimately be changed (such as age, sex, race, or ethnicity).

Association A formally organized secondary group which performs some relatively specialized function or set of functions.

Autocracy Rule by one man.

Autogeneous Self-generated; produced independently of external influences.

Band A nomadic community at the hunting and gathering level.

Biological progress A raising of the upper level of the capacity of populations to mobilize energy and information in the adaptive processes.

495

Brokerage-type parties Political parties whose leaders' chief goal is to win public office in order to trade favors with special interest groups, giving preferential legislative treatment in exchange for electoral and financial support (contrasted with *Ideological parties*).

Bureaucracy The administrative agencies of a government or other association.

Capitalism An economic system in which the basic problems of production and distribution are settled by means of the market system with minimal government regulation or control (see *Market economy*).

Caste A largely hereditary class; in extreme cases, there are no legitimate avenues of mobility into or out of the group.

Categoric concept A concept framed in either-or terms (contrasted with *Variable concept*).

Chief The head of a small, multi-community, preliterate society (compare with *Headman*).

Civilization An advanced sociocultural system; the term is usually reserved for societies which are literate and have urban communities.

Clan An extended family group claiming descent from a common ancestor, whether real or mythical.

Class (1) An aggregation or group of people whose overall status is similar; (2) an aggregation or group of people who stand in a similar position with respect to some specific resource which affects their access to power, privilege, or prestige.

Command economy An economy in which the basic questions of production and distribution are decided by political authorities (contrasted with *Market economy*).

Communication The exchange of information by means of signals or symbols.

Community A secondary group which is informally organized and performs a relatively wide range of functions. See *Geographical community* and *Cultural community*.

Correlation A measure of the degree of association between two variables; correlation coefficients range from 0.0 when there is absolutely no relationship between the variables to 1.0 when there is a perfect relationship (i.e., one value is a perfect function of the other).

Cultural community A community whose members are united by ties of a common cultural tradition (e.g., a racial or ethnic group).

Culture A society's symbol system and all the aspects of human life dependent on it.

Custom A durable pattern of action shared by some or all members of a group.

Demography The study of populations, their size, composition, and change.

Determinism The assumption that chance plays no part in causal relations in the natural world and that all causal relations are therefore potentially predictable (contrast with *Probabilism*).

Diffusion The transfer of cultural information from one group to another.

Discovery An innovation that provides men with new information.

Ecological community A population of plants and animals of diverse species that occupy a given territory and are bound together by ties of mutual dependence.

Ecology The science of the interrelationships of living things to each other and to their environment.

Economic surplus Production that exceeds what is needed to keep the producers alive and productive.

Endogamy The practice of marrying only within the group (whether society, tribe, community, or religious group).

Energy The capacity for performing work.

Environment Everything external to an organism or population that affects it in any way.

Era A period of time during which a particular type of society is the most advanced in existence (e.g., the agrarian era).

Ethnography A division of anthropology devoted to the *description* of sociocultural systems, especially those of primitive peoples.

Ethology The study of animal behavior.

Evolution A process of change in a definite direction, particularly from a simpler to a more complex state.

Exogamy The practice of marrying only outside one's group (contrast with *Endogamy*).

Extended family A group of related persons, larger and more inclusive than the nuclear family, who maintain meaningful ties.

Family See *Nuclear family* and *Extended family.*

Feedback The partial reversion of the effects of a given process to its source so as to modify or reinforce it (i.e., A influ-ences B, thereby causing B to exert an influence back on A).

Fishing society A society in which fishing or fishing and gathering are the chief means of subsistence.

Fixed costs Costs of production which remain more or less constant regardless of the number of units produced (contrasted with *Variable costs*).

Function (1) A characteristic activity of a person, thing, or institution; (2) a consequence of the actions of a person, thing, or institution; (3) a relationship in which changes in the magnitude of one variable are associated in a definite and determined way with changes in the magnitude of another variable.

Fundamental innovation An invention or discovery that either (1) opens the way for many other innovations or (2) alters the conditions of human life so that many other changes become either possible or necessary.

Gathering Collecting edible fruits and vegetables which grow wild.

Gene A segment of a chromosome with characteristic effects on the development of the individual bearing it; repository of a unit of genetic information.

Genetic drift Random fluctuations in the distribution of genes within a population.

Genotype The sum total of genetic materials found in an organism or population.

Geographical community A community whose members are united primarily by ties of spatial proximity.

Governing class A largely hereditary class from which the political authorities of a society are recruited.

Gross national product The total value of the goods and services produced in a nation during a specific period (usually a year).

Group An aggregation whose members (1) act together in a common effort to satisfy common, or complementary, needs; (2) share common behavioral expectations; and (3) have a sense of common identity.

Guild A mutual aid association of merchants and artisans in the same trade; found in agrarian and maritime societies.

Habit A conditioned response.

Headman The leader of a local community, usually in a preliterate society; one who leads rather than rules. The term is sometimes used (though not in this volume) to refer to the leader of a kinship group.

Herding society A society in which herding is the primary means of subsistence. *Advanced* herding societies are differentiated from *simple* by the use of horses or camels for transportation.

Hominid Men and manlike creatures, one of the Primate family of Hominidae; specifically Homo sapiens sapiens and his tool-making ancestors.

Horticultural era The period in history when there were no societies technologically more advanced than horticultural societies (c. 7000 B.C. to 3000 B.C.).

Horticultural society A society in which horticulture is the primary means of subsistence. *Advanced* horticultural societies are differentiated from *simple* by the manufacture of metal tools and weapons.

Horticulture The cultivation of small gardens using the hoe or digging stick as the chief tool; differentiated from agriculture by the absence of the plow.

Human nature Behavioral tendencies shared by mankind as a whole; a result of our common genetic heritage.

Hunting and gathering era The period in history when there were no societies more advanced than hunting and gathering (to c. 8000 B.C.).

Hunting and gathering society A society in which hunting and gathering are the primary means of subsistence. *Simple* hunting and gathering societies lack the spear-thrower and the bow and arrow; *advanced* have one or both of these weapons.

Hybridization The flow or transfer of genetic information from one species to another.

Hybrid society A society in which two or more modes of subsistence are intermingled.

Ideological parties Political parties with strong ideological commitments and definite political programs (contrasted with *Brokerage-type parties*).

Ideology A society's basic belief systems and their applications to daily life; made up of world views, values, and norms.

Industrial era The period in history when industrial societies have been dominant (from c. 1850 to the present).

Industrialization Increasing reliance on the newer inanimate sources of energy and the technological and economic consequences of this (compare with *Modernization*).

Industrial society A society in which industrial activities are the chief means of subsistence and the newer sources of energy (coal, petroleum, etc.) are dominant; a society that consumes at least 1,000 kilograms of coal equivalent per person per year.

Information Signal that is impressed on the memory system of an organism, population, or machine and influences its subsequent action.

Instinct Genetically programmed responses or response sets.

Intersocietal selection Spontaneous processes responsible for the survival of some societies and the extinction of others.

Intrasocietal selection Processes, both spontaneous and deliberate, which are responsible for different rates of survival among elements of a sociocultural system.

Invention An innovation that involves a useful new combination of existing information.

IQ or Intelligence quotient A measure of the combined effects of innate learning capacity and learning opportunities (particularly opportunities to learn test-relevant information); originally thought to be a measure of innate capacity alone.

Language A system of symbols capable of transmitting and storing information.

Laws Norms sanctioned by the state or society.

Learning A process which manifests itself by changes in behavior (usually adaptive in nature) based on prior experience.

Legitimate That which is morally and/or legally justified.

Legitimize To make legitimate; to provide an ideological or legal justification for a practice which would otherwise be regarded as objectionable.

Leisure Time free from the demands of providing subsistence.

Maritime society A society in which overseas commercial activity is the primary means of subsistence.

Market economy An economy in which the basic problems of production and distribution are settled by means of the market system (*see Capitalism* and contrast with *Command economy*).

Matrilineal kin group An extended family organized on the basis of common descent through the female line.

Matrilocality The practice of married couples living with or near the wife's female relatives; sometimes called uxorilocality.

Median The middle number in a series of numbers arranged in order from the highest to the lowest.

Meiosis Process by which the number of chromosomes is reduced by half to compensate for the chromosome-doubling effect of fertilization in sexually reproducing species.

Mesolithic The Middle Stone Age (from c. 10,000 B.C. to 7000 B.C.).

Mobility, vertical See *Vertical mobility*.

Modernization All the long-term social and political changes that have accompanied industrialization (compare with *Industrialization*).

Monopoly A commodity market with only a single seller.

Mutation A change in the number of chromosomes; or a change in the internal structure of chromosomes (other than by crossing over in meiosis); or a change in the internal structure of the genes themselves.

Nation A multicommunity society governed by full-time political leaders (i.e., a society with more than minimal political development).

Natural selection Spontaneous processes resulting in differential rates of reproduction, and hence in the eventual extinction of certain populations.

Neolithic The New Stone Age; this term is also used as an adjective to refer to horticultural societies.

Nomad A member of a group that has no permanent settlements and moves about periodically (usually in a well-defined territory) in order to obtain food and other necessities.

Normative Of, or pertaining to, norms (i.e., having a moral and/or legal character).

Norms Behavioral prescriptions and proscriptions for the incumbents of specific roles in specific situations.

Nuclear family A man, his wife or wives, and their unmarried children living with them.

Oligarchy The rule of the few.

Oligopoly A commodity market with only a few sellers.

Organization A structured entity (see also *Social organization*).

Paleolithic The Old Stone Age (from c. 2,000,000 B.C. to 10,000 B.C.); divided into three parts, Lower (the earliest), Middle, and Upper.

Patrilineal kin group An extended family organized on the basis of common descent through the male line.

Patrilocality The practice of married couples living with or near the husband's male kinsmen; sometimes called virilocality.

Patrimony Property transmitted within a family from father to son.

Peasant An agricultural worker in an agrarian society.

Per capita income National income divided by population. (This measure is somewhat misleading as a measure of the standard of living of the average person, since a small number of people with very large incomes usually pulls the average far above the median).

Phenotype The sum total of organic and behavioral characteristics of an organism or population.

Pleistocene The geologic era beginning about 2,000,000 years ago and ending about 10,000 years ago; an era characterized by repeated expansion of glaciers.

Polity The political system of a group, especially a society.

Polygyny The marriage of a man to two or more wives simultaneously.

Population An aggregation of organisms.

Priest A religious functionary whose supernatural powers are bestowed on him by an organized religious group; one who mediates between God, or a god, and man; not to be equated with a shaman.

Primary group A small group in which face-to-face relations of at least a fairly intimate and personal nature are maintained.

Primates An order of mammals which includes the prosimians (e.g., tarsiers and lemurs) and the anthropoids (e.g., baboons, chimpanzees, gorillas, and men).

Primogeniture The right of the eldest surviving son to inherit all real estate.

Probabilism The assumption that random events and chance factors (i.e., factors which are not predictable from a given theory) play a part in many causal relations in the natural world and that these causal relations, therefore, are *not* precisely predictable (contrast with *Determinism*).

Process A series of related actions with an identifiable outcome.

Progress A series of changes which show overall movement in a single direction (i.e., toward more, or less, of some quality like size, complexity, etc.). See *Biological progress* and *Sociocultural progress*.

Random The absence of statistical bias (i.e., each member of a set having the same probability of occurrence as every other member).

Recombination Regrouping of genes by crossing over in meiosis or the regrouping of chromosomes by conjugation of gametes with unlike chromosomes

Religion The world view of a group of people and the practices associated with that view (as used in this book, the term includes nontheistic religions such as Communism and humanism, as well as theistic religions like Christianity).

Retainer An individual who owes service to a person or household of high status, especially in horticultural and agrarian societies.

Role A position which can be filled by an individual and to which distinctive behavioral expectations and requirements are attached; *less formally*, the term is used to refer to the part which a group, institution, or other social unit plays in the life of a society.

Sanction (1) A reward or punishment; (2) to reward or punish.

Secondary group Any group that is larger and more impersonal than a primary group.

Selection See *Natural selection, Intersocietal selection,* and *Intrasocietal selection.*

Serf A peasant farmer who is bound to the land and is subject to the owner of the land.

Shaman A person who enjoys special powers because of the distinctive, personal relationship he has established with the spirit world; a medicine man; not to be equated with priest.

Sib See *Clan.*

Signal A genetically determined response to a stimulus and a means of transmitting information.

Slave A person who is legally the property of another and hence subject to his authority.

Social movement A loose-knit group that seeks to change the social order.

Social organization Any structured system of relationships among people.

Socialization The process by means of which a person acquires the culture of his society.

Society A territorially bounded and autonomous population of animals of a single species (e.g., men) maintaining ties of association and interdependence.

Sociocultural Contraction of social and cultural.

Sociocultural progress The raising of the upper level of the capacity of human societies to mobilize energy and information in the adaptive process.

Sociology The study of human societies.

Species An evolved or evolving, genetically distinctive, reproductively isolated population.

Status The relative rank of a person, role, or group.

Status group A class made up of members of a racial, ethnic, or religious group (i.e., a class in which the resource involved is the individual's *membership in the group*).

Stratification Class or status differentiation within a population.

Structure The arrangement of the parts of an entity.

Subculture The culture of a group within a society.

Subsistence The basic necessities of life; also the process by which they are obtained.

Surplus See *Economic surplus*.

Symbiosis A relationship of mutual interdependence of unlike organisms or populations.

Symbol A culturally determined vehicle for the transmission of information.

System A system exists to the degree that the actions of the parts of an entity are coordinated both with one another and with the actions of the entity as a whole.

Systemic Having the attributes of a system.

Taxonomy A system of classification (synonym for *Typology:* the term "taxonomy" has been used more often in the biological sciences, "typology" in the social sciences).

Technology The information, techniques, and tools by means of which men utilize the material resources of their environment to satisfy their varied needs and desires.

Technostasis The absence of either technological progress or regression.

Theocracy A society ruled by a priesthood in the name of some deity or by a ruler believed to be divine.

Tribe A preliterate group whose members speak a distinctive language or dialect, possess a common culture that distinguishes them from other peoples, and who know themselves, or are known, by a distinctive name.

Typology See *Taxonomy*.

Unilinear theories of evolution Theories which assume that all societies follow exactly the same path of evolutionary development.

Urban community A community is urban to the degree that its inhabitants are freed from the necessity of producing their own food and fibers.

Values The generalized moral beliefs to which the members of a group subscribe.

Variable concept A concept in which the property involved is conceived of as varying in degree (contrast with *Categoric concepts*).

Variable costs Costs of production which tend to vary in proportion to the number of units produced (contrasted with *Fixed costs*).

Vertical mobility Change of status, either upward or downward.

Working class A class of people in modern industrial societies who belong to families headed by manual workers.

World views Men's beliefs concerning the *ultimate* nature of reality; their interpretation of the totality of experience.

$\mathcal{A}$ppendix: Notes on Murdock's Sample

The classification of 696 of Murdock's first 915 societies, shown below, is the basis for Tables 6/2 through 6/8. The 221 societies omitted here fall into the residual category composed of hybrid, maritime, and industrial societies, as well as a few societies which could not be classified because of insufficient information.

Objections may be leveled against some of the individual classifications, owing either to errors in Murdock's codes or my reading of them. In view of the very large number of societies in the analysis, however, occasional lapses of this kind should not alter results to any significant degree.

The category most vulnerable to criticism is probably the agrarian. As some readers will recognize, it includes a number of groups that are no longer independent societies, groups that are now ethnic minorities within agrarian societies. The chief justification for including them is that the larger societies involved (especially India) are still societies in only a minimal sense. Since independence, India has already divided once (into India and Pakistan) and powerful centrifugal forces are still at work—in particular, ethnic cleavages which involve major language differences. Looking to the past (when the studies of these groups were made), an even stronger case can be made for their inclusion, since these ethnic groups commonly enjoyed a substantial degree of autonomy. In short, these groups are on the borderline which divides those that meet the minimal qualifications for societies from those that fall short.

Hunting and gathering societies:

Achomawi	Aranda	Beatty	Botocudo
Ainu	Atsakudokwa	Beaver	Cahuilla
Andamanese	Atsugewi	Bergdama	Callinago
Antarianunts	Aweikoma	Bororo	Carinya

Hunting and gathering societies: continued

Carrier
Chemehuevi
Chamacoco
Chichimec
Chimariko
Chipewyan
Choroti
Cree, Eastern
Cupeno
Diegueno
Dieri
Dorobo
Eskimo, Caribou
Gabrielino
Gosiute
Guahibo
Guato
Hamilton
Huchnom
Hukundika
Kaibab
Kariera
Katikitegon
Kawaiisu
Keweyipaya
Kidutokado
Kiliwa
Kindiga
Klikitat
Koso
Kung
Kutubu
Kuyuidokado
Kwoma

Lassik
Las Vegas
Luiseno
Mahaguaduka
Maidu
Maricopa
Mattole
Mbuti
Menomini
Mescalero
Miami
Micmac
Motilon
Miwok
Miwok, Lake
Moanunts
Moapa
Monachi
Mono, Eastern
Montagnais
Murinbata
Murngin
Nabesna
Nambicuara
Naron
Naskapi
Nipigon
Nisenan
Nomlaki
Nunamiut
Ojibwa
Ona
Ottawa
Panamint

Panguitch
Patwin
Penkangekum
Penobscot
Piaroa
Pomo, Eastern
Pomo, Northern
Pomo, Southern
Potawatomi
Purari
Rainy River
Ramcocamecra
Rossel
Salinan
Sanema
Saulteaux, N.
Sawakudokwa
Sekani
Semang
Serrano
Shasta
Sherente
Shiriana
Shivuits
Shoshoni, Elko
Shoshoni, Ely
Shoshoni, Lida
Shuswap
Sinkyone
Siriono
Slave
Spring Valley
Stalo
Tagotaka

Tahltan
Takelma
Taqamiut
Tiwi
Toedokado
Tolkepaya
Tolowa
Tubaduka
Tubatulabal
Tukudika
Tunava
Vedda
Wadaduka
Wadatkuht
Wadodokado
Waika
Wappo
Waropen
Washo
White Knife
Wikmunkun
Winnebago
Wintu
Wiyambituka
Wukchummi
Xam
Yagua
Yana
Yavapai
Yokuts
Yokuts, Lake
Yuki
Yuki, Coast

Simple horticultural societies:

Abelam
Amahuaca
Apinaye
Arapesh
Bacairi
Basketo
Camarocoto
Camayura
Camba

Campa
Chakma
Cherokee
Choco
Chorti
Cochiti
Coroa
Cubeo
Curipaco

Enga
Gond, Maria
Guanche
Hanunoo
Hasinai
Hawaiians
Hopi
Huichol
Huron

Isleta
Jivaro
Kapauku
Katab
Keraki
Kiwai
Kurtatchi
Laguna
Lamet

Simple horticultural societies: continued

Lau	Natchez	Saramacca	Trumai
Lifu	Orokaiva	Sia	Tsamai
Locono	Palikur	Siane	Ulawans
Macusi	Panare	Siuai	Vanua Levu
Makitare	Piapoco	Subanun	Waiwai
Mangaians	Picuris	Tapirape	Wantoat
Maue	Rengma	Tarahumara	Wogeo
Mentaweians	Rotumans	Taulipang	Yuchi
Miriam	Rucuyen	Tenetehara	Yupa
Motu	Samoans	Trobrianders	Zuni

Advanced horticultural societies:

Abor	Bira, Plains	Fur	Kela
Acholi	Birifor	Fut	Khasi
Aimol	Bolewa	Ganda	Kikuyu
Akha	Bombesa	Giriama	Kipsigis
Akyem	Bontok	Gisu	Kisama
Amba	Bubi	Gogo	Kissi
Ambo	Budja	Gurage	Koko
Anaguta	Budu	Gure	Kom
Anfillo	Bunda	Gusii	Kongo
Angami	Buye	Ha	Konjo
Ao	Chagga	Hadimu	Konkomba
Arbore	Chamorro	Haya	Konso
Ashanti	Chawai	Hehe	Kota
Azande	Chewa	Hunde	Kpe
Aztec	Chibcha	Iban	Kpelle
Babwa	Chiga	Ibo	Kuba
Bafia	Chin	Ifugao	Kumu
Bako	Chokwe	Igbira	Kunda
Bali	Coniagui	Ila	Kundu
Bambara	Darasa	Inca	Kutshu
Bamileke	Digo	Iwa	Kwere
Bamum	Dilling	Jukun	Lakher
Banda	Dime	Kachin	Lala
Banen	Dogon	Kamba	Lalia
Bari	Duala	Kanawa	Lamba
Bashi	Duruma	Kanembu	Lango
Baule	Dzem	Kanuri	Lele
Baya	Dzing	Kaonde	Lenge
Bemba	Ekonda	Kara	Lhota
Bena	Fang	Karekare	Lobi
Bende	Fipa	Karen	Lotuko
Bete	Fon	Karewe	Lovedu
Bira	Fungom	Kasena	Lozi

Advanced horticultural societies: continued

Luapula	Ndebele	Rundi	Tetela
Luba	Ndembu	Safwe	Thado
Luchazi	Ndob	Sahel	Thonga
Luguru	Ndoko	Sakata	Tikar
Lulua	Ngombe	Sandawe	Tiriki
Luo	Ngonde	Sanga	Tiv
Luvale	Ngoni	Sena	Toma
Luwa	Ngumba	Shambale	Tonga, Plains
Maguzawa	Ngumbi	Shangama	Topoke
Makonde	Nkundo	Sherbro	Toro
Makua	Nsaw	Shila	Tswana
Malinke	Nsungli	Shilluk	Tumbuka
Mam	Nupe	Shogo	Turkana
Mambila	Nyakyusa	Shona	Ubamer
Mamvu	Nyamwezi	Sidamo	Udalan
Mangbetu	Nyanja	Soga	Ungassana
Margi	Nyankole	Songe	Venda
Masa	Nyaro	Songhai	Vugusu
Matakam	Nyasa	Songo	Widekum
Maya, Yucatec	Nyoro	Sonjo	Wolof
Mbala	Otoro	Sotho	Wute
Mbundu	Oyo Yoruba	Suku	Xhosa
Mende	Pare	Sukuma	Yaka
Merina	Pedi	Sumbwa	Yako
Meru	Pende	Sundi	Yanzi
Miao	Pimbwe	Swazi	Yao
Mnong Gar	Pokomo	Tallensi	Yatenga
Mongo	Puku	Tanala	Yeke
Mpongwe	Rangi	Teda	Yombe
Mzab	Rega	Teita	Zermu
Nankanse	Rhade	Teke	Zigula
Navaho (1930)	Ruanda	Tera	Zinza
Ndaka	Rumbi	Teso	Zulu
Ndau			

Agrarian societies:

Algerians	Barea	Burji	Coorg
Amahara	Basques (1930)	Burmese	Dagur
Annamese	Batak	Burusho	Dard
Armenians (1900)	Bengali	Byelorussians	Druze
Babylonians	Beraber	(1910)	Dusun
(2000 B. C.)	Bhil	Cham	Egyptians, Ancient
Baiga	Bhuiya, Hill	Cheremis	Egyptians (1957)
Balinese	Brazilians (1940)	Cherkess	Falasha
Barabra	Bulgarians (1940)	Chinese, Min	Georgians (1850)

Agrarian societies: continued

Gheg	Kumyk	Nuri	Sindhi
Gibe	Kunama	Okinawans	Sinhalese
Greeks (1950)	Kurd	Oraon	Spaniards (1950)
Hebrews (800 B.C.)	Lebanese (1950)	Pahari	Syrians
Ho	Lepcha	Pathan	Tamil
Irish (1930)	Li	Portuguese (1950)	Tekna
Janjero	Lolo	Purum	Telugu
Javanese	Macassarese	Riffians	Tibetans
Jebala	Macha	Romans	Tigrinya
Jordanians (1950)	Malays	Sagada	Tristan
Kabyle	Manchu	Santal	Tunisians
Kafa	Minchia	Serbs (1950)	Turkmen
Kerala	Moghol	Shawiya	Turks
Khevsur	Monguor	Shluh	Ukranians
Kol	Moroccans	Siamese	Yemeni
Koreans			

Fishing societies:

Alacaluf	Conibo	Makah	Selung
Alsea	Coos	Mangarevans	Seri
Aleut	Ellice	Manus	Sivokakmeit
Angmagsalik	Eskimo, Copper	Netsilik	Songola
Attawapiskat	Haida	Nootka	Tareumiut
Baffinland	Ket	Nunivak	Tlingit
Bellacoola	Klallam	Paraujano	Tokelau
Bozo	Koryak	Poto	Tsimshian
Callinago	Labrador	Quileute	Tututni
Chinook	Lokele	Raroians	Twana
Chugach	Luimbe	Sehing	Yahgan

Herding societies:

Ababda	Buryat	Herero	Nail
Afar	Chaamba	Icelanders	Nuer
Ahaggaren	Chahar	(1100 A.D.)	Osset
Amarar	Chukchee	Ifora	Regeibat
Antessar	Daza	Kababish	Rwala
Arusi	Delim	Kalmyk	Saadi
Asben	Dinka	Kazak	Sangu
Aulliminden	Esa	Khalka	Sanusi
Azjer	Galab	Kunta	Shuwa
Banna	Gilyak	Lapps	Somali
Basseri	Gimma	Masai	Tigre
Berabish	Habbania	Mbugwe	Toda
Bisharin	Hamama	Messiria	Trarza
Bogo	Hammar	Midobi	Yurak
Bororo Fulani	Hamyan	Mutair	Zenaga

𝒫icture Credits

10/3 P. F. Mele, Photo Researchers, Inc.
10/4 Standard Oil Co. (N.J.)
10/5 Standard Oil Co. (N.J.)
10/6 By permission of Institut Français d'Archeologie, Beirut, Lebanon
10/7 Courtesy of the British Museum, London
10/8 Courtesy of the Metropolitan Museum of Art, Rogers Fund, 1906

11/1 The Smithsonian Institution
11/2 The Smithsonian Institution
11/3 The Smithsonian Institution
11/4 United Nations
11/5 Courtesy of Con Edison
11/6 The Granger Collection
11/7 Susan Johns, Picture Editor

12/1 United Nations
12/2 Standard Oil Co. (N.J.)
12/4 Standard Oil Co. (N.J.)
12/5 Erich Hartmann, Magnum Photos Inc.

12/6 Courtesy of the New York Public Library
12/7 Ian Berry, Magnum Photos Inc.
12/8 Wide World Photos

13/1 Standard Oil Co. (N.J.)
13/2 Courtesy of the New York Public Library
13/3 AT&T Photo Service
13/4 United Nations
13/5 By permission of Swedish Information Service
13/6 United Nations
13/7 Cornell Capa, Magnum Photos Inc.
13/8 Karsh, Ottawa. Submitted by Rapho-Guillumette
13/9 Cornell Capa, Magnum Photos Inc.
13/11 United Nations
13/12 Warner Bros.—Seven Arts, Inc.
13/13 United Nations

14/1 (Marx) Courtesy of the New York Public Library

(Tillich) Burt Glenn, Magnum Photos Inc.
(Russell) Magnum Photo Library Print
14/2 Burk Uzzle, Magnum Photos Inc.
14/3 Bill Brandt from Rapho-Guillumette

15/1 United Nations
15/2 Standard Oil Co. (N.J.)
15/3 (Nasser) Magnum Photo Library Print
(Nehru) Ernst Haas, Magnum Photos Inc.
(Shah of Iran) Lee Lockwood from Black Star
(Castro) Bruce Davidson, Magnum Photos Inc.
15/4 Standard Oil Co. (N.J.)
15/5 United Nations
15/6 United Nations
15/7 Standard Oil Co. (N.J.)
15/8 United Nations
15/9 United Nations
15/10 United Nations
15/11 Ian Berry, Magnum Photos Inc.
15/12 United Nations

$\mathcal{N}$ame Index

Abegglen, James, 402
Aberle, D. F., 29, 219, 221
Adams, Robert, 239, 242
Adams, Walter, 483
Aitchison, Leslie, 128, 202, 206, 250–251
Alford, Robert, 362, 391
Allardt, Erik, 362
Alle, W. C., 14, 52
Alliluyeva, Svetlana, 413
Alsop, Joseph, 375
Anderson, Jack, 355, 391
Andreades, A., 254
Andrzejewski, Stanislaw, 257
Apter, David, 439, 459, 461, 465
Aristotle, 111
Arth, M. J., 135

Baegert, Jacob, 184
Bagley, William C., 106
Bailey, F. G., 94, 451
Banfield, Edward, 285, 366
Barber, Elinor, 274
Barnett, H. G., 74
Barringer, Herbert, 10, 62
Bates, Marston, 57
Baumer, Franklin, 493
Baumhoff, Martin, 165–166
Becker, Howard, 119
Bell, Daniel, 461
Bell, Wendell, 439
Bellah, Robert, 283

Benedict, Ruth, 32
Bennett, H. S., 260, 269–272
Berger, Morroe, 266, 279
Berger, Peter, 44, 77, 415
Berle, A. A., 377
Berndt, Catherine, 159, 182–183
Berndt, Ronald, 159, 182–183
Berry, Brian, 64
Bhagwati, Jagdish, 437
Biggs, E. Power, 103
Birket-Smith, Kaj, 176, 179, 186–187
Bishop, C. W., 238
Blau, Peter, 397
Bloch, Marc, 261, 263, 271
Blum, Jerome, 253–254, 256, 258, 262, 267–270, 272
Blumenthal, Fred, 35
Boak, A. E. R., 257, 271
Boas, Franz, 120, 147
Bogardus, Emory, 400
Bourgeois-Pichat, J., 423
Brace, C. Loring, 96
Braidwood, Robert, 121, 158, 192–194, 196, 209–210
Brigham, Carl, 106
Bright, William, 37
Brown, B., 106
Brown, Emily Clark, 379
Brown, Harrison, 55, 280, 282, 479
Brzezinski, Zbigniew, 354, 360
Buah, F. K., 231
Buck, John Lossing, 275

Buer, M. C., 282
Bush, R. R., 135

Callender, Charles, 20
Campbell, Angus, 391, 395
Campbell, Donald, 62
Carcopino, Jerome, 254, 273
Carneiro, Robert, 25, 101, 130
Carr-Saunders, A. M., 344
Carson, Rachel, 484
Carstairs, G. M., 270
Carter, Gwendolen, 455, 464
Cayton, Horace, 406
Chagnon, Napoleon, 224
Chang, Chung-li, 254, 260, 267, 279
Chang, Kwang-chih, 121, 199–200, 204, 206–208
Chapin, F. Stuart, 66
Cheng, Te-k'un, 204–206
Childe, V. Gordon, 36, 61, 115, 120–123, 188, 193–198, 201, 203, 213, 238, 240, 244, 246, 248–249, 301
Childs, Marquis, 381
Clapham, J. H., 316
Clark, Grahame, 80, 147–148, 150, 153, 155–156, 159–161, 189
Clough, S. B., 256, 276, 317, 321, 328, 373, 376
Cohen, Ronald, 101, 130
Cole, C. W., 256, 276, 317, 321, 328, 373, 376
Cole, Sonia, 149–151, 228
Cole, W. A., 312, 315, 317–318, 344
Collier, Donald, 210, 215–216
Collver, O. Andrew, 279
Comte, Auguste, 22, 23, 119
Converse, Philip, 391, 395
Cooley, Charles Horton, 32
Coon, Carleton S., 150, 176, 184, 187, 295
Cooper, John, 176
Coult, Allan, 115
Coulton, G. G., 265, 270–271, 279
Cowell, F. R., 255, 271, 276
Curwen, E. Cecil, 128, 192, 194–195, 199, 237–238

D'Antonio, William V., 450
Darwin, Charles, 13, 50, 52, 55, 58, 62, 68, 93
Davidson, Basil, 231, 233, 235
Davis, Kingsley, 10, 31, 242, 254
Day, Clarence, 15
Day, Clive, 315
Deane, Phyllis, 312, 315, 317–318, 344

deCastro, Josue, 266
Deutsch, Karl, 477
Deutsch, M., 106
DeVore, Irven, 190–191
Dewhurst, J. Frederic, 322–323, 341, 381–382, 384
Dewitt, Nicholas, 388
Dixon, Roland, 176, 183
Djilas, Milovan, 394
Dole, Gertrude, 188
Douglas, Robert K., 258, 269
Drake, St. Clair, 406
Drucker, Philip, 293
Duncan, O. D., 397
Duverger, Maurice, 391, 395, 413

Eberhard, Wolfram, 258, 271, 279
Eggan, Fred, 67
Ehrmann, Henry, 355, 392
Eiseley, Loren, 55
Elkin, A. P., 164–165, 172, 174–175, 179, 181, 183–184
Emerson, Alfred E., xi, 10, 14, 20, 50, 52
Engels, Friedrich, 407, 412
Erman, Adolf, 248
Evans, Ivor, 173, 175, 179, 182–184, 186
Eversley, D. E. C., 279–280, 282, 423
Evtushenko, Evgeny, 412–413

Fainsod, Merle, 394
Fallers, Lloyd, 461, 465
Farmer, B. H., 195, 237–238
Faron, Louis, 215–216, 218, 222, 224
Feierabend, Ivo, 360
Feierabend, Rosalind, 360
Fisher, Sydney, 295, 438
Florence, P. Sargant, 377
Forbes, R. J., 202, 204, 215
Fortes, Meyer, 230, 231
Fraenkel, Merran, 459, 461, 463–464, 467
Franck, Peter, 438
Frankfort, Henri, 213
Freedman, L. Z., 33
Freeman, Linton, 101
Freud, Sigmund, 72, 413
Fried, Morton, 272

Galbraith, Kenneth, 374
Gamble, Sidney, 277–278
Garvan, John, 166–167, 170, 173, 175, 182, 475
Gayton, A. H., 177, 183

Geiger, Kent, 422
George, M. Dorothy, 278
Gibbs, James, 167–168, 234
Gil, Frederico, 266
Gillen, F. J., 177
Ginsberg, M., 92, 130
Ginsburg, Norton, 64
Glass, David V., 279–280, 282, 423
Goldman, Irving, 222
Goldschmidt, Walter, xi, 25, 90, 101–102, 121–123, 129, 131, 133–134, 168, 170, 172, 176, 179–180, 182
Goode, William J., 403, 415, 421
Goodenough, War, 186
Gordon, Milton, 400
Gordon, Robert A., 377
Gough, Kathleen, 219
Gouldner, Alvin, 64, 130, 301
Granick, David, 377
Groves, Reg, 258, 272
Gsovski, Vladimir, 422
Gurdon, P. R. T., 234

Habenstein, Robert, 115
Hagstrom, Warren, 110
Halpern, Manfred, 434, 439, 449
Halphen, L., 288
Hamburg, David, 16
Hammond, Barbara, 456
Hammond, J. L., 456
Hanson, A. H., 438
Harden, Donald, 301
Harris, Marvin, 25
Hatt, Gudmund, 128, 192, 194–195, 199, 237–238
Hawkes, Jacquetta, 96, 128, 150, 152, 154–156, 159–161, 163, 165, 195–199, 201
Hawley, Amos H., xi
Heilbroner, Robert, 263, 311, 371, 392
Heizer, Robert, 112, 147, 189, 193
Helleiner, F. K., 282
Herberg, Will, 400
Herrick, C. J., 58
Herskovits, Melville, 67
Hewes, Gordon, 292, 294
Higbee, Edward, 370, 383
Hobhouse, L. T., 92, 130
Hodges, Harold M., 405
Hoebel, E. Adamson, 98, 128, 150, 154, 181, 218
Hole, Frank, 112, 147, 189, 193
Hollingshead, A. B., 406
Hollingsworth, T. H., 280

Holmberg, Allan, 167, 170–172, 176, 181, 187
Homans, George, 271–272
Honigmann, John, 150, 178–179, 183
Horner, George, 452
Hose, Charles, 168, 171, 173, 176, 178, 180–182, 185–186
Howe, Bruce, 192–194, 196
Hsu, Cho-yun, 204–207
Hughes, Everett, 401
Hunter, Guy, 454–455, 457, 459–461, 464
Huntington, Ellsworth, 107–108
Huntington, Samuel, 354, 360
Huxley, Julian, 48, 55, 58, 61–62
Hymes, Dell, 37

Inkeles, Alex, 422
Issawi, Charles, 254, 345

Janowitz, Morris, 362, 402
Jennings, J. D., 159
Jones, A. H. M., 264
Jones, William O., 456

Kahn, Herman, 480–482
Kendall, Paul Murray, 272–274, 284, 287
Kennedy, Ruby Jo Reeves, 400
Key, V. O., Jr., 355, 391
Klema, Bohuslav, 158
Klineberg, Otto, 106
Kluckhohn, Clyde, 11
Krader, Lawrence, 295–296
Kraeling, Carl, 239, 242
Kramer, S. N., 240, 242, 245
Kraus, Bertram, 150
Krech, David, 482
Kroeber, A. L., 18, 67, 80, 109, 114
Kwan, Kian, 400

Laird, Charleton, 35
Lamarck, Jean Baptiste, 62
Lampman, Robert, 390, 402–403
Landtman, Gunnar, 218
Langley, Kathleen, 390
Langlois, Charles, 272
Lanternari, Vittorio, 464
Latourette, K. S., 282
Lee, Everett, 106
Lerner, Daniel, 357–358
Leslie, J. A. K., 456, 459, 463, 466–467
Lessa, William, 182–183

Levi, Carlo, 285
Lewis, David, 279, 345, 419–420, 423
Lewis, William H., 452
Liebow, Elliot, 406
Lindsay, Philip, 258, 272
Linton, Ralph, 84–85, 106, 256, 491
Lipset, S. M., 357–358, 362, 365, 439, 447–448, 450
Littunen, Yrjö, 362
Lloyd, P. C., 234
Loeb, Edwin, 166–167, 170
Lorenz, Konrad, 90
Lowie, Robert, 222
Lundberg, Ferdinand, 389
Lybyer, Albert, 260–261

McArthur, Margaret, 170, 180
McCarthy, Frederick, 159, 170, 180
McConnell, James, 225
McDougall, William, 168, 171, 173, 176, 178, 180–182, 185–186
Macintosh, N. W. G., 159
McKisack, May, 272
McNeill, William H., 128, 239, 243, 249, 299–300
Maine, Sir Henry, 119
Mair, Lucy, 231, 459, 473
Malthus, Thomas, 54–55, 93
Mandelbaum, David, 37
Mantoux, Paul, 314
Mariéjol, Jean Hippolyte, 262–263
Marshall, Lorna, 168, 170, 179
Marx, Karl, 119, 407, 412, 414
Maslow, A. H., 33, 47, 93, 470
Mason, E. S., 377
Matthews, Donald, 391, 402
Mattingly, Harold, 257–258
Maugham, W. Somerset, 273
Mayr, Ernst, 48–50, 52, 54–55, 60
Mead, Herbert, 32
Mead, Margaret, 222, 290
Means, Gardner, 377
Meggers, Betty, 108
Mehnert, Klaus, 394
Mellaart, James, 128, 160, 188, 192–198, 201–202
Menard, Wilmend, 295
Merrill, Robert S., 38
Métraux, Alfred, 222, 227
Michels, Robert, 111, 378
Miller, Warren, 391, 395
Mills, Lennox A., 438
Miner, Horace, 279
Misra, B. B., 261–262, 274

Misra, Shridhar, 266
Modge, Charles, 24
Montet, Pierre, 243
Moore, Barrington, 491
Moore, Wilbert, 110
Moreland, W. H., 260–261, 263, 268–269, 272
Morgan, Lewis Henry, 119–123, 147, 222
Morley, Sylvanus, 210–212, 216
Mosca, Gaetano, 249
Moskos, Charles, 439
Mountford, Charles, 170
Murdock, George Peter, 123, 130–134, 136–138, 140–142, 166, 174, 186, 217–219, 221, 229–230, 234, 290, 292, 296–297, 421, 503
Murray, Henry, 11
Murray, Margaret, 241
Myrdal, Gunnar, 270
Myres, John L., 296

Naroll, Raoul, 101, 130
Nash, Manning, 279
Nef, John, 113, 276–277, 312
Neumann, Franz, 375
Newcomer, Mabel, 402
Noss, John, 279
Notestein, Frank W., 436
Nove, Alec, 375, 382, 384
Nowak, Stefan, 386

Ogburn, William F., 82–83, 85, 109
Oppenheim, A. Leo, 241–244
Orenstein, Henry, 287
Orwell, George, 6

Painter, Sidney, 260–261, 263
Park, Orlando, 14, 52
Park, Thomas, 52
Parry, Albert, 360, 399
Parsons, Talcott, 24, 29, 104, 140, 258
Paul VI, Pope, 484
Pavlov, Ivan Petrovich, 72
Pearson, Drew, 355, 391
Pelsaert, F., 261
Perrot, Jean, 192, 195
Peterson, Richard, 64, 130
Piggott, Stuart, 115–116, 128, 147, 150, 153, 159–161, 189
Pike, Frederick, 450
Pirenne, Henri, 272, 288
Plato, 111
Polanyi, Karl, 371
Porter, John, 392

Pospisil, Leopold, 222
Post, Ken, 455
Postl, William, 83
Pritchard, E. E., 231
Putnam, Patrick, 187

Radcliffe-Brown, A. R., 174, 176, 178–180, 183–184
Ramsay, James H., 260–274
Ray, F., 222
Redfield, Robert, 119
Reichel-Dolmatoff, Gerardo, 210
Rivet, Paul, 214
Roberts, J. M., 135
Robinson, E. A. G., 454
Robinson, John A. T., 411, 415
Roe, Anne, 32, 48, 57
Rosenberg, Hans, 259, 263
Rostovtzeff, Michael, 258
Roth, H. Ling, 179
Russell, Bertrand, 413–414
Russell, J. C., 272, 279
Russett, Bruce, 330, 404, 432, 435, 445, 452, 455, 463
Rustow, Dankwort, 355, 360

Sahlins, Marshall, 25
Salzman, L. F., 287
Samuelson, Paul, 87
Sanders, Irwin T., 275
Sankalia, H. D., 121, 198
Sansom, George, 254, 268, 274
Sapir, Edward, 37
Sarapata, Adam, 386
Sawyer, Jack, 64
Schapera, I., 166, 170–171, 176–180, 182–183, 186–187, 233
Schmidt, K. P., 14, 52
Schneider, David, 219
Schnore, Leo, 64
Scott, Robert E., 450
Seele, Keith, 241, 243
Semenov, S. A., 153–155, 160–161
Serrano, Antonio, 166
Service, Elman, 25, 33, 40, 119, 174–175, 183
Shapiro, Harry, 194
Shell, Kurt, 360
Shibutani, Tamotsu, 400
Simirenko, Alex, 24, 376
Simmons, Leo, 137–139
Simpson, Alan, 262
Simpson, George Gaylord, 11, 13, 33, 48, 50, 52, 57–58, 62

Singer, Charles, 251–252, 328
Singh, Baljit, 266
Sjoberg, Gideon, 254, 267, 272–273, 286
Skinner, B. F., 72
Smelser, Neil, 447–448
Smith, John Maynard, 48, 55
Solari, Aldo, 450
Sorokin, Pitirim, 92, 119, 257–258
Southall, A. W., 473
Speck, Frank, 170, 176, 180, 185
Spencer, Baldwin, 177
Spencer, Herbert, 22, 23, 60, 110–111, 257
Spencer, R. F., 159
Srinivas, M. N., 270
Stanner, W. E. H., 182–183
Steindorff, George, 241, 243
Stern, Philip, 389, 391
Steward, Julian, 119, 166, 175–176, 215–216, 218, 222, 224, 227
Stokes, Donald, 391, 395
Stoney, Samuel G., 273
Storer, Norman, xi
Stubbs, William, 271
Sumner, William Graham, 34
Sutherland, Edwin, 409
Swanson, G. E., 134

Taeuber, Irene, 254, 279
Takekoshi, Yosoburo, 271, 274
Tawney, R. H., 329, 332–333
Tax, Sol, 20, 48, 55
Thomas, Dorothy, 109
Thompson, J. E. S., 210
Thompson, James Westfall, 261, 271, 278, 285
Thompson, Warren, 279, 281–282, 345, 419–420, 423
Thomsen, Christian J., 119–123
Thorpe, W. H., 13, 17
Thrupp, Sylvia, 277–278
Tilley, Arthur, 272, 288
Tillich, Paul, 411, 414
Toennies, Ferdinand, 119
Toynbee, Arnold, 311
Trevor-Roper, H. R., 263
Turnbull, Colin, 167, 173–175, 177–178, 181–182, 184, 187, 475
Turner, Ralph, 241, 243, 246–247, 253, 255, 258, 299
Turner, Ralph H., 39
Tylor, E. B., 18

Vallier, Ivan, 450
van Werveke, H., 288

Veblen, Thorstein, 33, 93, 115
Vogt, Evan, 182–183
von Frisch, Karl, 29
von Hagen, Victor, 211, 214–216

Walinsky, Louis, 438
Wallace, Alfred Russel, 55
Wallbank, T. W., 254
Warner, W. L., 366, 402
Washburn, Sherwood L., 16
Watson, James D., 110
Watson, William, 204–207
Watters, R. F., 211, 238
Weber, Max, 258, 330–333, 336
Weiner, Myron, 446
Weinstein, Brian, 459
Wheeler, G. C., 92, 130
Wheeler, Mortimer, 198
White, Leslie, 18, 19, 25, 34, 140
White, M. J. D., 50
Whiting, John, 186
Wiener, Anthony, 480–482

Willcox, Walter F., 344
Willey, Gordon, 121, 158, 192, 209–211
Williams, Philip, 392
Wilson, Everett, xi
Wilson, James, 366
Wilson, John A., 239
Winch, Robert, 101
Wittfogel, Karl, 262
Woodruff, William, 276
Woolley, Leonard, 240–241, 243
Woytinsky, E. S., 316, 320–324, 342, 344, 423
Woytinsky, W. S., 316, 320–324, 342, 344, 423
Wright, Quincey, 92
Wrigley, C. C., 461
Wrong, Dennis, 33

Yates, P. Lamartine, 383
Yerkes, R. M., 106

Zink, Harold, 395
Zolberg, Aristide, 459

Subject Index

Adaptation, 10, 16–17, 27, 54, 56, 59, 66, 69–70, 78, 97, 120, 150, 161, 304, 469, 492, 495
Africa, 98, 106, 126, 149, 164, 216, 228–235, 295, 299, 345, 451–467, 485–486
  North, 198, 255, 283, 295, 450
    (*See also* Egypt)
Age distinctions, 170, 224, 402, 425–427, 456, 465–466
Aggregations, 40, 43, 495
Aging, 187–188
Agrarian societies, 25–26, 112, 114–115, 122–139, 219–221, 237–289, 295, 305–307, 327, 360, 408–409, 415, 429, 471–472, 483, 495
  advanced, 125, 250–289, 495
  simple, 125, 238–250, 495
Agricultural revolution, 333–335
Agriculture, 316, 318, 370–371, 381, 432, 444–445, 495
  (*See also* Agrarian societies)
Alphabet, 71, 248
Alteration, 63, 66–67, 495
Aluminum, 313, 323
American society, 316, 318, 320–326, 340–343, 347, 350–353, 355, 358, 362–366, 370–371, 373–374, 377–381, 385–392, 394, 397–405, 419–423, 433, 436–438, 447, 472, 476

Andaman Islanders, 178–180
Animal domestication, 98–99, 121, 160, 162, 218, 224, 305
Anthropology, relation to sociology, 5, 25–26
Arabia, 295–296, 298, 431
Archaeology, 119–122, 147–163, 188–190, 192–216
Argentina, 325, 347, 354, 364
Armies, 242–243
Art, 86, 99, 102, 156–158, 162, 171, 184–185
Artisans, 241, 256, 276–278, 287, 306, 495
Asia, 84, 98, 216, 299, 345, 446, 457
  southeast, 164, 228, 234–235, 251, 266, 283, 433–434, 449–451, 453
Asia Minor, 193, 242
  (*See also* Hittites)
Associations, 40–41, 495
  (*See also* Corporations; Labor unions)
Athenian society, 301–302
Atomic energy, 125
Atomic warfare, 479
Australia, 115, 120, 159, 163–165, 174, 177, 182, 289
Authority, 425–426, 480
Automation, 313, 326, 481
Automobile, 313, 320–321
Autonomy, 9, 97
Aviation, 313, 323, 384

Babylonia, 242, 248, 272

Barbarian societies, 120

Behavioral expectations (*see* Norms)

Biology, 33

Biotic world, 7–8, 10–22
  universals, 13–14

Birth control, 346–347, 436, 484–485, 492

Birth rates, 185–186, 188, 272, 279–280, 307, 338, 345–347, 404, 406–407, 419–421, 433–436, 454, 484–485, 492

Blue-collar jobs, 351, 385–388, 407, 426

Bow and arrow, 124, 154–155, 162

Brazil, 266, 325, 344, 364, 442

Britain and British society, 149, 193, 198–199, 258, 261, 268–270, 273, 277, 279–282, 311–320, 322, 332, 342–344, 347, 354–356, 359, 361–363, 373, 379, 390, 392, 416, 419–420, 422, 437–438, 448

Bronze, 204–207, 222, 228, 250

Bronze Age, 119–120, 228

Buddhism, 282–283, 330, 411, 413, 422, 449–450

Bureaucracy, 397–398, 415, 428, 455, 496
  governmental, 243–245, 365–367

Bushmen, 169, 171, 173, 178–179, 181–182, 186–187, 289, 431

Calendar, 71, 211, 248

Calvinism, 330–333

Canadian society, 325, 347, 362–363, 392, 401, 422, 433

Cannibalism, 139, 152, 162, 225, 227, 236

Capitalism, 372, 376, 496

Castro, Fidel, 438, 440

Çatal Hüyük, 196–197, 199

Categoric concepts, 59, 70, 354, 496

Catholicism, Roman, 330–332, 422, 449–450
  (*See also* Christianity)

Chalcolithic Age, 119

Chance, 36, 54, 68, 80–81, 501

Chemical industry, 318, 338

Chiefs, 222, 224, 228, 474, 496

Chile, 266

Chinese society, 84, 98, 193, 198–200, 203–208, 239, 241, 252, 254, 257–258, 269, 274–275, 277–279, 299, 325, 344, 348, 427, 438, 454

Christianity, 103, 282–285, 298, 411–415, 450, 463–465

Classes, 42–44, 135–137, 189, 206, 287–288, 306, 361–363, 384–409, 443–445, 496
  (*See also* Inequality; Nobility; Slavery)

Cleavages, sociocultural, 246–248, 287–288, 445–447, 461–462

Cliques, 40

Clothing, 153, 162

Coal, 125, 312, 315, 318, 341–342

Command economies, 371, 392, 490, 496

Commerce (*see* Trade and commerce)

Communication, 30, 35–37, 61, 98, 105, 248, 251, 261, 338–339, 353, 365–366, 388, 479, 481, 486–488, 496
  (*See also* Mass media; Writing and literacy)

Communism and Communist countries, 77, 103, 354, 358–359, 375–376, 379, 386, 392–394, 412–413, 416, 422, 427–428, 438–439, 441, 448, 450–451, 488–490

Communities, 40–41, 43, 97, 131–133, 155, 160, 165–166, 189, 196–197, 210, 217, 221–222, 228–229, 296, 452
  permanence, 129, 133, 166–167, 209, 217–218, 235, 292, 305
  urban, 115, 205, 215, 234, 239, 242, 247, 254, 256–257, 263–266, 272–282, 287, 300–304, 306, 349–350, 358, 369–371, 466–467, 502

Competition, 13–14, 92–93
  (*See also* Scarcity)

Computers, 313, 324, 326, 339, 479, 481–482

Conditioning, 72, 89

Conflict, political, 257–258, 260–263, 360–363, 406, 445–447, 461–462

Conquest, 205–208, 216, 231–232, 242–243, 299, 306, 327, 485

Conservatism, 77–78, 102–103

Continuity, 49, 51, 61, 63, 65–66, 71–79

Control, social, 30, 39, 65, 178–179, 470, 482
  (*See also* Laws; Polity)

Cooperatives, 380–382

Copper, 201–203, 214–216, 228, 248

Corporations, 376–379, 482, 486

Corruption, 258, 438

Craftsmen (*see* Artisans)

Cranial capacity, 150, 152

Creativity, 32, 249, 339

Crete, 128, 300

Crime, 257, 407
  punishments for, 270, 473–474

Culture, 18–22, 32, 93, 496

Customs, 72–73, 496

Cyclical patterns of change, 110–112

Czechoslovakia, 155–156, 158, 347, 354, 489

Death, 476

Death rates, 186–187, 190, 280–282, 307, 345–347, 420, 423, 454, 485

Defense, 30, 37

Democracy, 336, 354–363, 366–367, 395, 397, 408–409, 416, 437–439, 442–444, 446, 459–460, 473, 475, 486, 488–490, 494
  ecclesiastical, 356–357
Demography (*see* Birth rates; Death rates; Population)
Denmark, 120, 187, 325–326, 347
Deterministic theory, 59–60, 70, 107–109, 478, 496
Diffusion, 61–63, 67, 84–85, 164, 198–200, 216, 228, 239, 251–252, 328, 430, 467, 496
Discoveries, 63, 66, 80–81, 109–110, 496
  (*See also* specific discoveries)
Distribution, 30–31
Diversification, 58, 69, 95–100, 486–487
Division of labor, 44, 89, 102, 129, 133–134, 170–172, 189, 193, 306, 350–353
  (*See also* Specialization)
Divorce, 175, 417–418, 421–423

Ecological communities, 7, 57, 484, 496–497
Ecological-evolutionary approach in sociology, 25, 60ff.
Ecological niches, 61
Economic growth rates, 442
Economics, 5, 25
Economizing, 33–34, 89, 105
Economy, 167–173, 224, 246, 263–279, 286, 328–333, 364, 369–384, 436–437, 454–457, 490
  planned, 375
  world, 436–437, 490
  (*See also* Trade and commerce; Technology)
Education, 41, 336–337, 357, 395–399, 416–417, 444, 447–449, 461, 483
Egalitarian trend, 407–409
Egypt, 84, 128, 228, 238–250, 253, 255, 258, 266, 325, 344, 422, 431, 434, 437, 440, 447, 450
Elections, costs, 390–391
Electrical industry, 313, 318, 321
Electronics, 313, 323–324
Elites, political (*see* Governing class)
Empires, 216, 239, 242–245, 283, 306
Energy, 59, 63, 70, 99, 105, 126, 154, 238, 248, 278, 299, 311–326, 340–342, 432, 469, 479, 481, 497
  consumption per capita, 325–326, 432
Engineering, 447–448
England (*see* Britain and British society)
Environment, 13–14, 20–21, 37, 49–50, 55–59, 62, 69, 78–80, 87–88, 98, 105, 107–109, 127, 132–133, 159–161, 189, 212, 234–235, 289–305, 314, 342, 410–411, 468, 483–484, 497

Eskimoes, 1, 186–187, 289
Ethnic stratification, 399–401
Ethnography, 131–139, 147–148, 163–190, 216–235, 497
Ethology, 33–34, 48, 190–191, 497
Europe, 84–85, 91, 94, 105–106, 113, 149, 160, 193–199, 203–204, 262, 276, 283, 323, 345, 436, 457, 459, 486
  backwardness, 252, 327–328
Evolution:
  organic: compared with sociocultural evolution, 60–63, 467, 469
    new synthetic theory, 48–62
  unilinear theories of, 205
Evolutionary approach in sociology, 22–25, 497
Exchange, 30
Exogamy, 175, 497
Exploitation, 45, 206, 265, 267–268, 270–271, 306, 394, 416, 425, 429, 437, 439, 475
Extinction, 49, 52–57, 61, 63, 67–69, 89–94, 105

Factories, 103, 311, 319, 369
Families, 40, 172, 174–175, 416–425, 491–492
  enterprises, 376, 382–383
  extended, 175, 218–219, 228, 231, 286, 416–417, 465–467, 491, 497
  (*See also* Kinship)
Famine, 54, 282, 346
Farmers, 370–371, 381–383, 386–388
  (*See also* Peasants)
Fascists, 354, 358, 375, 379, 413
Fatalism, 285, 411
Fertility cults, 156–157, 195
Feudalism, 206, 260–263
Fire, 151, 162, 191, 202
Fishing, 159, 162, 164–165, 189, 305
  societies, 123–137, 159, 290–295, 305, 430, 497
Fission, societal, 97, 181
France, 320–322, 324–325, 347, 349, 355, 362, 379, 392, 423, 438
Freedom, 178–179, 460, 470–473, 477, 493–494
Functional requisites, 29–30
Fundamental discoveries and inventions, 85, 483, 497
Future, 477–494

Games, 135
Generosity, 176, 180, 259, 285
  (*See also* Mutual aid)
Genetic code, 34

Genetic drift, 54, 67

Genetic systems, 18–22

Genetics, 33–34, 48–63, 481–482, 497

Genotype, 49–50, 63–64, 104, 492

Geographical determinism, 107–109

German society, 85, 92, 258, 262, 318, 320, 323–325, 347, 349, 354, 360, 362–363, 379, 399, 427, 489, 494

Ghana, 454, 460–461, 465

God, 71, 134, 298–299, 331, 413–415, 493

Gold, 214, 224, 250, 328–329, 372

Governing class, 206–208, 224, 241, 246–247, 250, 257–263, 266–268, 273–274, 284, 287, 306–307, 327, 329, 367, 392, 416, 437, 497

Government, growth of, 363–367
   (*See also* Polity)

"Great man" explanations, 109–110

Greek society, 107, 120, 300–302, 325, 344, 364, 442

Groups, 40–41, 43, 498

Guilds, 278, 372, 376, 498

Habits, 72–73, 497

Happiness, 475–477, 493–494

Headmen, 171–172, 176–178, 180–181, 222, 228, 498

Herding societies, 122–137, 295–299, 431, 498

Hierarchy of organization, 8

Hinduism, 283, 330, 411, 413, 449–450

History, its relation to sociology, 26

Hittites, 242, 250

Hoe, 126, 237–239

Hominids, 96–97, 149–150, 304, 498

Homo sapiens sapiens, 97, 152, 154–155, 481

Horse, 208, 297, 299

Horticultural societies, 122–139, 192–236, 259, 294, 305, 472, 475, 483, 498
   advanced, 125, 202–208, 214–216, 228–235, 498
   simple, 125, 193–201, 209–214, 216–228, 430, 498

Horticulture, 164–165, 189, 498
   (*See also* Horticultural societies)

Housing, 155–156, 162, 209, 381–382, 400

Human nature, 32–34, 47, 367, 486, 498

Humanism, 103, 413, 450, 493

Hunger, 170, 429

Hunting and gathering societies, 97–100, 114–115, 121–191, 219–220, 291–292, 304–305, 430, 471–472, 474–475, 483, 498

Hybrid societies, 125, 173, 216, 430–467, 498

Ideology, 34, 44–47, 64, 77, 86–87, 89, 98, 101–105, 116–117, 119, 121, 142, 211–213, 234, 248, 329–333, 335, 339, 355–357, 361, 366, 372, 395, 397, 427, 448–451, 462–465, 498
   (*See also* Norms; Religion; Values; World Views)

Incas, 107–108, 328

Income, 41, 461
   differences, 260, 385, 387, 398, 400, 404
   national, 408–409
   per capita, 343–344, 500
   per square mile, 453–454

India, 84, 94, 115, 203, 252, 254, 266, 283, 325, 344, 348, 423, 431–432, 439–440, 442, 446, 448, 451, 454

Indians, American, 84–85, 94

Industrial Revolution, 47, 311–339, 430, 474
   causes, 327–339
   concept of, 311–313

Industrial societies, 100, 105, 122–129, 311–429, 472, 477–494, 498–499

Industrialization, 147, 311–326, 343–344, 348–354, 357, 387–388, 421–423, 430–467, 498

Industrializing agrarian societies, 430–451, 453, 458, 461

Industrializing horticultural societies, 430, 451–467, 485

Industrializing societies, 364, 430–467, 483

Inequality, 136–137, 179–181, 190, 203, 216, 223–224, 228, 230, 236, 249, 292, 297, 361, 384–409, 416, 443–445

Infanticide, 187, 269, 307n

Infants, 32–33, 74

Information, 20–22, 35, 37–38, 59–62, 66–67, 70, 82–83, 86–89, 98, 247, 304–305, 335, 338–339, 397, 405, 410–411, 447, 469, 492–493, 499
   cumulation of, 335
   size of store, 82–83, 87, 114, 248, 251, 478–479
   (*See also* Technology)

Inheritance, 206–207, 261–263

Innovation, 49, 52, 61, 63, 66–67, 79–89, 104–105, 109–110, 142, 161–163, 249–250, 252, 303–304, 480–483
   attitude toward, 86, 249–250
   institutionalization of, 336–337
   rate of, 82–89
   (*See also* Progress, technological rates of)

Insect societies, 33

Instinctive (genetically programmed) behavior, 17, 19, 33–34, 72–74, 499

Integration, 39

Intelligence, 14, 106, 481, 492, 498
  (*See also* Learning)

Interaction, social (*see* Communication)

Interdependence, 57, 77, 86–88

Inventions, 63, 66, 81–83, 428, 498
  simultaneous, 109–110

Iron, 125, 228, 248, 250–251, 315, 317–318,
  320, 342

Iron Age, 120

Iroquois Indians, 119–120

Irrigation, 195, 208, 224, 248, 342

Islam, 282–283, 298–299, 330, 332, 411, 413,
  421–422, 449, 463–464

Isolation, 50–51, 60, 64–65, 98, 114–115, 430

Italian society, 323, 325, 347, 349, 354, 362–
  363, 379, 392, 422

Japanese society, 262, 279, 299, 322–323, 325,
  340, 347, 354, 392, 447

Jarmo, 196

Jericho, 196–199, 213

Jordan, 266

Judaism, 282–283, 285, 298–299, 332, 411,
  413–414

Justice, 71, 178, 408–409, 429, 473–474, 476–
  477, 493–494

Kenya, 454

Kings, 232, 242–245, 257–263, 354, 474

Kinship, 174–175, 195, 206–207, 218–219,
  222–223, 231, 285–287, 297, 416–425,
  461, 465–467, 473, 490–492
  (*See also* Families; Marriage)

Labor unions, 40, 103, 379–380, 460

Land owners and land ownership, 260–261, 263,
  266–268, 329, 333–334, 443–444, 450

Language, 34–37, 64, 96, 98, 181, 487–488, 498

Latin America, 251, 266, 325, 340, 345, 433–
  434, 446, 449–451, 454, 486

Laws, 47, 103, 138, 200, 245, 265, 379, 405,
  408–409, 498

Learning, 16–20, 22, 30, 59, 72, 81, 105, 480–
  481, 498
  (*See also* Socialization)

Lebanon, 242, 266, 325, 446

Legitimacy, 45, 241, 332, 355, 426, 498

"Leisure," 87, 102, 129, 203, 211, 224, 305, 498

Lenin, 438

Liberia, 454, 463

Life expectancy, 280, 346

Literacy (*see* Writing and literacy)

Love, 31, 47, 475–476

Luxury goods, 208, 264, 273–274, 299

Lydia, 84

Machine tools, 315–316

Magic, 156, 162, 250, 285, 327, 411

Mali, 232–233

Man, primate ancestry, effects of, 14–17

Managers, power of, 277–279

Manual jobs (*see* Blue-collar jobs)

Maritime societies, 123–125, 128–129, 300–
  304, 431, 499

Market economy, 189, 263, 371–375, 415, 456–
  457, 499

Markets, 209, 455

Marriage, 136, 175, 273, 278, 286–287, 292,
  297–298, 417, 426

Mass media, 36, 353, 357–358, 459, 487, 493–
  494

Material necessities, 13

Matrilineality, 199–200, 219–221, 499

Mayas, 209–216

Merchants, 246, 273–274, 276–278, 287, 300–
  304, 306, 329, 332–333, 355–356, 443

Mesolithic Age, 119, 121–122, 124, 128, 148–
  149, 161–163, 188–190, 291, 305, 499

Mesopotamia (*see* Middle East)

Metallurgy, 71, 119–120, 125, 128, 133, 202–
  206, 210, 213–215, 224, 250–251

Mexican societies, 85, 209–216, 239, 241, 325,
  328, 344

Middle East, 94, 120, 128, 149, 160, 192–204,
  213, 228, 238–252, 266, 283, 298–299,
  327, 446, 449–451, 454, 486
  (*See also* Egypt; Lebanon)

Migration, 97–98, 159, 335, 429

Military power, 91, 93

Minoan society, 128

Mixed economy, 372–375, 382

Mobility, vertical, 42, 406–407, 502

Mobs, 41

Modernization, 430, 437, 443–444, 448–451,
  461, 464–465, 499

Modernizers, 437–441, 448–451

Money, 208, 245–246, 328–329, 372, 455

Mongol empire, 299

Morality, 235–236, 474–475, 477, 493–494
  (*See also* Values)

Movements, 41

Mughal empire, 260–263

Multiplier effect, 86–88

Murdock's sample, 130–137, 503–507

Mutation, 52–54, 60, 63, 66, 483, 499
Mutual aid, 175, 179–180, 218–219, 236

Nasser, 438–440
Nationalism, 360, 451, 455, 465
Nature, human (*see* Human nature)
Neanderthal man, 152–153
Needs, human, 27–34, 37, 40, 47, 93, 105, 406, 470, 486
    derivative social, 28–30, 406
    elemental, 28
Negritos, 186
Neolithic Age, 119, 121–122, 193–201, 500
Netherlands, 160, 301–302, 325, 347, 349, 354, 363, 379, 487
New Guinea, 217
New World, 98, 120, 159, 163–164, 208–216, 232, 234, 251, 328–329, 451, 457
    conquest of, 328–329, 357, 372
Nigeria, 459, 461, 463–465
Nobility, 206, 216, 224, 233–234, 292
    (*See also* Governing class)
Nomadism, 166–167, 189, 295–296, 500
Nonmanual jobs (*see* White-collar jobs)
Norms, 39–40, 46–47, 73, 75, 500
Nuclear power, 313, 326, 341
Numeral system, 211, 248

Offices, 39, 206, 258, 260–261, 286, 366, 394–395, 438
Officials, 241, 243–245, 249, 258, 263, 273, 306, 359, 366, 438
    (*See also* Bureaucracy)
Oratory, 223
Organisms, 7–8
Organization, 500
    hierarchy of, 8
    social, 14, 28–30, 34, 38–44, 64, 86, 98, 101–104, 106, 142, 209, 238, 242–245, 248–249, 293, 307, 348–354
        scale of, 253–254, 286, 305–306, 348–350, 471, 485–486, 501
            (*See also* Economy; Polity)
    societal, 16, 190–191, 229
Organizations, economic, 376–384
    (*See also* Factories; Guilds; Labor unions)
Origins of mankind, 96–97
Ottoman empire, 260–261, 299

Paleolithic Age, 119, 122, 124, 126–127, 148–159, 161–163, 188–190, 291, 304, 469, 500

Palestine, 193, 196–199, 242
Peasants, 247–249, 264–272, 276, 279, 287, 444, 451, 500
    living conditions, 268–272
    revolts, 257–258, 265, 288, 356
    viewed as subhuman, 270–271
Peru, 214–216, 325, 442, 447
Petroleum, 125, 313, 320–322, 324, 341–342
Phenotype, 49–50, 62–64, 104, 500
Phoenecians, 301–302
Plant cultivation, 71, 98–99, 121, 125, 162, 192–194, 235, 237, 305
Plastics, 313, 324
Plow, 125–126, 128, 195, 204, 237–239, 248
Poland, 325, 347, 354, 489
Political parties, 358–363, 390–391, 400–401
    functionaries, 355, 393–395, 488
Political science, 5, 25
Polity, 99, 102–103, 106, 111, 138, 176–179, 195, 200, 217, 219, 222, 230–231, 241–245, 257–263, 292, 354–368, 408–409, 437–443, 457–460, 488–490, 500
Pollution, 342, 428, 480, 484
Polygyny, 136, 174–175, 190, 224, 421, 464, 467, 500
Population:
    distribution, 369–371
    excess, 278–279
    size and growth, 83–84, 87–88, 93, 97, 99, 105, 114, 129, 131–133, 164–166, 188–189, 198, 203, 209, 235, 248, 251, 279–282, 292, 296–297, 305, 307, 344–345, 348, 367, 433–436, 454, 479, 484–485
Populations, 49–51, 54–56, 64–65, 83–84, 500
    (*See also* Societies; Species)
Pottery, 195, 197, 199–200, 210, 218
Poverty, 268–269, 278, 439
Power, 31–32, 42–43, 176–180, 222–223, 249, 263, 392, 402, 404, 473–474
    (*See also* Authority; Stratification)
Prediction, 6, 477–494
Prestige, 42–43, 93, 180, 402, 404
    (*See also* Stratification)
Priests, 211–214, 235, 240–241, 306, 443, 462, 500
    (*See also* Religion)
Primary groups, 40, 500
Primates, 14–17, 190–191, 468–469, 500
    (*See also* Hominids; Homo sapiens sapiens)
Primogeniture, 261, 500
Privilege, 42–43, 402, 404
    (*See also* Stratification)
Probabilistic theory, 59–60, 70, 140, 478, 501
Problems, social, origins of, 306–307, 428–429

Production, 30, 37, 99, 101–102, 108, 113, 159, 167–173, 177, 203, 218, 239, 249, 305–307, 327, 335, 416–417, 431–433, 447, 452–454
Professional associations, 380
Professions, 380, 444, 450–451, 461
Progress:
   nontechnological, 469–477
   technological, 52, 54, 58–59, 61, 69–70, 101–110, 200–201, 235–236, 304–307, 428–429, 447–448, 469, 501
   rates of, 62, 150, 154, 161–163, 194, 198, 209, 248–250, 469, 478–480
   slowdown, 248–250
Property, 139, 167–169, 179–180, 189, 209, 305, 389–392, 473, 476
   (*See also* Land owners and land ownership; Wealth)
Proprietary theory of the state, 258–259, 416
Prostitution, 278–279, 307*n.*, 407
Protestantism, 329–333, 356–357, 372, 422, 450
   (*See also* Christianity)
Psychology, 33
   social, 5, 25
Punan, 178, 186
Punishments, 30, 473–475

Race, 105–107
Racialist explanations, 105–107
Racial stratification, 399–401
Radiation, adaptive, 58, 161
Radiocarbon dating, 193
Railroads, 312, 384
Random processes (*see* Chance)
Rationality, 331
Recombination, 52–53, 63, 66, 82–83, 501
Regression, 112–116
Religion, 44–45, 86, 99, 102–103, 134, 152, 156–158, 162, 182–184, 195–196, 207, 210–214, 222, 224, 235, 240–241, 250, 279, 282–285, 288, 298–299, 306, 329–333, 356–357, 411–416, 448–451, 456, 462–465, 493, 501
Religious stratification, 399–401
Reproduction, 13–14, 30, 50–52, 54–55, 57, 63, 65, 93, 417
   (*See also* Birth rates)
Republics, 257, 302–303
Requisites, functional, 29–30
Research, 336–337, 479
Resources, 33, 42, 54, 62, 93, 105, 108, 116–117, 258, 260, 297, 305, 479
Respect, 31

Retainers, 231, 259–260, 306, 501
Revolution, social, 121, 195, 235, 360–361, 374, 407, 439, 444
   (*See also* Industrial Revolution)
Rewards, 30, 33
Roles, 39–41, 75, 174, 501
   (*See also* Offices)
Roman society, 84, 106, 112–115, 120, 128, 254–255, 257, 263, 272–273, 276, 282, 412
Russian society, 253–254, 257–258, 266
   (*See also* Soviet society)

S-curve, 85–86
Sacrifice, human, 139, 208, 214, 236, 474
Salvation, 32
Sanctions, 75–77, 178–179, 501
Sanitation, 280–282, 345, 485
Savage societies, 120
Scalp taking, 139, 236
Scandinavia, 84, 325, 354, 361–362, 379, 392, 416, 487–488
   (*See also* Denmark; Swedish society)
Scarcity, 13–14, 33, 43, 93, 105, 494
Science, 38, 44, 81, 86, 320, 337, 364, 398–399, 410–411, 415, 427, 447–448, 479, 493
Scribes, 244–245
Secondary groups, 40, 501
Secularization, 284
Selection:
   intersocietal, 63, 67–69, 90–94, 114, 180, 205–208, 306, 477, 494, 498
   intrasocietal, 63, 67–69, 89–90, 498
   natural, 13–14, 54–57, 109, 500
Self-interest, 33–34, 47, 105, 258, 368, 428, 438, 493
Self-respect, 32
Self-sufficiency, 113, 172, 197, 217
Servants, 273, 306
Sex distinctions, 170–172, 180, 193, 220–221, 287, 298, 402–404, 456, 491
Shamans, 158, 171, 183–184, 399, 501
Sharing (*see* Mutual aid)
Shen-nung, 199–200
Siberia, 155, 159
Signals, 19, 65*n.*, 235, 501
Simmons' data, 137–139
Siriono, 176, 187
Skills, 32
Slavery, 205, 230, 236, 292, 297, 372, 409, 471, 491, 501
Smelting, 203, 214, 248, 250, 315
Smiths, 203

Social control (*see* Control, social)

Socialism and socialists, 358–359, 450

African, 460–461

Socialization, 30–31, 63, 65–66, 74–77, 501

Social organization (*see* Organization, social)

Societies:

basic function, 10

defined, 9–10, 501

human; expansion, 205–208, 348

imperfect systems, 90–91

their place in nature, 7–8

Sociocultural drift, 67

Sociology:

goal, 5

history of, 22–26

Soldiers, 241, 249, 306

Soviet society, 322–326, 347–348, 354, 375–376, 382, 384, 392–394, 404, 412, 416, 422, 437–438, 447, 487, 489

(*See also* Communism and Communist countries; Russian society)

Spanish society, 85, 254, 325, 347, 354, 364, 392

Spear, 124, 151, 154–155, 162

Spear-thrower, 124, 154–155, 162

Specialization, 30, 39, 102, 133–134, 158, 171–172, 189–190, 197, 203, 208–209, 222, 229–230, 235, 241, 249, 254–257, 276–278, 306, 350–353, 365, 455–456

community, 255–256, 352–353

national, 436–437, 490

organizational, 352

(*See also* Division of labor)

Specialized societal types, 125–126, 290–304

Species, 7–8, 50–52, 60–61, 95, 502

Spinning machines, 251, 313–314

State, 208

Status groups, 399, 502

Statuses, 41–42, 44, 502

Steam engine, 251, 311–312, 314–317, 341–342

Steel, 250, 312, 317–318, 320, 342

Stratification, 41–44, 384–409, 443–445, 460–461, 490, 502

consequences of, 404–406

(*See also* Classes; Inequality)

Structural-functional approach in sociology, 24–25, 27–47

Students, 425–427, 447

Subsistence, 13, 55, 108, 121–142, 164, 166–167, 170, 172, 188, 191, 205, 211, 220–221, 224, 249, 291–292, 298, 306, 431, 457, 469, 494, 502

Sumer, 84, 203

Superstition, 247

Surplus, economic, 213, 232, 235–236, 238–241, 247, 259, 264–265, 273, 276, 305–306, 327, 392, 497, 502

Survival, 10, 13–14, 29–30, 44, 74, 90–91, 101, 147, 159, 306, 492

(*See also* Selection)

Swedish society, 325, 343–344, 347, 364, 420, 423

(*See also* Scandinavia)

Symbols, 18–22, 35–37, 61–62, 96, 150, 152, 235, 304, 469, 502

(*See also* Culture; Language)

Systems, 90–91, 502

Tanzania, 456, 463–464

Taxes, 235, 249, 263–264, 267–268, 306, 391–392, 395, 456

Taxonomies, 104, 502

(*See also* Typologies)

Technological determinism, 139–142

Technology, general, 34, 37–38, 64, 69–70, 78, 86, 90, 93, 96, 98, 100–106, 112–117, 119–142, 168–170, 173, 188–190, 198–199, 203, 209, 218, 235, 241, 248–252, 295, 304–307, 311–326, 340–345, 357, 367, 431–433, 452–454, 470–494, 502

(*See also* specific modes of subsistence)

Technostasis, 112–116, 502

Telephones, 313, 322, 339

Temples, 201, 210–214

Territories, 179, 198, 232–233

Textile industry, 311–316

Theocracies, 213, 240–241, 284, 502

Tool-making primates, early, 96, 191, 304

Tools (*see* Technology; *and* specific tools)

Towns (*see* Communities, urban)

Trade and commerce, 113, 172–173, 196–197, 201, 203, 209, 218, 246, 263–265, 300–304, 430, 455

Transportation, 61, 98, 232, 234, 261, 299, 316–317, 364–365, 388, 430, 486

costs, 275–276

Tribal religions, 462–464

Tribalism, 457–459

Tribes, 181–182, 222, 502

Typologies, societal, 118–126

Ubaid culture, 200–201, 203

Umayyad empire, 254

Unions (*see* Labor unions)

United Nations, 349

United States (*see* American society)

Universities, 410–411, 447–448, 482, 487
  (*See also* Students)
Urban communities (*see* Communities, urban)
Urbanization, 203, 353, 369–371, 452, 454
  (*See also* Communities, urban)

Values, 30, 45–47, 86–87, 235–236, 246–247, 249, 298, 303, 405, 426–427, 447, 502
Variable concepts, 59, 70, 140, 354, 502
Variations within societal type, 288–289, 427–428
Vietnam, 266, 446

War, 54, 91–93, 99, 111, 138, 197–198, 205–207, 210, 218, 224–225, 227, 249, 258, 280, 298, 303, 306, 327, 337, 367–368, 475, 479, 494

Wealth, 32, 41, 188, 190, 198, 209, 224, 231, 235, 263, 273–274, 306, 355, 389–392, 402, 488
  (*See also* Property)
Weapons, 154–156, 178–179, 197–198, 202–203, 205–207, 215–216, 222, 224, 251
Wheel, 232, 248
White-collar jobs, 351–352, 385–388, 407
Work, attitudes toward, 249, 303–304, 330–333, 455–456
World views, 44–45, 405, 411–416, 502
  (*See also* Religion)
Writing and literacy, 36, 203, 208, 211, 216, 239, 244–245, 247–248, 287–288, 357–358, 396–397, 455

Yugoslavia, 325, 347, 354, 359, 375, 382–383, 416, 489

Zulus, 233